# STAR WARS™

# FORCE AND DESTINY™

## ROLEPLAYING GAME

CORE RULEBOOK

A long time ago in a galaxy far, far away....

## FORCE AND DESTINY

*Darkness* covers the galaxy. The evil **GALACTIC EMPIRE** rules through fear, *holding countless planets in an iron grip.*

*The dreaded* DARTH VADER and his agents have destroyed the JEDI—guardians of order and justice. The forces of evil have *triumphed, crushing the forces of good.*

*Now, a few brave souls band together, arming themselves with the legacy of the Jedi. They stand ready to fight the darkness and restore peace to the galaxy....*

# CREDITS

### STAR WARS: FORCE AND DESTINY DESIGNED BY

Jay Little

### LEAD DEVELOPER

Sam Stewart

### WRITING AND ADDITIONAL DEVELOPMENT

Max Brooke, John Dunn, Daniel Lovat Clark, Andrew Fischer, Michael Gernes, Sterling Hershey, Keith Kappel, Monte Lin, Jason Marker, Jason Mical, and Christopher Rowe with Katrina Ostrander

### EDITING AND PROOFREADING

Christine Crabb, Molly Glover, and David Johnson

### MANAGING RPG PRODUCER

Chris Gerber

### GRAPHIC DESIGN

Chris Beck with Shaun Boyke, Samuel Shimota, and Evan Simonet

### GRAPHIC DESIGN MANAGER

Brian Schomburg

### MANAGING ART DIRECTOR

Andy Christensen

### ART DIRECTION

Zoë Robinson

### COVER ART

Darren Tan

### INTERIOR ART

Andrius Anezin, Cristi Balanescu, Ryan Barger, Chris Beck, Arden Beckwith, Dimitri Bielak, Cassandre Bolan, Alberto Bontempi, Matt Bradbury, Dmitry Burmak, Rovina Cai, JB Casacop, Anna Christenson, Alexandre Dainche, Christina Davis, Anthony Devine, Florian Devos, Sara K. Diesel, Tony Foti, Michele Frigo, Zachary Graves, David Griffith, Clark Huggins, Joel Hustak, Lukasz Jaskolski, Tomasz Jedruszek, Andrew Johanson, Jeff Lee Johnson, Katayanagi, David Kegg, Romana Kendelic, Julian Kok, Leonid Kozienko, Kate Laird, Adam Lane, Ignacio Bazán Lazcano, Jorge Maese, Kate Maximovich, Brynn Metheney, Aaron B. Miller, Victor A. Minguez, Scott Murphy, Jake Murray, David Nash, Mike Nash, David Ogilvie, Claudio Pozas, Maciej Rebisz, Adam Schumpert, Carmen Sinek, Beth Sobel, Anna Steinbauer, Matthew Starbuck, Darren Tan, Tiffany Turrill, Ryan Valle, Jose Vega, Magali Villeneuve, Christer Wibert, Jarreau Wimberly, Sara Winters, Richard Wright, Ben Zweifel, and the Lucasfilm art archives.

### PRODUCTION MANAGEMENT

Megan Duehn, Simone Elliott, and Eric Knight

### EXECUTIVE GAME DESIGNER

Corey Konieczka

### EXECUTIVE PRODUCER

Michael Hurley

### PUBLISHER

Christian T. Petersen

### PLAYTESTERS

For a complete list of playtesters, please see page 444.

# LUCAS LICENSING

### CREATIVE DIRECTOR

Michael Siglain

### SENIOR EDITOR

Jennifer Heddle

### LUCASFILM STORY GROUP

Leland Chee and Pablo Hidalgo

FANTASY FLIGHT GAMES

Fantasy Flight Games
1995 West County Road B2
Roseville, MN 55113
USA

ISBN: 978-1-63344-122-4     Product Code: SWF02

Printed in China

For more information about the *Star Wars*: FORCE AND DESTINY line, free downloads, answers to rule queries, or just to pass on greetings, visit us online at

**www.FantasyFlightGames.com**          **www.starwars.com**

# CONTENTS

# INTRODUCTION

**W**hat secrets lie in the Well of Shadows? Let's find out."

Kasuni Tamm set her back against the rock and pushed. With a grating rumble, the capstone slid aside. The weak rays of the winter sun danced across the layers of hoarfrost that covered the rough-hewn stones. Kasuni peered over the edge, then lit a glow rod and tossed it in. The brilliant green light fell through the shaft, briefly illuminating the walls before vanishing into the depths.

Kasuni Tamm pursed her lips and glanced over at Vaxim. "I guess they weren't kidding when they said 'bottomless,' huh?"

The bogwing seemed to laugh, a blend of chirps and croaks. Kasuni grinned. "Maybe you could fly down there, and see what's at the bottom?"

Vaxim turned away and started scratching for insects in the gorse around the rim. "Coward."

Twenty minutes later, Kasuni hung fifty meters down the well, staring intently at a patch of stonework. It looked no different than any of the other rocks she'd rappelled past, but something about it spoke to her. The Togruta closed her eyes and ran her free hand across the rough surface, tracing the whorls of frost. Vaxim chirped.

"Yeah, there is something here," Kasuni murmured. "It feels...old. Like the rock is asleep. But something about this stone..."

She pushed, and the stone slid inwards. A roughly circular portion of the wall followed suit, revealing the passageway beyond. "Yes! Vaxim, we're in!"

Kasuni swung into the entrance, deftly detaching her climbing gear and securing the rope. She made her way through the cramped passage, crouching to avoid scraping her montrals on the low ceiling. Vaxim swooped on ahead, and in a few moments, she heard his triumphant chirp.

The passageway opened up to a vast cavern. The cave had once been natural; flowstone formations and stalagmites still lined the walls. However, someone had hewn steps into the floor—steps that led to an octagonal pedestal in the cavern's center. And on the pedestal...

Kasuni's breath caught in her throat. Vaxim swooped around the cavern and settled onto her shoulder, quietly burbling in satisfaction. She walked up the steps and stared down at the pedestal, studying the small, ornate cube. She reached down to pick it up.

"I would appreciate if you did not touch that." The measured voice echoed through the chamber.

Kasuni whirled around, her hand moving to the carbine slung over her shoulder. Three figures stepped out of the passageway. The first two were humans: one an older man with a gray beard and black combat armor, the other a small woman with an intense, unsettling expression and thick brown robes. The last, the one who spoke, was a Kel Dor, who towered over his companions.

"I recognize you," Kasuni said, nodding toward the older man. "You're the traveling merchant I met in the village. I don't remember the armor, though."

The man looked slightly embarrassed. "Yes. A necessary deception, I'm afraid, Mistress Tamm. My name is actually Markus Dorivonn. This is Zora," he gestured to the woman, "and Dal Kir."

The Kel Dor nodded. "We have been looking for this item for quite some time. Strange that you should have found it so quickly."

Kasuni shrugged. "Just lucky, I guess."

Markus raised an eyebrow. "Perhaps; perhaps not. In any case, we can't let the holocron fall into Sor Venge's hands. You need to give it to us."

From Kasuni's shoulder, Vaxim hissed. Kasuni shook her head. "Sorry, people. This box is the map to a place I desperately want to find. Besides, what's a 'Sor Venge,' anyway?"

Markus was about to respond, when Zora placed a hand on his shoulder. "She's not one of Venge's people," she said.

"How do you know?"

Zora looked coolly at Kasuni. "She's not lying; I can tell." Suddenly she paused, head cocked. "I hear someone in the passageway." A small metal cylinder dropped out of the sleeve of her robe and into her hand, and she whirled around.

A volley of blaster bolts exploded out of the passage, only to be deflected in mid-air as a double-bladed lightsaber ignited in Dal Kir's hands. More bolts shot toward the Kel Dor, who spun the weapon in flashing arcs. The shots ricocheted away, scorching stone and throwing up chips of rock.

Behind the blaster bolts, a dark-robed figure charged from the opening, howling a challenge as it swung a crimson lightsaber in sweeping arcs. Zora ignited her own blade, flicking it up in a perfunctory salute before meeting her opponent with a crushing overhead strike. The figure sidestepped the blow, only to stagger backward when Zora redirected her momentum and shouldered him viciously in the chest.

Kasuni unslung her carbine and snapped off a shot at the stormtroopers now starting to pour out of the passage. She saw one go down, the rest taking cover behind the flowstone formations. Markus, his own lightsaber ignited, was backing towards her while deflecting any shots that came in his direction. "These are Venge's agents! I think it's safe to say they want all of us dead."

Kasuni kept up her fire from behind the protection of his blade. "Well, given the circumstances, I'm willing to work with you three—for now. Do you know a way out of here?"

Markus shook his head. "Just up the Well, and that's going to be crawling with stormtroopers." Zora drove her opponent back with a furious swing, quickly raising her guard to block the equally savage riposte. The two lightsabers flashed and hissed as the duel continued. "We'd never make it up."

"Hm." Kasuni closed her eyes for a moment, concentrating. Then she pointed at one of the stone steps before the pedestal. "There. Cut through that!"

Markus's saber flashed down, slicing through rock in three controlled swings. The step crumbled, revealing darkness below: a hidden passage. "We've got an exit!"

Dal Kir had dropped at least one stormtrooper with reflected blaster shots. Now he lowered his lightsaber and raised his free hand. Kasuni felt her skin tingle and she stared, wide-eyed, as all around the chamber, small rocks and stones began to rise into the air.

Suddenly, the Kel Dor dropped into a fighting crouch and thrust his fist forward. The stones, the stormtroopers, and even the dark figure flew backward as if struck by a blast of wind, landing in the passageway in a tangle. Dal Kir straightened, then ran for the steps. Zora spat at her prone opponent and followed.

As the four climbed into the secret passage, Markus paused for a moment and looked at Kasuni. "Just lucky, huh?"

Kasuni smirked. "I guess I make my own luck."

Markus returned her grin as they jumped into the darkness. "Right. Have you ever heard of something called the Force?"

# WELCOME TO ROLEPLAYING IN FORCE AND DESTINY!

A roleplaying game is a cooperative improvisational storytelling experience you play with up to six friends. During the game, players take on the role of a character or characters, each of which contributes to the telling of an exciting story set in the rich fabric of the *Star Wars* galaxy. You and your friends create the story as you play, using the fantastic *Star Wars* setting to create sprawling adventures filled with drama, suspense, humor, and combat. You have more than a few opportunities to cross paths with Rebel heroes while combating stormtroopers, bounty hunters, and Imperial villains in your hero's journey to bring peace to the galaxy and discover a deeper understanding of the Force.

To play the game, you need your imagination, this book, paper and pencil, some *Star Wars* ROLEPLAYING DICE, and a few other players. Before you begin, you need to decide which member of your group will play as the Game Master (GM). While this does not need to be a permanent decision, the role of the GM does not generally change from one game session to the next,

## WHERE DO I START?

Different parts of the FORCE AND DESTINY Core Rulebook serve as good starting points, depending on whether you are playing FORCE AND DESTINY as the Game Master or as a Player Character.

Players should begin by reading **Chapter I: Playing the Game** and can then dive right into **Chapter II: Character Creation**.

The Game Master should also begin with **Chapter I: Playing the Game** but can then move on to **Chapter IX: The Game Master**. It is also advisable for new GMs to familiarize themselves with **Chapter VI: Conflict and Combat**.

and the Game Master has several responsibilities that the rest of the players do not.

## I'M THE GAME MASTER! WHAT DO I DO?

Running a roleplaying game is a lot of fun. Game Masters are part narrator, part actor, part storyteller, and part referee. You provide the initial plot to draw the players into the story, and you describe the beautifully unique, exciting environments *Star Wars* is famous for. While the other players each have their own character, as GM you portray supporting characters, antagonists, and anyone else the players might meet along the way. The GM keeps the plot moving forward and provides plot twists and side quests, while collaborating with players in the moment to keep them engaged in the story. Finally, the GM is the ultimate arbiter of how the rules are interpreted during the course of the game, using them or breaking them as necessary to maximize fun and enhance the story.

The best GMs can think on their feet and improvise new plans and directions for a story on the fly. Players are often unpredictable, and frequently perform unexpected actions that might threaten to derail a GM's plans for an adventure. Good GMs are flexible and can shuffle their plans around in the moment, incorporating new elements in ways that keep the experience organic and fresh. Your number one job as GM is to make sure everyone has a good time. Fun first, rules second.

## I'M A PLAYER! WHAT DO I DO?

Players each portray an individual character in the game, referred to as a Player Character (PC). The PCs are the main characters of the story. Usually, you create your own PC before the first session of play, although the GM may provide you with a pre-generated character instead, particularly if it is your first time playing FORCE AND DESTINY. PCs in FORCE AND DESTINY are Force-sensitive heroes trying to find their place in the galaxy and to restore the power of the Jedi Knights.

Your PC joins the other players in Force-powered *Star Wars* adventures, which typically last one to four sessions of play. Each adventure is a complete story,

with a beginning, middle, and end, not unlike the individual episodes of the *Star Wars* trilogies. With each adventure, characters grow both as individuals and in their understanding of the Force, improving their ability to complete increasingly difficult tasks successfully.

In FORCE AND DESTINY, the PCs typically battle Emperor Palpatine's sinister agents as would-be Jedi Knights, but they don't have to. The players and the Game Master work together to develop the most interesting story they can. You use the rules presented in **Chapter II: Character Creation** to construct the kind of character that interests you.

During character creation, you develop a background unique to your character. What kind of person is your character? Where is your character from? How did your character discover the ability to use the Force? You might be a heroic Jedi Knight who somehow survived the Clone Wars, or a Podracer pilot who uses the Force to win heats. You might even be a princess whose family has a long, secret tradition of Force adepts; anything is possible in the galaxy of FORCE AND DESTINY!

You also create a unique personality for your character, which can be as similar to or different from your own as you like. Games like FORCE AND DESTINY work best when players inhabit their characters, taking into account the events of their past, their hopes for their future, and the realities of their present. FORCE AND DESTINY includes rules to help bring your character's history, goals, and personality to life, creating a rich sense of immersion in the game. FORCE AND DESTINY includes rules governing PC backgrounds and Morality, which helps define how your character might behave at his best, and at his worst.

Once your PC is created, you join the other players, usually three to five people, and meet their PCs. A group of players is generally referred to as a "party." Before play begins, the players work with the Game Master to determine how the party meets. The characters might have all been drawn together by the Force, remaining allies ever since. Alternatively, the PCs could meet in an Imperial Inquisitor's dungeon, having been captured in locations throughout the galaxy, and find they must work together to escape. Maybe one of the PCs has a reputation as a powerful Force adept, and the rest of the group has sought that PC out. Players also work with the GM to develop any special relationships between PCs. Two of the PCs might be married to each other, siblings, old or former partners, former enemies, or anything else that interests the players.

When the game starts, each player controls his own PC, while the Game Master portrays all the other characters the PCs encounter, including allies, enemies, and those caught in the middle. (These are called Non-Player Characters, or NPCs.) During the adventure, you tell the GM what you want your Player Character to do. You might use an accent or unusual voice like an improvisational actor, but it's also acceptable to

# EXAMPLE OF PLAY

Ryan, Monica, Josh, Phil, and Diana have gathered to play FORCE AND DESTINY around Ryan's kitchen table. Ryan is acting as the GM. Josh is playing Markus, a human Guardian. Monica is playing Zora, a human Warrior. Phil is playing Dal Kir, a Kel Dor Consular. Diana is playing Kasuni, a Togruta Seeker.

We join the group mid-session as they attempt to escape the Well of Shadows...

**Ryan** (GM): All right, so now you're in the secret passageway beneath the Well. It's dark and cramped. I don't suppose any of you remembered to bring a light?

**Josh** (Markus): Um...I have my lightsaber?

**Diana** (Kasuni): Put the glowstick away, Josh. Kasuni rummages through her pack and pulls out a glow rod.

**Phil** (Dal Kir): Nice! I'm glad someone in our party believes in being prepared.

**Ryan** (GM): The light illuminates the rock passageway. The passage goes on in front and behind you, well beyond the range of your lights.

**Monica** (Zora): Hm, we need to figure out which way gets us out of here. Zora is going to glare at Kasuni and Markus. "Now that you two got us into this mess, can you get us out?"

**Diana** (Kasuni): Hey, Ryan. Can I use my Perception skill to figure out which direction to go?

**Ryan** (GM): Absolutely. That's going to be an **Average (◇◇) Perception check** to study your surroundings. Normally, I'd add two Setbacks ■ ■ because of the darkness, but since you have a glow rod, I'll drop that to one Setback ■.

**Diana** (Kasuni): And my one rank of the Keen Eyed talent removes that Setback ■ from the pool. (Diana builds a dice pool based on her skill and other factors and rolls.) Let's see...two Successes ✹ ✹ and one Advantage ☻.

**Ryan** (GM): Nice roll. So, you close your eyes and focus. After a long minute, you feel a slight breeze from the tunnel behind you.

**Diana** (Kasuni): "Hey, everyone. The way out is that way." Kasuni feels relieved, so I spend the Advantage ☻ to recover one strain.

**Phil** (Dal Kir): "The Force is strong with you, Kasuni."

**Diana** (Kasuni): "Um, if you say so." Kasuni isn't sure what the Force is, yet, so she sounds skeptical.

**Ryan** (GM): After a few minutes, the passage slopes upward. You push your way through a curtain of vines. The good news is that you're outside. The bad news is that you're on a ledge in the middle of a cliff, overlooking the valley below—

**Monica** (Zora): Whoops! "I hate heights."

**Ryan** (GM): —and the worse news is that below you, maybe ten meters, is a much larger ledge. On it are two squads of stormtroopers, an airspeeder, and your old "friend" Sor Venge.

**Josh** (Markus): Well, I don't think we want to start a fight with him. Has he seen us?

**Ryan** (GM): Let me see... (Since Venge isn't looking for the group, Ryan makes a Vigilance check for the NPC. Venge ends up with three Failures ▼ ▼ ▼.) He's so busy yelling at his soldiers, he doesn't notice you.

**Josh** (Markus): Perfect. I'm going to climb up and rig a rope to the top of the cliff. Then we can climb up and leave before he sees us.

**Ryan** (GM): Discretion is the better part of valor. That's a **Hard (◇◇◇) Athletics check**. But I'm going to flip a Destiny Point to upgrade one of the Difficulty die ◇ into a Challenge die instead ⬡.

**Josh** (Markus): Oh, great. No pressure. (Josh assembles his dice pool and rolls). Well, I got two Successes ✹ ✹...and uh oh. One Despair ▽.

**Ryan** (GM): All right. You make it to the top of the cliff with the rope, Markus, secure it, and throw it down to your friends. Unfortunately, the Despair ▽ means that when you drop the rope, it falls past your friends and ends up hanging in front of Venge's face.

**Monica** (Zora): Well, so much for sneaking. I draw my lightsaber.

**Ryan** (GM): Venge hops on the airspeeder with one of the stormtrooper squads and flies up to your level, staying a good distance from the ledge. You see a smug smile on his face as he shouts, "Surrender, or I'll blast you off the ledge!"

**Monica** (Zora): I'm tired of running from this guy, but I don't think he's going to come within reach of my lightsaber if I ask nicely.

**Phil** (Dal Kir): Maybe you just need to take the lightsaber to him. Ryan, how wide is the gap between us?

**Ryan** (GM): Not too wide. Call it short range.

**Phil** (Dal Kir): Perfect. I'd like to throw Zora onto the airspeeder with the Force. (Phil assembles his dice pool and rolls.) Two Light Side results ●●. I generate two Force Points ◐◐, which is enough to pick up Zora and move her.

**Ryan** (GM): OK, then! Zora, you suddenly feel your feet lift off the ground, and you go flying toward the airspeeder. You land on the back of the speeder, standing above Venge, saber raised. He stumbles backward, shocked, and I think it's time to roll for Initiative.

simply tell the GM what action you want your PC to take. Don't worry if you don't know all of the rules your first time playing; just explain what you want to accomplish, and allow the GM to explain how the rules function for that activity. The most important thing is to enjoy yourself playing **FORCE AND DESTINY**!

# WELCOME TO THE GALAXY!

It is a time of upheaval in the galaxy, and in the Force. Every day, the agents of the Galactic Empire viciously hunt the few remaining Force users in known space and strive to end the influence of the Jedi forever. Already reduced to myth and legend in the public eye, the Jedi Order is nearly wiped out. Save for a lonely few—a wise master and a young farm boy turned Rebel hero—their legacy is all but extinct.

Yet, not everyone has forgotten the Jedi and their selfless guardianship of galactic civilization. Others protect their legacy, storing forbidden artifacts, documents, or holorecordings, awaiting some sign that the light side is ascendant in the galaxy once again. The Empire is distracted from its crusade against the Jedi by the growing Rebel Alliance. Now is the time for a group of brave individuals bound together by a dream of a free and just galaxy without the Empire, inspired by the legends of the Jedi, to band together and fight against the forces of evil.

## THE EMPEROR RULES

Emperor Palpatine dominates much of the galaxy from Imperial Center, once known as Coruscant. Initially known for his media presence and powerful oratory, the Emperor has grown reclusive in recent years, relying on his chief aides and administrators to carry out his instructions and handle more routine matters of governance. To avoid questions about his lack of public life and appearances, the Emperor claims complete focus on liberating the Rim from lawless piracy and crushing the growing Rebellion arrayed against him.

However, the truth is much more sinister. Having finally achieved the Sith dream of ruling the galaxy, Palpatine fears losing it to the cold embrace of death. The Emperor has left Lord Vader and other agents to deal with the Rebellion while he probes the mysteries of the Force. In particular, he is continuing the work of his master, Darth Plagueis, and trying to learn the secrets of immortality, that he might rule the Empire forever.

## THE JEDI ARE NO MORE

The Empire has destroyed the guardians of peace and justice, the Jedi Knights! For almost two decades, the once bright, warm light of the Jedi has gone out of the galaxy, snuffed out by Palpatine's betrayal when he crushed the ancient Republic and created his Galactic Empire. Emperor Palpatine's agents, led by the sinister Darth Vader, have systematically hunted down, destroyed, and erased all remaining traces of the Jedi from the galaxy. With the destruction of Jedi Master Obi-Wan Kenobi on board the Death Star, Lord Vader struck a fatal blow against the hopes of those who would see the Jedi Order rise once more.

## TRUST IN THE FORCE

**FORCE AND DESTINY** begins as the time of the Jedi is ending...or is it? Jedi training dictates trust in the will of the Force, a mystical energy field created by life that binds the galaxy together. The Force is what gives Jedi their power: the ability to influence the weak-minded; to perform amazing feats of strength, speed, and agility; and even to manipulate objects from a distance with the power of the mind. Trust in the Force, and the Force will reveal a path.

The Emperor and Lord Vader failed in their quest to rid the galaxy of the Jedi before they even began. The Jedi can never truly be extinguished from the galaxy as long as there are those who believe in peace and justice. The Force selects its adepts from the farthest reaches of the Empire and leads them to develop their skills until they are ready to help restore balance to the Force.

## RESTORING BALANCE TO THE GALAXY

The Force is out of balance, and the dark side clouds everything, making the future uncertain. The role of those able to feel the Force is to serve its mysterious will. Those who give in to their selfish, base natures are lost to the dark side, trapped in an endless cycle of fear, anger, hate, and suffering. To serve the light side of the Force is to break that cycle wherever it can be found.

### BEGINNER GAME

New to roleplaying games? One easy way to learn how to play roleplaying games (and **FORCE AND DESTINY** specifically) is to play through the **FORCE AND DESTINY BEGINNER GAME**. This product teaches roleplaying to new players over the course of an adventure and contains everything a group needs to get started.

## WHAT ABOUT EDGE OF THE EMPIRE AND AGE OF REBELLION?

Edge of the Empire and Age of Rebellion are other *Star Wars* roleplaying games made by Fantasy Flight Games. Edge of the Empire focuses on the shadier side of life in the *Star Wars* galaxy. Age of Rebellion details the struggle between the brave freedom fighters of the Rebel Alliance and the tyrannical Galactic Empire.

Edge of the Empire, Age of Rebellion, and Force and Destiny are all completely compatible. Characters, careers, species, and items from each may be used together or separately. The Force and Destiny Core Rulebook contains all of the rules needed for play and does not require the Edge of the Empire or Age of Rebellion Core Rulebook (and vice versa). For more information, see page 338.

What this means for Player Characters is that they have to choose. Are the PCs committed to serving the light, working to emulate and restore the Jedi Order? Or are they servants of evil working toward selfish ends and lashing out at those around them? This isn't a choice made once, but every session, with every action. Those sensitive to the Force are constantly tested and tempted by the dark side.

The Player Characters may seek to mend the scars the dark side has left across the galaxy. Seeking out and studying long-lost Jedi artifacts is a way to gain critical knowledge that might one day lead to the restoration of the Jedi Order. Meditating at tainted vergences in the Force can restore them to their natural state. Of course, the most natural solution for many Force users is to attack the source of the dark side's growing influence, the Galactic Empire.

The Empire not only betrayed and murdered the Jedi, but destroyed everything they stood for. The Jedi were dedicated to preserving individual freedom and the galaxy's right to self-govern through a representative democracy, but the Emperor rules from his throne, listening only to trusted advisors. The Jedi were keepers of the peace, but the Imperials wage war throughout the Rim to expand Palpatine's domain. The Jedi used the Force for knowledge and defense, never to attack unprovoked. However, Emperor Palpatine, Lord Vader, and a slew of Force-powered Imperial Inquisitors and Emperor's Hands twist the Force to dark and violent ends.

To contribute to the fight against the Empire, either on the side of the Rebel Alliance or on one's own, is a noble goal for any hopeful Jedi. However, there are other evils in the galaxy independent of the Empire. Greedy corporations have committed atrocities, strip-mining or enslaving entire planets. Criminal syndicates prey on the weak and fearful who have only the Empire to depend on for help. As vast as the galaxy is, there are ancient evils: hidden and forgotten things that have been awaiting the right moment to return.

Force and Destiny campaigns can go in any of these directions or none of them. The temptations of the dark side may prove too much for the PCs, and they may shortly find themselves running a criminal syndicate, or even an empire of their own. The characters may track lost artifacts around the galaxy not to safeguard them, but to unleash their power for personal gain. Anything is possible in *Star Wars*.

# PLAYING
# THE GAME

*"Remember, concentrate on the moment.*
*Feel, don't think. Trust your instincts."*

–Qui-Gon Jinn

The FORCE AND DESTINY Roleplaying Game focuses on the deepest conflict in the *Star Wars* galaxy: the struggle between the light and dark sides of the Force. In a FORCE AND DESTINY campaign, many different characters, from lightsaber-wielding warriors and would-be Jedi to cunning shamans and intuitive pilots, all work together to learn to master their unique abilities. In the process, they struggle with their own personal choices between good and evil.

During these adventures, characters find themselves facing any number of challenges, from repairing their damaged starship or slicing their way past a security panel to fighting in a furious lightsaber duel against agents of the dreaded Emperor. The characters must rely on their innate abilities, trained skills, and special talents to survive, but in the end, they must also trust in the power of the Force.

This chapter provides a broad overview of the basics of FORCE AND DESTINY. First, it discusses what players need when preparing to play the game. The chapter then explores the various elements of the game's core mechanic and special dice. It continues with additional rules that govern the core of FORCE AND DESTINY's gameplay. **Chapter I** ends with a discussion on the general makeup of characters in FORCE AND DESTINY. Overall, this chapter covers the core rules of FORCE AND DESTINY, while other chapters cover rules dealing with specific situations in the game.

## WHAT PLAYERS NEED

Beginning a FORCE AND DESTINY game requires very few materials. Besides at least one copy of this rulebook for their group, players will need pencils or pens and copies of the character sheets found on page 445 to record information about their characters. The group will also need access to one or more standard ten-sided dice. Two dice per player is recommended.

Everyone involved in the game should also use the special custom *Star Wars* ROLEPLAYING DICE designed specifically to manage the unique task resolution system used in the game. The dice are described in detail later in this chapter.

- Packs of *Star Wars* **ROLEPLAYING DICE** are available for purchase at local hobby game retailers or can be ordered online from Fantasy Flight Games.
- Each **FORCE AND DESTINY** Beginner Game comes with a set of dice.
- Fantasy Flight Games offers a *Star Wars* Dice app for iOS and Android devices.

However, if these dice are not available, a chart on page 18 shows how players can instead use standard six-sided, eight-sided, and twelve-sided dice, which are readily found at most hobby game retailers.

## NARRATIVE PLAY

**FORCE AND DESTINY** asks the players to step into their characters' roles and use dramatic narrative to describe events and advance a story. In this manner, the players experience the excitement, drama, and epic scope of the *Star Wars* universe from the perspectives of their characters. While this rulebook provides specific rules for how to resolve actions, the game relies heavily on both the Game Master and the players to use their imaginations—tempered with common sense—to explain what happens.

In **FORCE AND DESTINY**, combat and other situations are represented in an abstract fashion. The game focuses on the characters and the heroic actions they take rather than on measurements, statistics, or other minutiae. Instead of taking a ruler and measuring the distance between characters on a map, it's preferable for a player to simply state, "I'm ducking behind the computer console to get some cover while I return fire." That sort of description paints a much better picture of the action taking place. Action resolution also has a narrative element. **FORCE AND DESTINY** uses a unique dice system to determine if a given task succeeds or fails. However, the dice reveal more than whether or not the Player Characters succeed. The different dice and their varied symbols tell a larger story, adding depth and detail to the scene in which the PCs find themselves. The variety of results allows for interesting and compelling encounters. It's possible for a character to fail at a task but still receive some benefit or find a brief respite. Likewise, a character can succeed at a task but at a certain cost or with unforeseen complications.

# THE CORE MECHANIC

Whether flying a speeder bike through the deadly swamps of a far-off world or using the Force to throw a rock at an Imperial stormtrooper, characters often find themselves performing actions that require skill and no small amount of luck. To determine whether these actions succeed or fail—or if they have any other unforeseen consequences—characters in **FORCE AND DESTINY** perform **skill checks**. Skill checks are easy to use, and they are broken into two key elements:

1. Roll a pool of dice.
2. After all factors have been accounted for, if at least one Success symbol remains, the task succeeds.

When a character attempts an action, the first step is to gather a number of dice and assemble the dice pool. The number and type of dice in the pool are influenced by several factors, including the

Each dice pool is made up of a number of dice from several different sources. Essentially, these dice pools are composed of "positive dice" and "negative dice."

Positive dice are added to the pool to help accomplish a task or achieve beneficial side effects. These may reflect innate talents or abilities, spe-cial training, superior resources, or other advantages that affect the specific task. Negative dice are added to the pool to hinder or disrupt a task, or to introduce the possibility of complicating side effects. These may reflect the inherent difficulty of the task, obstacles, additional risks, or the efforts of another character to thwart the task.

## TABLE 1-1: POSITIVE AND NEGATIVE DICE

| Positive Dice Come From | Negative Dice Come From |
|---|---|
| The skill used to accomplish a task | The difficulty of the task attempted |
| The characteristic being applied | An opponent's special abilities, skills, or characteristics |
| An applicable talent or special ability | Opposing forces at work |
| Equipment or gear being used by the character | Inclement weather or environmental effects |
| The use of light side Destiny Points | The use of dark side Destiny Points |
| Tactical or situational advantages | Tactical or situational disadvantages |
| Other advantages, as determined by the GM | Other disadvantages, as determined by the GM |

character's innate abilities, skill training, and equipment, as well as the inherent difficulty of the task being attempted. The GM may decide that the environment or the situation warrants the addition of certain dice; repairing a starship with ample time and the proper tools is one thing, but attempting repairs in the pouring rain, without tools, and under a hail of blaster fire is quite different. Once all the necessary dice have been assembled, the player attempting the task rolls all of the dice in the pool.

The second step involves interpreting the results on the dice. The player looks at the symbols on the face-up sides of the dice. Certain symbols work in pairs, one type canceling out another. Other types of symbols do not cancel each other out, and their effects are applied regardless of the outcome of the task. After comparing the first set of paired symbols—Success and Failure—the player can determine if the task succeeds. The player then compares the second set of symbols—Advantage and Threat—to determine if there are any beneficial side effects or negative consequences. Finally, any other symbols are resolved to add the last details to the outcome.

This core mechanic, the skill check, forms the foundation of the game. Other rules and effects either modify or interact with one of these two fundamental elements—the assembly of the dice pool and the interpretation of the results after the dice are rolled.

# THE DICE

This section takes a closer look at the special dice and their symbols. When the blaster bolts start flying, just about anything can happen. Dice symbols provide a narrative framework for the action—did a character hit the stormtrooper or force him to scramble for cover, throwing off his next shot? By understanding these dice and symbols, players will have a better understanding of the core mechanic. This section also discusses how to assemble a dice pool and when to introduce extra dice based on the circumstances. Dice sets can be purchased separately, or players may use the *Star Wars* Dice app to roll them electronically.

When a character makes a skill check in **FORCE AND DESTINY**, the dice allow the player and GM to quickly determine a task's success or failure, as well as its magnitude and narrative implications. To accomplish this, **FORCE AND DESTINY** uses seven types of dice. Each die has a specific function and purpose. Each die face is either blank or features one or more symbols that represent various positive or negative effects.

A typical dice pool can contain from five to eight dice. This pool size covers the majority of situations. Difficult, complex, or epic situations may include more dice, while mundane situations may involve fewer dice. If a task is so easy that success is virtually guaranteed, dice might not even be rolled at all. The impact of generating and rolling a dice pool is best reserved for important tasks that can influence the story.

Dice are divided into three categories. The first type features dice with symbols beneficial to accomplishing tasks. The second type has symbols that cancel those beneficial symbols and hinder the accomplishment of tasks. The third type is Force dice, which are used somewhat differently than the other dice.

Boost, Ability, and Proficiency dice are the beneficial, positive dice. Setback, Difficulty, and Challenge dice are the negative, disruptive dice. Force dice are distinct; while used for a number of situations, they are not usually used in a standard skill check.

## POSITIVE DICE

There are three types of positive dice with symbols that improve the odds of successfully completing a task or achieving beneficial side effects.

### BOOST DICE ☐

Special advantages, or "boosts," are represented with light-blue six-sided dice. Boost dice represent benefits gained through luck, chance, and advantageous actions taken by the characters. They can be added to a pool for a wide variety of reasons. Boost dice are most often used to reflect the character's possession of some sort of benefit or advantage, such as having ample time to complete the task or having the right equipment. Boost dice and Setback dice are thematic opposites of each other. Boost dice are represented by ☐ in text.

### ABILITY DICE ◆

Ability is represented with green eight-sided dice. Ability dice form the basis of most dice pools rolled by the players. They represent a character's aptitude or skill used when attempting a skill check. These dice possess positive, beneficial symbols. Ability dice are opposed by Difficulty dice. Ability dice are represented by ◆ in text.

### PROFICIENCY DICE ⬡

Proficiency is represented with yellow twelve-sided dice. Proficiency dice represent the combination of innate ability and training. They are most often used when a character is attempting a skill check using a skill in which he has trained. Proficiency dice can also be added to a pool when a player invests a Destiny Point for an important skill check. These dice possess a greater likelihood of success, and they are the only dice that feature the potent Triumph symbol (see page 20). Proficiency dice are the upgraded version of Ability dice (for more on upgrades, see page 30). Proficiency dice are represented by ⬡ in text.

## CONVERTING STANDARD DICE TO *STAR WARS* ROLEPLAYING DICE

When playing **Force and Destiny**, the GM and players ideally have access to a full complement of the special dice described here. However, there might be times when the dice are not available. This should not stop the game from continuing. Players may use several standard six-sided, eight-sided, and twelve-sided dice to generate the results found on the custom dice by referring to the chart below. Players simply convert the numerical results generated to the chart's associated symbols, which are the same as the symbols on the special game dice.

### TABLE 1–2: STANDARD TO STAR WARS ROLEPLAYING DICE CONVERSION

| Die Type | 1 | 2 | 3 | 4 | 5 | 6 | 7 | 8 | 9 | 10 | 11 | 12 |
|---|---|---|---|---|---|---|---|---|---|---|---|---|
| Boost die (d6) | Blank | Blank | ☆ | ☆○ | ○○ | ○ | | | | | | |
| Setback die (d6) | Blank | Blank | ▼ | ▼ | ⚙ | ⚙ | | | | | | |
| Ability die (d8) | Blank | ☆ | ☆ | ☆☆ | ○ | ○ | ☆○ | ○○ | | | | |
| Difficulty die (d8) | Blank | ▼ | ▼▼ | ⚙ | ⚙ | ⚙ | ⚙⚙ | ▼⚙ | | | | |
| Proficiency die (d12) | Blank | ☆ | ☆ | ☆☆ | ☆☆ | ○ | ☆○ | ☆○ | ☆○ | ○○ | ○○ | ⊕ |
| Challenge die (d12) | Blank | ▼ | ▼ | ▼▼ | ▼▼ | ⚙ | ⚙ | ▼⚙ | ▼⚙ | ⚙⚙ | ⚙⚙ | ▽ |
| Force die (d12) | ● | ● | ● | ● | ● | ● | ●● | ○ | ○ | ○○ | ○○ | ○○ |

# NEGATIVE DICE

There are three types of negative dice that have symbols that undermine success or introduce unwanted complications.

### SETBACK DICE ■

Certain complications, or "setbacks," are represented with black six-sided dice. Setback dice represent problems or minor obstacles during task resolution. Setback dice are often used to represent relatively minor conditions that impair or hinder a character, such as poor lighting, obstructive terrain, insufficient resources, or the fact that he is facing a robust, hungry rancor instead of an old, decrepit one. Setback dice are not as potent as Difficulty dice. They are added to represent additional circumstances or environmental effects that would not in and of themselves increase the base difficulty of the task. Setback dice and Boost dice are thematic opposites of each other. Setback dice are represented by ■ in text.

### DIFFICULTY DICE ◆

Difficulty is represented with purple eight-sided dice. Difficulty dice represent the inherent challenge or complexity of a particular task a character is attempting. In simplest terms, the more Difficulty dice in a dice pool, the more challenging it is to succeed. Difficulty dice possess negative, harmful symbols that cancel out the positive, beneficial symbols found on Ability, Boost, and Proficiency dice. Difficulty dice oppose Ability dice. Difficulty dice are represented by ◆ in text.

### CHALLENGE DICE ⬠

Challenge is represented with red twelve-sided dice. Challenge dice represent the most extreme adversity and opposition. These dice may be featured in place of Difficulty dice during particularly daunting challenges posed by trained, elite, or prepared opponents. Challenge dice can also be added to a pool when the GM invests a Destiny Point for an important skill check. These dice feature primarily negative, obstructive results, such as Threat and Failure, but they also feature the potent Despair result (see page 21). Challenge dice are the upgraded version of Difficulty dice (for more on upgrades, see page 30). Challenge dice are represented by ⬠ in text.

## FORCE DICE

The Force is abstracted using white twelve-sided dice. These Force dice represent the power and pervasiveness of the Force. They are generally only used in dice pools by Force-sensitive characters (or creatures) or under special circumstances. One of these special cases is when the players generate their starting Destiny pool at the beginning of a session (see **Destiny Points**, page 35).

Unlike the other dice used for task resolution, which generate results that impact success and failure or magnitude and complication, the Force dice generate resources. Each die features both dark side and light side points. There are no blank sides on a Force die. When players roll Force dice, they always generate a number of resources—but the resources can be dark side, light side, or a combination of the two.

Force dice are represented by ◯ in text. See **Chapter VIII: The Force** for more on using Force dice.

## TEN-SIDED DICE

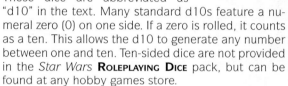

In addition to the custom dice described above, the game also uses standard ten-sided dice. These dice are abbreviated as "d10" in the text. Many standard d10s feature a numeral zero (0) on one side. If a zero is rolled, it counts as a ten. This allows the d10 to generate any number between one and ten. Ten-sided dice are not provided in the *Star Wars* ROLEPLAYING DICE pack, but can be found at any hobby games store.

In FORCE AND DESTINY, a more common roll using d10s is called the percentile roll. When making a percentile roll, the player rolls two dice, designating one die as the tens digit and the other die as the ones digit. A result of zero on either die means that the corresponding digit is zero in the two-digit number rolled. A result of "00"—zero on both dice—indicates a roll of 100. The percentile roll is abbreviated as d100. It is used most often as a randomizer, generating a number between 1 and 100. Percentile rolls are used to generate numbers that correspond to particular results on lookup tables, such as the severity of a Critical Injury effect or whether or not a character's Morality is triggered and comes into play (see page 323).

### EXAMPLE

Ellie's character inflicts a Critical Injury on a stormtrooper. Ellie rolls percentile dice to determine how severe the Critical Injury is. She chooses one green d10 and one blue d10. She designates the green die as the tens digit. After she rolls the dice, the green die shows a 4 and the blue die a 7. The percentile roll is read as 47. If the green die showed a zero instead, the percentile roll would be read as 7 (zero-seven).

# DICE SYMBOLS & RESULTS

The dice used in **Force and Destiny** feature a number of unique symbols used to determine success or failure, as well as to provide additional context and consequences during task resolution. Understanding these symbols allows the players to more fully contribute to the story, generating memorable details and describing cinematic actions over the course of their adventures. This section introduces and defines the different symbols, then describes how they are used in play.

Just like the special game dice, these symbols can be classified into several broad categories. The three types of symbols represent positive results, negative results, and Force resources.

## POSITIVE RESULTS

A character was able to slice into the Imperial security network while infiltrating a heavily guarded cell block, but how successful was that action? Did the character succeed by the skin of his teeth, or was the success so complete that all of the facility's security systems, not just those governing the cell block, were quietly deactivated? These sorts of specific results of character skill checks are determined by interpreting positive dice symbols.

Three positive symbols are found on the *Star Wars* **Roleplaying Dice**. These symbols represent Success, Advantage, and Triumph.

### SUCCESS ✻

Success symbols ✻ are critical for determining whether a skill check succeeds or fails. Success is undermined by Failure. Mechanically, one Success symbol ✻ is canceled by one Failure symbol ▼. Based on the core mechanic, if at least one Success remains in the pool after all cancellations have been made, the skill check succeeds. In **Force and Destiny**, Success symbols ✻ can also influence the magnitude of the outcome. For example, in combat, each net Success is added to the damage inflicted on the target. Generating four net Successes inflicts four additional damage.

Success symbols appear on ◆, ■, and ⬡ dice.

### ADVANTAGE ❂

The Advantage symbol ❂ indicates an opportunity for a positive consequence or side effect, regardless of the task's success or failure. Examples of these positive side effects include slicing a computer in far less time than anticipated, finding unexpected cover during a firefight, or recovering from strain during a stressful situation.

It's possible for a task to fail while generating a number of Advantage symbols, allowing something good to come out of the failure. Likewise, Advantage can occur alongside success, allowing for significantly positive outcomes. It's important to remember that Advantage symbols do not have a direct impact on success or failure; they affect only their magnitude or potential side effects. Advantage is canceled by Threat. Each Threat symbol ◉ cancels one Advantage symbol ❂.

Characters may use Advantage results in a wide variety of ways; this is known as "taking the Advantage." If a skill check generates one or more net Advantage symbols ❂, the player can spend that Advantage to apply one or more special side effects. These could include triggering a Critical Hit, activating a weapon's special quality, recovering strain, or even performing additional maneuvers. The applications of Advantage are covered in more detail on page 210.

Advantage symbols appear on ◆, ■, and ⬡ dice.

### TRIUMPH ✪

The Triumph symbol ✪ is a powerful result indicating a significant boon or beneficial outcome. Each Triumph symbol ✪ provides two effects:

First, each Triumph symbol ✪ also counts as one Success, in every way Success ✻ has previously been defined. This means that the Success generated by a Triumph symbol ✪ could be canceled by a Failure symbol ▼ generated during the same skill check.

Second, each Triumph symbol can be used to trigger incredibly potent effects. Two common uses are to trigger a Critical Injury upon a successful attack and to activate a weapon's special quality. Effects generated by a weapon's special quality usually require multiple Advantage symbols ❂ to activate. Triumphs may activate other potent effects as well, including effects above and beyond those triggered by Advantage. These effects may be set by the GM, or they may defined by the environment, a piece of equipment, or a special character ability. See page 210 for more information on using the Triumph symbol ✪ to trigger effects.

Players gain both effects with each Triumph symbol; they don't have to choose between the Success and the special effect trigger. Although the Success aspect of the Triumph symbol ✪ can be canceled by a Failure symbol ▼, the second aspect of the ✪ result cannot be canceled. Multiple Triumph symbols are cumulative: each Triumph adds one Success, and each can be used to generate its own special effect.

The Triumph symbol only appears on the ⬡ die.

## NEGATIVE RESULTS

While evading a squad of Imperial scouts aboard a stolen speeder bike, a character unsuccessfully attempts to weave between two massive rock formations. Is the failure severe, resulting in a terrible crash? Or does it result in little more than a scratch on the speeder's fuselage? Such details are provided by interpreting negative dice symbols.

Three negative symbols are found on the task resolution dice. These results are Failure, Threat, and Despair.

## FAILURE ▼

Failure symbols ▼ are critical for determining whether a skill check succeeds or fails. Failure undermines Success. Mechanically, one Failure symbol ▼ cancels one Success symbol ☼. Based on the core mechanic, if at least one Success symbol ☼ remains in the pool after all cancellations have been made, the skill check succeeds. Fortunately for characters, multiple net Failure symbols ▼ do not influence the magnitude of the failure.

Failure symbols appear on ■, ◆, and ⬢ dice.

## THREAT ۞

The Threat symbol ۞ is fuel for negative consequences or side effects, regardless of the task's success or failure. Examples of these negative side effects include taking far longer than expected to slice a computer terminal, leaving an opening during a firefight that allows an enemy to duck into cover, or suffering additional strain during a stressful situation.

It's possible for a task to succeed while generating a number of Threat symbols, tainting or diminishing the impact of the success. Likewise, Threat can occur alongside Failure, creating the possibility for some significantly dire outcomes. It's important to remember that Threat symbols ۞ don't directly impact success or failure, only their magnitudes or potential side effects. Threat cancels Advantage. Each Threat symbol ۞ cancels one Advantage symbol ⚝.

The GM generally resolves Threat effects. There are a wide variety of possible effects that Threat may trigger. If a skill check generates one or more net Threat symbols, the GM generally applies one or more special side effects. These could include being knocked prone, losing the advantage of cover, taking more time than anticipated, suffering strain during a normally routine action, or giving an enemy an opportunity to perform a maneuver. The applications of Threat are covered in more detail on page 211.

Threat symbols appear on ■, ◆, and ⬢ dice.

## DESPAIR ▽

The Despair symbol ▽ is a powerful result, indicating a significant bane or detrimental outcome. Each Despair symbol imposes two effects:

First, each Despair symbol ▽ also counts as one Failure ▼, in every way Failure ▼ has previously been defined. This means that the Failure represented by a Despair symbol could be canceled by a Success symbol ☼ generated during the same skill check.

Second, each Despair can be used to trigger potent negative effects. A Despair symbol ▽ may be used to indicate a weapon has jammed or run out of ammunition or energy cells. Despair may activate other potent effects as well, including effects above and beyond those triggered by Threat. These effects may be determined by the GM or defined by the environment, an adversary, or a special character ability. See page 211 for more information on using a Despair symbol ▽ to trigger effects.

Players suffer both effects of each Despair symbol; they do not get to choose between the Failure and the special effect trigger. The Failure aspect of the Despair symbol can be canceled by a Success symbol ☼; however, the second aspect of a Despair symbol ▽ result cannot be canceled. Multiple Despair symbols ▽ are cumulative; each Despair imposes one Failure, and each can be used to generate its own special effect.

The Despair symbol only appears on the ⬢ die.

## FORCE RESOURCES

The final category of dice symbols represents resources generated by the Force. There are two types of Force symbols: Light Side Force Points ◯ and Dark Side Force Points ●. The generic symbol for a Force point, whether light side or dark side, is ◖.

◯ and ● appear on Force dice ◇, which are used frequently for characters who are Force users, struggling with the balance of the light and dark sides of the Force. Force-sensitive characters can use these resources to help fuel special abilities such as telekinesis and precognitive combat awareness.

Unlike the positive and negative dice used for task resolution, Force dice generate resources that are spent to fuel a power's effects, such as its magnitude, range, or duration. The Force die ◇ and the mechanics that govern it are very different from the core skill check mechanics of FORCE AND DESTINY. They are discussed in greater detail in **Chapter VIII: The Force**.

There are other uses for the Force dice besides employing Force powers. Another common application of Force dice in FORCE AND DESTINY is their use to determine a group's starting pool of Destiny Points at the beginning of each session (see page 35).

# LIGHTS, CAMERA, ACTION!

During the course of a FORCE AND DESTINY adventure, characters find themselves in countless situations, attempting a variety of tasks. In everything from seemingly mundane actions, such as repairing a damaged starship or negotiating the price of a crate of rations, to extraordinary feats, like balancing on the edge of a skyscraper in a rainstorm while fighting a deadly bounty hunter, characters will inevitably be put to the test. When the outcome of a PC's attempt at a task is uncertain, the player usually needs to roll a skill check to determine the task's success or failure. These skill checks hinge upon a number of different character attributes, including skills, special talents, and inherent abilities.

The GM decides which type of skill check is required for a given task. Once the type of check and its difficulty have been set, the player assembles a pool of dice based on the different factors involved. The pool can be a combination of many types of dice, which vary depending on the characters involved and the specific situation.

After the dice pool has been assembled, the player rolls all of the dice in the pool. The dice results are evaluated to determine which symbols cancel each other out and which ones are cumulative. Once all evaluations have been made, the player and GM resolve the skill check by determining the action's success or failure. The information obtained from the dice results is used to describe not only the outcome of the check, but also any additional effects, complications, or surprises.

# THE BASIC DICE POOL

**F**ORCE AND DESTINY uses a concept known as a dice pool, which is a collection of the dice needed to determine the outcome of any given situation in the game (see **The Dice** on page 17). While advanced or complex actions may require a large dice pool, the basic dice pool is quite simple. It relies on three factors: the PC's inherent ability, any specialized training the character has, and the difficulty of the task being attempted.

Following a more detailed look at these three factors, this section describes how players assemble and resolve basic dice pools and rolls, discusses other types of dice pools, and examines the kinds of checks players might make during a game session.

## CHARACTERISTICS

In FORCE AND DESTINY, a character's intrinsic abilities are defined by six **characteristics**: Agility, Brawn, Cunning, Intellect, Presence, and Willpower.

Brawn and Agility are measures of the character's physical abilities: strength, flexibility, athletic prowess, skill with weapons, and general toughness. Intellect and Cunning are the character's mental abilities, reflecting the PC's knowledge, analytical skill, cleverness, and deductive reasoning. Willpower and Presence represent the character's personality and force of spirit, including such aspects as charisma, mental fortitude, and facility in relating to and interacting with others.

A character's species determines that character's starting characteristic ratings. After all, Mirialans tend to be quick, while Twi'leks tend to be charming. Each player has the opportunity to increase these default characteristics during character creation by investing a portion of the PC's starting experience points. It is important to note that after character creation, increasing characteristics is a significant in-game investment and can only be done by purchasing a specific and expensive talent—something that might happen only a few times over the course of an entire campaign. **Players need to think carefully about their characteristic ratings, and should consider investing a significant portion of their starting experience points in improving their characteristics**. More on character creation is covered on page 42.

Although it does make sense to focus on characteristics that improve the character's core skills and talents (for instance, an Advisor character might invest in a high Presence, or an Ataru Striker in a high Agility rating), the game system offers a great deal of flexibility. Both going against stereotype and planning ahead in anticipation of purchasing specializations in other careers over the course of a campaign are acceptable options for characters. For example, a player whose Starfighter Ace character is big and hulking might elect to increase the character's Brawn, with an eye toward eventually having the character become a Shii-Cho Knight as well. Likewise, a Shadow with a high Presence rating could be just as deft with words as with stealth, opening up the opportunity to perhaps become an Advisor.

### CHARACTERISTIC RATINGS

Characteristic ratings for both PCs and NPCs generally range from 1 to 6. Some exceptions exist, especially in powerful or unique cases. For example, a rancor likely has a Brawn rating much higher than that of a PC. NPCs like Yoda, Han Solo, Darth Vader, and other exceptional individuals from the *Star Wars* universe likely have abilities well beyond the scope of a typical starting NPC.

A typical humanoid has an average characteristic rating of 2. A rating of 1 is weak and below average. A characteristic rating of 3 or 4 is significantly above average, while ratings of 5 and 6 represent exceptional performance and ability. During character creation, no characteristic can be increased above 5. Once play begins, PC characteristics are capped at 6. Each species has a default characteristic profile that reflects particular strengths and weaknesses. This profile is then augmented and improved during creation by investing experience points.

To find the default characteristic profiles of each playable species, see **Chapter II: Character Creation**. The six characteristics are defined below.

### AGILITY

The Agility characteristic measures a character's manual dexterity, hand-eye coordination, and body control. Characters with a high Agility have flexibility, a good sense of balance, and deft hands. Agility is used for a number of physical skills, such as Coordination, and it is key to ranged combat skills such as Ranged (Light) and Ranged (Heavy).

### BRAWN

A character's Brawn represents a blend of brute power, strength, and overall toughness, as well as the ability to apply those attributes as needed. Characters with a high Brawn are physically fit and hardy, rarely get sick, and have strong constitutions. Brawn is used for a number of physical skills, such as Athletics and Brawl. Brawn is also used to determine a character's starting wound threshold.

### CUNNING

Cunning reflects how crafty, devious, clever, and creative a character can be. Characters with a high Cunning are savvy, quickly pick up on vital social and environmental clues, and can more readily come up with short-term plans and tactics. Cunning is used for a number of mental skills, including Deception, Perception, and Survival.

### INTELLECT

The Intellect characteristic measures a character's intelligence, education, mental acuity, and ability to reason and rationalize. Characters with a high Intellect can extrapolate and interpolate data, can recall details and draw from previous experience, and can think of long-term strategies and envision the ramifications of present actions. Intellect is used for a number of mental skills, including Astrogation, Computers, and all of the Knowledge skills, such as Lore and Xenology.

### PRESENCE

A character's Presence characteristic is a measure of moxie, charisma, confidence, and force of personality. Characters with a high Presence make natural leaders, draw attention when they enter a room, can easily strike up a conversation with nearly anyone, and are quick to adapt to social situations. Presence is the key characteristic for interpersonal skills such as Charm and Leadership.

### WILLPOWER

The Willpower characteristic reflects a character's discipline, self-control, mental fortitude, and faith. Characters with a high Willpower can withstand stress and fatigue, remain composed during chaotic situations, and exert influence over the weaker-willed. Willpower is used for skills such as Coercion and Vigilance. Willpower is also used to determine a character's starting strain threshold.

### CHARACTERISTICS IN PLAY

Various careers and professions rely on certain characteristics more than others. Characteristics also influence skills, a wide variety of character abilities, and some derived statistics. For example, in addition to being used for Athletics and Melee combat skill checks, Brawn is used to determine a character's starting wound threshold and forms the basis of a character's soak value.

As mentioned previously, characteristics are one of the three factors that affect the composition of a dice pool for a check (the other factors being skill training and task difficulty).

## SKILLS AND TRAINING

While characteristics create the foundation of a character's abilities, skills and specialized training are what really make a PC stand out from the crowd. Skills represent the character's training and experience in performing specific tasks and actions. Although a character can attempt almost anything even without

the proper training or skill, a PC is far more effective and capable if trained to perform the task at hand.

Skills, the second factor influencing a dice pool, represent specific training, hands-on experience, and focused knowledge in a certain area. Each skill is linked to a specific characteristic, which is the default ability a character uses when performing a task with that skill. For example, the Athletics skill is based on Brawn, Deception relies on Cunning, and Lore uses Intellect. Proper skill training can compensate for a character's low characteristic rating. However, the most proficient characters are those who have both the proper training and a strong linked characteristic.

A character's career choice provides **career skills**. Characters start out with training, or "ranks," in some of their career skills. As time passes during a campaign, a character can learn and improve any skills the player likes; however, improving career skills costs fewer experience points than increasing skills outside the PC's career.

For a more in-depth look at skills and their applications, see **Chapter III: Skills**.

## DIFFICULTY

The third factor in composing a dice pool (in addition to the relevant characteristic and related skill) is the difficulty of the task being attempted. The characteristic and skill ranks add positive dice to the dice pool. Difficulty adds negative dice, making success more challenging. In addition to dice that represent the task's inherent difficulty, other dice are added to reflect further complications based on the environment or specific situation.

While the characteristic and related skill are derived from the character attempting the task, the difficulty of a task is set by the GM. There are six basic difficulty levels. Some modifiers and situations may warrant checks higher than the sixth level, Formidable, subject to the GM's discretion (see the **Impossible Tasks** sidebar on page 27 for an optional seventh difficulty level).

In addition to providing a general classification that describes a task's inherent challenge, the difficulty level also indicates how many purple Difficulty dice ◆ are added to the dice pool when that particular task is attempted. A task attempted against a set difficulty level is referred to as a **standard check**.

### DEFINING TASK DIFFICULTY

When used in a check to represent the challenge posed by a task, the difficulty level is indicated with one of the following labels: **Simple**, **Easy**, **Average**, **Hard**, **Daunting**, or **Formidable**. This label is followed in parentheses by the number of Difficulty dice ◆ to be added to the dice pool. For example, a player

## TABLE 1-3: DIFFICULTY LEVELS

| Difficulty Level | Dice | Example |
|---|---|---|
| Simple | — | Routine, with the outcome rarely in question. Usually not rolled unless the GM wishes to know the magnitude of success, or unless Setback dice indicate the possibility of complications. |
| Easy | ◆ | Picking a primitive lock, tending to minor cuts and bruises, finding food and shelter on a lush planet, shooting a target at close range. |
| Average | ◆◆ | Picking a typical lock, stitching up a small wound, finding food and shelter on a temperate planet, shooting a target at medium range, trying to strike a target while engaged. |
| Hard | ◆◆◆ | Picking a complicated lock, setting broken bones or suturing large wounds, finding food and shelter on a rugged planet, shooting a target at long range. |
| Daunting | ◆◆◆◆ | Picking an exceptionally sophisticated lock, performing surgery or grafting implants, finding food and shelter on a barren desert planet, shooting a target at extreme range. |
| Formidable | ◆◆◆◆◆ | Picking a lock with no comprehensible mechanism, cloning a new body, finding food and shelter on a planet without breathable atmosphere. |

might face an **Easy (◆) Perception check** or a **Hard (◆◆◆) Mechanics check**. More detailed examples of each difficulty level are provided next to give players a clear idea of what the different levels represent.

### SIMPLE TASKS (–)

A Simple task is something so basic and routine that the outcome is rarely in doubt. Success is assumed for the majority of attempts at Simple tasks. If failure is virtually impossible, the task won't even require a check: the GM may simply state that the proposed action succeeds. If circumstances make the outcome uncertain, then a Simple task may require a roll. This may be the case only if one or more ■ are introduced—due to injuries, environmental factors, or opposition by foes, for example.

A Simple task adds no Difficulty dice to the skill check's dice pool.

### EASY TASKS (◆)

An Easy task poses little challenge to most characters, but something could still go wrong, and failure is still possible. A typical character with the proper training, resources, and tools for a

situation can expect to succeed at most of the Easy tasks he attempts. Often, the magnitude or potential side effects are more uncertain than the success itself.

An Easy task adds one Difficulty die (◆) to the skill check's dice pool.

### AVERAGE TASKS (◆◆)

An Average task represents a routine action for which success is common enough to be expected, but failure is not surprising. A typical character with the proper training, resources, and approach to the situation might expect to succeed at Average tasks slightly more often than he fails.

An Average task adds two Difficulty dice (◆◆) to the skill check's dice pool.

### HARD TASKS (◆◆◆)

A Hard task is much more demanding of a character. Success is certainly feasible, but failure is far from surprising. A typical character with the proper training, resources, and tools for the situation should expect failure at Hard tasks more often than success—especially without Destiny or other advantages on his side.

A Hard task adds three Difficulty dice (◆◆◆) to the skill check's dice pool.

## DAUNTING TASKS (◆◆◆◆)

A Daunting task taxes a character, pushing him to his limits. Success may be difficult to achieve, but it's certainly possible. A typical character with the proper training, resources, and tools for the situation will likely experience failure more often than success at Daunting tasks and may wish to look for some beneficial circumstances to aid him.

A Daunting task adds four Difficulty dice (◆◆◆◆) to the skill check's dice pool.

## FORMIDABLE TASKS (◆◆◆◆◆)

Formidable tasks seem nigh impossible. In fact, if casually approached, a Formidable task is most likely impossible. However, with proper planning, a well-trained and well-equipped character has a chance at success. Typical characters almost always fail at Formidable tasks. Even trained veterans fail Formidable tasks more often than they succeed. Failure seems inevitable unless the character can apply one or more advantages, such as Destiny Points or bonuses from specific equipment, talents, or assistance.

A Formidable task adds five Difficulty dice (◆◆◆◆◆) to the skill check's dice pool.

## IMPOSSIBLE TASKS

There are some situations in which the chance of success is impossibly low. In almost all cases, the GM simply states that any such check automatically fails without needing the player to assemble and roll a pool of dice.

However, the GM may decide to allow a PC to attempt a check where success is extremely improbable—throwing a grenade in hopes that it puts out a fire; scaling a perfectly smooth wall; or using reason to calm a rampaging rancor. Allowing PCs to attempt an impossible task should be relegated to critical moments in a story's arc or truly life-or-death situations only.

To prevent players from abusing these opportunities, attempting an impossible task automatically requires the player to spend one Destiny Point. The player gains no benefits for doing so, beyond being able to attempt the task in the first place. The player also may not spend any additional Destiny Points on the check. For simplicity, an impossible task imposes the same number of Difficulty dice as a **Formidable** (◇◇◇◇◇) task.

# BUILDING A BASIC DICE POOL

Now that the three primary building blocks of a skill check's dice pool have been discussed, all that remains is to show how the dice pool is actually assembled.

When a character wants to attempt some sort of action that might have a chance of failure, the player makes a skill check. The skill check uses the character's appropriate skill: Athletics for breaking down doors, Knowledge for recalling facts, or Charm for convincing a guard to let the character enter, for example. Each skill also has a linked characteristic: Brawn for Athletics, Intellect for Knowledge, and Presence for Charm, for instance. To make a skill check, the character assembles a dice pool.

There are two sides to every basic dice pool: the side to which the player contributes (in the form of Ability dice ◆ and Proficiency dice ◯) and the side to which the GM contributes (in the form of Difficulty dice ◆, Challenge dice ⬡, Boost dice ☐, and Setback dice ■). Additional factors may modify the number and type of dice for a check. When building a dice pool, every aspect of the player's and GM's contributing dice should be explained and defined before the roll is made. The GM sets the difficulty level of the task once, prior to the roll. After creating the base dice pool, either side may have the opportunity to upgrade dice.

## APPLYING SKILLS AND CHARACTERISTICS

A character's skill training and the associated characteristic are equally important in building a dice pool. When a task is attempted, the GM determines which skill is most appropriate. The skill used determines which characteristic is used. For example, if the character is attempting to bypass a security terminal by slicing its alarm system, the skill check would use the Computers skill, which is linked to the Intellect characteristic. The ratings for these two attributes determine the number of Ability and Proficiency dice that are added to the dice pool.

A player can start building the dice pool once the proper skill and characteristic are determined. To add dice to the pool, the player compares the PC's ranks of skill training to the linked characteristic's rating.

The higher of the two values determines how many Ability dice are added to the skill check's dice pool. Then the player **upgrades** a number of those Ability dice equal to the lower of the two values. If a character is unskilled (possesses no ranks) in the necessary skill, then zero is automatically the lower value, and the character will rely solely on the appropriate characteristic. (This also applies if the character has a zero in the corresponding characteristic; however, in practice, it's almost impossible for a character to have a zero in a characteristic.)

## APPLYING TASK DIFFICULTY

After determining which skill and related characteristic the character uses to attempt the task, the GM then chooses the level of difficulty for the task by consulting **Table 1–3: Difficulty Levels**, on page 26.

The difficulty level of the task determines the number of Difficulty dice that the player must add to the pool. For example, an **Average (◆ ◆) skill check** means the player adds two Difficulty dice to the dice pool.

In some cases, the GM may upgrade one or more of these Difficulty dice by removing them from the dice pool and replacing them with an equal number of Challenge dice ⬟. Difficulty dice are usually upgraded into Challenge dice when a character faces skilled opposition or particularly challenging circumstances, or when the GM invests Destiny Points to make a check more challenging.

After setting the difficulty level for the task, the GM adds the corresponding number of Difficulty dice to the task's dice pool. If no other factors are deemed to influence the outcome of the attempt, the basic dice pool is now complete and can be rolled to determine success or failure, as well as any potential side effects.

## MODIFYING A DICE POOL

If there are no other influences or contributing factors that may impact the outcome of a check, the dice pool may consist solely of dice representing the acting character's skill and characteristic, along with the dice representing the difficulty level set by the GM. However, the *Star Wars* universe is a vast place where any number of environmental effects can impact the actions taken by the characters. Howling gale-force winds caused by atmosphere escaping through a breach in a starship hull can negatively impact any action, while a motionless space pirate silhouetted by a bright light is a much easier target to hit. If an action is important enough to assemble and roll a dice pool, there's a good chance other factors are involved.

These other factors affect or modify the dice pool in a number of ways. The most common ways are by adding dice, upgrading/downgrading dice, and removing dice. These modifications may be triggered by the players or the GM, or they may simply make sense given the environment and situation. Examples of factors that warrant modification of the dice pool include obstructing terrain, poor lighting, tactical advantages, time constraints, superior equipment, special talents, unlocked career abilities, investment of Destiny

There may come times when the GM is unsure whether a situation should have the difficulty level increased or whether dice should be added or upgraded. The difficulty should be set based on the task itself, not on the circumstances surrounding that specific attempt at the task. In general, once set, the difficulty level remains the same, regardless of who, what, when, or why that particular task is attempted.

Upgrading (or downgrading) dice is not usually necessary unless a specific rule or ability calls for it. These situations are defined by the individual abilities, and are generally not applied arbitrarily by the GM.

If the circumstances for a particular execution of a task are unique, then the GM may decide the task warrants the addition of Boost or Setback dice. Added dice should reflect the elements that make this attempt distinct or special. As a general rule, if the GM feels that a skill check has distinct factors that could modify the outcome, he should consider using Boost and Setback dice.

multiple Setback dice to the dice pool. It's important to note that while these dice are essentially mirror opposites in their use, **Boost dice and Setback dice do not cancel each other out**. If the situation warrants the addition of two Boost dice and one Setback die, all three dice (☐ ☐ ■) are added to the dice pool.

The use of Boost dice and Setback dice is a common device all players can use to help reinforce important elements of the story. Players should describe their characters' actions in detail, pointing out both advantages and disadvantages that may influence a particular action.

Some equipment may add Boost dice ☐ to a pool to reflect superior craftsmanship, while talents may allow a player to add Boost dice ☐ to a pool to reflect special training or aptitudes that apply to the situation. Maneuvers like aiming may also allow a player to add Boost dice ☐ to a pool. Conversely, some effects may specifically impose Setback dice ■, such as the defined effects of a Critical Injury or a penalty for using inferior tools for a delicate task.

While the players may suggest the addition of Boost or Setback dice, the GM is the final arbiter, deciding which and how many dice are added to the pool. The GM does have access to helpful guidelines when making those decisions and should use common sense depending on the way the scene and action have been described. See the **Positive Dice and Negative Dice** sidebar on page 17 for examples of the types of situations that may warrant the addition of Boost or Setback dice.

Points, and Critical Injuries. The following sections describe these modifications in more detail.

It's also important to note that when modifying a dice pool, players perform the modifications in a specific order. First, players assemble the basic pool, and then they add additional dice. Next, they upgrade dice. Then they downgrade dice. Finally, they remove dice.

## ADDING DICE

One way to modify the basic dice pool is to add dice to reflect environmental conditions or various advantages and disadvantages. This is done primarily through the use of Boost and Setback dice. As a general rule, one Boost die ☐ is added to the dice pool for each bonus that would help the character succeed, and one Setback die ■ is added for each disadvantage impeding success.

A single Boost die ☐ is often enough to represent the benefits provided by useful gear, ample time, superior position, or the element of surprise. If more than one of these advantages is applicable, the GM may allow multiple Boost dice to be added to the dice pool.

Likewise, a single Setback die ■ is usually enough to reflect the impact of detrimental or obstructing effects like poor lighting, inferior supplies, harsh environments, or outside distractions. If more than one of these disadvantages is applicable, the GM may add

## UPGRADING AND DOWNGRADING DICE

Game effects can improve dice, making a weaker die stronger. Likewise, circumstances can turn a potent die into a weaker one. Improving a die is called upgrading, while weakening a die is called downgrading. Beyond the upgrading based on a character's ranks

Certain rules may call for a player to upgrade or downgrade the ability or difficulty of a dice pool. For example, the Dodge talent allows a character to upgrade the difficulty of a combat check made against him by a certain value. Upgrading or downgrading the ability of a pool refers to upgrading Ability dice ◆ into Proficiency dice ⬡ or downgrading Proficiency dice ⬡ into Ability dice ◆. Likewise, upgrading or downgrading the difficulty of a pool refers to upgrading Difficulty dice ◇ into Challenge dice ⬡ or downgrading Challenge dice ⬡ into Difficulty dice ◇.

in a skill or characteristic (see **Applying Skills and Characteristics**, page 27), upgrading and downgrading dice most often occur when one of the participants invests a Destiny Point in a skill check. Certain talents and special abilities also allow a character to upgrade or downgrade dice.

## UPGRADING DICE

Upgrading dice is a mechanic specific to Ability dice and Difficulty dice, and these are the only two types of dice that can be upgraded. When an Ability die ♦ is upgraded, it is converted into a Proficiency die ⬡. When a Difficulty die ♦ is upgraded, it is converted into a Challenge die ⬣.

When a special talent or effect calls for one or more dice to be upgraded, the player first determines how many dice are to be upgraded. Once this is determined, the player removes that number of Ability dice ♦ or Difficulty dice ♦ from the pool and replaces them with an equal number of either Proficiency dice ⬡ or Challenge dice ⬣. When an effect requires a player to upgrade dice, the rules always state whether Ability dice ♦ or Difficulty dice ♦ are being upgraded.

## UPGRADING MORE DICE THAN AVAILABLE

Sometimes a player may need to upgrade Ability dice into Proficiency dice but has no more Ability dice left in the pool. In this case, the player performs the following steps. First, he determines how many die upgrades remain. Then, using one upgrade, he adds one additional Ability die ♦ to the pool. If any upgrade opportunities remain, he then upgrades the newly added Ability die ♦ into a Proficiency die ⬡. This process is repeated until all remaining upgrades have been applied.

Likewise, if a player needs to upgrade Difficulty dice into Challenge dice but there are no more Difficulty dice in the pool, the same process is followed. First, one additional Difficulty die ♦ is added; then, if any more upgrades remain, the Difficulty die ♦ is upgraded into a Challenge die ⬣, and so on.

## DOWNGRADING DICE

Downgrading dice is also a specific mechanic, and it applies only to Proficiency dice and Challenge dice. When a Proficiency die ⬡ is downgraded, it becomes an Ability die ♦. When a Challenge die ⬣ is downgraded, it becomes a Difficulty die ♦.

Special talents or effects may call for one or more dice to be downgraded. The player first determines how many dice are to be downgraded. Once this is determined, the player removes that number of Proficiency dice ⬡ or Challenge dice ⬣ from the pool and replaces them with an equal number of either Ability dice ♦ or Difficulty dice ♦. When an effect requires a character to downgrade dice, the rules always state whether Proficiency dice ⬡ or Challenge dice ⬣ are being downgraded.

## DOWNGRADING MORE DICE THAN AVAILABLE

There may be situations in which a player needs to downgrade more Proficiency dice ⬡ into Ability dice ♦ or Challenge dice ⬣ into Difficulty dice ♦ than are available. If all of the potential dice are already in their downgraded form, any further downgrades are ignored.

## UPGRADES AND DOWNGRADES IN THE SAME POOL

Sometimes abilities will call for both upgrades and downgrades in the same dice pool. When this occurs, all upgrades are applied first. Then, any downgrades are applied. This is important, since upgrading dice could add more dice to the overall pool.

## REMOVING DICE

Just like some effects add Boost dice ▢ or Setback dice ▪ to a pool, some effects remove dice from the pool before they are ever rolled. Most often, this is a result of character talents that allow the removal of Setback dice ▪ to reflect a level of expertise in overcoming minor distractions or disadvantages that would rattle a less experienced character. In a similar fashion, a skilled enemy may have a talent that removes Boost dice ▢ from skill checks made against that enemy.

The individual talent or effect describes what circumstances warrant the removal of dice, as well as the number and type of dice to be removed. If an ability would remove more dice of a type than there are in the dice pool, the maximum number of dice available are removed, and any additional removals are ignored.

Removing dice is done after all other dice have been added and all upgrades and downgrades have been applied.

# INTERPRETING THE POOL

After a dice pool is rolled, the players and GM evaluate the results to resolve the outcomes. The first outcome to resolve is the success or failure of the skill check. Then, the players can determine if any significant side effects—good, bad, or both—are triggered. Whether the task is attempted amidst the chaos of a punishing planetary bombardment or in an Imperial interrogation room, nearly anything can happen.

## SUCCESSES AND FAILURES

If the roll for a skill check results in both Success symbols ✷ and Failure symbols ▼, the total number of each type of symbol is compared. Each Failure symbol ▼ cancels one Success symbol ✷. After the cancellations due to Failure symbols ▼ have been made, a pool will have one or more Success symbols ✷ or one or more Failure symbols ▼ remaining, or those symbols will be evenly canceled out.

During this step, it's important to note that a Triumph symbol ❖ contributes one Success ✷ to the pool, in addition to any special effects it may trigger. Likewise, a Despair symbol ▽ contributes one Failure ▼ to the pool, in addition to its special effects.

If all Successes ✷ and Failures ▼ in the pool are canceled out, or if there are any net Failures ▼ remaining, the skill check fails. If at least one Success ✷ remains, the skill check succeeds. **Remember, a dice pool must have at least one Success symbol ✷ remaining for a skill check to succeed.**

## ADVANTAGE AND THREAT

It's also likely for a skill check to result in Advantage symbols ❂, Threat symbols ⬡, or both. The player adds up the total number of Threat symbols ⬡ and compares that number to the total number of Advantage symbols ❂. Each Threat symbol ⬡ cancels one Advantage symbol ❂. After all Threat symbols ⬡ have canceled Advantage symbols ❂, a pool will have one or more Advantage symbols ❂, or one or more Threat symbols ⬡ remaining, or those symbols will be evenly canceled out.

Having one or more net Advantage symbols ❂ indicates a positive side effect or benefit. Having one or more net Threat symbols ⬡ indicates a negative side effect or complication. If all the Advantage ❂ and Threat ⬡ symbols cancel each other out, there are no additional effects. The positive and negative side effects can occur regardless of whether the task succeeds or fails.

Advantage ❂ and Threat ⬡ can be used to fuel a wide variety of side effects. The player rolling the skill check generally chooses how to spend Advantage ❂, such as by triggering a weapon's special quality, performing an additional maneuver, or recovering some strain. Various weapons, talents, and equipment may have special uses for Advantage ❂.

Threat ⬡ is generally spent by the GM to impose some sort of complication, with more severe complications requiring more Threat ⬡. Threat ⬡ can result in side effects such as suffering strain, providing an opportunity to an opponent, falling prone, being subjected to environmental effects, or a task taking longer to complete than expected. Various talents, environments, and opponents may have special uses for Threat ⬡.

For more about using Advantage or suffering from Threat, see page 210 and 211.

## TRIUMPH AND DESPAIR

Two symbols represent far more potent effects than the others. Triumph ❖ and Despair ▽ indicate special cases and operate slightly differently than the other symbols. Unlike Success and Failure (✷ and ▼) or Advantage and Threat (❂ and ⬡), Triumph and Despair (❖ and ▽) do not completely cancel each other out. Rather, they indicate an especially positive or unfortunately dire side effect.

Remember that it's possible for a skill check to result in both ❖ and ▽ symbols. In this case, **both results are interpreted separately**. As with Threat, it's possible for a skill check to succeed but still impose a Despair effect, or fail but still trigger a Triumph effect. For more about the specific applications of Triumph and Despair, see page 210 and 211.

### TRIUMPH ❖

A Triumph symbol ❖ has two effects. First, each Triumph symbol ❖ counts as one Success symbol ✷. Second, a Triumph result indicates an unexpected boon or significantly beneficial effect related to the task. Many weapons and talents have side effects that can be triggered using a Triumph result. Otherwise, the scenario or GM may present further options for using Triumph. It's important to keep in mind that while a Triumph symbol ❖ does add a Success symbol ✷ to the pool, the presence of one or more Triumph symbols ❖ does not automatically make the skill check successful.

Triumph can be thought of as an enhanced, more powerful version of Advantage. For example, a single Triumph symbol ⊕ can trigger any weapon's special quality or inflict a Critical Injury, while without a Triumph, these effects require a certain number of Advantage symbols ❂. Or, while Advantage may allow a character to recover strain, in the right situation, a Triumph ⊕ may allow him to heal a wound.

### DESPAIR ▽

A Despair symbol ▽ also has two effects. First, each Despair symbol ▽ counts as one Failure symbol ▼. Second, a Despair result indicates an unfortunate consequence, significant complication, or dire effect related to the task. The opponent's abilities, the environment, or the encounter description may offer different options for using Despair. Otherwise, the GM adjudicates the results of Despair symbols ▽ based on the situation. It is important to keep in mind that while a Despair symbol ▽ does add a Failure symbol ▼ to the pool, the presence of one or more Despair symbols ▽ does not automatically mean the skill check has failed.

Despair can be viewed as an upgraded, more potent form of Threat. For example, a single Despair symbol ▽ may trigger effects that would normally require several Threat symbols ❂. Despair may be significant enough to inflict wounds instead of strain,

cause an important piece of equipment to break, make a weapon jam or run out of ammo, or, when coupled with failure, make a grenade explode in the user's hand.

### UNLIMITED POSSIBILITIES

With the opportunity for success or failure, as well as the myriad side effects made possible through one or more Advantage, Threat, Triumph, or Despair symbols, no two skill checks are the same. Hundreds of outcomes are possible with almost every skill check. A character may achieve a high-magnitude success with no other complications, a low-magnitude success with Advantage, or a moderate success with Advantage that is tempered with Despair. Likewise, a failed check may have a silver lining if accompanied by Advantage or Triumph, or it may create a truly dire situation when accompanied by both Threat and Despair.

The sheer number of possibilities provides opportunities to narrate truly memorable action sequences and scenes. Nearly anything can happen in the heat of the moment; even a single shot fired at an Imperial Star Destroyer might hit some critical component that results in its destruction. Players and GMs alike are encouraged to take these opportunities to think about how the symbols can help move the story along and add details and special effects that create action-packed sessions.

# OTHER TYPES OF CHECKS

The standard skill check using a basic dice pool can be used to resolve the vast majority of tasks in a game session. However, there may be some situations that require a slightly different approach to properly resolve. Are the characters involved in a high-stakes negotiation, competing with multiple factions for their goal? Or are they racing to escape the clutches of Imperial agents hot on their trail? In addition to the standard skill check, FORCE AND DESTINY uses opposed checks, competitive checks, and assisted checks.

**Opposed checks** are often used when the success or failure of a task is strongly influenced by an opponent. **Competitive checks** can be used to determine which character performs better when two or more characters are attempting the same task. **Assisted checks** are simply variations of other checks but with two or more characters working together.

# OPPOSED CHECKS

An opposed check occurs when someone is actively trying to prevent a character from succeeding, or when one character is trying to overcome or get past another. For example, a Force-sensitive Sentinel lies to an Imperial governor, claiming to know nothing about the ancient Jedi holocron that recently vanished from the governor's collection. The Sentinel's Deception check might be opposed by the governor's Vigilance.

Opposed checks are most often applicable when a task involves directly opposing the task that another character is performing, or when a task involves trying to go unnoticed, undetected, or undiscovered by someone else.

Like standard checks, opposed checks add ◆ and potentially ⬡ to the skill check's dice pool. However, rather than simply being assigned by the GM, the difficulty of an opposed check is determined by a quick comparison of the opposing character's relevant characteristic and skill ranks.

Building the active character's dice pool starts out following the same procedures as those for a basic dice pool. Based on the character's relevant characteristic and skill ranks, ◆ are added, and some may be upgraded into ⬡. The opposition then introduces ◆ and ⬡ based on its own relevant characteristic and skill ranks. The higher of the opposition's characteristic and skill values determines how many ◆ are added to the pool, while the lower value indicates how many of those dice are upgraded into ⬡ (see **Upgrading Dice**, on page 30).

---

### EXAMPLE: OPPOSED CHECKS

Kaveri Ra, a Togruta Seeker, is trying to sneak up on a wild nexu without being detected. Kaveri has Agility 4 and Stealth 2, building an initial dice pool of four Ability dice, two of which are upgraded to Proficiency dice (◆◆○○ in total). The nexu has Cunning 2 and Perception 1. Therefore, the opposition adds two Difficulty dice (◆◆) to the check, one of which is subsequently upgraded to a Challenge die (⬣). If there are no other factors, the skill check has six dice: ◆◆○○◆◆.

---

# COMPETITIVE CHECKS

Competitive checks occur when several people are trying to accomplish the same goal at the same time or are trying to determine who performs a task better than another. When multiple characters are attempting the same task and the players need to determine who accomplishes the task first or performs it better, or to measure some other outcome, they are engaging in a competitive check.

For example, two characters engage in a friendly arm-wrestling contest aboard their starship. Each one has the same goal: to win the match by pinning the opponent's arm. The winner can be determined through a competitive check to see who outperforms the other. Additional examples include several pilots navigating an asteroid training course, or two politicians trying to win over an undecided crowd during a council hearing.

For a competitive check, the GM assigns a difficulty level for the task, and each character involved in the competition makes a skill check based on that difficulty. When characters make a competitive check, it's important to track how many total ✬ they generate with their respective dice pools. The character with the most total ✬ "wins" the check. If none of the characters succeed at the check, then none win, and the competitive check results in a draw. If two or more characters generate the same number of ✬, the check goes to a tiebreaker to see if the draw can be resolved.

Although ✪ and ⊕ still provide their customary effects in these situations, they also provide one additional benefit. If the two characters tie with the number of net ✬ they generate, the character with the greater number of ⊕ becomes the winner. If the characters are also tied for number of ⊕, the character with more total ✪ is declared the winner.

If the characters are still tied after evaluating these categories, the competitive check is a draw. In this case, the GM may simply appoint a winner, declare that all tied parties have lost, resolve the draw with another competitive check, or find some other way to settle the competition.

---

### EXAMPLE: COMPETITIVE CHECKS

Belandi the Mirialan Consular and Pon the Nautolan Warrior are each attempting to convince a local antiquities dealer that he should sell one of them a crystal that either could use in constructing a lightsaber. The GM decides that making their arguments will require a **Hard (◆◆◆) Leadership check**. Belandi has Presence 3 and Leadership 2, while Pon has Presence 2 and Leadership 1. Belandi generates ✬ ✬ ✪ ✪. Despite his inferior Presence and Leadership, however, Pon manages to succeed, generating ✬ ⊕ ❂ ❂ ❂. Pon wins the competitive check based on the tiebreaker (since the ⊕ also counts as a Success), convincing the dealer to tell him where the dealer got the crystal in addition to selling the crystal to him. However, Belandi also has ✪ ✪ to resolve, while Pon must contend with ❂ ❂ ❂. Perhaps even though Pon won the argument, the dealer saw how desperate he was to get the crystal, and gouged him on the price. Meanwhile, the dealer took a liking to Belandi and gave her a discount on anything else she wanted to purchase from his shop.

---

## ASSISTED CHECKS

Some tasks are important or challenging enough that help is required—or at the least appreciated. Fortunately, characters can—and should—provide assistance to each other in performing a variety of tasks. Over the course of normal narrative play, providing assistance is easy. A player explains how his character wants to help with the task. If the explanation is reasonable, the GM may allow that assistance. There are two types of assistance that can be provided: skilled assistance and unskilled assistance.

### SKILLED ASSISTANCE

Assistance works best when the assisting party brings additional insight or expertise to the task. When a character with a higher characteristic or skill rating provides assistance to another character, the dice pool may use one character's characteristic and the other character's skill rating.

> **EXAMPLE: SKILLED ASSISTANCE**
>
> Belandi the Consular is assisting Kaveri the Seeker with an Astrogation check to set hyperdrive coordinates. Kaveri has Intellect 2 and Astrogation 3, and Belandi has Intellect 4 and Astrogation 0. Kaveri's player chooses to use Belandi's Intellect 4 and Kaveri's Astrogation 3 when making the skill check, resulting in the following dice pool: ◆ ⬡ ⬡ ⬡.

### UNSKILLED ASSISTANCE

If the assisting party does not have a higher characteristic or skill rating, so that using either rating would provide no benefit to the other character, the GM may add ☐ to the dice pool (representing the fact that the additional assistance is still providing some benefit).

> **EXAMPLE: UNSKILLED ASSISTANCE**
>
> Later, Kaveri finds herself needing to assist Belandi in tending to a comrade's wounds. Belandi has Intellect 4 and Medicine 2, while Kaveri has Intellect 2 and no ranks in Medicine. Kaveri cannot provide skilled assistance, so Belandi gains one Boost die on the skill check to reflect Kaveri's attempts to help, resulting in the following dice pool: ◆ ◆ ⬡ ⬡ ☐.

### ASSISTANCE RESTRICTIONS

The GM can require that certain conditions be met in order for Player Characters or other parties to offer assistance. To assist in tending to an injury, the assisting character might need to be next to the patient, or to assist with translating an ancient holocron, the assisting character might need to have access to the holocron.

Generally, only one character can provide assistance at a time. However, the GM may decide that certain situations can accommodate more people. In this case, only one assisting character can offer his characteristic or skill rating, and all other participating characters contribute ☐ to the check.

### ASSISTANCE AND TIMING

During combat or structured encounters, when initiative and the order in which characters act is more important, assistance can be accomplished by performing the assist maneuver. The assist maneuver allows an engaged ally to benefit from assistance provided by the acting character on the ally's next skill check. Assistance lasts only until the assisted character's next activation.

For more on the assist maneuver, see **Chapter VI: Conflict and Combat**.

# OTHER KEY ELEMENTS

Even when things are at their worst, Player Characters are capable of rising above adversity to face challenges head-on. Whether they are able to shrug off wounds that would kill lesser folk, focus their will to manipulate the Force in some way, or call upon their experiences to fuel higher levels of proficiency, Player Characters are a breed apart. This section describes a number of these key elements, including character talents, Destiny Points, experience and development, and derived attributes such as wound and strain thresholds.

## TALENTS

Whereas skills represent what a Player Character knows, his practiced disciplines, or the experience he applies in a particular area, talents are a much broader class of special ability. Talents represent various tricks, techniques, and knacks PCs pick up over the course of their careers, or reflect their sheer determination to get things done. Each talent is a distinct special ability that provides the PC with an edge in certain situations. Keeping a rickety old freighter together with a combination of determination and baling wire, inspiring allies in the

The majority of talents are specific to a PC's given profession. Talent trees represent the natural flow of learning and experience that a Player Character gains throughout adventures. Talent trees are divided into five tiers, with the higher tiers representing remarkable abilities. Some talents may appear across multiple specializations, but at different tiers or costs.

# DESTINY POINTS

Player Characters are cut from a different cloth than most NPCs that populate the galaxy. Not only do they have access to skills and special talents to help them succeed, but PCs are also intimately connected to destiny. Destiny is that special spark that elevates heroes above commoners, imbuing an individual with enough significance in the galaxy's events to be a Player Character. Over the course of the PCs' adventures, destiny can intervene on their behalf for good or ill. Destiny might manifest in a positive way and provide a temporary advantage or boost to a PC's abilities. Or destiny might prove an ill omen and impose additional hardships and complications.

The concept of destiny and the Player Characters' ability to tap into and influence this resource is represented by Destiny Points. Destiny is interwoven with the Force, which pervades the galaxy with both light energy and dark energy. Destiny is one way the Force guides and surrounds the Player Characters.

Destiny Points are resources that can be invested by the players and GM for a variety of different effects. For example, Destiny Points may be used to upgrade Ability dice or Difficulty dice, or to trigger certain talents or special abilities.

face of a Force storm summoned up by a crazed dark side acolyte, and knowing just where to hit a rampaging rancor in order to take it down are all examples of talents at work.

While characteristics and skills are fairly universal—every PC has six characteristics, and everyone has access to all of the skills—talents are far more specific. Each career is defined by a series of unique talents bundled together in a format called a talent tree. These talent trees define specializations within each career, helping to distinguish the ways in which Player Characters advance along separate career paths.

Talents are divided into several categories and are either active or passive. Active talents typically require the player to state that his PC is using them. Some active talents have a cost or requirement associated with them, such as investing a Destiny Point, suffering strain, or using the talent as part of an attack action. Other talents are passive, meaning they are always "on" and don't need to be activated by the player. Passive talents either constantly provide their benefit or are automatically triggered under certain circumstances.

Some talents belong to a series of related talents. These may comprise either lower-level talents and their improved versions or identical talents taken multiple times for a cumulative effect. In the former case, an improved version of a talent completely replaces or upgrades the lower-level version. In the latter case, the talent is measured with a series of ranks. The more times that talent is taken, the more ranks it has and the greater the magnitude of its effects.

## THE POOL OF DESTINY

Like the Force, destiny has both a light side and a dark side. Light side Destiny Points favor the Player Characters and can be used to aid them in their actions. Dark side Destiny Points impede the PCs and are used by the GM to imperil and complicate their actions. The light side and dark side are two sides of the same coin, struggling for balance, each enduring the effects of the other side's strengths and exploiting the other side's weaknesses. As the pool of light side destiny ebbs, the dark side's Destiny pool grows. As dark side Destiny Points are consumed, light side Destiny Points are replenished.

### PREPARING THE DESTINY POOL

Each player with a PC rolls one Force die ⬡ (the GM does not roll a ⬡) to determine the current Destiny pool before the start of each game session. The results of the Force dice are tallied to become the starting Destiny pool for that session. For example, a player who rolls one light side symbol (○) adds one light side Destiny Point to the session's Destiny pool. A player who rolls two dark side symbols (● ●) adds two dark side Destiny Points to the Destiny pool.

Once set, the size of the Destiny pool does not change for that session. Before the next session begins, players roll to generate a new Destiny pool, which may have a different number and composition of Destiny Points. While the Destiny pool size is fixed for a session, the number of light side and dark side Destiny Points available can change frequently as players and GM call on destiny to influence their actions.

### TRACKING DESTINY POINTS

Destiny Points are easily tracked using the Destiny Point tokens found in the Star Wars ROLEPLAYING DICE pack. Players can also use gaming tokens, glass beads, or any other convenient method. Two-sided tokens or chips work especially well. Ideally, one side is colored or designated to represent light side Destiny Points, and the other side to represent dark side Destiny Points.

## HOW DESTINY POINTS ARE USED

All players and the GM can tap into destiny by using the Destiny Points in the pool. There are several distinct ways players and GMs spend Destiny Points. The players may only spend light side Destiny Points, and the GM may only spend dark side Destiny Points.

When a player spends a light side Destiny Point, it's converted into a dark side Destiny Point once the current action is resolved. When the GM spends a dark side Destiny Point, it's then converted into a light side Destiny Point. Conversion takes place at the end of the action during which the Destiny Point was used, preventing players or GMs from immediately spending a just-converted Destiny Point. Destiny is a powerful resource, but it's limited. A player can spend only one light side Destiny Point during a single action, and so should think carefully about how to use destiny before doing so. The GM likewise is limited to spending only one dark side point per action.

The following section explains some of the ways in which Destiny Points can be used. Unless noted otherwise in an option's description, both the players and the GM have access to that option.

### A HELPING HAND

All characters have the opportunity to call on destiny to enhance any skill check they are about to attempt. A player may spend one Destiny Point to upgrade his starting dice pool by one. In other words, the player may upgrade ◆ into the superior ⬡. The GM may spend a dark side Destiny Point in this way to upgrade

an NPC's dice pool. Additional information on upgrading dice can be found on page 30.

### RAISING THE STAKES

Destiny can also be used to help keep characters out of harm's way. Characters can call on destiny to make an opponent's skill check more challenging. A single player may spend one light side Destiny Point to upgrade the difficulty of any NPC's skill check by one. This refers to upgrading a ◆ into the more potent ⬢. The GM may spend a dark side Destiny Point in this way to upgrade difficulty in a PC's dice pool. Additional information on upgrading dice can be found on page 30.

### SPECIAL ABILITIES AND TALENTS

Many powerful talents allow characters to spend Destiny Points for various effects. For example, a savvy Ambassador can spend a Destiny Point to immediately recover from strain equal to his Presence rating. Many other uses exist as well—see the individual talent descriptions for details.

### LUCK AND DEUS EX MACHINA

Destiny can also be used by the players to introduce "facts" and additional context directly into the narrative. The GM already does this by managing and directing the story, but this use of Destiny Points provides the players with a means to make contributions as well.

Imagine the Player Characters land on a planet they expected to have a breathable atmosphere, only to find that a leak at the gas mining facility has rendered the air toxic. One of the players suggests spending a Destiny Point, saying, "Good thing you remembered to pack those rebreathers last time we were in dry dock, Arkhan." While none of the players may have specifically mentioned or listed rebreathers before, it's a sensible and creative addition to the game. If the GM agrees, the Destiny Point is spent, and the player's suggestion becomes a true statement—there are rebreathers handy.

Similarly, a player may spend a Destiny Point in this manner to suggest finding a spare stimpack while quickly scavenging through a medical facility, or to propose introducing a terrain feature the Player Character can duck behind for cover.

Using Destiny Points narratively is a great way to keep all of the players involved and the story moving forward. However, the GM has final say over what is and is not acceptable. Players should not abuse this use of Destiny Points; the more outrageous or unlikely the suggestion, the more likely it is that the GM will curtail Destiny Point use. Ultimately, narrative use of Destiny Points allows the players to feel empowered as active participants in the game and story by rewarding their creativity and roleplaying. If a requested use of a Destiny Point would contribute toward this goal, the GM should consider allowing it.

## DESTINY POINT ECONOMY IN GAMEPLAY

All players and the GM are encouraged to use Destiny Points regularly, creating an ebb and flow of destiny over the course of a session. While the players could theoretically "lock" all the Destiny Points and simply not spend any light side Destiny Points to prevent the GM from using dark side Destiny Points against them, this works both against the spirit of the mechanics and the setting. Players who horde their Destiny Points may find the GM using other methods of putting pressure on the group, forcing them to reconsider their plan. It's perfectly acceptable for the GM to remind the players about using Destiny Points in play, such as by suggesting the use of Destiny Points if they are feeling overmatched by a tough enemy.

The Player Characters are wrapped up in the fate of the galaxy, and through their adventures, destiny will work both for and against them. When used wisely, Destiny Points provide tension and excitement by making routine checks more significant, adding an element of drama to the mundane, or helping provide a boost when the Player Characters are overwhelmed.

## THE LIMITS OF LUCK

Destiny is a powerful resource that must be used wisely—each player can invest only one Destiny Point in any single check. If a player chooses to invest a Destiny Point to upgrade an ◆ into a ⬡, for example, that player cannot also invest a Destiny Point to trigger one of his character's talents. The GM may also choose to invest one Destiny Point per skill check. This does introduce the possibility that both the player and the GM invest destiny in the same skill check, resulting in no net difference to the overall Destiny pool balance.

The active player (the player or GM forming the dice pool) always has the first chance to use a Destiny Point. Once that player has decided whether or not to use a Destiny Point, the other party involved in the check (the targeted player, or the GM in the case of an NPC) has the opportunity to respond and spend a Destiny Point as well. For example, if the GM declares he will spend a Destiny Point to upgrade an enemy's Ability die into a Proficiency die for an attack against a PC, that PC's player has the opportunity to then use a Destiny Point, either to upgrade one of the pool's ◆ into a ⬣, or perhaps to trigger one of the PC's talents.

# EXPERIENCE AND DEVELOPMENT

After surviving everything the Empire and the dark side of the Force has to throw at them, Player Characters are liable to learn from their successes—and mistakes—in order to better themselves in preparation for even greater challenges. Experience is the primary means by which players customize their characters. Each PC starts with a beginning pool of experience points that can be spent during character creation to train skills, improve characteristics, or acquire talents. During each session of a **FORCE AND DESTINY** campaign, Player Characters receive additional experience, which can also be spent to improve their skills, talents, and characteristics.

## STARTING EXPERIENCE POINTS

Player Characters begin with a number of experience points (XP) based on their species. The experience points used during character creation are the same "currency" as experience points received during play. If a player chooses to spend fewer experience points than budgeted during character creation, those points carry over into the game, and the PC has more experience points to spend once the adventures begin. More information on spending starting experience points can be found in **Chapter II: Character Creation**, on page 102.

## IMPROVING CHARACTERISTICS

Raising a characteristic during character creation costs ten times the value of the next highest rating. During character creation, no characteristic can be increased to higher than 5. During the course of play, no characteristic can be increased to higher than 6. Characteristics may only be purchased with experience points during character creation, not at any later time. During gameplay, characteristics can only be increased by acquiring specific high-tier talents. For more on raising characteristics, see page 102.

## SKILL TRAINING

Each skill has five ranks of training available. A Player Character may have already acquired several ranks of skill training from his starting career and specialization for free. PCs may train additional skills and gain additional ranks during character creation. Regardless of any species or career bonuses, no skill can be raised higher than rank 2 during character creation.

The cost for training skills falls into one of two categories: career skills and non-career skills. Training a career skill costs five times the value of the next highest rank. Training a non-career skill costs five times the value of the next highest rank plus 5 additional experience points. Players may purchase ranks in skills for their PCs during character creation or later during gameplay.

## ACQUIRING TALENTS

Talents are acquired from a Player Character's available talent trees, generally provided by their specialization choices. A PC can purchase any talents for which he is eligible. An eligible talent is any talent in the top row (which cost 5 experience points each), or any talent that is directly connected to an already-acquired talent. The cost of a talent varies according to which tier it occupies. Similar talents may have different costs for different PCs, based on their specializations. Player Characters may purchase talents during character creation or later during gameplay.

### ACQUIRING NEW SPECIALIZATIONS

Each Player Character starts with a single specialization within his chosen career. However, PCs may purchase additional specializations in order to gain access to a broader range of skills and talents. There is no limit on the number of specializations a PC may possess.

Acquiring a specialization allows a Player Character to spend experience points in the new specialization's talent tree, in addition to any he was able to access before. Most specializations have one or more bonus career skills as well. These skills now count as career skills for the PC. Player Characters can purchase specializations from any career. Purchasing an additional specialization within a PC's career costs ten times the total number of specializations he would possess after adding this new specialization. Purchasing non-career specializations costs ten times the total number of specializations he would possess after adding this new specialization, plus an additional 10 experience.

# DERIVED ATTRIBUTES

S ome character attributes are based on other choices made during character creation or over the course of a campaign. Some of these attributes may change frequently over the course of play or may be modified by talents, equipment, or various special abilities.

## WOUND THRESHOLD

A character's wound threshold represents how much physical damage he can withstand before he is knocked out. Wounds can be serious and lead to a Critical Injury. They can be treated with the Medicine skill, but it may take time to recover (droids use Mechanics to repair wounds).

A character's starting wound threshold is based on species and Brawn rating. After this initial value is determined, increases to Brawn rating do not increase a character's wound threshold; wound threshold improvements can then be acquired only by purchasing the appropriate talent, such as Toughened.

## STRAIN THRESHOLD

A character's strain threshold represents how much stress a character can withstand before becoming stunned, dazed, or otherwise incapacitated. Strain represents psychological or mental damage to the character. Strain is more easily suffered than wounds, and can even be used as a resource by players to trigger certain character abilities. Thankfully, characters recover from strain more quickly than from wounds.

A character's starting strain threshold is determined based upon species and Willpower rating. After this initial value is determined, increases to Willpower rating do not increase the character's strain threshold; strain threshold improvements are then acquired only by purchasing appropriate talents, such as Grit.

## DEFENSE

Defense determines how difficult a character is to hit in combat situations. Characters have both a ranged defense and a melee defense. A character's default value in both ranged defense and melee defense is zero. If a character's defense value is listed simply as "Defense" and not specifically defined by separate ranged and melee values, then the same value is applied to both ranged and melee defense.

Defense is most commonly gained by wearing armor or by adopting a defensive position in combat, such as taking cover. Some special talents may also increase one of a character's defense ratings.

## SOAK VALUE

A character's soak value determines how much incoming damage the PC can shrug off before taking real damage. The soak value is subtracted from any incoming damage to the character. Any damage remaining after subtracting the soak value becomes wounds applied against the character's wound threshold.

A character's default soak value is equal to his Brawn rating. After this initial value is determined, increases to Brawn rating **do** increase the character's soak value. Additional soak value bonuses are most often gained by wearing armor. Some talents may also increase a character's innate soak value.

# CHARACTER CREATION

*"There is another."*

–Yoda

**F**ORCE AND **D**ESTINY recounts the dark days when the evil Empire focused on destroying everyone who dabbled with the Force. Those Force-sensitives who hoped to survive had no choice but to remain hidden. Thus, in play, while some characters may attempt to recover lost information and embrace their connections to the Force, others may maintain that they have no such talents. Regardless of their beliefs, the inherent abilities of Force-sensitives can draw unwanted attention. Those who are strong in the Force become drawn to oppose the Galactic Empire—either out of a sense of conviction or a drive for survival.

Almost any living being in the galaxy can manifest affinity for the Force. Before beginning the process of generating the numbers and selecting the gear for each character, players and the Game Master should discuss the core concept for the campaign and consider what might bring together the group of Force-sensitive Player Characters.

## CREATING A HERO

Creating a character for FORCE AND DESTINY is done in just a few short steps (presented here), allowing players to get involved in the action right away. To create a character, each player needs access to this rulebook, a character sheet (found at the end of this book), and a pencil. Players also need access to ten-sided (d10) dice for rolling on certain charts. Finally, a few sheets of note paper are not necessary, but might be helpful.

Character generation uses a point-buy system, meaning each player has a budget of experience points he can invest in different aspects of his character. Selecting a character's species and career determines the character's starting characteristics and skills, as well as the character's starting experience points. After those initial choices, players invest their experience points to improve starting characteristics, acquire training in key skills, learn special talents, and even unlock additional talent trees.

# CHARACTER CONCEPT

The section that follows provides a way for a player to delineate a character via numbers and game mechanics. The central core of the idea for the character, however, must come from the player. Each person participating in the game needs to start out with the seed of a concept for a character who can manipulate the Force and travel throughout the *Star Wars* galaxy. Perhaps the character is an old hermit, someone who was once a Jedi who fought in the defense of the galaxy, but has since gone into hiding and seen his skills dwindle with disuse. Or the character might be a naive youth growing up on a homestead on the Outer Rim. He may not even realize the power that he can control, and the upcoming adventures will be a chance for him to grow into a hero who might save the galaxy.

At the earliest stages of character creation, the players and Game Master should have a detailed discussion about the types of characters to be created. If the GM has a specific campaign framework in mind, it could require the presence of specific types of skills or even focus on a limited subset of species. A campaign that takes place exclusively on the Core Worlds might have less need for the Survival skill, while one centered on the Galactic Civil War might focus more on combat skills than on skills related to diplomacy. Sometimes the GM might want to adjust the campaign based on the players' wishes, and the players are likely to appreciate the opportunity to tweak their initial character ideas. Information shared at this stage can help the players and Game Master work together to create characters that complement the types of stories envisioned for the campaign.

While some character concepts can be a better fit for a campaign, seldom is a concept truly wrong. Roleplaying games often work best when everyone is willing to work in a collaborative fashion. Constructive criticism as well as meaningful compromises during character creation can lead to a more fulfilling gameplay experience. Group members should be open to one another's ideas at this stage. Working together to bring out the most fun and entertaining aspects of different characters can be a great way for the players to establish a rapport that lasts throughout a campaign.

# GENERATION STEPS

To create a character, a player follows ten steps. Each step is summarized here and then fully explained later in the chapter.

### STEP 1: DETERMINE BACKGROUND

Each character starts as an idea. Does a player want to play a noble and aspiring knight working to save the poor and oppressed, a backwater shaman with mystical powers, or a deadly and feared warrior? Before starting the game, the player should take a few minutes to think about the character he wants to build and what he wants that character's background to be. Where did the character come from, what inspired him to leave his former life and pursue a life of adventure, and when did he first realize he might have a connection to the Force?

Perhaps the character lived a quiet life of luxury as an heir to a fortune in the Core Worlds. Alternatively, he could have been a struggling farm boy on the Outer Rim. The circumstances of his childhood—as well as the way he first encountered the Force—are certain to have colored his maturation process and his goals.

More information on developing the character's background begins on page 45.

### STEP 2: DETERMINE MORALITY

When creating a character in **FORCE AND DESTINY**, determining the character's Morality is a key decision made early in character creation. Force-sensitives must carefully consider the implications of the choices they make, particularly as they reflect the use of their Force abilities. Morality tracks how "good" and "evil" a character is. A character's starting Morality can affect other decisions a player makes during character creation, such as the type of character to play, the overall moral compass of the group, and the character's starting skills, characteristics, and gear.

Morality is presented in detail starting on page 48.

### STEP 3: SELECT A SPECIES

The Force interacts with all living things, regardless of their world of origin. Many are drawn to travel the breadth of the galaxy, interacting with other species as they answer the Force's call. Once players determine their characters' starting Morality, they choose what species their characters will be. A character's species establishes initial ratings in the characteristics of Brawn, Agility, Intellect, Cunning, Willpower, and Presence. Secondary characteristics, including wound and strain thresholds, are also determined by species. Finally, species have unique intrinsic abilities that further set them apart. Of course, once chosen, characters cannot change species.

More on the various species options for characters in **FORCE AND DESTINY** can be found on page 54.

### STEPS 4 AND 5: SELECT A CAREER AND SPECIALIZATION

Steps 4 and 5 are handled together, but represent two distinct choices that shape a Player Character: career and specializations.

## CAREER

After choosing a species, a player must next select the PC's career, choosing one of the six options presented. The career chosen reflects the character's philosophical approach to overcoming challenges, and can be thought of as a broad archetype of related skills and abilities. Each career can be explored through a range of specializations that share a common set of initial skills and focus on similar talents.

The choice of career establishes the central focus of the character's training, practices, and even professional experience. While not intended to limit a character, the choice of career does establish what kinds of skills and talents are going to be most readily available, as well as the roles the PC is likely to excel at within a group. Players should think of their character's career as an archetype that forms the initial framework for constructing their PC.

Each career has six associated career skills. These skills should be marked on the character sheet to indicate that they are career skills. During this step of character creation, the player may choose three of the six starting career skills and have his character gain one rank in each of the selected skills free (experience points are not spent to gain these ranks). The player may not choose the same skill more than once. Each career also gives the player character Force rating 1.

During play, career skills are less expensive to train and improve than non-career skills. As with species, players cannot change a character's career during gameplay.

The six careers in **Force and Destiny** begin on page 63.

## SPECIALIZATIONS

If a career is the broad framework for a Player Character's construction, specializations can be viewed as the materials added to the framework to fill it in and give it detail and distinction. As their name implies, specializations are specific areas of focus within a career. While linked by the career's common philosophy, each specialization takes a different, more focused approach to a particular aspect of the career. For example, while the Warrior career focuses on combat, the Warrior's Starfighter Ace specialization emphasizes space combat, while the Shii-Cho Knight specialization allows a character to focus on lightsaber fighting.

Each specialization within a career possesses a unique talent tree, available only to those who have chosen that specialization. The specialization also gives players access to certain career skills, allowing ranks in these skills to be purchased for fewer experience points. **Each character gains access to one specialization without spending experience at character creation. That specialization must be one of the specializations within the chosen career.**

Specializations grant the character access to four additional career skills, which should be marked on the character's sheet as career skills if they are not already marked. During this step of character creation, the player may choose two of the four additional career skills from his character's first specialization (and only his first) and gain one rank in each without spending experience. The same skill may not be chosen more than once. Remember, even if the player purchases additional specializations during Step 6, only the specialization selected during this step counts as the character's "first" specialization. Therefore, this is the only specialization that will grant the PC a free rank in two of its career skills.

Specific specializations are presented within the context of their associated career, beginning on page 67. A full list and descriptions of each talent in this book can be found starting on page 136.

## STEP 6: INVEST EXPERIENCE POINTS

The species a player selects for his character also establishes an initial pool of experience points (XP). These experience points can be spent to improve certain aspects of the character: to increase characteristics, purchase additional ranks in skills, acquire talents, learn new specializations, or even gain new Force powers. Players may spend their points in any combination of these areas, meaning that two Player Characters with the same species, career, and specialization still may end up very different from one another. During gameplay, characters will earn additional experience points based on their achievements and successes. Those points can also be spent to purchase new skill ranks, specializations, Force powers, and talents.

Information about spending experience points begins on page 102.

## STEP 7: DETERMINE DERIVED ATTRIBUTES

This step must be taken only after the player completes the previous steps. Several attributes can only be determined after a player fully establishes a character's starting characteristics and talents. The derived attributes are wound threshold, strain threshold, defense, and soak value.

Full information on calculating these attribute values can be found on page 104.

## STEP 8: DETERMINE MOTIVATION

A character's Motivation is his primary call to take action and experience adventures. For Force-sensitives, the Force is often linked to their calling, as it guides and motivates them just as it shapes the galaxy around them. In some instances, a character's primary Motivation is an overarching philosophical belief. Other characters focus on more concrete objectives, often associated with the desire to aid family or close allies. A few choose a specific cause that they hope to achieve within their lifetime, possibly moving on to another one should they ever achieve it.

There are three general categories of Motivation: Ambition, Cause, and Faith. Each of these Motivations has a list of specific manifestations. Alternatively, a player may obtain the Game Master's permission and create a different Motivation and its specific details.

Motivation has an important role to play in a character's progression. If a character acts true to Motivation, that PC may earn additional experience points at the end of a game session.

Different Motivations are presented on page 105.

## STEP 9: CHOOSE GEAR AND APPEARANCE

Once a player has defined his character's species, background, career, specialization, and any other important attributes, he can begin determining the descriptive details of his character. Height, weight, eye color, hair color and style (or tentacle or horn color), skin color, build, distinguishing features such as scars and tattoos, and choice of clothing are all descriptive details that can be determined narratively. This information can and often should be linked to the previous choices made for the PC; a character with a high Brawn may be more muscular, for instance, while a character raised on a desert planet may have skin that's weathered and darkened by the punishing sun.

Each PC also starts the game with 500 credits' worth of personal gear and weaponry. At this stage, the PC may select this gear.

Equipment selection is presented on page 107.

## STEP 10: DETERMINE GROUP RESOURCE

At the conclusion of the Clone Wars, the Jedi were eliminated from the galaxy. In the years that followed, Force practitioners needed to conceal their abilities or face extreme consequences. Information about the Force, particularly as encrypted in holocrons, represents a critical learning tool to any individual who wishes to learn the ways of the Jedi. Alternatively, the group may start with a ship, or even a mentor. This resource, shared among the group, is one of the things that has brought them together.

Information about starting resources begins on page 109.

# STEP 1: DETERMINE BACKGROUND

The Force fills the galaxy, from the most cosmopolitan Core World to the farthest outpost in the Outer Rim. Those who can hear the call of the Cosmic Force may come from anywhere; they hail from wildly diverse walks of life. When it comes to choosing a character's background, a player's options are limitless.

A significant portion of a Force initiate's attitudes can be based on the philosophy and background of his youth. Characters who enjoyed a comprehensive education while interacting with people of other cultures and worlds are likely to be more open-minded than those raised in a single culture. Individuals from primitive worlds, where each day's food depended on a successful hunt, likely see the world differently than those raised in a high-tech environment.

If the Force was considered a key part of the character's culture, there may have been a great deal of reverence and respect toward teachings associated with it. Other cultures may have treated the Force as nothing more than an old myth. Every character must come from somewhere, and the story of that origin is likely to have repercussions that affect career choice as well as Morality and Motivation.

A character's game statistics need not all directly reflect his background. Instead, the background is meant to provide depth to the character, offering insights on personality and mindset that are not evident in skills, talents, and Force abilities. Knowing a character's origin can often provide a useful framework for determining what goals the PC might have as well as the paths he might pursue to achieve those goals.

## CULTURAL BACKGROUND

Characters' cultural backgrounds frame many of the decisions they make. Backgrounds can determine the types of skills characters possess at the beginning of play as well as the types of solutions they bring to challenges. If they are accustomed to living in the natural world, they may not be as quick to look for technological solutions. Similarly, if every resource was precious during their youth, their attitude toward wealth and conservation is certainly different than that of characters who came from privilege.

If a character came from the homeworld of his species, some of these answers may be determined at the same time the species is chosen. However, most worlds have some variation in culture types and levels, particularly between different population centers. Alternatively, a character might have come from a colony world or could even have grown up on a world completely different from his homeworld, surrounded by an alien culture.

### COMFORTABLE WITH TECH

Many of the worlds and cultures across the galaxy have a high level of technological sophistication. Droids and the HoloNet are tools that many sentients use on a daily basis. Starships and repulsorlift craft are a common sight on many worlds, and characters are likely comfortable using these fantastic devices. Most adult individuals from these sorts of worlds enjoyed an education that included a solid grounding in engineering and the hard sciences. This level of technological familiarity is considered the norm for the civilized galaxy.

Most of the planets from the Core Worlds to the Outer Rim fall into this category. Even frontier and colonial worlds tend to have denizens familiar with standard galactic technologies, even if said technologies are rare or unavailable. These planets are typically a part of wider galactic society. Citizens of these worlds who wish to avoid technology must make a deliberate effort to do so.

### PRIMITIVE BACKWATER

Within the Outer Rim and the Unknown Regions, there remain worlds and civilizations isolated from the greater galaxy. Even among those that are aware of other worlds and cultures, many have only limited access to technologies. Some cultures—regardless of their location within the galaxy—choose to avoid technology or interaction with other worlds. Many of these hold a particular reverence for the natural world. Others simply feel that an overdependence on any but the most rudimentary of tools can be a corrupting influence.

A character from a primitive world often lacks a full understanding of the scope of technology. Some may routinely expect a device to be able to do virtually anything. Others may have little appreciation for a tool's abilities, preferring to perform tasks manually. Often, the attitude the character feels for devices is proportionate to his loyalty toward his homeworld. If he holds it in reverence, he may be reluctant to learn about tools and techniques from other places.

### THE PRIVILEGED FEW

Even on affluent worlds, there are individuals who enjoy lives of greater privilege than most. On worlds where basic necessities are precious, there exist some members of society who never want for those essentials. For children, a life of privilege is most often a quirk of birth. Generally, their family somehow earned the rank and lifestyle, and they benefit immensely from being born into it.

Characters with this background have had opportunities that most have not enjoyed. This typically includes a thorough education and can also encompass other life opportunities, such as travel and cultural interactions. This background colors the character's attitude toward wealth and material possessions. Some who choose to abandon these comforts look down upon others who continue to enjoy them.

### THE POOR AND HUNGRY

On some worlds, resources are so scarce that everyone must constantly scramble to obtain the basic necessities of life. From early childhood, individuals are expected to contribute in a meaningful way to increase their family's odds of survival. On worlds where resources are more readily available, there still exist subcultures where families live in desperation, constantly in search of their next meal.

Individuals who live in constant want may be able to accept this situation as the norm, readily learning to make do with the assets that are available and living this way for the rest of their lives. Alternatively, some become obsessed with material possessions, spending all of their time focused on obtaining more. Characters with either outlook often work carefully to plan and manage their resources. When someone isn't sure where the next meal may be coming from, it helps encourage them to be cautious in their actions. Of course, some characters with this background may be exceptionally cavalier in their endeavors, secure in the knowledge that they have nothing to lose.

## EXPERIENCING THE FORCE

The environment and circumstance of a character's youth can play a major factor in how that character interacts with the world and can inform the player's selection of skills. A society's attitude toward the Force frames the lives of those who are sensitive to its presence. Depending on their culture, characters' sensitivity to the Force could be a major blessing to display or a horrible secret to conceal. These early attitudes often play a major factor in determining the types of Force talents a character might have studied, as well as the amount of effort put into developing them.

### AN ANCIENT RELIGION

More than twenty years ago, then–Supreme Chancellor Palpatine wiped out the Jedi. Before he did so, the Jedi were figures of whom many people had heard, but with whom few had ever interacted. To most, they were a tiny and aloof band of warriors and peacekeepers, not people one interacted with on a daily basis.

After the purge, those few who had formerly had the most opportunity to interact with the Jedi, the people engaged in the work of galactic governance, worked directly for the man responsible for wiping out those same Jedi. Some dismissed the Jedi as a dangerous cult that had almost overthrown the galactic government. Some figured the best way to survive in the growing Galactic Empire was to forget the Jedi had ever existed. Some refused either of these paths, only to vanish quietly as they drew the attention of the Imperial Security Bureau. Many beings in the rest of the galaxy had never even seen a Jedi or experienced the Force. For them, it was all too easy to believe the Force was a hoax, and the Jedi were gone.

Now, the Galactic Empire works tirelessly to stamp out the last rumors and legends of the Jedi's existence. Many who live under the Empire's dominion believe the Force is little more than an outdated legend. Citizens who have the potential to use the Force almost never come to recognize their inborn talents. Instead, they simply attribute any signs of their ability to luck, spiritual favor, or some other natural ability. Most vigorously deny any connection to the Force, insisting that their skills and abilities are not enhanced by its influence. Learning to embrace the Force as well as to use his abilities deliberately could be a central part of a character's initial development.

### THE DUTY TO TRADITION

Even at the height of the Empire's power, the Force still plays a major cultural role on some worlds. In less sophisticated cultures, Force-sensitives may occupy leadership roles as shamans or spiritual advisors. Individuals could be inducted into an order during their early childhood, so that they could engage in a rigorous course of study. Such trainees are seldom given any other option but to embrace their education. The ability to manipulate the Force provides them with a moral obligation to use it for the betterment of their culture and the greater galaxy beyond it. The character may be selfless in making decisions to help others and may face the consequences which come from intuitive self-sacrifice.

### PRAGMATIC POWER

Characters who recognize their Force potential do not always readily acknowledge its spiritual associations. Some see their powers and talents as tools they can use to advance their lives or accomplish their goals. This may help them to be more successful in their career of choice, enabling them to transform the world in a way that fits with their personal philosophies.

Many deny the fundamental goodness or evil of the Force, insisting that consequences for success and failure are far more important than any spiritual elements. Such characters are no more or less likely to make choices or perform actions that could be classified as "good" than those that could be classified as "evil." However, in their minds, their preference for a certain moral choice is independent of the powers they wield. This can prove problematic if, for example, a character believes his righteous anger is a reasonable motivator for his actions. Such a character may constantly flirt with the dark side of the Force and never realize it.

Learning or denying Force philosophies and histories invariably plays into the stories of characters from this background. Eventually, the character likely learns of the truth of the Force. Whether he embraces this knowledge or denies it and continues on his chosen path can prove to be a very interesting opportunity for character development.

### ONE WITH THE FORCE

Some adepts are so deeply grounded in the Force that it influences their every action. These characters constantly perceive the world through its lens, and it decides their every thought. Often, their education has included a thorough grounding in Force philosophies, so that they choose to act with deliberate devotion to the light (or dark) side of the Force.

Such knowledge is deliberately suppressed in the Empire and thus incredibly hard to come by. However, it is not impossible. A character with this background may have been raised by one of the last Jedi to escape the purges, who, before dying, passed on a measure of knowledge of the Force to the character. Alternatively, the character may have known someone

who would have reason to be familiar with the Jedi and their knowledge. A former Republic soldier or sympathetic Senator, an old friend of the Jedi, or even an ally who worked with the Jedi but was not Force-sensitive may have escaped the Emperor's purges and passed on what he has learned. It may be that the character is one of those individuals, and as he has aged, he has realized that he too can tap into the power of the Force.

# HEEDING THE CALL

Whatever the character's background or understanding of the mysterious powers he can wield, eventually something occurred to inspire him to leave his former life behind and seek a life of adventure in the wider galaxy. The options for this turning point are limitless; below are a few possibilities.

### FLEEING THE EMPIRE

The Empire hunts down Force users diligently and enthusiastically. The character may have betrayed his affinity to the Force in some way, perhaps by anticipating someone's thoughts or saving someone's life by stopping a crashing speeder with his mind. Whatever the cause, the character is now hunted by Imperial agents and must flee his former life or be destroyed.

### DESIRE FOR UNDERSTANDING

Having realized he has some untapped power at his disposal, the character now wishes to know what this power is. Simple research on his home planet or via the HoloNet has yielded nothing, so he must set out into the wider galaxy to see what he can learn about his odd abilities.

### WITH GREAT POWER...

Some individuals cannot stand idly by while watching the evils the Empire inflicts on the galaxy. The character knows he's been given a gift that few others have. To squander it while innocents suffer would be the height of irresponsibility.

### ULTIMATE ABILITIES

Some characters see their strange abilities as a sign that they are destined for greatness. They can do things that others around them cannot. Clearly, this means they are a cut above the general population. To leave their life behind is merely the first step in a journey that may see them rise to become the ultimate power in the universe. Whether or not they use that power for good—or for evil—remains to be seen.

# STEP 2: DETERMINE MORALITY

**M**orality is, simply put, the measure of right and wrong. Though the *Star Wars* universe has shades of moral relativism, it is primarily a universe of good and evil. Morality measures how good or evil characters are. It is a measure of their actions, thoughts, and attitudes, and how they have helped, harmed, or hindered those around them. In addition, a character's Morality can often be shaped and guided by his personality, and therefore a character's emotional strengths and weaknesses can contribute to and affect his overall Morality. Most importantly, a character's Morality affects his use of the Force, and the Force can in turn affect a character's Morality. Thus in **Force and Destiny**, Morality is a character's single most important defining characteristic.

During character creation, players get the chance to customize their characters not only by selecting careers, skills, and specializations, but also by determining their characters' Moralities. Although some aspects of a character's Morality may change over time—allowing the character to become a better or worse person throughout the course of his adventures—some aspects also remain set, continuing to influence the character's thoughts and actions throughout his life.

Over the course of a campaign, a character's Morality not only greatly defines his personality, but it also can drastically affect his relationship with the Force. Those who inflict pain on others wantonly, who make selfish decisions, who act out of anger or fear, and who seek power and glory for themselves risk falling to the dark side of the Force. On the other hand, those who remain at peace with themselves, sacrifice their own well-being to help others, and seek to improve the lives of those around them rather than benefit themselves may become paragons of the light side.

## WHAT IS MORALITY?

Each Player Character in **Force and Destiny** has a Morality, a value that measures how "good" or "evil" that character is. This value changes over the course of a campaign, reflecting a character's choices and actions as adventures progress. In addition, each character's Morality includes an emotional strength and an emotional weakness that help define the character's personality. These personality traits are key to the character's Morality, as a character's moral decisions may be greatly affected by them.

The Morality mechanic is based on a number that represents a character's Morality within the game rules. This is meant to encourage the character's player to make interesting and even risky choices, and to give something that is inherently narrative (making decisions about right and wrong) mechanical benefits and repercussions. In *Star Wars*, the dark side of the Force is very real, and it is quite possible for people to fall to evil, and even later to be redeemed. The gameplay aspects of Morality represent that within the framework of the rules.

The Morality system is not, however, intended to spawn arguments between players as to whether an action is "evil" or not and whether a character should be penalized for engaging in it. In fact, the Morality system is designed to avoid that in two ways. First, the system has a specific set of guidelines as to what actions may penalize a character's Morality (see page 324), and second, it has a randomizing element that means players do not know for certain if their moral choices will penalize their characters or not in the course of the game.

Players may select their character's Morality from those presented in **Table 2–1: Morality**, page 50. Each entry presents an emotional strength and an emotional weakness for the character. Often, characters' emotional strengths and weaknesses can play a major part in the choices they make.

## SHARED MORALITY

It is perfectly acceptable for more than one Player Character in a group to have the same emotional strengths and weaknesses and goals. Often, this simply means that they have similar backgrounds and mindsets—even if they originated on different worlds and in vastly different cultures. Their methods for attempting to achieve their goals could be identical, or they could be vastly different. This provides a means for the characters to complement one another as they work cooperatively. Of course, at times, even characters with the same Morality could believe that there are different ways to achieve their objectives. This could introduce discussion, as the characters' different methods might be at odds with one another.

Alternatively, a player may generate Morality randomly by rolling percentile dice and comparing the result generated with the corresponding entry on the table. Although the Morality selections are designed to be paired, the table is also set up so that a player may roll once to generate an emotional strength, and a second time to generate an emotional weakness. This can create interesting and creative combinations for a character to roleplay.

Some players may even have a specific set of emotional strengths and weaknesses in mind for their character. They may, with their GM's permission, create a completely new Morality entry that is better suited to their vision of the character.

Each character's Morality is described in two ways:

- **A strength, a weakness, and a description of both:** These do not have specific rules effects. Instead, they offer an explanation that allows the player to develop the character's personality and temperament.

- **A numeric value:** This represents the character's moral standing and determines the PC's relationship with the light side and dark side of the Force. It is tracked on a scale of 1 to 100. The mechanical elements associated with shifting up and down this scale are described in detail on page 51.

### PLAYER CHARACTER STARTING MORALITY VALUES

Although these characters may have led exciting and adventurous lives before the game begins, and may have even started to explore their relationship with the Force, they have not had the chance to embrace the light or dark side of the Force. At this point, they have likely performed both good deeds and bad, and while they could still be fundamentally decent people, they probably aren't perfect.

Initially, each character begins with a Morality of 50. However, to represent their prior experiences in the galaxy, they can choose to modify their starting Morality or to gain additional experience points or credits with which to purchase additional gear. When creating a character, each player may select one of the following options for that character.

- Gain +10 starting XP. This XP increases the starting XP the PC gains when the player selects a species, and it can be spent to increase skills or characteristics, purchase talents, or obtain new specializations or Force powers. More on spending XP is covered on page 102.

- Gain +2,500 starting credits. This money may be spent on the PC's starting gear or saved to be spent during gameplay. More on spending starting credits is covered on page 107.

- Gain +5 starting XP and +1,000 starting credits.

- Increase or decrease the PC's starting Morality by 21. This gives the PC the option of beginning with a Morality of 29 or a Morality of 71. More on Morality thresholds can be found on page 52.

## TABLE 2-1: MORALITY

| d100 | Emotional Strength | Emotional Weakness |
|---|---|---|
| 01–08 | **Bravery:** The character's bravery is quite remarkable. Whether facing down a charging rancor or racing into a burning building to save innocents, he is always willing to take risks to help others. | **Anger:** Hot blood, however, can easily lead to hot tempers. The character is quick to anger, and what he cannot deal with face-to-face can often frustrate him to the point of rage. |
| 09–16 | **Love:** The character has an open heart. While he may hold a special place in his heart for his companions or a significant other, he tends to genuinely like most individuals he meets. His love for others can make him charming and affable, and exceedingly tolerant. | **Jealousy:** Love, if not given selflessly, can quickly turn to jealousy. The character's personality tends toward envy if his love is not reciprocated, or sometimes he simply envies others' accomplishments or possessions. |
| 17–24 | **Caution:** The character possesses commendable prudence, willing to always look before he leaps into a new situation. His forward-thinking ways may have saved his fellows from dangerous situations on numerous occasions. | **Fear:** The line between caution and fear is a thin one. Sometimes the character spends too much time concerned about the potential problems of a situation to act in that situation at all. At other times, his caution causes him to flee when danger presents itself, through bolder action might reap real rewards. |
| 25–32 | **Enthusiasm:** The character is always ready to try something new, and he approaches all of his tasks, even mundane ones, with excitement. He's not one to overthink a situation, lest he miss a great new opportunity. | **Recklessness:** Of course, a little thought can go a long way towards saving someone from a major mistake, which this character may find out to his sorrow on more than one occasion. Reckless behavior can leave him in dangerous situations or at the mercy of more calculating individuals. |
| 33–40 | **Compassion:** The character cares about the tribulations others face, and wants to help those he comes across. His compassion may lead to self-sacrifice in order to aid those who need it. | **Hatred:** The galaxy can be a cruel and heartless place, and compassion can quickly turn to hatred of the individuals or situations that cause others to suffer. When a character's mind roils with simmering hatred, that hatred may be all too slow to fade. |
| 41–48 | **Mercy:** The character shows mercy toward his foes, dealing with them fairly and honorably. He can spare the defenseless, will help a helpless enemy, and generally does not abuse a position of strength. | **Weakness:** There is a fine line between showing mercy to one's foes and letting evil fester because one does not want to engage with it. The character may let bad things happen simply because it is too hard to deal with them. |
| 49–56 | **Curiosity:** The character is driven to learn new things, to seek out and discover new information, and to expand his knowledge and understanding of those things that interest him. | **Obsession:** Sometimes, interest in something can turn to obsession if not tempered with reason. The character can slip into an obsessive state about his need to discover information, accomplish a goal, or even defeat a rival, and he may ignore all else until success is his. |
| 57–64 | **Pride:** Pride can be a powerful emotion, and can push a character to impressive feats of personal accomplishment. He strives to be the best and to take pleasure in his skills. | **Arrogance:** Pride, among all emotions, is perhaps the easiest to fall to a darker form. Arrogance mirrors pride, but satisfaction in one's accomplishments is replaced with contempt for others' failings. It is not enough to succeed; the character also expects all others to fail. |
| 65–72 | **Independence:** The character believes in relying on himself. He does not count on others to perform tasks for him; instead, he ensures he can handle any situation he encounters. He refuses to be a burden on others. | **Coldness:** Self-reliance can slip into isolation if one is not careful. A cold character doesn't just desire to rely only on himself, but has nothing but disinterest for anyone else. If they can't help themselves, why should he aid them? |
| 73–80 | **Ambition:** An ambitious character sets a lofty goal for himself and then strives to accomplish it. The harder the task, the more willing the character is to take it on, and the greater the triumph when he finally succeeds. | **Greed:** An ambitious character is only as selfless as his goals. Those who strive for worldly pleasures, whether power, wealth, or personal comforts, can quickly find their ambition turning to simple greed. |
| 81–88 | **Justice:** The character strives for just and deliberate actions in his life, and in his interactions with others. He attempts to make the objectively right choice every time, knowing that justice is more likely to guarantee positive outcomes than sympathy or other emotional displays. | **Cruelty:** All too often, the cruel use justice to excuse their actions. If one stops himself from tempering justice with empathy and understanding, he can inflict great harm on others and feel justified doing it. Eventually, he can grow to revel in the suffering of others, even as he deludes himself into thinking he makes the "just" choice. |
| 89–96 | **Discipline:** Rigorous mental and physical discipline comes naturally to the character. He does not make choices rashly, and every action is precise and selected. Those who think they can goad the character into making foolish choices are sorely mistaken. | **Obstinance:** Disciplined characters may fall into the trap of simple stubbornness if they are not careful. An obstinate character often refuses to consider any course of action other than the one he chooses, unwilling to accept that someone else may have conceived of a better option. |
| 97–00 | Roll twice on this chart. The PC has multiple emotional strengths and weaknesses. | |

# MORALITY IN PLAY

The implications of Morality extend far beyond the character's initial experiences with the Force. Throughout a Force adept's lifetime, he must constantly ensure that he is acting in a manner consistent with his personal ethos. Decisions to respect that moral code can offer the character rewards that have a meaningful game effect. Actions taken that violate it can reduce the character's Morality, which can have lasting negative consequences.

## TRIGGERING MORALITY

Triggering Morality is an optional rule the GM can use if he wants to have a Player Character's moral choices take center stage during the game session. How the GM triggers Morality is covered on page 323 of **Chapter IX: The Game Master**. If the GM uses this rule, a character can have narrative opportunities to play up his emotional strengths and weaknesses, and also see his Morality increase or decrease significantly at the end of a session.

## MORALITY AND CONFLICT

During gameplay, each player is responsible for tracking his PC's Morality. Morality can increase or decrease during the course of a campaign as the PC becomes a paragon of virtue or risks falling to the dark side.

A Player Character's Morality has a chance of changing at the end of each game session. A PC's actions during the session may increase the probability that his Morality will rise or fall. Whether or not a PC's Morality increases or decreases is determined through **Conflict**.

Conflict is a resource that Player Characters can accumulate throughout a game session based on choices they make and actions they perform. The more Conflict a PC accumulates, the greater the chance his Morality will decrease at the end of the session. Conflict is tracked publicly by each PC's controlling player. A player can track Conflict by writing the current total on his character sheet or by using tokens, beads, or coins.

Player Characters earn Conflict in several ways:

- Using dark side results to generate Force points when activating a Force power or Force talent.

- Performing certain narrative actions.

- Generating certain results when failing a fear check.

Any time a character uses one or more Dark Side results ● to generate Force Points ◐, he accumulates 1 Conflict per Dark Side result ● used (in addition to any other penalties, such as strain, that the character may accrue).

The character can also accumulate Conflict for performing immoral actions, as determined by the GM. Extreme actions, including taking lives, can give a PC a significant amount of Conflict. However, the GM should always inform players if their characters are about to perform an action that would cause them to earn Conflict. The GM does not have to tell players the exact amount of Conflict their characters would earn, but should give them an idea of the severity of the penalty. More information on earning Conflict by performing actions can be found on page 324.

When a Force-sensitive Player Character fails a fear check, the GM can choose to have the PC suffer a number of Conflict equal to the difficulty of the check instead of the normal penalties. Generating ▽ on a fear check may cause this to happen automatically, and may have other effects as well. See page 326 for more details.

Over the course of a game session, a PC may earn no Conflict at all, as much as 10 Conflict, or even more. At the end of the session, each player tallies up the Conflict his character has earned and then rolls 1d10. If the roll result is less than the amount of Conflict he earned during that session, he subtracts the roll result from his Conflict, and then decreases his PC's Morality by the difference. If the roll result is greater than the amount of Conflict he has earned, he subtracts his Conflict from his roll result and increases his Morality by that number. (If the roll and Conflict earned are the same, Morality neither increases nor decreases.)

### EXAMPLE

At the end of the game session, Sarah tallies up her Conflict and discovers that her character has earned 3. She rolls 1d10, and gets a 1. Her character's Morality is reduced by 2. If she had instead rolled a 6, her Morality would have increased by 3.

### ENGAGING A TRIGGERED MORALITY

In addition to their narrative changes, games using the optional triggering Morality rule have specific mechanical effects. If the GM chooses to have a character's Morality trigger and if the character successfully engages his triggered Morality, then at the end of the game session, when the player checks for a Morality increase or decrease by rolling a d10 and subtracting Conflict (see above), he should double that value. For example, if the character had earned 2 Conflict, and then an 8 was rolled on the d10, his Morality would normally increase by 6. If the PC's Morality was triggered, he would instead increase his Morality by 12.

**S**hifting allegiance to the dark side requires deliberate and continued choices. Similarly, characters must focus and act in a consistent manner over an extended period of time to recover their allegiance to the light.

Once a character's Morality drops below 30, he becomes a dark side Force user. Once a character has become a dark side Force user, he remains a dark side Force user, even if his Morality increases above 30 at a later point.

There is only one way a Player Character who has become a dark side Force user can become a light side Force user again and redeem himself. He must increase his Morality to above 70. When his Morality increases above 70, the character is redeemed and mechanically, he functions as a light side Force user again. This applies even if his Morality later drops to below 70 (although if it drops below 30 after he becomes a light side Force user, he falls to the dark side again).

Note that although these are the mechanical steps for returning to the light, there should always be a strong narrative component to redemption as well. The GM and player should always work together to craft the story of the PC's penance and restoration. He may have to perform tasks to redeem himself in the eyes of his fellows, seek forgiveness from those he has wronged, or even perform some heroic sacrificial task to correct some terrible consequences of his existence within the dark side.

Players should also keep in mind that, mechanically, redemption is no simple matter, either. To reach 70 Morality, the PC not only must consistently make decisions that will let him avoid earning additional Conflict, but he must also refrain from using ◯ to generate ◑, as each of the ◑ generated from ◯ generates Conflict as well.

Redemption is not easy.

Once the player has determined how much his character's Morality has increased or decreased, he resets his Conflict amount to zero. This way, PCs start with no accumulated Conflict at the beginning of each session.

### CASES WHEN MORALITY SHOULD NOT INCREASE

Although generally players will resolve their characters' Morality at the end of each session, there are some cases when they should not do so.

If a player was not present for a session, his character's Morality should not have a chance to increase. Similarly, if a character had no chance to do anything in a session or spent an entire session incapacitated, then his Morality should not increase. This may be the case if a character spends the entire session healing in a bacta tank or stuck in a coma, for example. These cases are likely to be very rare, but a good overall guideline should be that Player Characters should have a chance to earn Conflict (even if they don't take it) if their Morality will have a chance to change.

## MORALITY THRESHOLDS

At character creation, most PCs begin play as light side Force users. Some may have dabbled in the dark side of the Force earlier in their careers, while others may have remained resolute in their allegiance to their moral code. They remain light side users until their Morality drops beneath the dark side threshold.

### DARK SIDE THRESHOLD

If a character's Morality drops below 30, he has crossed the dark side threshold. At this point, he becomes a dark side Force user. Being a dark side Force user adds significant narrative effects to a character's ongoing story. These effects are usually determined by the GM or by the GM and player working together. Becoming a dark side Force user also has several mechanical effects:

- The character generates Force points ◑ using Dark Side results ●.
- The character's presence in the group alters the starting Destiny Point pool.
- The character's strain threshold may decrease and wound threshold may increase.

One crucial effect of being a dark side Force user involves how the character generates Force points on checks. Instead of using Light Side results ◯ from the Force dice ◇ to generate Force points ◑, the character must use Dark Side results ●. This works following the same rules governing a regular Force user's generation of Force points ◑ from Light Side results ◯, as described in **Force Power Checks**, page 280. It also means that if the dark side Force user wants to generate Force points ◑ from Light Side results ◯, he must flip a Destiny Point and suffer strain equal to the number of Force points ◑ generated.

In addition, as long as the character remains a dark side Force user, his presence influences the party's Destiny pool. At the beginning of each game session, after the entire group rolls for Destiny Points, the player flips one light side Destiny Point to the dark side. If there are no light side Destiny Points to flip, this has no effect.

Allegiance to the dark side also reduces the Force user's strain threshold. This reflects the character's

dependence on Conflict. At the same time, his wound threshold increases as he becomes inured to pain.

- When the character's Morality score falls below 20, the dark side Force user's strain threshold is decreased by 1 and his wound threshold is increased by 1.

- If the character's Morality score falls below 10, the dark side Force user's strain threshold is decreased by another 1 and his wound threshold is increased by another 1, for a total increase and decrease of 2.

A character remains a dark side Force user even if his Morality later climbs above 30. A PC can seek redemption and try to become a light side Force user again; this is described in the **Redemption from the Dark Side** sidebar on the preceding page.

## LIGHT SIDE PARAGON THRESHOLD

Characters who remain consistently loyal to their Morality can reap additional benefits. If a Force user's Morality score increases above 70, he becomes a true champion of goodness and a paragon of the Force. Though this does not intrinsically change how his character works mechanically, it does confer certain benefits which can aid his character in ongoing adventures.

As long as the character's Morality score remains above 70, at the beginning of every session, when generating the Destiny pool (but before any players roll to determine starting Destiny Points), the character adds one light side Destiny Point to the pool. In addition, as the character's Morality score continues to rise above certain thresholds, he gains additional benefits:

- As long as his Morality score is above 80, the light side Force user's strain threshold is increased by 1.

- As long as his Morality score is above 90, the light side Force user's strain threshold is increased by 1 additional point, to a total of 2.

# STEP 3: SELECT A SPECIES

The Force binds all living things. Throughout the billions of planets in the galaxy, there are a functionally limitless number of different species from which a player could select for his character, from the ever-present human to the much less common Togruta. In the ways of the Force, all of these are equal, as each displays its own unique connection to the Force. Some cultures have an ingrained connection to the Force, including those with an affinity for the dark side. For others, any association or knowledge of the Force is anathema. Either of these approaches—along with the huge array of intermediate ones—can play a major role in establishing a character's background.

This section presents eight species found in the *Star Wars* universe. All of these examples have had one or more well-known members who were strong in the Force—and several have included members who served in prominent roles on the Jedi Council. Of course, some players or Game Masters may wish to pursue alternative options. In some instances, players with access to the other game lines could select from those species presented in **Age of Rebellion** or **Edge of the Empire**. The only species that players should avoid in these cases are those who cannot use Force talents or Force powers (such as droids). Since a large part of **Force and Destiny** is playing a Force user, this would only hamper the PC.

## CHOOSING A SPECIES

A player must choose a species for his character, even before he commits to a career. The choice of species and career can go hand-in-hand and is informed by a character's background story above all else.

Each species has idiosyncratic abilities and characteristics that influence the next stage of character creation, the picking of careers. Species selection determines the PCs' initial ratings for characteristics, like Brawn and Cunning, as well as their starting experience points (XP). Players use their XP allotments to modify characteristics or acquire new skills and talents appropriate to their characters' backgrounds and careers.

Remember, a wide range of characteristic distributions can be created by spending starting XP, so do not feel forced to choose a specific species because of its baseline characteristic ratings. Moreover, characteristics do not define a character completely. Good roleplaying and storytelling do more to create a distinctive personality than numbers ever do.

## CEREAN

Cereans are a distinctive species. Though they are similar in appearance to humans, their one noticeable difference comprises their extended, almost cone-like skulls, which house large, binary brains (in essence, two brains closely linked together). Because of their binary brains, members of this humanoid species can simultaneously pursue multiple lines of thought and have extraordinary mental aptitude. The species is also known for attention to detail as well as a cultural tendency toward extended contemplation.

**Physiology:** Cereans are mammalian, with anatomy very similar to that of humans. The most notable differences are the presence of the enlarged, conical cranium—to accommodate the binary brain structure—as

---

## USING LANGUAGES IN FORCE AND DESTINY

Language has always been a vital scene-setting tool in *Star Wars*. The animalistic roars of a Wookiee, the bird-like twittering of an astromech droid, or the guttural rumblings of a Hutt crime lord serve as reminders that the *Star Wars* universe is a vast place with countless species and cultures. For this reason, nearly every species in **Force and Destiny** has its own language, and in the case of wildly diverse species like humans, they may actually have many different languages.

While all of these varied languages exist, they are not intended to provide a barrier to understanding or comprehension. *Star Wars* has a wide variety of tools for language interpretation, from protocol droids that are fluent in over six million forms of communication to the simple fact that most galactic citizens utilize the pan-

galactic language known as Basic, which nearly everyone understands even if unable to speak it.

Each species entry lists the languages unique to that species. However, all Player Characters are able to understand Basic, and they are not required to track the different languages they speak. Every PC in a group can understand fellow PCs. In addition, the GM should endeavor to make any individuals the PCs encounter comprehensible, by whatever means the GM deems appropriate. For example, one of the PCs may speak the individual's language, or vice versa. There may be a protocol droid available, or perhaps everyone involved speaks Basic. The one exception to this should be if the lack of comprehension is itself a major plot point; otherwise, the issue of language should never hamper the ongoing story.

well as a pair of hearts to improve blood circulation. Cereans are generally regarded as somewhat less physically coordinated than humans.

Cereans exhibit an unusual sexual dimorphism. Female births outnumber male births by a ratio of twenty to one. Further, males age more rapidly than females. Consequently, female Cereans dominate the world's population.

**Society:** Cerean culture is focused on preserving the undamaged portions of their homeworld and living in harmony with the natural world. Meditation is a central part of their lives, often in conjunction with kasha crystals. These stones aid in calming and cleansing the mind, helping users to harness their natural energies.

Partly due to their imbalanced sexual ratio, Cerean society is primarily matriarchal. The government is ruled by a president who works with a Council of Elders. Decisions are made only after lengthy discussions that thoroughly analyze both sides of an issue, with concerted efforts toward achieving objectivity. Notably, once the council makes a resolution, its decision is final, with no opportunity for appeal. Cereans believe so absolutely in their infallibility that they assume all decisions made by the council are correct. Revisiting such a decision may only happen due to changing circumstances or new, previously unknown information.

Tradition plays a major role in Cerean life. This begins with an individual's name. Most Cereans have three names, derived from their parents and grandparents. Clothing styles are also highly traditional, established over centuries. Many Cereans train in the use of an ancient, curved sword known as the shyarn. Duelists often focus on a highly artistic and stylized combat style as a means of releasing their aggression. Some argue that this catharsis plays a critical role in maintaining their peaceful society.

**Homeworld:** Cerea is a Mid Rim world with strong isolationist tendencies. Historically a verdant paradise, Cerea chose a neutral stance during the Clone Wars. However, it allowed large numbers of refugees displaced by the fighting to settle in its enclaves, creating tremendous population pressures and cultural clashes. Since the Clone Wars, Cerea has attempted to remain isolated from the galaxy at large.

**Language:** All Cereans learn Basic during their childhood, as well as native Cerean. Cerean uses glottal stops and a large number of lengthy compound words.

**Perception of the Force:** Cereans have a cultural predisposition for meditation and contemplation, which can be linked to a tendency to embrace the Force. Their inherent knack for analysis also grants them a degree of insight comparable to the precognition that some talented Force users can master. Legends suggest that some accomplished Cerean Jedi were able to use their binary brains to simultaneously explore both the dark and light sides of the Force.

## OUTSIDER CITADELS

After the Battle of Cerea and the later killing of Cerean Jedi Master Ki-Adi-Mundi by his own troops during the Jedi Purges, Cerea withdrew inward to nurse its wounds and tend to itself. However, Cereans historically have had a suspicious attitude toward outsiders.

Cereans have always worked to maintain harmony with themselves and their environment. Consequentially, they limit the amount of technology they use in their everyday life, especially if that technology could harm the planetary ecology. The Cereans have also generally made a point to limit the impact non-Cereans can have on their planet. Thus, outsiders and immigrants may only settle in the so-called Outsider Citadels. These vast structures tower over the surrounding landscapes. Within the Citadels' often cramped and squalid confines, non-Cereans are free to live without following the Cereans' strict rules concerning offworld technology and non-polluting lifestyles. Needless to say, this has led to the Outsider Citadels' having become havens of vice and criminal enterprise.

### SPECIES ABILITIES

| BRAWN | AGILITY | INTELLECT | CUNNING | WILLPOWER | PRESENCE |
|:---:|:---:|:---:|:---:|:---:|:---:|
| 2 | 1 | 3 | 2 | 2 | 2 |

- **Wound Threshold:** 10 + Brawn
- **Strain Threshold:** 13 + Willpower
- **Starting Experience:** 90 XP
- **Special Abilities:** Cereans begin the game with one rank in Vigilance. They still may not train Vigilance above rank 2 during character creation.
- **Binary Processing:** Cereans treat all Knowledge skills as career skills.

# HUMAN

Humans are the most common form of sentient life in the galaxy. Characterized by an exceptional degree of adaptability, they have come to reside on most of the galaxy's habitable worlds. Human cultures have explored much of the galaxy and established many colonies.

**Physiology:** Humans are oxygen-breathing omnivores, capable of consuming a broad range of animal and plant products for food. A mammalian species, they have internal biology adaptable to a wide array of environmental conditions, and they tend to use clothing and technology to further extend their ability to survive and thrive in all sorts of places. Males average just

Cerean       Human       Kel Dor       Mirialan

under two meters in height, while females are slightly shorter. Human skin is mostly hairless, and comes in colors ranging from off-white to very dark brown. Hair color can vary even more wildly, running the gamut from shades of red and yellow to solid black.

**Society:** Humans are far too broadly spread throughout the galaxy to constitute a single cultural entity. Instead, the species embraces an extraordinary range of different cultural norms. Humans live under virtually every known or imaginable political system. Economic and sociological attitudes vary substantially between places where humans dwell in peace and areas where they wage war with other sentient species or human factions.

During the time of the Galactic Empire, humans are unquestionably the most powerful force in the galaxy. They control the military and political forces of the Imperial government. However, just as many humans work together against the Empire's tyranny.

**Homeworld:** The precise origin of human life has been lost to the ages. Most scholars believe that the species originated from somewhere within the Core Worlds—arguably Coruscant. However, humanity embraced star travel a very long time ago, founding colonies on every habitable world they could. Human cultures now exist on countless different planets.

**Language:** Human cultures invented Basic, and many use it. Some cultures, however, may speak different dialects of Basic, or entirely unique languages.

**Perception of the Force:** Humanity exhibits a broad range of attitudes toward the Force. Some deny its existence completely, while others insist on seeing its influence upon all things. Extreme attitudes can often exist together, even within the constraints of a single

## A GALAXY OF HUMANS

Even in a galaxy of countless stars and planets containing potentially millions of species, one can find humans just about everywhere. Some say humans were the first explorers to venture out into the darkness of space before the dawn of the Republic. They say these early humans were bold explorers who colonized the rest of the galaxy while most species were still striking flint to rock. Others, notably early spacefaring pioneers like the Duros, claim humanity simply has a penchant for expanding as fast as possible and sticking its collective nose where it doesn't belong.

## BARAN DO

Thousands of years before Dorin became aware of the Galactic Republic, the Kel Dor had already discovered the power of the Force and crafted their own traditions. A group of skilled and powerful mystics known as the Baran Do Sages studied the Force so that they could expand their abilities to predict danger for their people. The Sages delved deeply into the ability to foresee events, whether those events were in the past, in the future, or in faraway lands. Soon, they not only became an invaluable resource for criminal investigations, but also served as advisors to Dorin's leadership. Their predictive abilities helped Dorin avoid natural disasters, famines, diplomatic incidents, and even outright wars.

With the coming of the Republic and the Jedi Order, the Baran Do's influence dwindled. Many Force sensitives joined the Jedi, and thus the ranks of the Sages quickly shrank. By the time of the Clone Wars, most Kel Dor had forgotten the Baran Do ever existed, and the few who know about them are unsure whether any Sages have passed on their traditions to the modern age. This may be a boon in disguise, however. As the Empire hunts down Force-sensitives across the galaxy, obscurity could prove the best defense.

planet's culture. Currently, the Galactic Empire's heavy-handed approach toward the Force informs most human opinions.

### SPECIES ABILITIES

- **Wound Threshold:** 10 + Brawn
- **Strain Threshold:** 10 + Willpower
- **Starting Experience:** 110 XP
- **Special Abilities:** Humans start the game with one rank each in two different non-career skills of their choice. They still may not train these skills above rank 2 at character creation.

## KEL DOR

Best known as a kindly and soft-spoken species, Kel Dors are most easily identified by the protective eyewear and rebreather masks that they must wear when outside of their native environments. In spite of Kel Dors' gentle natures, they are renowned for their sense of justice and willingness to enforce it with great prejudice.

**Physiology:** Near-hairless humanoid mammals, Kel Dors average 1.7 meters in height. Their respiratory systems are well adapted to Dorin's unusual atmosphere of helium and unique gas compounds, so that they must make use of filtration masks in order to survive in other environments. This, combined with innate toughness, does allow them to survive hard vacuum for a short time, an extraordinarily useful ability.

Similarly, they wear protective and enhancing goggles because their black eyes are sensitized to the dim light and unusual atmospheric conditions of Dorin. A highly developed extrasensory organ is located at the back of the Kel Dor skull, tightly linked to the brain. Kel Dor skin tone ranges from a pale orange to a dark red.

**Society:** Kel Dors are tightly linked into their extended families. Several generations of a family often live together by choice. This offers an opportunity to share responsibility for the extended family's younglings and ease in consulting the family's elders for advice. Often, entire families share a common career, which can lead to family-owned businesses that span successive generations.

Technological advancement drives Kel Dor society strongly. Due to its own specialized needs, the species has become particularly adept at designing environmental systems. These include individual and large-scale systems suited to a wide variety of environments.

Justice is certain and swift on Dorin. Security workers are quick to offer assistance to those in need, but they are also unwilling to wait long to see justice delivered. Instead, they interpret legal and moral issues in stark black-and-white terms, ignoring any potentially mitigating factors.

**Homeworld:** Dorin is located in the Expansion Region. Due to its location between two black holes, it remained isolated from the rest of the galaxy until only a few centuries before the start of the Galactic Civil War. Dorin's atmosphere is composed largely of helium and a second unidentifiable gas that is unique to the system. Dorin's oxygen levels are low enough that most non-natives require technological assistance to venture there.

**Language:** Kel Dors learn both Kel Dorian and Basic from childhood. They speak Basic as well as any native speaker and seldom speak Kel Dorian off-world. Their native language is easier to speak and understand when they are breathing Dorin's native atmosphere.

**Perception of the Force:** The Kel Dors have had a strong connection to the Force that predates their association with the greater galaxy. For millennia, Sages of the obscure Baran Do tradition served as advisors to Kel Dor leaders. Depending on sensory deprivation to offer a greater insight into the Force, these practitioners refined skills that were later practiced by the most talented of Jedi. Whereas most Kel Dors have black eyes, those with the strongest connections to the Force frequently have silvery eyes, a fact that can be exceptionally dangerous for practitioners. Since the rise of the Empire, more than a few Kel Dor Force-sensitives have been identified by their distinctive eyes and killed by Imperial agents.

## SPECIES ABILITIES

- **Wound Threshold:** 10 + Brawn
- **Strain Threshold:** 10 + Willpower
- **Starting Experience:** 100 XP
- **Special Abilities:** Kel Dors begin the game with one rank in Knowledge (Education). They still may not train Knowledge (Education) above rank 2 during character creation.
- **Dark Vision:** When making skill checks, Kel Dors remove up to ■ ■ imposed due to darkness.
- **Atmospheric Requirement:** Kel Dors must wear a specialized mask to breathe and see outside of their native atmosphere. A Kel Dor character starts the game with an antitox breath mask and treats oxygen as a dangerous atmosphere with Rating 8 (see page 220). However, Kel Dors may survive in vacuum for up to five minutes before suffering its effects.

# MIRIALAN

Mirialans are a near-human species from the planet Mirial. Their culture is characterized by a deep-seated faith and respect for an individual's destiny. Mirialans undergo ritual tattooing to represent the ways that they have overcome the obstacles that fate placed before them.

**Physiology:** Mirialans are physiologically extremely similar to humans. Their most obvious departure from human norms is in their skin tone, which ranges in color from green to a paler yellow-green. Hair color tends toward blacks and browns, while eye color can encompass human tones in addition to yellow, orange, and red. They are generally regarded as capable martial artists, as Mirialans are typically both faster and more agile than humans.

**Society:** Mirialan culture is defined by its religious beliefs. Mirialans believe that an individual's destiny is defined by the decisions he makes and the actions he takes. Every decision builds upon those that have gone before to determine each person's ultimate outcome. Because these choices embody an individual's personal integrity, Mirialans choose to express this

## MIRIALAN MARKINGS

A full lexicon of Mirialan tattoos and their various meanings would be extensive beyond the imagining of other species, and even most Mirialans cannot memorize the entirety of the tattoo lexicon. Part of the reason of this is the subtle interactions between the placement and positioning of different geometric shapes. A slight variation in spacing or placement on an individual's face can drastically change the meaning of a tattoo set. While this ensures the Mirialans can portray the entirety of their life histories on their faces, it also means very few non-Mirialans can decipher the markings.

visually as well. Every significant event in a Mirialan's life is illustrated by a tattoo inscribed upon his face, hands, or other commonly visible location. As Mirialans age, the pattern of tattoos becomes increasingly intricate and detailed. The different geometric patterns and locations of the tattoos form a visual representation of each Mirialan's life story and suggest the role that the individual is likely to play in the planet's future.

Because Mirialans are so open about their personal histories, their society holds an inherent level of stratification. Those who have enjoyed past successes are automatically recognized and lauded for their success, and trusted with greater opportunities. In contrast, an individual who has made poor choices early in life is less likely to receive opportunities for redemption. After all, anyone who meets an individual can immediately recognize the Mirialan's past transgressions. Many who have made poor choices feel constrained to paths that limit them to an unfortunate ultimate outcome. However, for many, their faith in fate can provide the motivation to transform their lives. Some believe that their mistakes serve as learning experiences for later challenges.

**Homeworld:** Mirial is located near the Hydian Way, not far from the Corporate Sector. The world is both dry and cold, which has forced the Mirialans to go to great lengths just to survive its challenges. Prior to the Clone Wars, the Trade Federation used Mirial's need for imports to keep its inhabitants under its sway.

**Language:** Mirialan is the native tongue of Mirial, though most Mirialans also learn Basic during childhood.

**Perception of the Force:** Mirialan religion is based upon their limited understanding of the Cosmic Force, which they identify as fate. Even those incapable of directly interacting with the Force have faith in fate's presence and recognize that it is a guiding force in their lives. Because of this, Mirialans hold a deep-seated respect for Force practitioners. Before the Clone Wars, there was always at least one Mirialan Jedi in residence at the Jedi Temple.

- **Wound Threshold:** 11 + Brawn
- **Strain Threshold:** 10 + Willpower
- **Starting Experience:** 100 XP
- **Special Abilities:** Mirialans begin the game with one rank in Discipline and one rank in Cool. They still may not train Discipline or Cool above rank 2 during character creation.

# NAUTOLAN

Nautolans are an amphibious species native to Glee Anselm. They are renowned for empathetic and cheerful natures and for enjoying everyday activities. Though generally peaceful, they are also tough and strong.

**Physiology:** Nautolans are a natively aquatic humanoid species capable of breathing underwater. Webbed toes and fingers aid them in swimming through the depths. A dense cartilaginous support network combines with a bony endoskeleton to make them exceptionally tough. Lengthy green tendrils emerge from their heads, serving as sensory organs that detect the pheromones of nearby sentients. Their large black eyes are adapted to pierce the murkiest underwater environments. However, Nautolans are capable of surviving for extended periods on dry land.

Nautolans are an egg-laying species. When hatching, they emerge from the eggs as tadpoles. Arms, legs, and head-tails begin to emerge during the second year of life, at which point they are roughly the same size as a human infant. Initially, these limbs are

## STRUGGLES WITH THE ANSELMI

The Nautolans are one of several species to evolve sharing their planet with another sentient species. Some of these species, such as the Utai and the Pau'ans, evolved to live together in harmony. Unfortunately, the Nautolans and the Anselmi have not been so lucky.

The Anselmi evolved as a land-based species on an oceanic planet. Thus, their entire history has been spent in intraspecies warfare over the few landmasses available. Meanwhile, the Nautolans developed unmolested in the oceanic depths. As the Nautolans adapted to an amphibious lifestyle, their numbers and natural strength gave them crucial advantages against the severely depleted Anselmi. After centuries of conflict they dominate Glee Anselm, leaving the Anselmi marginalized and torn by warfare.

not strong enough to support their weight on land, so most spend their early years in aquatic environments.

**Society:** An elected Council of Elders forms the centralized government for Nautolan settlements. On Glee Anselm, representatives from each settlement cooperate to form an overarching centralized government. Notably, "elder" is a title of respect, as representatives are elected based upon merit rather than age.

Nautolans mate for life and are extremely loyal to their families. Both parents contribute equally to raising their young. Historically, Nautolan parents arranged marriages for their children, but in modern times this has become much less common.

Nautolan moods often reflect those of nearby sentients due to the pheromone sensitivity of their tendrils. As a broad generalization, Nautolans are happy and free-spirited, particularly when given an opportunity to pursue their interests. However, when confronted with anger or despair, members of this empathetic species are prone to respond in kind.

**Homeworld:** Glee Anselm is a Mid Rim world filled with a broad range of aquatic environments. Its few landmasses are largely archipelagos. While Nautolans evolved in Glee Anselm's oceans, another unrelated species—the Anselmi—arose to dwell upon its landmasses. Constant fighting over the land turned the Anselmi into a warlike people. This has led to many conflicts throughout the world's history.

**Language:** Nautolans' native language is Nautila, which was originally created for underwater use. In atmosphere, the language is largely unpronounceable, as it is dependent upon pheromones that are dispersed through the water in conjunction with spoken sounds. Consequently, Nautolans invariably learn to speak another language, most commonly Basic or Anselmian.

**Perception of the Force:** Many Nautolans recognize the significance of the Force, and there were numerous Nautolan Jedi. However, the Force does not play a central role in Nautolan culture.

- **Wound Threshold:** 11 + Brawn
- **Strain Threshold:** 9 + Willpower
- **Starting Experience:** 100 XP
- **Special Abilities:** Nautolans begin the game with one rank in Athletics. They still may not train Athletics above rank 2 during character creation.
- **Amphibious:** Nautolans may breathe underwater without penalty and never suffer movement penalties for traveling through water.

# TOGRUTA

A carnivorous humanoid species from the planet Shili, Togrutas are easily recognized by the combination of their head-tails and hornlike montrals. Only Togrutas who are independent-minded—a relatively rare trait for them—travel off-world.

**Physiology:** Togrutas are a near-hairless, mammalian, humanoid species that average 1.7 meters in height. Their skin tones tend towards bold colors like orange or red, and most individuals have contrasting white pigmentation patterns scattered across their bodies. They have three—or rarely, four—head-tails. Two are normally draped across the front of the body, while the other falls to the back. Above these, they have two hollow montrals, which are used for a simple form of echolocation that enhances their keen senses.

**Society:** Togrutas evolved from pack hunters, and their society continues to demonstrate this heritage. While urban life has begun to emerge, the majority of Togrutas still live in dense communal villages within Shili's forested canopies and hidden valleys. In these places, they live in harmony with nature. Every member of a community is expected to learn to work in concert with other members of the pack, contributing to everyone's overall success.

Togrutas have little sympathy for those who can't contribute to society. However, most Togrutas quickly point out that contributions in the modern world can be wide and varied, ranging from the ability to construct valuable tools to the ability to entertain the rest of the pack through song or storytelling. This holds especially true in Shili's growing urban areas, where keen minds can be more valuable than strong arms.

Most Togrutas consider excessive expressions of individuality to be a sign of social deviance. Yet in many instances, this same deviation is rewarded, as distinctive individuals can rise to positions of authority within Togrutas communities. Some outsiders have observed that the willingness for Togruta culture to excuse individuality generally depends on how successful and valuable those individuals are to the greater whole. If independent-minded Togrutas cannot succeed among their peoples, they tend to travel off-world, where they may find the attitudes of the wider galaxy more accepting.

**Homeworld:** Shili is in the Expansion Region, located near the Hydian Way. Shili's natural environment features many scrublands and dense, canopied forests. Both feature the red-and-white-colored turu-grass, which matches a Togruta's natural coloration. The world's wildlife includes a broad range of prey animals and other predators, including the savage akul. In the past, whole tribes of Togrutas frequently worked together to overcome prey and then proudly incorporated portions of their kills into their wardrobes.

However, many Togrutas have traveled off-world to establish colonies in the years since they became aware of wider galactic society. Freed from some of the traditions of their homeworld, these Togruta colonies have developed wildly different cultural paths. The artisan colony of Kiros, for example, focuses on nurturing creative expression and peaceful coexistence, along with a higher level of individuality among its citizens. Colonial Togrutas can thus differ greatly in outlook and attitudes from their cousins on Shili.

**Language:** The Togrutas were members of the Old Republic for thousands of years. While all speak the native tongue of Togruti, most also speak Basic. Togruti incorporates trills, which have varied meanings depending upon tremors from a speaker's head-tails.

**Perception of the Force:** Togrutas do not have a native Force tradition, but numerous members of the species did travel off-world to join the Jedi Order. Jedi scholars believe that Togrutas have a heightened affinity for the Force. This is most commonly demonstrated through their exceptional spatial senses, which play a major role in their ability to respond to their environment.

## SPECIES ABILITIES

- **Wound Threshold:** 10 + Brawn
- **Strain Threshold:** 10 + Willpower
- **Starting Experience:** 100 XP
- **Special Abilities:** Togrutas begin the game with one rank in Perception. They still may not train Perception above rank 2 during character creation.
- **Pack Instincts:** When performing the assist maneuver, Togrutas grant ☐☐ instead of ☐.

## TOGRUTA TROPHIES

Traditionally, Togruta hunters take the teeth of an akul after defeating it. They craft these into jewelry, most commonly in the form of a headdress, interworking the teeth with precious metals and stones. Some Togrutas who travel offworld adapt this practice with trophies taken from other opponents.

Some individuals who meet Togrutas make the mistake of assuming their trophy-taking implies they are primitive savages. Of course, this assumption could not be further from the truth, as such people often find out to their detriment.

# TWI'LEK

Twi'leks are a common sight throughout the galaxy, particularly within less reputable locales. This is largely because the species has sold their young into slavery for many millennia. They are easily recognized by their twin head-tails, also known as lekku or tchun-tchin.

**Physiology:** Twi'leks are an omnivorous, hairless, humanoid species. Their lengthy lekku are prehensile but also serve additional functions. These include playing a role in sensory input as well as providing a location for their brains to store memories. Their smooth skin comes in a broad range of colors, which are commonly associated with ancestry and clan. Some individuals even have natural striped patterns. Their orange or yellow eyes offer exceptional night vision, and their flexible fingers terminate in clawlike nails.

**Society:** Twi'lek society is tightly linked to an ancestral structure of clans. In the lack of a central planetary government, each city is instead ruled by a head clan made up of five Twi'lek males. Each group of leaders is born to assume this role. Notably, the head clan serves as a city's leadership until a member of the clan dies, at which point the surviving members are deposed so that the next generation can assume the leadership roles. As these roles are hereditary, there are strong rivalries surrounding each appointment.

Twi'leks entered galactic society soon after the medicinal—and recreational—values of the mineral ryll were discovered. At that time, Twi'leks had no native spacefaring capability. Partly because of this limitation, their world soon became dominated by the Hutts, who seized control of ryll mining and production. In short order, this led to the Twi'leks' involvement in the slave trade.

Twi'leks are generally regarded as being cunning and manipulative, conducting subterfuge within their clans and in the service of other causes. However, they are not particularly confrontational, preferring to avoid taking a stand on an issue whenever possible.

**Homeworld:** Ryloth is an Outer Rim world located on the Corellian Run. Its seasons are violent and its environments extreme, ranging from snowy wastelands to scorching deserts. The majority of the native Twi'leks live within a narrow temperate band. For millennia, Ryloth's primary export has been slaves. As a consequence, Twi'leks can be found throughout the galaxy, and many have never visited the Twi'lek homeworld.

Nautolan        Togruta        Twi'lek        Zabrak

**Language:** The primary native spoken language of Twi'leks is Ryl, and the vast majority are fluent in it. In addition, Twi'leks can communicate with one another using their lekku. The head-tails can be used to accentuate spoken languages, but they may also be used in a nonspoken sign language. Because of their galactic presence, most Twi'leks also know Basic, while those who are active in the slave trade invariably learn Huttese.

**Perception of the Force:** Twi'leks do not profess any particular faith in the Force in a religious manner, nor do they have any native Force traditions. However, conversations between Twi'leks who use their lekku are believed to have spiritual connotations. Some scholars of Jedi lore believe that the lekku have a degree of inherent Force sensitivity. This suggests that Twi'leks could have at least a limited connection to the Force, though they may not necessarily recognize it.

## TWI'LEK SLAVERY

Much of the galaxy finds Twi'leks and slavery to be synonymous. To many Twi'leks' shame, slavery is one of their homeworld's chief exports, and far too many of their fellows are complicit in this reprehensible business. Many Twi'leks are born into slavery. Some become slaves far from Ryloth, while others are sold into slavery at a young age by their homeworld. Under Imperial control, Twi'lek slavery has become even more prevalent, as the Empire is perfectly happy to encourage the deplorable practice through neglect. Even for those who escape, their time spent in captivity often defines their lives. Some former slaves revel in their freedom, while others embark upon personal crusades to free others from such a thankless existence.

## SPECIES ABILITIES

- **Wound Threshold:** 10 + Brawn
- **Strain Threshold:** 11 + Willpower
- **Starting Experience:** 100 XP
- **Special Abilities:** Twi'leks begin the game with one rank in either Charm or Deception. They still may not train Charm or Deception above rank 2 during character creation.
- **Desert Dwellers:** When making skill checks, Twi'leks may remove ■ imposed due to arid or hot environmental conditions.

# ZABRAK

Zabrak resemble humans in skin tone and physique, but they are easily distinguished by their vestigial horns. They are renowned for both their inherent confidence and their martial prowess.

**Physiology:** Zabrak physiology is similar to human, with several notable differences, including the presence of a second heart and a heightened resistance to physical pain. Zabrak vestigial horns emerge at puberty; they are a sign that an individual is reaching maturation and nearing the age of the traditional rite of passage. Zabrak skin colors range from near-ivory through browns to near-black, in a broad range of tones. Some have hair, but many are completely bald. Eye colors include the common human range, but can also include yellow, red, and orange.

**Society:** Upon completing the rite of passage, Zabrak adopt a pattern of facial tattoos. These are generally made up of a pattern of thin lines and elegant designs. They are often based on family tradition, but can also incorporate personal designs or representations associated with significant events.

Zabrak are renowned for their self-assurance and independent natures. The harsh conditions of their homeworld, Iridonia, led to a particularly competitive and warlike nature in its inhabitants. Thus, study in martial arts is common throughout Zabrak cultures. The bladed quarterstaff—known as a zhaboka—is a culturally significant weapon to Zabrak; historically, Zabrak would wield zhabokas while riding reeks, their war mounts. The combination of determination and military prowess has made Zabrak culture extremely resistant to Imperial domination.

In concert with their militaristic tendencies, Zabrak have established a reputation as exceptional weaponsmiths. They craft both traditional melee weapons and reliable blasters. While none of these armaments are mass-produced, they can still be found throughout the galaxy (sometimes when Zabrak surreptitiously arm other oppressed species).

**Homeworld:** Zabrak are native to Iridonia, a world located in the Mid Rim. Because its environment is so hostile to life—conditions include brutal weather, acidic seas, and a host of predatory wildlife—many Zabrak were quick to embrace spacefaring and migrate to other worlds. Consequently, many Zabrak identify themselves with their colony world rather than the homeworld of their species. Zabrak colonies can now be found spread across the galaxy, from established colonies on major metropolitan worlds to enclaves in entirely unexpected locations, such as the mountain colonies found on Dathomir. The Dathomirian Zabrak emphasize their culture's warlike tendencies to the exclusion of all else, and tend to be even more violent and dangerous than their off-world kin.

## THE ZHABOKA

Traditionally, Zabrak fought with a stylized quarterstaff called a zhaboka. Modern zhabokas are two meters long and feature a detachable central grip. Each end is a metal blade crafted from tempered durasteel. Zabrak learn to use a zhaboka afoot as well as while riding a reek war mount.

Council profited tremendously from the mercenary contracts, and a degree of savagery that appealed to the Sith became an ingrained part of Zabrak martial culture. It has remained in place long after the Sith vanished.

### SPECIES ABILITIES

**Language:** The native language of Zabrak from Iridonia is Zabraki. However, because of their long association with broader galactic civilization, almost all Zabrak also speak Basic.

**Perception of the Force:** Even before the Zabrak mastered interstellar travel well enough to establish colonies, their civilization came into contact with the dark side of the Force. The ancient Sith hired numbers of Zabrak mercenaries to use within their armies. The Zabrak High

- **Wound Threshold:** 10 + Brawn
- **Strain Threshold:** 10 + Willpower
- **Starting Experience:** 100 XP
- **Special Abilities:** Zabrak begin the game with one rank in Survival. They still may not train Survival above rank 2 during character creation.
- **Fearsome Countenance:** Zabrak add automatic ⚜ to all Coercion checks they make.

# STEPS 4 AND 5: SELECT A CAREER AND SPECIALIZATION

The first several steps in character creation determine a character's origin story. During these next two steps, the character's life decisions start to truly come into play. Players must select their character's permanent career as well as starting specialization (note that a character can gain additional specializations over the course of his adventures). These two choices reflect a character's natural aptitudes as well as life goals.

As each player undertakes this step, it is a worthwhile investment of time to review skill lists and talent trees associated with all of the careers and specializations before coming to a final choice. A selection should be based on the abilities available initially, as well as those that require a significant investment of experience points. Characters can later purchase a specialization from outside of their career, but doing so requires an investment of additional experience points and should not be taken lightly. It is far easier for a player to make an informed decision now, making sure that the career offers the abilities that he envisions his character using.

## WHAT'S THE DIFFERENCE?

A career represents a character's general approach to living life and overcoming challenges. Some individuals are oriented toward physical conflict, while others focus on acquisition of knowledge or social manipulation.

A specialization represents greater refinement of this overall approach. While many Force-sensitive individuals have trained to be Warriors, those who have chosen this path may be further classified into ones who are particularly adept at lightsaber combat and ones who specialize in flying a starfighter.

An important consideration at this stage is the fact that a character's career does not change. This is a reflection of the PC's central personality. The overall approach toward challenges and confrontations remains consistent, even as a character learns new techniques and occupations through one or more specializations. A great many of a character's choices and achievements are based upon initial career selection, and it may prove to be the cause of the PC's triumphs and failings as well.

Obi-Wan Kenobi is, ultimately, a Guardian. When he began his career, he focused on becoming a talented duelist, believing that this was the best way for him to serve the Jedi Order. Eventually, he became an accomplished general as well as a capable negotiator. Finally, as he moved into hiding from the Galactic Empire, he focused on surviving in the wastelands of Tatooine.

Each of these roles could be explained as the result of a decision by Obi-Wan to pursue a different specialization within the Guardian career. During his time as a Padawan, the young Jedi focused on refining his lightsaber expertise as a Soresu Defender. Then, when the Clone Wars erupted, he had no choice but to transfer to the Peacekeeper path as he led units into battle and negotiated treaties. Finally, as he entered hiding and attempted to live outside of civilization, he embraced the Protector path.

Not every character needs to follow a range of specializations. Many may identify a single path as ideal for their needs and pursue it to its very end, becoming particularly adept within a single field. Others, however, may wish to follow a broader range of approaches. This can include a familiarity with specializations from outside of their initial career as well.

# CHOOSING A CAREER

Selecting a character's career should always take into consideration more than the simple numbers. Different players often derive greater enjoyment from different styles of play. Two key questions can quickly narrow down the important decision of which career to choose.

## WHICH ROLE?

Most campaigns benefit from characters with a broad variety of backgrounds. With this approach, each player's character has an opportunity to assume the central focus of gameplay as different types of challenges arise. Of course, groups of complementary characters are unlikely to arise by random chance. To facilitate this, it is important for the players to discuss their selections with one another and the Game Master at this stage.

In specialized circumstances, a campaign could be built around a batch of characters who all share the same career. This might work if the characters are all from a common Force tradition, embracing the same teacher and philosophy. However, that is a restricted and atypical approach. In most cases, players like to approach the setting from different play styles, and a range of careers is key to addressing that.

When choosing a career for a new character, there are a few questions that can be instrumental in making a good choice:

- **Is this character's first instinct to fight?** Force techniques can make any character a capable combatant, and all of the careers include a lightsaber specialization, which reinforces this. The Warrior career, however, makes combat a primary focus. Seekers and Guardians are also skilled fighters, though they choose different approaches. Some Seeker specializations tend toward ranged combat, and some Guardian specializations tend toward toughness and resilience.
- **Is this character a negotiator?** In the days of the Old Republic, Jedi were often called upon to

settle conflicts, negotiate, and keep the peace. Mind tricks can make this easier, but empathy and logic are longer-term solutions. Mystics are particularly capable in this field, but both Consulars and Guardians have effective techniques as well.

- **Is this character an academic?** Through mental discipline and meditation, some Force practitioners can absorb and retain huge amounts of information. This can be a valuable resource in the field, particularly when a holocron is unavailable. Consulars are the characters most likely to master a range of fields of study, though Sentinels often become adept in this area as well.
- **Is this character an infiltrator?** Reconnaissance builds the foundation for successful conflicts, whether those conflicts are physical or social. A character who can discreetly investigate an organization may uncover information that becomes critical. Sentinels are the sneakiest within settled areas, while Seekers are more capable in less civilized areas.
- **Is this character an explorer?** The galaxy is unspeakably vast and filled with life. Many of its worlds are civilized and populous, but others remain unexplored or are occupied by unsophisticated peoples. Missions can draw characters into these environments. When they do, a Seeker is extremely capable, though some Mystics also learn such techniques.
- **Is this character a team player?** A successful mission is far more important than any personal glory. Working together, Force wielders can transform galactic culture. Guardians often master teamwork, while Consulars often pursue related paths.

These questions can help players choose a character's specializations as well. The career choice simply narrows the options for specializations. Choosing a good option at this stage can smooth later steps.

## WHAT'S THE STORY?

The outcome of a roleplaying campaign is seldom apparent at character creation. Different choices made in play can have major ramifications such that even the Game Master is left surprised at the plot's eventual direction.

Characters, likewise, can change and evolve such that their beginnings may bear little resemblance to what they eventually become. Individuals from mundane origins could become renowned heroes like Luke Skywalker or notorious villains like Darth Vader. Characters who have been separated from their Force traditions might emerge as some of the Force's preeminent masters, like Obi-Wan Kenobi. As a campaign develops, characters grow and adapt, and they

FORCE AND DESTINY is tightly focused on Player Characters who have an affinity for the Force. Because of this, every career includes a Force rating of 1. However, some players may want to play characters who are not Force-sensitive. One possible solution is that such characters could be in denial about their abilities, believing their connection to the Force to be instead simply a particular aptitude. Alternatively, Game Masters can permit players to select careers and specializations presented in EDGE OF THE EMPIRE and AGE OF REBELLION as well as in supplements for both of those lines.

A notable concern, however, is that characters who do not have a Force rating have a harder time interacting with the Morality system (see page 48). While it is possible for these players to use the system, since they do not have Force powers, they do not have access to one of the major means by which Player Characters gain Conflict. Game Masters who choose to allow careers that do not include a Force rating should consider implementing the Obligation or Duty systems from the other Star Wars Roleplaying Games.

become something different. Selecting a career provides a basis for that growth, but does not dictate it.

Characters' backgrounds and training still provide the foundation for their involvement in the story. Throughout the course of gameplay—in addition to the remaining steps in character creation—a distinct character emerges. Specializations, in conjunction with other advances, combine to mold and refine the character's abilities. The player's choices on how to use these abilities determine the character's ultimate fate.

# CHOOSING A SPECIALIZATION

Specialization selection is simply a further refinement of the career choice. After players read through the descriptions and talent trees, three questions can make this decision more clear for them.

## HOW DID THE CHARACTER LEARN THIS?

Often, characters' initial specializations are best linked to their backstories. In many cases, characters select careers based upon their predilections or their environment during their youth. A character from a primitive world is much less likely to begin play as a Starfighter Ace or a technology-oriented Artisan. Conversely, one who matures on Coruscant is less likely to begin as a Seer or Pathfinder.

## WHAT DOES THE CHARACTER DO?

Knowing the character's focus—particularly as it is related to the abilities of any other characters in the gaming group—can make the specialization choice easier. Initially, it is often effective to have each character focus on a specific skill—ideally, one of interest to the player controlling the character. The choice of a specialization can then be made based on access to that skill as well as associated talents. Skills that are core to a career are always available to all specializations, but each specialization can emphasize different ways of using them. The different styles can be tailored as keys to developing the character's personality.

## WHAT DOES THE CHARACTER WANT TO BE?

Sometimes, knowing what a character is going to become can help determine a good starting specialization. For example, even though starting characters cannot begin the game with a lightsaber, a player who wants his character to become a famed lightsaber duelist can still choose a lightsaber-focused specialization. The specialization may not provide abilities that are immediately useful, but those early purchases can pay off as the character grows and matures.

# THE CONSULAR
ᒑᓭᐯ ᔜᒍᐸᘝᐱᒍᒍᐘᒐ

The Consular's six career skills are **Cool**, **Discipline**, **Knowledge (Education)**, **Knowledge (Lore)**, **Leadership**, and **Negotiation**. A Consular automatically gains a rank in three of these skills without spending experience, as well as a discount on increasing them with future experience points. **The Consular begins play with a Force rating of 1.**

## A CONSULAR'S ROLE

The Consular focuses on the goal of achieving peace and harmony through positive discourse. Followers of this career try to avoid physical conflict whenever possible. Instead, they have faith in the Force to fuel basic compassion in all sentient beings. They believe that it is always more effective to have an intelligent discussion about a problem and then solve it through negotiations and other peaceful means than to engage in conflict to resolve it. They are opposed to needless violence but know that when confronting true evil, they must be willing to take decisive action. A Consular prides himself in knowing when to speak words of peace, and when the time for words is over.

Followers of this career are not Jedi Consulars of the now-fallen Republic, but they do embrace some of the same philosophies and practices. During the time of the Galactic Civil War, Consulars are a relatively rare breed. Imperial negotiations are most commonly handled through a position of vastly superior military might. Consequently, the Empire has little use for their peaceful approaches.

In contrast, the Rebel Alliance has a far greater need for Consulars. As the various smaller Rebel groups come into contact with one another, they need negotiators capable of building a foundation for an alliance. Consulars have helped build the foundations for the fight for freedom, bringing groups of diverse backgrounds and needs together and joining them in common cause against injustice.

Even as the Rebel Alliance becomes a well-established entity, the need for Consulars continues. Maintaining the Rebellion's push against the Empire requires assistance from a broad range of different groups. Consulars are capable of working with planetary governments—and even large corporations—to procure the equipment necessary to maintain and grow the Rebellion. They are also instrumental in persuading worlds to risk attempts at throwing off the shackles of the Empire.

Of course, not every Consular has necessarily played a role on the galactic stage. In fact, many help settle disputes closer to home, in small villages or planetary governments. Most Consulars see helping two feuding families find peace to be as rewarding as convincing an entire world to join the fight against the Empire.

Beginning characters—particularly those who are cognizant of their Force abilities—are most likely to have learned their techniques from relatively obscure traditions. Alternatively, characters who do not recognize their abilities could be extremely competent negotiators, such as accomplished political, religious, and business leaders. Any of these individuals might unwittingly tap into their Force abilities during the course of their work. This could provide the basis for a character who denies any knowledge of Force techniques while simultaneously depending on them.

# CONSULAR SPECIALIZATIONS

Those who select the Consular career must choose at least one of the following specializations. While each of these employ different techniques, all remain true to the Consular's overall goal of forging peace and understanding while standing against evil and injustice.

### HEALER

Consulars are often drawn to their career by a strong sense of compassion. In many, this is expressed by a desire to mitigate bodily harm and cure the sick. A Healer trains to do so, recognizing that helping the individual can be just as important as helping the entirety of galactic civilization.

Healers gain access to the additional career skills of **Discipline**, **Knowledge (Education)**, **Knowledge (Xenology)**, and **Medicine**. If this is the character's starting specialization, he may choose two of these

skills and gain one free rank in each without spending starting experience.

For some physicians, healing is focused entirely on the problems of the body. They treat injuries with a detached, clinical approach. A Healer, however, is driven by compassion and affinity with the Force. Because of this, a Healer takes a holistic approach toward medicine. Many Healers learn techniques that use the Force to fuel the body's natural recuperative abilities—sometimes transforming a potentially lethal injury into one that is survivable. They also seek to calm and heal the wounded spirit just as thoroughly as healing the wounded physical form.

Many Healers have very strong philosophical compunctions against physical violence. As they spend so much of their lives attempting to heal injuries, they can be extremely reluctant to inflict them. Consequently, those who study this specialization exclusively are less likely to gain abilities that are devoted to combat. Some Healers, however, can take the time to develop defensive techniques, believing that dangerous situations are often the ones in which they are most needed.

### NIMAN DISCIPLE

Even the most accomplished of negotiators can see negotiations fail and come to violence. In the time of the Republic, many Jedi peacemakers trained with the lightsaber to prepare themselves for that eventuality. Today, Consulars who wish to do the same can focus on self-defense and gain a working knowledge of lightsaber combat by following the path of the Niman Disciple.

Niman Disciples gain the additional career skills of **Discipline**, **Leadership**, **Lightsaber**, and **Negotiation**, and if this is the PC's starting specialization, the PC gains one rank in each of two of these skills. They remain focused on working with groups of individuals to come to a peaceful accord, but they acknowledge that the road to that accord may be fraught with danger. These skills can make surviving in a treacherous environment much more possible.

Due to Consulars' naturally compassionate nature, this path centers on developing defensive measures in concert with negotiation techniques. In general, the associated combat techniques are focused on survival and defense instead of attack. Also, due to the Consular's emphasis on mental discipline and self control, the Niman Disciple puts more emphasis on integrating his Force abilities into his fighting style, using the Force as his ally to defeat dangerous foes.

### SAGE

Many Consulars know the universal truth: knowledge is power, and understanding a situation can give one a decisive advantage. This holds just as true when resolving disputes or negotiations as it does on the

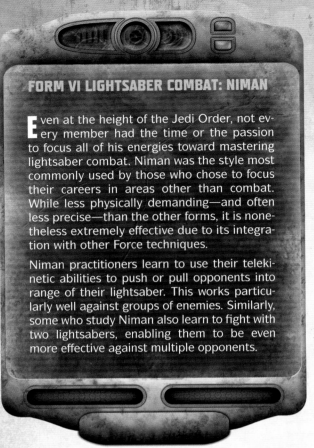

## FORM VI LIGHTSABER COMBAT: NIMAN

Even at the height of the Jedi Order, not every member had the time or the passion to focus all of his energies toward mastering lightsaber combat. Niman was the style most commonly used by those who chose to focus their careers in areas other than combat. While less physically demanding—and often less precise—than the other forms, it is nonetheless extremely effective due to its integration with other Force techniques.

Niman practitioners learn to use their telekinetic abilities to push or pull opponents into range of their lightsaber. This works particularly well against groups of enemies. Similarly, some who study Niman also learn to fight with two lightsabers, enabling them to be even more effective against multiple opponents.

battlefield. A Sage focuses on studying the world around him, recognizing that information offers tremendous advantages to himself and his allies. He then uses that power to help change the hearts and minds of others to achieve his goals.

Equal parts scholar and diplomat, Sages gain the additional career skills **Astrogation**, **Charm**, **Cool**, and **Knowledge (Lore)**. If this is a PC's first specialization, the PC gains one rank in each of two of these skills. Sages see knowledge and understanding as the basis for long-term peace and harmony. It is their belief that hatred often springs from ignorance. When a sentient comes to appreciate the backgrounds of another being's beliefs and practices, it becomes far easier not only accept that being but to feel compassion for him.

Some researchers may become lost in their academic pursuits, obsessing over dry facts while blind to the plight of the weak and helpless. Not so a Sage, who maintains connections to those around him via the Living Force. The Force provides a means of grounding Sages' studies so that they keep what they learn in perspective, always mindful of how they can use their knowledge to help others.

## CONSULAR STORIES

Consulars can emerge from nearly anywhere in the galaxy. Often, those who have escaped suffering maintain a strong sense of compassion for those who remain in need. Beings from more luxurious backgrounds may also feel the need to help the less fortunate. Sometimes, the Force can serve as a guide, drawing the right person instinctually to the path of the Consular.

- **Duty:** Some who undertake the role of a Consular do so because they believe no one else is capable of performing the task as well as they can. In many cases, this is a sign of characters who recognize his natural affinity for the Force. Such individuals know how rare that ability can be and thus feel an obligation to be a Consular and embrace the Force.

- **Compassion:** Characters who have an affinity for the Force are often also particularly empathetic. They can feel the suffering of those nearby and at times can recognize emotional turmoil from a very great distance. Many who have this natural sensitivity live their lives trying to comfort others, as they simply cannot tolerate the idea that other sentients must suffer. Such characters may go to great lengths in order to help others. In some cases, the character may have worked hard to learn the abilities necessary in order to be helpful. Others act more impulsively, simply traveling to a place where they can offer aid, depending entirely upon the Force to guide them.

- **Understanding:** Individuals who have spent much of their lives studying a situation often long for an opportunity to put their knowledge into action. In some cases, this wish can be fulfilled when the character discovers that he has critical knowledge that could transform a situation. Those who are able to put that information to practical use could become Consulars, particularly if they feel that they have been compelled by the Force to choose their particular field of study. In some cases, their natural affinity might then guide them to a situation where they can best exploit their knowledge.

- **Hope:** The Force is present throughout the galaxy, even in the bleakest of places. Sometimes, sentient beings who dwell in abject squalor can become inspired in ways that can transform their worlds. Those with Force affinity can at times overlook the challenges they face and dare to dream of a better existence. By exploiting their connections to the Force, they may be able to convince their neighbors to also ignore their difficulties and work together for the common good. A series of negotiations under such dire conditions can be enough to launch a character onto the Consular's path.

# CONSULAR: Healer

**Career Skills:** Cool, Discipline, Knowledge (Education), Knowledge (Lore), Leadership, Negotiation
**Additional Career Skills:** Discipline, Knowledge (Education), Knowledge (Xenology), Medicine

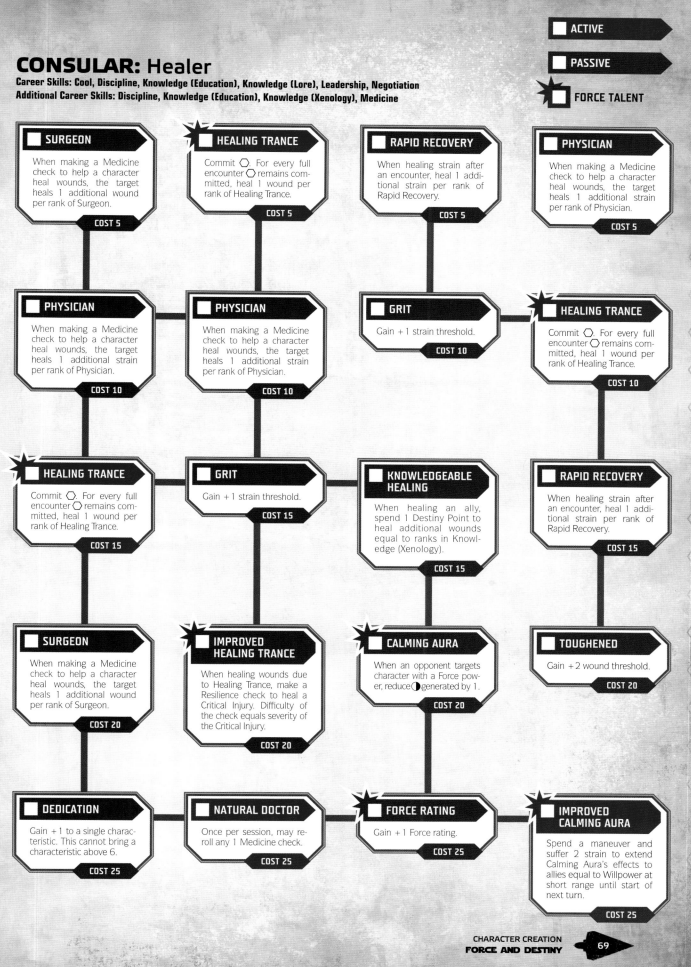

ACTIVE

PASSIVE

FORCE TALENT

**SURGEON**
When making a Medicine check to help a character heal wounds, the target heals 1 additional wound per rank of Surgeon.
COST 5

**HEALING TRANCE**
Commit ⬡. For every full encounter ⬡ remains committed, heal 1 wound per rank of Healing Trance.
COST 5

**RAPID RECOVERY**
When healing strain after an encounter, heal 1 additional strain per rank of Rapid Recovery.
COST 5

**PHYSICIAN**
When making a Medicine check to help a character heal wounds, the target heals 1 additional strain per rank of Physician.
COST 5

**PHYSICIAN**
When making a Medicine check to help a character heal wounds, the target heals 1 additional strain per rank of Physician.
COST 10

**PHYSICIAN**
When making a Medicine check to help a character heal wounds, the target heals 1 additional strain per rank of Physician.
COST 10

**GRIT**
Gain +1 strain threshold.
COST 10

**HEALING TRANCE**
Commit ⬡. For every full encounter ⬡ remains committed, heal 1 wound per rank of Healing Trance.
COST 10

**HEALING TRANCE**
Commit ⬡. For every full encounter ⬡ remains committed, heal 1 wound per rank of Healing Trance.
COST 15

**GRIT**
Gain +1 strain threshold.
COST 15

**KNOWLEDGEABLE HEALING**
When healing an ally, spend 1 Destiny Point to heal additional wounds equal to ranks in Knowledge (Xenology).
COST 15

**RAPID RECOVERY**
When healing strain after an encounter, heal 1 additional strain per rank of Rapid Recovery.
COST 15

**SURGEON**
When making a Medicine check to help a character heal wounds, the target heals 1 additional wound per rank of Surgeon.
COST 20

**IMPROVED HEALING TRANCE**
When healing wounds due to Healing Trance, make a Resilience check to heal a Critical Injury. Difficulty of the check equals severity of the Critical Injury.
COST 20

**CALMING AURA**
When an opponent targets character with a Force power, reduce ● generated by 1.
COST 20

**TOUGHENED**
Gain +2 wound threshold.
COST 20

**DEDICATION**
Gain +1 to a single characteristic. This cannot bring a characteristic above 6.
COST 25

**NATURAL DOCTOR**
Once per session, may re-roll any 1 Medicine check.
COST 25

**FORCE RATING**
Gain +1 Force rating.
COST 25

**IMPROVED CALMING AURA**
Spend a maneuver and suffer 2 strain to extend Calming Aura's effects to allies equal to Willpower at short range until start of next turn.
COST 25

# CONSULAR: Niman Disciple

**Career Skills:** Cool, Discipline, Knowledge (Education), Knowledge (Lore), Leadership, Negotiation
**Additional Career Skills:** Discipline, Leadership, Lightsaber, Negotiation

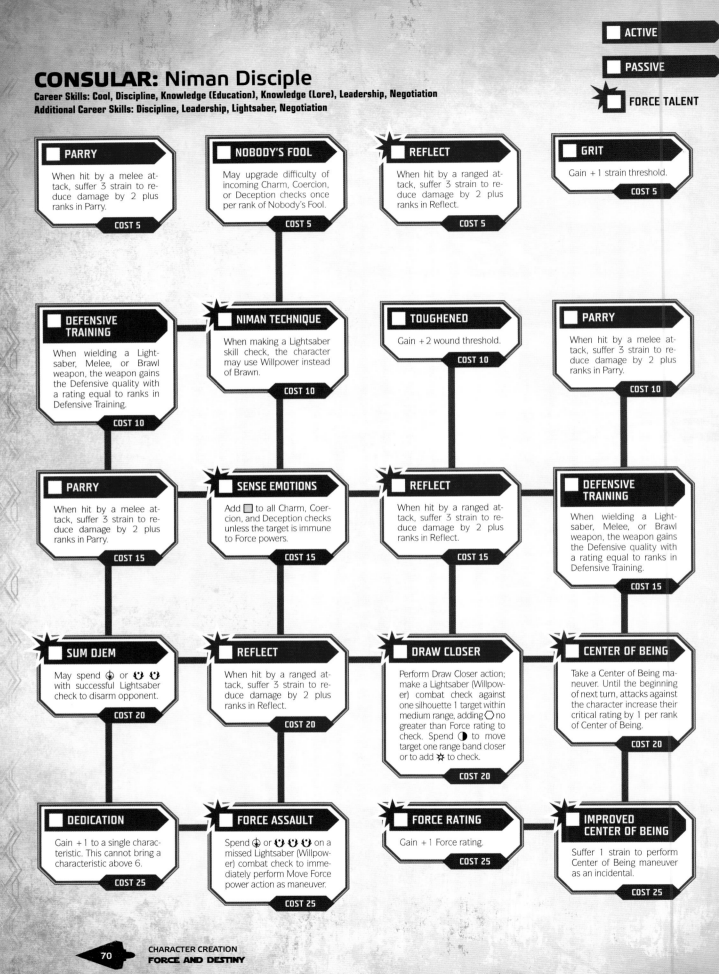

**ACTIVE**

**PASSIVE**

**FORCE TALENT**

---

**PARRY**

When hit by a melee attack, suffer 3 strain to reduce damage by 2 plus ranks in Parry.

COST 5

**NOBODY'S FOOL**

May upgrade difficulty of incoming Charm, Coercion, or Deception checks once per rank of Nobody's Fool.

COST 5

**REFLECT**

When hit by a ranged attack, suffer 3 strain to reduce damage by 2 plus ranks in Reflect.

COST 5

**GRIT**

Gain +1 strain threshold.

COST 5

---

**DEFENSIVE TRAINING**

When wielding a Lightsaber, Melee, or Brawl weapon, the weapon gains the Defensive quality with a rating equal to ranks in Defensive Training.

COST 10

**NIMAN TECHNIQUE**

When making a Lightsaber skill check, the character may use Willpower instead of Brawn.

COST 10

**TOUGHENED**

Gain +2 wound threshold.

COST 10

**PARRY**

When hit by a melee attack, suffer 3 strain to reduce damage by 2 plus ranks in Parry.

COST 10

---

**PARRY**

When hit by a melee attack, suffer 3 strain to reduce damage by 2 plus ranks in Parry.

COST 15

**SENSE EMOTIONS**

Add ☐ to all Charm, Coercion, and Deception checks unless the target is immune to Force powers.

COST 15

**REFLECT**

When hit by a ranged attack, suffer 3 strain to reduce damage by 2 plus ranks in Reflect.

COST 15

**DEFENSIVE TRAINING**

When wielding a Lightsaber, Melee, or Brawl weapon, the weapon gains the Defensive quality with a rating equal to ranks in Defensive Training.

COST 15

---

**SUM DJEM**

May spend ◈ or ❂ ❂ with successful Lightsaber check to disarm opponent.

COST 20

**REFLECT**

When hit by a ranged attack, suffer 3 strain to reduce damage by 2 plus ranks in Reflect.

COST 20

**DRAW CLOSER**

Perform Draw Closer action; make a Lightsaber (Willpower) combat check against one silhouette 1 target within medium range, adding ○ no greater than Force rating to check. Spend ◑ to move target one range band closer or to add ✪ to check.

COST 20

**CENTER OF BEING**

Take a Center of Being maneuver. Until the beginning of next turn, attacks against the character increase their critical rating by 1 per rank of Center of Being.

COST 20

---

**DEDICATION**

Gain +1 to a single characteristic. This cannot bring a characteristic above 6.

COST 25

**FORCE ASSAULT**

Spend ◈ or ❂ ❂ ❂ on a missed Lightsaber (Willpower) combat check to immediately perform Move Force power action as maneuver.

COST 25

**FORCE RATING**

Gain +1 Force rating.

COST 25

**IMPROVED CENTER OF BEING**

Suffer 1 strain to perform Center of Being maneuver as an incidental.

COST 25

---

# CONSULAR: Sage

**Career Skills:** Cool, Discipline, Knowledge (Education), Knowledge (Lore), Leadership, Negotiation
**Additional Career Skills:** Astrogation, Charm, Cool, Knowledge (Lore)

## GRIT
Gain +1 strain threshold.
**COST 5**

## KILL WITH KINDNESS
Remove ■ per rank of Kill with Kindness from all Charm and Leadership checks.
**COST 5**

## RESEARCHER
Remove ■ per rank of Researcher from all Knowledge checks. Researching a subject takes half the time.
**COST 5**

## GRIT
Gain +1 strain threshold.
**COST 5**

## SMOOTH TALKER
When first acquired, choose 1 skill; Charm, Coercion, Deception, or Negotiation. When making checks with that skill, spend ⊕ to gain additional ☼ equal to ranks in Smooth Talker.
**COST 10**

## RESEARCHER
Remove ■ per rank of Researcher from all Knowledge checks. Researching a subject takes half the time.
**COST 10**

## CONFIDENCE
May decrease difficulty of Discipline checks to avoid fear by 1 per rank of Confidence.
**COST 10**

## KNOWLEDGE SPECIALIZATION
When acquired, choose 1 Knowledge skill. When making that skill check, may spend ⊕ result to gain additional successes equal to ranks in Knowledge Specialization.
**COST 10**

## VALUABLE FACTS
Once per encounter, perform Valuable Facts action; make an **Average (◆ ◆) Knowledge check**. If successful, add ⊕ to one ally's skill check during the encounter.
**COST 15**

## SMOOTH TALKER
When first acquired, choose 1 skill; Charm, Coercion, Deception, or Negotiation. When making checks with that skill, spend ⊕ to gain additional ☼ equal to ranks in Smooth Talker.
**COST 15**

## KNOWLEDGE SPECIALIZATION
When acquired, choose 1 Knowledge skill. When making that skill check, may spend ⊕ result to gain additional successes equal to ranks in Knowledge Specialization.
**COST 15**

## ONE WITH THE UNIVERSE
Once per session, meditate, then perform One with the Universe action; make **Average (◆ ◆) Astrogation check**. If successful, add ○ to all Force power checks in next encounter. If successful with ⊛, add ● instead.
**COST 15**

## FORCE RATING
Gain +1 Force rating.
**COST 20**

## GRIT
Gain +1 strain threshold.
**COST 20**

## PREEMPTIVE AVOIDANCE
May spend 1 Destiny Point to disengage from engaged enemy as an out-of-turn incidental.
**COST 20**

## KNOWLEDGE SPECIALIZATION
When acquired, choose 1 Knowledge skill. When making that skill check, may spend ⊕ result to gain additional successes equal to ranks in Knowledge Specialization.
**COST 20**

## BALANCE
When the character recovers strain at the end of the encounter, he may add ○ per Force rating. He recovers additional strain equal to ◗ generated.
**COST 25**

## THE FORCE IS MY ALLY
Once per session, may suffer 2 strain to perform Force power action as maneuver.
**COST 25**

## NATURAL NEGOTIATOR
Once per session, may reroll any 1 Cool or Negotiation check.
**COST 25**

## FORCE RATING
Gain +1 Force rating.
**COST 25**

# THE GUARDIAN
## ⃕⊒⌐ ⊍⊐⌐⊀⊀⊼⌐⋀

The Guardian's six career skills are **Brawl**, **Cool**, **Discipline**, **Melee**, **Resilience**, and **Vigilance**. A character who chooses this career automatically gains a rank in three of these skills without spending experience and gains a discount on increasing them with future experience points. **The Guardian begins with a Force rating of 1.**

## A GUARDIAN'S ROLE

Adherents of the Guardian career are driven by a strong sense of responsibility and compassion. They recognize their affinity for the Force gives them the power—and responsibility—to help the helpless and aid the oppressed. Guardians tend to be blunt and forthright, using their prodigious combat prowess and natural leadership skills to directly intercede where they are needed most.

Most Guardians have a swagger about them, a cool confidence coupled with an air of nobility and authority. This poise is often well deserved. Guardians are capable of surviving and winning battles against overwhelming odds. Their martial training tends to focus almost exclusively on defense and resilience, leaving a Guardian as hard as granite. Hordes of opponents break upon a Guardian like waves upon shoreline rocks, leaving themselves exhausted and open to devastating counterattacks.

Alone, this combat prowess would be impressive, but a Guardian couples his abilities with his connection to the

Force. This combination makes the Guardian far more than a mere thug, inspiring compassion and concern for those he protects. A Guardian's defensive combat style matches this concern for life. Rather than make aggressive moves, he gives his opposition every chance to relent and choose a peaceful resolution. However, if they attack, the Guardian quickly demonstrates why their choice was the wrong one.

In many cases, a Guardian becomes established within a particular geographic region. This might be as large as a group of planets within a sector or as small as a neighborhood in a large city. A Guardian who focuses on a region in this way can choose to take stewardship of it. Notably, such stewardship comes out of a sense of responsibility and duty rather than any actual authority. Guardians seldom assume political power. Instead, they act in accordance with their internal moral compass, as guided by the Force, to ensure that everyone under their protection receives the justice they deserve.

Other Guardians follow the calling of the Force to travel and aid beings in need wherever they might find them. Many such Guardians wander in a seemingly aimless fashion, apparently letting random chance direct them where they might need to go. Almost invariably, their voyages soon lead them to people who desperately need help.

# GUARDIAN SPECIALIZATIONS

Each of the specializations within the Guardian career focuses on using the Force to aid others. Each pursues a different path, though they are complementary, so that an accomplished Guardian may rely on lessons from each specialization.

## PEACEKEEPER

Across the galaxy, there are always tyrants, and those unlucky enough to suffer under their rule. Some Guardians take direct action through military force to attempt to overthrow such despots. Other Guardians see wars ravaging planets and harming the weak and defenseless. They step in to defend those innocents, and enforce peace at the tip of a lightsaber. These Guardians are often known as Peacekeepers.

Peacekeepers acquire **Discipline**, **Leadership**, **Perception**, and **Piloting (Planetary)** as additional career skills, and if this is the PC's starting specialization, the PC gains one rank in each of two of these skills. This combination ensures that they can recognize threats and respond to them in an effective and timely manner. Skilled Peacekeepers must be able to effectively delegate assignments to allies while reserving themselves to confront the challenges for which they are most adept.

Many Peacekeepers only assume this specialization after they have been thrust into a position of authority—sometimes repeatedly. Because of their naturally protective personalities, these Guardians want to do everything in their power to protect their friends. Often, they decide the best choice is to become the best leader they can, out of a sense of responsibility rather than a desire for power.

Characters who pursue the Peacekeeper's path seldom limit their activities to a single region. Often once one region has been pacified or a tyrant overthrown, a Peacekeeper sets his sight on the next challenge and leads his friends and fellow freedom fighters to overcome it. Under the shadow of the Empire, Peacekeepers are always needed.

## PROTECTOR

Guardians are often driven by their compassion for the plights of those who cannot protect themselves. Protectors ensure these innocents never come to harm. Few are tougher than a Protector, and even fewer can get through his guard to attack those he defends. Even if his charges do suffer harm, the Protector possesses basic medical knowledge to heal their wounds.

Protectors gain the additional career skills of **Athletics**, **Medicine**, **Ranged (Light)**, and **Resilience**. If this is the character's starting specialization, he may choose two of these skills and gain one free rank in each, without spending starting experience. This combination enables the character to assist those who are in need during a crisis. These skills complement many of the talent selections, so that the Protector remains capable of effectively shielding others from suffering harm without sacrificing his own capabilities.

Protectors could be considered bodyguards, but their efforts are seldom limited to protecting a single individual. Instead, Protectors are more likely to defend the needy on a larger scale. Often, they function as rescue workers, using their medical knowledge to stabilize injuries in the field and then providing additional protection. In other cases, Protectors may shelter refugees or other victims fleeing terrible situations, holding the line until the innocents can escape to safety. When a Protector does defend a single individual, it is likely because a great threat—even another Force user—pursues the person.

Some Protectors might come to master their abilities while working in a military or law enforcement role. Some Force techniques might manifest spontaneously as they instinctively act to keep companions safe. This could be particularly relevant for individuals who have not recognized their connection to the Force. Its presence might enable them to save an ally from danger in a seemingly inexplicable fashion. However, once these individuals realize the power they have, they must decide whether to continue their career and keep it a secret, or leave the life they've known and explore their new abilities.

## FORM III LIGHTSABER COMBAT: SORESU

Also known as the Resilience Form, Soresu is a style of lightsaber combat focused on defensive maneuvers. Jedi who train in the Soresu form spend much of their time in deep meditation. Those who master this combat style consider themselves to be the calm eye of the attacking storm. From this position, they can easily deflect any incoming attacks.

Soresu is adept at intercepting blaster fire as well as the lightsabers of multiple opponents. When practicing this technique at the highest level of competence, the Jedi enter into a precognitive state, knowing the precise move required to deflect each attack. However, in order to prepare him to defend, Soresu limits the combatant's ability to counterattack.

### SORESU DEFENDER

Guardians frequently and deliberately put themselves in harm's way in order to aid others. However, just as the Protector is unmatched at keeping others safe, the Soresu Defender has mastered the art of self defense. With lightsaber in hand, Soresu Defenders can fend off hordes of enemies or stand firm against hails of blaster fire, surviving the worst the enemy can throw at them.

A Soresu Defender earns additional career skill access to **Discipline**, **Knowledge (Lore)**, **Lightsaber**, and **Vigilance**. If this is the character's starting specialization, he may choose two of these skills and gain one free rank in each, without spending starting experience. With this combination of skills, the character can maintain constant vigilance, recognize threats, and remain resolute in the face of danger.

Soresu Defenders depend on the Force to guide them through dangers. Their techniques rest almost entirely on knowing how best to use their weapons for defensive purposes. In many ways, this style approaches the level of precognition, as the Force guides its practitioners to use their weapons to deflect an incoming attack or to move out of the way of an assault. Individuals who are unaware of their Force potential can become accomplished martial artists using these techniques, but true Soresu Defenders must be sensitive to the Force.

## GUARDIAN STORIES

Guardians can emerge from nearly any environment. These characters act out of a strong compulsion to see justice and fairness throughout the galaxy. While they are often physically strong, Guardians use their strength as a tool to help those in need, rather than as a means to force their beliefs on others.

- **Justice:** Guardians often emerge from cultures or communities where there is a clear case of inequality. The character may draw upon the Force instinctively to see to it that a tyrant is overthrown or conditions are improved for the needy victims. Such individuals may live out their lives fighting crusade after crusade against injustice, always striving to offer assistance to those who cannot help themselves.

- **Selflessness:** Most Guardians are extremely self-assured, but they are also willing to act without fear of personal consequence. Throughout their lives, they have shown that they can overcome the most dramatic of challenges. Because of their past successes—as well as their connection to the Force—they are often comfortable with the idea of taking extreme personal risks in ways that others find unacceptable. They know that they're the only ones who can help in dire situations, and they throw themselves into those situations selflessly. All of their training and study becomes focused on helping others.

- **Zeal:** Enthusiasm can be a driving factor in a Guardian's life and career choices. Characters who experience success when they take risks can come to love the thrill of danger and sweet rush of victory. A commitment to travel across the galaxy righting wrongs and saving people from misfortune can be extremely tempting to an individual who laughs in the face of danger. Guardians who embark upon their career due to such a drive must sometimes depend on their companions and allies to steer them toward more moderate solutions to their challenges. Otherwise, even beings with the advantages they possess may find themselves overwhelmed.

- **Wanderlust:** Rarely, those who pursue a Guardian career also have a tremendous desire to travel the galaxy. This can be a fortunate combination, as their travels may be punctuated by opportunities to use their abilities to ease suffering. Countless planets are littered with oppressors and people living under persecution. For many Guardians, their travels may never actually come to an end, as they meditate on the Force and depend on it to draw them to the places and peoples who need help.

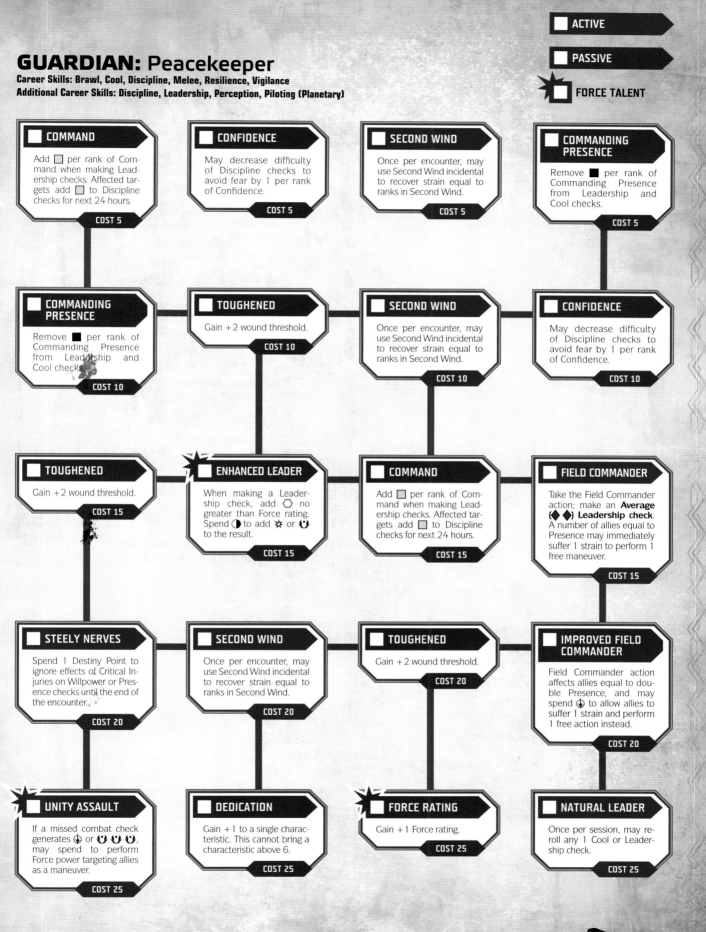

# GUARDIAN: Peacekeeper

**Career Skills:** Brawl, Cool, Discipline, Melee, Resilience, Vigilance
**Additional Career Skills:** Discipline, Leadership, Perception, Piloting (Planetary)

☐ ACTIVE
☐ PASSIVE
☐ FORCE TALENT

### COMMAND
Add ☐ per rank of Command when making Leadership checks. Affected targets add ☐ to Discipline checks for next 24 hours.
**COST 5**

### CONFIDENCE
May decrease difficulty of Discipline checks to avoid fear by 1 per rank of Confidence.
**COST 5**

### SECOND WIND
Once per encounter, may use Second Wind incidental to recover strain equal to ranks in Second Wind.
**COST 5**

### COMMANDING PRESENCE
Remove ■ per rank of Commanding Presence from Leadership and Cool checks.
**COST 5**

### COMMANDING PRESENCE
Remove ■ per rank of Commanding Presence from Leadership and Cool checks.
**COST 10**

### TOUGHENED
Gain +2 wound threshold.
**COST 10**

### SECOND WIND
Once per encounter, may use Second Wind incidental to recover strain equal to ranks in Second Wind.
**COST 10**

### CONFIDENCE
May decrease difficulty of Discipline checks to avoid fear by 1 per rank of Confidence.
**COST 10**

### TOUGHENED
Gain +2 wound threshold.
**COST 15**

### ENHANCED LEADER
When making a Leadership check, add ◯ no greater than Force rating. Spend ◐ to add ✹ or ✪ to the result.
**COST 15**

### COMMAND
Add ☐ per rank of Command when making Leadership checks. Affected targets add ☐ to Discipline checks for next 24 hours.
**COST 15**

### FIELD COMMANDER
Take the Field Commander action; make an **Average (◆ ◆) Leadership check**. A number of allies equal to Presence may immediately suffer 1 strain to perform 1 free maneuver.
**COST 15**

### STEELY NERVES
Spend 1 Destiny Point to ignore effects of Critical Injuries on Willpower or Presence checks until the end of the encounter.
**COST 20**

### SECOND WIND
Once per encounter, may use Second Wind incidental to recover strain equal to ranks in Second Wind.
**COST 20**

### TOUGHENED
Gain +2 wound threshold.
**COST 20**

### IMPROVED FIELD COMMANDER
Field Commander action affects allies equal to double Presence, and may spend ⦿ to allow allies to suffer 1 strain and perform 1 free action instead.
**COST 20**

### UNITY ASSAULT
If a missed combat check generates ⦿ or ✪ ✪ ✪, may spend to perform Force power targeting allies as a maneuver.
**COST 25**

### DEDICATION
Gain +1 to a single characteristic. This cannot bring a characteristic above 6.
**COST 25**

### FORCE RATING
Gain +1 Force rating.
**COST 25**

### NATURAL LEADER
Once per session, may reroll any 1 Cool or Leadership check.
**COST 25**

# GUARDIAN: Protector

**Career Skills:** Brawl, Cool, Discipline, Melee, Resilience, Vigilance
**Additional Career Skills:** Athletics, Medicine, Ranged (Light), Resilience

■ ACTIVE

■ PASSIVE

✦ FORCE TALENT

---

**TOUGHENED**

Gain +2 wound threshold.

COST 5

**BODY GUARD**

Once per round, perform the Body Guard maneuver to guard an engaged character. Suffer a number of strain no greater than ranks of Body Guard, then until the beginning of the next turn upgrade the difficulty of combat checks targeting the character by that number.

COST 5

**GRIT**

Gain +1 strain threshold.

COST 5

**TOUGHENED**

Gain +2 wound threshold.

COST 5

---

**PARRY**

When hit by a melee attack, suffer 3 strain to reduce damage by 2 plus ranks in Parry.

COST 10

**PHYSICIAN**

When making a Medicine check to help a character heal wounds, the target heals 1 additional strain per rank of Physician.

COST 10

**STIMPACK SPECIALIZATION**

Stimpacks heal 1 additional wound per rank of Stimpack Specialization.

COST 10

**FORCE PROTECTION**

Perform the Force Protection maneuver; suffer 1 strain and commit ◯ up to ranks of Force Protection. Increase soak by number of ◯ committed until beginning of next turn. Suffer 1 strain every turn ◯ remains committed.

COST 10

---

**REFLECT**

When hit by a ranged attack, suffer 3 strain to reduce damage by 2 plus ranks in Reflect.

COST 15

**STIMPACK SPECIALIZATION**

Stimpacks heal 1 additional wound per rank of Stimpack Specialization.

COST 15

**HEIGHTENED AWARENESS**

Allies within short range add ■ to Perception or Vigilance checks. Engaged allies add ■■.

COST 15

**CENTER OF BEING**

Take a Center of Being maneuver. Until the beginning of next turn, attacks against the character increase their critical rating by 1 per rank of Center of Being.

COST 15

---

**CIRCLE OF SHELTER**

When an engaged ally suffers a hit, may use Parry or Reflect incidental against the hit.

COST 20

**FORCE PROTECTION**

Perform the Force Protection maneuver; suffer 1 strain and commit ◯ up to ranks of Force Protection. Increase soak by number of ◯ committed until beginning of next turn. Suffer 1 strain every turn ◯ remains committed.

COST 20

**GRIT**

Gain +1 strain threshold.

COST 20

**BODY GUARD**

Once per round, perform the Body Guard maneuver to guard an engaged character. Suffer a number of strain no greater than ranks of Body Guard, then until the beginning of the next turn upgrade the difficulty of combat checks targeting the character by that number.

COST 20

---

**CENTER OF BEING**

Take a Center of Being maneuver. Until the beginning of next turn, attacks against the character increase their critical rating by 1 per rank of Center of Being.

COST 25

**FORCE RATING**

Gain +1 Force rating.

COST 25

**DEDICATION**

Gain +1 to a single characteristic. This cannot bring a characteristic above 6.

COST 25

**IMPROVED BODY GUARD**

Once per session, when an ally protected by the Body Guard maneuver suffers a hit, suffer the hit instead.

COST 25

# GUARDIAN: Soresu Defender

**Career Skills:** Brawl, Cool, Discipline, Melee, Resilience, Vigilance
**Additional Career Skills:** Discipline, Knowledge (Lore), Lightsaber, Vigilance

**PARRY**
When hit by a melee attack, suffer 3 strain to reduce damage by 2 plus ranks in Parry.
COST 5

**PARRY**
When hit by a melee attack, suffer 3 strain to reduce damage by 2 plus ranks in Parry.
COST 5

**TOUGHENED**
Gain +2 wound threshold.
COST 5

**DEFENSIVE STANCE**
Once per round, may perform Defensive Stance maneuver and suffer a number of strain to upgrade difficulty of all incoming melee attacks by an equal number for the next round. Strain suffered this way cannot exceed ranks in Defensive Stance.
COST 5

**SORESU TECHNIQUE**
When making a check using the Lightsaber skill, the character may use Intellect instead of Brawn.
COST 10

**REFLECT**
When hit by a ranged attack, suffer 3 strain to reduce damage by 2 plus ranks in Reflect.
COST 10

**GRIT**
Gain +1 strain threshold.
COST 10

**GRIT**
Gain +1 strain threshold.
COST 10

**CONFIDENCE**
May decrease difficulty of Discipline checks to avoid fear by 1 per rank of Confidence.
COST 15

**IMPROVED PARRY**
When parrying a hit that generated ▽ or ⚙ ⚙ ⚙, may hit attacker once with Lightsaber, Brawl, or Melee weapon (dealing base damage) after original attack resolves.
COST 15

**DEFENSIVE CIRCLE**
May take the Defensive Circle action, making a **Hard (◆◆◆) Lightsaber (Intellect) check**. The character, plus one ally within short range per ✦, gains X defense until the beginning of next turn. X equals 1, plus 1 per 🟢 🟢.
COST 15

**PARRY**
When hit by a melee attack, suffer 3 strain to reduce damage by 2 plus ranks in Parry.
COST 15

**PARRY**
When hit by a melee attack, suffer 3 strain to reduce damage by 2 plus ranks in Parry.
COST 20

**REFLECT**
When hit by a ranged attack, suffer 3 strain to reduce damage by 2 plus ranks in Reflect.
COST 20

**REFLECT**
When hit by a ranged attack, suffer 3 strain to reduce damage by 2 plus ranks in Reflect.
COST 20

**DEFENSIVE STANCE**
Once per round, may perform Defensive Stance maneuver and suffer a number of strain to upgrade difficulty of all incoming melee attacks by an equal number for the next round. Strain suffered this way cannot exceed ranks in Defensive Stance.
COST 20

**SUPREME PARRY**
If the user did not make a combat check during his previous turn, may suffer 1 strain to use Parry.
COST 25

**DEDICATION**
Gain +1 to a single characteristic. This cannot bring a characteristic above 6.
COST 25

**IMPROVED REFLECT**
When reflecting a hit that generated ▽ or ⚙ ⚙ ⚙, may hit one target in medium range with the same damage as the initial hit, after original attack resolves.
COST 25

**STRATEGIC FORM**
May take the Strategic Form action, making a **Hard (◆ ◆ ◆) Lightsaber (Intellect) check**, rolling ⬡ no greater than Force rating. If successful, 1 target within short range may only attack character for 1 round. Spend ◖ to extend effects for 1 target for 1 round.
COST 25

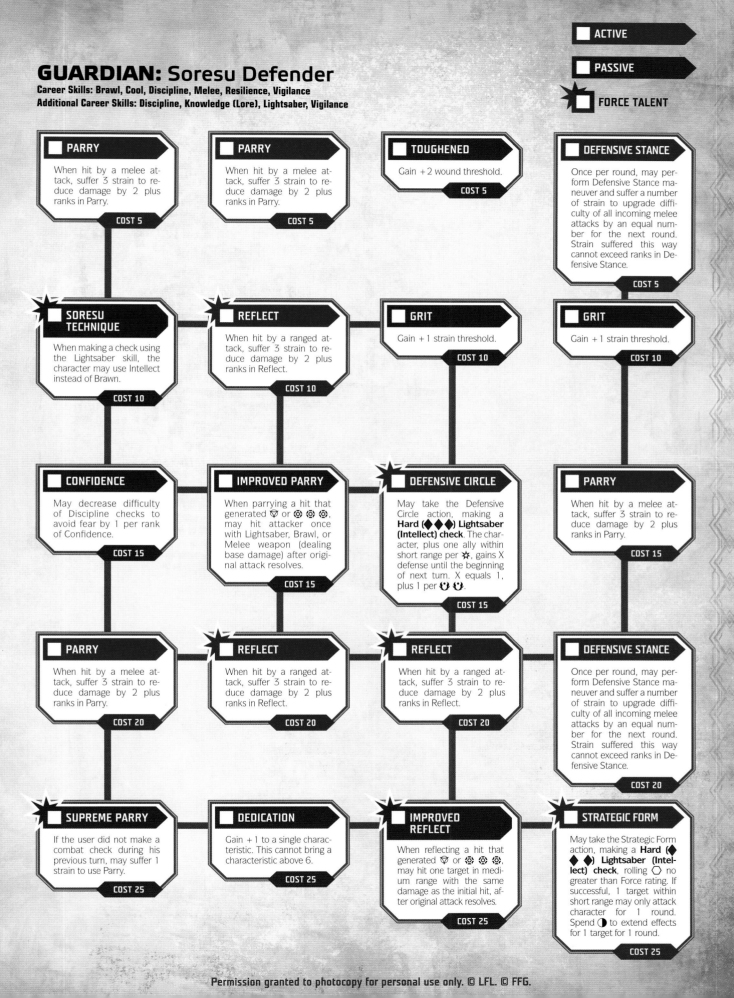

# THE MYSTIC
ᒡᓓᐯᒐ ᒐᐁᐁᒐᒡ1ᔦ

The Mystic's six career skills are **Charm**, **Coercion**, **Knowledge (Lore)**, **Knowledge (Outer Rim)**, **Perception**, and **Vigilance**. A Mystic automatically gains a rank in three of these skills without spending experience and gains a discount on increasing them with future experience points. **A Mystic begins play with a Force rating of 1.**

## A MYSTIC'S ROLE

Characters who follow the Mystic career are typically born to accept this mantle. From the time they first open their eyes, a strong connection to the Force colors their perception of the world surrounding them. They constantly perceive the ebb and flow of its energies between all living things. To many Mystics, the Force is as important a guide and mentor as their family and trusted friends. It teaches them to trust their instincts more than any training or instruction, for those instincts come from the Force.

Because Mystics dwell so deeply in the Force, they often learn to master a broad range of Force powers. Training and practice can, of course, enhance their aptitude, but not all of them require a teacher. Rather, many Mystics simply intuit their powers through experience and their connection to the Force. Many Mystics accept this as the natural way of things. They strongly believe that the Force guides and provides for them as long as they remember to remain open and aware of its presence.

Many Mystics come from a culture where their connection to the Force has made them a person of importance. In some instances, they might have served as an advisor or even a magistrate. In other cases, their role could have been more religious or shamanic. They are likely to expect a certain degree of deference because of their previous experiences. This means many Mystics develop a powerful charisma and captivating presence. Some Mystics come by this naturally, able to convince others of what they have seen using soft words and persuasive arguments. Others work tirelessly to develop these personality traits, knowing that a compliment (or even a lie) in the right ear at the right time can quickly advance their goals.

# MYSTIC SPECIALIZATIONS

Each of the specializations of the Mystic career are linked to Mystics' natural comfort with the Force and natural or cultivated charisma. Their assurance and confidence flows from the Force and, through the Force, Mystics know they can guide others to a desired outcome.

## ADVISOR

Not everyone who is skilled in the ways of the Force seeks to hold a position of tremendous authority. In fact, some believe they would find it too easy to abuse their unique abilities if they placed themselves in a position of leadership. Instead, they choose to accept the Advisor's role to ensure they cannot be corrupted by the lure of power. Others feel their advice too valuable to limit to one planet or region and wander the stars, sowing the guidance of the Force wherever they might go. Socially adept and Force-sensitive characters with either of these philosophies can be excellent fits for the Advisor specialization.

Advisors acquire **Charm**, **Deception**, **Negotiation**, and **Streetwise** as additional career skills. If this is the character's starting specialization, he may choose two of these skills and gain one free rank in each, without spending starting experience. This combination enables Advisors to take a very pragmatic approach in working with others and offering them the guidance of the Force. An accomplished Advisor can quickly analyze the risks of a situation and then, using the necessary tools, influence the involved parties so that a desired outcome is rapidly achieved. A less scrupulous individual with these techniques could become a successful con artist. Advisors must be careful to avoid that fate.

Some Advisors attach themselves to a planetary government, helping to shape the rule of law and ensure fairness and justice for all. Many popular rulers have had wise Advisors at hand, helping ensure their policies do the most good for the greatest number. Other Advisors choose to work in less glamorous roles—often among the poor and the desperate. There, they try to counsel and guide individuals in dire straits, sometimes providing salvation to those who have lost all hope.

## MAKASHI DUELIST

The presence and showmanship that can come naturally to all Mystics reflects itself in the way of a duelist.

For practitioners of Makashi, dominating a combat through one's presence is just as important as dominating it through martial prowess, and the Makashi Duelist is the ultimate expression of that art.

Makashi Duelists acquire **Charm**, **Cool**, **Coordination**, and **Lightsaber** as additional career skills. If this is the character's starting specialization, he may choose two of these skills and gain one free rank in each, without spending starting experience. This combination reflects the showmanship and presentation so intrinsic to the duelist's art. A true Makashi Duelist must always fight with poise and grace, never showing the slightest strain and keeping complete control over his facial expressions and his body's most minute movements.

Though some detractors may dismiss this fighting style as overly foppish and vain, a Makashi Duelist remains an exceptionally potent combatant. Those detractors forget that the Makashi form was developed to fight against other lightsaber-armed opponents. At its heart, Makashi focuses on one goal: to meet an enemy with a sword or lightsaber and slay him. A true Makashi Duelist never loses sight of this goal, and all his flourishes and feints are but means to an end. Movements that work to deflect and exhaust an opponent—particularly if the foe is not prepared for battle with a Force-sensitive—can soon leave an enemy frustrated with the entire experience. As the opponent becomes increasingly worn down, the Makashi Duelist soon finds an opportunity to exploit the foe's exhaustion.

A Makashi Duelist's force of personality, rather than natural athleticism, often drives his combat technique. Elements of personal flair become an effective means of disorienting and distracting an opponent during a battle. Sometimes a verbal misdirection can be every bit as effective as a physical one, leaving an opponent open to a single master stroke.

## SEER

Some individuals are able to remain constantly aware of the Force's presence, even as they go about their daily lives. They recognize its influence in the subtlest of ways. For them, minor ripples in the Force reveal deep meanings and forewarn of critical events far in the future. However, this quantity of information—particularly in environments filled with other sentients—can become overwhelming. Because of this, many who follow the path of the Seer choose to live lives of relative isolation, far from crowded towns and cities.

Seers acquire **Discipline**, **Knowledge (Lore)**, **Survival**, and **Vigilance** as additional career skills. If this is the character's starting specialization, he may choose two of these skills and gain one free rank in each, without spending starting experience. Successful Seers

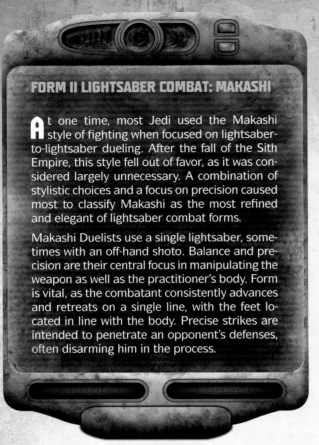

## FORM II LIGHTSABER COMBAT: MAKASHI

At one time, most Jedi used the Makashi style of fighting when focused on lightsaber-to-lightsaber dueling. After the fall of the Sith Empire, this style fell out of favor, as it was considered largely unnecessary. A combination of stylistic choices and a focus on precision caused most to classify Makashi as the most refined and elegant of lightsaber combat forms.

Makashi Duelists use a single lightsaber, sometimes with an off-hand shoto. Balance and precision are their central focus in manipulating the weapon as well as the practitioner's body. Form is vital, as the combatant consistently advances and retreats on a single line, with the feet located in line with the body. Precise strikes are intended to penetrate an opponent's defenses, often disarming him in the process.

must be able to maintain focus on daily life even as they also observe the Force. They must learn to recognize a broad range of subtle signs. They must also be prepared to dwell in a potentially hostile environment, apart from civilization, so that they can be spared from information overload.

Among Force-sensitive individuals, Seers are arguably the ones who feel the strongest sense of guidance from the Force. Dwelling within the Force at all times, they can recognize even minor ripples and follow them to their source to stop a small problem from turning into a major crisis. Similarly, they may recognize an event that occurs far away and advise those nearby to take action so they can be prepared well in advance of an upcoming crisis. Seers' abilities often give them insights into the future, guiding them to places and people who most need their wisdom and advice. This sometimes enables Seers to be in just the right place at the right time to take action that proves to be pivotal.

The challenge for many Seers is to know the best time to move into a civilized area. As their sensitivity can become muddled, they may miss a sign of great import. Consequently, some prefer to remain apart from society for as long as possible, depending on allies to carry their missives. Seldom, however, are others capable of communicating a warning as effectively as the Seer who initially sensed the danger.

## MYSTIC STORIES

Mystics often emerge from isolated environments, where they have been able to hone their Force abilities from an early age. However, a Mystic's mindset and philosophy is often far more important than his personal history. In essence, his ability to sense the power of the Force and to communicate its message to others is the very heart of a Mystic.

- **Insights:** Individuals with a strong connection to the Force often view the world around them through its lens. This alternative perspective sometimes reveals information that is concealed from others. Whether recognizing that such individuals are using the Force or not, others can soon come to appreciate and even rely on their keen perception. The character's particular knack effectively drives him to the Mystic career.

- **Hereditary:** In some cultures, a Force-sensitive may play a critical role as a spiritual advisor to an entire community. Sometimes the role is hereditary, passed from parent to child. In other instances, the character might have been anointed as a successor from an early age due to evidence of unusual abilities. Typically, such individuals train from the time they can walk in preparation for assuming their position of authority upon the passage of their predecessor. This can thrust them into the Mystic career without ever having had another option.

- **Secrets:** Information can shape people and cultures. Understanding, or a lack of it, often drives belief systems as well as political structures. In some instances, a Force-sensitive character—and possibly the character's teacher—can be privy to information that is hidden from a wider culture. Through initiation into the ways of the Force, the character may discover facts that could completely transform his native culture. Strictures of training—or fear of cultural transformation—may compel the character to keep this information hidden. The trappings of this approach could reveal his career as a Mystic.

- **Foresight:** During times of deep meditation, even an untrained Force-sensitive can receive brief visions of possible futures. These visions—particularly if they are worrisome—can become a compelling element in the individual's life. Some might flee from these visions, attempting to find isolation from them. Others might try to direct peers to act in ways that could prevent unfortunate outcomes. In either of these cases, the character could begin to embrace the life of the Mystic as he uses the Force to provide others with guidance based on his divinations.

# MYSTIC: Advisor

**Career Skills:** Charm, Coercion, Knowledge (Lore), Knowledge (Outer Rim), Perception, Vigilance
**Additional Career Skills:** Charm, Deception, Negotiation, Streetwise

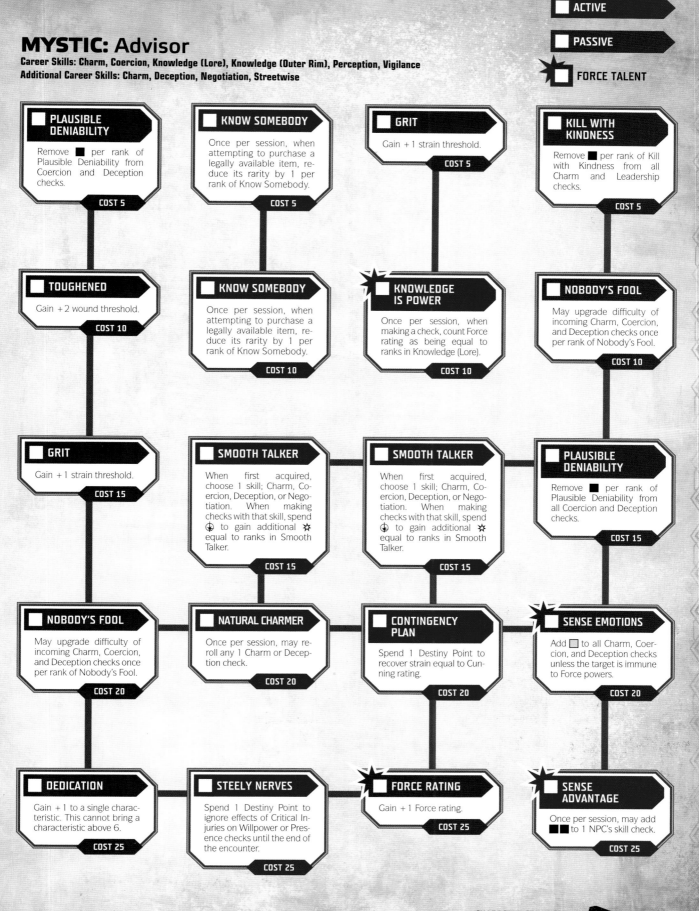

**ACTIVE**

**PASSIVE**

**FORCE TALENT**

### PLAUSIBLE DENIABILITY
Remove ■ per rank of Plausible Deniability from Coercion and Deception checks.
**COST 5**

### KNOW SOMEBODY
Once per session, when attempting to purchase a legally available item, reduce its rarity by 1 per rank of Know Somebody.
**COST 5**

### GRIT
Gain +1 strain threshold.
**COST 5**

### KILL WITH KINDNESS
Remove ■ per rank of Kill with Kindness from all Charm and Leadership checks.
**COST 5**

### TOUGHENED
Gain +2 wound threshold.
**COST 10**

### KNOW SOMEBODY
Once per session, when attempting to purchase a legally available item, reduce its rarity by 1 per rank of Know Somebody.
**COST 10**

### KNOWLEDGE IS POWER
Once per session, when making a check, count Force rating as being equal to ranks in Knowledge (Lore).
**COST 10**

### NOBODY'S FOOL
May upgrade difficulty of incoming Charm, Coercion, and Deception checks once per rank of Nobody's Fool.
**COST 10**

### GRIT
Gain +1 strain threshold.
**COST 15**

### SMOOTH TALKER
When first acquired, choose 1 skill; Charm, Coercion, Deception, or Negotiation. When making checks with that skill, spend ⬡ to gain additional ☼ equal to ranks in Smooth Talker.
**COST 15**

### SMOOTH TALKER
When first acquired, choose 1 skill; Charm, Coercion, Deception, or Negotiation. When making checks with that skill, spend ⬡ to gain additional ☼ equal to ranks in Smooth Talker.
**COST 15**

### PLAUSIBLE DENIABILITY
Remove ■ per rank of Plausible Deniability from all Coercion and Deception checks.
**COST 15**

### NOBODY'S FOOL
May upgrade difficulty of incoming Charm, Coercion, and Deception checks once per rank of Nobody's Fool.
**COST 20**

### NATURAL CHARMER
Once per session, may re-roll any 1 Charm or Deception check.
**COST 20**

### CONTINGENCY PLAN
Spend 1 Destiny Point to recover strain equal to Cunning rating.
**COST 20**

### SENSE EMOTIONS
Add □ to all Charm, Coercion, and Deception checks unless the target is immune to Force powers.
**COST 20**

### DEDICATION
Gain +1 to a single characteristic. This cannot bring a characteristic above 6.
**COST 25**

### STEELY NERVES
Spend 1 Destiny Point to ignore effects of Critical Injuries on Willpower or Presence checks until the end of the encounter.
**COST 25**

### FORCE RATING
Gain +1 Force rating.
**COST 25**

### SENSE ADVANTAGE
Once per session, may add ■■ to 1 NPC's skill check.
**COST 25**

# MYSTIC: Makashi Duelist

**Career Skills:** Charm, Coercion, Knowledge (Lore), Knowledge (Outer Rim), Perception, Vigilance
**Additional Career Skills:** Charm, Cool, Coordination, Lightsaber

### GRIT
Gain +1 strain threshold.

**COST 5**

### RESIST DISARM
Suffer 2 strain to avoid being disarmed or have weapon damaged or destroyed.

**COST 5**

### GRIT
Gain +1 strain threshold.

**COST 5**

### PARRY
When hit by a melee attack, suffer 3 strain to reduce damage by 2 plus ranks in Parry.

**COST 5**

### PARRY
When hit by a melee attack, suffer 3 strain to reduce damage by 2 plus ranks in Parry.

**COST 10**

### MAKASHI TECHNIQUE
When making a check using the Lightsaber skill, the character may use Presence instead of Brawn.

**COST 10**

### DUELIST'S TRAINING
Add ☐ to Melee and Lightsaber checks when engaged with only one opponent.

**COST 10**

### FEINT
Spend ⊕ or ♥♥♥ generated on a missed melee attack to upgrade difficulty of opponent's next attack targeting character by ranks in Feint.

**COST 10**

### PARRY
When hit by a melee attack, suffer 3 strain to reduce damage by 2 plus ranks in Parry.

**COST 15**

### FEINT
Spend ⊕ or ♥♥♥ generated on a missed melee attack to upgrade difficulty of opponent's next attack targeting character by ranks in Feint.

**COST 15**

### PARRY
When hit by a melee attack, suffer 3 strain to reduce damage by 2 plus ranks in Parry.

**COST 15**

### PARRY
When hit by a melee attack, suffer 3 strain to reduce damage by 2 plus ranks in Parry.

**COST 15**

### INTENSE PRESENCE
Spend 1 Destiny Point to recover strain equal to Presence rating.

**COST 20**

### IMPROVED PARRY
When parrying a hit that generated ▽ or ✸✸✸, may hit attacker once with Lightsaber, Brawl, or Melee weapon (dealing base damage) after original attack resolves.

**COST 20**

### GRIT
Gain +1 strain threshold.

**COST 20**

### DEFENSIVE TRAINING
When wielding a Lightsaber, Melee, or Brawl weapon, the weapon gains the Defensive quality with a rating equal to ranks in Defensive Training.

**COST 20**

### DEDICATION
Gain +1 to a single characteristic. This cannot bring a characteristic above 6.

**COST 25**

### SUM DJEM
May spend ⊕ or ♥♥ with successful Lightsaber check to disarm opponent.

**COST 25**

### MAKASHI FINISH
Take the Makashi Finish action. Perform a Lightsaber (Presence) combat check against engaged target, adding ◯ no greater than Force rating. Spend ◑ to add +10 to any resulting Critical Injury rolls.

**COST 25**

### MAKASHI FLOURISH
Once per encounter, perform Makashi Flourish action. Make an **Average (◆ ◆) Lightsaber (Presence) check**. 1 engaged opponent suffers strain equal to ✸, and heal an equal amount of strain.

**COST 25**

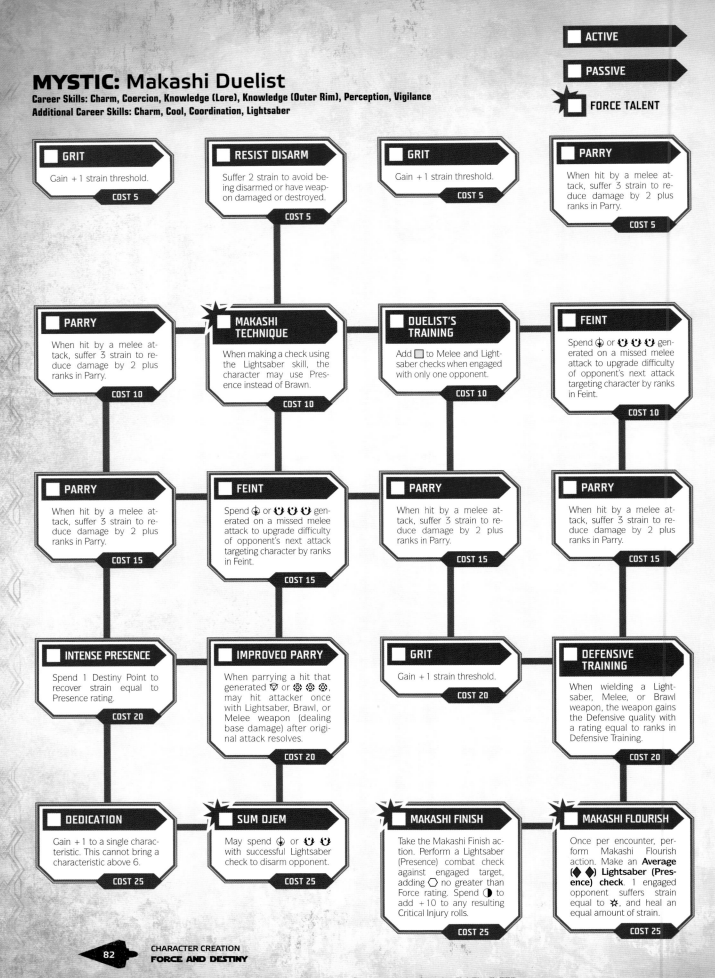

# MYSTIC: Seer

**Career Skills:** Charm, Coercion, Knowledge (Lore), Knowledge (Outer Rim), Perception, Vigilance
**Additional Career Skills:** Discipline, Knowledge (Lore), Survival, Vigilance

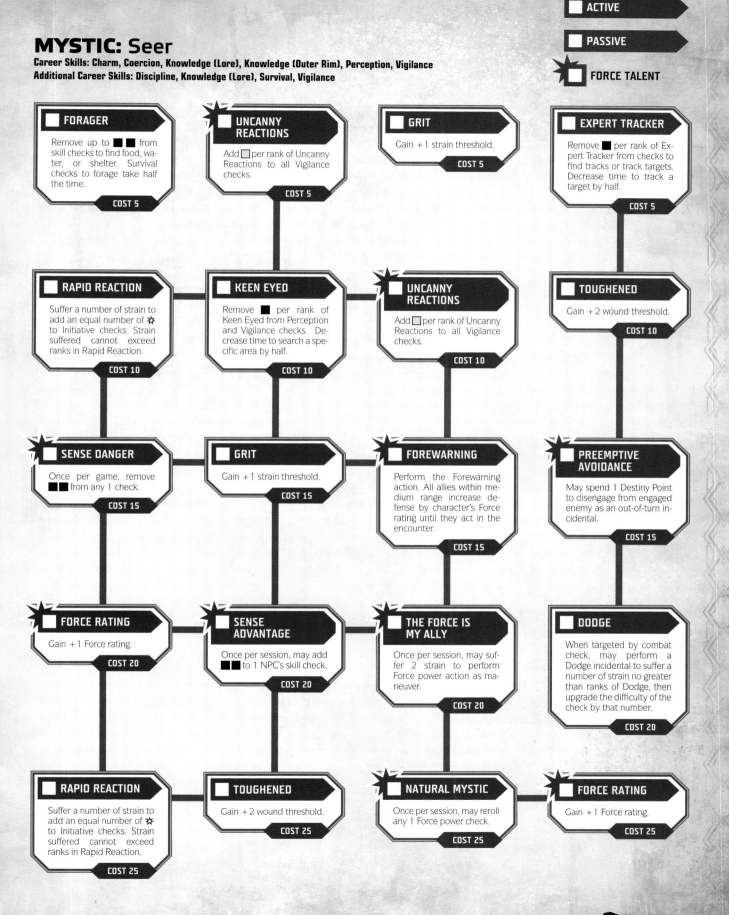

☐ ACTIVE

☐ PASSIVE

☐ FORCE TALENT

**FORAGER**

Remove up to ■ ■ from skill checks to find food, water, or shelter. Survival checks to forage take half the time.

COST 5

**UNCANNY REACTIONS**

Add ☐ per rank of Uncanny Reactions to all Vigilance checks.

COST 5

**GRIT**

Gain +1 strain threshold.

COST 5

**EXPERT TRACKER**

Remove ■ per rank of Expert Tracker from checks to find tracks or track targets. Decrease time to track a target by half.

COST 5

**RAPID REACTION**

Suffer a number of strain to add an equal number of ☆ to Initiative checks. Strain suffered cannot exceed ranks in Rapid Reaction.

COST 10

**KEEN EYED**

Remove ■ per rank of Keen Eyed from Perception and Vigilance checks. Decrease time to search a specific area by half.

COST 10

**UNCANNY REACTIONS**

Add ☐ per rank of Uncanny Reactions to all Vigilance checks.

COST 10

**TOUGHENED**

Gain +2 wound threshold.

COST 10

**SENSE DANGER**

Once per game, remove ■ ■ from any 1 check.

COST 15

**GRIT**

Gain +1 strain threshold.

COST 15

**FOREWARNING**

Perform the Forewarning action. All allies within medium range increase defense by character's Force rating until they act in the encounter.

COST 15

**PREEMPTIVE AVOIDANCE**

May spend 1 Destiny Point to disengage from engaged enemy as an out-of-turn incidental.

COST 15

**FORCE RATING**

Gain +1 Force rating.

COST 20

**SENSE ADVANTAGE**

Once per session, may add ■ ■ to 1 NPC's skill check.

COST 20

**THE FORCE IS MY ALLY**

Once per session, may suffer 2 strain to perform Force power action as maneuver.

COST 20

**DODGE**

When targeted by combat check, may perform a Dodge incidental to suffer a number of strain no greater than ranks of Dodge, then upgrade the difficulty of the check by that number.

COST 20

**RAPID REACTION**

Suffer a number of strain to add an equal number of ☆ to Initiative checks. Strain suffered cannot exceed ranks in Rapid Reaction.

COST 25

**TOUGHENED**

Gain +2 wound threshold.

COST 25

**NATURAL MYSTIC**

Once per session, may reroll any 1 Force power check.

COST 25

**FORCE RATING**

Gain +1 Force rating.

COST 25

# THE SEEKER

The Seeker's six career skills are **Knowledge (Xenology)**, **Piloting (Planetary)**, **Piloting (Space)**, **Ranged (Heavy)**, **Survival**, and **Vigilance**. Characters with this career automatically gain a rank in three of these skills without spending experience and gain a discount on increasing them with future experience points. **Seekers begin the game with a Force rating of 1.**

## A SEEKER'S ROLE

It is not uncommon for some Force adepts to feel compelled to travel throughout the galaxy to aid those in need and to oppose those who use the dark side. While some might focus their attentions in cities and urban centers, the need can be just as great far from the heart of galactic civilization. A Force adept who is willing and able to travel and work in these environments can help ease crushing poverty or crippling plagues of hunger and disease. He can also discover new Force techniques, find sensitives in need of training, and at times halt dangerous threats that could otherwise fester in isolation. A Seeker must be capable of doing all of these things, while traveling far from any meaningful support network.

Seekers generally take a very pragmatic view toward the Force. Operating independently, they consider it to be one of the tools in their arsenal, but not the only one. For a Seeker, preparedness and adaptability are paramount. They cannot count on finding the right tools for the job in the isolated areas in which they travel. As such, they learn to be flexible and adapt quickly to find the best equipment from what is available. In some environments, this may mean discovering information about flora and fauna that is previously undocumented. In such situations, the Force can be the most reliable asset, and its flexibility can aid them in selecting and using whatever else is at hand.

This flexibility is vital for a Seeker. Some of these characters travel at the direction of the Force, allowing fortune and chance to select their destinations and their traveling companions. Others work within the confines of larger groups. They may be troubleshooters, bounty hunters, envoys, or even traveling merchants. The variety of work means the Seeker must be prepared to quickly adapt to these changing situations and to make the most effective use possible of the tools that are at hand.

# SEEKER SPECIALIZATIONS

Each of the Seeker's specializations focuses on the ability to survive within savage and hostile environments. In many ways, these specializations center around the necessity for this character to be the apex predator at all times. However, they also reflect the character's intrinsic competence when operating in isolation.

## ATARU STRIKER

When working alone in a hostile environment, every physical conflict must be resolved quickly and decisively. Frequently, an uncivilized planet completely lacks any sort of medical facilities. In fact, at times, an isolated explorer could be the only sentient being on the world. In such a situation, a minor injury can be deadly. If a conflict is necessary, it is better to resolve it quickly, taking whatever risks are involved, than to fight more conservatively and prolong the risk of injury. The Ataru Striker embraces this approach, throwing himself into combat with every fiber of his being.

Ataru Strikers acquire **Athletics**, **Coordination**, **Lightsaber**, and **Perception** as additional career skills. If this is the character's starting specialization, he may choose two of these skills and gain one free rank in each, without spending starting experience. This fighting style is highly dependent on the combatant's ability to quickly assess a situation and use natural athleticism to exploit the environment. In this way, the combatant is able to gain every possible advantage over an opponent. The combination of these edges and the rapid attacks that characterize Ataru martial arts can force a combat to a very quick resolution.

Practitioners of the Ataru fighting style must be supremely confident in their abilities. They must also be exceptionally athletic and capable of committing all their energy into a very brief conflict. When engaged in a physical conflict, Ataru Strikers fight without remorse but also with little concern for their own safety. Every motion is designed to inflict a flurry of rapid and overpowering attacks against their opponents from myriad angles. Their vicious and unrelenting offense is their best (and sometimes only) defense—most opponents are so busy defending themselves that they have no time to attack in turn.

However, this style of unrelenting attack can have its disadvantages. An Ataru Striker needs to see his opponent defeated quickly, before he exhausts himself. An individual who can outlast an Ataru Striker can prove to be his deadliest enemy.

## HUNTER

Far from the civilized parts of the galaxy, there are many predators that can endanger sentient life. Some of these are animals that prey upon anything digestible. Others are malicious and twisted individuals who enjoy a savage and bloodthirsty existence. Hunters are Force adepts who are uniquely capable of tracking, confronting, and slaying these creatures, particularly those who hide in the wilds, far from civilization.

Hunters acquire **Coordination**, **Ranged (Heavy)**, **Stealth**, and **Vigilance** as additional career skills. If this is the PC's starting specialization, he chooses two of these skills and gains one free rank in each. These ranks do not cost experience. Hunters need to be able to sneak up on their targets, move through difficult terrain, and be constantly alert to their surroundings. Many hunters train with ranged weapons so that they can strike their targets from far away.

Most Hunters initially embark upon their careers focused on animal prey. Few, however, engage in this practice out of a desire to prove their mettle or a thirst for blood. Rather, their connection to the Force often lets them differentiate between predators that hunt out of necessity from those that are actively malicious. A Hunter does not normally interfere in the natural cycle of life, but he's more than willing to restore balance by eliminating a predator that kills needlessly and destroys natural habitats. Sadly, these foul and twisted animalistic intelligences also have their parallels within sentient beings. All too often, a Hunter finds himself hunting intelligent quarry; this can prove to be the most dangerous game of all.

## PATHFINDER

Few are as capable of exploring a planet and discovering its secrets as a Pathfinder. The combination of Pathfinders' Force talents and their training enables them to quickly and precisely complete a search, even under the most adverse conditions. A Pathfinder can survive in a hostile wilderness for weeks or months, living off the land with minimal supplies and possibly a faithful companion animal. In fact, some Pathfinders are said to be able to bond with their companions through the Force, communicating with them mentally, seeing through their senses, and even directing their actions.

Pathfinders acquire **Medicine**, **Ranged (Light)**, **Resilience**, and **Survival** as additional career skills. If this is the character's starting specialization, he may choose two of these skills and gain one free rank in each, without spending starting experience. These skills are focused on complementing the Seeker's career skills, so that the character becomes even more capable of operating independently. The addition of Medicine is primarily for personal benefit but can also be useful in aiding the character's companions.

Some Pathfinders follow this career because they discover they have a knack for independent survival. This is most commonly true for Force-sensitive individuals who matured on primitive and uncivilized planets.

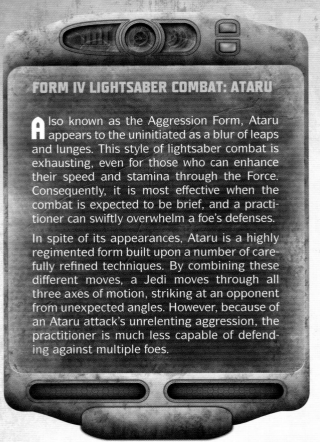

## FORM IV LIGHTSABER COMBAT: ATARU

Also known as the Aggression Form, Ataru appears to the uninitiated as a blur of leaps and lunges. This style of lightsaber combat is exhausting, even for those who can enhance their speed and stamina through the Force. Consequently, it is most effective when the combat is expected to be brief, and a practitioner can swiftly overwhelm a foe's defenses.

In spite of its appearances, Ataru is a highly regimented form built upon a number of carefully refined techniques. By combining these different moves, a Jedi moves through all three axes of motion, striking at an opponent from unexpected angles. However, because of an Ataru attack's unrelenting aggression, the practitioner is much less capable of defending against multiple foes.

If his small community was surrounded by hostile wilderness, a character is certain to have spent his youth exploring that environment—likely making friends with many of the wild animals present there. Pathfinders' natural abilities likely led them to a position of some responsibility within their tribe. Their roles might have included securing the safety of the surrounding wilderness and maintaining any trails leading to agricultural resources or other necessities needed by the community's residents.

Others who follow the Pathfinder career do so out of a preference for the company of animals over that of sentient beings. Through their Force abilities, some learn to establish effective communications with the relatively primitive minds. In these interactions, they find that they enjoy the sincerity and straightforward nature of wild creatures.

# SEEKER STORIES

Seekers are best characterized by their preference for working in isolation, as well as by their knack for surviving in hostile and isolated situations. While there are exceptions to this rule, their origins tend to begin with situations that strongly depend on self-sufficiency.

- **Exploration:** The desire to be the first to visit a new place, to see something that has never been seen before, can be a powerful draw. Some enter into this field with hopes of achieving fame and fortune. Others, however, are simply drawn by the idea of a completely novel experience. Jaded by life within more civilized environments, they wish to see the portions of the galaxy that remain wild and untamed, far from places they consider dull and traditional.

- **Sole Survivor:** Perhaps, during childhood, the Seeker's escape pod crashed on an isolated world. Maybe his colony met with disaster. Or he could have become lost and separated during a tribal migration. In any case, the character learned to live apart from civilization at an early age. Through his Force sensitivity, he not only survived, but thrived in the isolation. Soon, he became as capable of living in the environment as any native animal. Even after reestablishing contact with the civilized world, the Seeker enjoys spending time outside of it.

- **The Natural World:** While cities have myriad conveniences as well as social connections, there is a different splendor that can be found in the untamed hinterlands. These environments are a powerful draw to some individuals, whether they grew up in a city or a wilderness. Some characters discover that these places complement their Force talents, and they attempt to spend as much time as possible working and thriving within them. A simple appreciation for natural beauty and the joy of isolation from the pressures of civilized life can be transformative for some.

- **Escape:** Throughout the galaxy, there are slave owners and tyrants who make life miserable for their victims. Many children dwelling in abject terror prefer to flee and attempt to survive apart from society rather than continue to fall prey to cruelty. A Force-sensitive individual who escapes from such a place could develop talents that enable him not only to survive, but to thrive within the wilderness. With animals as his allies and the wilderness as his pantry, the character could eventually become a virtual lord in his isolation. Even after reestablishing contact with civilization, such a character might prefer to dwell apart in the wilds whenever possible.

# SEEKER: Ataru Striker

**Career Skills:** Knowledge (Xenology), Piloting (Planetary), Piloting (Space), Ranged (Heavy), Survival, Vigilance
**Additional Career Skills:** Athletics, Coordination, Lightsaber, Perception

### CONDITIONED
Remove ■ per rank of Conditioned from Athletics and Coordination checks. Reduce the damage and strain suffered from falling by 1 per rank of Conditioned.
**COST 5**

### PARRY
When hit by a melee attack, suffer 3 strain to reduce damage by 2 plus ranks in Parry.
**COST 5**

### JUMP UP
Once per round, may stand from seated or prone as an incidental.
**COST 5**

### QUICK DRAW
Once per round, draw or holster a weapon or accessible item as an incidental.
**COST 5**

### DODGE
When targeted by combat check, may perform a Dodge incidental to suffer a number of strain no greater than ranks of Dodge, then upgrade the difficulty of the check by that number.
**COST 10**

### REFLECT
When hit by a ranged attack, suffer 3 strain to reduce damage by 2 plus ranks in Reflect.
**COST 10**

### ATARU TECHNIQUE
When making a check using the Lightsaber skill, the character may use Agility instead of Brawn.
**COST 10**

### QUICK STRIKE
Add □ per rank of Quick Strike to combat checks against targets that have not acted yet this encounter.
**COST 10**

### QUICK STRIKE
Add □ per rank of Quick Strike to combat checks against targets that have not acted yet this encounter.
**COST 15**

### REFLECT
When hit by a ranged attack, suffer 3 strain to reduce damage by 2 plus ranks in Reflect.
**COST 15**

### PARRY
When hit by a melee attack, suffer 3 strain to reduce damage by 2 plus ranks in Parry.
**COST 15**

### IMPROVED PARRY
When parrying a hit that generated ▽ or ⚙ ⚙ ⚙, may hit attacker once with Lightsaber, Brawl, or Melee weapon (dealing base damage) after original attack resolves.
**COST 15**

### DODGE
When targeted by combat check, may perform a Dodge incidental to suffer a number of strain no greater than ranks of Dodge, then upgrade the difficulty of the check by that number.
**COST 20**

### HAWK BAT SWOOP
Take the Hawk Bat Swoop action. Perform a Lightsaber (Agility) combat check against target within short range, adding ○ no greater than Force rating. Spend ◗ to engage target and spend ◖ to add 🗘 to check.
**COST 20**

### SABER SWARM
Perform the Saber Swarm maneuver; suffer 1 strain, to make next Lightsaber (Agility) combat check this turn gain the Linked item quality equal to Force rating during check.
**COST 20**

### CONDITIONED
Remove ■ per rank of Conditioned from Athletics and Coordination checks. Reduce the damage and strain suffered from falling by 1 per rank of Conditioned.
**COST 20**

### PARRY
When hit by a melee attack, suffer 3 strain to reduce damage by 2 plus ranks in Parry.
**COST 25**

### DEDICATION
Gain +1 to a single characteristic. This cannot bring a characteristic above 6.
**COST 25**

### SABER THROW
Perform Saber Throw action; make Lightsaber combat check as ranged attack at target within medium range, adding ○ no greater than Force rating. Must spend ◗ and succeed to hit target; spend ◖ to have weapon return to hand.
**COST 25**

### BALANCE
When the character recovers strain at the end of the encounter, he may add ○ per Force rating. He recovers additional strain equal to ◗ generated.
**COST 25**

# SEEKER: Hunter

**Career Skills:** Knowledge (Xenology), Piloting (Planetary), Piloting (Space), Ranged (Heavy), Survival, Vigilance
**Additional Career Skills:** Coordination, Ranged (Heavy), Stealth, Vigilance

■ ACTIVE ►
■ PASSIVE ►
✦ FORCE TALENT

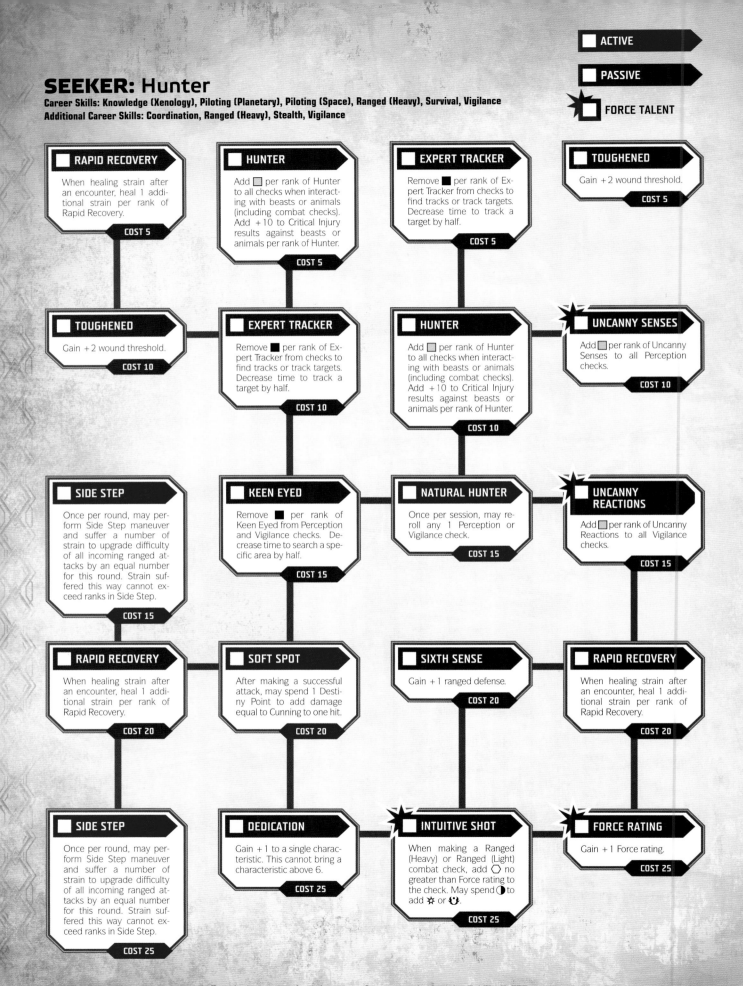

**RAPID RECOVERY**
When healing strain after an encounter, heal 1 additional strain per rank of Rapid Recovery.
COST 5

**HUNTER**
Add ■ per rank of Hunter to all checks when interacting with beasts or animals (including combat checks). Add +10 to Critical Injury results against beasts or animals per rank of Hunter.
COST 5

**EXPERT TRACKER**
Remove ■ per rank of Expert Tracker from checks to find tracks or track targets. Decrease time to track a target by half.
COST 5

**TOUGHENED**
Gain +2 wound threshold.
COST 5

**TOUGHENED**
Gain +2 wound threshold.
COST 10

**EXPERT TRACKER**
Remove ■ per rank of Expert Tracker from checks to find tracks or track targets. Decrease time to track a target by half.
COST 10

**HUNTER**
Add ■ per rank of Hunter to all checks when interacting with beasts or animals (including combat checks). Add +10 to Critical Injury results against beasts or animals per rank of Hunter.
COST 10

**UNCANNY SENSES**
Add ■ per rank of Uncanny Senses to all Perception checks.
COST 10

**SIDE STEP**
Once per round, may perform Side Step maneuver and suffer a number of strain to upgrade difficulty of all incoming ranged attacks by an equal number for this round. Strain suffered this way cannot exceed ranks in Side Step.
COST 15

**KEEN EYED**
Remove ■ per rank of Keen Eyed from Perception and Vigilance checks. Decrease time to search a specific area by half.
COST 15

**NATURAL HUNTER**
Once per session, may re-roll any 1 Perception or Vigilance check.
COST 15

**UNCANNY REACTIONS**
Add ■ per rank of Uncanny Reactions to all Vigilance checks.
COST 15

**RAPID RECOVERY**
When healing strain after an encounter, heal 1 additional strain per rank of Rapid Recovery.
COST 20

**SOFT SPOT**
After making a successful attack, may spend 1 Destiny Point to add damage equal to Cunning to one hit.
COST 20

**SIXTH SENSE**
Gain +1 ranged defense.
COST 20

**RAPID RECOVERY**
When healing strain after an encounter, heal 1 additional strain per rank of Rapid Recovery.
COST 20

**SIDE STEP**
Once per round, may perform Side Step maneuver and suffer a number of strain to upgrade difficulty of all incoming ranged attacks by an equal number for this round. Strain suffered this way cannot exceed ranks in Side Step.
COST 25

**DEDICATION**
Gain +1 to a single characteristic. This cannot bring a characteristic above 6.
COST 25

**INTUITIVE SHOT**
When making a Ranged (Heavy) or Ranged (Light) combat check, add ○ no greater than Force rating to the check. May spend ◑ to add ✦ or ☻.
COST 25

**FORCE RATING**
Gain +1 Force rating.
COST 25

# SEEKER: Pathfinder

**Career Skills:** Knowledge (Xenology), Piloting (Planetary), Piloting (Space), Ranged (Heavy), Survival, Vigilance
**Additional Career Skills:** Medicine, Ranged (Light), Resilience, Survival

## GRIT
Gain +1 strain threshold.
**COST 5**

## KEEN EYED
Remove ■ per rank of Keen Eyed from Perception and Vigilance checks. Decrease time to search a specific area by half.
**COST 5**

## FORAGER
Remove up to ■ ■ from skill checks to find food, water, or shelter. Survival checks to forage take half the time.
**COST 5**

## SWIFT
Does not suffer usual penalties for moving through difficult terrain.
**COST 5**

## KEEN EYED
Remove ■ per rank of Keen Eyed from Perception and Vigilance checks. Decrease time to search a specific area by half.
**COST 10**

## OUTDOORSMAN
Remove ■ per rank of Outdoorsman from checks to move through terrain or manage environmental effects. Decrease overland travel times by half.
**COST 10**

## TOUGHENED
Gain +2 wound threshold.
**COST 10**

## OUTDOORSMAN
Remove ■ per rank of Outdoorsman from checks to move through terrain or manage environmental effects. Decrease overland travel times by half.
**COST 10**

## ANIMAL EMPATHY
When making checks to handle or tame animals, add ○ no greater than Force rating to the check. Spend ◗ to add ✬ or ☽ to the check.
**COST 15**

## ANIMAL BOND
Develop long-term bond with single animal of silhouette no greater than half Force rating rounded down.
**COST 15**

## GRIT
Gain +1 strain threshold.
**COST 15**

## SLEIGHT OF MIND
Add □ to all Stealth checks unless the opposition is immune to Force powers.
**COST 15**

## MENTAL BOND
May perform the Mental Bond action. Commit ○. While committed, may communicate with bonded animal at long range and see and hear through its senses.
**COST 20**

## FORCE RATING
Gain +1 Force rating.
**COST 20**

## QUICK MOVEMENT
Suffer 2 strain to perform the Quick Movement incidental; add ○ no greater than Force rating to next check. May spend ◗◗ to perform one additional Move maneuver after action.
**COST 20**

## TOUGHENED
Gain +2 wound threshold.
**COST 20**

## SHARE PAIN
May perform the Share Pain incidental when bonded animal suffers wounds. Reduce wounds suffered to half, then character suffers wounds equal to number reduced.
**COST 25**

## ENDURING
Gain +1 soak value.
**COST 25**

## NATURAL OUTDOORSMAN
Once per session, may reroll any 1 Resilience or Survival check.
**COST 25**

## DEDICATION
Gain +1 to a single characteristic. This cannot bring a characteristic above 6.
**COST 25**

# THE SENTINEL
𐌋𐌄𐌅𐌕 𐌀𐌕𐌂𐌀𐌋𐌉𐌀𐌅𐌕𐌋

The Sentinel's six career skills are **Computers**, **Deception**, **Knowledge (Core Worlds)**, **Perception**, **Skulduggery**, and **Stealth**. These characters automatically gain a rank in three of these skills without spending experience and gain a discount on increasing them with future experience points. **Sentinels begin the game with a Force rating of 1.**

## A SENTINEL'S ROLE

Every city has its secrets, and every shining beacon of civilization has its seedy underworld. Within these shadowy depths, miscreants and malcontents prey on the helpless, committing heinous crimes and leaving misery and chaos in their wake.

Most law enforcement agencies try to combat criminals without violating the very laws the agencies exist to uphold. Thus, their agents must abide by strict regulations that restrain their behavior. Even institutions that exist to uphold evil laws, such as the Empire, have codes of conduct that apply to their enforcers. The Sentinel, however, plays by his own rules.

During the time of the Old Republic, the Jedi Sentinels were Force adepts who blended combat expertise and training in the Force with a more pragmatic approach to their duties. Sentinels embraced practical technologies and utilized techniques borrowed from police forces, skip tracers, spies, and even lawbreakers. Sentinels relied on quick thinking and cunning to accomplish their tasks, and they quickly found their calling in the depths of urban environments. On the streets, Sentinels could fight criminals by using their own tactics against them.

Such an approach was not without risk. Even as Sentinels skirted the law to enforce justice, they skirted the dark side of their own morality as well. A Sentinel had to maintain constant vigilance over his own actions, analyzing each choice he made to ensure it was the right one. The best Sentinels avoided falling to the dark side by cultivating a fierce intellect and a brilliant cunning—to see all sides of a no-win situation and find the unexpected solution.

Although the Empire has long since wiped out the Jedi Order, and with it the Jedi Sentinels, some remain who follow these guiding principles. Many quick-witted Force-sensitives living in urban areas find themselves unconsciously adopting a Sentinel's tactics as they unlock their own hidden potential.

Characters with a strong moral imperative may see these crusading skills as a means of investigating powerful individuals. If they find powerful villains who are above the law, then employing less ethical approaches might be the only means to bring these rogues to justice. Under these circumstances, a Sentinel could readily justify deception and even minor crimes if they were undertaken to assure that a tyrant's excesses could be curbed.

# SENTINEL SPECIALIZATIONS

In each of their different specializations, Sentinels are pragmatic in their approach. They work with the available assets to resolve whatever challenge they face, whether physical, mental, or social.

## ARTISAN

Some Force users have an innate skill with tools and machines. These skilled artificers can use their skill with the Force to enhance their abilities, and even intuitively understand a machine's form and function. After all, while tools and machines may not be alive, the Force envelopes everything in the galaxy. Artisans feel the Force that surrounds their tools and the items they work on, using this connection to build creations of wondrous beauty and precision. An Artisan does not create scores of the same item for sale or distribution. Instead, each of his creations is individual and iconic, a true work of art.

Artisans acquire **Astrogation**, **Computers**, **Knowledge (Education)**, and **Mechanics** as additional career skills. If this is the character's starting specialization, he may choose two of these skills and gain one free rank in each, without spending starting experience. In order to fully integrate their Force abilities with the devices they manipulate, Artisans must first have a solid understanding of how those tools work. This requires a fundamental educational grounding in the principles of technology.

Within urban environments, individuals who never learn to recognize their Force talents are prone to follow the Artisan's path. This is because they are surrounded by technology, and if these individuals take an interest in how things work and how to repair them, their Force abilities may naturally develop in concert. When faced with a broken machine, they can often identify the problem in an intuitive way—some even claim that the machines "speak" to them. Some Artisans live up to the stereotype of the messy inventor, while others remain meticulously neat or even take pains to disguise their craftsmanship from casual observers.

## SHADOW

In the ancient days of the Jedi Order, Sentinels worked tirelessly to police the galaxy's criminal underbelly. However, a small subset of these enforcers focused their attentions on a far greater and more dangerous threat. They trained tirelessly to find and eliminate those who had fallen to the dark side of the Force and willingly embraced corruption. These Sentinels were called Shadows, and they hunted the Sith.

For many years, the Sith were thought destroyed, and the Jedi Shadows gave up their calling or pursued other dark side Force users. They never realized that the Sith had not been eliminated, and were hiding right under their noses.

Now, with the Jedi Order destroyed and a Dark Lord of the Sith ruling the Galactic Empire, those who would follow the path of the Shadow find their roles reversed. No longer the secret investigators of an established order who searched the shadows of civilization, they are now the ones who must stay hidden. However, within these dark corners, Shadows still work tirelessly to bring justice to untouchable criminals and dark side Force users alike.

Shadows acquire **Knowledge (Underworld)**, **Skulduggery**, **Stealth**, and **Streetwise** as additional career skills. If this is the character's starting specialization, he may choose two of these skills and gain one free rank in each, without spending starting experience. These characters recognize that stealth and deception are integral to finding the targets they hunt. Criminal organizations are often mired in secrecy, and uncovering these secrets requires underhanded methods. While their techniques are frequently of questionable moral character, Shadows firmly believe

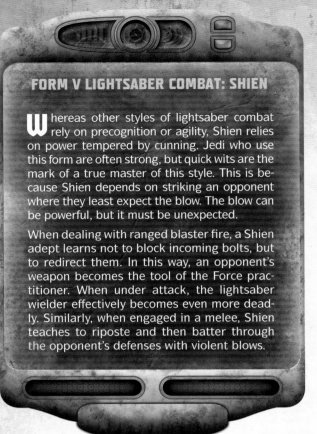

## FORM V LIGHTSABER COMBAT: SHIEN

Whereas other styles of lightsaber combat rely on precognition or agility, Shien relies on power tempered by cunning. Jedi who use this form are often strong, but quick wits are the mark of a true master of this style. This is because Shien depends on striking an opponent where they least expect the blow. The blow can be powerful, but it must be unexpected.

When dealing with ranged blaster fire, a Shien adept learns not to block incoming bolts, but to redirect them. In this way, an opponent's weapon becomes the tool of the Force practitioner. When under attack, the lightsaber wielder effectively becomes even more deadly. Similarly, when engaged in a melee, Shien teaches to riposte and then batter through the opponent's defenses with violent blows.

their ultimate accomplishments more than justify the tools that they must use.

Of course, an initiate who has turned to the dark side can prove a powerful opponent for a Shadow. Working against such an adversary can require all of an adept's mundane and Force talents. A Shadow's willingness to examine and utilize every tool and asset can play a major factor in overcoming such capable foes.

### SHIEN EXPERT

A lightsaber is a potent weapon. When wielded forcefully, it can even overpower an opponent who has a weapon capable of parrying it. Further, its ability to deflect blaster bolts can make it an effective ranged weapon as well. Those who consider themselves Shien Experts—masters of the Shien lightsaber form—embrace the seeming contradiction between those two uses. They know that true lightsaber masters must possess the cunning to use such weapons to their full potential. It takes clever precision to reflect a ranged attack back toward an adversary, but just as much shrewd brilliance to recognize the right time to overpower adversaries through raw force.

Shien Experts acquire **Athletics**, **Lightsaber**, **Resilience**, and **Skulduggery** as additional career skills. If this is the character's starting specialization, he may choose two of these skills and gain one free rank in each, without spending starting experience. In order to effectively follow this path, a character needs to be flexible and to recognize the best approaches for different types of physical conflicts. Resilience and Athletics are critical

tools for engaging in and enduring a prolonged battle, while Skulduggery enables the character to case out and prepare possible combat locations ahead of time to exploit the environment against an opponent.

Whenever possible, a Shien Expert prepares a battleground well in advance of a conflict. Often, these individuals take the time to study a range of different locations soon after they arrive in a city. Once combat begins, they can carefully exploit the environment and trigger any traps they may have prepared to unleash upon their opponents.

During combat, Shien Experts continue to constantly analyze the situation. While they take advantage of the terrain throughout a battle, they are also selective in choosing the best way to use their training as well as their lightsaber. This can change with each passing instant, in reaction to the armament, position, and stance of their enemies. For these individuals, an extended conflict is a sure route to victory as they react to every move their opponents make with a clever counter or powerful strike. .

## SENTINEL STORIES

Among Force-sensitive characters, Sentinels are often the ones who are most willing to examine and make use of assets that are not directly associated with the Force.

- **Delinquent:** Every crowded urban environment has individuals who fall outside of the social safety net. Characters from this environment are likely to have had little opportunity and vast personal responsibility—even as they watched others enjoy lives of luxury. They might appreciate every item they accrue even while resenting those whose lives were "easier."

- **Prodigy:** Characters with Force potential often find unusual ways to express that talent, even without realizing the basis for their abilities. Some individuals express their knack in the ability to work with particular technological devices. They might be particularly adept at repairing broken machines or at devising new ones. Some are even regarded as one of the galaxy's experts within a field of study.

- **Victim:** Within the economically depressed sections of the galaxy's cities, there are countless petty criminal tyrants. Many of these individuals are seemingly immune to law enforcement as they inflict countless small cruelties upon the already-suffering individuals who live near them. Characters raised under these circumstances have likely lived in a state of constant need. Throughout childhood and adolescence, they observed these cruelties and dreamt of a day when they could stop them. Along the way, they learned some of the techniques that a criminal could use. Now, they have gained the Force as an ally and can use it to make a difference.

# SENTINEL: Artisan

**Career Skills:** Computers, Deception, Knowledge (Core Worlds), Perception, Skulduggery, Stealth
**Additional Career Skills:** Astrogation, Computers, Knowledge (Education), Mechanics

## SOLID REPAIRS
When repairing hull trauma on a starship or vehicle, repair 1 additional hull trauma per rank of Solid Repairs.
**COST 5**

## FINE TUNING
When repairing system strain on a starship or vehicle, repair 1 additional system strain per rank of Fine Tuning.
**COST 5**

## MENTAL TOOLS
Always count as having the right tools for the job when performing Mechanics checks.
**COST 5**

## TECHNICAL APTITUDE
Reduce time needed to complete Computers-related tasks by 25% per rank.
**COST 5**

## GRIT
Gain +1 strain threshold.
**COST 10**

## SOLID REPAIRS
When repairing hull trauma on a starship or vehicle, repair 1 additional hull trauma per rank of Solid Repairs.
**COST 10**

## FINE TUNING
When repairing system strain on a starship or vehicle, repair 1 additional system strain per rank of Fine Tuning.
**COST 10**

## GRIT
Gain +1 strain threshold.
**COST 10**

## INVENTOR
When constructing new items or modifying attachments, add ▢ or remove ■ per rank of Inventor.
**COST 15**

## IMBUE ITEM
Take the Imbue Item maneuver; suffer 1 strain and commit ◯ to grant one weapon, piece of armor, or item an improvement while ◯ remains committed. Suffer 1 strain every round ◯ remains committed.
**COST 15**

## NATURAL TINKERER
Once per session, may reroll any 1 Mechanics check.
**COST 15**

## DEFENSIVE SLICING
When defending computer systems, add ■ per rank of Defensive Slicing to opponents' checks.
**COST 15**

## SOLID REPAIRS
When repairing hull trauma on a starship or vehicle, repair 1 additional hull trauma per rank of Solid Repairs.
**COST 20**

## FORCE RATING
Gain +1 Force rating.
**COST 20**

## DEFENSIVE SLICING
When defending computer systems, add ■ per rank of Defensive Slicing to opponents' checks.
**COST 20**

## MENTAL FORTRESS
Spend 1 Destiny Point to ignore effects of Critical Injuries on Intellect and Cunning checks until end of encounter.
**COST 20**

## MASTER ARTISAN
Once per round, may take the Master Artisan incidental; suffer 2 strain to decrease the difficulty of next Mechanics check by 1, to a minimum of **Easy (◆)**.
**COST 25**

## INTUITIVE IMPROVEMENTS
When making check to craft or repair item, may add ◯ no greater than Force rating to check. Spend ◯◯ to increase hard points by 1, to max of +2.
**COST 25**

## DEDICATION
Gain +1 to a single characteristic. This cannot bring a characteristic above 6.
**COST 25**

## COMPREHEND TECHNOLOGY
Take Comprehend Technology action; make an **Average (◆ ◆) Knowledge (Education) check** to use Force rating as ranks in skills to use a single item.
**COST 25**

# SENTINEL: Shadow

**Career Skills:** Computers, Deception, Knowledge (Core Worlds), Perception, Skulduggery, Stealth
**Additional Career Skills:** Knowledge (Underworld), Skulduggery, Stealth, Streetwise

☐ ACTIVE ▶
☐ PASSIVE ▶
⭐☐ FORCE TALENT

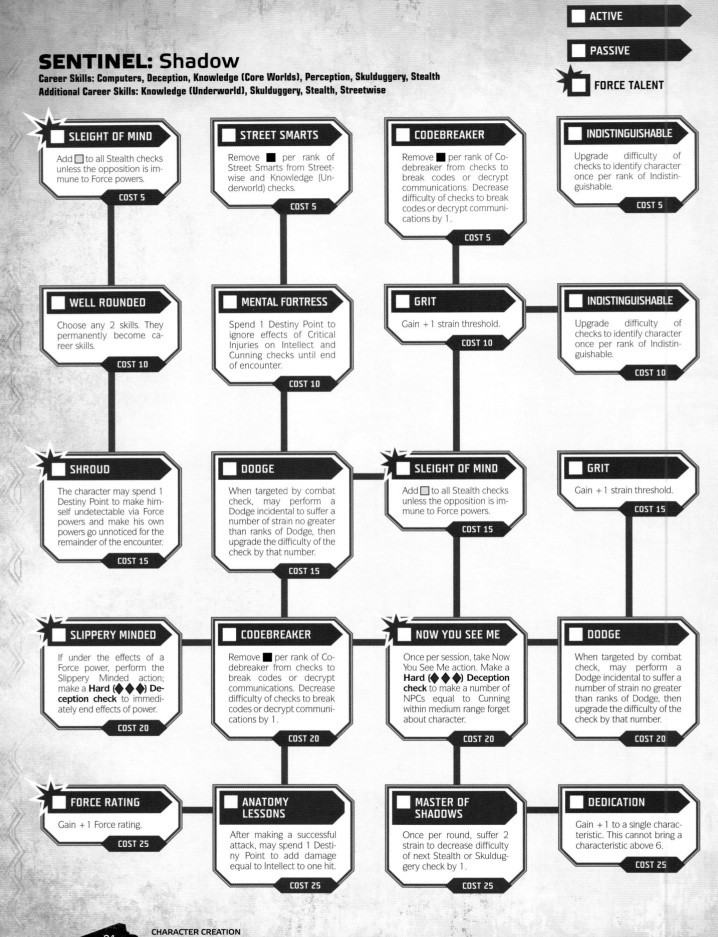

### SLEIGHT OF MIND
Add ☐ to all Stealth checks unless the opposition is immune to Force powers.
**COST 5**

### STREET SMARTS
Remove ■ per rank of Street Smarts from Streetwise and Knowledge (Underworld) checks.
**COST 5**

### CODEBREAKER
Remove ■ per rank of Codebreaker from checks to break codes or decrypt communications. Decrease difficulty of checks to break codes or decrypt communications by 1.
**COST 5**

### INDISTINGUISHABLE
Upgrade difficulty of checks to identify character once per rank of Indistinguishable.
**COST 5**

### WELL ROUNDED
Choose any 2 skills. They permanently become career skills.
**COST 10**

### MENTAL FORTRESS
Spend 1 Destiny Point to ignore effects of Critical Injuries on Intellect and Cunning checks until end of encounter.
**COST 10**

### GRIT
Gain +1 strain threshold.
**COST 10**

### INDISTINGUISHABLE
Upgrade difficulty of checks to identify character once per rank of Indistinguishable.
**COST 10**

### SHROUD
The character may spend 1 Destiny Point to make himself undetectable via Force powers and make his own powers go unnoticed for the remainder of the encounter.
**COST 15**

### DODGE
When targeted by combat check, may perform a Dodge incidental to suffer a number of strain no greater than ranks of Dodge, then upgrade the difficulty of the check by that number.
**COST 15**

### SLEIGHT OF MIND
Add ☐ to all Stealth checks unless the opposition is immune to Force powers.
**COST 15**

### GRIT
Gain +1 strain threshold.
**COST 15**

### SLIPPERY MINDED
If under the effects of a Force power, perform the Slippery Minded action; make a **Hard (◆◆◆) Deception check** to immediately end effects of power.
**COST 20**

### CODEBREAKER
Remove ■ per rank of Codebreaker from checks to break codes or decrypt communications. Decrease difficulty of checks to break codes or decrypt communications by 1.
**COST 20**

### NOW YOU SEE ME
Once per session, take Now You See Me action. Make a **Hard (◆◆◆) Deception check** to make a number of NPCs equal to Cunning within medium range forget about character.
**COST 20**

### DODGE
When targeted by combat check, may perform a Dodge incidental to suffer a number of strain no greater than ranks of Dodge, then upgrade the difficulty of the check by that number.
**COST 20**

### FORCE RATING
Gain +1 Force rating.
**COST 25**

### ANATOMY LESSONS
After making a successful attack, may spend 1 Destiny Point to add damage equal to Intellect to one hit.
**COST 25**

### MASTER OF SHADOWS
Once per round, suffer 2 strain to decrease difficulty of next Stealth or Skulduggery check by 1.
**COST 25**

### DEDICATION
Gain +1 to a single characteristic. This cannot bring a characteristic above 6.
**COST 25**

# SENTINEL: Shien Expert

**Career Skills:** Computers, Deception, Knowledge (Core Worlds), Perception, Skulduggery, Stealth
**Additional Career Skills:** Athletics, Lightsaber, Resilience, Skulduggery

ACTIVE

PASSIVE

FORCE TALENT

### SIDE STEP
Once per round, may perform Side Step maneuver and suffer a number of strain to upgrade difficulty of all incoming ranged attacks by an equal number for this round. Strain suffered this way cannot exceed ranks in Side Step.
**COST 5**

### CONDITIONED
Remove ■ per rank of Conditioned from Athletics and Coordination checks. Reduce the damage and strain suffered from falling by 1 per rank of Conditioned.
**COST 5**

### STREET SMARTS
Remove ■ per rank of Street Smarts from Streetwise and Knowledge (Underworld) checks.
**COST 5**

### REFLECT
When hit by a ranged attack, suffer 3 strain to reduce damage by 2 plus ranks in Reflect.
**COST 5**

### TOUGHENED
Gain +2 wound threshold.
**COST 10**

### PARRY
When hit by a melee attack, suffer 3 strain to reduce damage by 2 plus ranks in Parry.
**COST 10**

### SHIEN TECHNIQUE
When making a check using the Lightsaber skill, the character may use Cunning instead of Brawn.
**COST 10**

### REFLECT
When hit by a ranged attack, suffer 3 strain to reduce damage by 2 plus ranks in Reflect.
**COST 10**

### PARRY
When hit by a melee attack, suffer 3 strain to reduce damage by 2 plus ranks in Parry.
**COST 15**

### COUNTERSTRIKE
When an attack misses the character and generates ▽ or ⚙ ⚙, may upgrade next Lightsaber (Cunning) check against attacker during encounter once.
**COST 15**

### GRIT
Gain +1 strain threshold.
**COST 15**

### IMPROVED REFLECT
When reflecting a hit that generated ▽ or ⚙ ⚙ ⚙, may hit one target in medium range with the same damage as the initial hit, after original attack resolves.
**COST 15**

### DJEM SO DEFLECTION
After using Reflect, may spend 1 Destiny Point to perform Move maneuver as out-of-turn incidental to close distance with or engage opponent.
**COST 20**

### DEFENSIVE STANCE
Once per round, may perform Defensive Stance maneuver and suffer a number of strain to upgrade difficulty of all incoming melee attacks by an equal number for the next round. Strain suffered this way cannot exceed ranks in Defensive Stance.
**COST 20**

### SABER THROW
Perform Saber Throw action; make Lightsaber combat check as ranged attack at target within medium range, adding ◯ no greater than Force rating. Must spend ◑ and succeed to hit target; spend ◑ to have weapon return to hand.
**COST 20**

### REFLECT
When hit by a ranged attack, suffer 3 strain to reduce damage by 2 plus ranks in Reflect.
**COST 20**

### FALLING AVALANCHE
Suffer 2 strain to add damage equal to Brawn to next Lightsaber combat check made that turn.
**COST 25**

### DEDICATION
Gain +1 to a single characteristic. This cannot bring a characteristic above 6.
**COST 25**

### DISRUPTIVE STRIKE
Perform Disruptive Strike action; make a Lightsaber (Cunning) combat check, adding ◯ no greater than Force rating. Spend ◑ to add ▼ to the next combat check the target makes.
**COST 25**

### SUPREME REFLECT
If the user did not make a combat check during previous turn, may suffer 1 strain to use Reflect.
**COST 25**

# THE WARRIOR

The Warrior's six career skills are **Athletics**, **Brawl**, **Cool**, **Melee**, **Perception**, and **Survival**. Characters with this career automatically gain a rank in three of these skills without spending experience and gain a discount on increasing them with future experience points. **Warriors begin the game with a Force rating of 1.**

## A WARRIOR'S ROLE

Though the lightsaber is an iconic weapon for many Force users, some dedicate themselves wholly to becoming paragons of strife. These dangerous individuals are known as Warriors.

At their most basic, Warriors are focused combatants who use the Force to augment their prodigious martial prowess. Whether flying in the pilot's seat of a starfighter, wielding a lightsaber on the field of battle, or blazing away with a blaster pistol, Warriors excel in combat of all types.

Legends indicate that the Jedi Order's origins began with warriors who worked to integrate Force techniques into their physical training. Even in the absence of the Old Republic's guardians, this association remains. The Force can give strength to those who need it, and Warriors excel at exploiting that strength. They become a physical manifestation of the Force, willing and ready to overcome those who would inflict harm.

The Warrior's greatest strength, however, can also be his most dangerous weakness. Endless aggression can be a path toward the dark side. A wise individual must recognize that violence has its place but is not the only possible answer. A Warrior can inflict substantial and precise damage. However, even carefully applied attacks can still have far-reaching consequences. Because of this, it can be every bit as important for a Warrior to recognize when it is more appropriate not to attack. Some individuals who follow this career consider this sense of judgment to be the most important aspect of their training.

Warriors can come from a broad range of different cultures and environments. Physical conflict is every bit as common within the civilized and technologically advanced worlds of the Core as it is within the less structured societies of the Outer Rim. Combat styles and the tools employed within conflicts may change, but the motivations and final outcomes are often similar. Ultimately, Warriors must be willing to risk their own lives so that they can overcome threats to themselves and to those they hold most dear.

# WARRIOR SPECIALIZATIONS

Each of these paths focuses on a different aspect of conflict. With the aid of the Force, the Warrior can apply his instinctual knowledge of combat to any and every fight he finds himself in.

### AGGRESSOR

The Aggressor relies on fear to intimidate his opposition into surrender or retreat. Aggressors tend to be tough and dangerous combatants, able to dish out brutal damage to anyone who fights them, while surviving the same. They use their confident, terrifying attitudes to convey this to their opponents. Some Aggressors hope their enemies back down without a fight, but others fall into the trap of relishing the fear they inspire.

Aggressors acquire **Coercion**, **Knowledge (Underworld)**, **Ranged (Light)**, and **Streetwise** as additional career skills. If this is the character's starting specialization, he may choose two of these skills and gain one free rank in each, without spending starting experience. These skills enable Aggressors to recognize the bravado shown by criminal enforcers and thugs. It also aids them in cowing these individuals, assuring these predators that the Force-sensitive character is a far scarier and more potent individual than they have previously faced.

Tempered by the Force, some characters who undertake this specialization prefer to use their abilities to intimidate foes into surrender so they don't have to kill needlessly. While they are extremely capable in this regard, they frequently learn the techniques required to cause the bare minimum of damage necessary. Precision is important, as every life still holds value in the Force.

When confronted by a foe that seems irredeemable, however, the Aggressor's attitude shifts appropriately. All elements of self-restraint are discarded, and the Aggressor is able to simply punish his foes, inflicting devastating blow after devastating blow. Often, opponents simply flee rather than engage an Aggressor. Stories told by survivors—and sometimes allies—add to the character's reputation, making it even easier to intimidate future enemies.

### SHII-CHO KNIGHT

The ancient lightsaber fighting style of Shii-Cho is said to be the first lightsaber form taught to the Jedi and their predecessors. It focuses on the essentials of saber fighting and borrows heavily from other sword fighting techniques. Appropriately, the modern practitioners of this form focus on perfecting the core tenants of sword fighting, recognizing the strength of simplicity. Shii-Cho Knights eschew fancy maneuvers, preferring to focus on the fundamentals of block, parry, and strike.

Shii-Cho Knights acquire **Athletics**, **Coordination**, **Lightsaber**, and **Melee** as additional career skills. If this is the character's starting specialization, he may choose two of these skills and gain one free rank in each, without spending starting experience. These skills provide them with a solid grounding in the core techniques of any physical conflict. They are familiar with the weapon they wield, but they are also very comfortable exploiting their natural athleticism and flexibility. Because of this, they can not only avoid an enemy's attack, but also make certain that they are able to strike effectively when their target is at a disadvantage.

Followers of this path are seldom concerned with personal appearances or the style that they exhibit in a conflict. Instead, they are focused on precision and on achieving their ultimate goal of victory. For them, a solid grounding in the basics is something they can

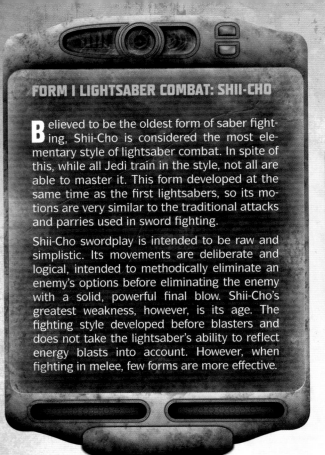

## FORM I LIGHTSABER COMBAT: SHII-CHO

Believed to be the oldest form of saber fighting, Shii-Cho is considered the most elementary style of lightsaber combat. In spite of this, while all Jedi train in the style, not all are able to master it. This form developed at the same time as the first lightsabers, so its motions are very similar to the traditional attacks and parries used in sword fighting.

Shii-Cho swordplay is intended to be raw and simplistic. Its movements are deliberate and logical, intended to methodically eliminate an enemy's options before eliminating the enemy with a solid, powerful final blow. Shii-Cho's greatest weakness, however, is its age. The fighting style developed before blasters and does not take the lightsaber's ability to reflect energy blasts into account. However, when fighting in melee, few forms are more effective.

rely on in any situation. When lives are on the line, they devote their attention to executing their maneuvers in a traditional way, using them to counter an opponent while simultaneously restricting his options.

### STARFIGHTER ACE

Starfighter pilots enthusiastically engage in one of the most dangerous forms of battle imaginable. Their shields and armor—for starfighters that have either—offer virtually no resistance to the weapons of the capital ships they oppose. Instead, they must trust in the Force to protect them as they launch their daring assaults. Those who embrace the risks of space combat may pursue the Starfighter Ace specialization.

Starfighter Aces acquire **Astrogation**, **Gunnery**, **Mechanics**, and **Piloting (Space)** as additional career skills. If this is the character's starting specialization, he may choose two of these skills and gain one free rank in each, without spending starting experience. These provide the essentials needed to successfully pilot a starfighter in combat. Force adepts who acquire these skills most often control single-passenger craft, in which they must assume responsibility for weapons at the same time that they handle navigation.

While this style of combat is dependent on a vehicle, it remains physically exhausting. Even with a full range of technological enhancements, effective pilots must be capable of enduring rapid and extreme shifts in velocity and direction. They must also remain ready to strike a deadly blow against an opponent at just the right instant, even while struggling to endure extreme physiological conditions.

# WARRIOR STORIES

Violence draws characters to the Warrior's path. For some, it is a natural aptitude due to their physical gifts and Force talents. For others, it is the only possible option, due to childhood tragedies.

- **Discipline:** Some sentients have a natural call to battle and physical violence. In many species, their physiological evolution leaves them needing an outlet for such physical exertions. In others, martial arts form a central cultural element. Ultimately, interaction with galactic civilization requires individuals with such tendencies to constantly restrain themselves. For many, an outlet for these energies and emotions is necessary so they can live in "civil" society. Some embark upon the Warrior path seeking such an outlet, and discover that it is a natural path for them.

- **Vengeance:** Violence often begets even greater measures of savagery. Children who have seen their peers, or even their guardians, suffer at the hands of others sometimes swear to avenge these tragedies. Force-sensitive individuals who encounter such challenges during their childhood can spend much of their life honing their physical and Force abilities to pursue their revenge.

- **Survival:** Even under the constraints of urban civilization, there are neighborhoods ruled by savagery. Within such locales, the most dominant individuals are truly urban predators. They can be every bit as dangerous as an apex predator on a frontier world. Some who have suffered at the hands of such monsters recognize that the only way to defeat them is to become an even more fearsome combatant. Force adepts who suffer through such conditions can learn to channel their talents toward violence and intimidation, as it may be the only way to escape.

# WARRIOR: Aggressor

**Career Skills:** Athletics, Brawl, Cool, Melee, Perception, Survival
**Additional Career Skills:** Coercion, Knowledge (Underworld), Ranged (Light), Streetwise

"1" />

■ **ACTIVE**

■ **PASSIVE**

■ **FORCE TALENT**

---

### INTIMIDATING

May suffer a number of strain to downgrade difficulty of Coercion checks, or upgrade difficulty when targeted by Coercion checks, by an equal number. Strain suffered this way cannot exceed ranks in Intimidating.

**COST 5**

### PLAUSIBLE DENIABILITY

Remove ■ per rank of Plausible Deniability from all Coercion and Deception checks.

**COST 5**

### GRIT

Gain +1 strain threshold.

**COST 5**

### TOUGHENED

Gain +2 wound threshold.

**COST 5**

---

### FEARSOME

When an adversary becomes engaged with the character, the character may force the adversary to make a fear check, with the difficulty equal to the character's ranks in Fearsome.

**COST 10**

### INTIMIDATING

May suffer a number of strain to downgrade difficulty of Coercion checks, or upgrade difficulty when targeted by Coercion checks, by an equal number. Strain suffered this way cannot exceed ranks in Intimidating.

**COST 10**

### PREY ON THE WEAK

Add +1 damage to one hit of successful combat checks against disoriented targets per rank of Prey on the Weak.

**COST 10**

### SENSE ADVANTAGE

Once per session, may add ■■ to 1 NPC's skill check.

**COST 10**

---

### FEARSOME

When an adversary becomes engaged with the character, the character may force the adversary to make a fear check, with the difficulty equal to the character's ranks in Fearsome.

**COST 15**

### TERRIFY

Take the Terrify action; make a **Hard (◆◆◆) Coercion check**, adding ◯ no greater than Force rating. Disorient one target within medium range per ☼. Spend ۞ ۞ to extend duration and spend ◖ to immobilize affected target.

**COST 15**

### CRIPPLING BLOW

Increase the difficulty of next combat check by 1. If check deals damage, target suffers 1 strain whenever he moves for the remainder of the encounter.

**COST 15**

### TOUGHENED

Gain +2 wound threshold.

**COST 15**

---

### GRIT

Gain +1 strain threshold.

**COST 20**

### IMPROVED TERRIFY

Reduce the difficulty of Terrify's check to **Average (◆◆)** and may spend ۞ to stagger an affected target.

**COST 20**

### PREY ON THE WEAK

Add +1 damage to one hit of successful combat checks against disoriented targets per rank of Prey on the Weak.

**COST 20**

### HEROIC FORTITUDE

May spend 1 Destiny Point to ignore effects of Critical Injuries on Brawn or Agility checks until the end of the encounter.

**COST 20**

---

### FORCE RATING

Gain +1 Force rating.

**COST 25**

### FEARSOME

When an adversary becomes engaged with the character, the character may force the adversary to make a fear check, with the difficulty equal to the character's ranks in Fearsome.

**COST 25**

### DEDICATION

Gain +1 to a single characteristic. This cannot bring a characteristic above 6.

**COST 25**

### AGAINST ALL ODDS

When incapacitated, perform Against All Odds action; making **Hard (◆◆◆) Resilience check** with ◯ equal to Force rating. Heal wounds equal to ☼, spend ◖ to add ☼.

**COST 25**

---

CHARACTER CREATION
**FORCE AND DESTINY**  99

Permission granted to photocopy for personal use only. © LFL. © FFG.

# WARRIOR: Shii-Cho Knight

**Career Skills: Athletics, Brawl, Cool, Melee, Perception, Survival**
**Additional Career Skills: Athletics, Coordination, Lightsaber, Melee**

☐ ACTIVE
☐ PASSIVE
☐ FORCE TALENT

## ☐ PARRY
When hit by a melee attack, suffer 3 strain to reduce damage by 2 plus ranks in Parry.
**COST 5**

## ☐ SECOND WIND
Once per encounter, may use Second Wind incidental to recover strain equal to ranks in Second Wind.
**COST 5**

## ☐ TOUGHENED
Gain +2 wound threshold.
**COST 5**

## ☐ PARRY
When hit by a melee attack, suffer 3 strain to reduce damage by 2 plus ranks in Parry.
**COST 5**

## ☐ SECOND WIND
Once per encounter, may use Second Wind incidental to recover strain equal to ranks in Second Wind.
**COST 10**

## ☐ CONDITIONED
Remove ■ per rank of Conditioned from Athletics and Coordination checks. Reduce the damage and strain suffered from falling by 1 per rank of Conditioned.
**COST 10**

## ☐ MULTIPLE OPPONENTS
Add ☐ to Lightsaber, Brawl, and Melee checks when engaged with multiple opponents.
**COST 10**

## ☐ DURABLE
May reduce any Critical Injury suffered by 10 per rank of Durable, to a minimum of 1.
**COST 10**

## ☐ QUICK DRAW
Once per round, draw or holster a weapon or accessible item as an incidental.
**COST 15**

## ☐ GRIT
Gain +1 strain threshold.
**COST 15**

## ☐ PARRY
When hit by a melee attack, suffer 3 strain to reduce damage by 2 plus ranks in Parry.
**COST 15**

## ☐ DEFENSIVE TRAINING
When wielding a Lightsaber, Melee, or Brawl weapon, the weapon gains the Defensive quality with a rating equal to ranks in Defensive Training.
**COST 15**

## ☐ NATURAL BLADEMASTER
Once per session, may reroll any 1 Lightsaber or Melee check.
**COST 20**

## ☐ SARLACC SWEEP
Increase difficulty of Lightsaber check by 1 to perform Sarlacc Sweep action. May spend 🕱🕱 to hit additional engaged targets.
**COST 20**

## ☐ IMPROVED PARRY
When parrying a hit that generated 🛇 or ⚙⚙⚙, may hit attacker once with Lightsaber, Brawl, or Melee weapon (dealing base damage) after original attack resolves.
**COST 20**

## ☐ SUM DJEM
May spend ⊕ or 🕱🕱 with successful Lightsaber check to disarm opponent.
**COST 20**

## ☐ CENTER OF BEING
Take a Center of Being maneuver. Until the beginning of next turn, attacks against the character increase their crit rating by 1 per rank of Center of Being.
**COST 25**

## ☐ DURABLE
May reduce any Critical Injury suffered by 10 per rank of Durable, to a minimum of 1.
**COST 25**

## ☐ DEDICATION
Gain +1 to a single characteristic. This cannot bring a characteristic above 6.
**COST 25**

## ☐ PARRY
When hit by a melee attack, suffer 3 strain to reduce damage by 2 plus ranks in Parry.
**COST 25**

# WARRIOR: Starfighter Ace

**Career Skills:** Athletics, Brawl, Cool, Melee, Perception, Survival
**Additional Career Skills:** Astrogation, Gunnery, Mechanics, Piloting (Space)

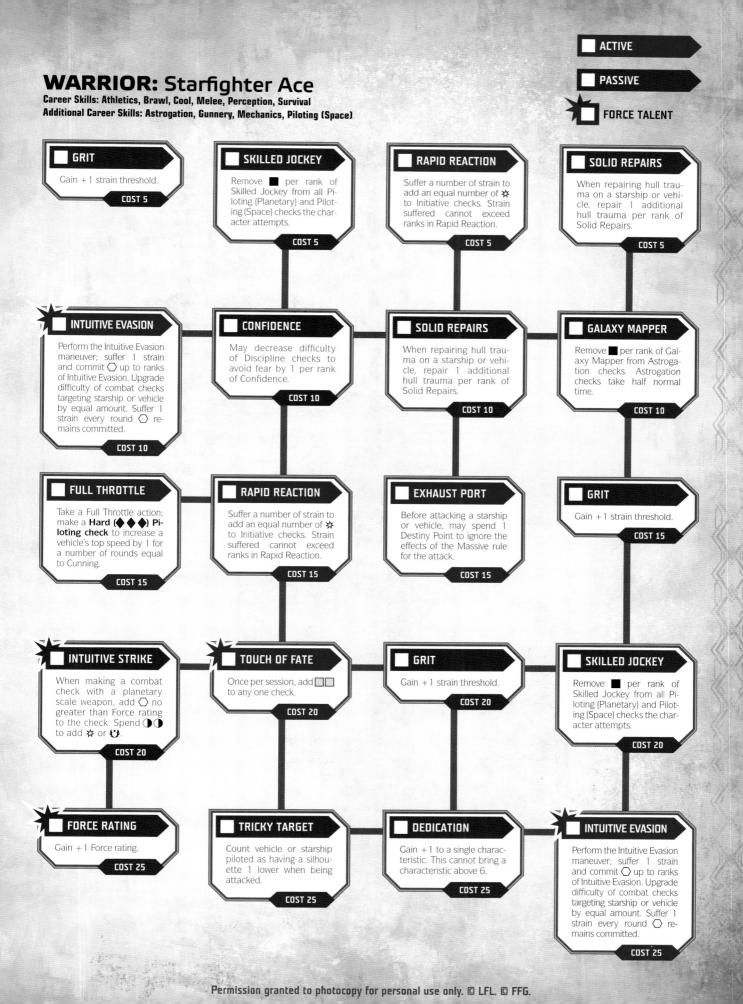

**ACTIVE**

**PASSIVE**

**FORCE TALENT**

**GRIT**
Gain +1 strain threshold.
COST 5

**SKILLED JOCKEY**
Remove ■ per rank of Skilled Jockey from all Piloting (Planetary) and Piloting (Space) checks the character attempts.
COST 5

**RAPID REACTION**
Suffer a number of strain to add an equal number of ✫ to Initiative checks. Strain suffered cannot exceed ranks in Rapid Reaction.
COST 5

**SOLID REPAIRS**
When repairing hull trauma on a starship or vehicle, repair 1 additional hull trauma per rank of Solid Repairs.
COST 5

**INTUITIVE EVASION**
Perform the Intuitive Evasion maneuver; suffer 1 strain and commit ◯ up to ranks of Intuitive Evasion. Upgrade difficulty of combat checks targeting starship or vehicle by equal amount. Suffer 1 strain every round ◯ remains committed.
COST 10

**CONFIDENCE**
May decrease difficulty of Discipline checks to avoid fear by 1 per rank of Confidence.
COST 10

**SOLID REPAIRS**
When repairing hull trauma on a starship or vehicle, repair 1 additional hull trauma per rank of Solid Repairs.
COST 10

**GALAXY MAPPER**
Remove ■ per rank of Galaxy Mapper from Astrogation checks. Astrogation checks take half normal time.
COST 10

**FULL THROTTLE**
Take a Full Throttle action; make a **Hard (◆◆◆) Piloting check** to increase a vehicle's top speed by 1 for a number of rounds equal to Cunning.
COST 15

**RAPID REACTION**
Suffer a number of strain to add an equal number of ✫ to Initiative checks. Strain suffered cannot exceed ranks in Rapid Reaction.
COST 15

**EXHAUST PORT**
Before attacking a starship or vehicle, may spend 1 Destiny Point to ignore the effects of the Massive rule for the attack.
COST 15

**GRIT**
Gain +1 strain threshold.
COST 15

**INTUITIVE STRIKE**
When making a combat check with a planetary scale weapon, add ◯ no greater than Force rating to the check. Spend ◖◗ to add ✫ or 🝆.
COST 20

**TOUCH OF FATE**
Once per session, add ▢▢ to any one check.
COST 20

**GRIT**
Gain +1 strain threshold.
COST 20

**SKILLED JOCKEY**
Remove ■ per rank of Skilled Jockey from all Piloting (Planetary) and Piloting (Space) checks the character attempts.
COST 20

**FORCE RATING**
Gain +1 Force rating.
COST 25

**TRICKY TARGET**
Count vehicle or starship piloted as having a silhouette 1 lower when being attacked.
COST 25

**DEDICATION**
Gain +1 to a single characteristic. This cannot bring a characteristic above 6.
COST 25

**INTUITIVE EVASION**
Perform the Intuitive Evasion maneuver; suffer 1 strain and commit ◯ up to ranks of Intuitive Evasion. Upgrade difficulty of combat checks targeting starship or vehicle by equal amount. Suffer 1 strain every round ◯ remains committed.
COST 25

# STEP 6: INVEST EXPERIENCE POINTS

Experience is the primary means by which players customize their characters. Each Player Character starts with a beginning pool of experience points which can be used to improve aspects of the character. As they progress in **FORCE AND DESTINY**, PCs receive additional experience which also can be spent to improve themselves.

## STARTING XP

Characters begin with a budget of experience points based on their species. The experience points used during character creation are the same as experience points received during play. If a player chooses to spend fewer experience points during character creation than his budget, those points carry over into the game, and the Player Character starts with more experience points to spend once the adventures begin.

Players may spend experience points in the following ways to improve their characters. These are also detailed in **Table 2–2: Spending Starting Experience**.

### NEED MORE EXPERIENCE?

Remember, a player can always increase his character's starting experience when determining his starting Morality, as described under **Player Character Starting Morality Values**, on page 49.

## IMPROVING CHARACTERISTICS

During character creation, raising a characteristic to the next highest rating costs ten times the value it is being raised to. For example, raising a character's Brawn from 3 to 4 would require 40 experience points.

Each improvement must be purchased sequentially. This means that raising a character's Brawn from 3 to 5 would cost 90 experience points: 40 for raising it from 3 to 4, then 50 more for raising it from 4 to 5.

During character creation, no characteristic can be increased to higher than 5. During the course of play, no characteristic can be increased above 6. Characteristics may only be purchased with experience points during character creation, not at any later time. (During gameplay, however, characteristics can be increased by purchasing specific talents.)

## SKILL TRAINING

Each skill has five ranks of training available. A character may have already acquired one or more ranks of skill training from a starting career and specialization for free. Characters may train additional skills and gain additional ranks during character creation. However, it is important to note that regardless of any species or career bonuses, no skill can be raised higher than rank 2 during character creation unless specifically stated otherwise.

The cost for training skills falls into one of two categories: career skills and non-career skills. The character should have check marks next to a number of skills based on starting career and specialization.

Training a career skill to the next highest rank costs five times the rank to which it is being raised. For example, training a career skill from rank 0 (untrained) to rank 1 requires 5 experience points. Improving a rank 1 career skill to rank 2 requires 10 experience points. Each rank must be purchased sequentially. This means that acquiring a rank 2 career skill during creation costs 15 experience points (5 for raising it from zero to rank 1, then 10 more for raising it from rank 1 to rank 2).

## TABLE 2–2: SPENDING STARTING EXPERIENCE

| Options | Cost | Character Creation Limits |
|---|---|---|
| May spend experience to increase characteristics. Character creation is the only time players can increase characteristics with experience points. | Ten times the purchased rating in experience. Each rating must be purchased sequentially. | May not raise any characteristic above rank 5 during character creation. |
| May spend experience to purchase ranks in skills. | Five times the purchased rank in experience. Each rank must be purchased sequentially. (Each rank in a non-career skill costs 5 additional XP.) | May not raise any skill above rank 2 during character creation. |
| May spend experience to purchase talents within specializations. | Depends on talent's position within specialization tree. | No special limits; only standard limits apply. |
| May spend experience to purchase Force powers. | Initial purchase of a Force power costs points listed in Force power. Additional power abilities depend on the position within the tree. | No special limits; only standard limits apply. |
| May spend experience to purchase new specializations. | Ten times the total number of character's specializations, including new specialization (non-career specialization costs 10 additional XP). | No special limits; only standard limits apply. |

A character can also purchase ranks in non-career skills. Each rank of a non-career skill costs five times the rank it is being raised to, plus 5 additional experience points. For example, training a non-career skill from rank 0 (untrained) to rank 1 requires 10 experience points. Improving a rank 1 non-career skill to rank 2 requires 15 experience points. Each rank must be purchased sequentially. This means that acquiring a rank 2 non-career skill during creation costs 25 experience points (10 for raising it from zero to rank 1, then 15 more for raising it from rank 1 to rank 2).

Characters may purchase ranks in skills during character creation or later during gameplay.

# ACQUIRING TALENTS

Talents are acquired from characters' available talent trees, which are generally provided by their career. Talent trees provide a unique format for purchasing talents that comes with several rules and restrictions.

Each specialization talent tree has four columns and five rows. This means each talent tree has a total of twenty talents that players may purchase. The cost of each talent depends on the row it occupies. The talents in the topmost row are the cheapest, costing 5 experience points each. The next row's choices cost 10 experience points each; the third row costs 15; the fourth row costs 20; and the fifth and final row's choices cost 25 experience points each.

Note that the choices on each tree are connected by a series of lines that link some talent choices with others. Characters may only purchase talents for which they are eligible. Characters are eligible to select any talents in the topmost row, plus any talents that are connected via one of the aforementioned links to a talent the character has already acquired.

When selecting talents on a talent tree, remember that each selection on the tree may only be purchased once. In the case of ranked talents (talents that may be purchased multiple times and have effects that stack the more times they are purchased), the only way to purchase them multiple times is if there are multiple selections of the same talent on the available talent trees. In some cases, a character may have already acquired a talent in one specialization, but needs to purchase it again in another specialization in order to reach further into the tree. If it is a ranked

talent, the character must purchase it again (gaining another rank in the talent). If it is not a ranked talent, he counts as already having purchased it, and he may continue to proceed through the second talent tree.

Characters may purchase talents during character creation or later during gameplay.

# BUYING FORCE POWERS

Force powers—as distinct from Force talents—are described more thoroughly in **Chapter VIII: The Force**, on page 282. Characters do not begin with any Force powers, but they may purchase them using experience points during character creation or later in gameplay.

# ACQUIRING NEW SPECIALIZATIONS

Each character starts with a single specialization within his chosen career. However, the player may purchase access to additional specializations.

Purchasing a specialization means basically that the player may buy the ability to purchase talents within that specialization. Also, each specialization has four additional career skills. These skills now count as career skills for the character (although the PC does not gain free advances in rank in them, as with a first specialization). Characters may purchase any specialization in any career.

Purchasing an additional specialization within a character's career costs ten times the total number of specializations he would possess with this new specialization. So, a character with one specialization could purchase a second career specialization for 20 experience points. If he wished to purchase a third career specialization, it would cost another 30 XP.

Characters may also purchase additional specializations outside of their careers. Purchasing non-career specializations costs ten times the total number of specializations the character would possess with this new specialization, plus an additional 10 XP. So, a character with one specialization could purchase a second non-career specialization for 30 experience. If the PC has two specializations already, a third specialization that is also a non-career specialization would cost another 40 experience.

Characters created following the steps in this chapter have begun their journey through the Force, but they are far from mastering it. Most are likely to have a limited selection of abilities from their career, and few have more than a single specialization. This is a far more approachable style of play for groups new to the game system or even to roleplaying games. However, some groups may wish to begin their play with characters who are more accomplished.

"Knight-level play" is an alternative approach that gets the characters involved in more complicated situations. At this stage, the Player Characters are significantly more accomplished and likely to immediately assume a larger role in galactic-scale conflicts. Knight-level is intended to depict PCs who are have received additional training or benefited from their experiences, and are close to having abilities comparable the Jedi Knights of old. (But not so powerful that they don't have plenty of room to grow and improve!) To reflect this, Player Characters gain an extra 150 XP. These experience points cannot be spent on characteristics, as they are intended to reflect the character's training and worldly experiences rather than inherent abilities. Characters also may not train any skills above rank 3 while building their Knight-level PC.

Further, characters constructed for this gameplay approach gain access to a basic lightsaber, (see page 176) or 9,000 credits' worth of starting gear (this can include a vehicle).

More information on Knight-level play is presented on page 322.

# STEP 7: DETERMINE DERIVED ATTRIBUTES

Some attributes of a character are derived from a player's other choices during character creation.

## WOUND THRESHOLD

A character's **wound threshold** represents, basically, how many wounds—how much physical damage—a character can withstand before becoming incapacitated. A character's starting wound threshold is determined by adding the wound threshold for his species to his Brawn rating (after spending starting XP). After determining this initial value, further increases to a character's Brawn rating do not increase his wound threshold—wound threshold improvements are acquired by purchasing talents, such as Toughened.

## STRAIN THRESHOLD

A character's **strain threshold** determines how much strain—psychological and mental damage—a character can withstand before becoming stunned, dazed, or incapacitated. A character's starting strain threshold is determined by adding the strain threshold for his species to his Willpower rating (after spending starting XP). After determining this initial value, further increases to a character's Willpower rating do not increase his strain threshold—strain threshold improvements are acquired by purchasing appropriate talents, such as Grit.

## DEFENSE

**Defense** determines how difficult a character is to hit in combat situations, either as a product of the PC's own training or the protective equipment he employs. Defense is divided into ranged defense and melee defense. A character's default value in each defense rating is zero.

Defense is most commonly gained by wearing armor or by adopting a defensive position in combat (such as gaining cover). Some talents may also increase one of a character's defense ratings.

## SOAK VALUE

**Soak value** determines how much incoming damage a character can shrug off before being seriously wounded. A character's soak value is subtracted from any incoming damage. Any remaining damage after subtracting soak becomes wounds, and is applied toward the character's wound threshold.

A character's default soak value is equal to his Brawn rating. After determining this initial value, subsequent increases to a character's Brawn rating *do* increase his soak value. An addition to soak value is most often gained by wearing armor. Some talents, such as Enduring, may also increase a character's innate soak value.

# STEP 8: DETERMINE MOTIVATION

otivation provides a means to link all of the different elements of a PC into one coherent persona.
It serves to differentiate characters with similar careers
by providing different reasons for their decisions. Often, Motivation also sets up a thread that recurs across
multiple adventures as the character continues to work
toward achieving some lofty goal.

Players can either select a Motivation from **Table
2–3: Random Motivation**, particularly if there is
one that seems well-suited to their character concept,
or they can roll on that table to determine a primary
Motivation. Once the primary Motivation is selected,
a further roll—or deliberate selection—on the relevant
table in the following pages provides added detail. Of
course, with the GM's permission, players can simply
create their own Motivation, as long as it is consistent
in tone with the ones presented here.

Whereas Morality has distinct game effects, Motivation is intended to add depth to the character's
roleplaying. Players should focus on linking the character's species, career, Morality, and background together with Motivation to create a detailed persona.
For more information on Motivation and how it's used
in play, see **Chapter IX: The Game Master**.

## TYPES OF MOTIVATION

**FORCE AND DESTINY** presents Ambition, Cause, and Faith
as the three primary categories of Motivation. After determining the primary category, players can then roll
or select from the specific category tables that follow.
These are intended to offer an array of different options.

### AMBITION

A character with this Motivation is driven by a specific
goal. This Motivation
is internal, often

### TABLE 2–3: RANDOM MOTIVATION

| d10 | Motivation Result |
|-----|-------------------|
| 1–3 | Ambition |
| 4–6 | Cause |
| 7–9 | Faith |
| 10 | Roll once on each of any two categories |

abstract, and possibly selfish in nature. A character
with the Ambition Motivation wants to better himself
in some way—gaining love, status, power, or spiritual
knowledge, for example. The player should determine
the character's ultimate goal and why he does things
the way he does to get there.

### CAUSE

Many characters prefer to have a discrete and attain-
able goal toward which they devote their lives. Even
generalized ideas can have incremental steps that can
be achieved over time. Characters devoted to a Cause
often remain focused on it throughout their lives. On
those rare occasions when the cause might be accomplished, they typically either begin to work to expand
it or to see that its existence is maintained.

### FAITH

Characters who select this Motivation have a deep and
abiding trust in some recurring facet of galactic existence. They dedicate their lives to spreading this belief,
in the hope that they can bring other beings to come to
a similar understanding. In many cases, their proselytiza-
tion becomes a central focus. In other cases, spreading
their belief is far less important than simply reveling in it.

## MOTIVATIONS IN PLAY

Motivations exist to offer a player an additional framework for how the PC interacts with the world. They establish the character's priorities, but they need not
be a restriction. Rather, Motivations help to suggest the character's intuitive response to the
challenges he encounters. Notably, a PC's
reactions must be colored by mitigating
factors, so that a response is seldom
based solely on a Motivation.

### CHANGING MOTIVATIONS

Over time, a character's attitudes
can shift. Sometimes a single

## TABLE 2-4: SPECIFIC AMBITION

| d10 | Ambition Result |
|---|---|
| 1 | **Revenge:** At some point in the character's past, he was brutally wronged. Now he seeks vengeance, and he has a hard time focusing on anything else. |
| 2 | **Wealth:** Money motivates this character. Often, his choices are based less on the consequences of right and wrong, and are based more on what will be best for his credit account. |
| 3 | **Power:** The character wants to amass power and authority. His aspiration to rule may be linked to altruism or despotic desire, but in either case he wants to control both his situation and those around him. |
| 4 | **Become a Jedi:** The character wants nothing more than to become a Jedi Knight, though he may not be sure how to do so. |
| 5 | **Survival:** In a galaxy where simply being a Force user can be a death sentence, the character's primary concern is survival. He's willing to do what it takes to make sure he lives another day. |
| 6 | **Glory:** Fame and the spotlight beckon to this character. He wants to perform great deeds, and be celebrated for them. |
| 7 | **Destroy the Sith:** Through ancient texts or diligent research, the character has learned of the Jedi's ancient enemies: the Sith. He has set out to defeat and destroy their order, or at the very least, do what he can to hinder them. |
| 8 | **Enlightenment:** The character seeks spiritual and intellectual enlightenment above all else. He does not seek to bring enlightenment to others, for he realizes that such a goal is innately personal. |
| 9 | **Expertise:** The character wants to excel in his chosen work or area of expertise, and constantly practices to achieve perfection. |
| 10 | **Discovery:** Seeking out and discovering new worlds, information, or the wondrous secrets hidden among the galaxy's countless stars drives this character's actions. More than anything, he wants to find and experience things nobody else has. |

dramatic event can force the character to reprioritize. Alternatively, an extended series of minor frustrations can be enough to change how the character views the world. Of course, if a player discovers that he does not enjoy his character's Motivation, this can also be an important reason to justify the change. Ultimately, changing Motivations is simply a matter of discussing the issue with the GM, so that he can offer input, and then making the appropriate change. New Motivations should be selected or created rather than determined randomly.

## SECRET MOTIVATIONS

Players can choose to share their characters' Motivations with one another or to keep them secret. Motivations for different characters can, at times, be in direct conflict. By keeping these secret from one another, the players create opportunities for potentially intense roleplay between their characters. Alternatively, by sharing their Motivations, the characters can better focus on the times when their characters can collaborate.

## TABLE 2-5: SPECIFIC CAUSE

| d10 | Cause Result |
|---|---|
| 1 | **Freedom:** All sentient beings must have the opportunity to make their own decisions, for good or for ill, and the right to face the consequences or receive the just rewards for their actions. The character seeks freedom for the enslaved and oppressed, and fights against organizations that promote slavery or subjugate their people. |
| 2 | **Restore the Jedi:** The character wants to see the Jedi Order restored and rebuilt, although what he knows of the Jedi may be limited or even inaccurate. He may want to be a Jedi, or just want to see them return to being a presence in the galaxy. |
| 3 | **Galactic Peace:** The galaxy has been torn and shattered by decades of warfare. The character wants nothing more than to see peace restored to the galaxy, and recognizes that concerted efforts must be made to resolve galactic warfare. |
| 4 | **Justice:** In a galaxy full of wrongdoing, justice must be done. The character seeks to bring justice to those who deserve it, while helping victims of injustice to right the wrongs done to them. |
| 5 | **Stop the Rebellion:** The Rebel Alliance is an organization of outlaws and malcontents who fight against their legitimate government. The character may not like the Empire, but he dislikes the Alliance more, and wants to see it stopped. |
| 6 | **Equality:** All sentient beings deserve the right to be treated with respect and as peers by other beings, regardless of their state of technological sophistication. When the character finds those who do not possess equality, he seeks to better their lot in life. |
| 7 | **Help the Helpless:** In a galaxy full of momentous events and desperate struggle, it is all too easy to forget the poor, the weak, and the downtrodden. The character seeks to give voice to the voiceless, and help those who cannot help themselves. |
| 8 | **Free Enterprise:** Free and unimpeded trade between cultures can create opportunity, innovation, and understanding. Governments cannot be permitted to impede such interactions, and the character seeks to do what he can to support this. |
| 9 | **Overthrow the Empire:** The Galactic Empire has created a civilization based on inequality and injustice. The character seeks to end its tyranny, possibly in cooperation with the Alliance. |
| 10 | **Knowledge:** All sentient beings deserve an education that gives them a broader view of the galaxy. This character promotes the discovery and dissemination of all knowledge, to improve the lives of everyone in the galaxy. |

## TABLE 2-6: SPECIFIC FAITH

| d10 | Faith Result |
|---|---|
| 1 | **Natural World:** The character believes in the spirits of the living things around him. Whether he recognizes this as the Living Force or has a more shamanistic approach to his beliefs, he respects the spirits of nature and even prays to them. |
| 2 | **Goodness of People:** The character believes in the inherent goodness of most people. He believes that together, the majority of different beings in the galaxy can interact to create an all-encompassing civilization that is greater than the sum of its parts. |
| 3 | **Friends and Family:** The character believes in, and trusts, his close friends and family. He knows that unlike lofty ideals or strange religions, those close to him will always support him, and he supports them in turn. |
| 4 | **The Cosmic Force:** The character understands on some level that everything that happens, has happened, or will happen in the galaxy is part of the Cosmic Force. The Force guides the galaxy and the individuals within it, and things happen for a reason. |
| 5 | **Science and Reason:** The character believes in reason, knowledge, and scientific understanding. Everything, even the Force, has a logical explanation and works according to certain rules, even if he doesn't understand what those rules are. |
| 6 | **The Jedi Code:** Though the Empire strives to suppress knowledge of the Jedi, the character knows the code of this ancient order. He follows it, feeling that it is something worth his belief and devotion. |
| 7 | **Imperial Rule:** Though the Empire has done some terrible things, the order it brings to galactic society is still better than the moribund Republic that came before. The character believes that the Galactic Empire is the best thing for the galaxy. |
| 8 | **The Rebellion:** The sooner the Galactic Empire is defeated, the better. The character believes absolutely that the Rebel Alliance is in the right and is doing what must be done to free the galaxy from tyranny. |
| 9 | **Religious Code:** There are countless religions in the galaxy, and the character adheres to one of his choice. Perhaps this is the religion of his family or his people. Perhaps he is a more recent convert. In any case, he adheres to it faithfully. |
| 10 | **Nothing:** The character refuses to put his faith in something greater. The galaxy is a chaotic and random place, and the only thing that someone can trust in is himself. |

# STEP 9: CHOOSE GEAR AND APPEARANCE

By this point, the Player Characters' game statistics and personalities should be well established. The key remaining issues are to determine their personal equipment and physical appearances. These combine to add visual elements to the characters' personae. Players should consider this an opportunity to add additional depth to their characters.

## STARTING GEAR

Player Characters start out with 500 credits to spend on personal gear. Characters may also have earned additional credits if they reduced their Morality modifier in Step 2. Refer to **Chapter V: Gear and Equipment** for a thorough listing of available options. Note that players may not elect to purchase anything that is listed as Restricted (R) without the Game Master's explicit approval. Player Characters are assumed to have miscellaneous incidental sundries that are not listed on their character sheet. This could include personal mementos as well as routine items like a journal or a chrono. While these items are of sentimental value, they seldom have financial value, nor are they likely to affect game mechanics.

Characters may keep any credits that are not spent on gear as part of their starting equipment. In addition, after all spending is complete, each player rolls 1d100. The value of the die roll is added to any remaining starting funds, and represents the "pocket money" characters may possess. This total represents the character's initial spending money at the beginning of the first game session. Note that these additional starting funds cannot be spent until gameplay actually begins.

## PHYSICAL DESCRIPTION

There is little uniformity of appearance within a group of FORCE AND DESTINY characters. The anatomical features of the different species vary significantly. Even within a species, there exists a broad range of different colorations and physiques. Players are encouraged to have fun with this range, creating appearances that reflect their characters' personalities.

An important first step is referring to the descriptions of the different species. A Nautolan's tendrils are very different in appearance from a Twi'lek's lekku. Each of the species has distinctive features that should play an

### SHORT ON CASH?

Remember, a player can always increase his character's starting credits when determining his starting Morality, as described under **Player Character Starting Morality Values**, on page 49.

important role in describing their physical appearance. Any significant departures from those descriptions are certainly worth mentioning, and may be a way of further distinguishing the character.

Keep in mind that a character's appearance should also mesh with his personality. A particularly flamboyant character is likely to reflect that personality in style of dress as well as in body modifications—possibly including dye, tattoos, or other permanent modifications. Conversely, characters who are more conservative only have modifications that are a traditional part of their native culture.

- **Height, weight, and build:** A character's physical build is primarily determined by his species. All of the species presented in FORCE AND DESTINY are typically 1.5 to 2 meters high, with Cereans tending toward 2 meters and Twi'leks tending toward the shorter 1.5 meters. However, even within the norms of a species, there can be a great deal of variation. Players should endeavor to keep their characters' builds within reasonable limits, of course; a 4-meter human would be well outside the realms of believability. But within those limits, players are free to choose whether their characters appear thin, fat, muscular, tall, short, or any combination thereof. If players like, they can also tailor their characters' physical appearances to match the characters' physical characteristics: Agility and Brawn.

- **Hair, horns, and eye color:** Not all species in the galaxy have hair, or even eyes. For example, Nautolans, Twi'leks, and Kel Dors do not have hair at all, while Cereans tend to only have hair growing in a fringe around the edges of their cone-shaped heads. In addition, Nautolans have black eyes without pupils. However, among those species who do have variations in eye and hair color, almost infinite variations are possible. Players can freely decide what color eyes and hair—as applicable—are appropriate for their characters. They can also decide how the characters choose to style and decorate such attributes, or if they have any particular accessories that they choose to wear.

- **Skin, scale, or fur color:** Some species in FORCE AND DESTINY tend to have consistent skin coloration; for example, Kel Dors almost always have orange-brown skin. Others, such as the Twi'leks and humans, can possess a wide range of skin pigmentation, ranging from albino white through all manner of flesh tones to stranger hues such as blue or green. Other species—including the Togruta—can even have patterns in their pigmentation. Fur or hair can have even wider variance. Some individuals may even dye their hair or fur with hues that are subtle or outlandish, depending on the individual.

- **Scars, tattoos, and other identifying marks:** This is an opportunity for players to get especially creative, because scars, tattoos, and other markings have little to do with a species' physiology, and everything to do with an individual PC's experiences and backstory. A tattoo may possess a deep cultural significance for the character, or it could be something the PC got as a lark after a long night at a cantina. Scars could come from exciting adventures, childhood events, or embarrassing accidents the character would prefer to forget. Characters may also possess piercings, brands, implanted corporate or government identification marks, subdermal cybercircuits, or nearly anything else the players can think of.

# PERSONALITY

A character's personality is another place where players can really get creative. Traits, quirks, habits, likes and dislikes—players can be as thorough or as concise as they wish.

A great starting point for a character's personality is the emotional strengths and weaknesses that come with his Morality. These choices can form the core of the character's personality, providing a solid foundation as the player creates a well-rounded and interesting character. Motivations can also provide a good basis for determining personality traits; after all, what the character is driven to accomplish can say a lot about how he acts. Morality and Motivations can be chosen so that they complement each other and work together to form a coherent personality type, but they don't have to. Having a personality and emotions that conflict with a character's Motivation can be a classic character trope. If a character's Emotional Weakness is anger but his Motivation is galactic peace, that character could be fun to play as he finds himself torn between his ideals and his base instincts.

Alternatively, another good way to develop a personality for a character is to start with a base (such as the choices made with Morality) and then let the broader personality evolve over time. Sometimes the best character personalities develop over the course of the game, evolving out of the decisions the player makes naturally. Don't be afraid to leave a character with room to grow and change.

# STEP 10: DETERMINE GROUP RESOURCE

Under the tyranny of the Galactic Empire, everyone with Force sensitivity must take extraordinary care in exhibiting and even admitting to their abilities. Without the Jedi Order to identify and educate young Force-sensitives, some do not even come to recognize that they possess such abilities. Those who do have abilities must train themselves, learn through associations with another, less well-known Force tradition, or study from materials that the Empire believes destroyed.

At this point, the group should have some idea as to what has brought them together and caused them to join forces against galactic tyranny. Selecting a group starting resource helps cement this bond. While this should not be the sole reason the group works together, it can provide a springboard or convenient initial excuse.

During this step, the group should jointly select one of the three options from the following list. It could be that they trained under the same master, or possibly they are from the same small community and learned about the Force together. Perhaps the group discovered each other while all were trying to track down an obscure Jedi relic, such as a holocron. Or maybe the group initially joined forces simply because fate and the Force worked to have them all aboard the same vessel.

## JEDI HOLOCRON

The character came into possession of a Jedi holocron. Perhaps it was found among an ancestor's possessions or among a hidden trove that the characters discovered. Information from the holocron guided the characters in developing their Force abilities, likely providing information about the Jedi philosophy in the process. The holocron is not all-knowing, as it contains only a limited amount of information, likely from the perspective of a single Jedi. However, it represents a valuable resource.

The group starts with one holocron (see page 190). The holocron the group starts with is a more basic example of its kind, and the only mechanical benefit it provides is giving the group access to two skills as career skills. The GM can either roll randomly on **Table 2-7: Holocron Skills** or choose from the table to determine what pair of career skills the holocron makes accessible to the players. Alternatively, the GM can choose any two skills from **Table 3-1**, on page 113.

## STARSHIP

Having a starship at a group's disposal can allow them to slip through Imperial blockades and avoid unnecessary and unpleasant complications. They can also use their ship to explore strange new worlds and travel beyond known space.

## TABLE 2-7: HOLOCRON SKILLS

| d10 | Skills |
|-----|--------|
| 1 | Knowledge (Outer Rim) and Piloting (Space) |
| 2 | Computers and Perception |
| 3 | Brawl and Streetwise |
| 4 | Mechanics and Ranged (Light) |
| 5 | Astrogation and Gunnery |
| 6 | Discipline and Medicine |
| 7 | Knowledge (Lore) and Lightsaber |
| 8 | Cool and Coordination |
| 9 | Skulduggery and Vigilance |
| 10 | Knowledge (Xenology) and Survival |

If the group selects this option, they begin the game with one G-9 Rigger light freighter on page 262 (or another starship that can transport everyone in the group and costs 70,000 credits or less).

## MENTOR

The characters trained in the ways of the Force with a mentor. Perhaps this mentor was a former Jedi now exiled, or even a Padawan who never completed his training. Perhaps he came of age after the Purges and is self taught. The mentor may even belong to a Force tradition other than the Jedi Order. If so, the tradition is most likely limited to members of a particular species, and it is probably from only one particular world.

The mentor does not travel with the group, and it is up to the GM as to whether he is alive or dead. If he is alive, he can contact the group to give them advice or help with their ongoing training. If he is dead, he may still appear to the group in dreams or visions. In either case, the particulars of the mentor's species, gender, Force tradition, and other pertinent information are left to the GM's discretion. However, he should only facilitate and aid the group's adventures: not dominate sessions or control the group's actions.

The mentor makes it easier for members of the group to obtain Force powers. When a Player Character purchases the basic version of a Force power, he may decrease the cost of the basic power by 5 XP. This discount does not apply when purchasing upgrades to Force powers. This discount only applies after the character has spent their initial XP during character creation.

# III

# SKILLS

*"If you spent as much time practicing your saber techniques as you did your wit, you'd rival Master Yoda as a swordsman."*

–Obi-Wan Kenobi

hen playing **FORCE AND DESTINY**, characters have plenty of opportunities for bold and exciting action, from flying a starfighter through a solar storm to dodging traps in the depths of an ancient evil temple. Whether characters succeed or fail in these actions is determined by their skills.

The vast majority of characters' actions are governed by abilities they have acquired through education or experience. Any time PCs attempt an action that has a reasonable chance of success or failure, their skills come into play as a means of determining the result. In some instances, the task may be so trivial, or the character so capable, that the Game Master may not call for a check. At other times, the task might be so outlandish that the player might choose to act differently once the odds are calculated. Ultimately, when there is a reasonable chance of failure, players must depend on their characters' skills to see them through to success.

Skill values fulfill this role in conjunction with characteristics. These two values interact to establish the number of Ability and Proficiency dice used when

attempting any action. A character's innate abilities are generally described by characteristics, while skills require learning and practice. In this way, the intersection of education and natural ability contributes to a character's chances of success or failure.

## WHAT ARE SKILLS?

Anything that a character might learn could be considered a skill. The galaxy is a vast place, however, and not everything a person might learn has applications that fit well within a dramatic game. To reflect this, **FORCE AND DESTINY** includes a list of the skills that are most likely to be useful in the course of dramatic adventures set within the *Star Wars* galaxy. The list may not cover every imaginable situation, but it should address the majority of actions that occur often during a typical game session.

Skills are divided into three categories based on their general application and use. Knowledge skills are entirely cerebral. They do not govern action—only understanding. Combat skills deal with how a character may act and react in a direct physical confrontation. Other skills may be useful during an altercation, but Combat skills can seldom be employed without violence. All skills that deal with non-combat actions are considered General skills.

## SKILL RANKS

When a character chooses to attempt an action, the player begins by forming a dice pool. The higher of the relevant characteristic and skill values is used to determine the total number of Ability dice in the pool. The smaller of these two values indicates how many of those dice are upgraded to Proficiency dice. A character who has no ranks in a skill is considered to be unskilled. This character has a value of 0 for the skill in question, so his checks for that skill are made without upgrading any Ability dice to Proficiency dice.

Aside from the game terms, it may also be useful to consider what skill ranks represent in a more narrative sense. Even a single rank in a skill represents a significant amount of time spent learning and practicing its use. It's generally reasonable to assume that other characters in the game world rely heavily on their characteristics for actions outside their field of expertise. For example, almost everyone can pilot a speeder in routine traffic, but most characters do not have a rank of Piloting (Planetary). Instead, they default to using their Agility characteristic for this type of routine task.

Each rank of a skill represents a substantial degree of training and practice. Further, that practice must often come under strenuous conditions. A character who spends endless days performing the same task on a droid assembly line does not improve his Mechanics skill. However, if that same character were regularly working on a range of different droids that came in for repairs after being exposed to harsh environmental conditions, it's likely that he could soon improve his skill rank.

The first two ranks of a skill represent a thorough grounding in that skill but little practical experience. Such a character may have just completed a formal education, taken part in an apprenticeship, or begun an entry-level job. At this level of competency, the PC knows the basics of the skill but hardly realizes how little he knows. He may accomplish routine tasks on a regular basis, but he is often overwhelmed by complex ones.

The third and fourth ranks are indicative of a true professional. These are individuals who have honed the skill thoroughly and can make their living at it. They might be talented and capable physicians, respected pilots, or gifted mechanics. They are aware of how much more they have to learn, but they are quite capable of handling most tasks when they have prepared for them.

Only a handful of individuals attain the fifth rank of a skill. Few can adequately appreciate the artistry of a master's craft, so those who attain this level must deliberately challenge themselves to perfect their expertise. Characters with this degree of proficiency may have a reputation for their particular talents that extends far beyond their community. These individuals are generally driven and passionate about the skill that they have mastered.

## SKILL DESCRIPTIONS

This section details all of the skills used throughout the game. Each skill is presented with clarifications on how it may best be used, along with notes on its key differences from similar skills. In addition, examples are provided highlighting potential ways that a skill might use ⚙.

---

### CUSTOM SKILLS

At the Game Master's discretion, new skills may be introduced to a campaign. The most common of these might pertain to Knowledge. The six Knowledge skills included in this book represent a broad overview, but a campaign focused within a particular portion of the galaxy or on a particular style of play might benefit from alternative options. Similarly, games that focus on other aspects of *Star Wars* might also consider alternative General skills. If the Player Characters regularly visit worlds where beasts serve as the primary form of transportation, then Animal Handling might be in order. Alternatively, if the characters travel incognito as a troupe of actors, then Perform might be an appropriate skill. Before adding such skills, Game Masters should carefully consider whether an addition is critical for the campaign tone and how often it might come into play. Each new skill rank that a character needs to purchase represents XP that might have been spent on existing skills.

When adding a new skill, the Game Master and players work together to decide which careers and specializations might offer it as a career skill. In some cases, it might be most effective to remove a standard skill from the list prior to adding a new skill, so as to maintain comparable levels of flexibility between archetypes. In other cases, a more generalized skill might be available to everyone at career skill pricing.

## TABLE 3-1: SKILL LIST

| Skill | Characteristic | Type | Page |
|---|---|---|---|
| Astrogation | Intellect | General | 114 |
| Athletics | Brawn | General | 115 |
| Brawl | Brawn | Combat | 129 |
| Charm | Presence | General | 116 |
| Coercion | Willpower | General | 116 |
| Computers | Intellect | General | 118 |
| Cool | Presence | General | 118 |
| Coordination | Agility | General | 119 |
| Core Worlds | Intellect | Knowledge | 132 |
| Deception | Cunning | General | 120 |
| Discipline | Willpower | General | 120 |
| Education | Intellect | Knowledge | 132 |
| Gunnery | Agility | Combat | 130 |
| Leadership | Presence | General | 121 |
| Lightsaber | Brawn | Combat | 130 |
| Lore | Intellect | Knowledge | 132 |
| Mechanics | Intellect | General | 122 |
| Medicine | Intellect | General | 122 |
| Melee | Brawn | Combat | 131 |
| Negotiation | Presence | General | 123 |
| Outer Rim | Intellect | Knowledge | 133 |
| Perception | Cunning | General | 124 |
| Piloting (Planetary) | Agility | General | 124 |
| Piloting (Space) | Agility | General | 125 |
| Ranged (Heavy) | Agility | Combat | 131 |
| Ranged (Light) | Agility | Combat | 131 |
| Resilience | Brawn | General | 125 |
| Skulduggery | Cunning | General | 126 |
| Stealth | Agility | General | 126 |
| Streetwise | Cunning | General | 127 |
| Survival | Cunning | General | 128 |
| Underworld | Intellect | Knowledge | 133 |
| Vigilance | Willpower | General | 129 |
| Xenology | Intellect | Knowledge | 133 |

Sometimes, through particular fortune, a character's check may generate more ✸ than are needed to accomplish a task. Each entry presents ways in which these additional ✸ may be used. These are not necessary, but are intended to add additional flavor. Game Masters and players are encouraged to work together to create alternative ways in which extra ✸ might appropriately and dramatically modify a given situation.

# CHOOSING SKILLS

**D**uring character creation, it's vital that each player select the skills that cover his character's core area of expertise. A Warrior must be able to use his weapon, a Consular must be able to negotiate, and a Peacekeeper must be able to lead. This doesn't mean that every Player Character should maximize his core skills, but those who fail to take at least one rank are likely to regret it.

Skills beyond a Player Character's central focus must be chosen carefully. Those related to a PC's profession are substantially more economical than those outside his career. Players who spread their characters too thin at the early stages may discover that the sacrifices necessary were not worthwhile. Routine uses of a skill do not generally require a check. A retired Sage may not need to be a talented pilot if he only uses his speeder for transport and is unlikely to be piloting in a high-speed chase.

At the same time, some skills are much more likely to come up during the course of a hero's adventures. Injuries that require Medicine are common. In some situations, it can be critical to move with Stealth. At other times, a PC's life may depend upon his Vigilance or Athletics. Often, it's in a group's best interest to discuss skills collectively, so that the players and the Game Master have a shared expectation about how often particular skills are likely to be used.

# GENERAL SKILLS

**T**his group of skills represents the majority of the actions a character attempts. In dramatic situations, the entire success or failure of a mission might ride on how effectively a given character uses one of these skills. Though General skills do not focus on violent pursuits or combat, life and death can certainly hinge on the success of an Athletics check or an effective application of medical expertise.

## ASTROGATION (INTELLECT)

There are many billions of stars populating the galaxy, all of which are in motion relative to one another. Planets and smaller masses are in constant orbit around many of these stars. Vast numbers of nebulae and other astronomical anomalies are also present throughout the galaxy. Traveling between the worlds of the galaxy requires at least a rudimentary knowledge of the galaxy's organization and composition. It also requires a navicomputer that is up to date on the current time and relative motion of all of these objects. The Astrogation skill represents a character's ability to use his knowledge of the galaxy to most effectively program the hyperspace coordinates for any jump. It can also represent a character's knowledge of stellar locations, astronomy, and the formation of the galaxy.

- Programming a navicomputer for a hyperspace jump requires a successful Astrogation check.
- Astrogation governs a character's basic knowledge of galactic geography. It may be checked any time a character wonders what other systems are nearby.

- In the event that characters arrive in an unknown system, they may use a navicomputer and their Astrogation skill to identify their location.
- Astrogation also covers familiarity with the galaxy's hyperspace routes and the types of craft and commerce most common along those routes.

The difficulty of a hyperspace jump is based on the area targeted and the distance traveled. Travel to a nearby system along a well-established route is generally an **Easy (◆) check**. The difficulty increases based on the accuracy of navigational information and other factors. See page 252 for more information on hyperspace travel.

Additional ☼ beyond those required to calculate a hyperspace jump may be used to better target the location. While a single net ☼ reaches the target system without incident, extras might place the character's vessel directly into orbit around the target planet. Alternatively, characters may use additional ☼ to reduce the time spent calculating, when rushed.

❂ generated as part of an Astrogation check are most commonly used to reduce travel time. On extended journeys, they might be used to identify convenient stopovers en route, where the vessel can resupply or conduct additional business to help defray the cost of the trip. ⊕ could be spent either to complete Astrogation calculations in the minimum amount of time, or to greatly reduce the travel time involved. It could also reveal some highly valuable but previously unknown information, such as a safer or quicker alternative route.

Conversely,  generated on an Astrogation check could decrease the accuracy or increase the travel time of a hyperspace jump, or it could simply cause a character to miss relevant details when analyzing hyperspace routes or galactic maps. ▽ could be spent in the same way but to greater magnitude, or it could trigger some truly disastrous occurrence, such as jumping out of hyperspace into the path of an asteroid.

# ATHLETICS (BRAWN)

Player Characters lead dramatic lives filled with constant physical confrontation. Often, that confrontation comes from an enemy with a blaster, but sometimes it may be a mountain to be scaled, a river to be swum, or a chasm that must be leapt. The Athletics skill governs these actions. It serves as a measure of the character's overall fitness and physical conditioning. Those who actively engage in a regimen of physical training, such as field infantry or scouts, are the most likely to have a high rank in Athletics.

- All aspects of climbing—including rappelling and swinging on a line—fall under the purview of the Athletics skill. The difficulty of these tasks is calculated based on the surface, incline, and other basic conditions of the surface being climbed.

- Characters who attempt to swim in difficult conditions must check their Athletics. Water conditions—particularly waves, current, and tides—dictate the overall challenge of any effort to swim.

- A character's vertical and horizontal jump are both determined through use of an Athletics check. Gravitational conditions and the distance required factor into the difficulty.

- Most characters can run, but sprinting or running for an extended time falls under the purview of an Athletics check.

The difficulty of an Athletics check is set by the severity of the task. Attempting to perform a routine task under normal conditions should never require a check. A more demanding task—jumping more than a person's body length or staying afloat for hours—should require ◆ commensurate with the difficulty of the task. Adverse conditions—extreme rain, rough winds, or aggressive pursuit—could impose one or more ■. A combination of these elements can make a check significantly more challenging. Extremely adverse conditions—hurricane force winds or a surface covered in oil—and attempts at superhuman feats may introduce one or more ⬡, in addition to increasing the difficulty.

Additional ✦ on an Athletics check can either reduce the time required to make the check or increase the distance traveled with that check.

⊕ ⊕ on an Athletics check may be used to grant the character an additional maneuver during the course of his turn. The maneuver should be one that involves movement or some sort of physical activity. See page 206 for more information, and remember that characters can take a maximum of only two maneuvers during their turn. ⊕ can also generate bonus ☐ on other physical checks performed by allies during that round, or on physical checks the character performs later.

⊛ results on successful checks should allow the character to perform the check with a truly impressive outcome. Instead of heaving a boulder aside, he hurls it into the air; instead of grabbing onto the edge of a hovering platform, he uses his momentum to flip atop it, landing on his feet.

As Athletics is generally used to perform physical actions, ⊚ and ▽ results should most often result in physical penalties. Small amounts of ⊚ may cause the character to suffer strain, while larger amounts of ⊚ may cause the character to fall prone, or even suffer a wound from sprains and bruises. ▽ could even inflict a Critical Injury, either chosen by the GM to fit the circumstances or rolled randomly.

# CHARM (PRESENCE)

For a character with a kind smile and a silver tongue, it might be possible to travel the galaxy simply by depending on the kindness of others. An individual with this knack is capable of giving just the right compliment to his target—often by deciphering the subject's social and cultural background. Note that the use of the Charm skill requires the acting character to maintain a degree of sincerity in his statements. A character who employs flagrant flattery with no basis in reality would be better suited to the Deception skill. See **Social Skill Interactions**, on the next page, for more information. Politicians, salespeople, and con artists are all renowned for their Charm.

- Persuading an individual to make a special exception to his usual practices through flattery, flirtation, and grace typically relies on Charm.

- Appeals to a target's better nature—even if it does not exist—generally require a character to use Charm. These sorts of requests may require the target to go out of his way to aid the characters, without any hope of remuneration.

- Seduction attempts for most species typically rely on Charm, but for situations in which the interest is entirely feigned, it is usually more appropriate to use Deception.

Charm is often an opposed check against the subject's Cool. An exception is a situation in which the PC is trying to Charm a large group, in which case a set difficulty is usually employed. Of course, situational modifiers may also apply based upon the character's style of dress, species, and other characteristics. For instances in which the desired outcome is directly opposed to the target's interests, an additional ◆ may be added.

For situations involving multiple subjects or a target predisposed to react favorably toward the character, the character does not make an opposed check. Instead, the difficulty of the check is determined by the number of subjects and their disposition. Larger crowds or groups who are predisposed against the character's desired outcome require a more difficult check, while charming those already partial to the character may require few, if any, ◆.

Extra ✬ on a Charm check may be used to extend the target's support for additional scenes. Each ✬ spent in this way gains the character an extra scene in which the target is willing to support him.

⊕ may be spent to affect unexpected subjects beyond the original target. These may be bystanders or others who are not directly involved in the scene, but who may be able to aid the character in their own way. With ⊛, the player may choose to have a target NPC become a recurring character who remains predisposed to assist his character. This NPC may not join the character's crew, but might offer a better than usual price for fencing goods, or may share certain Imperial secrets.

⊚ and ▽ are, conversely, harmful to a character's standing with those he is trying to sway. ⊚ may be spent to reduce the number of people the character is able to influence or to turn those affected negatively against the character. The GM may use ▽ to turn a single NPC against the character and to make that NPC a minor recurring adversary.

# COERCION (WILLPOWER)

Some people believe that the only way to maintain respect is to be feared. Others may only grant respect to those whom they fear. When characters attempt to instill obedience in a target through the use of threats or acts of physical intimidation, they use Coercion. A Sith Lord or an Imperial interrogator may use Coercion to frighten the weak or force innocents to do his bidding. However, even decent individuals may use Coercion to intimidate opponents into surrendering rather than fighting and killing their enemies. See **Social Skill Interactions** sidebar, on the next page, for more information. Imperial Intelligence agents, dark side Force adepts, and organized crime leaders are all known for their ability to coerce their subjects.

- Any time a character issues a threat, whether or not accompanied by hostile actions, he is using Coercion against the subject. An implied threat—

# SOCIAL SKILL INTERACTIONS

Not every conflict must be resolved by force of arms. In fact, it can often be in a character's best interest to resolve a situation amicably.

Whenever one character attempts to convince another character to act in a specific way, it requires a check, often referred to as a social skill check. Social skill checks generally use one of the following skills: Charm, Coercion, Deception, Leadership, or Negotiation. These checks are commonly used to determine how the target reacts to the attempt. They are often opposed checks, although not when dealing with groups. If the acting character is successful, the target is swayed to his point of view—at least for the duration of the scene. Upon failure, the arguments presented fail to influence the opposing character.

If the characters have a previous relationship, this may add ▨ or ☐ to the check. If the target has prior evidence that the acting character is trustworthy, then he is much more likely to cooperate. However, if there are prior acts of betrayal, the situation may become far more challenging.

Ultimately, the different social skills are indicative of the way that a character might attempt to manipulate his target. Charm governs trying to persuade a target by being nice to him. Coercion represents efforts to scare an opponent into submission. Deception entails lying to the target so that he might cooperate. Leadership reflects the use of authority, real or imagined. Negotiation covers persuading someone to cooperate by offering him something that he wants. **Table 3–2: Social Skill Interactions** illustrates the social skill oppositions. Refer to the individual skill descriptions for additional details on the various social skills involved.

## TABLE 3-2: SOCIAL SKILL INTERACTIONS

| Acting Skill | Opposing Skill |
| --- | --- |
| Coercion, Deception, Leadership | Discipline |
| Charm | Cool |
| Negotiation | Negotiation or Cool |

such as gesturing toward a weapon—is sufficient to invoke Coercion.

- If a target is questioned or persuaded under conditions of physical captivity, the acting character should make a Coercion check.

- Acts of physical torture always invoke Coercion. Of course, physical violence may also induce strain or wounds in a subject. Such actions are separate from the actual Coercion attempt.

Coercion is an opposed check, resisted by the subject's Discipline. Situational modifiers, such as the degree to which a subject is helpless or a degree of threat that is less significant than expected, may significantly affect the dice pool. Attempting to persuade a subject to betray his core beliefs should always add ◆ to the pool.

In situations in which the character is attempting to intimidate multiple subjects or a target who is already threatened by the character, the character need not make an opposed check. In such circumstances, the difficulty of the check is determined by the number of subjects and their disposition. Larger crowds or groups that are more likely to resist authority require a more difficult check, while using Coercion on those already cowed by the character may require few, if any, ◆.

Extra ✵ on a Coercion check may be used to inflict strain upon the target at a rate of 1 strain per ✵ ✵.

By spending ۞ ۞, the character may affect unexpected subjects beyond the original target. These may be bystanders or others not directly involved in the scene, but who may be cowed by the character as a result of witnessing the Coercion attempt. With ⊕, the character may completely break the subject's will. The target's allegiance shifts, and he becomes a subjugated ally of the acting character, at least temporarily. The newfound follower may be exploited to gain additional information or assets, or even to serve as a spy within the ranks of a foe. However, if the follower's betrayal is discovered by the foe, this forced loyalty may not prove permanent.

Intimidation and strong-arm tactics are only as successful as the strength and thought behind the attempt. The GM may spend ۞ and ▽ to undermine the outcome of a character's Coercion attempt. Extra ۞ may be spent by the GM to represent a building resentment toward the coercing character. Regardless of the success or failure of the Coercion attempt, the subject may grow to despise the character as a result of having been strong-armed. ▽, on the other hand, may be spent to represent the character's slipping up and revealing something about his goals and motivations to the target. For instance, a character attempting to coerce a target to give up security codes for an Imperial detention facility might let slip that he is looking to rescue Force-sensitive prisoners, and he is also Force-sensitive.

# COMPUTERS (INTELLECT)

The galaxy could scarcely function without the constant assistance of computers. Devices everywhere are linked together and coordinated by computers and droid brains. Those talented in computing can sometimes exploit these resources, or they might know how best to avoid those systems under computer control. Many people are so unconsciously dependent upon computers that those who can cleverly manipulate them may commit crimes without their victims even becoming aware of the offenses. Even using the HoloNet for communications or entertainment requires the use of computers—particularly if there are forces interfering with the system. This skill also governs the repair of a damaged computer system, defensive actions against an intruding slicer, and routine maintenance necessary to keep the software on a computer or droid running effectively.

- Attempts to open a locked door, control an elevator, or bypass a security system make use of the Computers skill.

- Searching through a subject's records, particularly if those notes are encrypted, makes use of Computers to overcome any security measures and interpret the material's organizational structure and any external links.

- Investigating what actions a slicer might have taken against a computer system requires the Computers skill to identify the files that have been accessed or altered.

- Efforts to alter a droid's programming or gain access to its memories require the acting character to make a Computers check.

- Characters must make a Computers check to recover data from a system that has suffered physical damage.

The difficulty for a Computers check is calculated based on any defenses present within the system and the inherent sophistication of the system against intrusion. Slicing into a tapcafé's systems to alter a transaction might be trivially easy, while a military outpost could be hardened and prepared for a slicer's assault. In general, the more vital the materials protected by the system, the more difficult the system should be to overcome.

Additional ✵ may be spent to reduce the time required for the action undertaken. This is generally representative of the character's extensive familiarity with systems of the type targeted.

✪ may be spent to uncover additional information about the system. The character might discover additional assets that could be targeted, the owner's personal journal entries, or the presence of well-concealed defenses. Once the presence of such systems is discovered, a character may attempt to gain access to them with further Computers checks. ⊕ may be spent to conceal any actions the character may have taken while slicing the system. Each ⊕ may be spent to add ⬤ to the check if another slicer should attempt to detect or identify the character's actions with a Computers check.

The GM may spend ⬡ generated on a character's Computers check to represent the character's doing a poor job of concealing his presence in the system. Security systems are alerted to the electronic intrusion, while other slicers attempting to discover evidence of the character's actions may add ◻ to their check for each ⬡ generated by the character's initial Computers check.

▽ may be spent by a GM to represent the character's leaving behind of trace information about his own system in the system he was attempting to slice. For each ▽ generated by the character's Computers check, the GM may add ◻ to any future Computers checks in which an NPC uses the target system to slice the character's own system.

# COOL (PRESENCE)

The life of a Force-sensitive within the Empire is never easy. The ability to stay calm and think while one's life hangs in the balance can be essential for survival amid the constant stream of Imperial threats. By maintaining a calm and placid temperament, the character is much more likely to be able to effectively prioritize issues and solve the most critical problems first. These characters are also better able to remember and focus on achieving their goals, allowing outside influences to have much less effect.

- In some combat situations, a character's Initiative may be determined by his Cool skill. This is applicable under circumstances in which the acting character has calmly prepared to take action. See page 204 for full details.

- A character's Cool is used to resist Charm and Negotiation, and may permit him to ignore many of the lies that come as part of a discussion. See **Social Skill Interactions**, on page 117, for more information.

- Often, when someone is trying to be overly kind, authenticity becomes lost among the niceties. Characters can use Cool to resist these efforts, penetrating through to the truth.

- If a character has set a trap for a target, carefully lining up a shot on an unsuspecting foe, he may check for Initiative using Cool, as he calmly selects the optimal time to begin the engagement.

- If multiple characters are engaging another in a debate in which the timing of the argument matters, Cool may be used to determine Initiative, as that character is better prepared.

There is rarely any extra ✵ on a Cool check, as it's generally used to oppose another's actions or to determine Initiative, which takes all ✵ into account.

An ❂ from a Cool check may be spent to give the character an additional insight into the situation at hand. He may notice an extra complication before it comes into play against him or identify an object that can be used directly against his opponent. The character might spot a rogue asteroid during a dogfight, notice a security officer near a sniper's target, or pick up on a magistrate's predilection for a particular style of argument.

A character who generates a ✦ result during a Cool check has not only stood unflinching as chaos erupts around him, but has actually come away the better for it. For each ✦ result on a Cool check, the character may recover 3 strain.

Sometimes a situation is so frantic that it can overwhelm even the most steadfast of souls. The GM may spend ✧ generated as a result of a Cool check to cause the character to miss a vital detail or event. For instance, if a character generates ✧ during a duel, he may be so focused on his target that he fails to notice the target's ally on the sidelines pulling a weapon of his own. If the situation goes badly enough, the character may lose all sense of where he is and what he is doing, effectively succumbing to minor shell shock. The GM may spend any ▽ generated on a Cool check to stagger the character for one round as he is overwhelmed by the chaos around him.

# COORDINATION (AGILITY)

When a character needs to go somewhere without being seen, it often requires him to remain stable on unsteady surfaces, crawl through narrow openings, or even tumble down safely from a dangerous height. Overcoming these types of challenges requires a tremendous sense of balance and a heightened degree of flexibility. While both of those abilities depend heavily on a person's natural characteristics, they can be further developed through regimens of practice and exercise.

Any time a character needs to contort his body into an unusual position, Coordination is used to calculate the dice pool. Note that some species may be inherently more flexible than the norm. This benefit is discussed in their species description, where applicable.

Many Shadows and Hunters become known for their natural flexibility and grace. For some, their lives may frequently depend on their expertise in the skill. For others, the skill serves as an important complement to their other abilities.

- A character may attempt to reduce damage suffered from falling, diminishing the impact by rolling into a tumble upon a successful Coordination check. See **Falling**, on page 221, for more information.

- Walking across a narrow surface, whether a wide beam or a thin pipe, requires a tremendous sense of balance and a successful Coordination check.

- Characters can use Coordination to escape from restraints, contorting their limbs at unusual angles so that bindings slip free.

- Crawling through the twists and turns of a sewage pipe, ventilation duct, or garbage chute may require a successful Coordination check to avoid a sudden fall or—worse yet—becoming stuck in place.

Any additional ✵ received when using Coordination may be spent to increase the distance traveled during the action or to decrease the time it takes to perform the action. Each ✵ spent in this way can increase the distance moved by 25%, up to a maximum of ✵ ✵ ✵ ✵.

❂ ❂ on a Coordination check may be used to grant the character an additional maneuver during the course of his turn. (However, during an encounter, a character can only use two maneuvers per turn.) ✦ on a Coordination check may be spent to accomplish the task with truly impressive results, either with narrative flair or granting additional benefits in the course of completing it. For example, instead of walking across a rope to get across a chasm, the character could cut the rope, swing across, and in doing so deny anyone the ability to follow him.

To represent harm done to a character's body in the process of a Coordination check, the GM could spend ✧ generated during that check to cause the character to lose his free maneuver for one round per ⬡. ▽ represents something truly harmful happening to the character during his check. The character could suffer a wound as a result of ▽ during a Coordination check or could lose a vital piece of equipment.

# DECEPTION (CUNNING)

Sometimes a character needs to persuade someone to act a certain way but lacks any leverage for the discussion. In times like this, a certain degree of moral flexibility may be necessary. Whether it's an effort to persuade someone to make a purchase, do a favor, or simply go somewhere else, a well-timed and convincing lie can make the difference between success and failure. When a falsehood plays the central role in a persuasive effort, the character making use of it is employing the Deception skill. Advisors, Shadows, and many less-than-reputable merchants are all masters of Deception. Many individuals outside of these fields make use of this skill, but it's seldom a critical focus of their development.

Attempts to deceive are subject to the perceptions of the target. Deception is opposed by the subject's Discipline; see **Social Skill Interactions**, on page 117, for more information. In situations in which the character is attempting to trick multiple subjects or a target who believes that character to be trustworthy, the character need not make an opposed check. In such circumstances, the difficulty of the check is determined by the number of subjects or their disposition (or both). Larger crowds or groups that are more likely to disbelieve the character require a more difficult check, while deceiving those already fooled by the character may require a lower difficulty.

- If a character wishes to mislead a buyer or seller about an object's value so that he may adjust the purchase price to his advantage, he uses Deception.

- Any time a character wishes to distract an opponent through guile—even within the context of a physical confrontation—he may make use of Deception.

- When pursued, a character may choose to use Deception as a means to lay a false trail, in the hope that the tracker might make a wrong turn, thus leaving the character ample time to escape.

Extra ✶ on a Deception check may be spent to extend the duration of the Deception. This could give the acting character ample time to travel offworld before the treachery is discovered, or it might even leave the target less likely to notice the fraud and more susceptible to further deceptions.

✦ may be used to increase the value of any goods or services gained through the action. The subject might simply believe that he is agreeing to fair terms with the liar. ✦ may be spent to fool the target into believing that the character is a trustworthy sort. Future

Deception checks against the target do not require an opposed check; they are simply made at a baseline difficulty depending on the nature of the lie.

⬡ during a Deception check gives away a portion of the lie. Perhaps the target realizes that he has been lied to but is unable to identify how much of the interaction is false, thereby prompting him to become more suspicious of the character. ▽ may represent a more extreme example of this phenomenon; for instance, the target not only distrusts the character, but spreads the word of his deceit and harms his reputation among a small community of people. Additionally, the target may realize that he is being lied to and use the situation to his advantage, perhaps to insert some false information of his own. Perhaps the target is able to slip shoddy gear past the character by playing along with the lie.

# DISCIPLINE (WILLPOWER)

The ability to focus one's mind is vital to a Force user. Though one must be sensitive to the Force in order to use it, if a character has no Discipline, he can never hope to master his abilities. In addition, characters may confront countless horrors as they explore the galaxy. Some of these are natural, if terrifying: the rancor, the krayt dragon, and the wampa, to name a few. Others, such as the Death Star, may be constructions or artifacts, and still others—such as a vergence of the dark side of the Force—may be supernatural. The ability to maintain composure and react in an effective manner is also governed by Discipline. This skill represents a character's ability to control his biological instincts so that he can overcome things that might induce abject panic in a person of lesser resolve.

A character's Discipline is used to resist Leadership, Coercion, and Deception checks targeting him, and may enable him to overcome treachery and threats that others attempt to impose upon him. See **Social Skill Interactions**, on page 117, for more information.

Discipline plays a key role in the development of Force abilities. See **Chapter VIII: The Force** for a full explanation.

- If a character is pinned down by heavy fire, he may need to pass a Discipline check in order to act normally.

- Often, when summoning the Force in order to throw objects at people, influence the mental state of others, or otherwise affect individuals, a character may also need to succeed on a Discipline check.

- When confronted by a creature with inherently horrifying aspects, a character's ability to engage the foe rather than flee before its might is governed by the Discipline skill.

- Sometimes, a business contact might offer a character a deal that seems far too good to be true. The ability to resist such temptations is based upon Discipline.

- Mentally sorting truth from fiction and determining when someone is lying (and not letting oneself be swayed by lies), is often a function of Discipline.

- Discipline is often used to oppose another's actions—thus, the roll is made by the opposing player—so it may not always be possible to generate an extra ✲. In situations in which an extra ✲ can be earned, one may be spent to downgrade a ⬡ to a ◆ on the character's next action.

❂ from a Discipline check may be spent to give the character an additional insight into the situation at hand. He might notice a particular vulnerability on a seemingly indomitable foe or an unusual pattern to the suppressing fire that gives the character a moment to leap from cover. Often, the sight of an ally looking danger in the eye and refusing to blink is all it takes to bolster one's resolve. ⊕ generated during a Discipline check may be spent to add ☐ to any Discipline checks made by the character's allies during the following round.

The GM may spend ❂ generated during a Discipline check to undermine the character's resolve, perhaps inflicting a penalty on further actions in the face of distressing circumstances. ▽ may be spent to overwhelm the character entirely. In this case, the character is unable to perform more than a single maneuver during the following round of combat.

# LEADERSHIP (PRESENCE)

Even great heroes sometimes need the assistance of others to complete their goals. Certainly the foulest villains consistently use legions of flunkies to assist them in their schemes. The ability to lead such companions and devotees can play a crucial part in the success or failure of any endeavor. While some may follow out of fear or the promise of tremendous riches, ultimately most individuals choose to work with a person in whom they have faith and trust. The Leadership skill represents a character's ability to instill that belief in the people with whom he chooses to interact. Politicians, military officers, and crime bosses all determine their degree of success based upon their abilities to lead others.

Leadership is a combination of making smart decisions, being firm and decisive when doing so, and instilling a sense of loyalty and respect in one's subordinates. See **Social Skill Interactions**, on page 117, for more information.

- If a character's allies have become subject to the effects of fear (see page 326), they may be rallied through a Leadership check.

- When acting in a public venue, a character may use Leadership to sway a crowd to take action, most commonly of a political nature.

- If a character's underlings have fallen to the guile of an opponent, the character may realign their loyalty to his cause by making a successful Leadership check.

The difficulty of a Leadership check is based on the complexity of the orders a character is attempting to convey. It is also based on the intelligence and professionalism of the subjects he is attempting to command. Particularly complex orders, or stubborn or particularly dull subjects, require a larger number of ◆, while a simple order given to a loyal servant may require few, if any, ◆.

When a character attempts to command a target to perform an action that could result in harm to the target, or is in some other way against the target's nature or best interest, an opposed check is required. The character's Leadership check is opposed by the Discipline of the target, depending on the particulars of the order given.

Extra ✬ on a Leadership check may be used to extend the target's support for additional scenes or may increase the efficiency or effectiveness of the target during the ordered actions.

❂ may be used to affect bystanders in addition to the target. With ⊕, the player may choose to have the target NPC become a recurring character who decides to faithfully follow the acting character. This individual may decide to join the character's crew, offering his services as a permanent *aide-de-camp*.

The GM may spend ❂ generated during a Leadership check to decrease the efficiency of the ordered actions, causing them to take longer or be done poorly. ▽ may be used to undermine the character's authority, damaging the character's ability to command the target or those who witnessed the attempt. Should a character accrue multiple ▽ on a single Leadership check, the target may become a recurring thorn in the character's side, either by refusing future orders outright or turning others against the character.

# MECHANICS (INTELLECT)

Space travel is fraught with dangers. A failed life-support system can leave a crew desperate to find any haven where they might safely land. A failed hyperspace engine might strand them hopelessly far from the nearest repair yard. Individuals who accept these dangers need to have tremendous faith in either the quality of their craft or the mechanical skills of its crew. Even in those cases where confidence is based upon a craft's quality and maintenance regimen, the presence of a capable mechanic can still be crucial to the ship's ultimate survival.

Planetary and atmospheric craft, droids, and even a trusty blaster can break down at the least convenient moment possible. These devices use vastly different technologies, but they share core concepts that any technical expert can carry over from one device to another. The Mechanics skill represents the expertise required for these repairs. The skill plays a critical role for any Artisan, but is also relevant for pilots and support staff who serve in the field.

- Any device that suffers physical damage can be repaired using this skill, with the proper tools.
- Droids are repaired with this skill.

- A character may use Mechanics prior to beginning a repair job so that he can identify the parts and tools necessary for the job, along with their approximate cost. This information may be particularly useful to a character seeking to pay for repairs.
- Sometimes, a character may have access to an extensive supply of discrete components or damaged devices. In this situation, attempts to construct a completely new device are dependent on the Mechanics skill.

At the Game Master's discretion, it might be impossible to complete a repair without the necessary tools or components. Alternatively, the Game Master may choose to apply additional ◆ to represent the instability of temporary fixes.

Additional ✬ on a Mechanics check may be used to increase the efficiency of the action. Each additional ✬ may be used to reduce the time required to make the check by 10 to 20%.

❂ generated during a Mechanics check can mean especially high-quality repairs, possibly making the item higher in quality than it originally was. This may grant □ when using the item or may even make the item count as having the Superior quality for a session. ⊕ earned on a Mechanics check may give a device an additional function that is good for only a single use. Examples might include a temporary engine speed boost or a more powerful blaster shot. The nature and precise details of this temporary function are subject to the Game Master's discretion. Mechanics checks may have specific rules when applied to the repair of starships and vehicles (see page 249).

❂ generated during a Mechanics check may represent particularly shoddy repairs or temporary measures. The GM may spend ❂ to cause the target object or system to malfunction shortly after the Mechanics check is completed. ▽ may be spent to cause further harm to the target object or system, or to cause other components of the target to begin to malfunction.

# MEDICINE (INTELLECT)

Through the course of their travels, characters are certain to suffer injuries. Minor injuries may not require medical intervention, but more serious ones may need the attentions of a trained professional. The Medicine skill constitutes that training and can be used to heal cuts and bruises as well as life-threatening injuries.

- Routine first aid, including use of medpacs, depend upon a character's abilities in Medicine. Medpacs are mercifully simple to use, but the difficulty may be complicated by the severity of the wound.
- The ability to treat for poison—or to inflict it—falls under the Medicine skill. This also governs the use of pharmaceutical and recreational drugs.

- Many planets harbor unique infectious diseases as well as parasites. A well-traveled medical technician may become familiar with both the symptoms and treatments for many such planetary syndromes.

- More serious treatments, such as surgeries, cybernetic augmentations, and psychotherapy, are governed by Medicine, but they generally require additional pharmaceuticals and medical instruments.

The difficulty of the check is based on the target's current state of health. See **Table 3–3: Medicine Check Difficulty**. On a successful check, the target recovers a number of wounds equal to the number of ✵ generated by the roll, as well as an amount of strain equal to the number of ❂ generated. Note that a character may attempt only one Medicine check per week when helping a character to recover from Critical Injuries. Note also that droids may not benefit from Medicine but they may substitute the Mechanics skill for these same healing checks. Characters attempting to treat their own injuries increase the difficulty of the Medicine check by ◆◆.

## TABLE 3–3: MEDICINE CHECK DIFFICULTY

| State of Health | Difficulty |
|---|---|
| Current wounds equal half or less of wound threshold | Easy (◆) |
| Current wounds equal more than half of wound threshold | Average (◆◆) |
| Current wounds exceed wound threshold | Hard (◆◆◆) |
| Recover Critical Injury | Critical Injury severity rating |

Each ✵ on a Medicine check normally heals a single wound, up to the maximum number of wounds the target is currently suffering. Beyond that, additional ✵ have no mechanical effect but may represent particularly competent medical aid.

❂ generated during a Medicine check may be spent to eliminate 1 strain from the target. ⊕ generated during a Medicine check to heal a Critical Injury may also heal additional wounds, or vice versa.

A GM may use ✷ during a Medicine check to increase the amount of time the procedure takes or to inflict strain on the target to represent the shock of the procedure. ▽ represents a truly terrible accident: perhaps the character unintentionally inflicts further wounds on a target whom he was attempting to heal.

# NEGOTIATION (PRESENCE)

Often, the easiest way to get someone's cooperation is by giving him exactly what he wants. The art of Negotiation deals with determining exactly how much of what a subject wants must be surrendered in order to get a particular good or service in return. A master negotiator might need to make only the most minimal of sacrifices in exchange for a vital service, while a novice could be forced to dramatically overpay— particularly if he lets his desperation show. This skill is essential for anyone who regularly acquires new equipment, and it is vital to characters who must mediate between warring parties.

Characters need to effectively negotiate at times to accomplish their goals and, potentially, to avoid gaining Conflict through needless bloodshed. Negotiation is opposed by the subject's Negotiation or Cool. See **Social Skill Interactions**, on page 117, for more information.

- Any time a character wishes to purchase goods or services, he must either pay the seller's asking price or use the Negotiation skill to haggle.

- If a character wishes to sell goods or services, the final price is determined by a Negotiation check.

- When two individuals create an agreement or treaty, they may make an opposed or competitive Negotiation check. The winner gains the better end of the resulting agreement.

Negotiation is usually an opposed check, using the target's Cool or Negotiation. Situational modifiers may also apply, based on any past relationship between the characters involved and the desirability of the goods and services. The cases in which this skill may be used without an opposed check are exceedingly rare.

Extra ✸ on a Negotiation check may be used to increase the acting character's profit by 5% per ✸. It may alternatively be used to modify the scope of the agreement, so that the contract can extend for a longer period of time or so more goods may be obtained for a given price. Additional rules for how extra ✸ may benefit characters when buying or selling goods can be found on page 158.

✪ generated during a Negotiation check may be spent to earn unrelated boons from the target, either concessions if the check is failed, or extra perks if it is passed. With ⊕, the player may choose to have the target NPC become a regular client or specialist vendor. The NPC might thereafter keep an eye out for specific goods the PC may be interested in, or may refer other potential clients to the PC, emphasizing to them the quality of the PC's goods or services.

◎ during a Negotiation check may be spent to increase the cost of goods the character is attempting to purchase, to decrease the value of those he is trying to sell, or to shorten contracts he is trying to negotiate. A GM may spend ▽ to seriously sabotage the character's goals during the interaction.

# PERCEPTION (CUNNING)

Characters must often maintain a careful awareness of their environment. Subtle clues can hint at imminent danger or unexpected advantage. The Perception skill represents the character making an active attempt to study his surroundings. This is how a character notices concealed or inconspicuous signs of danger or other items of significance when actively seeking them out. The skill is critical for anyone who faces peril on a regular basis—whether they are in the wilds of a frontier world or among the urban jungle of a sprawling city.

Note that Perception encompasses all of a character's natural senses. Humans without cybernetic augmentation are limited to five. However, many alien races have additional means to perceive their surroundings.

- A character who is unprepared for a trap or an ambush may have an opportunity to make a Perception check to avoid being surprised. Alternatively, this might oppose an attacker's Stealth check.

- Skulduggery checks are often opposed by a target's Perception.

- The character can make a Perception check if he wants to check his surroundings for a subtle clue—an overheard conversation, the telltale scent of explosive materials, or a drug introduced to a beverage.

- Perception can be used in surveillance situations, in which the user is trying to observe an unaware target from a distance.

Perception may be opposed by skills used for concealment, or it might have a difficulty set by the environment. The noise of a loud factory could conceal a conversation, just as a spicy drink might prevent a character from noticing a poison.

Extra ✸ on a Perception check may be spent to reveal additional details. Perhaps the character recognized the speaker's accent, the flash burns from a certain kind of blast, or the number of attackers lying in ambush.

An ✪ may be spent to recall additional information associated with the object noticed. Perhaps a passing familiarity with a field of study is the reason why the character initially realized that something was out of place. A ⊕ may be spent to notice details that could be useful later, allowing characters to gain ▢ on all future interactions with the noticed element.

◎ resulting from a Perception check may be spent by the GM to conceal a vital detail about the situation or environment from the character. ▽ may be spent to cause the character to obtain false information about the surroundings or the target in question.

# PILOTING (PLANETARY) (AGILITY)

When characters travel across the surface of one of the galaxy's numerous worlds, they often stray far from their spacecraft. Smaller craft, particularly ones best suited to a given planet's habitats, are commonly used for surface transportation. These can include repulsorlift vehicles, watercraft, and aircraft. No matter how the vehicle moves—by rolling, gliding, walking, flying, or floating—the skill that governs its use is Piloting (Planetary).

Under normal traffic and environmental conditions, a character should never need to actually check the Piloting (Planetary) skill. Its use is reserved for more extreme conditions. These might include a high-speed pursuit, travel in treacherous weather conditions, the use of a failing vehicle, or any combination of such complications. For some, this skill is a passion and a livelihood; for others, it's simply a necessity of their lifestyle.

- If a character is confronted by a completely foreign type of atmospheric craft, he must make a Piloting (Planetary) check to decipher its basic controls.

- Any time two characters are involved in a vehicle race upon a world's surface, the results are determined by a competitive check using Piloting (Planetary).

- If chasing or being chased by another vehicle, losing the follower or maintaining the tail is done through an opposed Piloting (Planetary) check.

The difficulty of a Piloting (Planetary) check may be determined based on the difficulty of the relevant maneuver, the size and speed of the vehicle being piloted, and any features or failures of the vehicle involved.

Extra ✵ on a Piloting (Planetary) check allows the acting character to gain insights into the situation. Alternatively, the PC might deduce a way that the vehicle could be modified so that it could be more effective in the future.

❂ generated during a Piloting (Planetary) check may be spent to reveal a vulnerability in an opponent's piloting style or vehicle, giving the character a benefit in later rounds of combat. ⊕ on a Piloting (Planetary) check may be used to let the character take an additional maneuver while continuing to pilot the vehicle.

A GM may spend ❁ ❁ during a Piloting (Planetary) check to give opponents ☐ on checks against the character and vehicle to represent a momentary malfunction in one of the vehicle's systems. ▽ may be spent to deal actual damage to the vehicle, as the character strains systems throughout the vehicle during the check.

# PILOTING (SPACE) (AGILITY)

Those involved in the conflict between the stars often find the ability to pilot a starship paramount. Some use starships to travel to distant planets and explore long-lost regions of space. Others fly in swift snubfighters or even heavily armed patrol boats, fighting with laser cannons and torpedoes in the cold void. Whether a crew is attempting to bring down enemy fighters or slip past a blockade undetected, its success or failure most often depends upon the person at the helm.

Routine actions—like taking off or landing without additional complications—do not require a Piloting (Space) check. When those actions are complicated by such conditions as a choking nebula, a failed motivator, or enemy fire, then skill checks come into play.

- Whenever two or more spaceships race, a competitive Piloting (Space) check determines the results.

- Chases, whether they are through asteroid belts, within a crowded battlefield, or skirting the edge of a gravimetric instability, are resolved with an opposed Piloting (Space) check.

- During a space conflict, pilots may jockey for position to determine which shields face the enemy and which weapons may be brought to bear. When opponents attempt to negate these efforts and the ships are too large, slow, or cumbersome to benefit from certain specific vehicle maneuvers or actions, the winner can be determined via an opposed Piloting (Space) check.

The difficulty of a Piloting (Space) check may be determined based on the difficulty of the particular maneuver, any unusual navigational hazards, and any features or failures on the spacecraft involved.

Extra ✵ on a Piloting (Space) check allow the acting character to gain insights into the situation. Alternatively, the character might deduce a clever way that his vehicle could be modified so that it could be more effective in the future.

❂ generated during a Piloting (Space) check may be spent to reveal a vulnerability in an opponent's piloting style or vehicle, giving the character a benefit in later rounds of combat. ⊕ may be used to let the character take an additional maneuver action while continuing to pilot the vehicle.

A GM may spend ❁ ❁ during a Piloting (Space) check to give opponents ☐ on checks against the character and vehicle to represent a momentary malfunction in one of the vehicle's systems. ▽ may be spent to deal actual hull trauma to the vehicle, as the character strains systems throughout the vehicle during the check.

# RESILIENCE (BRAWN)

The galaxy doesn't stop moving just because a character needs a break. To achieve their objectives, characters must have the perseverance to overcome the most challenging obstacles. These can include sleep deprivation, hideous climates, and malnutrition. Characters might also ingest toxins, either inadvertently when scavenging for food or due to the malicious actions of an infiltrator.

Resilience represents a character's physical fortitude against all threats of this sort. This skill reflects the body's ability to be pushed beyond reasonable limits. When characters make a Resilience check, their actions are typically taking them into situations that most would consider bad ideas.

- When a character attempts to go without sleep for significantly longer than is healthy for his species, he must make a Resilience check to remain awake.

- If a character ingests a toxin, he uses Resilience to resist its effects.

- When a character endures prolonged exposure to a hostile environment—such as heat, cold, or toxic pollution—the consequences may be mitigated with a successful Resilience check.

- Dehydration and malnutrition can quickly leave a character badly fatigued, and Resilience protects against this.

The difficulty for a Resilience check is based on the severity of the effects that the character is attempting to overcome. Going twenty-four hours without sleep could add only a single ◆, but marching across Hoth in a vicious blizzard should be far more difficult.

Extra ✷ on a Resilience check may be used to extend the effects of the success, so that the character may persevere for a longer period of time before needing to make an additional check.

❂ earned on a Resilience check may be used to identify a way for the character and his allies to reduce the difficulty of future checks against the same threat, while ⊕ may be spent to recover 3 strain as the character resolves to work through the adversity.

The GM may spend ❖ generated during a Resilience check to overburden the character, inflicting penalties on subsequent checks. ▽ may be spent to inflict a wound or a minor Critical Injury on the character as he succumbs to harsh conditions.

# SKULDUGGERY (CUNNING)

Skulduggery encompasses a broad range of skills that are used to engage in covert or criminal activity. These skills encompass both the physical abilities to perform such actions and the mental familiarity needed to execute various techniques. Activities covered by Skulduggery include picking locks, breaking into and out of secure facilities, covert operations, disguise, setting traps, and other underhanded actions. At the Game Master's discretion, particular Skulduggery checks may use Agility instead of Cunning, to reflect a more physical approach.

- If a character attempts to pick a lock or pocket, he usually uses Skulduggery. Some electronic locks could require Computers, Skulduggery, or both.

- Once an imprisoned character slips his bonds using Coordination, escaping from a cell depends on Skulduggery for picking locks and avoiding any security systems he might encounter.

- Identifying the most vulnerable aspects of a security scheme can be nearly intuitive for a character who has become practiced in Skulduggery.

- Skulduggery is often opposed by a target's Perception. In instances in which another character is not directly involved, the quality of the object being overcome should determine the check's degree of difficulty.

One or more ✷ on a Skulduggery check should indicate additional insights that the acting character gains about the nature of the opposition. This might suggest that a Shadow could better plan a strategy against a current foe to avoid future complications.

A character may spend ❂ earned on a Skulduggery check to identify an additional target or gain additional items. Perhaps as the characters make their escape, they discover their captor's cache of Imperial Intelligence reports. ⊕ may be spent to earn the character an unexpected boon. For instance, the value of an item stolen might exceed his original estimation, and the item might also provide vital information. When using Skulduggery to pick a lock, the character might devise a near-permanent means of overcoming it, perhaps by crafting a makeshift key or by obtaining access to the actual key itself.

By generating ❖ during a Skulduggery check, a character gives an NPC the opportunity to catch him immediately after the act. Depending on the amount of ❖ spent by the GM, the character will be in varying degrees of danger: the more ❖, the more immediate the discovery and the greater the ensuing jeopardy and difficulty of escape. The GM may spend ▽ to cause the character to leave behind some evidence of his larceny that directly ties him to the crime. Perhaps a recognizable piece of equipment traceable by its serial numbers slips off into the target's pocket as the character attempts to pick it.

# STEALTH (AGILITY)

Often, a character may have business to conduct that is best completed with a certain degree of privacy. It might be that there are powerful individuals—perhaps Imperial agents or dangerous dark side adepts—who are directly opposed to his choice of actions. At other times, a character might be avoiding an Imperial bounty hunter. Under such conditions, a successful mission may depend entirely on how talented the character is at not being noticed. The Stealth skill reflects this ability in virtually all situations.

- Any Shadow or other stealthy character who depends upon physical insertion must be a master of this skill. Stealth also encompasses wilderness camouflage skills, which may be crucial to any Hunter.

- Attempts to hide from all of an opponent's senses are dependent upon Stealth, though difficulties may be modified by ambient conditions and any applicable gear.

- Stealth can allow characters to shadow or follow other individuals without being detected.

- Characters may attempt to hide people or objects from the attentions of others, either through concealment or misdirection. Such actions are dependent upon their Stealth skill.

The difficulty of a Stealth check often depends on the abilities of those the character is attempting to avoid. Members of species that are more dependent upon smell, hearing, or other senses may be more susceptible to Stealth under different weather conditions or distracted by events that seem trivial to a species focused on visual cues.

Stealth checks are typically opposed by Perception, based on whether the opponent is passively or actively searching for the hidden character. If the opponent is actively searching for the character, the character's Stealth check would be opposed by the opponent's Perception. Otherwise, it would be opposed by the opponent's Vigilance.

Extra ✸ on a Stealth check may be used to aid any allied characters who are infiltrating at the same time. Effectively, the successful character points out a factor that might otherwise have caused the ally to fail.

⚡ may be spent to decrease the amount of time required to perform a given task while using the Stealth skill. This could represent the character's finding superior cover, enabling him to move faster while remaining out of sight, or successfully distracting a key figure to obtain access to his target. Under the right circumstances, a character may spend ⊕ to identify a way to completely distract an opponent for the duration of the scene. This could allow the character to drop all pretense of Stealth in favor of completing a task faster.

The GM may spend ✪ generated during a Stealth check to hinder the character as he attempts to remain hidden. The character may need to overcome a particularly unpleasant obstacle or take extra time to remain out of sight. The GM may increase the time it takes for the PC to perform the desired action while

remaining hidden by 25% per ✪ spent in this way. The GM may spend ▽ to cause the character to leave behind some evidence of his passing by. While this has no bearing on the success or failure of the Stealth check, some object, clue, or information about the character's identity, and possibly even motive, is accidentally left behind.

# STREETWISE (CUNNING)

The Streetwise skill represents the instinctive understanding that comes from many years of living in the less-than-savory parts of the galaxy. While a few manage to learn the signs and develop gut instincts through careful study and association with those who have lived this hard life, most come about this information through the school of hard knocks. If a character expects to use the complex network of the criminal underworld (and survive), he must learn to speak its language and recognize the roles of those involved.

- If a character is looking for a merchant who specializes in unsavory goods or illicit services, such a merchant may be located through a Streetwise check.

- Streetwise represents a character's instinct for picking up on subtle cues in the language and attitudes of those who operate outside of legal structures. It may be used to understand particular references within conversations.

- When dealing with criminals or underworld elements, knowing how to approach them and open a conversation without coming across as a threat uses Streetwise.

Generally, Knowledge (Underworld) governs specific information and facts involving criminals and underworld elements. Streetwise governs how to use that information effectively and how to operate in any criminal environment. Extra ✸ on a Streetwise check may be used to reduce the time or funds required to obtain the item, service, or information sought.

⚡ may reveal additional rumors or alternative sources that can be used to find something. ⊕ may be spent to earn the character a semipermanent contact on the street, someone to whom the character may turn for information regularly.

The GM may spend ✪ generated during a Streetwise check to seed the gathered information with minor falsehoods, representing the ever-changing nature of information passed by word of mouth on the street. ▽ may be spent to represent a character letting slip details about himself or the information he seeks, information that may be picked up by an adversary.

# SURVIVAL
# (CUNNING)

It's not uncommon for characters to become isolated far from civilized worlds. Sometimes this is by choice; at other times, they could be stranded on a world, hoping for some sort of rescue. Learning to recognize the dangers of the natural environment, as well as determining how to exploit its resources, is dependent upon the Survival skill.

Characters who spent their formative years on wilderness planets often have this skill as part of their background. Others may learn it as part of military training. Some may be completely dependent upon it, as their jobs focus on traveling to untamed worlds.

- Identifying safe food, potable water, or shelter in a natural environment requires the character to make a Survival check.

- Characters who are skilled at Survival understand weather patterns and the signs of imminent dangerous conditions, and know how to prepare.

- Tracking a subject through the wilderness— whether the subject is wild game or an enemy combatant—is dependent upon Survival.

Survival governs a character's ability to handle domesticated animals, so that they may be used as beasts of burden or as transport.

The difficulty of a Survival check is dependent upon the severity of the environment. Key factors are the biocompatibility of a world's native life with the PC, the type of local environment (a desert versus a forest, for example), and the basic tools on hand.

☼ that exceed the difficulty on a Survival check may be used to assist other characters in surviving or to grant additional supplies, food, and water.

✪ may be spent to gain an insight into the environment that makes future Survival checks easier. Examples include locating a watering hole where prey is common, an abandoned cave that makes an excellent shelter, or a grove of biocompatible fruit trees. When tracking, ✪ may be spent to learn a detail about the target, its numbers, its species, or how recently tracks were made. ✪ generated during a Survival check to handle animals may be spent to permanently predispose the target animal toward the character in a positive way, effectively earning the character a loyal companion. While tracking, ✦ may be spent to learn a clue about the target: its destination, disposition, or the presence of prisoners or cargo.

The GM may spend ✦ generated on a Survival check to represent the character's spending of vital resources during the check, perhaps using food as bait to catch game or losing fuel in an attempt to make a fire. ▽ may be spent to inflict wounds, Critical Injuries, or high levels of strain on the character as he succumbs to one of the untamed environments of the galaxy.

# VIGILANCE (WILLPOWER)

In uncertain times, individuals who are constantly prepared to face a variety of challenges are far more likely to succeed than those who simply react to the ever-changing circumstances. This sort of preparedness requires mental discipline, and it can facilitate the making of sound instantaneous decisions when disaster or unexpected events suddenly strike. Characters who must remain alert because of the nature of their lifestyles are often particularly vigilant. This includes those who live within hostile environments—either urban jungles or dangerous wildernesses—and those who live as professional soldiers.

- In combat situations, outside of those times when a character has patiently prepared to begin the engagement, Vigilance is used to calculate Initiative.
- Vigilance represents how fastidious a character is about preparing for unexpected crises. If there's a question about preparedness, a Vigilance check can be made to confirm preparedness retroactively.

- Sometimes a character may have a chance to notice small but important details in his surroundings while not specifically looking for them. In this case, the GM might have the player make a Vigilance check to see if his character notices this.

The difficulty for a Vigilance check is typically modified by the likelihood of the incident that occurs. A character might be prepared for an ambush when traveling through a darkened alley, but he is unlikely to expect a groundquake in the middle of the night. A poor result on such a check might leave the character momentarily unable to act as he mentally attempts to decipher the current situation.

When calculating Initiative, all ✦ are generally used as part of the calculation. In other situations for which this check is critical, extra ✦ may indicate that the character was particularly well-prepared for that sort of conflict. Alternatively, it could indicate that an important resource might be readily accessible.

Characters may spend ✧ on a Vigilance check to notice an environmental factor that could play a key part in the relevant scene. This might be excellent cover, a convenient escape route, or something that could be used to distract a foe. ✦ may be spent to allow the character to take an extra maneuver at the beginning of the first round of combat, as his keen awareness alerts him to danger. See page 204 for more on Initiative checks.

The GM may spend ✦ generated during a Vigilance check to cause the character to miss a piece of information about the situation or environment, blinding him to an advantage. The GM may spend ▽ to cause the character to lose his free maneuver on his first turn.

# COMBAT SKILLS

Skills that are tightly focused on use during physical confrontations are considered Combat skills. Full details on using Combat skills during conflicts are presented in **Chapter VI: Conflict and Combat**. **Chapter VI** also contains information concerning how a character may make use of extra ✦, ✧, and ✦ generated during a Combat skill check, as well as how the GM may spend ✦ and ▽ in such circumstances.

## BRAWL (BRAWN)

During some physical confrontations, a character seeks to incapacitate a foe without causing serious injury. At other times, a fight erupts with little preparation, and a character may not have any weapon at hand. Some individuals are trained in unarmed combat, or have natural weapons that they prefer to use during altercations. In any of these situations, Brawl is the skill used to determine success or failure in the combat.

Most characters who grew up in a hostile environment have some knack for Brawl. All wildlife, particularly creatures with natural weapons, use Brawl to fight. Anyone who participates in military or law enforcement training learns some basic or advanced martial arts, which fall under the Brawl skill. However, improvised weapons—such as a bottle or a table leg—require the Melee skill. Of course, any fighting with fists or feet is covered by Brawl.

The Brawl skill is most often used to make combat checks in melee combat while unarmed or using a weapon specifically designed to augment unarmed combat (see page 218), though there may be other uses for this skill, at the GM's discretion. The difficulty of Brawl checks is **Average (◆ ◆)**, the difficulty of all melee attacks. If the opponent is incapable of resisting, the check might be easier, at the GM's discretion. See page 210 for more details on melee attack difficulties.

# GUNNERY (AGILITY)

Many weapons are simply too large for a person to carry. In order to bring such a weapon to bear against an opponent, it may be mounted aboard a vehicle, hastily assembled where needed, or even built into a defensive emplacement. Weapons of this sort might require a team to transport, assemble, and ultimately operate.

Characters seldom gain experience with weapons of this magnitude outside of military training. Weapons of this caliber are also difficult to acquire by anything but government entities. Only the most dangerous worlds have natural predators that require a weapon of this power as a proportionate response. Gunnery applies to laser cannons and proton torpedoes mounted on starships. Larger mounted weapon systems like heavy laser turrets and ion cannons are also fired using this skill.

- If a character is piloting a starfighter, the ship may have weapons that are mounted on it with a fixed orientation. Prior to making a Gunnery check, the pilot may need to maneuver the craft in order to achieve a firing solution.

- Characters using Gunnery to fire turret-mounted weapons may need to hold their action until a pilot can maneuver the vehicle such that targets are within the weapon's firing arc.

- Complex targeting computers and automated weapons mounts are often used with large-scale weapons. Operating this equipment also falls under Gunnery.

The Gunnery skill is most often used to make combat checks while using an appropriate ranged weapon, though there may be other uses for this skill, at the GM's discretion. Gunnery check difficulties are determined by the distance to the target or by relative silhouettes, depending on the weapon fired. The difficulty may be modified by maneuvers the character makes and specific combat situational modifiers, as described in **Chapter VI: Conflict and Combat**.

# LIGHTSABER (BRAWN)

Lightsabers (and their derivatives) are quite unlike any other weapons in the galaxy. While most close-combat weapons have some sort of blade or striking edge attached to a grip or handle, an inactive lightsaber seems to be nothing more than a simple weapon hilt. However, when activated, the hilt projects a humming "blade" of intense energy. Such weapons are difficult for even an accomplished swordfighter to use and require a very unique set of skills.

Although the Lightsaber skill is linked to the Brawn characteristic, many characters may have access to talents that can link the skill to a different characteristic instead, representing unique forms and fighting styles. The Lightsaber skill governs melee attacks made with lightsabers as well as with derivative weapons such as lightwhips, guard shotos, and training sabers.

The Lightsaber skill is most often used to make combat checks while using these weapons, though there may be other uses for this skill, at the GM's discretion. The difficulty of Lightsaber combat checks is **Average (◆ ◆)**, the difficulty of all melee attacks. If the opponent is incapable of resisting, the check might be easier, at the GM's discretion. The difficulty may

be modified by maneuvers the character makes and specific combat situational modifiers, as described in **Chapter VI: Conflict and Combat**.

# MELEE (BRAWN)

All ranged weapons require some sort of ammunition, and many are loud. They typically have fragile components or require regular maintenance, which may require its own set of tools. By contrast, most Melee weapons are inexpensive, virtually silent, and require little maintenance and no power beyond the strength of their wielder's limbs.

The majority of Melee weapons depend upon the wielder's strength to inflict damage, but a few have their own energy sources. However, their core principles remain the same. Mastering one type of Melee weapon can help master most types.

Any military training includes at least a basic course in melee combat preparation. In addition, characters who have spent time on primitive worlds may have learned to defend themselves with Melee weapons. Aristocrats and nobles, in some systems, may also learn a number of melee techniques as part of their cultural traditions.

The Melee skill is most often used to make combat checks while using a Melee weapon, though there may be other uses for this skill, at the GM's discretion. The difficulty of Melee checks is **Average (◆◆)**, the difficulty of all melee attacks, including Brawl and Lightsaber. If the opponent is incapable of resisting, the check might be easier, at the GM's discretion. The difficulty may be modified by maneuvers the character makes and specific combat situational modifiers, as described in **Chapter VI: Conflict and Combat**.

# RANGED (HEAVY) (AGILITY)

When fired upon a target at range, weapons that are held with two hands offer a more stable firing platform than those that are held in a single hand. These also often have longer barrels, providing a consistent fire pattern out to a much longer range. In the larger space required for such armaments, designers can often include a significantly larger ammunition reserve and may also make the weapon far more potent than smaller weapons. This combination can yield weapons that are substantially more deadly and accurate.

Countless varieties of rifles are used throughout the galaxy. Some are simple slugthrowers, while common blaster rifles range in size from carbines to extended barrel sniper rifles. There are also a number of unique weapons, such as the Wookiee bowcaster. Any of these weapons requires Ranged (Heavy) to operate.

In addition to combat uses, Ranged (Heavy) weapons are commonly employed for hunting purposes. As a result, these types of weapons are seen on frontier worlds far more frequently than Ranged (Light) weapons. Characters who are focused on wilderness survival skills may prefer the additional range that a rifle offers when confronting predators.

- Ranged (Heavy) weapons inflict wounds upon targets by default. A subset of the weapons in this category may have a Stun option, as do some specialized Stun-only weapons.

The Ranged (Heavy) skill is most often used to make combat checks while wielding an appropriate ranged weapon, though there may be other uses for this skill, at the GM's discretion. Ranged (Heavy) check difficulties are determined by the distance to the target. The difficulty may be modified by maneuvers the character makes and specific combat situational modifiers as described in **Chapter VI: Conflict and Combat**.

# RANGED (LIGHT) (AGILITY)

Many characters prefer to use a weapon that can be wielded effectively with one hand, rather than carrying something larger. This may be a preference based on the ease of concealment, or it could be simply a stylistic choice. Alternatively, some individuals feel that they must be able to keep a hand free, allowing them to, for example, pilot a speeder bike and fire a blaster pistol at the same time.

A broad selection of weapons falls under the category of the Ranged (Light) skill. It includes any weapon that can be fired with one hand without the benefit of a brace or other support element. Specific examples include countless pistols, spears, nets, and grenades. Some are so small as to be easily concealed, while others can only be wielded by the strongest individuals.

The Ranged (Light) skill reflects the hand-eye coordination that a character has developed in conjunction with an intuitive grasp of wind resistance, gravity, and distance. Upon first arriving on a planet, an expert in this field may wish to practice his abilities so that he can learn how the world's environs might affect them.

- The vast majority of Ranged (Light) weapons inflict wounds on targets. Those that are capable of inflicting strain are specifically indicated and typically must be adjusted for use in that firing mode.

- Characters may wield a Ranged (Light) weapon in each hand, or a one-handed Melee weapon and a Ranged (Light) weapon in the other hand. See page 217 for more information.

The Ranged (Light) skill is most often used to make combat checks while wielding an appropriate ranged weapon, though there may be other uses for this skill, at the GM's discretion. Ranged (Light) check difficulties are determined by the distance to the target. The difficulty may be modified by maneuvers the character makes and specific combat situational modifiers, as described in **Chapter VI: Conflict and Combat**.

# KNOWLEDGE SKILLS

Players can never be expected to know as much about life in the game setting as the characters who live there. Knowledge skills serve to bridge this gap. They enable a player to make decisions about his character's actions informed by what his character might know.

✵, ✷, ✦, ✧, and ▽ may be spent among the different Knowledge skills with similar results for each. Additional ✵ represents the character's recalling information or completing research with remarkable haste, while ✷ may be spent to learn minor but possibly useful information about the subject. ✦ may be spent to learn relevant, beneficial information concerning the subject, perhaps an understanding of a beast's particular weakness in the case of Knowledge (Xenology), or information concerning the familial strife between crime syndicates in the case of Knowledge (Underworld). ✧ may be spent by the GM to omit a vital detail about the subject at hand, while ▽ may be used to seed the character with misinformation and outright falsehoods.

## CORE WORLDS (INTELLECT)

Those worlds closest to the Galactic Core are generally considered to represent the pinnacle of galactic culture and civilization. A few notions are particularly common among the worlds of the Core, but even with those, there are distinct exceptions. Perfectly acceptable behavior on one planet may be considered grossly disruptive manners on another, even within this culturally distinct region of the galaxy. Many hyperlanes connect the Core Worlds with the other portions of the galaxy. The Core Worlds represent centers of trade and diplomacy that can connect planets in disparate portions of the galaxy.

- If a character needs to identify a person's planet of origin without asking, he may make a Core Worlds check. This allows him to recognize accents, dress, and mannerisms that are associated with a particular world.

- When interacting with someone from a Core World, a character might make a Core Worlds check to know what behaviors are considered necessary and polite and what could be considered offensive.

- Characters who specialize in the acquisition and delivery of goods can make this check to identify which markets are the best places to sell or purchase a particular cargo. They may also recognize any worlds where such goods could be illegal.

The difficulty of a Core Worlds check is generally proportionate to the rarity of the information involved. Common knowledge about Coruscant, for example, is far easier to recall than an obscure fact about a minor moon.

## EDUCATION (INTELLECT)

Among most of the races and cultures of the galaxy, achieving literacy is a crucial first step toward adulthood. Once literacy is attained, an individual's education generally expands to cover additional areas of expertise. Typically, such an education includes at least a basic grounding in mathematics, science, and engineering. Many also study philosophy, politics, and galactic history. Characters often rely on these essentials to appropriately interact with the broader galaxy.

- Any time a character needs to interact with a government entity, an Education check may be made to identify the best way to proceed.

- If a character needs to employ basic scientific knowledge in an analysis, his understanding of this field is represented by his Education skill.

Education also represents a default Knowledge skill. Any time a question comes up that doesn't obviously fall under one of the other Knowledge skills, an Education check may be used to determine the character's understanding of a particular subject matter.

The difficulty for an Education check is typically represented by the rarity of the data in question. A reference document may provide bonuses, but even using such a work requires an understanding of core principles.

## LORE (INTELLECT)

Parts of the galaxy have been inhabited for more than a million years. During that time, countless civilizations have arisen, and many have gone extinct. Over the millennia, some of these civilizations' histories changed and grew into myths and legends. However, some of these stories still conceal a great deal of valuable information. Characters with a particular interest in lost cultures and ancient legends may decide to try to turn this interest into a profession. At other times, a character might stumble across an artifact whose utility could far exceed its initial appearance. Lore is also the skill often related to knowledge of the Force and ancient Jedi traditions.

- Any time a character needs to decipher an ancient piece of writing, he must make a Lore check.

- A character's knowledge of the exploits of an ancient hero is represented by the Lore skill.

- A character trying to learn about ancient Jedi traditions or attempting to master a Force technique must make a Lore check.

A Lore check's difficulty is assigned by the obscurity of the information. Well-known legends may not even require a check, but the tales of a race that died out millennia ago may be nearly forgotten.

# OUTER RIM (INTELLECT)

The systems of the Outer Rim are filled with independent worlds exhibiting an incredibly diverse mix of species, cultures, and political systems. Because the range of cultures is so great, anything learned about the culture of one world is not necessarily relevant to those of other systems in the Outer Rim. Learning about this scattered and often mysterious region of space can be a full-time job. However, this also makes mastery of this subject extremely valuable.

- If a character needs to find a planet with a particular resource or service in the Outer Rim, he could make an Outer Rim check.

- When determining the best location to acquire critical supplies, an Outer Rim check might reveal locations where the goods can be found at a reasonable price without Imperial scrutiny.

- At times when a character must interact with a person from the Outer Rim, this skill could be used to determine appropriate customs or traditions.

The difficulty for an Outer Rim check is based upon the obscurity of the world and goods in question. This may also be modified based upon the specificity of the question posed.

# UNDERWORLD (INTELLECT)

In some places, criminal elements control the government through less-than-legal machinations. In more traditionally governed areas, seedier elements depend on secrecy and deception to survive. The galactic underworld is as varied and scattered as the cultures of any collection of planets; learning the facts and history of criminal enterprise in the galaxy is a hard discipline to master. Knowledge (Underworld) covers this discipline.

- The Underworld skill may be used to know what illegal activities take place on a world and who coordinates them.

- A familiarity with Underworld may be useful if the characters need to determine the most common methods that an opponent might use for a particular type of criminal activity.

When the criminal nature of a location or individual is well known, recalling the relevant data should be relatively simple. The difficulty of the task should be much more challenging if the individual has gone to lengths to conceal illegal activities.

# XENOLOGY (INTELLECT)

The motivations, biological origins, and philosophies of the galaxy's varied species are highly divergent. An object that is desirable to members of one species could be repugnant to another. Those who have mentally cataloged the different species of the galaxy and learned their distinctive traits are skilled in Xenology. Anyone who regularly interacts with the inhabitants of the galaxy's varied worlds must become adept at Xenology. This is particularly vital for anyone who might need to offer medical treatment to members of varied species, as basic anatomy and biochemistry can vary wildly. Knowledge of various cultural traits is also vital for a character who interacts in a social fashion. A bargaining tactic that is perfectly effective with a Twi'lek might be disastrous when used on a Wookiee.

- When a character first encounters a member of an unfamiliar race, a Xenology check can be made to figure out how to interact with that individual.

- If a character needs to either help or harm a member of another species, Xenology may assist in identifying a type of injury or in pointing out a characteristic vulnerability.

- Different species need substantially different environmental conditions and foodstuffs. A Xenology check may allow a character to offer the appropriate considerations to a guest.

The difficulty for a Xenology check should be based both on how often the acting character interacts with the members of the species and the relative rarity of that species.

# TALENTS

*"I used to bull's-eye womp rats in my T-16 back home. They're not much bigger than two meters."*

–Luke Skywalker

In a galaxy filled with bold heroes and terrible villains, Player Characters are distinguished by their special abilities. Where a minor character might surrender to overwhelming odds, a hero is expected to dramatically defeat the foe and triumph. Talents set the PCs apart from the galaxy's rank and file, providing a game mechanic by which Player Characters may perform tasks with superhuman flair and ability.

Talents generally represent specialized techniques that a character has mastered, typically through intense practice and study. A character is likely to be more successful when engaged in actions for which he has appropriate skills and talents.

It's important to note also that talents are focused for situational use. Generally speaking, talents have more narrow applications than skills. A character who intends to use a particular skill in a broad variety of ways might be better suited by advancing the skill as opposed to learning a talent. At the same time, a character involved in a situation for which his talents are appropriate could enjoy exceptional degrees of success.

## TALENT TYPES

There are many different types of talents. Some are associated with an individual skill or closely related group of skills. These tend to be particular knacks that a character has acquired through the process of mastering that skill. In many cases, talents represent operational shortcuts—corners an experienced individual knows can be safely cut or particularly effective methods he can follow. Other such talents are simply natural abilities that fit in especially well with the use of that skill. These could include a certain mental process, a physical technique, or a learned pattern.

A number of talents are specifically associated with physical conflict. These combat talents represent techniques that a character likely learned through practice and experience. The presence of combat talents within a particular talent tree reinforces the archetypal nature of a particular specialization. Specializations that focus on avoiding physical conflict have fewer combat talents than those that are devoted to it, for example.

Every specialization has access to **Force talents**, talents that may only be used by Force-sensitive characters (see page 282 for more information about these talents). Force talents may grant new abilities related to the Force, provide bonuses to skill checks due to the character's innate Force sensitivity, or do anything else a talent could do. Force talents may not be used by characters who are not Force-sensitive.

Most specialization trees offer access to Dedication. This talent is the only means by which a character can increase a characteristic rating after character creation is complete. In addition, most specialization trees in **Force and Destiny** offer access to the Force Rating talent. This talent permanently increases a character's Force rating by 1 and is the only way a character can increase his Force rating.

## TALENT RANKS AND PURCHASING THE SAME TALENT MULTIPLE TIMES

Many trees have multiple entries for a single talent. This is because many of the talents can be learned repeatedly. When characters learn a talent for the second—or later—time, they gain an additional rank in the talent. With few exceptions, there is no set limit to the number of ranks a character can possess in a given talent. Instead, characters can purchase as many ranks of each talent as are present on their currently available talent trees.

Talents that are not ranked can only be purchased a single time. If a character is advancing through a specialization's talent tree and reaches a talent without ranks

that he has already acquired from another specialization's talent tree, then he counts as having purchased that talent on his new talent tree for the purpose of purchasing additional talents in that tree. (This does not require him to spend any experience points.)

---

### EXAMPLE: PURCHASING RANKED TALENTS

Wendy's character, Sarenda, has two ranks of Parry from the Soresu Defender specialization tree. When she later selects the Shii-Cho Knight specialization tree, she may purchase up to four additional ranks of Parry, bringing Sarenda to a total of six ranks of Parry. However, if she had purchased the Improved Parry talent (which is not ranked), she would not have to spend XP for Improved Parry again when she reached it on the second tree.

---

## TALENT TREES

Any time a player wishes to select a new talent for a character, he must first make certain that it is currently accessible from one of the character's available specialization trees. Initially, characters can only purchase talents in the top row of the tree. In order to navigate to a new talent, the character must have already purchased all of the preceding talents listed on the tree, so that he can draw a "line" from the top of the tree, through purchased talents, to the new talent. All such descents must follow the available lines shown on each tree. Note that for some trees, directly descending a column is not possible, because there is a break in the listing. In these cases, the character must first descend a neighboring column, and then follow the line over before moving up or down the tree to access a desired talent.

# TALENT DESCRIPTIONS

A description for each of the talents used in **Force and Destiny** follows. Every entry includes the information required for game play:

- **Activation** explains whether a talent is always in use (Passive) or if a character must take action to activate it (Active). If activation is required, the type of action necessary is indicated (see **Actions**, page 209). Some talents can be activated on other characters' turns. If this is the case, the Activation line also includes the "Out of Turn" note.

- **Ranked** indicates whether a talent can be purchased multiple times (Yes) or only once (No).

- **Trees** references the specialization talent trees that provide access to the particular talent. Note that for ranked talents, some of these trees may

allow the character to purchase the talent more than one time.

- **Force talent** indicates that a character must be Force-sensitive (have a Force rating of 1 or higher) to use the talent. The mechanics that govern Force talents are discussed in **Chapter VIII: The Force**. Some Force talents involve the use of Force powers (which are described in the same chapter), the Force die ◇, or spending Force Points ◗. Note that a character without a Force rating (a non–Force-sensitive) can purchase a Force talent; however he cannot use it or gain any benefits from it.

The final paragraph in each entry details the specific game mechanics involved in using the described talent.

## TABLE 4-1: TALENT LIST

| Name | Activation | Ranked | Name | Activation | Ranked |
|------|-----------|--------|------|-----------|--------|
| Adversary | Passive | Yes | Field Commander (Improved) | Passive | No |
| Against All Odds | Active (Action) | No | Fine Tuning | Passive | Yes |
| Anatomy Lessons | Active (Incidental) | No | Forager | Passive | No |
| Animal Bond | Passive | No | Force Assault | Passive | No |
| Animal Empathy | Passive | No | Force Protection | Active (Maneuver) | Yes |
| Ataru Technique | Passive | No | Force Rating | Passive | Yes |
| Balance | Active (Maneuver) | No | Forewarning | Active (Action) | No |
| Body Guard | Active (Maneuver) | Yes | Full Throttle | Active (Action) | No |
| Body Guard (Improved) | Active (Out of Turn) | No | Galaxy Mapper | Passive | Yes |
| Calming Aura | Passive | No | Grit | Passive | Yes |
| Calming Aura (Improved) | Active (Maneuver) | No | Hawk Bat Swoop | Active (Action) | No |
| Center of Being | Active (Maneuver) | Yes | Healing Trance | Active (Action) | Yes |
| Center of Being (Improved) | Passive | No | Healing Trance (Improved) | Passive | No |
| Circle of Shelter | Passive | No | Heightened Awareness | Passive | No |
| Codebreaker | Passive | Yes | Heroic Fortitude | Active (Incidental) | No |
| Command | Passive | Yes | Hunter | Passive | Yes |
| Commanding Presence | Passive | Yes | Imbue Item | Active (Maneuver) | No |
| Comprehend Technology | Active (Action) | No | Indistinguishable | Passive | Yes |
| Conditioned | Passive | Yes | Intense Presence | Active (Out of Turn) | No |
| Confidence | Passive | Yes | Intimidating | Active (Out of Turn) | Yes |
| Contingency Plan | Active (Out of Turn) | No | Intuitive Evasion | Active (Maneuver) | Yes |
| Counterstrike | Passive | No | Intuitive Improvements | Passive | No |
| Crippling Blow | Active (Incidental) | No | Intuitive Shot | Passive | No |
| Dedication | Passive | Yes | Intuitive Strike | Passive | No |
| Defensive Circle | Active (Action) | No | Inventor | Passive | Yes |
| Defensive Slicing | Passive | Yes | Jump Up | Active (Incidental) | No |
| Defensive Stance | Active (Maneuver) | Yes | Keen Eyed | Passive | Yes |
| Defensive Training | Passive | Yes | Kill with Kindness | Passive | Yes |
| Disruptive Strike | Active (Action) | No | Know Somebody | Active (Incidental) | Yes |
| Djem So Deflection | Active (Out of Turn) | No | Knowledge Is Power | Active (Incidental) | No |
| Dodge | Active (Out of Turn) | Yes | Knowledge Specialization | Active (Incidental) | Yes |
| Draw Closer | Active (Action) | No | Knowledgeable Healing | Passive | No |
| Duelist's Training | Passive | No | Makashi Finish | Active (Action) | No |
| Durable | Passive | Yes | Makashi Flourish | Active (Action) | No |
| Enduring | Passive | Yes | Makashi Technique | Passive | No |
| Enhanced Leader | Passive | No | Master Artisan | Active (Incidental) | No |
| Exhaust Port | Active (Incidental) | No | Master of Shadows | Active (Incidental) | No |
| Expert Tracker | Passive | Yes | Mental Bond | Active (Action) | No |
| Falling Avalanche | Active (Incidental) | No | Mental Fortress | Active (Incidental) | No |
| Fearsome | Passive | Yes | Mental Tools | Passive | No |
| Feint | Passive | Yes | Multiple Opponents | Passive | No |
| Field Commander | Active (Action) | No | Natural Blademaster | Active (Incidental) | No |

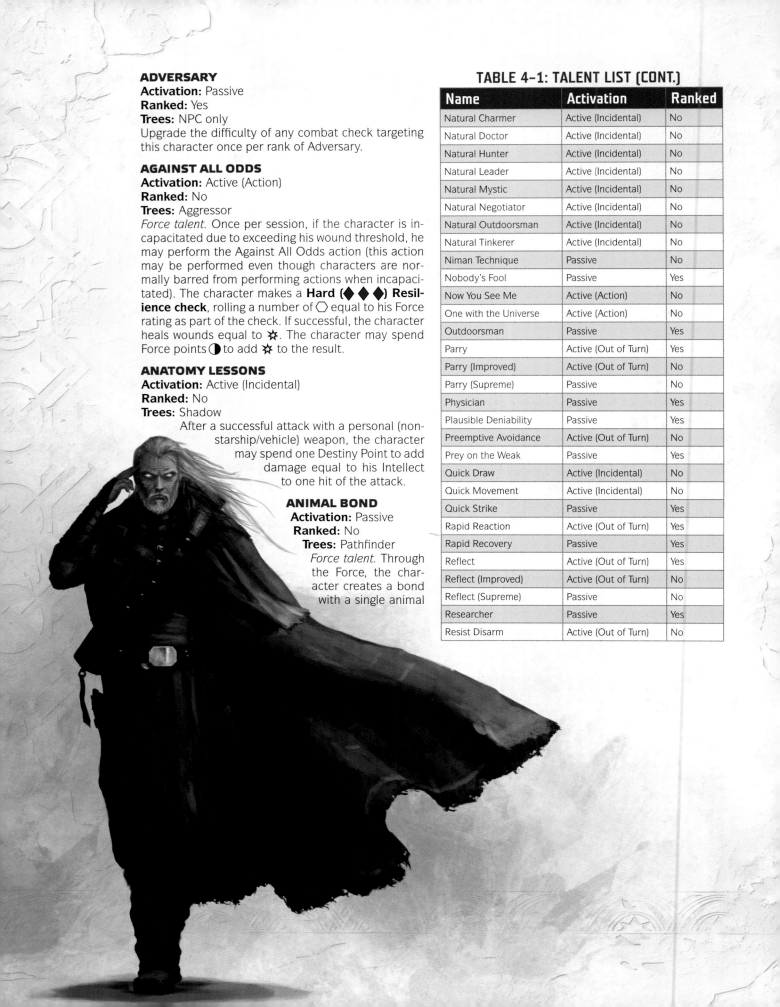

## ADVERSARY
**Activation:** Passive
**Ranked:** Yes
**Trees:** NPC only
Upgrade the difficulty of any combat check targeting this character once per rank of Adversary.

## AGAINST ALL ODDS
**Activation:** Active (Action)
**Ranked:** No
**Trees:** Aggressor
*Force talent.* Once per session, if the character is incapacitated due to exceeding his wound threshold, he may perform the Against All Odds action (this action may be performed even though characters are normally barred from performing actions when incapacitated). The character makes a **Hard (◆ ◆ ◆) Resilience check**, rolling a number of ⬡ equal to his Force rating as part of the check. If successful, the character heals wounds equal to ✸. The character may spend Force points ◗ to add ✸ to the result.

## ANATOMY LESSONS
**Activation:** Active (Incidental)
**Ranked:** No
**Trees:** Shadow
After a successful attack with a personal (non-starship/vehicle) weapon, the character may spend one Destiny Point to add damage equal to his Intellect to one hit of the attack.

## ANIMAL BOND
**Activation:** Passive
**Ranked:** No
**Trees:** Pathfinder
*Force talent.* Through the Force, the character creates a bond with a single animal

## TABLE 4-1: TALENT LIST (CONT.)

| Name | Activation | Ranked |
|------|-----------|--------|
| Natural Charmer | Active (Incidental) | No |
| Natural Doctor | Active (Incidental) | No |
| Natural Hunter | Active (Incidental) | No |
| Natural Leader | Active (Incidental) | No |
| Natural Mystic | Active (Incidental) | No |
| Natural Negotiator | Active (Incidental) | No |
| Natural Outdoorsman | Active (Incidental) | No |
| Natural Tinkerer | Active (Incidental) | No |
| Niman Technique | Passive | No |
| Nobody's Fool | Passive | Yes |
| Now You See Me | Active (Action) | No |
| One with the Universe | Active (Action) | No |
| Outdoorsman | Passive | Yes |
| Parry | Active (Out of Turn) | Yes |
| Parry (Improved) | Active (Out of Turn) | No |
| Parry (Supreme) | Passive | No |
| Physician | Passive | Yes |
| Plausible Deniability | Passive | Yes |
| Preemptive Avoidance | Active (Out of Turn) | No |
| Prey on the Weak | Passive | Yes |
| Quick Draw | Active (Incidental) | No |
| Quick Movement | Active (Incidental) | No |
| Quick Strike | Passive | Yes |
| Rapid Reaction | Active (Out of Turn) | Yes |
| Rapid Recovery | Passive | Yes |
| Reflect | Active (Out of Turn) | Yes |
| Reflect (Improved) | Active (Out of Turn) | No |
| Reflect (Supreme) | Passive | No |
| Researcher | Passive | Yes |
| Resist Disarm | Active (Out of Turn) | No |

## TABLE 4-1: TALENT LIST (CONT.)

| Name | Activation | Ranked |
|------|-----------|--------|
| Saber Swarm | Active (Maneuver) | No |
| Saber Throw | Active (Action) | No |
| Sarlacc Sweep | Active (Action) | No |
| Second Wind | Active (Incidental) | Yes |
| Sense Advantage | Active (Out of Turn) | No |
| Sense Danger | Active (Incidental) | No |
| Sense Emotions | Passive | No |
| Share Pain | Active (Out of Turn) | No |
| Shien Technique | Passive | No |
| Shroud | Active (Incidental) | No |
| Side Step | Active (Maneuver) | Yes |
| Sixth Sense | Passive | Yes |
| Skilled Jockey | Passive | Yes |
| Sleight of Mind | Passive | Yes |
| Slippery Minded | Active (Action) | No |
| Smooth Talker | Active (Incidental) | Yes |
| Soft Spot | Active (Incidental) | No |
| Solid Repairs | Passive | Yes |
| Soresu Technique | Passive | No |
| Steely Nerves | Active (Incidental) | No |
| Stimpack Specialization | Passive | Yes |
| Strategic Form | Active (Action) | No |
| Street Smarts | Passive | Yes |
| Sum Djem | Passive | No |
| Surgeon | Passive | Yes |
| Swift | Passive | No |
| Technical Aptitude | Passive | Yes |
| Terrify | Active (Action) | No |
| Terrify (Improved) | Passive | No |
| The Force Is My Ally | Active (Incidental) | No |
| Touch of Fate | Active (Incidental) | No |
| Toughened | Passive | Yes |
| Tricky Target | Passive | No |
| Uncanny Reactions | Passive | Yes |
| Uncanny Senses | Passive | Yes |
| Unity Assault | Active (Maneuver) | No |
| Valuable Facts | Active (Action) | No |
| Well Rounded | Passive | Yes |

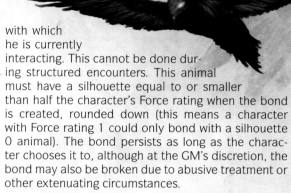

with which he is currently interacting. This cannot be done during structured encounters. This animal must have a silhouette equal to or smaller than half the character's Force rating when the bond is created, rounded down (this means a character with Force rating 1 could only bond with a silhouette 0 animal). The bond persists as long as the character chooses it to, although at the GM's discretion, the bond may also be broken due to abusive treatment or other extenuating circumstances.

As long as the bond persists, the animal remains near the character, and the controlling player dictates the animal's overall behavior (although, since the animal is only bonded with the character, not dominated, it may still perform certain inconvenient actions such as scratching furniture, consuming rations, and marking territory). Once per round in structured encounters, the character may spend one maneuver to direct his animal in performing one action and one maneuver. The animal must be within hearing and visual range of the character (generally medium range) to do this. Otherwise, the animal does not contribute to the encounter. The specifics of its behavior are up to the player and GM.

### ANIMAL EMPATHY
**Activation:** Passive
**Ranked:** No
**Trees:** Pathfinder
*Force talent.* When making checks to handle, tame, or control animals, the character may add a number of ⬡ no greater than his Force rating to the check. The character may spend ◗ to add ✷ or ۞ (character's choice) to the result.

### ATARU TECHNIQUE
**Activation:** Passive
**Ranked:** No
**Trees:** Ataru Striker
*Force talent.* When making a Lightsaber skill check, the character may use Agility instead of Brawn.

### BALANCE
**Activation:** Active (Maneuver)
**Ranked:** No
**Trees:** Ataru Striker, Sage
*Force talent.* When the character recovers from strain at the end of each encounter, he may roll ⬡ no greater than his Force rating. He recovers additional strain equal to the ◗ generated.

## BODY GUARD

**Activation:** Active (Maneuver)
**Ranked:** Yes
**Trees:** Protector

Once per round on the character's turn, the character may perform a Body Guard maneuver to protect one ally with whom he is engaged. He then suffers a number of strain no greater than his ranks in Body Guard. Until the start of the character's next turn, upgrade the difficulty of all combat checks targeting the protected ally a number of times equal to the strain suffered by the character.

## BODY GUARD (IMPROVED)

**Activation:** Active (Incidental, Out of Turn)
**Ranked:** No
**Trees:** Protector

Once per session, when an ally protected by the character's Body Guard maneuver would suffer a hit from a combat check, the character may choose to suffer that hit instead of the ally.

## CALMING AURA

**Activation:** Passive
**Ranked:** No
**Trees:** Healer

*Force talent.* When an opponent targets the character with a Force power, after the opponent generates ◑, reduce the total ◑ generated by one, to a minimum of 0.

## CALMING AURA (IMPROVED)

**Activation:** Active (Maneuver)
**Ranked:** No
**Trees:** Healer

*Force talent.* The character may spend a maneuver and suffer 2 strain to extend the effects of Calming Aura to a number of allies within short range equal to his Willpower. This lasts until the beginning of his next turn.

## CENTER OF BEING

**Activation:** Active (Maneuver)
**Ranked:** Yes
**Trees:** Niman Disciple, Protector, Shii-Cho Knight

*Force talent.* Once per round, when wielding a lightsaber, the character can make a Center of Being maneuver. Until the beginning of his next turn, whenever an enemy makes a melee attack targeting the character, the critical rating of the enemy's weapon counts as one higher per rank of Center of Being.

## CENTER OF BEING (IMPROVED)

**Activation:** Passive
**Ranked:** No
**Trees:** Niman Disciple

*Force talent.* The character may voluntarily suffer 1 strain to perform Center of Being as an incidental instead of a maneuver.

## CIRCLE OF SHELTER

**Activation:** Passive
**Ranked:** No
**Trees:** Protector

*Force talent.* When an ally engaged with the character suffers a hit from a combat check, the character may use a Parry or Reflect incidental to reduce the damage the hit deals (even though he is not the target of the combat check).

## CODEBREAKER

**Activation:** Passive
**Ranked:** Yes
**Trees:** Shadow

The character removes ■ per rank of Codebreaker from his attempts to break codes or decrypt communications. In addition, the character decreases the difficulty of his Computers and Intellect checks made to break codes or decrypt communications by one (this does not increase with additional ranks of Codebreaker).

## COMMAND

**Activation:** Passive
**Ranked:** Yes
**Trees:** Peacekeeper

The character gains □ per rank of Command when making Leadership checks (or other checks to inspire, lead, or rally an audience). Inspired targets also add □ per rank to any subsequent Discipline checks they make over the next twenty-four hours (this does not increase with additional ranks of Command).

## COMMANDING PRESENCE

**Activation:** Passive
**Ranked:** Yes
**Trees:** Peacekeeper

The character removes ■ per rank of Commanding Presence from his Leadership and Cool checks.

## COMPREHEND TECHNOLOGY

**Activation:** Active (Action)
**Ranked:** No
**Trees:** Artisan

*Force talent.* Once per session, the character may take the Comprehend Technology action, making an **Average (◆ ◆) Knowledge (Education) check** to intuitively understand one weapon, armor set, or other piece of personal gear. Success means that for the remainder of the encounter, when the character makes any skill checks to use or repair the item, he may count his ranks in the applicable skill as equal to his current Force rating.

For example, a character may use Comprehend Technology to count his ranks in Mechanics as equal to his Force rating when repairing a broken lightsaber, or he can count his ranks in Ranged (Light) as equal to his Force rating when firing a blaster pistol.

## CONDITIONED

**Activation:** Passive
**Ranked:** Yes
**Trees:** Ataru Striker, Shien Expert, Shii-Cho Knight

The character removes ■ per rank of Conditioned from his Athletics and Coordination checks. He reduces the damage and strain suffered from falling by 1 per rank of Conditioned.

## CONFIDENCE

**Activation:** Passive
**Ranked:** Yes
**Trees:** Peacekeeper, Sage, Soresu Defender, Starfighter Ace

The character may decrease the difficulty of any Discipline check to avoid the effects of fear by one per rank of Confidence. If he decreases the difficulty to zero, he does not have to make a Discipline check.

## CONTINGENCY PLAN

**Activation:** Active (Incidental, Out of Turn)
**Ranked:** No
**Trees:** Advisor

The character may spend one Destiny Point to recover strain equal to his Cunning rating.

## COUNTERSTRIKE

**Activation:** Passive
**Ranked:** No
**Trees:** Shien Expert

*Force talent.* Whenever an attack misses the character, the character may spend ✹ ✹ or ▽ to upgrade the next Lightsaber (Cunning) combat check he makes against the attacker during his next turn once.

## CRIPPLING BLOW

**Activation:** Active (Incidental)
**Ranked:** No
**Trees:** Aggressor

The character may voluntarily increase the difficulty of a combat check by one to deal a crippling blow. If

he succeeds and deals damage to the target's wound threshold, the target suffers 1 strain whenever he moves for the remainder of the encounter.

## DEDICATION

**Activation:** Passive
**Ranked:** Yes
**Trees:** Advisor, Aggressor, Artisan, Ataru Striker, Healer, Hunter, Makashi Duelist, Niman Disciple, Pathfinder, Peacekeeper, Protector, Shadow, Shien Expert, Soresu Defender, Starfighter Ace

Each rank permanently increases a single characteristic of the player's choice by 1 point. This cannot bring a characteristic above 6.

## DEFENSIVE CIRCLE

**Activation:** Active (Action)
**Ranked:** No
**Trees:** Soresu Defender

*Force talent.* While wielding a lightsaber, the character may take the Defensive Circle action, making a **Hard (◆ ◆ ◆) Lightsaber (Intellect) check**. If successful, the character plus one ally per ✷ within short range gains ranged and melee defense X until the beginning of the character's next turn. X equals 1, plus 1 for every ❂ ❂.

## DEFENSIVE SLICING

**Activation:** Passive
**Ranked:** Yes
**Trees:** Artisan

When attempting to defend a computer system against intrusion (or when an opponent attempts to slice a computer owned or programmed by the character), the character adds ■ per rank of Defensive Slicing to his opponent's checks.

## DEFENSIVE STANCE

**Activation:** Active (Maneuver)
**Ranked:** Yes
**Trees:** Shien Expert, Soresu Defender

Once per round on the character's turn, the character may perform a Defensive Stance maneuver to defend against incoming melee attacks. He then suffers a number of strain no greater than his ranks in Defensive Stance. Until the start of the character's next turn, upgrade the difficulty of all melee combat checks targeting the character a number of times equal to the strain suffered by the character in this way.

## DEFENSIVE TRAINING

**Activation:** Passive
**Ranked:** Yes
**Trees:** Makashi Duelist, Niman Disciple, Shii-Cho Knight

When the character wields a Lightsaber weapon, Melee weapon, or Brawl weapon, that weapon gains ranks in the Defensive item quality equal to the character's ranks in Defensive Training (this replaces any ranks in Defensive the weapon already has).

## DISRUPTIVE STRIKE

**Activation:** Active (Action)
**Ranked:** No
**Trees:** Shien Expert

*Force talent.* The character may take a Disruptive Strike action, making a Lightsaber (Cunning) combat check against one engaged target and adding ◯ no greater than Force rating to the check. The character may spend ◑ to add ▼ to the target's next combat check made during this encounter.

## DJEM SO DEFLECTION

**Activation:** Active (Incidental, Out of Turn)
**Ranked:** No
**Trees:** Shien Expert

*Force talent.* After using the Reflect incidental, the character may spend one Destiny Point to perform a Move maneuver as an out of turn incidental to move closer to or engage an opponent. This incidental may be performed once per round.

## DODGE

**Activation:** Active (Incidental, Out of Turn)
**Ranked:** Yes
**Trees:** Ataru Striker, Seer, Shadow

When targeted by a combat check (ranged or melee) the character may choose to immediately perform a Dodge incidental to suffer a number of strain, then upgrade the difficulty of the combat check by that number. The number of strain suffered cannot exceed his ranks in Dodge.

## DRAW CLOSER

**Activation:** Active (Action)
**Ranked:** No
**Trees:** Niman Disciple

*Force talent.* The character may take a Draw Closer action, making a Lightsaber (Willpower) melee combat check against one silhouette 1 (or smaller) target within medium range and adding a number of ◯ no greater than Force rating to the check. The character may spend ◑ before resolving the success or failure of the check to move the target one range band closer to the character (including from short to engaged). He may also spend ◑ to add ✸ to the combat check. If the character cannot move his target to engage him, the combat check automatically misses.

## DUELIST'S TRAINING

**Activation:** Passive
**Ranked:** No
**Trees:** Makashi Duelist

The character adds ■ to his Melee and Lightsaber checks when engaged with only a single opponent. A single minion group counts as multiple opponents.

## DURABLE

**Activation:** Passive
**Ranked:** Yes
**Trees:** Shii-Cho Knight

The character may reduce a Critical Injury result he suffers by 10 per rank of Durable, to a minimum of 1.

## ENDURING

**Activation:** Passive
**Ranked:** Yes
**Trees:** Pathfinder

The character gains + 1 soak value per rank of Enduring.

## ENHANCED LEADER

**Activation:** Passive
**Ranked:** No
**Trees:** Peacekeeper

*Force talent.* When making a Leadership check, the character may add ◯ no greater than Force rating to the check. The character may spend ◑ to add ✸ or ✪ (character's choice) to the result.

## EXHAUST PORT

**Activation:** Active (Incidental)
**Ranked:** No
**Trees:** Starfighter Ace

Before attacking a starship or vehicle, the character may spend one Destiny Point to ignore the effects of the Massive rule for the attack.

## EXPERT TRACKER

**Activation:** Passive
**Ranked:** Yes
**Trees:** Seer, Hunter

The character removes ■ per rank of Expert Tracker from his checks to find or follow tracks. Survival checks made to track targets take 50% less time than normal (this does not decrease with additional ranks of Expert Tracker).

## FALLING AVALANCHE

**Activation:** Active (Incidental)
**Ranked:** No
**Trees:** Shien Expert

*Force talent.* Once per round the character may suffer 2 strain to add additional damage equal to Brawn to one hit of a successful Lightsaber combat check.

## FEARSOME

**Activation:** Passive
**Ranked:** Yes
**Trees:** Aggressor

When an adversary becomes engaged with the character, the character may force the adversary to make a fear check (see page 326), with the difficulty equal to the character's ranks in Fearsome. At the GM's discretion, some adversaries may be immune to this talent based on the type of adversary or the ongoing circumstances.

## FEINT

**Activation:** Passive
**Ranked:** Yes
**Trees:** Makashi Duelist

Upon missing an opponent with a Lightsaber, Brawl, or Melee combat check, the character may spend ✦ or ✪ ✪ ✪ to upgrade the difficulty of the opponent's next combat check targeting the character during this encounter by the character's ranks in Feint.

## FIELD COMMANDER

**Activation:** Active (Action)
**Ranked:** No
**Trees:** Peacekeeper

The character may take a Field Commander action. By successfully passing an **Average (♦ ♦) Leadership check**, a number of allies equal to his Presence may immediately suffer 1 strain to perform one maneuver. This does not count against the number of maneuvers they may perform in their turn. If there are any questions as to the order in which allies act, the character using Field Commander is the final arbiter.

## FIELD COMMANDER (IMPROVED)

**Activation:** Passive
**Ranked:** No
**Trees:** Peacekeeper

When taking a Field Commander action, the character may affect allies equal to twice his Presence. In addition, he may spend ⊕ generated on his Leadership checks to allow one ally to suffer 1 strain to perform an action, rather than a maneuver.

## FINE TUNING

**Activation:** Passive
**Ranked:** Yes
**Trees:** Artisan

Whenever the character repairs system strain on a starship or vehicle, he repairs 1 additional system strain per rank of Fine Tuning.

## FORAGER

**Activation:** Passive
**Ranked:** No
**Trees:** Pathfinder, Seer

The character removes up to ■ ■ from his skill checks to find food, water, or shelter. Survival checks to forage take half the time.

## FORCE ASSAULT

**Activation:** Passive
**Ranked:** No
**Trees:** Niman Disciple

*Force talent.* Upon missing an opponent with a Lightsaber (Willpower) combat check, the character may spend ⊕ or 😈 😈 😈 to perform a Move Force power action as a maneuver this turn (the character must still be able to perform maneuvers and still may not perform more than two maneuvers in a turn).

The character must have already purchased the Move Force power to use it as part of this ability.

## FORCE PROTECTION

**Activation:** Active (Maneuver)
**Ranked:** Yes
**Trees:** Protector

*Force talent.* The character may take the Force Protection maneuver, suffering 1 strain and committing a number of ○ no greater than Force rating or ranks of Force Protection. The character then increases his soak value by an equal amount. The character suffers 1 strain at the beginning of each of his turns in which he keeps these dice committed.

## FORCE RATING

**Activation:** Passive
**Ranked:** Yes
**Trees:** Advisor, Aggressor, Artisan, Healer, Hunter, Niman Disciple, Pathfinder, Peacekeeper, Protector, Sage, Seer, Shadow, Starfighter Ace

*Force talent.* Each rank permanently increases the character's Force rating by 1.

## FOREWARNING

**Activation:** Active (Action)
**Ranked:** No
**Trees:** Seer

*Force talent.* The character may take the Forewarning action. All allies within medium range increase their melee and ranged defense by a number equal to the character's Force rating until they take their first turn during an encounter. If they have already taken their first turn, Forewarning has no effect.

## FULL THROTTLE

**Activation:** Active (Action)
**Ranked:** No
**Trees:** Starfighter Ace

The character may push a ship or vehicle past its limits of speed. He may perform the Full Throttle action, attempting a **Hard (♦ ♦ ♦) Piloting check**. With success, the ship's top speed increases by 1 for a number of rounds equal to Cunning. The ship still cannot perform actions or maneuvers it could not perform normally (e.g., actions that have a minimum speed requirement).

## GALAXY MAPPER
**Activation:** Passive
**Ranked:** Yes
**Trees:** Starfighter Ace
The character removes ☐ per rank of Galaxy Mapper from his Astrogation checks. In addition, Astrogation checks take 50% less time (this does not decrease with additional ranks of Galaxy Mapper).

## GRIT
**Activation:** Passive
**Ranked:** Yes
**Trees:** Advisor, Aggressor, Artisan, Healer, Makashi Duelist, Niman Disciple, Pathfinder, Protector, Sage, Seer, Shadow, Shien Expert, Shii-Cho Knight, Soresu Defender, Starfighter Ace
Each rank of Grit increases a character's strain threshold by 1.

## HAWK BAT SWOOP
**Activation:** Active (Action)
**Ranked:** No
**Trees:** Ataru Striker
*Force talent.* The character may take a Hawk Bat Swoop action, performing a Lightsaber (Agility) melee combat check against one target within short range and adding ⬡ no greater than Force rating to the pool. The character may spend ◑ before resolving the success or failure of the check to engage the target immediately as an incidental, and may spend ◑ to add 🜨 to the check. If the character cannot move to engage the target, the attack automatically misses.

## HEALING TRANCE
**Activation:** Active (Action)
**Ranked:** Yes
**Trees:** Healer
*Force talent.* The character may commit ⬤. For every full encounter ⬤ remains committed, the character heals 1 wound he is suffering per rank of Healing Trance. This is in addition to wounds healed due to natural rest or other abilities. If in a situation without defined encounters, the GM can have Healing Trance take effect every 12 hours.

## HEALING TRANCE (IMPROVED)
**Activation:** Passive
**Ranked:** No
**Trees:** Healer
*Force talent.* Whenever the character heals wounds as a result of Healing Trance, if the character is suffering from a Critical Injury, he makes a Resilience check with the difficulty equal to the Critical Injury's severity rating. On a successful check, the character recovers from the Critical Injury. If the character is suffering from multiple Critical Injuries, he chooses which one to attempt to recover from.

## HEIGHTENED AWARENESS

**Activation:** Passive
**Ranked:** No
**Trees:** Protector

Allies within short range of the character add ⬜ to their Perception and Vigilance checks. Allies engaged with him add ⬜⬜ instead.

## HEROIC FORTITUDE

**Activation:** Active (Incidental)
**Ranked:** No
**Trees:** Aggressor

The character may spend one Destiny Point to ignore the effects of ongoing Critical Injuries on any Brawn or Agility-related checks until the end of the encounter. He still suffers from the injury itself.

## HUNTER

**Activation:** Passive
**Ranked:** Yes
**Trees:** Hunter

The character adds ⬜ per rank of Hunter to all skill checks when interacting with wild beasts and animals, including combat checks. The character adds +10 per rank of Hunter to all of his Critical Injury rolls against animals.

## IMBUE ITEM

**Activation:** Active (Maneuver)
**Ranked:** No
**Trees:** Artisan

*Force talent.* The character may take the Imbue Item maneuver, suffering 1 strain and committing ◯. He then grants one weapon or item within short range a temporary enhancement chosen from the following options: increase weapon's damage by 1, decrease the 💠 cost for its Critical Hit or for any other single effect by 1, to a minimum of 1, or increase a piece of armor's ranged or melee defense by 1. Alternatively, the character can decrease an item's encumbrance by 2, to a minimum of 1. The character suffers 1 strain at the beginning of each of his turns in which he keeps this die committed.

## INDISTINGUISHABLE

**Activation:** Passive
**Ranked:** Yes
**Trees:** Shadow

The character's appearance is so common that people have a hard time identifying distinguishing traits. Opposing characters upgrade the difficulty of any checks made to identify him once per rank of Indistinguishable.

## INTENSE PRESENCE

**Activation:** Active (Incidental, Out of Turn)
**Ranked:** No
**Trees:** Makashi Duelist

The character may spend one Destiny Point to recover strain equal to his Presence rating.

## INTIMIDATING

**Activation:** Active (Incidental, Out of Turn)
**Ranked:** Yes
**Trees:** Aggressor

When attempting a Coercion check, the character may suffer a number of strain to downgrade the difficulty of the check a number of times equal to the strain suffered. This number cannot exceed his ranks in Intimidating. When the character is the target of a Coercion check, the character may suffer a number of strain to upgrade the difficulty of the check a number of times equal to the strain suffered. This number cannot exceed his ranks in Intimidating.

## INTUITIVE EVASION

**Activation:** Active (Maneuver)
**Ranked:** Yes
**Trees:** Starfighter Ace

*Force talent.* When piloting a vehicle of silhouette 5 or smaller, the character may take the Intuitive Evasion maneuver, suffering 1 strain and committing a number of ◯ no greater than his Force rating or his ranks of Intuitive Evasion. He then upgrades the difficulty of combat checks targeting his vehicle by an equal amount. The character suffers 1 strain at the beginning of each of his turns in which these dice remain committed.

## INTUITIVE IMPROVEMENTS

**Activation:** Passive
**Ranked:** No
**Trees:** Artisan

*Force talent.* When making a check to repair or craft a non-starship or vehicle item, the character may add ◯ no greater than Force rating to the check. The character may spend ◐◐ to permanently increase the number of hard points the item has by 1, to a maximum of 2 additional hard points. An item may only be improved in this way once.

## INTUITIVE SHOT

**Activation:** Passive
**Ranked:** No
**Trees:** Hunter

*Force talent.* When making a Ranged (Heavy) or Ranged (Light) combat check, the character may add ◯ no greater than Force rating to the check. The character may spend ◐ to add ✨ or 💠 (character's choice) to the result.

## INTUITIVE STRIKE

**Activation:** Passive
**Ranked:** No
**Trees:** Starfighter Ace

*Force talent.* When making a combat check with a planetary scale weapon, the character may add ◯ no greater than Force rating to the check. The character may spend ◐◐ to add ✨ or 💠 (character's choice) to the result.

## INVENTOR
**Activation:** Passive
**Ranked:** Yes
**Trees:** Artisan

When constructing new items or modifying existing attachments (see **Chapter V: Gear and Equipment**), the character may choose to add ☐ or remove ■ from the check per rank of Inventor.

## JUMP UP
**Activation:** Active (Incidental)
**Ranked:** No
**Trees:** Ataru Striker

Once per round on the character's turn, the character may stand up from prone or a seated position as an incidental.

## KEEN EYED
**Activation:** Passive
**Ranked:** Yes
**Trees:** Hunter, Pathfinder, Seer

The character removes ■ per rank of Keen Eyed from his Perception and Vigilance checks. Checks made to search a specific area take 50% less time than normal. This does not decrease with additional ranks of Keen Eyed.

## KILL WITH KINDNESS
**Activation:** Passive
**Ranked:** Yes
**Trees:** Advisor, Sage

The character removes ■ per rank of Kill with Kindness from his Charm and Leadership checks.

## KNOW SOMEBODY
**Activation:** Active (Incidental)
**Ranked:** Yes
**Trees:** Advisor

Once per game session, when attempting to purchase a legally available item, the character may reduce its rarity by one step per rank of Know Somebody.

## KNOWLEDGE IS POWER
**Activation:** Active (Incidental)
**Ranked:** No
**Trees:** Advisor

*Force talent.* Once per session, when making a single check, the character may treat his Force rating as being equal to his ranks in Knowledge (Lore).

## KNOWLEDGE SPECIALIZATION
**Activation:** Active (Incidental)
**Ranked:** Yes
**Trees:** Sage

When the character first acquires this talent, he may choose one Knowledge skill. When making checks with that skill, he may spend ⊕ to gain additional ✹ equal to his ranks in Knowledge Specialization.

## KNOWLEDGEABLE HEALING
**Activation:** Passive
**Ranked:** No
**Trees:** Healer

When the character performs a successful Medicine check to heal an ally, the character may spend one Destiny Point to allow the target to heal additional wounds equal to the character's ranks in Knowledge (Xenology).

## MAKASHI FINISH
**Activation:** Active (Action)
**Ranked:** No
**Trees:** Makashi Duelist

*Force talent.* The character may take the Makashi Finish action, making a Lightsaber (Presence) combat check against an engaged target, adding ◯ no greater than Force rating to the check. The character may spend ◐ to add +10 to any Critical Injury roll resulting from the check.

## MAKASHI FLOURISH
**Activation:** Active (Action)
**Ranked:** No
**Trees:** Makashi Duelist

*Force talent.* Once per encounter, the character may take the Makashi Flourish action, making an **Average (◆ ◆) Lightsaber (Presence) check**. If it is successful, one engaged opponent suffers strain equal to ✹ (ignoring soak), and the character recovers an equal amount of strain. The character may also spend ✪ ✪ ✪ or ⊕ generated on the check to stagger the opponent until the end of the target's next turn.

## MAKASHI TECHNIQUE
**Activation:** Passive
**Ranked:** No
**Trees:** Makashi Duelist

*Force talent.* When making a check using the Lightsaber skill, the character may use Presence instead of Brawn.

## MASTER ARTISAN
**Activation:** Active (Incidental)
**Ranked:** No
**Trees:** Artisan

Once per round, the character may voluntarily suffer 2 strain to decrease the difficulty of his next Mechanics check (or his next check to build or mod an item) by one, to a minimum of **Easy (◆)**.

## MASTER OF SHADOWS
**Activation:** Active (Incidental)
**Ranked:** No
**Trees:** Shadow

Once per round, the character may voluntarily suffer 2 strain to decrease the difficulty of the next Stealth or Skulduggery check by one, to a minimum of **Easy (◆)**.

## MENTAL BOND

**Activation:** Active (Action)
**Ranked:** No
**Trees:** Pathfinder

*Force talent.* The character may take the Mental Bond action, committing ◯. As long as ◯ remains committed, he may communicate mentally with an animal bonded to him via the Animal Bond talent. He can see and hear what it sees and hears, and in structured encounters, he may direct his animal (see the Animal Bond talent, page 138) at up to extreme range.

## MENTAL FORTRESS

**Activation:** Active (Incidental)
**Ranked:** No
**Trees:** Artisan, Shadow

The character may spend one Destiny Point to ignore the effects of ongoing Critical Injuries on any Intellect- or Cunning-related checks until the end of the encounter. He still suffers from the injury itself.

## MENTAL TOOLS

**Activation:** Passive
**Ranked:** No
**Trees:** Artisan

*Force talent.* The character always counts as having the right tools for the job (see page 181) when performing Mechanics checks.

## MULTIPLE OPPONENTS

**Activation:** Passive
**Ranked:** No
**Trees:** Shii-Cho Knight

The character adds □ to his Brawl, Melee, and Lightsaber combat checks when engaged with multiple opponents. This includes single groups of multiple minions.

## NATURAL BLADEMASTER

**Activation:** Active (Incidental)
**Ranked:** No
**Trees:** Shii-Cho Knight

Once per game session, the character may reroll any one Lightsaber or Melee check.

## NATURAL CHARMER

**Activation:** Active (Incidental)
**Ranked:** No
**Trees:** Advisor

Once per game session, the character may reroll any one Charm or Deception check.

## NATURAL DOCTOR
**Activation:** Active (Incidental)
**Ranked:** No
**Trees:** Healer
Once per game session, the character may reroll any one Medicine check.

## NATURAL HUNTER
**Activation:** Active (Incidental)
**Ranked:** No
**Trees:** Hunter
Once per game session, the character may reroll any one Perception or Vigilance check.

## NATURAL LEADER
**Activation:** Active (Incidental)
**Ranked:** No
**Trees:** Peacekeeper
Once per game session, the character may reroll any one Cool or Leadership check.

## NATURAL MYSTIC
**Activation:** Active (Incidental)
**Ranked:** No
**Trees:** Seer
*Force talent.* Once per session, the character may reroll any one Force power check.

## NATURAL NEGOTIATOR
**Activation:** Active (Incidental)
**Ranked:** No
**Trees:** Sage
Once per game session, the character may reroll any one Cool or Negotiation check.

## NATURAL OUTDOORSMAN
**Activation:** Active (Incidental)
**Ranked:** No
**Trees:** Pathfinder
Once per game session, the character may reroll any one Resilience or Survival check.

## NATURAL TINKERER
**Activation:** Active (Incidental)
**Ranked:** No
**Trees:** Artisan
Once per game session, the character may reroll any one Mechanics check.

## NIMAN TECHNIQUE
**Activation:** Passive
**Ranked:** No
**Trees:** Niman Disciple
*Force talent.* When making a Lightsaber skill check, the character may use Willpower instead of Brawn.

## NOBODY'S FOOL
**Activation:** Passive
**Ranked:** Yes
**Trees:** Advisor, Niman Disciple
The difficulty of any Charm, Coercion, and Deception checks attempted against the character is upgraded once for each rank of Nobody's Fool.

## NOW YOU SEE ME
**Activation:** Active (Action)
**Ranked:** No
**Trees:** Shadow
*Force talent.* Once per session, the character may take the Now You See Me action, making a **Hard (◆◆◆) Deception check**. If successful, a number of NPCs equal to his Cunning within medium range forget any interactions they had with the character during the last thirty minutes.

At the GM's discretion, multiple ⚙ or ⬡ may give the NPCs in question unpleasant side effects, such as confusion, nightmares, or a persistent and maddening suspicion that they've forgotten something important.

## ONE WITH THE UNIVERSE

**Activation:** Active (Action)
**Ranked:** No
**Trees:** Sage

*Force talent.* Once per session, the character may spend several minutes meditating, then take the One with the Universe action, making an **Average (◆ ◆) Astrogation check**. If successful, during the next encounter he adds ◯ to all Force power checks. However, if he succeeded with ⚙, he adds ● to all Force power checks instead.

## OUTDOORSMAN

**Activation:** Passive
**Ranked:** Yes
**Trees:** Pathfinder

The character removes ■ per rank of Outdoorsman from his checks to move through terrain or to manage terrain or environmental effects. Decrease overland travel times by 50% (this does not decrease with additional ranks of Outdoorsman).

## PARRY

**Activation:** Active (Incidental, Out of Turn)
**Ranked:** Yes
**Trees:** Ataru Striker, Makashi Duelist, Niman Disciple, Protector, Shien Expert, Shii-Cho Knight, Soresu Defender

When the character suffers a hit from a Brawl, Melee, or Lightsaber combat check, after damage is calculated (but before soak is applied, so immediately after step 3 of **Perform a Combat Check**, page 210), the character may take a Parry incidental. He suffers 3 strain and reduces the damage dealt by that hit by a number equal to 2 plus his ranks in Parry. This talent may only be used once per hit and when the character is wielding a Lightsaber or Melee weapon.

## PARRY (IMPROVED)

**Activation:** Active (Incidental, Out of Turn)
**Ranked:** No
**Trees:** Ataru Striker, Makashi Duelist, Shii-Cho Knight, Soresu Defender

When the character suffers a hit from a Brawl, Melee, or Lightsaber combat check and uses the Parry incidental to reduce the damage from that hit, after the attack is resolved, the character may spend ⬡ or ⚙ ⚙ ⚙ to automatically hit the attacker once with a wielded Brawl, Melee, or Lightsaber weapon. This hit deals the weapon's base damage plus any damage from applicable talents or abilities. This talent may not be used if the original attack incapacitates the character.

## PARRY (SUPREME)

**Activation:** Passive
**Ranked:** No
**Trees:** Soresu Defender

*Force talent.* If the user did not make a combat check during his previous turn, he suffers 1 strain when taking the Parry incidental, instead of 3.

## PHYSICIAN

**Activation:** Passive
**Ranked:** Yes
**Trees:** Healer, Protector

When this character makes a Medicine check to help a character heal wounds, the target heals one additional strain per rank of Physician.

## PLAUSIBLE DENIABILITY

**Activation:** Passive
**Ranked:** Yes
**Trees:** Advisor, Aggressor

The character removes ■ per rank of Plausible Deniability from his Coercion and Deception checks.

## PREEMPTIVE AVOIDANCE

**Activation:** Active (Incidental, Out of Turn)
**Ranked:** No
**Trees:** Sage, Seer

*Force talent.* Immediately after an opponent moves to engage the character, the character may spend one Destiny Point to disengage from that opponent as an out-of-turn incidental.

## PREY ON THE WEAK

**Activation:** Passive
**Ranked:** Yes
**Trees:** Aggressor

The character deals +1 damage to one hit on all successful combat checks against disoriented targets per rank of Prey on the Weak.

## QUICK DRAW

**Activation:** Active (Incidental)
**Ranked:** No
**Trees:** Ataru Striker, Shii-Cho Knight

Once per round on the character's turn, he may draw or holster an easily accessible weapon or item as an incidental, instead of a maneuver. This talent also reduces the amount of time to draw or stow a weapon that usually requires more than one maneuver to properly prepare or stow, by one maneuver.

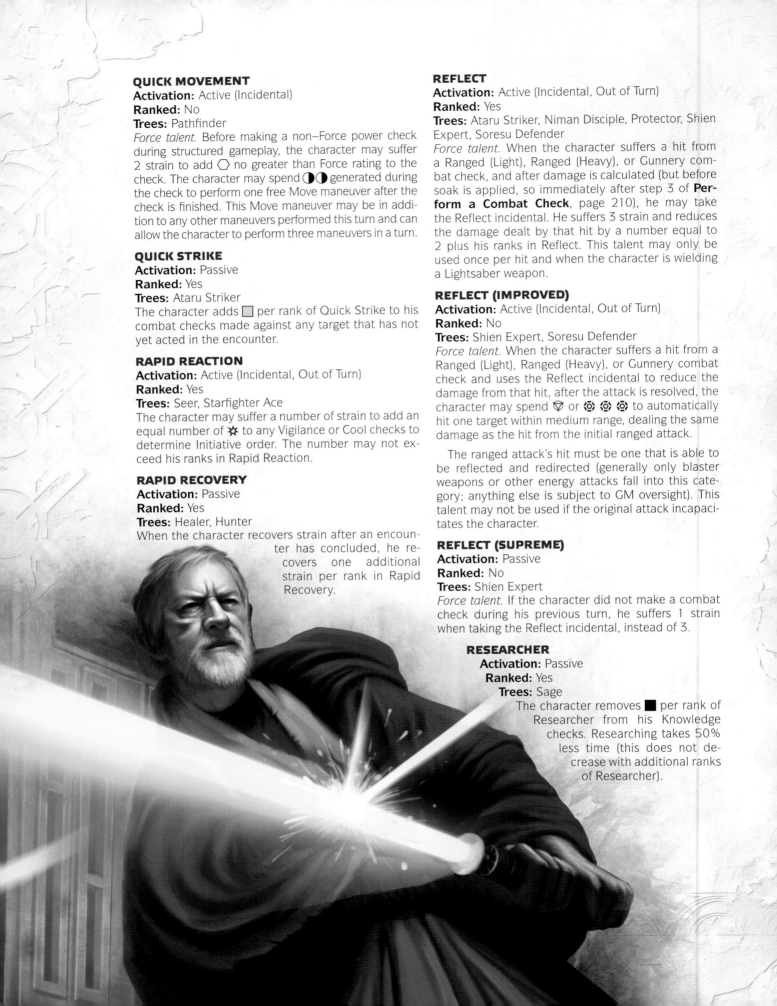

## QUICK MOVEMENT
**Activation:** Active (Incidental)
**Ranked:** No
**Trees:** Pathfinder
*Force talent.* Before making a non–Force power check during structured gameplay, the character may suffer 2 strain to add ○ no greater than Force rating to the check. The character may spend ○○ generated during the check to perform one free Move maneuver after the check is finished. This Move maneuver may be in addition to any other maneuvers performed this turn and can allow the character to perform three maneuvers in a turn.

## QUICK STRIKE
**Activation:** Passive
**Ranked:** Yes
**Trees:** Ataru Striker
The character adds ▢ per rank of Quick Strike to his combat checks made against any target that has not yet acted in the encounter.

## RAPID REACTION
**Activation:** Active (Incidental, Out of Turn)
**Ranked:** Yes
**Trees:** Seer, Starfighter Ace
The character may suffer a number of strain to add an equal number of ✯ to any Vigilance or Cool checks to determine Initiative order. The number may not exceed his ranks in Rapid Reaction.

## RAPID RECOVERY
**Activation:** Passive
**Ranked:** Yes
**Trees:** Healer, Hunter
When the character recovers strain after an encounter has concluded, he recovers one additional strain per rank in Rapid Recovery.

## REFLECT
**Activation:** Active (Incidental, Out of Turn)
**Ranked:** Yes
**Trees:** Ataru Striker, Niman Disciple, Protector, Shien Expert, Soresu Defender
*Force talent.* When the character suffers a hit from a Ranged (Light), Ranged (Heavy), or Gunnery combat check, and after damage is calculated (but before soak is applied, so immediately after step 3 of **Perform a Combat Check**, page 210), he may take the Reflect incidental. He suffers 3 strain and reduces the damage dealt by that hit by a number equal to 2 plus his ranks in Reflect. This talent may only be used once per hit and when the character is wielding a Lightsaber weapon.

## REFLECT (IMPROVED)
**Activation:** Active (Incidental, Out of Turn)
**Ranked:** No
**Trees:** Shien Expert, Soresu Defender
*Force talent.* When the character suffers a hit from a Ranged (Light), Ranged (Heavy), or Gunnery combat check and uses the Reflect incidental to reduce the damage from that hit, after the attack is resolved, the character may spend ▽ or ⚙⚙⚙ to automatically hit one target within medium range, dealing the same damage as the hit from the initial ranged attack.

The ranged attack's hit must be one that is able to be reflected and redirected (generally only blaster weapons or other energy attacks fall into this category; anything else is subject to GM oversight). This talent may not be used if the original attack incapacitates the character.

## REFLECT (SUPREME)
**Activation:** Passive
**Ranked:** No
**Trees:** Shien Expert
*Force talent.* If the character did not make a combat check during his previous turn, he suffers 1 strain when taking the Reflect incidental, instead of 3.

## RESEARCHER
**Activation:** Passive
**Ranked:** Yes
**Trees:** Sage
The character removes ▉ per rank of Researcher from his Knowledge checks. Researching takes 50% less time (this does not decrease with additional ranks of Researcher).

## RESIST DISARM

**Activation:** Active (Incidental, Out of Turn)
**Ranked:** No
**Trees:** Makashi Duelist

If the character would be disarmed or his weapon would be damaged or destroyed, he may choose to suffer 2 strain to ignore the effect.

## SABER SWARM

**Activation:** Active (Maneuver)
**Ranked:** No
**Trees:** Ataru Striker

*Force talent.* The character may take the Saber Swarm maneuver, suffering 1 strain. His next Lightsaber (Agility) combat check this turn gains the Linked item quality, with ranks equal to Force rating.

## SABER THROW

**Activation:** Active (Action)
**Ranked:** No
**Trees:** Ataru Striker, Shien Expert

*Force talent.* The character may take the Saber Throw action, making a Lightsaber combat check as a ranged attack at one target within medium range, adding ◯ no greater than his Force rating to the check. The character must spend ◑ and succeed on the check to hit his target; he may spend ◑ to have his weapon return to his hand after resolving the attack.

## SARLACC SWEEP

**Activation:** Active (Action)
**Ranked:** No
**Trees:** Shii-Cho Knight

*Force talent.* The character may take the Sarlacc Sweep action, making a Lightsaber combat check with +1 difficulty against one engaged target. The character may spend ✪ ✪ generated by this combat check to hit one additional target he is engaged with. He may do this once per engaged target, paying ✪ ✪ for each additional hit.

When performing a Sarlacc Sweep action, the character must always target the opponent with the highest difficulty and highest defense (if two targets have the same difficulty and defense, the GM chooses which target is the initial target).

## SECOND WIND

**Activation:** Active (Incidental)
**Ranked:** Yes
**Trees:** Peacekeeper, Shii-Cho Knight

Once per encounter, the character may use a Second Wind incidental to recover an amount of strain equal to his ranks in Second Wind.

## SENSE ADVANTAGE

**Activation:** Active (Incidental, Out of Turn)
**Ranked:** No
**Trees:** Advisor, Aggressor, Seer

*Force talent.* Once per game session, the character may add ■ ■ to the skill check of one NPC within extreme range.

## SENSE DANGER

**Activation:** Active (Incidental)
**Ranked:** No
**Trees:** Seer

*Force talent.* Once per game session, the character may remove ■ ■ from any one skill check.

## SENSE EMOTIONS

**Activation:** Passive
**Ranked:** No
**Trees:** Advisor, Niman Disciple

*Force talent.* The character adds ☐ to all Charm, Coercion, and Deception checks unless the target is immune to Force powers.

## SHARE PAIN

**Activation:** Active (Incidental, Out of Turn)
**Ranked:** No
**Trees:** Pathfinder

*Force talent.* When an animal bonded to the character by the Animal Empathy talent suffers wounds, the character may take the Share Pain incidental. He reduces the wounds the animal suffered by half (rounded up), then suffers a number of wounds equal to the number reduced.

## SHIEN TECHNIQUE

**Activation:** Passive
**Ranked:** No
**Trees:** Shien Expert

*Force talent.* When making a Lightsaber skill check, the character may use Cunning instead of Brawn.

## SHROUD

**Activation:** Active (Incidental)
**Ranked:** No
**Trees:** Shadow

*Force talent.* Once per session, the character may spend one Destiny Point to make himself undetectable via the Force (through abilities such as the Sense power) and to make his own Force powers unnoticeable for the remainder of the encounter.

What this entails exactly is up to the player and the GM, and the GM may rule that some actions (such as lifting an X-wing with one's mind) are too obvious to be ignored. However, abilities such as manipulating control panels, lifting small objects, or using Force powers to affect someone physically or mentally go unnoticed, or the effects are attributed to something else.

## SIDE STEP

**Activation:** Active (Maneuver)
**Ranked:** Yes
**Trees:** Hunter, Shien Expert

Once per round on the character's turn, the character may perform a Side Step maneuver to try to avoid incoming ranged attacks. He then suffers a number of strain no greater than his ranks in Side Step. Until the start of the character's next turn, upgrade the difficulty of all ranged combat checks targeting the character a number of times equal to the strain suffered by the character.

## LIGHTSABER (CHARACTERISTIC) CHECKS

Several talents require the character to make a Lightsaber skill check with a specific characteristic—a Lightsaber (Cunning) check, for example. The character must already have a talent allowing him to use the alternate characteristic with the Lightsaber skill in order to make this check.

### SIXTH SENSE
**Activation:** Passive
**Ranked:** Yes
**Trees:** Hunter
The character gains +1 ranged defense.

### SKILLED JOCKEY
**Activation:** Passive
**Ranked:** Yes
**Trees:** Starfighter Ace
The character removes ■ per rank of Skilled Jockey from his Piloting (Planetary) and Piloting (Space) checks.

### SLEIGHT OF MIND
**Activation:** Passive
**Ranked:** Yes
**Trees:** Pathfinder, Shadow
*Force talent.* The character adds □ per rank of Sleight of Mind to his Stealth checks unless the being attempting to detect the character is immune to Force powers.

### SLIPPERY MINDED
**Activation:** Active (Action)
**Ranked:** No
**Trees:** Shadow
*Force talent.* On any turn in which the character is under the effects of a Force power, he may perform the Slippery Minded action (this action may be specifically performed even if the Force power would normally bar him from performing actions). He makes a **Hard (◆ ◆ ◆) Deception check**. If he succeeds, he is no longer under the effects of the Force power.

### SMOOTH TALKER
**Activation:** Active (Incidental)
**Ranked:** Yes
**Trees:** Advisor, Sage
When a character first acquires this talent, he chooses one skill: Charm, Coercion, Negotiation, or Deception. When making checks with that skill, he may spend ⊕ to gain additional ☼ equal to his ranks in Smooth Talker.

### SOFT SPOT
**Activation:** Active (Incidental)
**Ranked:** No
**Trees:** Hunter
After making a successful attack with a non-starship/vehicle weapon, the character may spend one Destiny Point to add damage equal to his Cunning to one hit of the successful attack.

### SOLID REPAIRS
**Activation:** Passive
**Ranked:** Yes
**Trees:** Artisan, Starfighter Ace
Whenever the character repairs hull trauma on a starship or vehicle, he repairs 1 additional hull trauma per rank of Solid Repairs.

### SORESU TECHNIQUE
**Activation:** Passive
**Ranked:** No
**Trees:** Soresu Defender
*Force talent.* When making a Lightsaber skill check, the character may use Intellect instead of Brawn.

### STEELY NERVES
**Activation:** Active (Incidental)
**Ranked:** No
**Trees:** Advisor, Peacekeeper
The character may spend one Destiny Point to ignore the effects of ongoing Critical Injuries on any Presence or Willpower-related checks until the end of the encounter. He still suffers from the injury itself.

### STIMPACK SPECIALIZATION
**Activation:** Passive
**Ranked:** Yes
**Trees:** Protector
Whenever the character uses a stimpack, the target heals an additional wound per rank of Stimpack Specialization. The sixth stimpack and beyond each day still have no effect.

### STRATEGIC FORM
**Activation:** Active (Action)
**Ranked:** No
**Trees:** Soresu Defender
*Force talent.* While wielding a Lightsaber weapon, the character may take the Strategic Form action, making a **Hard (◆ ◆ ◆) Lightsaber (Intellect) check** and rolling ○ no greater than Force rating as part of the check. For each ☼, one target within short range of the character may only make combat checks if those combat checks target the character until the end of the following round. The character may spend ◖ to cause Strategic Form to affect a target for one additional round. The effects of Strategic Form end if the character is incapacitated.

### STREET SMARTS
**Activation:** Passive
**Ranked:** Yes
**Trees:** Shadow, Shien Expert
The character removes ■ per rank of Street Smarts from his Streetwise and Knowledge (Underworld) checks.

### SUM DJEM
**Activation:** Passive
**Ranked:** No
**Trees:** Makashi Duelist, Niman Disciple, Shii-Cho Knight
*Force talent.* When the character makes a successful Lightsaber combat check, he may spend ⊕ or ⟁ ⟁ to disarm his opponent (with GM's approval). The

disarmed weapon lands anywhere within short range of the engagement (character's choice).

## SURGEON
**Activation:** Passive
**Ranked:** Yes
**Trees:** Healer
When this character makes a Medicine check to help a character heal wounds, the target heals 1 additional wound per rank of Surgeon.

## SWIFT
**Activation:** Passive
**Ranked:** No
**Trees:** Pathfinder
The character does not suffer the penalties for moving through difficult terrain (he moves through it at normal speed, without spending additional maneuvers).

## TECHNICAL APTITUDE
**Activation:** Passive
**Ranked:** Yes
**Trees:** Artisan
For each rank, the character reduces the amount of time needed to complete computer-related tasks by 25%.

## TERRIFY
**Activation:** Active (Action)
**Ranked:** No
**Trees:** Aggressor
*Force talent.* The character may take a Terrify action, making a **Hard (◆ ◆ ◆) Coercion check** and rolling ⬡ no greater than Force rating as part of the check. If successful, one target per ☼ within medium range of the character is disoriented until the end of the next round. The character may spend ✹ ✹ to increase the duration of disorientation for all affected targets by one round, and may spend ◗ to immobilize an affected target until the end of the next round. A character who has purchased this talent automatically gains 1 Conflict at the beginning of a game session.

## TERRIFY (IMPROVED)
**Activation:** Passive
**Ranked:** No
**Trees:** Aggressor
*Force talent.* The difficulty of the Terrify action decreases to **Average (◆ ◆)**. In addition, the character may spend ✦ generated on the check to stagger an affected target until the end of the next round.

## THE FORCE IS MY ALLY
**Activation:** Active (Incidental)
**Ranked:** No
**Trees:** Sage, Seer
*Force talent.* Once per session, the character may suffer 2 strain to perform a Force power action as a maneuver.

## TOUCH OF FATE
**Activation:** Active (Incidental)
**Ranked:** No
**Trees:** Starfighter Ace
*Force talent.* Once per game session, the character may add ☐☐ to any one skill check.

## TOUGHENED
**Activation:** Passive
**Ranked:** Yes
**Trees:** Advisor, Aggressor, Healer, Hunter, Niman Disciple, Pathfinder, Peacekeeper, Protector, Seer, Shien Expert, Shii-Cho Knight, Soresu Defender
The character increases his wound threshold by 2 per rank of Toughened.

## TRICKY TARGET
**Activation:** Passive
**Ranked:** No
**Trees:** Starfighter Ace
Any vehicle the character pilots counts as having a silhouette one lower than normal when being attacked, to a minimum of 0.

## UNCANNY REACTIONS
**Activation:** Passive
**Ranked:** Yes
**Trees:** Hunter, Seer
*Force talent.* The character adds ☐ per rank of Uncanny Reactions to his Vigilance checks.

## UNCANNY SENSES
**Activation:** Passive
**Ranked:** Yes
**Trees:** Hunter
*Force talent.* The character adds ☐ per rank of Uncanny Senses to his Perception checks.

## UNITY ASSAULT
**Activation:** Active (Maneuver)
**Ranked:** No
**Trees:** Peacekeeper
*Force talent.* Whenever the character misses an opponent with a combat check and generates ✪ or ✹ ✹ ✹, the character may spend this to perform a Force power action that targets one or more allies as a maneuver (he must still be able to perform maneuvers, and may not perform more than two maneuvers in a turn).

## VALUABLE FACTS
**Activation:** Active (Action)
**Ranked:** No
**Trees:** Sage
Once per encounter, the character may take a Valuable Facts action, making an **Average (◆ ◆) Knowledge check** (the GM and player should determine which Knowledge skill is most applicable in the given situation). If successful, the character may add ✪ to any one check made by an allied character during the encounter.

The subsequent check should relate in some way to the facts the character learned, or the player should come up with an explanation for why the information the character learned is instrumental in the success of the ally's check.

## WELL ROUNDED
**Activation:** Passive
**Ranked:** Yes
**Trees:** Shadow
The character chooses any two skills. They permanently become career skills.

# GEAR AND EQUIPMENT

**T**he ancient Jedi knew that the most powerful weapon they could wield was the Force. More than a simple tool of destruction, the Force is a mighty ally for anyone who can call upon its aid. However, those same Jedi still wielded lightsabers, flew starships, and carried medpacs and datapads. No matter who they are, characters rely on gear and equipment to carry out tasks from the trivial to the vital. Comlinks enable communications, scanners detect hidden dangers, and good luck surviving in the cold void of outer space without a spacesuit. And some Force users still carry a trusty blaster, as clumsy and random as it may be.

In the *Star Wars* galaxy, the most important thing for a fugitive Force user to be is prepared. Luckily, in the time of the Empire, the equipment characters need to handle mundane problems can be purchased on most civilized planets. Glow rods, macrobinoculars, and stimpacks are generally readily available, and most worlds even have specialized gear like fusion lanterns and blaster rifles for sale. Smart adventurers should be sure to spend a few credits on medical supplies, survival gear, some heavy clothing or padded armor,

and a weapon of some type. After all, who knows what they might encounter on their journeys?

While much of their equipment is relatively easy to procure, some items Force users may be interested in can be both exceedingly valuable and vanishingly rare. Ancient Jedi records, mystical holocrons, and the renowned lightsabers are not things one can buy at the corner shop. The Empire enthusiastically hunts items like these and those who carry them, making the few that exist even more valuable. The unscrupulous criminal dealers and taciturn private collectors who might possess one of these items would only sell them for a veritable fortune. Thus, obtaining one is rarely a matter of payment, and much more often a matter of danger and adventure.

In the following chapter, players can find information on common personal weapons, armor, and gear critical for adventures from the Core Worlds to the Outer Rim. They can also learn rules on buying, selling, and modifying their equipment. Finally, they can obtain data on some of the rare weapons and items used by Force-sensitives, the Jedi, and the Sith.

# THE GALACTIC ECONOMY

Even under the iron fist of the Empire, trade continues on most worlds much as it did in the days of the Galactic Republic. Hundreds of worlds produce myriad products that are shipped to all sectors of the galaxy along busy hyperspace routes. Traders and manufacturers regard the Imperial regime as both a threat and an opportunity. While the Empire is more exacting when collecting taxes and far more punitive in punishing those who fail to pay such dues, it is also less concerned with regulation and the exploitation of new markets and natural resources. Unscrupulous corporate interests can make plenty of credits under the Empire's lax stewardship.

Force-sensitive adventurers have to be very careful when dealing with the representatives of trade guilds and shipping consortiums. Many wealthy traders have enriched themselves due to relaxed regulations and are staunchly loyal to the Empire as a result. These individuals would like nothing better than to curry favor with the Empire (and reap the huge bounties) by turning in a captured Force user. Even those who are not supporters of the Imperial regime are often so cowed by the Empire's military might that they would not risk an association with outlaws. Thus, no matter who they deal with, Force-sensitives must always remain on their guard.

## IMPERIAL CREDITS

There are a number of different currencies and financial systems at work in the galactic economy, but only Imperial credits are so widely accepted as to be considered a truly galactic currency. The Galactic Credit Standard was initially backed by the immense wealth of the InterGalactic Banking Clan (IGBC) of the planet Scipio. The Muuns, who run most of the IGBC and tend to occupy most of the positions on its governing council, display prodigious talents for mathematics and finance. Coupled with the incredibly vast wealth found in Scipio's impenetrable vaults, these skills saw them grow rich enough to back a currency that could be used throughout the galaxy. The Empire dare not destroy the IGBC, lest it be blamed for plunging the civilized galaxy into a deep recession, thereby losing support from the important Core Worlds. However, it does place its own administrators in positions where they can keep a close eye on the IGBC's business, and it favors human-controlled banking organizations. Meanwhile, administrators and

the might of the Imperial military keep a close eye on Scipio, to ensure total compliance with Imperial law. This effectively limits the influence of the Muuns over the Imperial economy for the time being.

Credits come in the form of chips, bills, and coins, though the popularity of chips is declining, as investors and consumers fear that they may become worthless should the Empire suffer defeat. Credit chips and coins come in a number of denominations, ranging from one decired (a tenth of a credit) to 5,000 credits. Some branches of the IGBC and its affiliates issue credit sticks which hold varying amounts of credits depending on the sales and purchases made by the holder. These credit sticks are notoriously hard to tamper with, and the penalties for forging credit are high, though that does not stop some scoundrels from trying.

There are alternative economic systems in the galaxy, though they are relatively parochial and easily ignored. Indeed, some of those doing business within such a system may well prefer to take credits rather than local currency. Most parts of the galaxy deemed civilized will accept credits.

## LOOKING OUT FOR NUMBER ONE

The sad truth is, being a star-wandering adventurer and possible do-gooder doesn't pay very well. The heroes of **FORCE AND DESTINY** may have strange and mystical powers at their disposal. They may be able to win lightsaber duels, lift starships with their minds, and find the truth at the heart of thorny and violent disputes, but none of these things puts food on their tables or credits in their pockets.

Characters may approach this problem in several different ways. Some may use the gear and credits they obtain in the course of their adventures (perhaps stolen from Imperial supply depots or taken from the pockets of vile criminals) to keep themselves afloat. Though there is a certain poetic justice in using the resources of their enemies against them, characters who resort to this may find themselves borrowing additional trouble. Stolen items may be tracked, and characters who attempt to sell a cargo of Imperial thermal detonators may find the Imperial Security Bureau taking an inordinate interest in them. Likewise, most crooks react violently when people pilfer from them, and nobody holds a grudge like a Hutt crime boss or Black Sun enforcer.

Some characters prefer to accept payment for their good deeds instead, reasoning that accepting rewards for their actions helps facilitate helping others at a later time. This can work, although taking money for supposedly selfless acts tends to sour these deeds. More than a few dark side Force users started down the long and slippery road to damnation by rationalizing rewards for their mystical abilities.

Finally, some adventurers take on side jobs to pay the bills in-between their adventures. This can be mind-numbingly tedious, although generally these jobs don't come with life-threatening choices or moral quandaries. However, adventure can strike when one least expects it, and even a boring job can lead to something far more interesting.

# RARITY

Some items are naturally more difficult to purchase than others, depending on where characters find themselves at any given time. After all, the galaxy is a big place, and the vagaries and intricacies of galactic trade mean that some items that are easy to find in certain locations are very difficult to find in others. Of course, some items are rare no matter where one goes, and likewise, some items are always common and inexpensive.

Rarity in **FORCE AND DESTINY** is a simple way of measuring how difficult an item can be to find on a scale of 0–10, with 0 being the easiest to track down and 10 being the hardest. However, whether or not an item is available for purchase should never be solely a matter of rolling dice. Instead, the needs of the plot make it at least partially the Game Master's decision. Nevertheless, for simple items, rarity provides a simple way for the GM to determine whether something is available and to let the players easily track items down. Finding an item on a world requires a successful Negotiation check (although the GM may allow the character to use an appropriate Knowledge skill check instead).

**Table 5–1: Rarity** lists the rarities, the corresponding check difficulty to find items with those rarities, and examples of items with those rarities. **Table 5–2: Rarity Modifiers** on page 158 lists some general modifiers that can be applied to an item's rarity, based on the technological status and general type of the world where the item is being sought. Some worlds may impose their own individual modifiers as well. Modifiers can raise an item's rarity above 10. For rarities higher than 10, the difficulty remains at **Formidable (◆◆◆◆◆)**, but the GM may upgrade the difficulty once for every rarity beyond 10.

## TABLE 5–1: RARITY

| Rarity | Difficulty | Examples |
|---|---|---|
| 0 | Simple (–) | Glow Rod |
| 1 | | Long Range Comlink |
| 2 | Easy (◆) | Medpac |
| 3 | | Scanner Goggles |
| 4 | Average (◆◆) | Blaster Pistol |
| 5 | | Blaster Rifle |
| 6 | Hard (◆◆◆) | Cybernetic Limb |
| 7 | | Cortosis Gauntlets |
| 8 | Daunting (◆◆◆◆) | Thermal Detonator |
| 9 | | Dantari Crystal |
| 10 | Formidable (◆◆◆◆◆) | Lightsaber |

## THE BLACK MARKET

Not all goods are available on all planets. A city might outlaw weapons within its limits, and most planetary authorities forbid thermal detonators. Selling illegal goods is dangerous but lucrative, and finding them means dealing with greedy thugs and criminals.

Exactly what is illegal on each world is up to the Game Master or may be specified in that world's description. Finding an illegal item typically requires a Streetwise check. The difficulty generally depends on the rarity of the item (see **Table 5–1**), but the difficulty can increase based on the world's law enforcement capabilities (as determined by the GM).

## TABLE 5-2: RARITY MODIFIERS

| Rarity Modifier | Circumstances |
|---|---|
| –2 | Primary Core World such as Coruscant, Duro, or Corellia |
| –1 | Other Core World |
| –1 | World on primary trade lane |
| +0 | Colony or Inner Rim world |
| +0 | Civilized world |
| +1 | Mid Rim world |
| +1 | Recently settled world, out-of-the way-world |
| +2 | Outer Rim world |
| +2 | Frontier world |
| +3 | Wild Space world |
| +4 | Uncivilized world |

Selling illegal goods also requires a Streetwise check with the same difficulty as above. If three or more ✵ or a ⬙ are generated, something has gone wrong; the buyer tries to rob the characters, or the local police arrive to arrest these brazen criminals, for example.

Finding black market items always requires a Streetwise check, and the items may cost far more than the list price, depending on their scarcity on a particular world. This varies from place to place, so the Game Master should determine if an item is restricted in a particular location, to what degree, and what the difficulty is to track it down. Some items are marked with an (R) by their price, which means they are restricted and always count as black market items.

Most black marketeers have established patterns, customers, and habits that allow them to stay in business. While the Rebellion has been known to deal with the black market, the Player Characters might not have these connections; if they sell goods, they may even be selling to a criminal who plans on turning around and reselling the goods again. For that reason, PCs selling illegal items net one-quarter of the listed price with a successful Streetwise check, one-half with ✵ ✵, and three-quarters with ✵ ✵ ✵ or higher.

Truly extraordinary and illegal items, like rare animals or exotic pets, can be sold for higher values, but this is based on the story and the difficulty it took to find them. The rules above present the general guidelines for buying and selling most illegal items.

## SELLING AND TRADING

Selling legal items follows guidelines similar to those for selling illegal ones. Player Characters can generally sell an item for one-quarter of its cost upon a successful Negotiation check, increasing that to one-half with ✵ ✵ and to three-quarters with ✵ ✵ ✵ or more.

In some cases, the PCs might wish to engage in trade, buying multiple items at one location and then selling them at another location where they are rarer. These actions can be handled narratively, but if the GM wishes to use some mechanical guidelines for this process, following are some basic rules covering trading.

Trade works the same whether with black market (restricted) items or with legal items. Selling the items follows the rules listed previously, whether the items are black market or legal, with the caveat that trading in legal items requires a Negotiation check, while trading in illegal items requires a Streetwise check. However, when determining the sell price based on the success of the Negotiation check, first multiply the cost of the item by the difference between the item's rarity where it was bought and its rarity where it is to be sold, referring to **Table 5–2: Rarity Modifiers** and **Table 5–3: Increased Costs When Trading**. Then take the new, increased cost and determine the sell price by the results of the Negotiation check.

Of course, these rules do not account for all sorts of details, such as buying in bulk, marketing and advertising, and myriad other factors that may affect prices. This is why the rules for buying, selling, and trading are all modifiable by the GM, and subject to his judgment. It is also important to note that these rules only apply when engaging in commercial trade. If the PCs sell a cargo load of blasters on a world using these rules, then later one of them buys a blaster on that world, he would normally pay the listed cost, without any increases. Remember, these rules are for engaging in trade only.

Always remember when engaging in interstellar trade that the GM has final say as to how much an item is worth, which can also be based on narrative factors. For example, if the PCs collect some E-11 blaster rifles off dead stormtroopers, they may try to sell them. However, though a blaster rifle is not (R), it's still obviously an Imperial weapon. Some shopkeepers may refuse to purchase them, and others may offer a criminally low price for these goods, no matter how well the PCs roll on their Negotiation check. Finally, some may offer to buy the goods at a reasonable price, and then turn around and betray the PCs to the Empire.

## TABLE 5-3: INCREASED COSTS WHEN TRADING

| Rarity Increase | Cost Increase |
|---|---|
| +0 or +1 | x1 |
| +2 | x2 |
| +3 | x3 |
| +4 or higher | x4 |

# ENCUMBRANCE

**F**ORCE AND DESTINY emphasizes sweeping stories, epic tales, and fast action. Keeping track of the weight of every stimpack isn't fun, but knowing that a hero has to carry the child he just rescued from Imperial stormtroopers is an important story element; so is having some idea of how many days' worth of rations an explorer can carry while journeying in the wilderness.

In general, players and the Game Master won't need to track a character's encumbrance (how much he's carrying on his person). Occasionally, however, it may play an important part in the story, and a player needs to know if the weight, mass, and collective bulk of the items his hero is wearing inhibits his actions.

## ENCUMBRANCE VALUES

Every item of gear listed in this chapter has an encumbrance value. Most items that can commonly be carried have a value between 0 and 5—from relatively light objects (such as credit chips or light clothing) to heavier items (like blaster rifles or gaffi sticks). The encumbrance value of armor is discussed in more detail later, and is different when it's worn. When worn, the weight is distributed appropriately, and when armor is carried, it's treated as just another item.

Encumbrance doesn't strictly represent weight: it also represents mass, bulk, and how easy items are to carry. A well-fitting suit of armor adds very little encumbrance, while an armful of gimer sticks has a high encumbrance because they're tricky to carry.

Small items such as datapads, most pistols, and knives have an encumbrance value of 1 or 2. Medium items, such as blaster rifles, a satchel of thermal detonators, or a grappling hook and cord, have an encumbrance value of 3 or 4. Large or heavy items, such as cargo crates, repeating blaster rifles, or a heavy toolbox, are valued at 5 or 6.

If it becomes critical to the story to have more detail, ten loosely carried incidental items have an encumbrance value of 1. If they are stored in an effective manner—such as bowcaster quarrels in a quiver, or crystals in a pouch—then twenty incidental items have an encumbrance value of 1. If, for some reason, the character is unable to manage his gear in such a way, the GM may increase the items' overall encumbrance value by several points to reflect the difficulty in managing and carrying items by less efficient means. When carried, a living being generally has an encumbrance value of 5 plus Brawn. A typical human has a Brawn of 2, and therefore a total encumbrance value of 7. A scholar from Ryloth, with a Brawn of 1, has an encumbrance value of 6. This may be modified by specific species' features, such as the fatty bulk of a Hutt or the hollow bones of an avian.

## ENCUMBRANCE THRESHOLD

Characters have an "encumbrance threshold" of 5 plus their Brawn rating, which limits how much they can carry under normal conditions without penalty. A total encumbrance value over the threshold means the hero is "encumbered," and suffers ■ to all Agility and Brawn checks for every point of encumbrance over the limit. This is cumulative with any ■ suffered for strain or other conditions, should any be in play.

Further, if a character is encumbered by an amount equal to or greater than his Brawn rating, he no longer earns a free maneuver each turn. The character can still perform up to two maneuvers, but each maneuver costs 2 strain. With a Brawn of 2, for example, a character would not get a free maneuver each turn if he's carrying 9 or more points of encumbrance.

## LIFTING AND CARRYING EXCESSIVE ENCUMBRANCE

Characters shouldn't typically carry more than their encumbrance threshold. When necessity demands, however, they can do so for a short time (suffering the effects described above).

If a character needs to lift an object with an encumbrance value greater than his encumbrance threshold, such as an ally who has fallen off a gantry or ledge, he must make an Athletics check. The difficulty is **Simple (–)** if the object's encumbrance value is less than or equal to the character's encumbrance threshold. Increase the difficulty by one for every point over, up to a maximum additional encumbrance of 4 and difficulty of **Daunting (◆ ◆ ◆ ◆)**. A character with a Brawn of 2 and a threshold of 7, for example, tries to lift a rock with an encumbrance value of 10. That's 3 over, so the difficulty is **Hard (◆ ◆ ◆)**.

> ### EXAMPLE
>
> Sarenda and Pon have stolen a crate of supplies that they want to redistribute to starving refugees. Pon, who is trying to run with a crate of the food in his arms, has an encumbrance threshold of 8 (5 plus his Brawn of 3). The crate's encumbrance value is 6. Between the crate and Pon's blaster rifle and lightsaber (encumbrance value 5), he is carrying 3 over his threshold, and thus makes a **Hard (◆ ◆ ◆) Athletics check**, loses his free maneuver, and suffers ■ ■ ■ to all Agility and Brawn-based checks until he drops the crate.

Additional characters may help, adding their raw Brawn to the encumbrance threshold. In the example, a Nautolan with a Brawn of 3 adds +3 to the encumbrance threshold for that specific task.

Characters in **Force and Destiny** frequently carry small arsenals on their persons. Sometimes a character wants everyone to see the massive disruptor slung over his shoulder and the heavy blaster pistol at his hip, knowing that intimidation can often stave off a fight. But sometimes a character needs to slip in somewhere with a little extra help, such as when Artoo-Detoo entered Jabba's palace with Luke's lightsaber hidden in a secret compartment.

Items with an encumbrance value of 1 or less can be hidden on a person easily. No checks are required for successful concealment unless a foe inspects the target up close—usually with a physical pat-down. In the latter case, the searcher makes an **opposed Perception check** against the target's Stealth. Add ☐

to the searcher's check for every encumbrance point over 1 that is due to the hidden item. If there are multiple items, use the highest. The Game Master should adjust this based on the situation. An unusually large species might be able to easily conceal items with an encumbrance value of 2, for example.

The same rules can apply to similar situations—such as hiding a blaster rifle (encumbrance value 4) in a wagon of scrapped droid parts. The Game Master should decide what value of object can be hidden without being noticed, and add ☐ for every point over that.

### ENCUMBRANCE AND VEHICLES

A ship's cargo hold can house the amount of encumbrance listed in its vehicle profile. Smuggling panels have varying limits. These small caches are usually placed in secret locations around the ship to avoid detection. Most smuggling panels have an encumbrance limit of 2 to 30 depending on their size and location.

# COMBAT SKILLS

Skills represent the ability to use, identify, maintain, and care for the weapons in each category. For example, the Gunnery skill governs firing large mounted weapons such as a land-to-air laser turret or a starship's main guns—and is also used to diagnose problems, reset the system if it overheats, identify manufacturers, and so on. This section discusses Combat skills as they relate to various weapons.

## BRAWL

Brawl weapons are generally light and cover the wearer's hands. They are easy to wield in close quarters and often designed with handguards or grips to keep them from being dropped easily in a scuffle. Cesti, brass knuckles, metal claws, vibroknucklers, and weighted gloves are all examples of brawling weapons, as are the various disciplines of unarmed combat. Many beasts and several of the more savage races fight with talons or claws, and their attacks are covered by Brawl as well.

An attacker must be engaged with his target to attempt a Brawl attack.

## LIGHTSABER

Lightsabers and derivative weapons are covered under the Lightsaber skill. These weapons generate a blade of coherent energy that can cut through nearly everything except the blade of another lightsaber.

An attacker must be engaged with his target to attempt a Lightsaber attack.

## GUNNERY

Larger weaponry that generally requires a mount, turret, or placement to use effectively is covered by the Gunnery skill. Gunnery covers vehicle-mounted guns and most starship weapon systems, as well as stationary platforms for devices such as E-Web repeating blasters, ion cannons, missile banks, laser turrets, proton torpedoes, and other armaments and ordnance.

Gunnery weapons cannot be used against targets engaged with the weapon and its user.

## MELEE

Melee weapons can be either one-handed or two-handed and are generally more than half a meter in length. They vary greatly, from gaffi sticks and halberds to cortosis staves and vibroknives.

An attacker must be engaged with his target to attempt a Melee attack.

## RANGED (HEAVY)

Heavy ranged weapons are those that generally must be wielded in, or directed with, two hands, such as a bowcaster, heavy blaster rifle, or flame projector. Heavy ranged weapons also include larger thrown items, such as spears and throwing axes.

Using a heavy ranged weapon while engaged with an enemy increases the difficulty of the check by two.

# RANGED (LIGHT)

Light ranged weapons are those that can generally be wielded in one hand, such as a blaster pistol or other handgun. Light ranged weapons also include one-handed thrown items, such as bolas, knives, and grenades.

Using a light ranged weapon while engaged with an enemy increases the difficulty of the check by one.

# ITEM QUALITIES

Some equipment features special qualities that add variety and depth to the vast array of armaments in the *Star Wars* universe. Some special qualities are inherent to certain items, while others are general qualities that can be applied by the Game Master to specifically tailor an item to the story.

Special qualities are generally either passive or active. Passive qualities are always on and require no activation on the part of the user. Active qualities must be triggered by the user, often by spending one or more 💠 to activate the effect.

Item qualities usually have a number associated with them. This is their rating. Ratings affect qualities in different ways, depending on the quality in question.

Active qualities require 💠 💠 to activate unless otherwise stated in their description. Active item qualities on weapons can only trigger on a successful attack, unless specified otherwise.

## ACCURATE (PASSIVE)

Accurate weapons are easier to aim or wield, whether through design or technology. For each level of this trait, the attacker adds ■ to his attack dice pools while using this weapon.

## AUTO-FIRE (ACTIVE)

A weapon with Auto-fire can be set to shoot in rapid succession and potentially spray an area with bolts, flechettes, slugs, or other types of projectiles. The advantage in using Auto-fire is that it has the chance to hit multiple targets or to hit a single target multiple times.

As attacking with a weapon on Auto-fire is generally less accurate, the attacker must increase the difficulty of the attack check by ◇. The user may choose to not use the Auto-fire quality on a weapon; in this case, he cannot trigger the quality but also does not suffer the aforementioned penalty.

If the attack hits, the attacker can trigger Auto-fire by spending ⚡⚡. Auto-fire can be triggered multiple times. Each time the attacker triggers Auto-fire, it deals an additional hit to the target. Each of these counts as an additional hit from that weapon, and each hit deals base damage plus the number of uncanceled ✶ on the check.

These additional hits can be allocated to the original target, or to other targets within range of the weapon. If the attacker wishes to hit multiple targets, he must decide to do so before making the check. Furthermore, if he wishes to hit multiple targets, his initial target must always be the target with the highest difficulty and highest defense (if this is two separate targets, the GM chooses which target is the initial target). The initial hit must always be against the initial target. Subsequent hits generated can be allocated to any of the other designated targets.

Auto-fire weapons can also activate one Critical Injury for each hit generated on the attack, per the normal cost; the Critical Injury must be applied to the target of the specific hit.

### BLAST (ACTIVE)

The weapon has a large spread, an explosive blast, or similar area of effect, like the detonation of a grenade or a warhead fired from a missile launcher. If the attack is successful and Blast activates, each character (friend or foe) engaged with the original target suffers damage equal to the weapon's Blast rating (plus an additional wound per ✶ as usual).

In a relatively small and enclosed area, the Game Master might decide that everyone in the room suffers damage.

If the Blast quality doesn't activate, the ordnance still detonates, but bad luck or poor aim on the part of the firer (or quick reactions on the part of the victims) means the explosion may not catch anyone else in its radius. However, the user may also trigger Blast if the attack misses by spending ⚡⚡⚡. In this case, the original target and every target engaged with the original target suffers damage equal to the Blast rating of the weapon.

### BREACH (PASSIVE)

Weapons with Breach burn through the toughest armor; they are often heavy weapons or starship weapons.

Breach weapons ignore one point of armor for every rating of Breach (meaning they also ignore 10 points of soak for every rating of Breach).

### BURN (ACTIVE)

Weapons with Burn inflict damage over time. If the attack is successful, the target continues to suffer the weapon's base damage each round for a number of rounds equal to the weapon's Burn rating. Damage is applied at the start of each of the target's turns.

A victim might be able to stop the damage by rolling around on the ground and making an Agility check as an action. This is an **Average (◆ ◆) Coordination check** on hard surfaces such as the hall of a spaceship, or an **Easy (◆) Coordination check** on grass or soft ground. Jumping into a body of water stops the damage immediately. Both situations assume the flame is from actual combustion rather than a chemical reaction. With the latter, there is usually little the victim can do.

### CONCUSSIVE (ACTIVE)

The weapon's attack can leave the target shell-shocked from mighty blows or punishing shockwaves, unable to perform any but the most basic actions. The target is staggered (see page 223) for a number of rounds equal to the weapon's Concussive rating. A staggered target cannot perform actions.

### CORTOSIS (PASSIVE)

Cortosis is an ore principally found in the Outer Rim. Extremely rare and valuable, it was used primarily during the Clone Wars against the Jedi Knights. There are two varieties of cortosis ore. The rarest versions can actually short out a lightsaber's blade, causing it to fail temporarily. The far more common cortosis ore is still a miraculous substance, because when molded into armor, it forms an interlocking molecular bond that is extremely resistant to energy weapons.

Weapons with the Cortosis quality are immune to the Sunder quality. Armor with the Cortosis quality makes the wearer's soak immune to the Pierce and Breach qualities.

### CUMBERSOME (PASSIVE)

A Cumbersome weapon is large, unwieldy, awkward, or heavy. To wield a Cumbersome weapon properly, the character needs a Brawn characteristic equal to or greater than the weapon's Cumbersome rating. For each point of Brawn by which the character is deficient, he must increase the difficulty of all checks made while using the weapon by one.

### DEFENSIVE (PASSIVE)

Defensive weapons are particularly good at fending off incoming melee attacks. A character wielding a weapon with the Defensive quality increases his melee defense by the weapon's Defensive rating.

### DEFLECTION (PASSIVE)

An item with the Deflection quality increases the wearer's ranged defense by an amount equal to its Deflection rating.

### DISORIENT (ACTIVE)

A weapon with Disorient can daze an opponent. When Disorient is triggered, the target is disoriented (see page 224) for a number of rounds equal to the weapon's Disorient rating. (A disoriented target adds ■ to all skill checks he performs.)

### ENSNARE (ACTIVE)

A weapon with Ensnare binds a foe and restricts his movements. When Ensnare is triggered, the target is immobilized (see page 223) for a number of rounds equal to the weapon's Ensnare rating. An Ensnared target may attempt a **Hard (◆◆◆) Athletics check** as his action on his turn to break free from the effect. (An immobilized target cannot perform maneuvers.)

### GUIDED (ACTIVE)

Certain projectiles, such as guided missiles, may benefit from course alterations after being fired. If a character misses while firing a Guided weapon and if Guided is activated, he may make an attack check at the end of the round. The difficulty of the check is calculated by comparing the weapon's silhouette of 0 to the silhouette of the target (see page 242); the check's ◆ is equal to the weapon's Guided rating. If the check is successful, the weapon strikes the target, and damage is dealt normally.

Guided requires ⚜ ⚜ ⚜ to activate, unless otherwise specified in the weapon's description. Remember,

the Guided effect can activate on its subsequent attacks, representing the projectile continuing to track the target.

"Spoofing" is a countermeasure designed to work against a particular type of projectile, such as flares designed to draw off infrared missiles. Spoofing directly increases the defense of the target against attacks with the Guided quality.

### KNOCKDOWN (ACTIVE)

When Knockdown triggers, the target is knocked prone.

Unless specified otherwise, Knockdown requires ⚜ ⚜ to trigger, plus one additional ⚜ per silhouette of the target beyond one.

### INACCURATE (PASSIVE)

Inaccurate weapons are weapons of a shoddy or inferior construction, which means they are less likely to be accurate or precise. Alternatively, the weapon's nature may inhibit accuracy. Inaccurate weapons add ■ to the attacker's dice pool equal to their Inaccurate rating.

### INFERIOR (PASSIVE)

An Inferior item is a lackluster example of its kind, representing shoddy and poor craftsmanship. An Inferior weapon generates automatic ⚙ on all checks related to its use, and its base damage is decreased by one. Inferior armor has its encumbrance increased by one and its defense decreased by one. If it does not have defense, decrease its soak value by one, to a minimum of zero.

### ION (PASSIVE)

Ion weapons are designed to affect electrical systems instead of dealing raw damage. They are fitted to ships to knock out opponents' shields, sensors, and engines. They are shorter range than laser weapons and deal larger amounts of damage, but their damage is dealt to the target (usually a vehicle) as system strain. The damage is still reduced by armor and soak. Droids are affected by ion weapons, taking damage to their strain threshold.

### LIMITED AMMO (PASSIVE)

Some weapons fire particularly large or complex projectiles that cost significant numbers of credits or are themselves complete weapons that, once launched, are expended. A weapon with the Limited Ammo quality may be used to make a number of attacks equal to its Limited Ammo rating before it must be reloaded with a maneuver. In addition, each shot expends one of a limited number of rounds of ammo, which, once used, must be purchased or otherwise obtained before firing the weapon again. This also applies to grenades and other "one-use" weapons that have the Limited Ammo 1 quality (here, the user is not "reloading" the grenade, but drawing another to use—mechanically, they are equivalent).

### LINKED (ACTIVE)

Some weapons, like the laser cannons fitted to the X-wing, are designed to fire together at the same target. This increases the possibility of a hit as well as the damage dealt. When firing a linked weapon, on a successful attack, the weapon deals one hit. The wielder may spend 🙂 🙂 to gain an additional hit, and may do so a number of times equal to the weapon's Linked rating. Additional hits from the Linked weapon may only be applied against the original target. Each hit deals the weapon's base damage plus the total uncanceled ✵ scored on the check.

### PIERCE (PASSIVE)

An attack made with this weapon ignores one point of soak for each rank of Pierce. If the weapon has more ranks of Pierce than the target's total soak, it completely ignores the target's soak. For example, Pierce 3 against a soak of 2 ignores 2 points of soak, but the extra point of Pierce has no further effect.

### PREPARE (PASSIVE)

Weapons with this quality require time to set up before being used. The user must perform a number of preparation maneuvers equal to the weapon's Prepare rating before making attacks with that weapon.

### SLOW-FIRING (PASSIVE)

Slow-Firing weapons tend to be large, heavy, emplacement-mounted weapons such as planetary defense ion cannons and the turbolasers found on capital ships. While they deal incredible damage, they need time to recharge or cool down between shots. A weapon's Slow-Firing rating dictates how soon the weapon can be fired again after attacking. For example, a heavy turbolaser with Slow-Firing 2 must wait two rounds after being fired before it can be fired again.

### STUN (ACTIVE)

A weapon with Stun can deal strain to the target. When the Stun quality is activated, it inflicts strain equal to the weapon's Stun rating.

### STUN DAMAGE (PASSIVE)

Some weapons deal Stun damage instead of regular damage. In this case, the weapon deals damage as strain instead of wounds. This damage is still reduced by a target's soak.

A variant of this is a Stun setting. As an incidental, the wielder can choose to switch the setting of his weapon to "Stun." In this case, it does Stun damage as described previously. When weapons with a Stun setting are used to deal Stun damage, their range changes to short and cannot be increased.

### SUNDER (ACTIVE)

When activated, the attacker chooses one item openly wielded by the target (such as a weapon, shield, or item on a belt). That item is damaged one step: to minor if undamaged, from minor to moderate, or from moderate to major. If a weapon already suffering major damage is the target of a successful Sunder, it is destroyed.

Sunder requires 🙂 to activate. If activated multiple times in the same attack, each activation can be applied against the same weapon, potentially taking a weapon from undamaged to destroyed in a single attack.

### SUPERIOR (PASSIVE)

A Superior item is a sterling example of its kind, representing masterful craftsmanship. A Superior weapon generates automatic 🙂 on all checks related to its use, and its base damage is increased by one. Superior armor has its encumbrance reduced by one and its soak value increased by one.

### TRACTOR (PASSIVE)

Instead of firing searing beams of laser fire or crackling ion discharges, this weapon fires relatively harmless electromagnetic beams that ensnare ships and hold them fast in space. Tractor beams, like all weapons, are fired at their target using the appropriate skill check (generally Gunnery) with all suitable modifiers. Once the weapon hits its target, the target may not move unless its pilot makes a successful Piloting check with a difficulty equal to the tractor beam's rating.

### UNWIELDY (PASSIVE)

An Unwieldy weapon is a weapon that can be particularly awkward to use for those without impressive dexterity and hand-eye coordination. To wield an Unwieldy weapon properly, the character needs an Agility characteristic equal to or greater than the weapon's Unwieldy rating. For each point of Agility by which the character is deficient, he must increase the difficulty of all checks made while using the weapon by one.

### VICIOUS (PASSIVE)

When this weapon scores a Critical Injury or Hit, the character adds ten times the Vicious rating to the Critical roll. With Vicious 3, for example, the victim adds +30 to his Critical Injury or Hit result.

# WEAPON CHARACTERISTICS

**E**ach weapon is defined through a variety of characteristics that delineate its abilities and make it distinct. All weapons share several characteristic categories, while many feature special qualities that add additional rules to their operation.

## NAME

The general name of the weapon. This may be a broad label that applies to several closely related weapons.

## SKILL USED (SKILL)

The Combat skill used when attacking with this weapon.

## BASE DAMAGE (DAM)

The base damage the weapon inflicts. This is the minimum damage inflicted if the attack with this weapon hits. Each net ✷ generated during the attack check adds one point of damage to this base damage rating.

## CRITICAL RATING (CRIT)

Indicates the number of 💥 required to trigger Critical Injuries using this weapon. If the weapon's critical rating triggers, the character rolls percentile dice on the corresponding Critical Injury chart to determine the effect on the target. A Critical Injury can only be triggered on a successful hit that deals damage that exceeds the target's soak value.

Some weapons and talents modify this Critical Injury roll, potentially making a Critical Injury more or less effective. In addition, a character can only generate one Critical roll per hit on a target. However, if the roll generates enough 💥 to trigger the critical rating of the weapon multiple times, the character can choose to add +10 to the Critical Injury roll for each trigger after the first. More on Critical Injuries can be found on page 223.

### EXAMPLE

Kaveri the Seeker fires her blaster at a stormtrooper, generating a total of three Critical Injuries! Kaveri rolls once on the Critical Injury chart, but adds +20 to the result.

## RANGE

The range of the weapon. Range is measured in several broad range bands. Melee weapons require the attacker to be engaged with the target. Ranged weapons have ranges listed as short, medium, long, or extreme. See pages 213 and 244 for more information.

## ENCUMBRANCE (ENCUM)

Encumbrance is, in essence, an abstract measurement of how heavy and awkward something is to carry and transport. The higher the encumbrance, the more difficult the item is to carry. More details on encumbrance can be found on page 159.

## HARD POINTS (HP)

Many items can be customized to an extent determined by the number of hard points they have. The vast majority of weapons have a limited number of hard points that determine how many attachments can be mounted on them. This is covered in greater detail on page 191.

## PRICE

The price of the weapon on the open market. An (R) next to the price means the weapon is restricted and cannot be bought on the open market, in which case the price listed is the average black market price.

## RARITY

The rarity of the item, before modifiers (page 157).

## SPECIAL

These are the qualities or other special rules each weapon possesses. More in-depth descriptions of these qualities can be found on page 161, while rules specific to a certain type of weapon are detailed in the weapon's description, starting on page 167.

# WEAPON MAINTENANCE

Invariably, weapons start to wear down. Rolling ▽ results may indicate a weapon has malfunctioned, misfired, jammed, broken down, or otherwise been rendered inoperable or impaired until it can be repaired.

All weaponry, from low-tech weapons such as knives or slugthrowers to more sophisticated devices such as blasters and vibro-weapons, can be repaired with the Mechanics skill or the Combat skill used to wield the weapon. More sophisticated weapons that rely on programming, circuitry, or electronics (such as a laser turret or missile launcher) can also be repaired with the Computers skill or the Combat skill used to wield the weapon.

Weapon repairs are generally classified as minor, moderate, or major. The magnitude of the required repairs indicates two things: the severity of any penalties applied to the user when trying to operate the defective weapon, and the difficulty rating of the necessary repairs. Repairing a weapon requires adequate time and tools, generally one to two hours per difficulty level. If a character attempts repairs in less time, the difficulty increases by one. Likewise, if the character lacks the proper tools, the difficulty increases by one. These factors are cumulative, so when repairing a blaster without the proper tools and in less time, the difficulty is increased by two.

The cost of the repairs is equal to a percentage of the weapon's base cost: 25% if it's a minor repair, 50% if it's a moderate repair, and 100% if it requires major work. Reduce the total by 10% for each ✴ received on the repair check if the PC is doing it himself. (A Non-Player Character weaponsmith won't reduce his price for his skill.)

## TABLE 5–4: REPAIRING GEAR

| Repair Required | Difficulty | Penalty for Use |
|---|---|---|
| Minor | Easy (◆) | One additional ■ |
| Moderate | Average (◆ ◆) | One additional ◆ |
| Major | Hard (◆ ◆ ◆) | Unusable |

This does mean it's sometimes easier to buy a new weapon than to fix an existing one, but that isn't always possible. It also doesn't include the price of any modifications that have been made, which aren't figured into the repair cost.

### EXAMPLE

Kaveri's blaster rifle has suffered a major malfunction. The base cost of the rifle is 900 credits, so it costs her 225 credits to make a minor repair, 450 to make a moderate repair, and 900 to make a major repair. Unfortunately, she's currently journeying through the wilderness, so when she meets a wandering trader, she barters for 900 credits' worth of parts so that she can afford to attempt the **Hard (◆ ◆ ◆) Mechanics check** to fix the weapon.

## AMMO

The weapons in *Star Wars* are primarily energy-based. That, coupled with the action-packed and narrative-based gameplay in FORCE AND DESTINY, means that players do not need to track ammunition for their characters' weapons. They are always assumed to have enough power packs or clips to handle whatever firefights they encounter. This carries over to primitive weapons such as slugthrowers.

There are a few exceptions to this, of course, the primary one being weapons with the Limited Ammo quality. This quality is used to represent weapons with deliberately limited clips, such as missile tubes and proton torpedoes, as well as one-use weapons such as grenades and nets.

Another exception is when weapons do run out of ammo, such as when a combat check generates ▽ that the GM spends to make the character's ammo run out. In these cases, the weapon is out until the end of the encounter, unless the character thought ahead and brought along extra reloads (see page 189).

# WEAPON DESCRIPTIONS

Arms production is one of the most lucrative and powerful industries in the galaxy. The average galactic citizen has myriad choices for offensive and defensive weaponry. There is a blaster, bludgeon, or blade to suit nearly every requirement and taste. The following list of weapons comprises those most commonly found in the armories of the Imperial military, among the disparate operatives of the Rebel Alliance, and in the holsters of bounty hunters, wanderers, and civilians. It also includes a list of esoteric weapons used by elite Imperial agents, dark side adepts, and Force-sensitives.

## BLASTERS

Blasters are the most commonly used ranged weapon in the galaxy. They come in a dizzying array of shapes and sizes, from small holdout pieces that can be hidden in a sleeve or pocket to heavy repeaters that can destroy light vehicles. All blasters use a highly pressurized volatile combustible gas, such as Tibanna gas, as their propellant. When the weapon is fired, the gas is pushed through a second chamber that "excites" the gas. The next compartment converts the gas into energy particles, which are then focused through a lens of natural or synthetic crystal. The end result is a dense packet of charged particles that can tear through flesh, duracrete, and even armor alloys.

Most blasters can be set to Stun, a non-lethal, low-powered setting that overloads a target's nervous system and renders him temporarily paralyzed (see the Stun Damage item quality, page 164). Blasters with this ability have it noted in their special qualities, listed as "Stun setting." Stun beams may only be used at short range, no matter what the weapon's normal range is. Switching between "Stun" and "Kill" on such a weapon is relatively simple, and requires an incidental.

Some blasters that only fire stun beams are known as stingbeams or simply stun blasters. Stun blasters exchange the Stun setting of a standard blaster for the Stun Damage item quality. If a weapon doesn't usually feature a Stun setting, such as a heavy repeating blaster, it cannot be purchased as a stun blaster. Blaster carbines and all pistols, save for heavy blasters, can be purchased as stun blasters, with a cost equal to half the usual amount for the regular full-powered version.

### HOLDOUT BLASTER

Holdout blasters are lightweight, small-framed pistols designed for ease of handling and concealment. Their size makes them an excellent choice for an individual needing to travel light and to remain inconspicuous. While every bit as deadly as their larger cousins, holdout blasters suffer from reduced range

and stopping power thanks to the lighter charge and smaller amount of blaster gas they hold in their magazines. Holdout blasters are hard to find when concealed well, even with a physical pat-down.

Those searching an individual carrying a concealed holdout blaster add ■ to their Perception check.

**Models Include:** BlasTech HSB-200, Imperial Munitions Model 22T4 ISB Special, Gee-Tech No. 12 "Defender" Disposable MicroBlaster.

### LIGHT BLASTER PISTOL

Light blaster pistols combine the concealability of a holdout blaster with the performance of a standard blaster pistol. Larger than holdout blasters, they are still easily concealed in a bag or about one's person and are often carried by those who need a blaster but wish to be discreet about the fact. They are also quite easy to obtain, thanks to lighter regulations imposed on them and their classification as "sporting blasters" as opposed to combat weapons. Light blaster pistols are quite popular among sportsmen and competitive shooters, as well as the galaxy's wealthy and powerful elite, and are typically highly accurate and ornately detailed. In addition, members of smaller species carry light blaster pistols instead of larger models.

**Models Include:** Merr-Sonn Model 44, BlasTech DL-18, DDC Defender Sporter.

### BLASTER PISTOL

The ubiquitous blaster pistol is the standard by which energy-based sidearms are measured throughout the galaxy. Blaster pistols come in many styles, finishes, and configurations, from short-barreled belly guns used by back-alley killers to the sleek, efficient, deadly-looking sidearms carried by the officers of the Imperial Navy. They are produced by a number of well-respected companies, such as BlasTech and Merr-Sonn, and are carried by everyone from farmers and nomadic traders to politicians and captains of industry. In general, blaster pistols have a respectable range and stopping power, can penetrate most kinds of armor, and are versatile and reliable personal defense weapons.

**Models Include:** BlasTech DH-17, BlasTech SE-14c, Merr-Sonn Model 434.

### HEAVY BLASTER PISTOL

Nearly as powerful as most blaster rifles, heavy blaster pistols are large, bulky sidearms that are nearly impossible to conceal. With the ability to kill most sentients in one or two shots, and to penetrate even the

## TABLE 5-5: RANGED WEAPONS

| Name | Skill | Dam | Crit | Range | Encum | HP | Price | Rarity | Special |
|------|-------|-----|------|-------|-------|----|-------|--------|---------|
| **Energy Weapons** | | | | | | | | | |
| Holdout Blaster | Ranged (Light) | 5 | 4 | Short | 1 | 1 | 200 | 4 | Stun setting |
| Light Blaster Pistol | Ranged (Light) | 5 | 4 | Medium | 1 | 2 | 300 | 4 | Stun setting |
| Blaster Pistol | Ranged (Light) | 6 | 3 | Medium | 1 | 3 | 400 | 4 | Stun setting |
| Heavy Blaster Pistol | Ranged (Light) | 7 | 3 | Medium | 2 | 3 | 700 | 6 | Stun setting |
| Blaster Carbine | Ranged (Heavy) | 9 | 3 | Medium | 3 | 4 | 850 | 5 | Stun setting |
| Blaster Rifle | Ranged (Heavy) | 9 | 3 | Long | 4 | 4 | 900 | 5 | Stun setting |
| **Slugthrowers** | | | | | | | | | |
| Slugthrower Pistol | Ranged (Light) | 4 | 5 | Short | 1 | 0 | 100 | 3 | |
| Slugthrower Rifle | Ranged (Heavy) | 7 | 5 | Medium | 5 | 1 | 250 | 3 | Cumbersome 2 |
| **Explosives and Ordnance** | | | | | | | | | |
| Missile Tube | Gunnery | 20 | 2 | Extreme | 7 | 4 | (R) 7,500 | 8 | Blast 10, Breach 1, Cumbersome 3, Guided 3, Limited Ammo 6, Prepare 1 |
| Frag Grenade | Ranged (Light) | 8 | 4 | Short | 1 | 0 | 50 | 5 | Blast 6, Limited Ammo 1 |
| Stun Grenade | Ranged (Light) | 8 | NA | Short | 1 | 0 | 75 | 4 | Blast 8, Disorient 3, Limited Ammo 1, Stun Damage |
| Thermal Detonator | Ranged (Light) | 20 | 2 | Short | 1 | 0 | (R) 2,000 | 8 | Blast 15, Breach 1, Limited Ammo 1, Vicious 4 |

hard plastoid armor worn by Imperial stormtroopers, heavy blasters are favored mainly by bounty hunters and professional gunmen. The trade-off for all of this power in such a small package is that heavy blaster pistols use more power and gas per shot than lighter, more efficient models. In addition, thanks to their power and performance, the purchase and ownership of heavy blaster pistols is very heavily regulated by the Galactic Empire. Possession of a heavy blaster pistol without the proper permits carries both a large fine and, typically, a long stint in an Imperial prison.

Game Masters have the option to spend ⚙ ⚙ ⚙ or ◈ to force a heavy blaster pistol to run out of ammo (see page 212).

**Models Include:** BlasTech DT-57 "Annihilator," BlasTech DL-44, SoroSuub SSK-7.

### BLASTER CARBINE

Blaster carbines are small-framed versions of common blaster rifles, designed to deliver the power of a rifle in a smaller, easier-to-use package. Their smaller size and lighter frames make them especially useful in confined spaces, such as ship's corridors and inside buildings. Although they have the same level of stopping power as longer, bulkier rifles, they have shorter range and are typically not as accurate, thanks to their shortened barrels. Blaster carbines may be fired one-handed with no penalties at short range, just like heavy blaster pistols.

**Models Include:** BlasTech EE-3, BlasTech DC-15S, SoroSuub E-11 Carbine.

### BLASTER RIFLE

The tried-and-true blaster rifle rivals the blaster pistol in ubiquity and versatility throughout the galaxy. Countless civilian and military model blaster rifles are produced by every major arms manufacturer, from BlasTech to Zenoti Arms. At their most basic, they are large-framed, semiautomatic weapons that combine accuracy, range, and stopping power into an incredibly versatile package. Blaster rifles commonly feature long barrels; fixed alloy, composite, or wood stocks; and basic iron sights. A healthy aftermarket provides a wide variety of modifications to improve handling and accuracy. While ownership of blaster rifles is only lightly regulated, possession of military-grade blaster rifles by civilians is strictly prohibited, and being caught with a military rifle by Imperial authorities is cause for a very long stay at an Imperial prison.

**Models Include:** BlasTech E-11, BlasTech A280, Czerka Arms 84-U.

## SLUGTHROWERS

Considered crude and inefficient by most of the galaxy's inhabitants, slugthrowers possess a reputation as the weapon of provincials from exceedingly poor or isolated backwater planets. Despite this reputation, slugthrowers remain popular because they are among the most basic, easily produced, and easily maintained weapons in the galaxy. Thanks to their simplicity, slugthrowers can easily be mass-produced by any industrial or postindustrial society. They require little

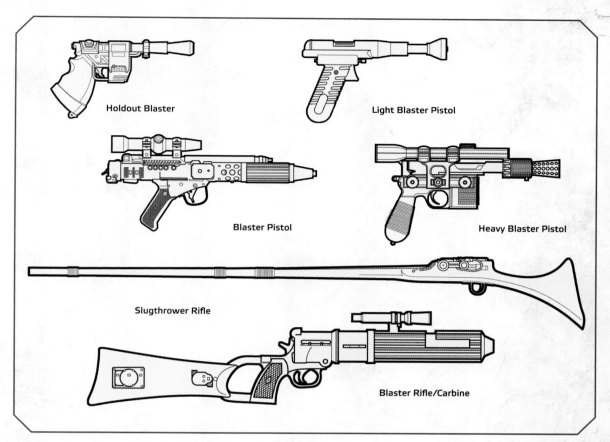

Holdout Blaster

Light Blaster Pistol

Blaster Pistol

Heavy Blaster Pistol

Slugthrower Rifle

Blaster Rifle/Carbine

in the way of modern infrastructure to build or maintain, and the tooling required to produce their inner workings can be created by even the most benighted Outer Rim world.

The downside to all of this is that slugthrowers are loud, dirty, relatively crude, and require a constant supply of finite ammunition. Whereas blaster gas can be found anywhere in the galaxy relatively easily, ammunition for slugthrowers can be terribly difficult to acquire, depending on the location. In addition, they rely on chemical combustion to propel their ammunition, which creates a deafening bang, bright flash, and cloud of smoke, depending on the propellant.

Despite their many shortcomings, slugthrowers are still popular among the occasional enthusiast or professional soldier. They are also easy to sneak past weapon scanners that look for blaster gas residue or energy signatures common to modern weapons, and they are rarely looked for in searches.

## SLUGTHROWER PISTOL

Like blaster pistols, slugthrower pistols are small, one-handed sidearms that fire lightweight ammunition over short distances. They are typically semiautomatic and magazine-fed, but a few are fed from open revolving cylinders. Slugthrower pistols are exceedingly

rare, thanks to the ubiquity of blaster technology, and they are rarely seen outside of backwater worlds and historical collections. Some professional soldiers carry a slugthrower pistol as a backup or concealed weapon, especially those individuals hailing from low-tech worlds who have a soft spot for their homeworld's technology.

**Models Include:** ODS Striker, Barimoq Industries "Protector" Revolver, Morellian Weapons Conglomerate "Enforcer" .48-caliber Pistol.

## SLUGTHROWER RIFLE

Slugthrower rifles are heavy, long-range weapons similar in size and use to blaster rifles. Although rare, they are occasionally used by professional killers, bounty hunters, and sportsmen. Rugged and reliable, slugthrower rifles are produced as either single-shot bolt-action weapons or magazine-fed semiautomatic weapons. While not as sophisticated or as potentially destructive as a blaster rifle, they are still lethal weapons with a long reach that can, depending on the properties of their ammunition, pierce even the heavy plastoid armor of Imperial stormtroopers.

**Models Include:** KiSteer 1284, Czerka Arms 6-2Aug2 Hunting Rifle, Czerka Arms Adventurer.

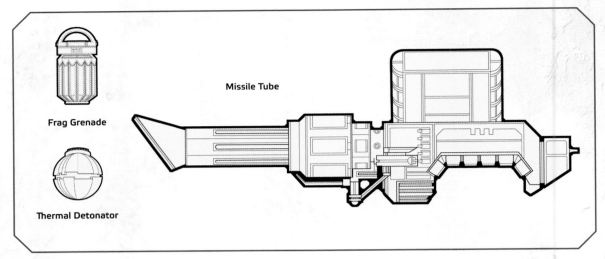

Missile Tube

Frag Grenade

Thermal Detonator

# EXPLOSIVES AND ORDNANCE

While many, if not most, adherents of the Force would prefer to use words or their elegant lightsabers to solve problems, there are occasional cases when heavier, more destructive firepower is required. For situations such as these, there are a number of heavy weapons and ordnance such as grenades and missile tubes that are perfect for tough jobs.

## MISSILE TUBE

Missile tubes are shoulder-fired, man-portable launchers capable of firing a variety of small and deadly rocket-assisted warheads. Equipped with microrepulsors and sophisticated targeting systems, missile tubes provide incredible punch in a small, easy-to-use package.

The most common models of missile tube feature three firing modes—infrared, grav-seeking, and line-of-sight—depending on the current warhead loaded. Infrared warheads home in on a vehicle's heat signature, which makes them especially useful against wheeled or tracked vehicles and walkers. Grav-seekers detect the gravity-repelling effect of a vehicle's repulsor engines and perform remarkably well against fast airspeeders. Line-of-sight, or direct-fire, warheads are typically used against slow-moving targets or fixed emplacements such as buildings, bunkers, and other fortifications. Infrared and grav-seeking warheads can be easily spoofed through the use of flares, smoke, repulsor decoys, or chaff dispensers, and use the Guided item quality in their attacks. Line-of-sight warheads are unguided, and although they require a much higher level of skill to use effectively, they cannot be spoofed by antimissile countermeasures. All missile tubes, no matter what mode they are firing in, require one preparation maneuver before firing.

**Models Include:** Golan Arms HH-15.

## FRAG GRENADE

At their most basic, frag grenades are little more than a disintegrating shell of hardened alloy or polycarbonate surrounding a small, wire-wrapped core of high explosives controlled by a simple timer. Upon detonation, frag grenades explode with a powerful blast and high-velocity cloud of razor-sharp shrapnel that proves deadly to anyone nearby.

Frag grenades can be set to detonate on impact or set with a timer to detonate up to 3 rounds after being activated at the beginning of the attacker's action. Some also have a "dead man's" or pressure switch that, once pressed, detonates immediately upon release.

**Models Include:** Merr-Sonn C-22 Fragmentation Grenade.

## STUN GRENADE

Stun grenades are effectively non-lethal defensive grenades used to disable, rather than kill, an opponent. They use a number of different technologies, ranging from sonic pulses and concussion waves to blinding phosphorous strobes, to disorient and confuse targets, allowing them to be taken alive or to be more easily restrained.

Like frag grenades, stun grenades can be set to detonate on impact or set with a timer to detonate up to 3 rounds after being activated. Stun grenades rarely have pressure detonators.

**Models Include:** Merr-Sonn C-10 Stun Grenade, Imperial Arms "Starfire" Flash Bang Grenade.

## THERMAL DETONATOR

About the size of a common frag grenade, thermal detonators are one of the most potent and feared destructive devices in the galaxy. Instead of a standard explosive core, thermal detonators use materials such as baradium to create a massive fusion detonation. This blast releases a burst of deadly radioactive particles, heat, and a shock wave that completely annihilates everything in the blast area. Thermal detonators are highly unstable and are often as much a danger to their users as their targets. Due to their instability and their sheer destructive potential, thermal detonators are strictly prohibited on many worlds. They have a reputation throughout the galaxy as terror weapons.

Any ▽ result on a check involving a thermal detonator means that the device explodes prematurely. If this should occur, the wielder takes full damage from the thermal detonator unless he has a maneuver with which he can attempt to avoid the blast. If this is the case, the wielder takes only the Blast damage from the explosion.

Thermal detonators can be set to detonate on impact or after a delay of up to 3 rounds by using the built-in timer. When used in delay mode, thermal detonators explode at the beginning of the attacker's turn when they reach their set time. Also, most thermal detonators are equipped with a dead man's switch, like that of frag grenades. Finally, thermal detonators are so potent that their Blast quality affects everyone and everything within short range of its intended target.

**Models Include:** Merr-Sonn Class-A Thermal Detonator.

# BRAWL WEAPONS

Brawl weapons are simple, often easily concealable weapons that are worn on the hands as both a means of protection and a way to increase the damage of physical blows. While there are many kinds of Brawl weapons in the galaxy, brass knuckles and shock gloves are the most common type available.

When using a Brawl weapon, users add their Brawn characteristic to the damage dealt, unless the weapon description indicates otherwise. When a Brawl weapon has its own stated damage, the inclusion of a plus sign next to the damage indicates that the user adds his Brawn to the damage dealt.

## BRASS KNUCKLES

Little more than a set of thick metal rings worn on the fingers and welded to a horizontal bar held in the fist, brass knuckles are the smallest, simplest, and easiest-to-conceal type of Brawl weapon available. Among the more civilized places of the galaxy, brass knuckles are looked down upon as the weapons of petty criminals, bounty hunters, and other undesirables.

One great advantage of brass knuckles is their ability to be concealed in a pocket or other compartment until they're needed. Add ■ to a character's Perception check when attempting to find brass knuckles on a person's body.

**Models Include:** Various models.

## REFINED CORTOSIS GAUNTLETS

Cortosis gauntlets are simply metal or composite gloves with thick forearm plates laced with cortosis ore. The cortosis in their construction allows them to block or even disrupt lightsaber blades.

When a character armed with a lightsaber makes a combat check targeting an opponent armed with refined cortosis gauntlets, ◎ ◎ ◎ or ▽ may be spent to cause a lightsaber to short out and deactivate after the combat check has been resolved. When a character armed with refined cortosis gauntlets makes a combat check targeting a character armed with a lightsaber, the attacking character may spend ♻ ♻ ♻ or ◈ to cause the lightsaber to short out and deactivate after the combat check has been resolved. The lightsaber may be reactivated as an incidental, but it may not be reactivated until after the last Initiative slot during the next round.

**Models Include:** Various models.

## SHOCK GLOVES

Produced in a variety of styles, from sleek hide gloves suitable for evening or formal wear to heavily armored gauntlets, shock gloves fit snugly over the hands and are threaded with tiny power systems that discharge powerful electric blasts. When an individual wearing shock gloves strikes a target, the gloves release stored energy in a burst of power that can knock even the toughest opponent out in an instant.

**Models Include:** Corellian Personal Defense X-21, Kamperdine "Slimline" Gloves.

# MELEE WEAPONS

In a galaxy full of deadly blasters and high-powered explosives, a Melee weapon seems an almost comical anachronism. In truth, however, the utility and deadliness of a well-honed blade or a heavy blunt object is as well-respected in modern times as at any point in galactic history. From the Rebel commando's deadly combat knife to the vibro-ax of a savage pirate on the bridge of a captured ship, Melee weapons still have their place on the modern battlefield.

Melee weapons can be useful to a well-equipped wanderer. They are typically silent, save for the high-tech vibro weapons, and they can even be improvised out of found materials in a desperate pinch. Those wandering the Outer Rim find Melee weapons' low cost and reliability extremely valuable. Larger weapons, such as force pikes and vibro-axes, have both a long reach and a high intimidation factor, often finishing an argument with their presence alone. Perhaps most importantly, Melee weapons are common, cheap, and usually not subject to the same kinds of legal restrictions that blasters and slugthrowers are.

When wielding a Melee weapon, users add their Brawn characteristic to the damage dealt, unless the weapon's description indicates otherwise. When a Melee weapon has its own stated damage, the inclusion of a plus sign next to the damage indicates that the user's Brawn is added to the damage dealt.

### ANCIENT SWORD

Some say the earliest precursors to the Jedi wielded true swords, not lightsabers, in their battles against evil. These weapons possessed strikingly shaped blades and a unique balance that made them difficult to master for those used to wielding more mundane weapons. Some whisper that those early Force-sensitive warriors could somehow imbue these weapons with the Force, making them stronger, keener, and more deadly. Whatever the truth of these rumors, there are still examples of such swords in the galaxy today. Some are artfully crafted replicas or commissioned by specific warriors, while a few are treasured heirlooms preserved from the mists of the distant past.

**Models Include:** None.

### COMBAT KNIFE

Part tool and part weapon, a good combat knife is a welcome addition to any traveler's gear. Produced in countless numbers in a dizzying array of styles, combat knives typically have a thin, razor-sharp, hardened metal clip-point blade roughly fifteen centime-ters long, mated to a polycarbonate or metal handle. The last few centimeters closest to the hand guard, if so equipped, feature a rugged serration that allows the knife to be used as a saw. Some complex knives feature built-in tools such as wire cutters, compasses, and fire starters. Whatever their features, combat knives are very handy tools for surviving in the wilder areas of the galaxy.

**Models Include:** Various models.

### CORTOSIS SHIELD

While law enforcement officers and some mercenaries might carry high-tech riot shields for use in crowd control situations, the common defensive shield is vanishingly rare on the battlefield. In the modern era of focused energy weapons, high-powered slugthrowers, and ship- and vehicle-mounted ordnance that can turn a sentient into a pile of ash in a heartbeat, even plastoid armor is of arguable value. In the face of heavy fire, most individuals prefer either to present an overwhelming force or to retreat. Those who deal with the remnants of the Jedi Order, such as the Inquisitors and the secret police units of the Galactic Empire, often have need of specialized equipment.

Cortosis shields are made from various alloys or synthetic compounds and are laced with a refined cortosis weave that absorbs blaster energy and can even turn or disrupt the blade of a lightsaber. Due to their inherent strength, cortosis shields can be used

## TABLE 5-6: MELEE WEAPONS

| Name | Skill | Dam | Crit | Range | Encum | HP | Price | Rarity | Special |
|------|-------|-----|------|-------|-------|----|-------|--------|---------|
| **Brawl Weapons** | | | | | | | | | |
| Brass Knuckles | Brawl | +1 | 4 | Engaged | 1 | 0 | 25 | 0 | Disorient 3 |
| Cortosis Gauntlets (Refined) | Brawl | +1 | 4 | Engaged | 3 | 2 | 1,000 | 7 | Cortosis |
| Shock Gloves | Brawl | +0 | 5 | Engaged | 0 | 1 | 300 | 2 | Stun 3 |
| **Melee Weapons** | | | | | | | | | |
| Ancient Sword | Lightsaber | +2 | 3 | Engaged | 3 | 1 | 350 | 8 | Defensive 1 |
| Combat Knife | Melee | +1 | 3 | Engaged | 1 | 0 | 25 | 1 | |
| Cortosis Shield | Melee | +0 | 6 | Engaged | 4 | 0 | 900 | 7 | Cortosis, Cumbersome 3, Defensive 2, Deflection 2 |
| Cortosis Staff (Refined) | Melee | +3 | 5 | Engaged | 4 | 2 | 2,500 | 7 | Cortosis |
| Cortosis Sword | Melee | +2 | 3 | Engaged | 3 | 2 | 1,350 | 7 | Cortosis, Defensive 1 |
| Electrostaff | Melee | +4 | 3 | Engaged | 4 | 3 | 4,500 | 6 | Cortosis, Cumbersome 3, Linked 1, Stun setting, Unwieldy 3 |
| Force Pike | Melee | +3 | 2 | Engaged | 3 | 3 | 500 | 4 | Pierce 2, Stun setting |
| Truncheon | Melee | +2 | 5 | Engaged | 2 | 0 | 15 | 1 | Disorient 2 |
| Vibro-ax | Melee | +3 | 2 | Engaged | 4 | 3 | 750 | 5 | Pierce 2, Sunder, Vicious 3 |
| Vibroknife | Melee | +1 | 2 | Engaged | 1 | 2 | 250 | 3 | Pierce 2, Vicious 1 |
| Vibrosword | Melee | +2 | 2 | Engaged | 3 | 3 | 750 | 5 | Defensive 1, Pierce 2, Vicious 1 |

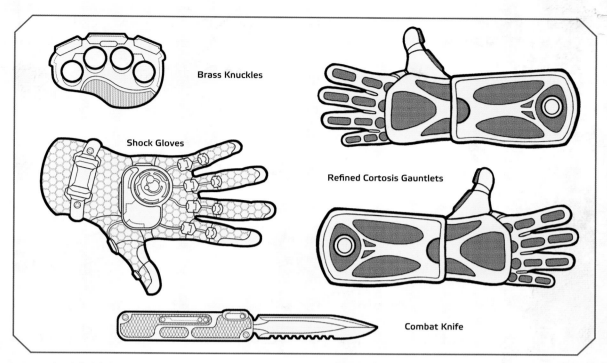

Brass Knuckles

Shock Gloves

Refined Cortosis Gauntlets

Combat Knife

as a makeshift Melee weapon, allowing a user to bash or push away an opponent.

**Models Include:** Arakyd Industries Special Order Model 3 Shield.

### REFINED CORTOSIS STAFF

From the basic, utilitarian staff of a nerf herder to high-tech weapons used to subdue unruly mobs, staffs are ubiquitous throughout the galaxy. However, what would normally be a simple and common tool can be modified into a uniquely effective weapon against Force users through the use of refined cortosis. In most forms, cortosis ore resists and absorbs energy, allowing items to withstand blows from weapons that would normally shatter them. However, specifically refined cortosis has a unique secondary effect: it can short out lightsaber blades on contact. Working with this refined cortosis is extremely difficult due to the properties of the ore, and even making a simple weapon like a staff is inordinately expensive. However, such weapons can prove a deadly advantage if someone has to face down a lightsaber-wielding enemy.

When a character armed with a lightsaber makes a combat check targeting an opponent armed with a refined cortosis staff, ✦ ✦ ✦ or ▽ can be spent to cause the lightsaber to short out and deactivate after the combat check has been resolved. When a character armed with a refined cortosis staff makes a combat check targeting a character armed with a lightsaber, the attacking character may spend ✪ ✪ ✪ or ✦ to cause the lightsaber to short out and deactivate after the combat check has been resolved.

The lightsaber may be reactivated as an incidental, but it may not be reactivated until after the last Initiative slot during the next round. Cortosis staffs require two hands to use.

**Models Include:** Various models.

### CORTOSIS SWORD

The making and use of cortosis swords is, perhaps, as old as the making and use of lightsabers. Cortosis swords were created to counter the elegant and deadly lightsabers wielded by Jedi and other Force adherents, and hopefully to grant their non–Force-using wielders some hope of survival against a determined lightsaber user. Built in a variety of styles, and using varying amounts of cortosis ore in their construction, cortosis-bladed swords, in the right hands, pose a decided threat to even the most powerful Force user.

**Models Include:** Barik Tarn Collective Razorblade.

### ELECTROSTAFF

Electrostaffs first saw widespread use during the Clone Wars among Separatist forces, especially among the personal guard droids of General Grievous. Over two meters long, electrostaves are designed to keep a Jedi or other lightsaber wielder at arms' length. Constructed from lightweight, highly durable phrik alloy, a mixture of phrikite, tydirium, and other trace ores, electrostaves can resist a lightsaber blade. In addition to their defensive capabilities, electrostaves are also equipped with small electromagnetic pulse generators at each end that constantly crackle and spit showers of sparks when active. Like force pikes, electrostaves can be set to a number of different power outputs: a mild shock used to control crowds; a powerful Stun setting that can sideline even the toughest opponent; or the full-power setting that can easily tear a sentient in half.

Electrostaves require two hands to use.

**Models Include:** Baktoid Armor Workshop vz. 890 Thunderer, Arakyd Industries Stryker.

## FORCE PIKE

Roughly two meters long, force pikes are long metal poles tipped with sharp prongs that continually spark and buzz when active. Built for crowd control and law enforcement, force pikes have two settings: vibrate and shock. On the vibrate setting, the prongs at the tip of the weapon generate a powerful vibro field that can rend flesh, shatter bone, and punch holes in artificial and natural materials. On the shock setting, the weapon generates a strong electrical charge that can

be set to various levels of intensity, from the lowest setting, used to herd crowds, to the full charge that can knock a Wookiee unconscious with one good hit.

Force pikes are very easy to use, as it takes little actual skill to swing a rod around, and they can cause incredible amounts of damage in the right hands.

When set to its Stun setting, a force pike does not benefit from the Pierce 2 quality. Force pikes require two hands to wield.

**Models Include:** SoroSuub Controller FP.

## TRUNCHEON

Made from a number of organic and inorganic materials such as metal, wood, and bone, truncheons are simple blunt weapons used by law enforcement agencies across the galaxy. These ostensibly non-lethal weapons are common in more enlightened areas where outright killing a criminal suspect is frowned upon.

**Models Include:** Various models.

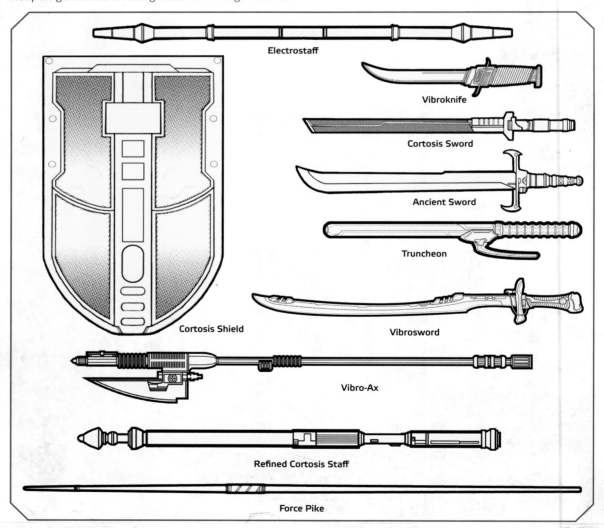

Electrostaff

Vibroknife

Cortosis Sword

Ancient Sword

Truncheon

Cortosis Shield

Vibrosword

Vibro-Ax

Refined Cortosis Staff

Force Pike

## VIBRO-AX

The average vibro-ax consists of a broad-bladed ax head mounted to a sturdy pole between one and two meters long. The ax head, typically built from sturdy and long lasting alloys and sharpened to a razor edge, is equipped with a small ultrasonic vibration generator that enhances the weapon's intrinsic combat effectiveness. The combination of the weapon's weight, the leverage from its long handle, the sharpness of its blade, and the ultrasonic generator allows users to cleave limbs and heads from even the most heavily armed opponents. While most sentients look down on the vibro-axe as a barbarian's weapon, many enforcers and self-proclaimed tough guys carry them, mostly for the intimidation factor.

Vibro-axes require two hands to wield.

**Models Include:** SoroSuub BD-1 "Cutter" Vibro-Ax.

### VIBROKNIFE

Little more than combat knives with onboard ultrasonic vibration field generators, vibroknives have evolved from individually crafted custom weapons to mass-produced commodities. The integrated ultrasonic generator causes the knife's blade to vibrate at incredibly high frequencies, greatly increasing its penetration and destructive potential. Vibroknives can saw through most materials, are easily concealed, and offer their users even more versatility than a standard combat knife.

**Models Include:** Merr-Sonn Treppus-2 Vibroblade.

### VIBROSWORD

While most cultures have moved beyond the use of bladed weapons for general use and protection, there are still some for whom intricate swordplay and the appreciation of a finely crafted blade are ingrained parts of their martial heritage. For these cultures, and for anyone who appreciates the value of a solid, well-built sword, there is the vibrosword. These weapons are a good compromise of form and function, combining the reach and weight of a traditional sword with the ultrasonic technology found in vibroknives and vibro-axes. They are produced in a variety of styles to meet the tastes and martial abilities of their users, and range from cheap, mass-produced pieces to handmade blades with ornate decoration that cost a year's wages. While not as powerful as the legendary lightsaber, vibroswords are still remarkably effective weapons that can cut through nearly any material and have the benefit of not requiring their users to be highly trained Jedi Knights.

**Models Include:** Merr-Sonn Damask-4 Duelist Sword, SoroSuub "Gladius" Vibro-Shortsword.

# LIGHTSABERS

More than any other item or cultural touchstone, the lightsaber was the symbol of the ancient Jedi Order throughout its long history. The first lightsabers were bulky, heavy affairs that bore little resemblance to the elegant weapons of today. Throughout the generations, lightsaber technology was refined from those first high-maintenance "captive bolt" lightsabers to the lightweight modern lightsaber, which utilizes a stabilized, massless plasma beam that burns as hot and bright as the core of a star.

Unlike other, lesser weapons, lightsabers were never mass-produced. Instead, lightsabers are constructed by a Force user from parts gathered or created by his own hand, and each individual lightsaber is a reflection of the builder and his connection to the Force. A basic lightsaber consists of a cylindrical hilt around 30 centimeters long. Contrary to the weapon's exotic, almost mythic nature, its base components are fairly commonplace. A diatium power generator produces an intense energy charge. This energy is routed through a series of focusing lenses and energizers that convert it into plasma, which is then projected through a kyber lightsaber crystal, which focuses the plasma in ways unique to the particular crystal. Once past the crystal, the plasma is routed through a series of field energizers and modulation circuitry within the emitter matrix, creating the final iconic humming lightsaber blade.

While they were never considered common, even at the height of the Jedi's power, today lightsabers are vanishingly rare. Thanks to Order 66 and the Empire's attempt to wipe the Jedi from the annals of history, very few lightsabers exist today. Those that do are in private collections or gathering dust on out-of-the-way worlds.

Although there are many different types of lightsabers, for rules purposes, any weapon that is listed in this section (Lightsabers) is considered a lightsaber.

Lightsabers cannot be Sundered.

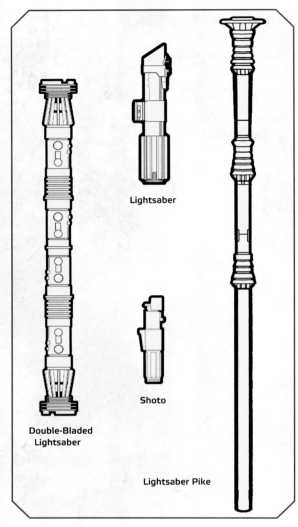

**Lightsaber**

**Shoto**

**Double-Bladed Lightsaber**

**Lightsaber Pike**

This lightsaber is a basic lightsaber hilt containing an unmodded Ilum lightsaber crystal (see page 197). This crystal occupies two of the weapon's hard points.

**Models Include:** None; each of these weapons is individually constructed.

## DOUBLE-BLADED LIGHTSABER

Known colloquially among Force adherents as light-staffs or Sith lightsabers, the dangerous double-bladed lightsabers were first designed by the Dark Lords of the Old Sith Empire. Double-bladed lightsabers consist of an oversized lightsaber hilt equipped with an upgraded power supply and twin emitter systems and crystals, one at either end of the hilt. When activated, a full-sized lightsaber blade springs from each emitter, making an exceptionally potent weapon nearly as long as a full-grown human. The weapon's twin blades allow a user to strike more rapidly, and sometimes fight multiple foes at once. Although quite dangerous and effective in combat, double-bladed lightsabers are also exceptionally difficult to master. Nevertheless, some Jedi constructed double-bladed lightsabers for themselves, including some notable figures in ancient Jedi myth.

Although technically, this weapon contains two lightsaber crystals (one for each blade), for the purposes of gameplay it is treated as having a single crystal. This lightsaber is a double-bladed lightsaber hilt containing an unmodded Ilum lightsaber crystal (see page 197). This crystal occupies two of the weapon's hard points.

When purchasing attachments for this weapon (including crystals), each attachment costs double the listed price. This represents the fact that the double-bladed lightsaber generally requires two of each attachment (one for each end). However, when installing and modding these attachments, follow all normal rules.

**Models Include:** None; each of these weapons is individually constructed.

## LIGHTSABER PIKE

Largely considered a ceremonial weapon, long associated with temple guards and Imperial bodyguards, lightsaber pikes are nevertheless potent and dangerous weapons in the right hands. Similar in construction to a force pike or electrostaff, a lightsaber pike consists of a long, sturdy haft typically made of composites or strong alloys. The haft, while a respectable weapon in its own right, contains the internal workings of a standard lightsaber. When activated, a shoto-length blade springs from the end of the haft, creating a weapon between two and three meters long. Its size gives the lightsaber pike incredible reach and respectable defensive capabilities.

This lightsaber is a basic lightsaber pike hilt containing an unmodded Ilum lightsaber crystal (see page 197). This crystal occupies two of the weapon's hard points.

## BASIC LIGHTSABER

The basic lightsaber is, in essence, the baseline to which all other lightsabers and their variants are compared. It consists of a basic hilt constructed from whatever material was available to the builder, typically metal or composites. Simple weapons, though still exceedingly elegant, all lightsabers are equipped with some form of kyber crystal. Kyber crystals are actually a broad family of different types of crystals. Though these can vary in shape and coloration, and even certain properties, kyber crystals share certain unique attributes. These attributes allow kyber crystals to be used within lightsabers, enabling them to focus the lightsabers' power into their signature energy blades. Prior to the rise of the Empire, nearly every lightsaber constructed by the Jedi Order during the Clone Wars contained a crystal gathered by a Padawan on the planet Ilum as part of the journey to become a Jedi Knight. These Ilum specimens are some of the best examples of kyber crystals.

## TABLE 5-7: LIGHTSABERS

| Name | Skill | Dam | Crit | Range | Encum | HP | Price | Rarity | Special |
|---|---|---|---|---|---|---|---|---|---|
| Basic Lightsaber | Lightsaber | 6 | 2 | Engaged | 1 | 5 | (R) 9,300 | 10 | Breach 1, Sunder |
| Double-Bladed Lightsaber | Lightsaber | 6 | 2 | Engaged | 2 | 4 | (R) 18,600 | 10 | Breach 1, Linked 1, Sunder, Unwieldy 3 |
| Lightsaber Pike | Lightsaber | 6 | 2 | Engaged | 3 | 3 | (R) 9,600 | 10 | Breach 1, Cumbersome 3, Defensive 1, Sunder |
| Shoto | Lightsaber | 5 | 2 | Engaged | 1 | 3 | (R) 9,300 | 10 | Accurate 1, Breach 1, Sunder |
| Training Lightsaber | Lightsaber | 6 | – | Engaged | 1 | 5 | 400 | 6 | Stun Damage |

**Models Include:** None; each of these weapons is individually constructed.

### SHOTO

Essentially miniaturized lightsabers, shotos are one of the more common lightsaber variants. A lightsaber created for duelists, the shoto was initially designed as an offhand weapon for individuals who practiced the two-handed Jar'Kai school of lightsaber combat. As they grew in popularity, shotos were adopted as a primary weapon by Jedi and Sith whose small statures made the use of a standard-sized lightsaber difficult or impossible. Some, especially students of the Ataru school, forsook standard-sized lightsabers altogether, instead wielding two shotos. This allowed these individuals to make good use of the acrobatic forms inherent in Ataru to deliver quicker and more accurate blows than an individual wielding a single full-sized lightsaber or even a lightsaber/shoto combination. Perhaps the most famous shoto user was the Jedi Master Yoda, who carried a green-bladed shoto which he used to shocking effect.

This lightsaber is a basic shoto hilt containing an unmodded Ilum lightsaber crystal (see page 197). This crystal occupies two of the weapon's hard points.

When installing a lightsaber crystal into a shoto, reduce the damage of that lightsaber crystal by 1.

**Models Include:** None; each of these weapons is individually constructed.

## LIGHTSABER HILTS

The soul of each lightsaber is its crystal. The Jedi of old tested their younglings by sending them to search for their lightsaber crystals. The process was as much a spiritual journey as a physical search, with the trainees confronting their inner demons as part of the process. In finding a crystal, they bonded with it in a way that transcended the physical realm.

The hilt of the lightsaber, on the other hand, is a primarily mechanical system. Individuals can customize a hilt, adding ornamentation or additional functionality just as they can with any weapon or item. In this way, an individual can make a unique hilt that is truly his, but it is still simply an item.

Provided here are the hilts for the lightsabers listed in this chapter. Each requires a crystal to become a true weapon (otherwise they deal no damage, have no critical rating, and do not have many of their item qualities). However, a PC wanting to construct their own lightsabers should start with a hilt. If the PC wants to construct his own hilt out of available materials, the GM can still have him make a check to find the hilt, based on its rarity, and pay the cost. This represents the PC finding and paying for the raw materials. Then it is simply a matter of spending a few hours putting the materials together to build the hilt—no checks are necessary.

### TABLE 5-8: LIGHTSABER HILTS

| Name | Skill | Dam | Crit | Range | Encum | HP | Price | Rarity | Special |
|---|---|---|---|---|---|---|---|---|---|
| Basic Lightsaber Hilt | Lightsaber | 0 | – | Engaged | 1 | 5 | 300 | 5 | |
| Double-Bladed Lightsaber Hilt | Lightsaber | 0 | – | Engaged | 2 | 4 | 600 | 6 | Linked 1, Unwieldy 3 |
| Lightsaber Pike Hilt | Lightsaber | 0 | – | Engaged | 3 | 3 | 600 | 7 | Cumbersome 3, Defensive 1 |
| Shoto Hilt | Lightsaber | 0 | – | Engaged | 1 | 3 | 300 | 6 | Accurate 1 |

### TRAINING LIGHTSABER

Designed to train Force users in lightsaber use, training lightsabers are low-powered, non-lethal variants of standard lightsabers. Equipped with an ultra-low-output power generator and either a kathracite or danite crystal, a training lightsaber produces a blade that, while possessing the same mass and energy characteristics as its full-powered cousins, does no lasting damage to living beings. Its permanent low-power setting allows younglings and initiates to practice their lightsaber techniques without the risk of maiming or killing their sparring partners. This is not to say that using a training lightsaber is without its risks: strikes from a training lightsaber cause heavy bruising, painful welts, and even mild burns. As they are simply common lightsabers with internal modifications, training lightsabers can be turned into full-powered lightsabers simply by changing out the power generator and replacing the crystal with a more formidable one.

This lightsaber is a basic lightsaber hilt containing an unmodded training lightsaber emitter (see page 200). This crystal occupies two of the weapon's hard points.

**Models Include:** None; each of these weapons is individually constructed.

# ARMOR

The usefulness of armor is hotly debated by those who live dangerous lives on the fringes of galactic society. A good flak vest or blast helmet can protect against splinters, shrapnel, and even glancing shots, but accurate hits can punch through most armor. Many Force-using individuals who live quiet lives in out-of-the-way corners of the galaxy prefer light and rugged pieces of armor, such as simple heavy robes or padded or heavy hide armors.

## ARMOR CHARACTERISTICS

Every piece of armor is defined through the following characteristics. Armor also shares some characteristics with weapons, notably price, encumbrance, hard points, and rarity. The descriptions of these characteristics can be found on page 165.

### DEFENSE

The armor's defense adds ■ equal to the defense rating directly to the attacker's dice pool. This reflects the armor's ability to deflect damage away from the wearer's body.

### SOAK

A suit of armor's soak is added to the wearer's Brawn and subtracted from any incoming damage suffered. If an attack causes 10 damage, for example, a soak of 2 plus a Brawn of 2 reduces the damage incurred by four, leaving a total of six points of damage.

### ENCUMBRANCE

Each full suit or discrete piece of armor has a listed encumbrance rating. Armor's encumbrance rating only comes into play when a suit or piece of armor is carried instead of worn. When worn, armor's encumbrance rating is reduced by 3 points.

## ARMOR TYPES

Below is a list of the most common types of armor worn by individuals throughout the galaxy.

### ADVERSE ENVIRONMENT GEAR

In the course of their wandering existence, Force adherents may find themselves in some of the most inhospitable environments the galaxy has to offer. Whether due to the blistering heat of Tatooine or the frigid cold of Hoth, many worlds require the use of adverse environment gear. Specialized clothing that wicks away sweat or retains body heat, respirators and gas masks, sealed environment suits, polarized goggles, and water recyclers are all examples of adverse environment gear.

Characters with this gear may ignore ■ imposed by the environment in which they find themselves. The gear must be appropriate for the environment at hand.

**Models Include:** Pretormin Environmental HS-90 Hazmat Suit, ScorSear 200 Survival Kit.

### ARMORED CLOTHING

Available in a variety of styles, armored clothing is an excellent option for those who prefer light, flexible protection. While bulkier than normal clothing, armored clothing can be tailored to fit any taste and retain its effectiveness. Lighter types typically rely solely on energy-dispersion mesh and the strength of the material to provide protection, but more advanced types offer additional protection in the form of strategically located plastoid or ceramic armor plates sewn into the clothing.

Detecting that clothing is armored requires an **Average (♦ ♦) Perception check**.

**Models Include:** Ayelixe Fabrico Armorweave, A/KT Tuff1 Combat Jumpsuit.

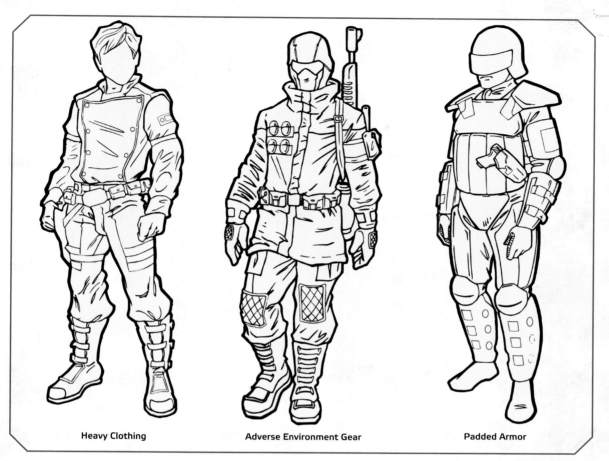

Heavy Clothing       Adverse Environment Gear       Padded Armor

## ARMORED ROBES

Often worn by Jedi engaging in dangerous activity during the Clone Wars, armored robes grant exceptional protection. Armored robes are distinct and unmistakable, however, making them uncommon in Imperial space. Durable, hard-wearing robes are draped over a variant on the standard Jedi tunic and pants. Attached to the tunic and pants are sets of plasteel plates that provide similar protection to heavy battle armor. Of course, such gear is highly illegal on any Imperial world.

**Models Include:** Various cuts and styles.

## CONCEALING ROBES

Many ancient Jedi Knights favored heavy concealing robes for their anonymity, and now Force users throughout the galaxy use them to avoid notice. While they can be made in a variety of styles from nearly any material, all concealing robes are many-layered, floor-length garments with deep hoods which can easily obscure an individual's shape and hide his face in shadow and folds of cloth.

Thanks to their cut and construction, concealing robes add ■ to checks to notice or recognize an individual wearing them.

**Models Include:** Various cuts and combinations.

## TABLE 5-9: ARMOR

| Type | Defense | Soak | Price | Encumbrance | Hard Points | Rarity |
|------|---------|------|-------|-------------|-------------|--------|
| Adverse Environment Gear | 0 | 1 | 500 | 2 | 1 | 1 |
| Armored Clothing | 1 | 1 | 1,000 | 3 | 1 | 6 |
| Armored Robes | 1 | 2 | (R) 4,500 | 5 | 2 | 8 |
| Concealing Robes | 0 | 1 | 150 | 1 | 0 | 2 |
| Heavy Clothing | 0 | 1 | 50 | 1 | 0 | 0 |
| Padded Armor | 0 | 2 | 500 | 2 | 0 | 1 |

## HEAVY CLOTHING

Heavy clothing typically consists of sturdy, well-made articles of clothing built to withstand the rigors of life in the galaxy. While a thick hide jacket, a reinforced mechanic's jumpsuit, or a thick woolen cloak doesn't offer much in the way of protection from blasters, it can absorb weak blows.

**Models Include:** Ayelixe Fabrico "Hard Wear" work clothes, Kamperdine Clothing Specialists ToughSuit adventuring gear.

### PADDED ARMOR

Made of thick, reinforced, wear-resistant textiles woven with energy-dispersion mesh, padded armor is a common form of personal protection. While it provides little protection from direct blaster hits, padded armor can shrug off glancing blows from energy weapons, and it absorbs shock waves and deflects shrapnel reasonably well. Pad-

Armored Robes

Concealing Robes

ded armor also has the benefit of being relatively comfortable to wear.

**Models Include:** Creshaldyne Industries Light Combat Armor.

# GEAR

While enlightenment and a connection to the Force is enough for some, there are those who need more than a rough-hewn brown robe and a trusty lightsaber. For those more worldly and connected Force adherents, the galaxy offers a dizzying array of gear, tools, and other sundries to help them in their daily work.

## COMMUNICATIONS EQUIPMENT

The following is a small selection of common communications devices used throughout the galaxy.

### COMLINK

Comlinks are the most common communication devices in the galaxy. Small, convenient, and easy to

use, they come in a variety of designs ranging from complex handheld devices that can transmit audio, video, and data to simple headset comlinks used to talk to nearby companions.

Most are simple two-way devices that can transmit and receive to a single mated unit at relatively long ranges over land and even into low orbit, but there are models that can transmit to multiple users at once or network whole groups together on the same frequency. Larger, longer-range models are carried in a satchel or backpack and can reach across entire planets. Most comlinks, especially those made specifically for military or law enforcement use, can be encrypted for secure lines of communications. While they are largely foolproof, comlinks can be disrupted by certain terrain features, atmospheric disturbances, and deliberate signal jamming.

### HOLO-MESSENGER

Small, complex devices roughly the size of a human hand, holo-messengers are used when a personal touch is needed in the sending of a message. Equipped with a small holographic display emitter, these devices can be used either to send a one-time recorded message or to act as a receiver and display device for holographic transmissions. When used, the messenger projects its hologram either directly over the user's hand or anywhere he wishes up to a meter away. Holo-messengers are easily concealed and transported, and are often used to send and receive secret messages.

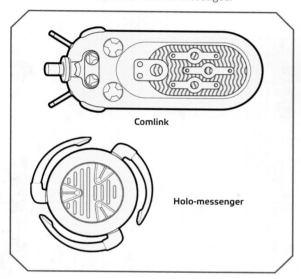

Comlink

Holo-messenger

# DRUGS AND POISONS

Despite a persistent and well-deserved negative reputation, drugs and poisons have been used to coerce, kill, or incapacitate for millennia. Produced in countless forms, from contact applications to aerosols to simple food additives, poisons and illicit drugs are highly restricted, and their possession and use carry harsh penalties. While some have more subtle effects and can be used to alter a target's mind or extract information, most are designed simply to kill as quickly and efficiently as possible.

Unless specified otherwise, characters use the Resilience skill to resist poisons.

### SYNTHETIC ANESTHETIC

This is a general anesthetic produced on many worlds for medical procedures and designed to render the user unconscious. This poison may be introduced into a target's body via aerosol deployment, food ingestion, or injection via an applicator or dart. A single dose has an **Average (◆ ◆)** difficulty, while two or more

doses combined into a single application have a **Hard (◆ ◆ ◆)** difficulty. The poison inflicts 5 strain if the target fails the check. If the check generates one to two ۞, the target must also give up his free maneuver during his next turn (he may still take two maneuvers, however); if it generates ۞ ۞ ۞ or more, he's staggered during his next turn. Finally, the GM can spend ▽ to make the target test against the poison again during the next round, as the poison remains in his system.

### SYNTHETIC NEUROPARALYTIC

Poisons that paralyze a target but leave higher cognitive functions intact (and do not kill the target) are difficult to create and administer. Certain types do exist, however, and are popular among Rebels tasked with infiltration and targeted kidnapping of Imperial officials. This poison may only be introduced into a target via injection, as with an applicator or dart. Any dose size has a **Hard (◆ ◆ ◆)** difficulty. The poison immobilizes the target for three rounds if the target fails the check. In addition, each ۞ generated inflicts 1 strain on the target, and the GM can spend ▽ to make the target test against the poison again during the next round, as the poison remains in his system.

### SYNTHETIC NEUROTOXIN

This is a general poison synthetically produced on hundreds of worlds (often illegally) that affects the

## CONSUMABLES

Shelter from the elements and the searching eyes of Imperial agents are only a part of day-to-day survival for a Force user. Even the great Jedi Master Yoda, safe and secure in the swamps of Dagobah, needed his three meals a day to live to the end of his nine-hundred–odd years. For an individual surviving on the fringes of society and hunted by the government, having a secure, or semi secure, source of food can mean the difference between life and death.

There are possibly more types of alcoholic beverages than any other type of food or drink in the galaxy. Most are created as a by-product of natural chemical reactions involving plant matter, though synthetic variants do exist as well. Depending on the world and culture, alcohol can be illegal, religiously taboo, included as ritual custom, commonplace, or even an established part of daily life. The price and quality of alcohol runs the gamut from deadly and nearly unpalatable rotgut distilled in a tramp freighter's head and almost guaranteed to blind or kill a drinker to rare and refined spirits that, by the bottle, sell for the cost of an Imperial cruiser.

The price and quality of food varies widely as well. From bland ration wafers to simple, hearty meals served in camps and spaceport cantinas to the luxurious spread of the Emperor's personal table, there exists something in the galaxy for every palate. Meals can range in cost from the incredibly inexpensive to the inordinately luxurious and costly, making the listing of prices for food or drink both unnecessary and largely impossible. Purchasing food or drink should seldom come up in a game, however, unless it adds to the narrative of the story.

biochemical reactions of most creatures, sometimes fatally. This poison may be introduced into the target's body via aerosol deployment, food ingestion, or injection via an applicator or dart. A single dose has an **Average (◆ ◆)** difficulty, while two or more doses combined into a single application have a **Hard (◆ ◆ ◆)** difficulty. The poison inflicts 5 wounds if the target fails the check. Each ✹ generated inflicts 1 strain on the target as the effort of fighting the poison overwhelms him. Finally, the GM can spend ▽ to make the target test against the poison again during the next round, as the poison remains in his system.

# CYBERNETIC ENHANCEMENTS AND REPLACEMENTS

Developed centuries ago, cybernetic and prosthetic technology returned sight to the blind and mobility to the grievously injured, and improved the lives of countless sentients. It also changed the face of medicine, labor, and even warfare, as organs and limbs could be replaced with stronger, hardier artificial systems. Some cybernetic enhancements are visible, either because the wearer cares little for the opinions of polite society or because he cannot afford better. Others are near-perfect duplicates of lost limbs or are hidden within the body, invisible to the casual observer.

Cybernetic enhancements and replacements increase skills or characteristics, providing raw bonuses to an individual character's abilities. The combination of XP-purchased increases and the increases provided by cybernetics can improve a character's skill or characteristic one step above the normal maximum (7 for characteristics, 6 for skills).

A character may only purchase and install a number of cybernetic enhancements and replacements equal to his Brawn rating.

The cybernetic enhancements listed here are obviously mechanical in nature, with the exception of BioTech Industries Repli-Limb Prosthetics. These do not enhance the user as the other cybernetic devices do, as they are designed to function identically to the original limb, and are covered with synthflesh so that they look virtually indistinguishable from that which they replace.

Cybernetic implants have a serious drawback in that they are affected by weaponry designed to disable technology, such as ionization blasters and ion cannons. If hit by a weapon that normally would only affect droids, a cybernetic enhancement temporarily stops working for the remainder of the scene or until repaired. The consequences depend on the enhancement in question and are left up to the GM, but should make sense. For example, a character with two malfunctioning cybernetic legs would not only lose any bonuses from the legs, but would also be unable to walk.

### CYBERNETIC ARMS (MOD V AND MOD VI)

Built by companies such as BioTech to fit nearly every sentient species in the galaxy, cybernetic arms are designed to increase an individual's strength or agility, depending on the model. While intended primarily as simple replacements for lost limbs, many are purchased by individuals seeking to increase their abilities by grafting technology directly to their bodies.

Mod V cyberams provide +1 Brawn, while Mod VI cyberarms provide +1 Agility. If a character replaces both arms with cybernetic enhancements, both arms

## TABLE 5-10: GEAR AND EQUIPMENT

| Item | Price | Encum | Rarity |
|---|---|---|---|
| **Communications Equipment** | | | |
| Comlink (Handheld) | 25 | 0 | 0 |
| Comlink (Long Range) | 200 | 2 | 1 |
| Holo-Messenger | 250 | 0 | 4 |
| **Drugs and Poisons** | | | |
| Synthetic Anesthetic (1 dose) | 35 | 0 | 4 |
| Synthetic Neuroparalytic (1 dose) | (R) 75 | 0 | 6 |
| Synthetic Neurotoxin (1 dose) | (R) 50 | 0 | 6 |
| **Cybernetic Enhancements and Replacements** | | | |
| Cybernetic Arms | 10,000 | – | 6 |
| Cybernetic Brain Implant | 10,000 | – | 6 |
| Cybernetic Eyes | 7,500 | – | 6 |
| Cybernetic Legs | 10,000 | – | 6 |
| Cyberscanner Limb | 4,000 | – | 7 |
| Prosthetic Replacement (Limb) | 2,000 | – | 4 |
| Prosthetic Replacement (Organ) | 1,000 | – | 4 |
| **Scanning and Surveillance Equipment** | | | |
| Electrobinoculars | 250 | 1 | 1 |
| Macrobinoculars | 75 | 1 | 2 |
| General Purpose Scanner | 500 | 2 | 3 |
| Hand Scanner | 100 | 0 | 2 |
| Scanner Goggles | 150 | 0 | 3 |
| **Medical Equipment** | | | |
| Bacta (Liter) | 20 | 1 | 1 |
| Bacta (Tank) | 4,000 | 12 | 1 |
| Emergency Medpac | 100 | 1 | 1 |

| Item | Price | Encum | Rarity |
|---|---|---|---|
| **Medical Equipment (Continued)** | | | |
| Physician's Kit | 400 | 2 | 2 |
| Stimpack | 25 | 0 | 2 |
| Synthskin/Synthflesh | 10 | – | 1 |
| **Security Equipment** | | | |
| Binders | 25 | 2 | 4 |
| Disguise Kit | 100 | 0 | 5 |
| Electronic Lock Breaker | (R) 1,000 | 1 | 5 |
| Restraining Bolt | 35 | 0 | 0 |
| **Survival Gear** | | | |
| Breath Mask/Respirator | 25 | 1 | 1 |
| Field Ration Pack | 5 | 0 | 0 |
| Spacesuit | 100 | 4 | 1 |
| Tent | 100 | 4 | 1 |
| Thermal Cloak | 200 | 2 | 1 |
| Wilderness Survival Kit | 350 | 5 | 2 |
| **Tools and Electronics** | | | |
| Backpack | 50 | – | 0 |
| Climbing Gear | 50 | 1 | 2 |
| Datapad | 75 | 1 | 1 |
| Extra Reload | 25 | 1 | 1 |
| Fusion Lantern | 150 | 2 | 2 |
| Glow Rod | 10 | 1 | 0 |
| Tool Kit | 350 | 4 | 2 |
| Utility Belt | 25 | – | 0 |

must be the same model, as they are designed to work in tandem. Modifiers from both arms do not stack.

**Models Include:** BioTech Industries Cyberarm Mod V and Mod VI.

### CYBERNETIC BRAIN IMPLANT

These enhancements are miniaturized computer implants designed to augment the user's brainpower. The implant fits around the user's ears and back of the head, granting superior reasoning and fast calculation as well as memory storage.

A cybernetic brain implant provides +1 Intellect and includes a comlink and computer access link.

**Models Include:** BioTech Borg Construct Aj^6 Cybernetic Implant.

### CYBERNETIC EYES

Cybernetic eyes were designed to restore sight to the blind. While they are obviously mechanical, which some species find unsettling, they grant the user increased visual acuity and recognition.

Cybernetic eyes provide +1 Vigilance and Perception.

**Models Include:** Athakam MedTech SharpEyes.

### CYBERNETIC LEGS (MOD II AND MOD III)

To assist those who have lost legs to accident or disease, many biotechnology companies produce replacement cyberlegs. Unlike cyberarms, cyberlegs must be purchased and installed in pairs. Most are simple replacements, tailored to the user's height, weight, and strength, but other, more advanced, models can increase strength and agility, just as cyberarms do.

Note that cyberlegs must be purchased as a pair. Mod II cyberlegs provide +1 Brawn, while Mod III cyberlegs provide +1 Agility. The wearer must have both legs replaced to receive the characteristic bonus.

**Models Include:** BioTech Industries Cyberleg Mod II and Mod III.

## CYBERSCANNER LIMB

More than a simple cybernetic replacement, this cybernetic arm includes a basic scanner for medium-range detection. Cyberscanner limbs typically display data on a holoprojector that appears above the user's open palm and can show nearby motion, life forms, energy signatures, and other common targets as desired. The Mod IV Scanner Limb incorporates a portable scanner and, unlike most cybernetics, is concealed by a synthflesh covering to disguise the fact that there is anything out of the ordinary about the limb.

**Models Include:** Neuro-Saav Technologies Cyber-Scanner Limb, NeuroFabritech ScanMaster Arm.

## PROSTHETIC REPLACEMENTS

Given the dangerous and often violent nature of the galaxy, the loss of limbs is relatively commonplace among those who operate outside of general galactic society. Internal organs, eyes, and other delicate and sensitive bodily systems are also often damaged or completely destroyed through accident, disease, or violence. While cloning technology and flesh regenerators can be used to repair such losses, these options are expensive and often highly illegal. Instead, many opt for mechanical replacements.

For those seeking high-quality, unobtrusive replacements for lost limbs, prosthetic replacements are among the more popular options. These systems are designed to provide functionality identical to that of the original limb or organ, and are installed with a synthflesh covering that makes them almost indistinguishable from the organic components they replace.

Limbs and major organs can all be replaced with prosthetics. Prosthetics do not provide any bonuses or enhancements to the character, but do restore the character to full functionality. There are two general cost entries for prosthetic replacements: the first is for limbs, the second for organs. However, the GM should feel free to increase or decrease costs depending on the specific circumstances.

**Models Include:** BioTech Industries Repli-Limb Prosthetic Replacements.

# SCANNING AND SURVEILLANCE EQUIPMENT

Scanning and surveillance equipment is designed to keep a watchful eye on a target or area, typically from far off or from within a concealed area, and to transmit that data back to its users. These items are commonly used by law enforcement agencies and others who need to keep a sharp eye on their surroundings.

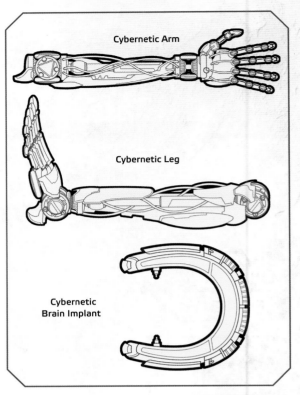

Cybernetic Arm

Cybernetic Leg

Cybernetic Brain Implant

## ELECTROBINOCULARS

Electrobinoculars are, at their most basic, a pair of macrobinoculars with one or more integrated optical enhancement systems, such as long-range digital zoom, passive light amplification, thermal imaging, ultrasound imaging, and the like. They are commonly equipped with filters to adjust for exceedingly high levels of light, and many are equipped with recording and playback systems for the collection of data.

Electrobinoculars allow the user to see normally in low light or extremely bright conditions. They also provide magnification of targets up to ten kilometers away. When using electrobinoculars, characters may also remove ■ imposed due to long range or poor light.

**Models Include:** Neuro-Saav Model TD2.3 Electrobinoculars, Fabritech "Longsight" Electrobinoculars, TaggeCo Model 3 Imperial Army Electrobinoculars.

## MACROBINOCULARS

Simpler, less expensive, and often more reliable than electrobinoculars, macrobinoculars are a common sight throughout the galaxy. Macrobinoculars use a combination of precision-ground magnifying lenses and simple technical upgrades such as image stabilization, light filtering, and image sharpening to magnify targets and allow users to see over long distances.

**Models Include:** Numerous variants.

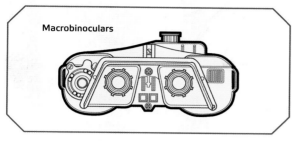

Macrobinoculars

## GENERAL PURPOSE SCANNER

Common scanners are usually small, handheld devices designed to sense and record a variety of data. Depending on the make and model, scanners can detect nearby life signs and heat signatures, different sources of radiation, the source and direction of different sounds, or any combination thereof. Some models scan in all directions, while others must be pointed in the desired direction for scanning. Some even have integrated metal detectors and the ability to intercept and record comlink traffic. Most scanners have an operational range of up to one and a half kilometers.

**Models Include:** Cryoncorp EnhanceScan General Purpose Scanner, Crozo Industrial Mineral Scanner, CUE GenScan.

## HAND SCANNER

The term "hand scanner" is a catchall designation used to describe a wide variety of handheld scanning devices used for specialized purposes. Medisensors, circuit tracers, materials fatigue and stress-fracture scanners, scanners designed to detect specific gasses or minerals, and narrow-band comlink scanners are all examples of devices that fall under the hand scanner banner. Most hand scanners can be connected to larger computer systems for the collection and analysis of data.

**Models Include:** BioTech RFX/K Medisensor, Soro-Suub Model 808 Materials Integrity Scanner.

## SCANNER GOGGLES

Scanner goggles are a lighter, wearable version of electrobinoculars that provide wearers with a suite of hands-free optical enhancements. Produced in a variety of styles, scanner goggles typically feature passive light amplification and thermal imaging, along with polarized lenses and a number of filters for different lighting situations.

When worn, scanner goggles allow the wearer to see normally in dark conditions.

**Models Include:** Fabritech X-2000 Scanner Goggles, Torjeka B3, TaggeCo Luminator Goggles.

# MEDICAL EQUIPMENT

Life in the wilder parts of the galaxy is, by nature, a rough-and-tumble existence. Whether living alone in the wilderness or wandering the stars aboard a tramp freighter, the galaxy's few remaining Force adherents are more prone to accident and injury than the average galactic citizen. The solitary lives of these gifted individuals are necessarily led far away from polite galactic society. Due to the nature of these locales, access to portable medical care and equipment is of paramount importance. While a dip in a bacta tank may be out of reach for many, items like stimpacks, synthflesh, and survival kits go a long way in easing the burdens of injury.

## BACTA

An ancient healing technology, bacta is nothing less than a miracle. Developed thousands of years ago, bacta is a viscous, clear liquid within which live millions of genetically altered and synthetic bacteria. Usable on nearly every species in the galaxy, bacta drastically increases the rate of healing and cures even the most grievous wounds with little-to-no scarring. Typically, patients are completely immersed in large bacta tanks, where they stay suspended in the thick liquid while hooked up to life-support systems. As this takes quite a bit of infrastructure, bacta tanks are relatively rare outside of large medical facilities. Bacta can be administered by injection or by pretreated patches, however, and is included in every medpac sold in the galaxy in one form or another.

Bacta provides greatly accelerated healing rates, as described on page 226.

**Models Include:** None.

## EMERGENCY MEDPAC

Small and easily stored in a backpack or small storage compartment, these lifesaving kits contain the basic supplies for healing small injuries as well as those needed to stabilize seriously wounded individuals for transportation to larger medical facilities. A standard emergency medpac contains a number of bandages and dressings; bacta patches; basic medical tools such as scalpels, syringes, and forceps; blood coagulators; synthflesh applicators; and other necessities. More advanced models include a limited-function medical scanner that can monitor vital signs and a small computer that includes a medical database and can suggest treatment options based on scan results.

Emergency medpacs allow characters to use the Medicine skill to heal others without penalty, as described on page 226.

**Models Include:** Athakam MedTech Survival Medpac, Chiewab GLiS Emergency Medpac.

## PHYSICIAN'S KIT

Carried by doctors and healers on backwater worlds, physician's kits are bigger and more comprehensive than their medpac cousins. While some contain the usual technological medical equipment such as mediscanners, diagnostic computers, spray splints, and the like, many users augment the included medical gear and medications with more holistic or natural healing products. It's not unknown for a physician's kit to include all manner of salves, tinctures, poultices, and special bandages made from local flora and fauna.

A physician's kit allows a user to perform relatively complex medical procedures in the field. Like emergency medpacs, physician's kits allow a character to use the Medicine skill without penalty, as per the rules on page 226, and in addition grant ☐ to all Medicine skill checks. Also, thanks to their stock of stimulants and other unguents, these kits add an automatic ✪ to successful Medicine checks made while using the kit.

**Models Include:** Numerous variants.

## STIMPACK

Stimpacks are small, single-use autoinjector systems containing a powerful cocktail of bacta, painkillers, anti-inflammatories, antibiotics, and other medications designed for quick healing in the field. Stimpacks are produced by most pharmaceutical corporations, especially Chiewab and Athakam.

It takes a maneuver for a character to inject a stimpack into himself or another. Stimpacks are one-use items, and they automatically heal 5 wounds. Characters can use stimpacks more than once, but each use heals one fewer wound (so the second use heals four, the third use heals three, and so on). The sixth stimpack heals no wounds—the character is already too oversaturated with the medicine for it to have any effect. It takes a day for the character's body to process the stimpacks and to be able to use them at full effectiveness. See page 227 for more information.

**Models Include:** Numerous variants.

## SYNTHSKIN/SYNTHFLESH

Synthskin and synthflesh are two versions of a synthetic, skinlike covering used in medicine and the production of cybernetic limbs. Sold as small patches, full sheets, or a thick gel, both are used to heal abrasions, cuts, and other minor wounds, as well as for skin grafts and cosmetic surgeries to replace large areas of dead or damaged skin. Synthskin is the more common type, and is used more often in emergency medical or surgical applications, while synthflesh is typically used to cover cybernetic limbs or even whole droids to disguise their artificial nature.

Synthskin applications are one-use items that can be used as first aid to treat cuts and bruises.

**Models Include:** BioTech FastFlesh Synthskin Slap Patch.

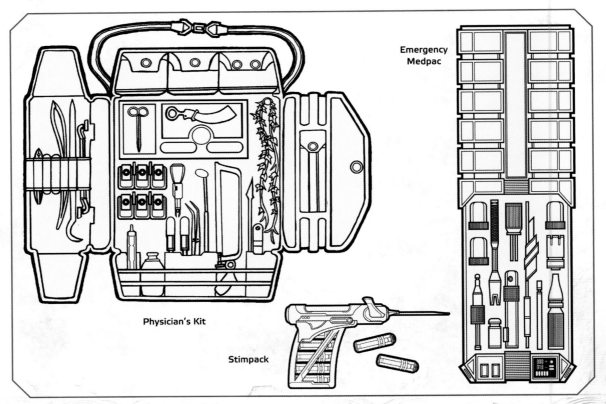

Emergency Medpac

Physician's Kit

Stimpack

Binders

Electronic Lock Breaker

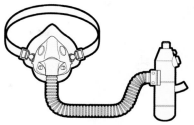

Breath Mask and Respirator

# SECURITY EQUIPMENT

While sneaking and skulduggery may seem unbecoming to Force users, there are times when secrecy and discretion are the better parts of valor. Avoiding Imperial attention often requires as much disguise and misdirection as being a guerrilla fighter or a common petty criminal, and many of the same tools are used.

## BINDERS

Binders are simple restraints used to keep prisoners subdued and manageable. They come in many shapes, sizes, and styles, and many are tailored to the strengths and weaknesses of different sentient species.

Breaking free from a set of binders requires either brute force or incredible feats of agility and flexibility. The difficulty varies by the make and model of binders, but the most common restraints require a **Daunting (♦♦♦♦) Athletics** or **Coordination check** to escape.

**Models Include:** LSS Bind-1.

## DISGUISE KIT

While use of Force abilities can cloud minds and obscure faces, even the most ardent follower of the Force enjoys the security of physical backups. Disguise kits are simple collections of makeup, wigs, hairpieces, prosthetic features, chromatic iris alternators, and even programmable skinweave for altering fingerprints and DNA cloaks to spoof advanced genetic scanners. In addition, they contain basic camouflage paints to help an individual blend more easily into the surroundings.

**Models Include:** LV Labs Flex-Mask Disguise System, Mehrak Corporation AlterEgo Street Makeup Kit.

## ELECTRONIC LOCK BREAKER

Much of the information and many of the artifacts so diligently sought after by those serving the Force, when they haven't been destroyed or lost forever, are kept behind securely locked doors by the Emperor and Lord Vader. Most locking mechanisms in the galaxy use complex electronic systems. Electronic lock breakers are small, powerful, limited-use slicing rigs designed to cut through the most common types of computerized locks. As with most equipment, lock breakers are available in a variety of models, from low-tech versions used to override simple civilian locks to heavily modified, military-grade lock slicers that can grant a user access to the bridge of an *Imperial*-class Star Destroyer.

**Models Include:** Locris Syndicated Securities "Skeleton Key" Locksmith's Tool.

## RESTRAINING BOLT

Restraining bolts are to droids what binders are to sentient creatures. Using magnetic clamps or chemical adhesives, restraining bolts attach to a droid's chassis and are used to control its actions, usually by means of a remote control. The most basic restraining bolts simply shut a droid down, allowing the user to bypass guards and incapacitate any droid witnesses. More advanced systems can be used to make a droid follow the orders of the person holding the restraining bolt controller.

Most droids cannot withstand the powerful programming overrides in a restraining bolt. However, Player Character droids are made of sterner stuff than their NPC comrades and can, with the right amount of effort, overcome a restraining bolt. PC droids may make a **Daunting (♦♦♦♦) Discipline check** to shake off the effects of a restraining bolt and act normally after one is applied. After a failed check, they may make another attempt at a later time at the Game Master's discretion.

**Models Include:** Industrial Automaton Master Control Restraining Bolt.

# SURVIVAL GEAR

Survival in the wilder parts of the galaxy requires great stamina, quick wits, and a sharp mind. Along with acquired knowledge, natural gifts, and a reliable weapon, specialized tools and equipment can contribute significantly to survival in any number of environments.

## BREATH MASK AND RESPIRATOR

Designed to allow sentient beings to breathe in dangerous atmospheres, respirators and breath masks are common pieces of survival gear. At their most basic, respirators are small plugs worn in the nose that filter atmospheric contaminants. More sophisticated versions feature partial or full face masks with on-board atmospheric gases and adjustments for pressure and gas mix. Some are even designed to be used underwater, employing a synthetic gill technology to allow air-breathing sentients to breathe water or to carry their required atmospheric gases with them into the deeps.

**Models Include:** Gandorthral Atmospherics Roamer-6.

## FIELD RATION PACK

Ration packs are typically bland, flavorless affairs that contain an entire meal packed with necessary nutrients and vitamins in a small, easily portable bag or box. They contain everything needed to heat and eat, with a chemical heater, an entree, sides, and often a dessert. Also included are disposable eating utensils and small single-serving packets of spices and condiments. Each ration pack is good for one meal. Ration packs are produced in a dizzying array of styles suited to the metabolisms of most species in the galaxy.

**Models Include:** Adventure Hiker and Hunter Trail Rations, Chiewab Nutrition ReadiMeal.

## SPACESUIT

Spacesuits are sealed, sometimes lightly armored full-body suits worn to protect individuals from the temperatures, extreme radiation, and vacuum of deep space. Spacesuits contain on-board life support systems as well as biomonitors that keep track of the wearer's physical state. Spacesuits have limited consumables, as they are typically designed for short operations; they generally have enough water and atmospheric gas on board for two or three hours of constant operation. Many variants also include a number of small, multidirectional maneuvering thrusters, built-in spotlights, comlinks, magboots, power couplings for hand tools, and any number of other convenient accessories. Every spacesuit sold comes with an emergency repair kit that allows for quick fixes of tears, leaks, and bad gasket seals.

**Models Include:** TaggeCo Standard X.

## WILDERNESS SURVIVAL KIT

Wilderness survival kits are a necessary precaution for those who regularly travel through inhospitable areas. Most survival kits include a thermal cloak, a multitool or survival knife, a distress beacon, two emergency comlinks, a spool of wire, ration bars, a basic med-pac, two respirators, a water jug with filter, a glow rod, fifty meters of high-tensile microfiber line, ten ration packs, and an emergency flare gun.

**Models Include:** Pretormin Environmental WanderKit.

## TENT

Found in larger survival kits and sold separately by a number of companies, tents are portable shelters used to provide protection from the elements. Depending on the model, a tent can hold one to six individuals. They can be made from materials ranging from simple canvas to advanced durasilk with internal memory supports that assemble themselves.

**Models Include:** Numerous variants.

## THERMAL CLOAK

Thermal cloaks are versatile pieces of equipment that can be worn or used as a blanket and provide protection from extreme heat or extreme cold.

Thermal blankets and thermal cloaks remove up to ■ ■ from any checks made to handle the effects of extreme heat or cold.

**Models Include:** Numerous variants.

# TOOLS AND ELECTRONICS

Tools are used to perform specific tasks or to aid in their performance, and can be anything from a simple hammer to an advanced handheld plasma cutter.

## BACKPACK

Most backpacks are simple textile constructs with a number of compartments and external pouches good for just about anything. More advanced models, such as those built for back-country adventuring or other strenuous outdoor activities, are reinforced and often have lightweight internal supports that allow for the easy carrying of heavy loads.

Backpacks increase the character's encumbrance threshold by 4.

**Models Include:** Adventure Hiker and Hunter Model 6 "Mule" Modular Backpack.

## CLIMBING GEAR

Climbing gear comprises tools used to scale steep or sheer surfaces. Whether for a stony cliff or office tower, climbing gear is essential for those who need to access otherwise unreachable places. Most sets of climbing gear include a few coils of synthrope or liquid cable, a hook or adhesive attachment, and a number of pitons, picks, hammers, and other tools used to secure lines.

**Models Include:** Pretormin Environmental Basic Climbing Gear.

## DATAPAD

A powerful combination of communications device, holo-messenger, handheld computer, and personal database, datapads are designed to combine a number of common consumer electronics in one small, easy-to-use package. Most have touch screens, but some more advanced models use holographic imaging devices to project their data, and all can be connected to the galactic HoloNet. All datapads can be encrypted, and many have emergency data destructs that wipe their memory if they are lost or stolen.

**Models Include:** SoroSuub MX Ultra Pocket Valet.

## EXTRA RELOAD

Although blaster weapons generally have large clips, it is a good idea to carry some reloads if those clips run out.

Extra reloads allow a character to overcome an "out of ammo" ⬙ result with a ranged weapon. By spending a maneuver, a character can switch out a power pack or reload a weapon to get back into the action.

**Models Include:** Numerous variants.

## FUSION LANTERN

Fusion lanterns are a combination power source, light, and area heater. Extremely durable and with a reputation for reliability, fusion lanterns can, with the right connecting cables, power all manner of electronics.

**Models Include:** SoroSuub Powermax Fusion Lantern.

## GLOW ROD

Glow rods are small, directional, handheld light sources used in many applications. They project a beam of bright light and can illuminate objects at respectable ranges.

**Models Include:** Numerous variants.

## ROBES, CLOTHES, AND SUNDRIES

Characters carry numerous pieces of gear that are too mundane or inexpensive to track on a character sheet. Chronos, journals, writing utensils, small multitools, credit chips, street clothing, shoes, fancy hats, inexpensive jewelry and decorations, snacks, mementos, holos of friends and family—all of these things and more are details that can embellish and add personality to a character but are not important enough to track. Player Characters can assume they have any number of miscellaneous sundries on them, depending on what they feel their characters would actually carry.

## TOOL KIT

Tool kits offer their users a wide variety of tools necessary for mechanical jobs. With the proper tools, there is little that a skilled and inventive technician can't accomplish, given the time and circumstances.

Tool kits allow mechanics and technicians to perform most mechanical checks to repair devices, as well as heal wounds on droids.

**Models Include:** Regalis Engineering QuikFix 20-Piece Portable Tool Kit.

## UTILITY BELT

Utility belts let travelers keep valuable tools and items close at hand. Contents and configurations vary by user, and many include integral holsters or gun belts.

Utility belts increase a character's encumbrance threshold by 1.

**Models Include:** Numerous variants.

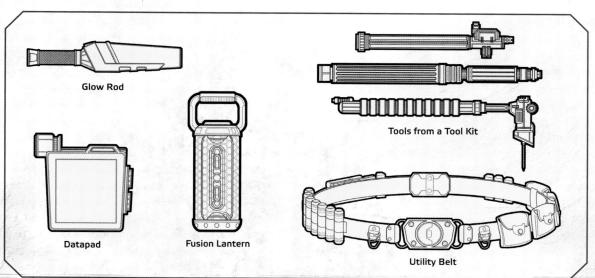

Glow Rod

Datapad

Fusion Lantern

Tools from a Tool Kit

Utility Belt

# HOLOCRONS AND OTHER ANCIENT TALISMANS

In the long history of the galaxy, many orders, traditions, and religions have perceived the Force in their own way. Though most of these organizations and faiths have long vanished from history, occasionally talismans or artifacts remain. While many of these artifacts are simply curiosities, some may have a measure of power imbued in them by some unknown means.

## MEDITATION FOCUS

Many of the Force and religious traditions throughout the galaxy develop some form of meditation focus, whether it be the prayer beads of the Solaran Hermetic Order, the Cosmic Wheel of the Voss Mystics, or Dagoyan incense. Although varied in form, these foci are allied in function, and aiding the user in finding inner peace and enlightenment.

A Force-sensitive character who has a meditation focus increases his strain threshold by 2 while he is a light side paragon.

## DEMON MASK

Every species and culture has scary stories of monsters with supernatural powers. While the stories are—usually—only stories, disciples of the dark side throughout history have found value in adopting the imagery of the mythical demons to spread fear in their enemies and fearlessness among their followers. Having been worn by these adepts for generations, some demon masks have become imbued with the dark side of the Force, and grant their wearers certain powers.

A Force-sensitive character wearing a demon mask increases his wound threshold by 2 while he is a dark side Force user. Furthermore, characters making Discipline checks to resist fear caused by a character wearing a demon mask add ■ equal to that character's Force rating.

## TALISMAN OF IRON FISTS

There have been many warrior traditions that have used the Force throughout the history of the galaxy, of which the Jedi are the most famous. Rather than the lightsabers of the Jedi and the Sith, some Force warrior traditions focus on turning the practitioner's body into a weapon. This talisman is from one such order, and it channels the Force into the wearer's body, making it hard as steel.

If the wearer of the Talisman of Iron Fists is Force-sensitive, he gains the Cortosis quality, which means that any armor he wears gains the Cortosis quality and his Brawl attacks gain the Cortosis quality. Furthermore, his Brawl attacks gain Pierce X, where X is his current Force rating.

## HOLOCRON

A holocron, or holographic chronicle, is an organo-mechanical data storage device capable of storing tremendous amounts of data in a small package. These fist-sized constructs were first created long ago by the Jedi and the Sith to record and store the knowledge and hard-won experience of members of their respective orders. Made from unique crystals encased in layers of precious metals and polycarbonites, these devices use advanced hologrammatic technology to map and store the contents of a single individual's neural pathways. In essence, holocrons record the memories and knowledge of a particular Jedi or Dark Lord of the Sith and store it for future reference.

Holocrons are accessed through an advanced holographic operating system based on the personality of the individual upon whom the holocron is imprinted. These gatekeepers act as a user interface, search-and-recovery program, and security system. Once activated, a small hologram of the holocron's namesake is projected above the device. The gatekeeper is then addressed, and can teach lessons, answer questions, or simply engage in conversation with the user. Remarkably intelligent

## TABLE 5-11: HOLOCRONS AND ANCIENT TALISMANS

| Item | Price | Encum | Rarity |
|------|-------|-------|--------|
| Demon Mask | (R) 4,000 | 1 | 10 |
| Holocron | (R) 100,000 | 1 | 10 |
| Meditation Focus | (R) 4,000 | 1 | 10 |
| Talisman of Iron Fists | (R) 8,000 | 1 | 10 |

and observant, holocron gatekeepers use latent Force energies to read the motives and personality of the user, in order to tailor the user's experience to his level of skill, experience, and trustworthiness. Some gatekeepers, especially those created by the Sith or who have become corrupt over the centuries, can even lie to and lead astray an unsuspecting user, often doing irreparable damage.

Most known holocrons were kept at the Jedi Temple on Coruscant, and the majority of those were lost during the Great Purge when Darth Sidious raided the Holocron Archives and either confiscated or destroyed everything he found there. Some few survived and are still at large throughout the galaxy, but with the proscription on the ownership of Jedi artifacts and rarity of holocrons, it's a rare person who has even heard of a holocron, let alone knows where to locate one.

In **Force and Destiny**, holocrons are more the goal of a quest or entire campaign rather than an item to be purchased or checked out of the local archives. Extremely rare and powerful, holocrons in a **Force and Destiny** game can have far-reaching consequences.

Game Masters should be extremely cautious when introducing a holocron into a game. The following guidelines are presented to assist Game Masters in introducing one of these powerful and desirable artifacts without ruining the tenor of the game.

Depending on its nature, a holocron can grant new Force powers, increase the damage of a specific kind of attack (Melee, Ranged, Gunnery, Lightsaber, etc.), grant basic or advanced talents, grant or increase a skill, or anything else a Game Master can imagine. On his first attempt to use a holocron, a character must make a **Hard (◆ ◆ ◆) Knowledge (Lore) check** to activate the device and summon the gatekeeper. Once the holocron is activated, the character who activated it must spend an amount of time dictated by the Game Master studying the holocron and conversing with the gatekeeper before benefiting from whatever bonuses the holocron provides. The character does not have to make the check to activate the holocron on subsequent uses.

All holocrons, unless noted otherwise, grant an ongoing benefit to the user. **Two skills, determined by the holocron, become career skills for the holocron's user as long as it remains in the user's possession.** What these skills are depends on the holocron in question (see **Table 2–7: Holocron Skills**, on page 109, for some examples of skill pairs). Further, some holocrons grant additional bonuses. Some bonuses are ongoing, but others take effect only once. In the latter case, the user may continue to consult the gatekeeper and even to search through the holocron for information, but the bonuses granted are not granted a second time.

# CUSTOMIZATION AND MODIFICATIONS

Equipment and weapons in the *Star Wars* galaxy are made in every conceivable way. Some are handcrafted, like Luke Skywalker's second lightsaber. Others are stamped out on assembly lines on industrial worlds. Even the latter may have a drastically different look from similar products made on other worlds, through variations in production or user modification. Jango Fett's armor is very different than Boba Fett's, for example.

The statistics and rules for gear in **Force and Destiny** are framed in fairly general categories to present clear, simple, and unified guidelines for their use, but the look of a character's gear can be tailored both cosmetically (meaning it has no game effect—for example, the color of a lightsaber) and mechanically (which changes its basic rules or statistics).

In general, characters can purchase attachments with which to customize their gear. Attachments are physical items that attach to or are installed in items, vehicles, and weapons to add capabilities or improve or change performance in some way. Attachments have a set of base modifiers that they automatically grant when installed. Installing an attachment is a fairly simple process (as they are designed for easy installation) and simply requires a few minutes of uninterrupted work.

Attachments slot into the hard points listed in a piece of equipment's stat block. Each attachment gives the ship, vehicle, or weapon some sort of bonus or edge (extra soak for a piece of armor, or extra damage for a weapon, for instance). In most cases, that's as far as it goes. The character spends money for his new attachment and gains an improved and unique piece of equipment specifically tailored to suit his needs. However, if the PC wishes to further customize and personalize an attachment, he uses the mod system.

# MODDING ATTACHMENTS

Most attachments have a listed series of **mods**. These are additional modifications that a skilled mechanic can make to the attachment to further improve the weapon or item's performance. These are listed under each attachment's **modification options**.

All of these modification options are potential mods for gear. Some of the modification options have a number listed before them, which indicates that the option can be installed multiple times. Otherwise, the option can only be installed once.

Modifications represent dedicated mechanics' and gearheads' ability to tweak and customize their gear. Of course, even the most talented mechanic can only do so much with a particular piece of tech, which is why each attachment has a discrete list of modification options.

## INSTALLING MODS

To install a mod, the user selects an uninstalled modification option from the attachment's available list. The character then spends 100 credits on components and supplies, makes sure he has a tool kit, spends a couple of hours at a workbench, and makes a **Hard (◆ ◆ ◆) Mechanics check**.

If he succeeds, he successfully installs the mod on his gear, and the item now benefits from the bonus provided by the mod. If he fails, however, the mod is not installed, and he may not attempt to install that mod again. If he failed and his check generated at least one ▽, the attachment is also rendered useless by his tinkering.

Each additional mod installed in an attachment beyond the first increases the difficulty of the Mechanics check by one, and costs an additional 100 credits beyond the base cost.

## TYPES OF MODS

There are several types of mods, each falling into one of the following broad categories:

- **Damage mods:** These mods increase the damage dealt by the weapon.
- **Item quality mods:** These mods add a listed quality to the weapon. Some qualities have values that can increase; if this is the case, then the mod lists it as "Quality (+1)," indicating that it increases an existing quality if the quality is already present or adds the quality at rating 1 if it's not there.
- **Innate talent mods:** These mods grant the user the listed talent only when wielding this gear, and it only affects this gear. For example, if a blaster had the innate talent Quick Draw, the user would be able to use Quick Draw to draw or stow his blaster but none of his other gear.

- **Skill and characteristic bonuses:** These mods grant the user a bonus in the listed skill or characteristic as if he had +1 ranks in that skill or characteristic when using the modded item.
- **Additional mod:** Some mods may not fall into any of the listed categories. If a mod does something specific and unique, it is described in the entry.

# WEAPON ATTACHMENTS

The longer a character uses a weapon, the more likely it is that he will modify it in some way to increase its performance or otherwise better suit his tastes or specific needs. The following is a selection of common attachments and modifications that can be installed on personal weapons. Due to the personal nature of equipment customization, it is nearly impossible to catalog every possible modification a character could make to his equipment. Thus, the following list, while detailed, is far from comprehensive.

It should be noted that, even taking a weapon's customization hard points into account, there is a limited amount of space on even the largest weapon, and only a few spots where attachments could be mounted. For example, under-barrel attachments such as bipods and auxiliary weapons can only be mounted to long arms like blaster rifles or slugthrower rifles. In addition, using under-barrel attachments as an example, rifle-sized weapons can only mount one under-barrel attachment, due to space limitations. Players and Game Masters should use common sense when choosing attachments, and they are advised to pay close attention to the attachment descriptions that note where attachments can be mounted and on what weapons they can be mounted.

## BIPOD MOUNT

Little more than a pair of folding or collapsible legs mounted beneath the barrel of a long arm, bipods are used to stabilize awkward or heavy weapons to improve their firing characteristics. Especially useful when firing from behind low cover or from a prone position, bipods are typically used on squad support weapons, or by sharpshooters and snipers to better steady their weapons. This attachment can only be applied to rifles, carbines, and light repeating blasters, and it takes one preparation maneuver to set up.
**Models Include:** Galactic Arms XA Classic Bipod, Czerka AA20 Marksman Bipod.
**Base Modifiers:** Decrease weapon's Cumbersome rating by 2 when firing from a prone or crouched position (or can otherwise brace the bipod on something).
**Modification Options:** None.
**Hard Points Required:** 1.
**Price:** 100 credits.

## TABLE 5-12: WEAPON, LIGHTSABER, AND ARMOR ATTACHMENTS

| Attachment | Price | Encumbrance | HP Required | Rarity |
|---|---|---|---|---|
| **Weapon Attachments** | | | | |
| Bipod Mount | 100 | – | 1 | 1 |
| Blaster Energy Dampener | (R) 750 | – | 1 | 4 |
| Mono-Molecular Edge | 1,000 | – | 1 | 5 |
| Night Vision Scope | 500 | – | 1 | 3 |
| Serrated Edge | 50 | – | 1 | 1 |
| Shadowsheath | (R) 1,500 | – | 1 | 5 |
| Stun Pulse | 250 | – | 1 | 4 |
| Superior Weapon Customization | 5,000 | – | 1 | 6 |
| Telescopic Optical Sight | 250 | – | 1 | 1 |
| Tripod Mount | 250 | – | 2 | 3 |
| Weapon Sling | 100 | – | 1 | 0 |
| Weighted Head | 250 | – | 2 | 3 |
| **Lightsaber Attachments** | | | | |
| Barab Ingot | (R) 15,000 | – | 2 | 8 |
| Curved Hilt | 1,000 | – | 1 | 6 |
| Dantari Crystal | (R) 12,000 | – | 2 | 9 |
| Dragite Gem | (R) 14,000 | – | 2 | 7 |
| Dual-Phase Modification | 4,500 | – | 2 | 6 |
| Extended Hilt | 3,800 | – | 1 | 7 |
| Ilum Crystal | (R) 9,000 | – | 2 | 10 |
| Krayt Dragon Pearl | (R) 15,000 | – | 2 | 10 |
| Lorrdian Gemstone | (R) 9,600 | – | 2 | 8 |
| Mephite Crystal | (R) 10,000 | – | 2 | 10 |
| Sapith Gem | (R) 18,000 | – | 2 | 10 |
| Superior Hilt Personalization | 5,000 | – | 1 | 6 |
| Training Lightsaber Emitter | 100 | – | 2 | 6 |
| **Armor Attachments** | | | | |
| Biofeedback System | 3,300 | – | 2 | 5 |
| Energy Dispersion System | 500 | – | 1 | 4 |
| Heating System | 1,000 | – | 1 | 3 |
| In-Helmet Scanner | 750 | – | 1 | 4 |
| Superior Armor Customization | 5,000 | – | 1 | 6 |
| Thermal Shielding System | 1,000 | – | 1 | 3 |

## BLASTER ENERGY DAMPENER

A blaster, with its focused energy, is one of the most powerful ranged weapons, but those who wish to conceal their shots are often forced to resort to other weapons if they want to pass unnoticed. Some assassins and spies prefer a blaster energy dampener, an attachment that significantly reduces the visibility of a blaster bolt, at the cost of stopping power. While dampened blaster fire is still noticeable in totally dark or very dim environments, an assassin can make a shot in a well-lit environment and not worry about attracting too much attention. This attachment is only for use on Ranged (Light) and Ranged (Heavy) blaster weapons.
**Models Include:** Czerka B78 Energy Dampener.
**Base Modifiers:** Increase the difficulty of checks made to detect this weapon's fire by 1. Decrease weapon damage by 1.
**Modification Options:** 1 Add ■ to checks made to detect this weapon's fire Mod.
**Hard Points Required:** 1.
**Price:** (R) 750 credits.

## MONO-MOLECULAR EDGE

All bladed weapons, even vibro weapons, can benefit from an edge sharpened to mono-molecular thickness and toughened through laser-forging techniques. This modification may be applied to Melee weapons that use a cutting edge.
**Models Include:** None.
**Base Modifiers:** Decreases the weapon's crit rating by 1 to a minimum of 1.
**Modification Options:** 2 Item Quality (Pierce + 1) Mods.
**Hard Points Required:** 1.
**Price:** 1,000 credits.

## NIGHT VISION SCOPE

This attachment uses an optical system similar to a set of electrobinoculars that shows infrared wavelengths of light, effectively allowing the shooter to track heat signatures in dark or concealed areas, or through walls. It does not differentiate between heat generated by life forms and other kinds of heat, whether from natural or manufactured phenomena. (It is blind to life forms that do not give off heat.) This attachment can be used on any ranged weapon, with the exception of single-use weapons and weapons that would not realistically benefit from a scope.
**Models Include:** Fabritech LRS Low-Light Scope, Zikon Optics Model 45 Infrascope.
**Base Modifiers:** Remove up to ■ ■ on any checks to use this weapon due to darkness.
**Modification Options:** None.
**Hard Points Required:** 1.
**Price:** 500 credits.

## SERRATED EDGE

The simplicity of this modification belies its viciousness. Adding a serrated edge to a weapon is something almost anyone can do, and giving a bladed weapon tearing edges ensures it does terrible damage to flesh and bone. This modification may be applied to Melee weapons that use a cutting edge.
**Models Include:** None.
**Base Modifiers:** Grants the weapon the Vicious (+1) quality.
**Modification Options:** None.
**Hard Points Required:** 1.
**Price:** 50 credits.

## SHADOWSHEATH

Bounty hunters, assassins, and other criminals often have a need to conceal weapons on their bodies to sneak them past guards or get close to a target without arousing alarm. A shadowsheath utilizes optical camouflage technology, but rather than conceal an entire body, its smaller projector is specifically designed to conceal a single weapon when kept in a holster or sheath. This attachment may be attached to any weapon with an encumbrance of 2 or less.
**Models Include:** Merr-Sonn Shadowsheath WCS.
**Base Modifiers:** Increase the difficulty of any checks made to detect the sheath or the weapon it holds by two.
**Modification Options:** None.
**Hard Points Required:** 1.
**Price:** (R) 1,500 credits.

## STUN PULSE

A stun pulse attachment deals an electric shock to the target, in addition to its weapon's normal damage. Generally attached to truncheons or bludgeoning weapons, stun pulses are often used by law enforcement to disable suspects without killing them. A stun pulse can be attached to any bludgeoning Melee or Brawl weapon.
**Models Include:** CoroTech EV45 Pulse Coil, SoroSuub "Enforcer" Stunner.
**Base Modifiers:** The weapon gains the Stun 2 quality.
**Modification Options:** 3 Item Quality (Stun + 1) Mods.
**Hard Points Required:** 1.
**Price:** 250 credits.

## SUPERIOR WEAPON CUSTOMIZATION

Even the simplest weapon can benefit from a craftsman's touch. A skilled weaponsmith can tweak a weapon to its owner's exacting specifications, turning a blunt instrument into a honed and deadly weapon of war.
**Models Include:** None.
**Base Modifiers:** Grants the weapon the Superior quality.
**Modification Options:** None.
**Hard Points Required:** 1.
**Price:** 5,000 credits.

## TELESCOPIC OPTICAL SIGHT

Popular with snipers and hunters, this attachment is essentially a long tube with a pair of telescopic lenses attached to the top of a weapon. The sight magnifies far-off objects, allowing a sharpshooter to hit distant targets with relative ease. This attachment can be used on any ranged weapon that could logically benefit from the addition of a sight.

**Models Include:** Zikon Optics Model 40 Marksman Scope, Merr-Sonn 80Z Telescopic Optical Sight.
**Base Modifiers:** Reduces the difficulty of ranged combat checks at long and extreme range by one.
**Modification Options:** None.
**Hard Points Required:** 1.
**Price:** 250 credits.

## TRIPOD MOUNT

Used in static weapon emplacements to augment heavy squad support weapons such as the Imperial Army's E-Web heavy repeating blaster, tripods use a number of different technologies—from self-extending hydraulics to tiny, low-output repulsorlift generators—to stabilize heavy weapons for firing. This attachment is only for use on light repeating blasters and heavy repeating blasters, as well as portable Gunnery weapons. Setting up a tripod takes two preparation maneuvers.

**Models Include:** BlasTech 3R Heavy Weapon Tripod Mount.
**Base Modifiers:** Decrease weapon's Cumbersome rating by 3 when set up. May not move the weapon (except to pivot) once tripod is set up.
**Modification Options:** 2 Item Quality (Cumbersome -1) Mods.
**Hard Points Required:** 2.
**Price:** 250 credits.

## WEAPON SLING

Slings are lengths of hide or synthetic fabric designed to allow easy handling of long arms like blaster rifles. They come in a dizzying array of styles, from the simplest adjustable single-strap leather sling for carrying a weapon off the shoulder to multi-strap slings that allow for any number of custom configurations. These attachments can only be used with Ranged (Heavy) weapons.

**Models Include:** Custom-Tooled Bantha Hide Sling, Quick-Release One-Point Drop Sling.
**Base Modifiers:** Decrease Cumbersome rating by 1.
**Modification Options:** 1 Innate Talent (Quick Draw) Mod.
**Hard Points Required:** 1.
**Price:** 100 credits.

## WEIGHTED HEAD

Bludgeoning weapons, such as truncheons, clubs, and staffs, deal damage through weight and impact. A simple modification to these weapons is to add heavier, denser materials to the head of the weapon, allowing for more powerful blows. Some enterprising sentients also add metal studs or ridges to the head of the weapon for particularly crippling strikes. This attachment may only be used on bludgeoning Brawl and Melee weapons.

**Models Include:** None.
**Base Modifiers:** Damage +1.
**Modification Options:** 1 Damage +1 Mod, 1 Item Quality (Concussive +1) Mod.
**Hard Points Required:** 2.
**Price:** 250 credits.

# LIGHTSABER ATTACHMENTS

Despite their unique construction and their status as the signature weapons of an ancient, outlawed religion, lightsabers are like any other weapon in that they can be modified to suit the tastes and needs of their users. The most important part of a lightsaber, and the one most likely to be modified, is the focusing crystal that transforms the weapon's powerful plasma energies into a crackling, coherent energy blade. Changing a lightsaber's crystal is, perhaps, the easiest and most cost-effective way of improving a lightsaber. Crystals come in all manner of shapes and sizes, and they are formed from a dizzying array of organic and inorganic materials. A new crystal can give a lightsaber the ability to create sonic blasts when struck, or increase its damage yield or ease of use. Lightsabers can only house one crystal at a time. While changing a crystal is a relatively easy process, it is still time-consuming and requires the correct tools and a not-insignificant investment of the user's Force energies.

The most common types of lightsaber crystals come from the planet Ilum and the areas in and around the Adega system. When the Jedi were at the peak of their powers during the Galactic Republic, lightsaber crystals were quite rare, and harvesting them took an inordinate amount of time and energy. Today, as the galaxy is firmly in the grasp of the Imperial regime, acquiring a lightsaber crystal is even more difficult. During the rise of the Empire, Emperor Palpatine closed or destroyed all known sources of lightsaber crystals, and his agents scoured the galaxy to remove as many crystals as they could from circulation. The acquisition of a lightsaber crystal is more akin to a quest or ordeal rather than a simple transaction. Those who wish to construct their own lightsabers are likely to encounter some difficult challenges during their searches.

Lightsabers can be modified not only through crystals, but also by means of different materials, hilt shapes, and other processes to improve their ease of use, potency, or nearly anything else their user desires. The following is a selection of lightsaber attachments, including various crystals, hilts, and internal systems, for use in FORCE AND DESTINY.

When a character modifies attachments on his own lightsaber, he decreases the difficulty of the Mechanics check by two, to a minimum of Simple (–). What constitutes a character's "own" lightsaber should be determined by the player and GM, but generally it should be limited to a weapon used and possessed by the character exclusively. "Loaning" a lightsaber to another character who's better at Mechanics is discouraged.

### BARAB INGOT

Rare variants of kyber crystals unique to the heavily irradiated world Barab I, home of the saurian Barabel people, Barab ingots are among the various crystals used in lightsabers. Found in small clusters in mountainous regions, Barab ingots are hot to the touch and glow with a fierce inner light. When installed in a lightsaber, they create a searing, fiery blade that burns so fiercely that it nearly loses cohesion. A lightsaber with an installed Barab ingot is slightly radioactive, and with a particularly good or lucky strike can set a target alight. A Barab ingot is a lightsaber crystal.

## LIGHTSABER CRYSTAL ATTACHMENTS

Lightsaber crystals are a special type of attachment unique to Lightsaber weapons. However, a lightsaber crystal is more than just an attachment. In many ways, it is the core of the weapon, defining each lightsaber's individual characteristics. Lightsabers have been constructed using a wide variety of crystals over the millennia. However, all crystals used in lightsabers are some form of kyber crystal. Something about kyber crystals' structural makeup enables them to withstand the energies run through them and focus that power into the blade of the lightsaber. While different variants of kyber crystals found on different worlds may have different shapes or colors, all share this unique trait.

A lightsaber can have one and only one crystal installed in it. If a lightsaber already has a crystal, the character may replace it with a new, different one. As noted in a lightsaber crystal's base modifiers, lightsaber crystals greatly affect the lightsaber's damage, critical rating, and item qualities.

When working with a kyber crystal, a Force-sensitive can use his connection to the Force to guide his hands. **When modding a lightsaber crystal attachment, a Force user may add ⬥ no greater than his Force rating to the check.** He may spend ◐ to add ✸ or ↻ to the check.

**Models Include:** None.
**Base Modifiers:** Installing this crystal changes a lightsaber's base damage to 8 and critical rating to 3. In addition, the lightsaber gains the Breach 1, Burn 1, and Sunder weapon qualities. If the crystal is ever removed, the lightsaber loses these qualities and reverts to its previous base damage and critical rating.
**Modification Options:** 2 Item Quality (Burn +1) Mods, 2 Item Quality (Vicious +1) Mods.
**Hard Points Required:** 2.
**Cost:** (R) 15,000 credits.

### CURVED HILT

The curved hilt is preferred by duelists and practitioners of the lightsaber combat form Makashi. This modification allows for both better control and better flexibility when handling the lightsaber, and for more force behind overhand strikes.
**Models Include:** None.
**Base Modifiers:** Adds automatic ↻ to successful Lightsaber combat checks when engaged with a single opponent.
**Modification Options:** 1 Item Quality (Defensive +1) Mod.
**Hard Points Required:** 1.
**Cost:** 1,000 credits.

### DANTARI CRYSTAL

As their name suggests, Dantari crystals are found on the Outer Rim world of Dantooine. Discovered within the eggs of the kinrath—giant, venomous, cave-dwelling arachnids—it is unknown how Dantari crystals come into existence. However, these multihued kyber crystals were once extremely popular among the Jedi. When installed in a lightsaber, a Force-reactive Dantari crystal helps the wielder maintain focus and calm. A Dantari crystal is a lightsaber crystal.
**Models Include:** None.
**Base Modifiers:** Installing this crystal changes a lightsaber's base damage to 7 and critical rating to 2, and the lightsaber gains the Breach 1 and Sunder weapon qualities. When making a Force power check as part of a combat check, a character using a lightsaber with a Dantari crystal may spend ◐ to recover 2 strain. If the crystal is ever removed, the lightsaber loses these qualities and abilities, and it reverts to its previous base damage and critical rating.
**Modification Options:** 1 Decrease the weapon's critical rating by 1 to a minimum of 1 Mod, 2 Damage +1 Mods.
**Hard Points Required:** 2.
**Cost:** (R) 12,000 credits.

### DRAGITE GEM

Small, dull, and brittle, Dragite gems are found in the caves and caverns of the D'olop mountain range on M'haeli, an agriworld in the Expansion Region. In their natural state, dragite crystals are one of the most brittle kyber crystals, and they produce a loud ringing when struck. Worked into a suitable lightsaber crystal, a difficult task due to the dragite gem's distressing tendency to fracture or shatter easily, it produces a blade that pulses and hums loudly. In addition to this noise, when a lightsaber equipped with a dragite gem strikes a solid target, it produces a deafening crack and a shock wave that can disorient and even cause bodily harm to its target. A dragite gem is a lightsaber crystal.

**Models Include:** None.
**Base Modifiers:** Installing this crystal changes a lightsaber's damage to 7 and critical rating to 3, and the lightsaber gains the Breach 1, Disorient 1, and Sunder weapon qualities. If the crystal is ever removed, the lightsaber loses these qualities and reverts to its previous base damage and critical rating.
**Modification Options:** 2 Item Quality (Disorient +1) Mods, 2 Item Quality (Concussive +1) Mods, 1 Damage +1 Mod.
**Hard Points Required:** 2.
**Cost:** (R) 14,000 credits.

## DUAL-PHASE MODIFICATION

Considered antiquated and outdated by the time of the Clone Wars, the dual-phase modification is an artifact of an older, more violent time. Designed to catch an opponent off guard, this modification allows the wielder to change the length of a lightsaber's blade with the push of a button. This causes an opponent's guard to falter momentarily as he adjusts to the new blade length, allowing the Jedi to press the advantage while his opponent is confused.

**Models Include:** None.
**Base Modifiers:** May change blade length once per encounter as an incidental. The next attack that turn made by the character using this weapon ignores the target's melee defense.
**Modification Options:** None.
**Hard Points Required:** 2.
**Cost:** 4,500 credits.

### EXTENDED HILT

The idea behind the extended hilt modification is to increase the lightsaber's striking and cutting power by using the leverage of the longer handle and a two-handed grip to help focus the wielder's strength into the force of the blow. The extended hilt modification is also popular among

Force users of unusual height or build as a way to capitalize on their size advantage in combat.
**Models Include:** None.
**Base Modifiers:** Increase weapon's damage by 1.
**Modification Options:** 1 Item Quality (Vicious +1) Mod.
**Hard Points Required:** 1.
**Cost:** 3,800 credits.

## ILUM CRYSTAL

The kyber crystals found deep within the caves of the icy planet Ilum were prized by the Jedi as some of the best crystals for constructing a lightsaber. Ilum featured heavily in Jedi tradition, with young Padawans traveling there as part of their training to commune with the Force and use its guidance to seek out the crystal that would go into the construction of their first lightsaber.

**Models Include:** None.
**Base Modifiers:** Installing this crystal changes a lightsaber's base damage to 6 and critical rating to 2, and the lightsaber gains the Breach 1 and Sunder weapon qualities. If the crystal is ever removed, the lightsaber loses these qualities and reverts to its previous base damage and critical rating.
**Modification Options:** 2 Item Quality (Vicious +1) Mods, 4 Damage +1 Mods, 1 Decrease the weapon's critical rating by 1 to a minimum of 1 Mod.
**Hard Points Required:** 2.
**Cost:** (R) 9,000 credits.

## KRAYT DRAGON PEARL

Highly sought after by jewelers, artisans, and wealthy collectors for their luster, color, and refractive properties, krayt dragon pearls are perhaps the rarest of the crystals used in the construction of lightsabers. The terrible krayt dragons of Tatooine tend to live for an incredibly long time, and over the course of their lives will ingest stones to aid with digestion. While the caustic digestive juices of the krayt dragon can even break down stone over time, every once in a while these stones contain some form of kyber crystal. Incredibly resilient, they remain in the creatures' guts for the entirety of the dragons' lives, slowly being polished and smoothed into small, dense spheres of crystal. The resulting "krayt dragon pearls" are vanishingly rare, hard to acquire, and demand exorbitant prices. Since they are a type of kyber crystal, they can be worked into powerful lightsaber crystals—ones which produce an exceptionally savage and destructive blade that makes an unsettling howling noise when swung about. A krayt dragon pearl is a lightsaber crystal.

**Models Include:** None.
**Base Modifiers:** Installing this crystal changes the lightsaber's damage to 9 and its critical rating to 1, and the lightsaber replaces its item qualities with the Breach 1, Sunder, and Vicious 1 item qualities.
**Modification Options:** 3 Item Quality (Vicious + 1) Mods, 1 Damage + 1 Mod.
**Hard Points Required:** 2.
**Cost:** (R) 15,000 credits.

## LORRDIAN GEMSTONE

Lorrdian gemstones are kyber crystals mined millennia ago by enslaved Lorrdians during the Kanz Disorders. Created by Force-sensitive Lorrdians to supplement the intricate kinetic communication developed among the slave populace, these gemstones were imbued with Force energies that allowed their possessors to read the emotions and actions of others. When installed in a lightsaber, a Lorrdian gemstone allows the wielder to predict the actions of an opponent, giving the wielder a decided edge in melee combat. A Lorrdian gemstone is a lightsaber crystal.

**Models Include:** None.
**Base Modifiers:** Installing this crystal changes the lightsaber's damage to 7 and its critical rating to 2, and the lightsaber gains the Breach 1, Defensive 1, and Sunder weapon qualities. If the crystal is ever

removed, the lightsaber loses these qualities and reverts to its previous base damage and critical rating.
**Modification Options:** 1 Item Quality (Defensive +1) Mod, 2 Item Quality (Deflection +1) Mods.
**Hard Points Required:** 2.
**Cost:** (R) 9,600 credits.

## MEPHITE CRYSTAL

Mephite crystals are rare, lustrous kyber crystals found in a handful of places in and around the Adega system. One of five types of crystal known collectively as "Adegan crystals," mephite crystals are well-suited for use in lightsabers due to their internal structure and light-modulating capabilities. Like all Adegan crystals, mephite crystals are Force-reactive and can be infused with a small amount of a Force user's power. When installed in a lightsaber and infused with the Force, mephite crystals give off a small but steady Force signature that can be sensed by any nearby Force user. A mephite crystal is a lightsaber crystal.
**Models Include:** None.
**Base Modifiers:** Installing this crystal changes the lightsaber's damage to 8 and its critical rating to 2, and the lightsaber gains the Breach 1 and Sunder item qualities. Force-sensitive characters using Force powers to sense their surroundings automatically detect a lightsaber using a mephite crystal if it is in range of the power. If the crystal is ever removed, the lightsaber loses these qualities and reverts to its previous base damage and critical rating.
**Modification Options:** 3 Damage +1 Mods, 1 Decrease the weapon's critical rating by 1 to a minimum of 1 Mod, 1 Item Quality (Vicious +1) Mod.
**Hard Points Required:** 2.
**Cost:** (R) 10,000 credits.

## SAPITH GEM

Said to originate from a strange and mysterious world called Lwhekk in the Unknown Regions, sapith gems are similar to krayt dragon pearls in that they were formed when rocks containing a kyber crystal were consumed by a great beast. In this case, the beast was a massive voilce worm, which died out long before the present day. Thus, the only way to find these vanishingly rare crystals is to dig them out from the fossilized remains of a voilce worm. Shaped like serpent scales, these smooth, lustrous crystals have an incredibly complex internal structure, which magnifies the intensity of any light that passes through them. When installed in a lightsaber, a sapith gem creates a powerful, intense beam that can pierce nearly anything with ease. A sapith gem is a lightsaber crystal.
**Models Include:** None.
**Base Modifiers:** Installing this crystal changes a lightsaber's damage to 7 and its critical rating to 2, and the lightsaber gains the Breach 1 and Sunder item qualities. If the crystal is ever removed, the light-

saber loses these qualities and reverts to its previous base damage and critical rating.
**Modification Options:** 1 Item Quality (Breach +1) Mod, 2 Damage +1 Mods, 1 Decrease the weapon's critical rating by 1 to a minimum of 1 Mod.
**Hard Points Required:** 2.
**Cost:** (R) 18,000 credits.

## SUPERIOR HILT PERSONALIZATION

While most lightsabers are austere and utilitarian, some Jedi have been known to personalize their weapons to better suit their tastes and styles. Numerous cosmetic or practical enhancements can be applied to a lightsaber, from rare metals and precious gemstones to customized grips and locking activating switches.
**Models Include:** None.
**Base Modifiers:** Grants the lightsaber the Superior quality.
**Modification Options:** None.
**Hard Points Required:** 1.
**Cost:** 5,000 credits.

## TRAINING LIGHTSABER EMITTER

In the days of the Republic, the Jedi allowed their younglings to train with "training sabers," non-lethal versions of their famous energy blades. A training lightsaber is almost the same as a standard lightsaber; however, the crystal is replaced with a training emitter. The training emitter creates a blade that is completely non-lethal, and at most can generate a stun shock. A training emitter is a lightsaber crystal.
**Models Include:** None.
**Base Modifiers:** Installing this crystal changes a lightsaber's damage to 6 and its critical rating to –, and the lightsaber gains the Stun Damage quality. If the crystal is ever removed, the lightsaber loses this quality and reverts to its previous base damage and critical rating.
**Modification Options:** None.
**Hard Points Required:** 2.
**Cost:** 100 credits.

# ARMOR ATTACHMENTS

Armor, like personal weapons, has a number of customization hard points and can be easily modified. By design, armor attachments are more defensive in nature, affording the user extra protection against enemies or the elements. A fair amount of common sense on the part of the players is required when modifying armor. Most suits of armor can only hold one environmental system, such as cold or heat resistance, or one type of optical enhancement in the helmet.

## BIOFEEDBACK SYSTEM

This system closely monitors the vital signs of the person wearing the armor. It can immediately identify when the user is hurt or experiencing elevated levels of adrenaline and administer minor sedatives, healing chemicals, and other drugs as needed. This attachment can be installed on any full-body armor suit.

**Models Include:** BioTech "Autodoc" Monitoring Network, Atlas Corp NG-7 Vital System.

**Base Modifiers:** Increase this character's strain threshold by 4 while wearing this armor.

**Modification Options:** 1 Innate Talent (Rapid Recovery) Mod.

**Hard Points Required:** 2.

**Price:** 3,300 credits.

## ENERGY DISPERSION SYSTEM

This minute metallic wiring is designed to distribute electrical shocks across the armor while grounding the user against the energy, reducing the potency of such attacks. It protects against electricity as well as weapons' Stun settings, although it does not effectively disperse blaster fire. This attachment can be installed on any armor.

**Models Include:** Atlas Corp Model 88 Electric Shield, Merr-Sonn AEGIS Nanoarray.

**Base Modifiers:** When using the wearer's soak to reduce damage dealt to the wearer's strain threshold, count the soak value as 2 higher.

**Modification Options:** None.

**Hard Points Required:** 1.

**Price:** 500 credits.

## HEATING SYSTEM

Heating systems are installed in armor to protect the wearer against dangerously low temperatures and frigid environments. Equipped with small, efficient heating elements and double-insulated against the cold, this attachment allows a wearer to survive in places where the ambient temperature can be dozens of degrees below freezing. Perhaps the most famous type of cold shielding is that built into the custom laminate armor worn by the Empire's snowtroopers. This attachment can be installed on any armor that covers the entire body and can be sealed.

**Models Include:** Atlas Corp DL87 "Frostback" Armor Enhancement, Min-Dal Model 00 Heating System.

**Base Modifiers:** Reduces the difficulty of Resilience checks made to resist effects of extreme cold by one. Removes up to ■ ■ added to checks due to extreme cold.

**Modification Options:** None.

**Hard Points Required:** 1.

**Price:** 1,000 credits.

## IN-HELMET SCANNER

An in-helmet scanner provides the usefulness of a general purpose scanner in a heads-up display splashed across the inside of the user's helmet. This feeds the user a constant stream of information about the surrounding environment. Depending on the specific model, an in-helmet scanner can indicate the presence of life forms or droids and display heat signatures, radiation sources, acoustic emissions, and more. Many can also scan and listen to nearby comlink frequencies. In-helmet scanners can be added to any helmet.

**Models Include:** CryonCorp GoScan, CUE Optical Information System (Mobile), Chedak Mk. 7 HUD-INFO.

**Base Modifiers:** Adds a general purpose scanner to the user's helmet. The scanner allows the user to remove ■ imposed on any checks due to darkness or environmental conditions such as smoke or fog. It also allows the user to detect heat sources and motion within medium range.

**Modification Options:** 1 Install a hands-free comlink within the user's helmet Mod.

**Hard Points Required:** 1.

**Price:** 750 credits.

## SUPERIOR ARMOR CUSTOMIZATION

Any piece of armor can benefit from retooling at the hands of a superior craftsman. A skilled armorsmith can add improved plastoid or even durasteel plating to increase the protection a piece of armor offers, even as he decreases its weight and bulk. Of course, such delicate and exacting work can make the armor less customizable in other respects.

**Models Include:** Numerous variants.

**Base Modifiers:** Grants the armor the Superior quality.

**Modification Options:** None.

**Hard Points Required:** 1.

**Price:** 5,000 credits.

## THERMAL SHIELDING SYSTEM

Utilizing both active and passive cooling systems, along with an insulated body glove and special coatings on the armor plates, this attachment allows a wearer to withstand dangerously high temperatures. This thermal shielding is proof against open flames, molten rock and steel, intense heat, and even some forms of radiation. This attachment can be installed on any armor that covers the entire body and can be sealed.

**Models Include:** Atlas Corp Model 451 Heat Exchanger, Min-Dal 3100 Firebrand Suit, Kaminoan Armorsmiths Thermal Shielding System.

**Base Modifiers:** Reduces the difficulty of Resilience checks made to resist the effects of fire and extreme heat by one. Removes up to ■ ■ added to checks due to extreme fire or heat.

**Modification Options:** None.

**Hard Points Required:** 1.

**Price:** 1,000 credits.

# VI

# CONFLICT AND COMBAT

*"Wars do not make one great."*

–Yoda

The galaxy is a dangerous place, especially for a Force user. War between the Galactic Empire and the Rebel Alliance overwhelms entire sectors; whole worlds burn in the fires of conflict. Crime lords, pirates, mercenaries, and brigands thrive in the dark and lawless reaches, playing both sides of the galactic conflict. Meanwhile, the Emperor's dark side minions stalk the shadows, hunting for those who can touch the Force. Against these adversaries, only the brave and the foolish fight to protect the helpless and struggle to bring light to the darkness.

## NARRATIVE AND STRUCTURED GAMEPLAY

Most of the gameplay in Force and Destiny is done on a narrative basis, with the GM describing events and the players describing their characters' actions and reactions to these events. Combat, however, requires more structured gameplay.

Narrative gameplay does not require the GM or players to keep track of the exact passage of time, and for the most part, this is perfectly acceptable.

It's usually enough to know that actions may take a few minutes, hours, days, or weeks (or any other amount of time). Narrative gameplay is most often used in any situation for which the precise order of actions is unimportant.

Conversely, structured gameplay is, at its heart, a rules system that breaks up a character's actions into what he could reasonably perform in a predetermined amount of time. It also gives each character in a scene the opportunity to perform actions in turn. It's most often used for playing through combat situations. However, the GM may decide to employ structured gameplay in certain non-combat scenes that he feels would benefit from requiring the players to clearly define their characters' actions within a rule set.

# STRUCTURED GAMEPLAY OVERVIEW

When using structured gameplay to describe the sequence of events during a firefight, lightsaber duel, or hectic chase through the crowded streets of Coruscant, the game is broken down into a series of **rounds**, each of which is further broken down into a series of **turns**. During a single round, each Player Character and Non-Player Character gets one turn, during which that character has the opportunity to accomplish tasks and perform various actions.

Rounds can represent roughly a minute or so in time, although the elapsed time is deliberately not specified. Players should keep in mind that a round lasts long enough for their character to move to a new location and perform an important action. They should also remember that although each round is broken up into turns that happen sequentially in gameplay, narratively the turns are occurring at roughly the same time.

Structured gameplay events (also called **encounters**), such as combat, follow these steps:

### STEP 1: DETERMINE INITIATIVE

At the beginning of the first round of combat, all players and the GM need to determine in what order the characters will take their turns. Do the stormtroopers ambush the refugees, or does the hidden Hunter get in the first shot? This is referred to as the **Initiative order**.

To determine the Initiative order, each Player Character and NPC makes a **Simple (–) Cool** or **Vigilance check** (for more information on which to use, see the **Cool or Vigilance?** sidebar). Once all Initiative checks have been made, the GM notes the results of each check and ranks them in order from the highest number of successes to the lowest. If two checks are tied, the check with more ⟨⟩ is ranked higher. If a Player Character and an NPC are still tied, the Player Character is ranked higher. This is the Initiative order.

### STEP 2: ASSIGN INITIATIVE SLOTS

Once the GM has determined the Initiative order, he notes which results were generated by Player Characters and which results were generated by NPCs. The results generated by Player Characters become Player Character Initiative slots. The results generated by NPCs become NPC Initiative slots.

## COOL OR VIGILANCE?

Two different skills in FORCE AND DESTINY can be used to determine Initiative: Cool and Vigilance. Which skill should be used in a particular circumstance is determined by the situation at hand.

Characters should determine their Initiative using the Cool skill when they are aware and ready for combat (or for whatever situation has resulted in the use of structured gameplay). For example, rolling to see who goes first in a quick-draw gunfight or springing an ambush on an unsuspecting enemy would require Cool, as Cool is a skill representing a character's ability to remain calm, collected, and focused on the task ahead.

Characters should determine their Initiative using the Vigilance skill when combat (or another situation resulting in structured gameplay) begins unexpectedly. Two enemies walking around a corner and running into each other would each use Vigilance to determine Initiative, for example. Likewise, someone being ambushed would also use Vigilance to determine Initiative (and if they ended up going earlier in the Initiative order than their ambusher, clearly they were vigilant enough to spot the ambush at the last second).

It's important to note that different characters may use different skills to determine Initiative during the same combat, depending on their differing circumstances. Also, if the GM and players are unsure as to which of the two skills best applies to a given situation, they should default to using Vigilance.

### STEP 3: PARTICIPANTS TAKE TURNS

Beginning at the top of the Initiative order, the players and GM fill each Initiative slot one at a time with a character turn. If the Initiative slot is a Player Character Initiative slot, then the players agree on one Player Character to fill the slot from among the Player Characters who have not acted yet that round. That Player Character then takes this turn.

If the Initiative slot is an NPC Initiative slot, then the GM chooses one NPC to fill the slot from among the NPCs who have not yet acted that round. That NPC then takes this turn.

### STEP 4: ROUND ENDS

Once all NPCs and Player Characters have taken a turn, the round ends. At this point, certain effects that last until the "end of the round" may end. The GM also determines if the ongoing action warrants additional rounds or if it has been resolved. If the ongoing action continues, repeat step 3 using the same Initiative order generated in step 1. If the action has been resolved and the encounter is over, proceed to step 5.

### STEP 5: ENCOUNTER ENDS

Once the action has been resolved, the GM ends the encounter. At this point, any character abilities that may only be used "once per encounter" reset, and any abilities that last "until the end of the encounter" expire. Player Characters also have a chance to catch their breath and recover strain, and may take steps to help heal any incapacitated characters.

# THE TURN

Each character (whether a Player Character or a Non-Player Character) gets one turn to act during each round. During this turn, the character can do any of a number of things, such as dash for cover, attempt to unlock a sealed blast door, or shoot a heavy blaster pistol at an opponent. The activities the character can perform during his turn are split into three categories: incidentals, maneuvers, and actions.

## CINEMATIC COMBAT

**F**ORCE AND **D**ESTINY strives to capture the pure cinematic thrill found in the *Star Wars* universe. Combat is frequent, fast-moving, and meant to showcase the talents and abilities of the Player Characters.

The unique dice system of FORCE AND DESTINY helps fuel the story-driven nature of the game. Even a single attack roll generates enough options (some good, some bad) to give the Game Master sufficient information to make combat far more than just a matter of rolling to hit and rolling to wound. In turn, the players are strongly encouraged to provide interesting detail before rolling on an attack, in order to give the GM ideas for describing the results. Combat is streamlined so the players do not bog down gameplay with too many tactical decisions; descriptions of their actions and the roll of the dice is sufficient to help visualize the violence.

### INCIDENTALS

Incidentals are minor activities characters can undertake that require extremely little time or effort. Dropping a broken comlink, speaking to a friend, or switching a blaster pistol to Stun mode are all incidentals. There is no hard limit to the number of incidentals a character may perform during his turn, although the GM may veto excessive numbers of them or decide they are complex enough to warrant counting as a maneuver. The following are examples of incidentals:

- Speaking to another character.
- Dropping an item held in one's hands.
- Releasing someone the character is holding.
- Minor movements such as shifting position, peeking around a corner, or looking behind a person.

### MANEUVERS

Maneuvers are activities that aren't complex enough to warrant a skill check, but which still involve time and effort on the part of a character. Characters are allowed one maneuver during their turn, and certain circumstances may allow them a second maneuver as well (see below). The following are some examples of maneuvers:

- Aiming a weapon.
- Moving one range band closer or farther away from an enemy (for more on range bands, see page 213).
- Opening a door.
- Diving behind cover.
- Standing up.

## ACTIONS

Actions are important activities that are vital to a character's accomplishment of a goal. Each character may normally only perform one action during his turn, and it will likely be the most important activity he undertakes during his turn. Actions almost always involve performing a skill check, although certain character abilities may require using an action to activate them. The following are some examples of actions:

- Slicing a computer.
- Unlocking a locked door.
- Firing a weapon.
- Punching or grappling an opponent.
- Instructing allies with a series of orders.
- Performing first aid on an ally.
- Sneaking up on a vigilant foe.
- Climbing a cliff.

Out of all of these options, the most common during combat are those that involve attacking an opponent. Attacking an opponent requires a combat skill check, sometimes referred to in shorthand as a **combat check** or simply an **attack**.

# MANEUVERS

**J**ust as **Force and Destiny** uses an abstract method of describing combat, movement is similarly described in broad strokes. Characters often do far more than shooting their blasters in combat, like pulling out stimpacks to heal a wounded comrade, activating the systems to open a blast door, or scaling a wall to gain an advantage over their opponents.

Not all undertakings require a check. These minor activities, known as maneuvers, cover a wide range of activities that any character can perform. They require an investment of time and effort on the character's part, but they are simple enough that there is no chance of failure when doing them. Technically, characters perform maneuvers during narrative gameplay as well as during structured gameplay, or encounters. However, maneuvers are tracked and defined during encounters, because characters' time and efforts are more limited by the frantic pace of conflict.

## MANEUVER LIMITATIONS

Whether taking careful aim at an Imperial officer, diving for cover behind a stack of cargo crates, or patching up a wounded friend, a character may perform one free maneuver on his turn. He may also perform a second maneuver by voluntarily suffering two points of strain, thereby stretching himself to his limits in order to get more done. (Characters may also perform a second maneuver through a particularly successful skill check, or by other means listed elsewhere.) However, regardless of the source, **a single character may not perform more than two maneuvers during his turn.**

## MANEUVERS OUTSIDE A CHARACTER'S TURN

In some cases, a character may even be able to perform a maneuver when it's not that character's turn. A stormtrooper rolling horribly on a Stealth check to ambush a PC may generate a number of failures on his check.

The GM may decide that the blunder allows the would-be victim the opportunity to perform a maneuver, even though it's the stormtrooper's turn.

Any bonus maneuvers gained outside of a character's turn do not count toward the aforementioned limit of two maneuvers a character may perform during his turn—specifically because they occur outside of the character's turn. These additional maneuvers are generally awarded at the providence of the GM, and thus there is no hard-and-fast limit to the number of maneuvers that can be awarded in this manner. However, the GM would be wise to limit the number of out-of-turn maneuvers any character performs each round to one or two at most.

# TYPES OF MANEUVERS

The following is a list of the maneuvers a character can perform during combat. Please note that this list is not exhaustive. The entire point of maneuvers is that they can cover any activity that is relatively easy to perform but still requires some amount of time and effort. While the maneuvers listed here are deliberately general to cover as many options as possible, if a player comes up with something he wants his character to do that is not covered by this list, he should not dismiss the idea out of hand. Instead, he should explain what he'd like to accomplish to the GM, who can decide if it can realistically be performed in a single maneuver.

Some activities may require multiple maneuvers to perform. Generally, these maneuvers must be performed sequentially, without being interrupted by the character performing other maneuvers or actions, for the task to be successful.

### AIM

Every shot counts once the blasters come out, and characters who eliminate their enemies first are more likely to walk away once the action dies down. During combat, a character can use the aim maneuver to steady a weapon or line up a hit before attacking, granting a bonus to his next combat check. A character only gains the benefit of aiming if he remains in his current position and does not perform any additional maneuvers or actions before his next combat check. Any damage taken that exceeds the character's soak also negates the benefit of aiming.

Aiming provides the character with one of the two following bonuses:

- Gain ▢ on the next combat check. If the character spends two consecutive maneuvers aiming, he gains ▢▢ on the next combat check.

- Target a specific item carried by the target, or a specific part of the target. This could allow the character to attempt to strike or shoot a weapon from an opponent's hand, for example, or target an opponent's limb to cripple him. If the character spends one maneuver aiming to do this, his next combat check suffers ■■. If he spends two consecutive maneuvers aiming, the combat check suffers ■ instead.

### ASSIST

Whether a character is trying to get a repulsorlift engine up and running or is using a medpac on a wounded comrade, it never hurts to have a little bit of help. Performing the assist maneuver allows an engaged ally to add ▢ to his next check. Several characters can use the assist maneuver to add more bonus ▢ to the engaged ally's next check. All awarded bonus dice must be used on the assisted character's next turn; otherwise, they are discarded. The Game Master should use his own discretion when allowing characters to assist one another. Some actions simply do not benefit from assistance.

### GUARDED STANCE

When a character is confronted by an angry Gamorrean with a vibro-ax, he may be inclined to defend himself rather than taking an ineffectual swing at his opponent. In such an instance, the character can take a maneuver to assume a guarded stance, which contributes to his defense against melee attacks. A character who performs this maneuver adds ■ to any combat checks he makes until the end of his next turn. However, he also gains melee defense +1 until the end of his next turn.

### INTERACT WITH THE ENVIRONMENT

Often, a single maneuver is enough to interact with the environment around a character. This is a broad category of possible interactions, such as opening a blast door, ducking behind a wall, pressing a specific button on a control panel, or grabbing a blaster off of the ground. The following are additional specifically designed examples of interacting with the environment:

- **Moving a large item.** Flipping over a table, shoving a barrel into a pursuer's path, hefting a crate: each of these takes a maneuver to perform.

- **Opening or closing a door.** Whether an electronic blast door or a primitive door with latches and hinges, opening or closing it takes a maneuver.

- **Taking cover.** Ducking behind a door jamb, crouching behind a crate, or peeking around a tree trunk: all of these allow the character to gain ranged defense 1 (and some cover can grant a ranged defense higher than 1, if particularly sturdy). It takes a maneuver to take cover, but once in cover, the character keeps the bonus unless the circumstances around him change such that he no longer benefits from cover, or he moves out of cover.

## MANAGE GEAR

Managing items and equipment is accomplished by this maneuver, which can cover the following options:

- **Draw, holster, ready, or load a weapon.** This maneuver covers the basic manipulations of most weapons, such as drawing a vibroknife from its sheath, reloading a blaster rifle's energy cells (provided the character has additional ammo at hand—see page 189), or drawing and arming a thermal detonator for use.

- **Draw something from storage or put it away.** A character can perform a maneuver to retrieve an item from a pouch, backpack, satchel, bandolier, or some other accessible container. This maneuver can also be used to stow items in a similar fashion.

## MOUNT OR DISMOUNT

Across the many worlds of the galaxy, beasts of burden are commonly used by characters to get from place to place. Mounting or dismounting a domesticated animal, such as a trained dewback or tauntaun, requires a maneuver. (Successfully mounting an **untrained** animal, however, requires an **Average [◆ ◆] Survival check**, which could be made harder depending on how ornery the GM feels the animal is.) Similarly, mounting a vehicle, sliding into a cockpit, or otherwise taking position to pilot a vehicle, crew a gunnery station, or the like requires a maneuver as well.

## MOVE

One of the most important maneuvers a character can make is to move—from one piece of cover to the next, to a wounded ally's side, away from an assassin droid's integrated vibroblade, or out of range of an enemy's blaster pistol. The game defines several different broad types of movement. When characters move, they do one of the following:

- **Change range increment.** Performing this maneuver allows a character to move between short and medium range relative to another person or object. Performing two move maneuvers allows a character to move between medium and long range or between long and extreme range. When covering long distances, multiple maneuvers do not have to be performed on the same turn, but the character is not considered to be in the new range increment until all required maneuvers have been performed. For more detail on determining range, see **Range Bands**, page 213.

## FLYING

**F**light in Force and Destiny is handled in two different ways. Vehicles and starships that fly use the rules found in **Chapter VII: Starships and Vehicles** to handle their flight. Some pieces of equipment allow individuals to mimic such flight and use these rules as well.

However, some creatures and individuals can fly, but not at the same speeds as vehicles or mechanical devices such as jump packs. In these cases, the creatures or individuals simply move from one place to the other by flying, but still use the rules presented in this chapter for situations such as combat. Their flight is handled mostly narratively, with a common-sense approach. For example, a flying creature could easily fly over difficult or impassable terrain, or fly over water without having to swim. It could cover vertical distances in the same way that individuals cover horizontal ones. However, there are some points to keep in mind concerning flying creatures.

Creatures and species that can hover (such as insects and Toydarians, for example) rely on swiftly moving wings, bags of lighter-than-air gas, or other systems to move while staying above the ground. This type of movement follows the same game rules as those for other creatures, with the following exceptions: hovering creatures ignore difficult or impassable terrain as long as they can reasonably stay above it, and they ignore the penalties for moving through water. They generally have to stay relatively close to the ground (within medium range) unless noted otherwise.

Creatures that can fly (such as most birds and mynocks) use aerodynamic principles such as lift to stay aloft. These follow all the same rules about terrain as creatures that hover. However, they have to maintain at least some speed to stay aloft, and thus while flying must spend one maneuver every turn to move (they can actually change position, or just circle or wheel in place and effectively remain where they are). Most flying creatures can move faster than hovering or ground creatures, and they can move from long range to short range using a single maneuver.

- **Engage or disengage from an opponent.** If a target is already within short range of a character, the character can perform a maneuver to engage that target. If the character is engaged with an opponent or adversary, he must perform a maneuver to disengage with that opponent before moving to any other location. This only changes his range relative to his opponent from "engaged" to "short" and represents the effort of backing away and avoiding his opponent's attacks. Characters do not need to perform this maneuver to leave an engagement consisting only of friendly characters or allies.

- **Moving within short range.** Performing this maneuver allows an unengaged character to move to another position that is currently within short range of the character.

## DROP PRONE OR STAND FROM PRONE

Dropping prone and standing from a prone position each requires a maneuver. Dropping prone allows the character to add ■ to all ranged attacks made against him, although he also must add □ to all melee attacks made against him.

## PREPARATION

Some actions require additional preparation to perform safely or effectively. The preparation maneuver is generally performed in conjunction with another ability to confer a bonus, offset a penalty, or fulfill a requirement. The individual talents or abilities that utilize the preparation maneuver define its specific effect. It is sometimes abbreviated under the requirements as "prepare."

# ACTIONS

During a character's turn, he generally has the chance to perform one primary activity. This is the character's action. Actions include any activity complex enough to warrant a skill check, such as slicing into a secured computer network, firing a blaster rifle, or leaping across a chasm.

## ACTION LIMITATIONS

A character may only perform one action in a turn. Some characters may have abilities allowing them to perform an action as a maneuver. This does not violate the limit of one action per turn, as the action now counts as a maneuver.

## TYPES OF ACTIONS

There are five major types of actions a character can perform during his turn: exchanging an action for a maneuver, spending the action to activate an ability or talent, activating a Force power, performing a skill check, and performing a combat check. The last, performing a combat check, is actually a variation on performing a skill check. However, enough unique circumstances surround it that it requires its own entry.

### EXCHANGE AN ACTION FOR A MANEUVER

A character may exchange his action for an additional maneuver during his turn. He may then perform any maneuver he would be able to perform normally, following all the rules that govern maneuvers. However, he still may not perform more than two maneuvers during his turn, no matter how he gained access to them.

### SPEND AN ACTION TO ACTIVATE AN ABILITY

Certain abilities and talents can require an action to activate. When a character spends an action to activate an ability or talent (even if spending the action does not require a check or any other activity on the character's part), he has used his action for his turn. He may not take a second action, unless he specifically has an ability that grants him a second action.

### ACTIVATE A FORCE POWER

Most Force powers require an action to use. These are covered in more detail in **Chapter VIII: The Force**.

### PERFORM A SKILL CHECK

The most common actions that most characters take during their turns are actions that require a skill check to resolve. In other words, these are activities for which success is not guaranteed or for which the failure of the task may be important to the ongoing story. For example, walking from one place to another does not bring with it any inherent risk of failure (the characters are assumed to be competent enough to handle walking from one location to another), and even if a character could fail, failing would not significantly change the ongoing story. However, trying to cross a chasm on a tightrope to escape pursuit brings an inherent risk of failure (falling and dying), and failing can advance the story (whether or not the character escapes pursuit). Therefore, a Coordination check would be called for, and if it occurred during an encounter, it would require an action to perform.

Most skill checks and what they can accomplish are covered in **Chapter III: Skills**. What a character can do with a skill outside of an encounter is the same as what he can do with it inside of an encounter. The only difference is that inside an encounter, he has certain time limits imposed. In fact, the GM can determine that certain activities may require more than one action to perform, if they would normally take a great deal of time. (If the activity is time-consuming enough that it cannot be performed while the encounter continues, the GM may require the character to wait for the encounter to end before attempting the activity.)

Combat checks, however, are unique enough that they require a separate description.

## PERFORM A COMBAT CHECK

A PC makes a **combat check** when he uses a combat skill to attack a target—by firing a blaster, throwing a punch, or swinging a lightsaber, for example. This is also referred to as an **attack**. The combat skills in **FORCE AND DESTINY** consist of the following: Brawl, Gunnery, Lightsaber, Melee, Ranged (Heavy), and Ranged (Light). All of these skills are covered in **Chapter III: Skills**. However, in brief, Brawl pertains to hand-to-hand combat without weapons; Melee governs fighting with close combat weapons such as vibro-axes; Lightsaber covers fighting with lightsabers and other similar weapons; Gunnery handles using heavy, crew-served weapons; Ranged (Light) covers fighting with pistols; and Ranged (Heavy) covers fighting with rifles and other ranged weapons.

First and foremost, keep in mind that a combat check is a skill check. It follows all of the rules and procedures for making a skill check, including the steps for assembling the dice pool. However, there are additional steps included in a combat check. All the steps a combat check follows are detailed here.

### 1. DECLARE AN ATTACK AND SELECT TARGETS

The character chooses to make an attack. He selects what skill he will use to make the attack and, if the skill requires a weapon to use, which weapon he will be using. He then declares the target of his attack.

### 2. ASSEMBLE THE DICE POOL

The character then assembles the dice pool based on the skill, its characteristic, and any applicable talents or other abilities. Certain conditions, such as the painful effect of a Critical Injury or an environmental effect such as fog or darkness, may also contribute dice to the dice pool. See page 27 for more information on building a dice pool.

The difficulty of a combat check depends on whether the attack is a ranged attack (using Ranged [Light], Ranged [Heavy], or Gunnery) or a melee attack (using Melee, Brawl, or Lightsaber). Melee attack difficulties are always **Average (◆ ◆)**. Ranged attack difficulties depend on the distance the target is from the active character, or in other words, the range band the target occupies. **Table 6–1: Ranged Attack Difficulties** lists difficulties as they relate to different range bands. See page 213 for more information about range bands. Once the pool is assembled, roll the dice.

## TABLE 6–1: RANGED ATTACK DIFFICULTIES

| Range Band | Difficulty |
|---|---|
| Engaged | **Easy (◆)** plus modifiers depending on weapon used; see page 217. |
| Short | **Easy (◆)** |
| Medium | **Average (◆ ◆)** |
| Long | **Hard (◆ ◆ ◆)** |
| Extreme | **Daunting (◆ ◆ ◆ ◆)** |

### 3. POOL RESULTS AND DEAL DAMAGE

Once the player rolls the dice pool for the attack, the player evaluates the results. As with any skill check, the check must generate more ☆ than ▼ to be successful.

When making a combat check, if the check is successful, each uncanceled ☆ adds +1 damage to a successful attack. If the attack affects multiple targets, the additional damage is added to each target.

### 4. RESOLVE ۞ AND ⊕

Just as they can be spent in a non-combat skill check, ۞ and ⊕ can be spent in a combat check to gain incidental beneficial effects. However, just as the rules

## RANGED ATTACKS AND MELEE ATTACKS

Ranged attacks and melee attacks are two different types of attacks, meaning they are also two different types of combat checks. A ranged attack is an attack made with a ranged weapon of some sort, most likely using the Ranged (Light), Ranged (Heavy), or Gunnery skill. A melee attack is an attack made in close combat with an opponent, and with a weapon designed for use in close combat. Such an attack is most likely to be made using the Melee, Brawl, or Lightsaber skill.

governing encounters are somewhat more regimented than the rules governing narrative gameplay, so some of the options governing the spending of ✹ and ✥ are more clearly defined. In encounters, the player controlling the active character determines how the character spends ✹ and ✥, unless the GM has a specific reason to decide instead.

The first and foremost ways to spend ✹ and ✥ in an attack are to activate a Critical Injury or active item quality. As described on page 165 and page 223, each weapon has a critical rating that consists of a numeric value. The user can spend that many ✹ to inflict one Critical Injury on the target, in addition to regular effects and damage. Remember, a Critical Injury can only be triggered upon a successful hit that deals damage that exceeds the target's soak value. For more information on Critical Injuries, see page 223.

Item qualities are special effects and abilities that apply only when a character is using that particular weapon—the vicious edge of a vibroblade, say, or the auto-fire capability of a heavy blaster rifle. Item qualities come in two forms: active and passive. Active qualities require the user to spend a certain number of ✹ to trigger them. Generally this is ✹ ✹, although some qualities may require more or fewer. Passive qualities always grant their effect. Some qualities may inflict effects on a target that, unless specified otherwise, are always applied in addition to other effects, Critical Injuries, and damage.

In addition to always counting as an additional ✶, ✥ can be spent to activate item qualities as well. A ✥ may be spent to inflict one Critical Injury (no matter what the critical rating of the weapon is). Alternatively, a ✥ may be spent to activate one item quality, no matter how many ✹ it would normally take to do so.

There are other options for spending ✹ and ✥ as well. A list of the most common can be found on **Table 6–2: Spending ✹ and ✥ in Combat**, on page 212. Keep in mind that these are not intended to be the only options available. As always, players and GMs may invent other ways to spend ✹ and ✥, depending on the specific circumstances of the encounter. Any option that the players and GM agree upon can be viable.

## 5. RESOLVE ⊚ AND ▽

In the same fashion in which the controlling player determines how to spend ✹ and ✥ in his combat check, the GM then determines how to spend any ⊚ or ▽ generated in the check. Much as fortune might favor the player, bad luck and circumstance can conspire against him. By default, the GM determines how ⊚ and ▽ are spent, although in some cases (such as checks made by NPCs) he may give the players the option to spend these instead.

Although many weapon descriptions include options for spending ✹ and ✥, most do not for ⊚ and ▽; however, this is not always the case. Some particularly volatile or dangerous weapons do have these options, and if they do, the options are detailed in the weapon's description. Specific options for spending ⊚ and ▽ in encounters do exist, however, and the most common of these can be found on **Table 6–3: Spending ⊚ and ▽ in Combat**, on page 212. As with ✹ and ✥, keep in mind that these are not intended to be the only options available. As always, GMs may invent other ways to spend ⊚ and ▽, depending on the specific circumstances of the encounter, and any option that the players and GM agree on can be viable.

## 6. REDUCE DAMAGE, APPLY TO WOUND THRESHOLD, AND APPLY CRITICAL INJURIES

When a character suffers damage, whether from a stormtrooper's blaster rifle or a rancor's claws, he reduces the damage received by his soak value. If any damage remains after this reduction, he suffers that many wounds. If the net result is zero or negative, the character suffers no wounds; his toughness and natural fortitude, in conjunction with any armor he might be wearing, have saved him from being injured. If the character suffers damage from multiple hits in an attack, he applies his soak value to each hit individually. For more information on damage and wounds, see **Wounds, Strain, and States of Health**, on page 222.

## CUSTOM SKILLS IN COMBAT

Some players may have characters who use custom Combat skills. This is acceptable within the game (as long as the GM is fine with it). However, many of the rules in this chapter are written with the six basic Combat skills in mind and do not mention custom Combat skills specifically. Thus, players need to determine beforehand whether these skills are used to make ranged attacks or close combat attacks. Ideally, they should determine to what existing skill their new, custom skill is most similar, and apply the same modifiers to their new skill that apply to the original skill.

## TABLE 6-2: SPENDING ⟐ AND ✦ IN COMBAT

| Cost | Result Options |
|---|---|
| ⟐ or ✦ | Recover 1 strain. |
| | Add □ to the next allied active character's check. |
| | Notice a single important point in the ongoing conflict, such as the location of a blast door's control panel or a weak point on an attack speeder. |
| | Inflict a Critical Injury with a successful attack that deals damage past soak (⟐ cost may vary). |
| | Activate an item quality (⟐ cost may vary). |
| ⟐ ⟐ or ✦ | Perform an immediate free maneuver that does not exceed the two maneuvers per turn limit. |
| | Add ■ to the targeted character's next check. |
| | Add □ to any allied character's next check, including that of the active character. |
| ⟐ ⟐ ⟐ or ✦ | Negate the targeted enemy's defensive bonuses (such as the defense gained from cover, equipment, or performing the guarded stance maneuver) until the end of the current round. |
| | Ignore penalizing environmental effects such as inclement weather, zero gravity, or similar circumstances until the end of the active character's next turn. |
| | When dealing damage to a target, have the attack disable the opponent or one piece of gear rather than dealing wounds or strain. This could include hobbling him temporarily with a shot to the leg, or disabling his comlink. This should be agreed upon by the player and the GM, and the effects are up to the GM (although **Table 6–10: Critical Injury Result** is a good resource to consult for possible effects). The effects should be temporary and not too excessive. |
| | Gain +1 melee or ranged defense until the end of the active character's next turn. |
| | Force the target to drop a melee or ranged weapon he is wielding. |
| ✦ | Upgrade the difficulty of the targeted character's next check. |
| | Upgrade any allied character's next check, including that of the current active character. |
| | Do something vital, such as shooting the controls to the nearby blast doors to seal them shut. |
| ✦ ✦ | When dealing damage to a target, have the attack destroy a piece of equipment the target is using, such as blowing up his blaster or destroying a personal shield generator. |
| | Destroy the lightsaber an opponent is wielding. At the GM's discretion, the crystal may be salvaged from the destroyed lightsaber and installed in a new hilt, with any modifications intact. |

## TABLE 6-3: SPENDING ⊛ AND ▽ IN COMBAT

| Cost | Result Options |
|---|---|
| ⊛ or ▽ | The active character suffers 1 strain. |
| | The active character loses the benefits of a prior maneuver (such as from taking cover or assuming a guarded stance) until he performs the maneuver again. |
| ⊛ ⊛ or ▽ | An opponent may immediately perform one free maneuver in response to the active character's check. |
| | Add □ to the targeted character's next check. |
| | The active character or an allied character suffers ■ on his next action. |
| ⊛ ⊛ ⊛ or ▽ | The active character falls prone. |
| | The active character grants the enemy a significant advantage in the ongoing encounter, such as accidentally blasting the controls to a bridge the active character was planning to use for his escape. |
| ▽ | The character's ranged weapon immediately runs out of ammunition and may not be used for the remainder of the encounter. |
| | Upgrade the difficulty of an allied character's next check or the next check of the current active character. |
| | The tool or Melee weapon the active character is using becomes damaged (see page 166). |

**EXAMPLE: APPLYING SOAK**

Dao Jodh is wearing heavy clothes, and with his natural Brawn, he has a total soak value of 4. A successful hit with a blaster pistol deals 9 points of damage. His soak value absorbs 4 points of that damage, resulting in 5 wounds.

An attack may also generate a Critical Injury. This may occur because the weapon's critical rating was triggered, or because the target suffered a number of wounds greater than its wound threshold. More about critical ratings is explained in **Step 4: Resolve ⟐ and ✦**.

When a Critical Injury is inflicted, the attacker rolls percentile dice on **Table 6–10: Critical Injury Result**, on page 225. The result of the dice roll indicates which Critical Injury is inflicted.

Some weapons and talents modify this Critical Injury roll, potentially making it more or less effective. If an attack generates enough ⟐ to trigger more than one Critical Injury, the character makes a single Critical Injury roll, adding +10 to the result for each additional time the critical rating is triggered.

# DEFENSE

Defense, or more specifically, **defense rating**, is one of the factors determining how difficult it is to land a successful attack during combat. Defense ratings represent the abilities of shields, armor, or other defensive systems to deflect attacks entirely, or to absorb or lessen incoming blows.

Defense ratings are most commonly provided by shields, and as such are usually limited to vehicles and starships. However, a character may gain a defense rating through talents that increase his ability to dodge and absorb blows, armor designed to deflect and diffuse shots, or even expensive personal shield generators.

**A character adds a number of ■ equal to his defense rating to all combat checks directed against him.**

## MELEE AND RANGED DEFENSE

A character's defense rating can be classified as one of three types: general defense rating, melee defense rating, or ranged defense rating. A general defense rating applies against all combat checks directed against the character. A melee defense rating only applies against close combat checks directed against the character (Brawl, Lightsaber, and Melee checks). A ranged defense rating only applies against ranged combat checks directed against the character (Ranged [Light], Ranged [Heavy], and Gunnery checks).

Multiple sources of defense do not stack. However, the character always uses the best defense rating available to him. If the PC possesses a defense rating of 1 against all attacks but a defense rating of 2 against melee attacks, he applies the defense 2 against all close combat attacks directed at him.

# SOAK

A character's soak value helps protect him from incoming wounds. Most creatures and characters have a default soak value equal to their Brawn rating. Most types of armor and other forms of protection provide additional soak (see **Chapter V: Gear and Equipment**).

When taking damage from attacks (actions involving a combat skill check) or other sources of physical damage (such as being struck by a falling rock or being hit by a landspeeder), the character may reduce the damage taken by his soak value. After calculating the total amount of damage inflicted, subtract the total soak value from that damage total. The result is the number of wounds the character suffers. If the

soak reduces the damage to zero or less than zero, then the character takes no damage. If the character suffers multiple hits from a single attack (such as from a weapon with Auto-fire), he applies his soak to each hit separately.

Soak stacks when it is from different sources, such as heavy assault armor and subdermal plating. Multiple applications of the same source do not stack, however. A character cannot wear three suits of heavy assault armor and stack the soak bonuses from each.

Soak does not reduce strain inflicted on a target, except in specific instances (such as when hit by a weapon with the Stun Damage quality).

# RANGE BANDS

FORCE AND DESTINY relies on broad terms to describe ranges and distances. Rather than have a player's attention focused on a grid, counting squares, FORCE AND DESTINY uses more abstract means to represent positions, distances, and ranges, thus allowing the players to focus on the action and the adventure.

The distance between two points—people, objects, or adversaries—is defined by general range

categories. These range categories are used to determine how far a ranged attack can reach, how far apart two people are from each other, how much effort is needed to move between two places, and so on. The most common ranges are short, medium, long, and extreme range. Another relative position—engaged—exists to represent characters who are in extremely close proximity to each other.

# THE FIVE RANGE BANDS

For ease of play, distance in **Force and Destiny** is divided up into five different bands, from engaged to extreme. As always, the GM has the final say in determining the range between the attacker and the target.

With the engaged status and the range bands, the GM is free to describe things dynamically and set scenes without having to worry about exact distances. Exact distances in meters do not matter. The details and adventure come first, creating a vivid picture in the minds of the players while allowing the GM to quickly provide the mechanical information they need to use their actions and build strategies.

### ENGAGED

To reflect two or more targets who are grappling or otherwise engaged in hand-to-hand combat, there is a special range status called engaged. Two characters engaged with each other are in very close proximity. A Warrior needs to be engaged with a target to hit him with his lightsaber. When two or more characters are engaged with each other, it is called an engagement.

Engaged is also used to indicate that a person is close enough to an item to use it. An Artisan needs to be engaged with a security terminal to attempt to hack it. A Starfighter Ace needs to be engaged with his starfighter to board it. A Pathfinder needs to be engaged with a tree if he wants to hide behind it for cover while tracking his target. The engaged status simply indicates that two things are close enough to each other to directly interact.

Consider engaged as a subcategory of short range. Obviously, someone can be slightly farther away if they're at short range, instead of being engaged with someone else. However, the difference in distance is relatively minor. Thus, spending a maneuver to move to engage someone or something is as much a matter of moving into combat cautiously enough to avoid receiving a blow unnecessarily as it is moving a physical distance.

## RELATIVE POSITIONING

**B**ecause of the narrative, abstract way in which distance is measured, both the players and Game Master must be aware of how positioning relative to two or more targets is measured. Once combat begins, the Game Master will tell each player where his character is relative to the opponents. It's then up to the player to track his character's range relative to those opponents as the battle progresses.

For example, during a battle within a huge hangar bay, the PCs are ambushed by four stormtroopers. Two approach from one side and two from the other. The GM indicates that each pair of stormtroopers is in the medium range band with respect to the characters. During their turns, the PCs split up to attack. Two of the PCs move toward one group of stormtroopers, getting within short range, and the other group moves to the opposite set of stormtroopers. Both groups of characters are now within short range of their respective targets, but at medium range from the other group of targets.

Personal and planetary ranges of scale should be considered separately. At a planetary scale, two starships attacking each other at close range does not translate to being within short range of each other on the personal scale—rather, the distance is considered farther than extreme range on the personal scale. (Even the shots of Ranged [Heavy] weapons normally only reach long range on the personal scale.) Two ships docked together are considered engaged at a planetary scale, but a gun battle on the surface of either ship utilizes the personal range bands, in which characters may be at long or even extreme range from each other.

### SHORT RANGE

Short range indicates up to several meters between targets. Many thrown weapons and small firearms are most accurate at short range. Two people within short range of each other can talk comfortably without raising their voices. Moving to another spot within short range is usually easy to do and generally only requires one maneuver.

### MEDIUM RANGE

Medium range can be up to several dozen meters away. More reliable pistols can reach to medium range, but few thrown weapons can reach this far. Two people within medium range of each other need to talk loudly to hear each other. Moving from short range to medium range takes little exertion and generally requires one maneuver.

### LONG RANGE

Long range is farther than a few dozen meters. Blaster rifles, mounted weapons, and weapons that use the Gunnery skill can reliably reach this far without too much trouble. Two people within long range of each other need to yell loudly to hear each other. Moving from medium range to long range requires two maneuvers, as it involves a greater distance and takes more time than moving between medium range and short range. This means that in most cases, a character cannot close the distance between short and long range in a single round, as it would take three maneuvers (one for short to medium, plus two for medium to long).

### EXTREME RANGE

Extreme range is the farthest range at which two targets can interact. High-tech sniper weaponry and some vehicle-mounted armaments may reach out to this range. Two people at extreme range may not be able to hear each other even if they shout. Moving between long range and extreme range can be time-consuming and exerting, and it requires two maneuvers. This means that in most cases, a character can move the entire distance between long and extreme range in a single round, but will suffer strain or give up his action to do so.

## PLANETARY SCALE RANGE

The distances and range bands presented in this chapter are based on the personal scale for characters. Starships and vehicles may use these range bands or much larger range bands, based on the needs of the story. On a planet's surface, personal scale range bands may suffice, while in the midst of a heated starship battle in the depths of outer space, range bands represent much larger distances and positions.

A good guideline is that close range on the planetary scale picks up where the extreme range of personal scale ends—it's the next step in ranged bands. However, the scale is so much bigger that a single person could never use maneuvers to move next to a target that's "close" to him on a planetary scale; the distance may be up to several kilometers and take hours of walking. Further range bands on a planetary scale would be even more extreme. See page 244 in **Chapter VII: Starships and Vehicles** for more details on planetary and starship-based ranges and distances.

# ADDITIONAL COMBAT MODIFIERS

The prior sections cover the fundamentals of making a basic combat check. However, combat rarely occurs in a vacuum. Any number of things can modify a combat check, from environmental factors to actions the character chooses.

This section discusses those modifiers. The first part of this section covers conditional and situational modifiers; the second part covers outside factors such as environmental effects.

## CONDITIONAL AND SITUATIONAL MODIFIERS

Character choices can modify combat checks in many ways, some good and some bad. These choices often provide additional benefits as well.

### MAKING RANGED ATTACKS AT ENGAGED TARGETS

Sometimes, characters may want to attack a target engaged with another character. If the target and the character with whom he is engaged are both enemies of the attacker, the attacker may not worry about whom he might hit. However, if one of the characters is an ally, then things become more dangerous.

When attacking a target engaged with an ally, the attacker upgrades the difficulty of the check by one (for more on upgrading difficulty, see page 29). In addition, if the attacker's check succeeds but generates at least ◈, that ◈ is automatically spent to make the attacker hit one of the individuals engaged with the target (of the GM's choice), instead of hitting the target.

### MAKING RANGED ATTACKS WHILE ENGAGED

Sometimes, a character may want to make a ranged attack even though he's locked in hand-to-hand combat with an enemy. Such an action can be risky; a character may find it hard to take the time to line up a shot while an opponent is swinging a vibro-ax at him!

Any opponent engaged with a character when the character makes a ranged attack (no matter who the target is), may add ▢ to his next Brawl, Melee, or Lightsaber check against that character. He automatically loses this bonus if he and the character are no longer engaged with each other.

In addition, the difficulty of some ranged attacks increases while the attacker and an enemy are engaged, and other ranged attacks become impossible. See **Table 6—4: Ranged Modifiers** for more information.

## TABLE 6-4: RANGED MODIFIERS

| Condition | Modifier |
|---|---|
| Engaged w/Ranged (Light) | +1 difficulty |
| Engaged w/Ranged (Heavy) | +2 difficulty |
| Engaged w/Gunnery | May not make Gunnery checks when engaged with an opponent |

### ATTACKING PRONE TARGETS AND ATTACKING WHILE PRONE

A character who is knocked down, unconscious, or willingly drops prone is considered prone.

Prone characters are easier to hit with certain combat checks and find it harder to use certain combat skills. A character gains ▢ when attacking a prone target with a Melee, Brawl, or Lightsaber check. A prone character suffers ■ when making a Melee, Brawl, or Lightsaber check from a prone position.

Prone characters are harder to hit with ranged attacks but suffer no penalties when making ranged attacks. When a character attacks a prone target with a Ranged (Light), Ranged (Heavy), or Gunnery check, he suffers ■.

Some attacks or weapons may cause a character to become prone. This is indicated in the individual weapon, talent, or creature attack entries. Getting knocked prone may be the result of a failed Coordination check or of the activation of a weapon's special quality.

### TWO-WEAPON COMBAT

A character may opt to carry a pistol or a one-handed melee weapon in each hand, increasing his volume of attacks at the expense of accuracy.

When attacking with two weapons, the character must be using weapons that can each be reasonably held and wielded in one hand. Generally, these weapons are Ranged (Light) weapons—such as pistols and grenades—and one-handed Melee, Brawl, or Lightsaber weapons. If it's unclear whether or not a weapon can be wielded one-handed, the GM makes the final determination.

To make the attack, the player performs a **combined check**. First, the player designates one weapon as the primary weapon. When making the combined check, the character attacks with this weapon. The player then determines what skills and characteristics the character uses when making attacks with the primary weapon and which are used with the secondary weapon (the other weapon wielded). Finally, he determines the target.

## TABLE 6-5: IMPROVISED WEAPONS

| Size | Dam | Crit | Range | Encum | Special | Examples |
|------|-----|------|-------|-------|---------|----------|
| Small | +1 | 5 | Engaged | 1 | – | Bottle, fist-sized rock, hydrospanner |
| Medium | +2 | 5 | Engaged | 3 | Cumbersome 2 | Two-handed rock, chair, holovid screen |
| Large | +3 | 5 | Engaged | 4 | Cumbersome 4 | Shovel, large tree branch, table, crate |

To assemble the dice pool for this check, the player compares the skills that would be used to make an attack with each weapon by itself, and then compares the characteristics that would be used to make an attack with each weapon by itself. He then takes the skill that he has lower ranks in, and the characteristic that he has lower ranks in, and uses this skill and characteristic to assemble his dice pool. It's very possible that the ranks in either the skills or characteristics are equal, in which case he can use either. If both checks would use the same skill or characteristic, he simply uses that skill or characteristic.

He then compares the difficulty of the two combat checks he would make with each of his two weapons to hit his target, and selects the check with the higher difficulty. He then increases the difficulty by one if the two skills in the combined check were the same, and by two if they were different. He then makes the check.

If he succeeds, he hits with his primary weapon as normal. He may also spend 🔣 🔣 or ⬦ to hit with his secondary weapon as well. If both weapons hit, he may spend additional 🔣 or ⬦ to activate qualities from either weapon. Each hit deals its base damage, +1 damage per uncanceled success.

### UNARMED COMBAT

Although most characters probably feel more comfortable going into a fight with a good blaster in their hand, there are times they must rely on their fists, feet, or other appendages. Of course, some species, such as Nautolans, positively relish a good brawl.

Characters fighting unarmed generally use the Brawl combat skill. Unlike other combat skills, the Brawl skill is designed to be used independently of any weapons (although some weapons can be used in conjunction with the Brawl skill).

When making an unarmed combat check using Brawl, the character's attack has a base damage of his Brawn rating, a range of engaged, a critical rating of 5, and the Disorient 1 and Knockdown qualities. Finally, when making a Brawl attack, the attacker can choose to deal damage to the target's strain threshold instead of its wound threshold, still reducing the damage by the target's soak.

Unlike other weapons, Brawl weapons augment this basic attack. Brawl weapons can add damage to the attack (as indicated in the **Brawl** profile, on page 171) and may have an improved critical rating and additional item qualities. When using a Brawl weapon, the user can choose to use its critical rating instead of the standard Brawl critical rating. He also adds the additional weapon qualities to the qualities already provided by the Brawl attack. If the weapon provides an improved version of an existing quality, the character uses the improved version.

### IMPROVISED WEAPONS

Sometimes a character doesn't have a real weapon available and must make do with anything that is on hand. Swinging a broken bottle, heavy tool, large rock, or tree branch at a target are all examples of using an improvised weapon. Improvised weapons use the Melee skill, and as with all Melee weapons, the attacker adds his Brawn to the damage dealt. Just like weapons with the Inferior quality, improvised weapons generate one automatic ⚙ on any check. Improvised weapons deal damage based on their size and general weight, as described in **Table 6–5: Improvised Weapons**. Any attack roll that results in a 🜚 or ⚙ ⚙ indicates that the improvised weapon breaks and is useless in further rounds of combat. Large improvised weapons require two hands to use if the user is silhouette 1 or smaller.

### SIZE DIFFERENCES (SILHOUETTES)

Generally, it's a character's skill that governs his chances of hitting a target. However, some targets are easier to hit than others, usually because of their size. Size, or **silhouette**, is usually used to determine the difficulty of attacks made from vehicles or starships (as described in **Chapter VII: Starships and**

### GRAPPLING

**F**ORCE AND DESTINY, being a more narrative game, does not possess specific rules for grappling. Instead, the unarmed combat rules have been designed to narratively cover multiple unarmed fighting techniques, including grappling. For this reason, the basic Brawl attack allows characters to deal damage to the target's strain threshold, and to knock the target prone and disorient him. This allows for the narrative of a grapple (which is often intended to incapacitate without killing) without additional rules.

Vehicles), as vehicle weapons are powerful and long-ranged enough that relative sizes matter more than distance. However, silhouettes can affect attack difficulties in standard combat as well.

When a character makes an attack against a target with a silhouette 2 or more points larger than he is, he decreases the difficulty of the check by one. When a character makes an attack against a target with a silhouette 2 or more points smaller than he is, he increases the difficulty of the check by one. (Vehicles and starships can have an even more difficult time shooting at targets with greater differences in silhouette, but when it comes to characters, checks are only modified somewhat due to size.)

**Table 6–6: Silhouettes and Characters** has a list of example silhouettes that covers the size of most

## TABLE 6-6: SILHOUETTES AND CHARACTERS

| Silhouette | Examples |
|---|---|
| 0 | Jawas, Ewoks, astromech droids, any smaller creatures. |
| 1 | Humans, Cereans, Nautolans, Kel'Dor, Mirialans, Twi'leks, humanoid droids, Zabrak, Togrutas, and most humanoid species. |
| 2 | Dewbacks, wampas, tauntauns, banthas, most riding animals. |
| 3 | Rancors, krayt dragons, other large and dangerous creatures. |
| 4+ | There are some creatures in the galaxy even larger than those listed. |

creatures the PCs may encounter. The most important thing to remember is that most characters are silhouette 1.

# ENVIRONMENTAL EFFECTS

The galaxy is made up of countless environments, from the frozen wastes of Hoth to the steamy jungles of Yavin 4 and the kilometer-high skyscrapers of Coruscant. Characters can often find themselves fighting in hazardous or exotic circumstances ranging from the cold, hard vacuum of space to the infernal heat of a volcanic planet such as Mustafar. Canny combatants know that taking advantage of their environment can make all the difference between triumph and defeat in an engagement. The following sections cover rules imposed by those environments.

## CONCEALMENT (DARKNESS, SMOKE, AND INTERVENING TERRAIN)

Concealment is a situation that occurs when a character is hard to spot because of environmental effects such as darkness, smoke, tall grass, or mist. Concealment imposes penalties on ranged attacks and sight-based skill checks such as many Perception checks. Conversely, it can provide bonuses for checks on other skills, such as Stealth.

The exact bonuses and penalties can be modified by the GM if needed. However, in general, concealment can be divided into levels based on how obscuring the concealment is. See **Table 6–7: Concealment** for examples of different types of concealment. In each case, the type of concealment adds a number of ■ equal to the "Dice Added" entry to any Ranged (Light), Ranged (Heavy), Gunnery, and Perception checks against targets with concealment. Conversely, it adds a number of □ equal to the "Dice Added" entry to any Stealth checks made by a character with concealment. These bonuses or setbacks may also be added to other skill checks if the GM feels it's appropriate.

## TABLE 6-7: CONCEALMENT

| Dice Added | Examples |
|---|---|
| +1 | Mist, shadow, waist-high grass. |
| +2 | Fog; the darkness of early morning or late evening; thick, shoulder-high grass. |
| +3 | Heavy fog; thick and choking smoke; the darkness of night; dense, head-high underbrush; and thick grass. |

### COVER

When the blasters start firing, most characters dive for cover. To keep things simple, being behind some sort of cover—a rock, crate, wall, or vehicle, for example—allows the character to gain a ranged defense of 1 and adds ■ to certain skill checks, such as Perception. A single ■ is sufficient for most situations, although the GM may add additional ■ if the target is particularly well-covered, such if he is within a trench, blockhouse, bunker, or any other prepared position. The same holds true for the increase in ranged defense.

### DIFFICULT AND IMPASSABLE TERRAIN

Difficult terrain is a catchall description of terrain that is hard to move through or over. It can include tight passageways, slippery ice, thick undergrowth, loose rubble, shifting sand, or waist-deep water (or any number of other circumstances). Essentially, it's terrain that characters move through with difficulty. Characters entering or moving through difficult terrain must perform twice as many maneuvers to move the same distance they would in normal terrain.

Impassable terrain is a description of terrain that is simply impossible to move through via maneuvers. This includes sheer cliffs, walls higher than a character can jump, and deep pits. Impassable terrain is not always an insurmountable obstacle, but it's an obstacle that requires special skills to circumvent. Depending on the impassable terrain in question and the resources at the character's disposal, the GM may allow the character to overcome impassable terrain by using a skill, probably the Athletics or Coordination skill (see **Chapter III: Skills**). During an encounter, this means the character must spend at least one action (and possibly give up one or more maneuvers) to accomplish this.

## GRAVITY

Although antigravity has existed in the galaxy for thousands of years, characters might still find themselves in a situation where they are away from an antigrav device, floating in open space, or walking in the crushing gravity of a supergiant planet.

Normal gravity is the default and does not affect any skill checks, attacks, or the like. Most habitable planets possess gravity close enough to normal as to be unnoticeable. Starships and space stations also possess devices that provide normal gravity. However, sometimes the characters end up in an environment without normal gravity: a starship with artificial gravity that has been disrupted by damage or a large planet with a higher-than-normal gravitational pull, for instance.

Stronger-than-normal gravity adds up to ■ ■ ■ to any Brawn-based skill checks (except Resilience checks) and to Coordination skill checks, depending on how strong the gravity is. Weaker-than-normal gravity adds up to ☐ ☐ ☐ to any Brawn-based skill checks (except Resilience checks) and Coordination skill checks, depending on how weak the gravity is.

Zero gravity, on the other hand, does not grant any ☐ or ■ to skill checks, because moving in zero gravity is completely different than moving in a gravity field. Characters can move in three dimensions in zero gravity, but they count all movement as movement through difficult terrain, due to having to constantly grab handholds, evaluate angles, and so forth.

A character's encumbrance threshold does not change due to different gravity, and items still maintain their usual encumbrance. This is because an item's weight may change, but its size and mass (and therefore its inertia) do not. Those pesky details can prove an unpleasant surprise to inexperienced spacers who attempt to shift something large and heavy while in zero gravity.

## WATER AND SWIMMING

Bodies of water such as lakes, rivers, oceans, and swamps are types of terrain encountered on most planets in the galaxy, and sometimes characters must cross them. Most species have some ability to swim through liquid water, although some species, such as Mon Calamari, are more adapted to it than others. Unless otherwise noted, characters treat any body of water as difficult terrain. The GM may also decide that some bodies of water, such as a river with a swift current or an ocean in a storm, are so difficult to move through that they require a successful Athletics check to swim in. In this case, it requires at least one action as well as any number of maneuvers to swim through the water from one location to another.

If completely submerged in water, a character can hold his breath for a number of rounds equal to his Brawn characteristic. Once this number is reached, the character starts to drown and is treated as suffocating (see **Suffocation** on the next page) on each successive round until he surfaces or finds some other source of air.

## VACUUM

For spacers, vacuum is an all-too-familiar and extremely dangerous environment lurking just outside the protective hull of their starship. Vacuum is not just the lack of breathable air; the lack of pressure and extreme heat or cold can cause veins to rupture, blood to boil, and delicate membranes to freeze or tear.

When exposed to vacuum without protective gear, a character may hold his breath for a number of rounds equal to his Brawn characteristic. Once this number is reached, the character begins suffocating (see **Suffocation** on the next page). Furthermore, during each round in which a character is exposed to vacuum, he also suffers 3 wounds. When the character exceeds his wound threshold, he is incapacitated and suffers one Critical Injury as usual, plus one additional Critical Injury during each additional round in which he is exposed to vacuum (which likely will quickly result in death). This is in addition to the Critical Injuries he suffers from suffocating.

## FIRE, ACID, AND CORROSIVE ATMOSPHERES

Fundamentally, the effects of fire, acids, and corrosive atmospheres are treated with the same rules. When characters are exposed to a fire, acid, or a corrosive atmosphere, the GM determines how dangerous the situation is by applying a rating. This rating is generally between 1 and 10, although higher ratings may also apply. A lower rating typically indicates minor, low-heat fire or mildly corrosive liquid or atmosphere. The higher the rating, the hotter the fire or the more corrosive the atmosphere. See **Table 6–8: Fire, Acid, and Corrosive Atmospheres** on the next page, for some examples of different ratings.

Each round at the beginning of his turn, a character subjected to one of these hazards suffers wounds equal to its rating. This damage persists until he is no

## TABLE 6-8: FIRE, ACID, AND CORROSIVE ATMOSPHERES

| Rating | Examples |
|---|---|
| 1–2 | Campfires, mildly caustic substances such as concentrated industrial cleansers, air filled with ash and fumes from a heavy fire. |
| 3–5 | Flammable liquids and flame projectors, dangerous substances such as industrial acids, air contaminated by chemical leaks. |
| 6–9 | Welding torches, weaponized acids, atmospheres with substantial parts dangerous gases such as ammonia or chlorine. |
| 10+ | Lava, blast furnaces, atmospheres completely made of unbreathable and hazardous gases such as ammonia-methane mixes with acid vapors. |

longer exposed to the hazard. With some corrosive atmospheres, the GM may decide they do not cause damage unless inhaled. In this case, the character can hold his breath for a number of rounds equal to his Brawn before having to breathe and suffer damage.

It's primarily up to the GM to decide how long the damage from one of these sources lasts. Acids usually neutralize themselves after a certain period of time (as few as several rounds, or as long as several minutes or hours). Fires burn for as long as they have a fuel source, which again could be very briefly or for a very long time. A corrosive atmosphere, on the other hand, usually deals damage as long as the character is exposed to it.

**Putting out fire/neutralizing acid:** A victim might be able to stop the damage caused by these hazards by rolling around on the ground and making a Coordination

## TABLE 6-9: FALLING DAMAGE

| Range | Damage | Strain |
|---|---|---|
| Short | 10 | 10 |
| Medium | 30 | 20 |
| Long | Incapacitated, Critical Injury at +50 | 30 |
| Extreme | Incapacitated, Critical Injury at +75 (or death at GM's discretion) | 40 |

check. This is an **Average (◆ ◆) check** on hard surfaces such as the deck of a spaceship, or an **Easy (◆) check** on grass or soft ground. Jumping into a body of water stops the damage immediately. In the case of acid, it's up to the GM to determine if the same procedures negate the damage, or if the character must apply some neutralizing substance instead. The only way to stop taking damage from a corrosive atmosphere is to leave it.

### SUFFOCATION

A suffocating character suffers 3 strain each round at the beginning of his turn, until he is no longer suffocating (how to stop suffocating depends entirely on the circumstances that led to the suffocation in the first place, but it usually involves reaching a breathable atmosphere or removing something preventing the character from breathing). Once the character exceeds his strain threshold, he is incapacitated. In addition, at the beginning of each of his subsequent turns, if the character is still suffocating, he suffers one Critical Injury. This continues until the character stops suffocating or dies.

### FALLING

Gravity kills. If a character falls from a height, the GM should determine the distance between the location from which the character falls and his point of impact below, then apply the closest comparable range band. Next, the GM consults **Table 6–9: Falling Damage** to determine the damage suffered. Damage is reduced by soak; however, the strain suffered is not.

A character can reduce the damage taken from falling by making an **Average (◆ ◆) Athletics or Coordination check**. Each ✷ reduces the damage suffered by 1, while each 🝔 reduces the strain suffered by 1. A ⨁ could, at the GM's discretion, reduce the overall distance fallen by one range band as the character grabs onto a handhold or does something else to slow his fall.

# WOUNDS, STRAIN, AND STATES OF HEALTH

In the fast-paced, high-action setting of FORCE AND DESTINY, characters are sure to find themselves in the thick of things, and are likely to pick up a few cuts and bruises along the way. A character's health is tracked using two separate yet similar systems: strain and wounds.

## WOUNDS AND WOUND THRESHOLD

A wide variety of items and actions can inflict physical damage: blaster shots, an angry wampa's claws, frag grenades, falling, etc. Damage to a character's physical body is tracked using wounds. Each point of damage inflicts 1 wound on a character. A character can only withstand so many wounds before becoming incapacitated. This is represented by the character's wound threshold.

### EXCEEDING WOUND THRESHOLD

When a PC suffers wounds greater than his wound threshold, he is knocked out and incapacitated until his wounds are reduced so that they no longer exceed his wound threshold (likely through healing). **He also immediately suffers one Critical Injury.** In some rare and dire circumstances, this could result in the PC's death.

When Non-Player Characters and creatures suffer wounds greater than their wound threshold, they are defeated (unless they are a high-level opponent such as a nemesis). Being defeated by exceeding their wound threshold usually entails death, but the overall interpretation is up to the GM. The GM can decide that they pass out due to shock, are so crippled that they can no longer fight, are knocked unconscious, or any other option that fits his plans for the ongoing narrative. Since non-nemesis characters do not track strain separately, but apply strain damage as wounds to their wound threshold, what happens once they are defeated may also depend on whether they were defeated due to strain damage or wound damage.

When wounds exceed a character's wound threshold, the player should track the number of wounds by which his character has exceeded the threshold, to a maximum of twice the wound threshold. The character must heal wounds until his wounds are below his wound threshold before he is no longer incapacitated.

## STRAIN AND STRAIN THRESHOLD

While wounds and injury represent potentially life-threatening damage, a number of other stressors and effects can impair a character. Collectively, this is referred to as strain. Any effect that impairs the character, but does not inflict physical harm or wounds, is considered strain. Spending hours wandering through Tatooine's blistering deserts, suffering a minor shock from an electric console, being battered around the inside of a trash compactor—all of these could represent types of strain. Weapons with a Stun setting or other effects that impair or hinder a character also inflict strain.

Additionally, effects that cause stress, fear, anxiety, or emotional turmoil also generate strain. Losing one's cool in combat during a bombardment, being berated by a superior officer, waking up to realize one has been imprisoned by the Hutts, or being boarded by an Imperial

## STATES OF HEALTH

Player Characters may pass through several states of health over the course of their adventures. The state of health is a general representation of overall fitness or well-being.

A character is **unwounded** and operating at peak performance if he is currently suffering from no wounds and has no injuries.

A character is **wounded** if he has any number of wounds below his wound threshold. At this point, he's suffered a few cuts, bruises, and scrapes. However, he has not taken any permanent or incapacitating damage. He's a bit battered, but he's still hale and hearty overall.

A character is **critically injured** if he is currently suffering from any number of Critical Injuries, regardless of how many wounds he may have. Critical Injuries are actual injuries that have some sort of detrimental effect. A character may be critically injured and wounded.

A character is **incapacitated** once he has suffered more wounds than his wound threshold or more strain than his strain threshold. Incapacitation means that a character is unconscious and no longer able to act until the number of wounds he is suffering is decreased below his wound threshold.

Since exceeding a character's wound threshold triggers a Critical Injury, it's possible for an incapacitated character to also be critically injured.

## STRAIN DAMAGE AND CRITICAL INJURIES

Although not always likely, some attacks that deal strain damage (notably stun weapons) can also trigger Critical Injuries. Although this may seem odd, it actually makes sense. When a Player Character inflicts a Critical Injury on an adversary that can be incapacitated by a single Critical Injury (such as a minion), then the adversary is simply incapacitated by being rendered unconscious. If a PC or nemesis NPC suffers a Critical Injury from a stun weapon, the outcome can be anything from adverse long-term effects from the stun weapon to tangential injuries from being stunned (for example, the character could be knocked off balance and take a nasty crack on the skull when he hits the ground). Of course, since these Critical Injuries would have to be triggered by the players or GM, both parties can always decide that a Critical Injury would not make sense in that narrative, and choose not to trigger them.

search team while smuggling goods could all represent incidents that result in strain on a character.

Strain can accumulate slowly as environmental effects or be gained in chunks when a PC is rattled by an effect that doesn't cause damage but still impairs him.

Characters can also voluntarily suffer strain to trigger certain effects. The most common use is to voluntarily suffer 2 points of strain to gain one additional maneuver during a character's turn.

Some special talents may require the character to suffer 1 or more points of strain to activate.

### EXCEEDING STRAIN THRESHOLD

When a character has suffered strain greater than his strain threshold, he becomes incapacitated until his strain is reduced so that it no longer exceeds his strain threshold. He is likely unconscious, or he may just be so dazed and staggered that he's completely unaware of his surroundings and unable to interact with them.

When Non-Player Characters and creatures suffer strain, they generally apply the strain directly to their wound threshold (unless they are nemeses and track strain separately).

## CRITICAL INJURIES

A particularly dangerous type of wound is a Critical Injury. A Critical Injury is often the result of an attack during combat, but characters can also suffer one from exceeding their wound threshold or through other means. Each time a character suffers a Critical Injury, the player rolls d100 on **Table 6–10: Critical Injury Result**, on page 225, to determine the injury's severity rating and effects.

The short-term effects of some injuries are temporary, and may only disorient or afflict the character for a brief amount of time. Other injuries are more serious and represent some sort of long-term debilitation or impairment. These injuries continue to affect the character until he receives the proper medical treatment to recover from the injury.

Regardless, a Critical Injury remains with the character until it is properly healed; even if the short-term effect of the Critical Injury has passed, the status of having a Critical Injury remains. Each Critical Injury a character suffers from adds +10 to any subsequent Critical Injury check. Essentially, Critical Injury is cumulative and, left untreated, even a number of relatively minor Critical Injuries can lead to devastating results.

## OTHER ONGOING STATUS EFFECTS

Characters can suffer status effects beyond being wounded or incapacitated. These status effects can change what a character can do during an encounter, and can be very dangerous. Alternatively, the power to inflict them on others can be a very potent ability indeed.

### STAGGERED

A **staggered** character cannot perform actions (including downgrading actions to maneuvers). Most effects that stagger a character last for a set duration. If a set duration is not specified, the staggered effect lasts until the end of the character's next turn. If a character is staggered multiple times, each instance increases the total duration of the effect by the instance's specified duration, but may not increase the total duration beyond the scope of the present encounter.

### IMMOBILIZED

An **immobilized** character cannot perform maneuvers (including maneuvers purchased via strain or by spending 😧). Most effects that immobilize a character last for a set duration. If a set duration is not specified, immobilization lasts until the end of the character's next turn. If a character is immobilized multiple times, each instance increases the total duration of the effect by the instance's specified duration, but may not increase the total duration beyond the scope of the present encounter.

## DISORIENTED

A **disoriented** character adds ■ to all checks he makes. Most effects that disorient a character last for a set duration. If a set duration is not specified, disorientation lasts until the end of the character's next turn. If a character is disoriented multiple times, each instance increases the total duration of the effect by the instance's specified duration, but may not increase the total duration beyond the scope of the present encounter.

## DEATH

The dangerous galaxy of **Force and Destiny** puts the Player Characters in treacherous situations, and even the most stalwart character cannot survive everything. A time may come when a PC faces his ultimate fate and perishes.

If a character ever rolls (or, through multiple or untreated Critical Injuries, otherwise suffers) a result of 151 or higher on **Table 6–10: Critical Injury Result**, he dies. A dead character cannot be brought back to life. Similarly, a destroyed droid character may not be restored—it's assumed that his central processing unit was irrevocably damaged. Either way, the player should move on and create a new character to continue the adventure.

For more on the death of a Player Character, see **Chapter IX: The Game Master**.

# TABLE 6-10: CRITICAL INJURY RESULT

| d100 | Severity | Result |
|---|---|---|
| 01–05 | Easy (♦) | **Minor Nick:** The target suffers 1 strain. |
| 06–10 | Easy (♦) | **Slowed Down:** The target can only act during the last allied Initiative slot on his next turn. |
| 11–15 | Easy (♦) | **Sudden Jolt:** The target drops whatever is in hand. |
| 16–20 | Easy (♦) | **Distracted:** The target cannot perform a free maneuver during his next turn. |
| 21–25 | Easy (♦) | **Off-Balance:** Add ■ to the target's next skill check. |
| 26–30 | Easy (♦) | **Discouraging Wound:** Flip one light side Destiny Point to a dark side Destiny Point (reverse if NPC). |
| 31–35 | Easy (♦) | **Stunned:** The target is staggered until the end of his next turn. |
| 36–40 | Easy (♦) | **Stinger:** Increase difficulty of next check by one. |
| 41–45 | Average (♦♦) | **Bowled Over:** The target is knocked prone and suffers 1 strain. |
| 46–50 | Average (♦♦) | **Head Ringer:** The target increases the difficulty of all Intellect and Cunning checks by one until the end of the encounter. |
| 51–55 | Average (♦♦) | **Fearsome Wound:** The target increases the difficulty of all Presence and Willpower checks by one until the end of the encounter. |
| 56–60 | Average (♦♦) | **Agonizing Wound:** The target increases the difficulty of all Brawn and Agility checks by one until the end of the encounter. |
| 61–65 | Average (♦♦) | **Slightly Dazed:** The target is disoriented until the end of the encounter. |
| 66–70 | Average (♦♦) | **Scattered Senses:** The target removes all ▢ from skill checks until the end of the encounter. |
| 71–75 | Average (♦♦) | **Hamstrung:** The target loses his free maneuver until the end of the encounter. |
| 76–80 | Average (♦♦) | **Overpowered:** The target leaves himself open, and the attacker may immediately attempt another free attack against him, using the exact same pool as the original attack. |
| 81–85 | Average (♦♦) | **Winded:** Until the end of the encounter, the target cannot voluntarily suffer strain to activate any abilities or gain additional maneuvers. |
| 86–90 | Average (♦♦) | **Compromised:** Increase difficulty of all skill checks by one until the end of the encounter. |
| 91–95 | Hard (♦♦♦) | **At the Brink:** The target suffers 1 strain each time he performs an action. |
| 96–100 | Hard (♦♦♦) | **Crippled:** One of the target's limbs (selected by the GM) is impaired until healed or replaced. Increase difficulty of all checks that require use of that limb by one. |
| 101–105 | Hard (♦♦♦) | **Maimed:** One of the target's limbs (selected by the GM) is permanently lost. Unless the target has a cybernetic replacement, the target cannot perform actions that would require the use of that limb. All other actions gain ■. |
| 106–110 | Hard (♦♦♦) | **Horrific Injury:** Roll 1d10 to determine which of the target's characteristics is affected: 1–3 for Brawn, 4–6 for Agility, 7 for Intellect, 8 for Cunning, 9 for Presence, 10 for Willpower. Until this Critical Injury is healed, treat that characteristic as 1 point lower. |
| 111–115 | Hard (♦♦♦) | **Temporarily Lame:** Until this Critical Injury is healed, the target cannot perform more than one maneuver during his turn. |
| 116–120 | Hard (♦♦♦) | **Blinded:** The target can no longer see. Upgrade the difficulty of all checks twice. Upgrade the difficulty of Perception and Vigilance checks three times. |
| 121–125 | Hard (♦♦♦) | **Knocked Senseless:** The target is staggered for the remainder of the encounter. |
| 126–130 | Daunting (♦♦♦♦) | **Gruesome Injury:** Roll 1d10 to determine which of the target's characteristics is affected: 1–3 for Brawn, 4–6 for Agility, 7 for Intellect, 8 for Cunning, 9 for Presence, 10 for Willpower. That characteristic is permanently reduced by 1, to a minimum of 1. |
| 131–140 | Daunting (♦♦♦♦) | **Bleeding Out:** Every round, the target suffers 1 wound and 1 strain at the beginning of his turn. For every 5 wounds he suffers beyond his wound threshold, he suffers 1 additional Critical Injury. Roll on the chart, suffering the injury (if he suffers this result a second time due to this, roll again). |
| 141–150 | Daunting (♦♦♦♦) | **The End Is Nigh:** The target will die after the last Initiative slot during the next round. |
| 151 + | – | **Dead:** Complete, obliterated death. |

# RECOVERY AND HEALING

While characters can be afflicted with various ailments and types of damage, there are thankfully several options for recovery. Recovery can vary in time and effectiveness, based on the resources and expertise available to the characters. With the proper resources and sufficient time, characters can recover from virtually any encounter.

## HEALING WOUNDS

There are several ways that characters can heal wounds. Some allow for natural, if slow, healing; others require access to high-tech medical facilities.

### NATURAL REST

For each full night's rest, the character heals 1 wound, regardless of the character's current state of health. At the end of each full week of rest, the character may attempt a Resilience check to recover from one Critical Injury. The difficulty is equal to the Critical Injury's severity rating (see **Table 6–10: Critical Injury Result** on page 225). On a successful check, the character recovers from the Critical Injury and is no longer affected. On a failed check, the character retains the Critical Injury, but still heals 1 wound. A ✦ result means the character can heal one additional Critical Injury.

Droids benefit from natural rest like any other character, as their subroutines and automated systems attempt self-repairs.

### MEDICAL CARE

A character may attempt a Medicine check to help a character heal wounds. Each character may only receive one Medicine check each encounter, as there is only so much good that first aid can do to help a character.

The difficulty of the check is based on the target's current state of health (see **Table 6–11: Medical Check Difficulty**). On a successful check, the target heals a number of wounds equal to the number of ✷ generated by the Medicine roll and heals an amount of strain equal to the number of ❂ generated.

A character may also attempt to help someone recover from a Critical Injury by making a Medicine check with a difficulty equal to the severity rating of the Critical Injury (see **Table 6–10: Critical Injury Result**). A character may attempt one Medicine check per week per Critical Injury.

A character may attempt to heal his own wounds or Critical Injuries with Medicine, but doing this himself increases the difficulty of the Medicine check by two. In addition, attempting a Medicine check without the proper equipment (see page 185) increases the difficulty of the check by one.

Droids cannot benefit from medical care. However, they do receive the same benefits from Mechanics checks, based on the same guidelines and difficulty ratings as their Medicine-based equivalents. All of the guidelines and rules governing Medicine checks also govern Mechanics checks to heal droids, with the exception that a droid using Mechanics to heal himself only increases the difficulty by one, rather than two. Simply put, most droids can avoid feeling "pain" and have the self-diagnostic routines and programming to better understand how to repair themselves.

### BACTA TANKS

Characters can also heal using a bacta tank. The rate of recovery depends on the character's state of health. A wounded character heals at a rate of 1 wound every two hours. An incapacitated character heals at a rate of 1 wound every six hours.

At the end of each twenty-four-hour period, the character may attempt one Resilience check to remove one Critical Injury. The difficulty is equal to the Critical Injury's severity rating (see **Table 6–10: Critical Injury Result**). On a successful check, the character recovers from the Critical Injury and is no longer affected. On a failed check, the character retains the Critical Injury effect, but still heals 1 wound.

### OIL BATHS (DROIDS ONLY)

Droids cannot benefit from a bacta tank. However, droids can benefit from an oil bath. An oil bath is specifically designed to help droids recover from damage and ill effects. Every hour spent in an oil bath heals 1 wound, as the lubricant helps facilitate the droid's self-diagnostic systems. Oil baths do not remove Critical Injuries, which is instead done with Mechanics checks.

## TABLE 6–11: MEDICAL CHECK DIFFICULTY

| State of Health | Difficulty |
|---|---|
| Current wounds equal half or less of wound threshold | Easy (◆) |
| Current wounds equal more than half of wound threshold | Average (◆◆) |
| Current wounds exceed wound threshold | Hard (◆◆◆) |
| Heal Critical Injury | Critical Injury Severity Rating |

## STIMPACKS

Stimpacks are auto-injection tubes filled with medicine, bacta, and painkillers. They are field-ready emergency health recovery products. Stimpacks heal a fixed number of wounds, with no roll necessary. However, the drawback is that stimpacks offer diminishing returns over the course of a day. Characters must spend a full night's rest or wait at least twenty-four hours before stimpacks can be used at their full effectiveness again.

The first stimpack used on a character automatically heals 5 wounds. The second stimpack only heals 4 wounds, the third stimpack heals 3 wounds, and so on. This means that a sixth stimpack will have no effect, as the target's body is too oversaturated with the medicine for it to be effective.

It requires one maneuver to inject a stimpack. The character administering the stimpack must be engaged with the target to treat him. A character with a free appendage may apply a stimpack to himself with one maneuver as well.

To heal Critical Injuries, a successful Medicine check based on the injury's severity (see **Table 6–10: Critical Injury Result**) is required. Stimpacks have no effect on Critical Injuries.

### EMERGENCY REPAIR PATCHES (DROIDS ONLY)

Droids cannot use stimpacks. However, they use and benefit from repair patches in a manner similar to the way organic beings benefit from stimpacks, including the limit of five per day. Emergency repair patches only heal 3 wounds per use, but their viability does not diminish over time. Fixing a droid's Critical Injuries requires Mechanics checks with a difficulty set by the Critical Injury's severity rating. (Emergency repair patches are not included in this book, but this information is included for compatibility with other **Star Wars Roleplaying** games.)

## RECOVERING FROM STRAIN

Fortunately, recovering from strain is fairly easy. Taking a moment to catch one's breath, eating a good meal, or spending time relaxing with friends are all ways a Player Character might recover from strain.

At the end of an encounter, each player can make a **Simple (–) Discipline** or **Cool check**. Each ✶ recovers 1 strain. Furthermore, a good night's rest generally removes all strain a character has suffered. It's also rumored that some Jedi have mastered a technique that allows them to ignore the effects of strain, or to ease the minds of others to help them recover more quickly.

## RECOVERING FROM CRITICAL INJURIES

Since lingering Critical Injuries make subsequent injuries increasingly dangerous, they should be treated as quickly and efficiently as possible. Critical Injuries vary in severity, which represents the difficulty of any corresponding Medicine check to treat and remove the injury.

It's important to note that even if the effect of a Critical Injury has expired, the Critical Injury still persists until treated. For example, with a Critical Injury result of 23, which indicates the Off-Balance Critical Injury, the character adds ■ to his next skill check. Even after this effect has been applied, the Off-Balance Critical Injury still exists and will linger until treated, making subsequent Critical Injury rolls against the character that much more dangerous to him.

# VII
# STARSHIPS AND VEHICLES

*"Traveling through hyperspace ain't like dusting crops, boy!"*

–Han Solo

In *Star Wars,* agile landspeeders choke the streets of massive planet-sized cities, suspended in mid-air by antigravity repulsorlift generators. Graceful airspeeders patrol the skies of a thousand worlds, their powerful ion engines propelling them to breathtaking velocities. Starships great and small rocket into space from backwater starports and hurtle through hyperspace, making trips thousands of light-years long with little more effort or fanfare than if traveling to a marketplace.

The universe presented in FORCE AND DESTINY is so reliant on such transportation technologies as to be inseparable from them. Vehicles take on almost talismanic importance to their captains and crews, treated as living things by those who love them. A vehicle may be the only home some spacers have. Presented in this chapter are a number of the more common types of starships and vehicles found in the galaxy, together with the rules governing them.

## VEHICLE CHARACTERISTICS

From the fastest swoop bike to a lumbering Star Destroyer, all ships and vehicles share a number of characteristics. These characteristics delineate such attributes as the strength of a ship's shields or how quickly a speeder accelerates off the line. The characteristics described here cover the bulk of important mechanical information about starships and vehicles.

**Handling:** The measure of a ship or vehicle's agility and how well it responds to its pilot.

**Speed:** A ship or vehicle's raw speed and how quickly it accelerates.

**Silhouette:** An abstract of the general size of a vehicle.

**Defense:** A ship's first line of defense against attack and accident. Typically representative of a ship's ray shields and particle shields, defense also represents any factors, technological or otherwise, that prevent damage from reaching a vehicle's armor.

**Armor:** The measure of a ship or vehicle's armor, similar to soak on personal scale.

# STARSHIPS, VEHICLES, AND SCALE

Starships and vehicles follow the same basic rules for interaction and operation outlined in **Chapter I: Playing the Game** and **Chapter VI: Conflict and Combat**. However, due to their increased size and mass, starships and vehicles necessarily operate on a different scale, referred to as planetary scale.

When dealing with a vessel's weapons, armor, and hull trauma threshold, every point is equal to 10 points of the equivalent characteristic in personal scale. For example, a laser cannon with a base damage of 3, mounted to a starfighter, deals 3 points of damage when fired at another spacecraft, but 30 points of damage when fired at a human. Conversely, a human-sized blaster rifle would need to deal 10 points of damage to a starship to inflict even 1 point of damage on it.

Note that planetary scale weapons deal massive amounts of damage to individuals. Most hits automatically deal enough damage to far exceed a character's wound threshold, meaning the target will automatically be incapacitated for the remainder of the encounter. However, some GMs may feel this is insufficient to represent the fearsome power of a starship weapon when turned on an individual. In these cases, the GM should feel free to add +50 to the resulting Critical Injury roll. (Also, those hit by a planetary scale weapon might be on the periphery of the blast zone, explaining why they survived somewhat unscathed.)

Also note that to avoid having weapons such as blaster pistols dealing Critical Hits to starships, their damage must exceed a starship's armor before the shot can inflict a Critical Hit.

Planetary scale weapons that have the Blast quality are particularly effective at decimating ground targets, even if their explosive radius does not allow them to hit multiple targets in space. Against ground targets, starship blast weapons hit their primary target and every additional target within short range (at personal scale), instead of just every target engaged with the original target.

**Hull Trauma Threshold:** A reflection of the sturdiness of a ship or vehicle's construction and its ability to sustain damage and keep operating.

**System Strain Threshold:** The limit to which a ship or vehicle can be pushed or knocked about before important systems overload or shut down.

**Customization Hard Points:** The number of spots available on a ship or vehicle for customization and upgrade.

## HANDLING

Generally speaking, handling reflects a ship or vehicle's inherent agility and response to a pilot. While a huge capital ship may maneuver slowly, smaller and faster craft are likely to be much more agile. Handling is dictated by a number of factors. While size is certainly the most obvious—an Aethersprite starfighter is, by nature, more maneuverable than a *Victory*-class Star Destroyer—other factors such as shape, control systems, mass, or just general awkwardness all contribute to handling.

In game terms, a ship or vehicle's handling characteristic dictates the number of ☐ or ■ it adds to a player's dice pool when making Piloting checks. Baseline handling is 0, with extremely agile ships adding ☐ and slow or plodding ships adding ■ to all Piloting checks. Pilots add ■ equal to a ship's negative handling value or ☐ equal to a ship or vehicle's positive handling value.

## SPEED

An abstraction of both speed and acceleration, a ship or vehicle's speed characteristic dictates how fast an object moves relative to its environment and what maneuvers are available to the pilot. The listed speed is the maximum at which the ship or vehicle can travel. A pilot can always choose to go slower than the maximum speed. Speed 0 indicates a stationary ship or vehicle, with higher values indicating an increased speed. (Speed 1, for example, might be a slow-moving AT-AT walker or ponderous transport ship, while speed 5 might be a nimble TIE fighter or cloud car.)

## SILHOUETTE

Much like the speed characteristic, silhouette is an abstract number, used to describe a ship or vehicle's size and mass relative to other ships and vehicles. Silhouette factors heavily into scale and is used to calculate the difficulty of attacking targets of different sizes. Generally, large ships are easy to hit, and small ships are hard to hit. Some ships, such as the *Lancer*-class frigate, are exceptions to this rule, as they are large ships fitted with smaller, lighter guns than their size and class would suggest, filling specific roles within fleets.

Silhouettes range from 0 to 10 (or even higher). Silhouette 0 is smaller than a human (such as a specific starship component, a Jawa, or an astromech droid), and silhouette 1 is about the size of an adult human. Most starfighters and light freighters range from silhouette 3 to 4. Silhouettes 10 and up are reserved for the very largest of space stations and starships.

## HULL TRAUMA THRESHOLD

Hull trauma threshold is the only thing that stands between a starship pilot and the cold and unforgiving vacuum of space. It's a reflection of a ship or vehicle's sturdiness and resistance to damage. The strength of a capital ship's keel, the sturdiness of a speeder truck's chassis, and the general spaceworthiness of a starfighter's spaceframe are all measured by hull trauma threshold. Like the wound threshold of a Player Character, hull trauma threshold represents the amount of physical damage that a ship or vehicle can suffer before it is either incapacitated or destroyed. Hull trauma threshold is measured in planetary scale, meaning that 1 point of hull trauma equals 10 wounds on an individual.

## SYSTEM STRAIN THRESHOLD

System strain threshold represents how well a ship or vehicle's internal systems handle the workaday abuse heaped on them by their owners and the galaxy at large. It is an aggregate of the efficiency and status of computer and navigation systems, engines and hyperspace drives, power generators, and a host of other delicate systems necessary to ensure peak performance. Once a ship or vehicle suffers strain exceeding its system strain threshold, its systems begin overloading and shutting down until they can be repaired or rebooted. This negatively affects a vehicle's performance and can even temporarily disable it on occasion, causing larger complications for its crew and passengers.

The factors that can cause a ship or vehicle to suffer strain are numerous and varied. Most commonly, a vehicle suffers strain due to the actions of its crew as they push it to (or beyond) its breaking point. Pushing sublight engines past their safe operating limits

while outrunning a pursuer or firing weapons until their barrels glow are prime examples of this kind of strain. Vehicles also suffer strain due to freak accidents caused by excess ✸, environmental hazards like rogue asteroids or ionized nebulae, or the effects of special weapons such as ion cannons.

**One difference between system strain and regular strain is that system strain cannot be recovered by spending ✪.** It can only be restored through actions taken by the crew, or it is reduced by one point for every full day spent without suffering more system strain.

# CUSTOMIZATION HARD POINTS

Every starship and vehicle produced in the galaxy is customizable to some degree. While many, like starfighters and most military vessels, are built for specific purposes and have very little room for modification, other civilian and commercial ships and vehicles are designed to be modular for ease of personalization and customization. The majority of freighters and transports fall squarely into this latter group, with highly modular hulls that can be configured in myriad ways to carry virtually any kind of cargo imaginable. To this end, all ships and vehicles have a number of customization hard points that can be used to tweak a vehicle's performance, characteristics, or armament to suit the needs of its owners.

The number of customization hard points a ship or vehicle possesses is determined more by its make and model than by its size. A HWK-290 light freighter is relatively small, yet easy to customize due to its construction, while a massive, kilometer-long Star Destroyer has little-to-no customization potential, despite its size, due to the specialized nature of its mission and design.

# PROTECTION

To protect their passengers, crews, and precious cargos, ships and vehicles in the *Star Wars* galaxy use a number of methods to avoid or deflect damage. In general terms, a ship or vehicle's protection is an amalgam of its maneuverability, the durability of its hull or chassis, the strength of its shields, and the thickness of its armor. Some ships have obscure types of protection such as focused gravity waves, clusters of point-defense laser cannons, or launchers full of micro-missiles used to intercept incoming starfighters, shuttles, and ordnance. Whatever form these protections take, **Force and Destiny** divides them into two discrete statistics: defense and armor.

## DEFENSE

Defense reflects a ship or vehicle's ability to completely deflect or reduce the damage of incoming attacks or collisions through use of deflector shields, point defense systems, raw speed, or other, more esoteric technologies. This is a crucial protective system, the first line of defense for the majority of space-going vessels and even some ground vehicles. Defense works the same as described on page 213; each point of defense adds ■ to any incoming attack roll made against a ship or vehicle. The amount of ▼ generated by the ■ added to the attacker's dice pool has the potential to greatly reduce or even negate any damage from the attack or collision, and the ✷ generated also lessens the chance of Critical Hits.

### SILHOUETTE AND DEFENSE ZONES

Ships (and those rare vehicles with defense) have a number of defense zones dictated by their silhouette. Anything with silhouette 4 or lower has two defense zones: forward and aft. Ships with silhouette 5 or higher have four defense zones: forward, aft, port, and starboard. Every ship comes with a pre-set defense rating for each of its defense zones, dictated by its computer system and the factory settings of its shield generators. The maximum amount of defense a ship or vehicle can have in any of its defense zones is four points, regardless of its size. For example, the sturdy BTL-A4 Y-wing attack starfighter has a silhouette of 3 and two defense zones, forward and aft. The default setting of the Y-wing's defense rating is one point of defense to the forward zone, and one point aft.

Most types of defense, especially the common ray and particle deflector shields found on the ships of the majority of spacefaring species, can be assigned or "angled" to different zones to shore up defense where it's needed most. This is done by re-routing power from one zone to another, reducing the defense at one part of the ship to bolster it somewhere else. In the case of the Y-wing above, if it were being pursued by a TIE fighter, the pilot could re-route power from the forward defense zone to the aft defense zone, giving the Y-wing two points of defense aft and none forward until the power is reset. The Y-wing adds ■ ■ dice to the TIE fighter's attacks, but any attacks made against the forward defense zone suffer no ■.

Each ship and vehicle has a chart displaying its default shield settings by defense zone. For ships with silhouette 4 and lower, this is represented by two numbers: one for the forward zone and one for the aft zone. For ships of silhouette 5 or higher with multiple defense zones, this is represented by four numbers indicating the forward zone, port zone, starboard zone, and aft zone.

## ARMOR

Armor is a starship's second line of defense, and the only protection available to most ground vehicles. It soaks up damage from attacks and impacts that penetrate a ship's defense. The more passive of the two types of protection, starship and vehicle armor is made of a number of materials ranging from common durasteel to rare carbon composites and advanced polycarbonites. Much like personal body armor worn by Player Characters, a ship or vehicle's armor soaks a number of damage points equal to its rating. As it is based on planetary scale, one point of a ship's armor is equivalent to ten points of soak on a personal scale.

# SHIPYARD STANDARD SYSTEMS

The number and variety of starships at large in the galaxy is staggering. Despite this, nearly every starship shares a number of common components required to travel safely among the stars. Ground vehicles also share some of these systems, primarily comms and sensors.

**Sublight Engines:** Sublight engines drive starships through realspace at speeds approaching that of light. They provide both transatmospheric and intrasystem capabilities to ships of all sizes, from the tiniest starfighters to the massive, kilometer-long Imperial Star Destroyers. The most common sublight engine is the ion drive, a tried-and-tested technology that uses fusion reactors with hypermatter cores to produce highly charged ions for thrust.

**Hyperdrive:** These delicate drives allow a ship to enter hyperspace, an alternate state of reality that allows travel at speeds many times that of light. Hyperdrives are rated on a class scale of descending numbers that reflect the relative superluminal speed of a drive, with lower numbers denoting faster drives. Civilian hyperdrives are typically between class 3 and 4, although faster drives can be obtained. Most ships are equipped with a backup hyperdrive for use should the primary hyperdrive fail. These are typically exceedingly slow and are only really useful for short-range trips.

**Navicomputer:** Ranging from the sophisticated and powerful computer arrays used aboard military capital ships to the astrogation buffer in an R2 astromech droid, navicomputers are primarily used to generate and solve the incredibly complex calculations needed to make a safe jump through hyperspace.

**Escape Pods/Ejection Systems:** All ships, and many airspeeders, are equipped with emergency escape systems in case of catastrophic damage. Most airspeeders and starships up to silhouette 3 are equipped with ejection seats that blast the pilot and any crew free of the disintegrating ship. Ejection seats are equipped with tiny maneuvering thrusters and a small repulsorlift engine designed to bring a pilot safely back to land in the case of ejection. Use of ejection seats is common in atmosphere, and many flight suits offer limited vacuum protection. Ships of silhouette 4 or larger are equipped with enough escape pods to evacuate the ship's crew and any passengers. These escape pods have enough consumables to keep their occupants—typically four to six—alive for five standard days.

**Sensors:** Sensors grant a vehicle's crew a constantly updated, 360-degree view of their immediate surroundings. Sensors operate at different range bands depending on their relative strength. Although powerful, they can be fooled or jammed altogether by numerous technologies. Sensors operate in two modes: passive and active. Sensors operating in passive mode operate at low power and see everything around the ship up to their maximum range band. Using sensors in passive mode requires no skill check, as they are largely automatic and are relaying the minimum amount of data their programming provides. Sensors operating in active mode are more powerful and focused, however. When operating in active mode, sensors can see one range band farther than their listed maximum range, but can only see in one of the ship's fire arcs (forward, aft, port, or starboard). Using sensors in active mode requires an **Easy (◇) Computers check** modified by any ambient radiation, atmospheric disturbances, terrain such as forests or mountains (or asteroids or nebulae in space), or active jamming on the part of whatever is being scanned.

**Comms:** "Comms" is shorthand for a ship's or vehicle's means of communication. Standard comms are subspace transceivers with a range equal to that of the vehicle's sensors. If a ship has short-range sensors, for example, it also has short-range comms. Comms are typically unencrypted, easily intercepted, and easily jammed, although modifications can make any signals transmitted or received more secure.

**Transponder:** Every space-going vessel possesses a subspace transponder. The subspace transponder broadcasts the vessel's registry, hull number, ownership, and other pertinent information on a special frequency that can be picked up by any vessel or subspace comms array at close range. The transponder also operates as a distress beacon. It is considered a serious crime in the Empire to tamper with a transponder, and evidence of an altered transponder is probable cause for a ship to be stopped and boarded by Imperial officers. This doesn't stop those who value their anonymity from doing so, however.

# STARSHIP AND VEHICLE WEAPONS

Starship and vehicle weapons range from the light repeating blasters found on speeder bikes to the massive turbolaser batteries on the flanks of an Imperial Star Destroyer. However, in FORCE AND DESTINY, every ship or vehicle-class weapon shares a number of common characteristics. These weapons are very similar to the weapons found in **Chapter V**, with some noted differences.

- **Range:** This is the maximum range of the weapon. To measure ranges, starships and vehicles use planetary scale instead of personal scale.

- **Damage:** This number is the base damage the weapon inflicts with a successful attack. For every ✷ generated during the attack, the attacker adds +1 damage to the base damage.

- **Critical Hit Rating:** This number is the amount of ✪ required to trigger Critical Hits with the weapon. If enough ✪ is generated and a Critical Hit is triggered, the character firing the weapon rolls 1d100 on **Table 7–9: Critical Hit Result** on page 250 to determine the Critical Hit's effect on the target. Some weapons and talents modify this Critical Hit roll, potentially making it more or less effective. In addition, a character can only generate one Critical Hit per hit on a target. However, if the roll generates enough ✪ to result in multiple Critical Hits, the character can choose to add an additional +10 per additional Critical Hit to the roll result.

- **Fire Arc:** The direction or directions a weapon can be fired, based on its mounting. These are specified in individual vehicle profiles. Fire arcs are discussed in further detail in the **Fire Arcs** sidebar on the next page.

- **Special Qualities:** Many weapons, such as ion cannons, tractor beams, and repeating blasters, have additional special item qualities that affect their performance. Descriptions of these special effects are found on page 161 of **Chapter V: Gear and Equipment**.

## BLASTER CANNONS

Known colloquially as "flash cannons," blaster cannons are heavy, crew-served versions of the common personal blaster. Although they are less powerful than laser cannons, blaster cannons are highly effective against infantry and light vehicles. Blaster cannons come in several versions of varying power.

### AUTO-BLASTER

Auto-blasters are rapid-fire variants of common blaster cannons. Advanced XCiter technology and highly specialized actuating modules mean these weapons achieve high cyclical rates of fire, spraying a hail of shots with a single pull of the trigger or push of a button.

## TABLE 7–1: STARSHIP AND VEHICLE WEAPONS

| Name | Range | Dam | Crit | Qualities |
|---|---|---|---|---|
| Auto-Blaster | Close | 3 | 5 | Auto-fire |
| Blaster Cannon (Light) | Close | 4 | 4 | |
| Blaster Cannon (Heavy) | Close | 5 | 4 | |
| Concussion Missile Launcher | Short | 6 | 3 | Blast 4, Breach 4, Guided 3, Limited Ammo 3, Slow-Firing 1 |
| Ion Cannon (Light) | Close | 5 | 4 | Ion |
| Ion Cannon (Medium) | Short | 6 | 4 | Ion |
| Ion Cannon (Heavy) | Medium | 7 | 4 | Ion, Slow-Firing 1 |
| Ion Cannon (Battleship) | Medium | 9 | 4 | Breach 3, Ion, Slow-Firing 2 |
| Laser Cannon (Light) | Close | 5 | 3 | |
| Laser Cannon (Medium) | Close | 6 | 3 | |
| Laser Cannon (Heavy) | Short | 6 | 3 | |
| Proton Torpedo Launcher | Short | 8 | 2 | Blast 6, Breach 6, Guided 2, Limited Ammo 3, Slow-Firing 1 |
| Quad Laser Cannon | Close | 5 | 3 | Accurate 1, Linked 3 |
| Tractor Beam (Light) | Close | – | – | Tractor 2 |
| Tractor Beam (Medium) | Short | – | – | Tractor 4 |
| Tractor Beam (Heavy) | Short | – | – | Tractor 6 |
| Turbolaser (Light) | Medium | 9 | 3 | Breach 2, Slow-Firing 1 |
| Turbolaser (Medium) | Long | 10 | 3 | Breach 3, Slow-Firing 1 |
| Turbolaser (Heavy) | Long | 11 | 3 | Breach 4, Slow-Firing 2 |

## FIRE ARCS

Every ship and vehicle has four fire arcs: forward, aft, port, and starboard. Each fire arc covers an area of the ship in a ninety-degree arc extending from the center point of the ship. Depending on its location on a ship's hull and the manner in which it is mounted, a weapon can cover one or multiple fire arcs. Fixed weapons cover only one fire arc. For example, the laser cannons mounted in the nose of the BTL-A4 Y-wing are fixed forward and can only hit enemies in the forward fire arc. Turret-mounted weapons, such as the turbolasers mounted to the CR90 corvette, can traverse to cover any fire arc required, which is listed as "Fire Arc All" in the weapon's description.

Some ships also have dorsal (top) and ventral (bottom) fire arcs. Weapons mounted on a ship's dorsal surface cannot hit ventral targets, and ventral-mounted weapons cannot engage threats approaching from the ship's dorsal side. For example, the ventral-mounted laser cannon on a YT-1300 light freighter has a ventral fire arc of All, which means it can engage any threat approaching from below the ship, but the ship must reposition itself to engage enemies coming in from above.

## ION WEAPONS

Ion weapons are anti-ship and anti-vehicle weapons designed to disable rather than destroy their targets. They use ion turbine generators to create masses of negatively charged particles, which are fused with plasma and released as blasts or pulses. The negatively charged particles interfere with a target's electrical systems, shorting circuits, corrupting computers, and forcing system shutdowns in an effort to subdue it or make it easier to destroy via more traditional means. Although this weapon is designed to do almost no physical damage, collateral damage such as fried circuits, fused joints, and even fires may occur due to the intense energy surges.

## LASER WEAPONS

These weapons use focused light beams combined with charged particles to produce long-range, accurate, and incredibly damaging blasts of energy. The number one choice for anti-vehicle and anti-personnel work, laser weapons make a fine complement to the lower-yield blaster.

### LASER CANNON

The standard anti-ship weapons mounted to starships, laser cannons are found on nearly every class of ship from the smallest starfighter to the mightiest capital ship. Preferred over blaster cannons for their damage and accuracy, laser cannons can be paired in batteries or mounted separately. Light and medium laser cannons are often found on starfighters and freighters. Heavy laser cannons are mounted to capital ships as secondary weapons to deal with smaller ships. Lasers are also often mounted to military ground vehicles.

### QUAD LASER CANNON

Quad lasers are dedicated anti-starfighter weapons consisting of four small-caliber laser cannons linked to a single firing mechanism and slaved to a sophisticated fire-control system. They fire four laser blasts with every pull of the trigger and can quite easily fill the space around a ship with enough kilojoules of energy to destroy even the toughest starfighter or patrol boat.

### TURBOLASER

Massive, heavy-caliber weapons with incredible energy requirements, turbolasers are the largest weapons mounted to starships. Turbolasers can punch clean through an opponent's shields, armor, and hull with a single blast, the lightest easily hulling small ships and the heaviest battering down the defenses of the largest cruisers. The trade-offs are their heavy power requirements, their slow recharge time, and their difficulty in tracking and hitting small, fast targets like starfighters.

## TRACTOR BEAMS

Tractor beams are modified shield generators that project a beam of energy that can ensnare starships. Used on orbital shipyards, planetary starports, space stations, and many starships, tractor beams are commonly used to guide vessels safely into slips and docking bays, as well as to handle cargo. When mounted to warships, they can be used offensively to capture enemy vessels and draw them into docking bays for ease of boarding.

## ORDNANCE

Ordnance provides vehicles and starships with a powerful one-use weapon that can punch through armor or even lock on to opponents and track them. These projectiles are propelled by small sublight drives and carry high-yield warheads designed to give small ships a heavier punch against large ships or to take out enemy starfighters or airspeeders before the opponent can close to engage. Most ordnance contains a sophisticated guidance system and vectored thrusters that allow it to track its target and even come around for another pass if it misses the first time.

**S**ometimes starfighters or other small ships have weapons such as proton torpedoes or concussion missile launchers that have the Limited Ammo quality. Although normally Limited Ammo weapons can be reloaded with a maneuver once exhausted, starfighters generally carry only one payload of torpedoes or missiles, and must be reloaded back at a base or carrier starship. They cannot be reloaded in mid-flight, and especially not in mid-combat!

## CONCUSSION MISSILES AND GRENADES

The more common and less powerful of the two types of shipboard ordnance, concussion missiles are found on all manner of spacecraft, from tiny starfighters to capital ships. Roughly a meter long, a concussion missile employs special warheads, combining a hardened durasteel penetrator that uses kinetic force to pierce through a ship's armor and a shaped high-explosive charge that causes damage through both explosive force and concussive shock. Concussion missiles are primarily anti-fighter weapons used to quickly deal debilitating damage to starfighters and patrol boats, although they perform well against larger targets as well.

Concussion grenades are primarily personal-scale weapons, although many military ground vehicles mount concussion grenade launchers that fire larger anti-infantry or anti-armor versions. Concussion grenade launchers are typically relatively short-range ballistic weapons designed for ground vehicles, and thus are useless in space combat.

Additional concussion missiles cost 500 credits each and are restricted.

### PROTON TORPEDOES

Proton torpedoes are highly advanced anti-ship projectiles typically carried by starfighters and patrol boats. They are larger and bulkier than concussion missiles and have a squat, conical warhead, meaning their launchers carry fewer rounds than an equivalent concussion missile launcher. These weapons mount a deadly, irradiating, proton-scattering warhead detonated by a volatile Nergon-14 explosive charge. Proton torpedoes are designed to damage and destroy large vessels like bulk transports and capital ships. They allow small ships like starfighters and patrol boats to punch well above their weight.

Additional proton torpedoes cost 750 credits each and are restricted.

# STARSHIP AND VEHICLE COMBAT

**C**ombat engagements between starships and vehicles—from dogfights in space over a war-torn planet to speeder chases through the crowded streets of a Core World—function using the same basic combat rules as found in **Chapter VI: Conflict and Combat**. Starship and vehicle combat is not intended to be a completely separate rules system. Instead, it is designed to be an added layer of detail on the standard combat rules that allows players to run structured gameplay encounters using starships, vehicles, characters, or any combination thereof.

When running encounters using starships and vehicles, it is important to note that starships with silhouette 5 or higher have some different rules governing their actions. This is because these ships are quite a bit larger than starfighters and freighters, with crews of hundreds or even thousands of individuals.

## COMBAT OVERVIEW

Starship and vehicle combat in **Force and Destiny** follows the same basic order and rules as those detailed in **Chapter VI: Conflict and Combat**. They are listed again here for ease of reference.

### STEP 1: DETERMINE INITIATIVE

Before the first salvos are fired, all players and NPCs need to determine the order in which they will take their turns. This is referred to as the **Initiative order**.

To determine the Initiative order, each Player Character and NPC makes a **Simple (–) Cool** or **Vigilance check** (for more information on which to use, see the **Cool or Vigilance?** sidebar on page 204). Once all Initiative checks have been made, the GM notes the results of each check and ranks them in order from highest to lowest. If two checks are tied, the check with more ✪ is ranked higher, and if they are still tied, PCs are ranked higher than NPCs. This is the Initiative order.

### STEP 2: ASSIGN INITIATIVE SLOTS

As the GM determines the Initiative order, he notes which results were generated by Player Characters and which results were generated by NPCs. The results generated by Player Characters become Player Character Initiative slots. The results generated by NPCs become NPC Initiative slots.

### STEP 3: PARTICIPANTS TAKE TURNS

Beginning at the top of the Initiative order, the players and GM fill each Initiative slot one at a time with a character turn. If the Initiative slot is a Player Character Initiative slot, then the players agree on one Player Character to fill the slot from among the Player Characters who have not acted that round. That Player Character then takes this turn. If the Initiative slot is an NPC Initiative slot, then the GM chooses one NPC to fill the slot from among the NPCs who have not acted that round. That NPC then takes this turn. Note that some starships can have multiple crew members in them.

### STEP 4: ROUND ENDS

Once all NPCs and Player Characters have taken a turn, the round ends. At this point, any effects that last until the "end of the round" end. The GM also determines if the ongoing action warrants additional rounds, or if it has been resolved. If the ongoing action continues, repeat step 3 using the same Initiative order generated in step 1. If the action has been resolved and the encounter is over, proceed to step 5.

### STEP 5: ENCOUNTER ENDS

Once the action has been resolved, the GM ends the encounter. At this point, any character abilities that

can only be used "once per encounter" reset. Player Characters also have a chance to catch their breath and recover strain, and may take steps to help heal any incapacitated characters.

## SMALL CRAFT COMBAT

Combat between small, one-person ships like starfighters and patrol boats or speeder bikes and single-seat airspeeders is relatively straightforward. The pilot, as the sole crew aboard, has one starship maneuver and one starship action (or two starship maneuvers) during his turn. This means he can fly and fight aboard his ship, or concentrate solely on flying. Small craft combat (especially with high-speed vehicles like airspeeders, speeder bikes, or starfighters) is quite abstracted. As the vehicles are constantly moving and striving against one another for the upper hand (thanks to their incredible speed and agility), it would be nearly impossible to map out every move a starfighter makes. Instead, the Game Master and players describe the actions the characters and NPCs take, embellish them with narrative flair, then make their skill checks to resolve the actions.

## CAPITAL SHIP COMBAT

Combat in larger, capital-class starships of silhouette 5 or higher is, by necessity, even more abstract due to the complexity of the vessels and the number of crew members involved. Similar to combat in small craft, capital ships can only perform one starship maneuver and one starship action (or two starship maneuvers) during their pilot's turn. This is not an inherent quality of the ship, however; it's based on the pilot or captain's actions and starship maneuvers. Along with the pilot, each additional crew member aboard can use his actions and starship maneuvers to handle weapons, operate sensors, move about the ship, and generally engage in combat. This all happens in the same round, and is subject to Initiative order just like personal combat. Something to remember concerning ship combat with vehicles of this immense size is that each ship is likely to have hundreds or thousands of crew. GMs and players should not track all of their Initiative slots and actions during combat. Instead, only focus on those individuals who are actually doing things pertinent to the ongoing encounter, and feel free to ignore the rest.

## COMBAT TURNS

Much like personal combat, combat between starships and vehicles in **FORCE AND DESTINY** is largely an abstract, narrative-driven activity designed for quickness and ease of use. This is meant to better reflect the frenetic, cinematic, action-adventure style of *Star Wars* and to avoid bogging down a game session with the minutiae of charts and grid maps. This means that

### COMBAT AND THE PILOTING SKILL

During combat involving starships and vehicles, Player Characters and NPCs are often called upon to make Piloting checks to control their vehicles, take certain actions, or avoid disastrous outcomes. Whenever a Piloting check is called for, the piloting character or NPC must make a check using either Piloting (Planetary) or Piloting (Space), depending on the vehicle. For the sake of brevity, the specific version of the Piloting skill is not defined, and it is up to the GM to adjudicate which skill is more appropriate.

the maneuvers a starship performs are open to narration and the interpretation of both the Game Master and the players.

In **Force and Destiny**, Player Characters follow the rules of combat detailed starting on page 203. This means they can perform one action and one maneuver during their turn. They may also be able to perform a second maneuver by either suffering strain or spending 🌀, although no PC may ever take more than two maneuvers during his turn.

# MANEUVERS

Less involved than actions, maneuvers are simple activities that do not typically require a skill check. Beyond all the maneuvers in personal combat, there are several maneuvers that apply specifically to starships and vehicles. These additional maneuvers follow the usual rules governing maneuvers (see page 206). In addition (and especially in larger starships), characters are assumed to be able to perform personal maneuvers such as dropping prone, managing gear, or interacting with the environment (although the GM and players should use common sense as to what a character can and cannot do given the situation). This also includes maneuvers such as aiming, since a character can aim with a quad laser turret just as he can aim with a blaster. In general, all of the maneuvers listed starting on page 207 apply in all forms of combat (with a certain level of common sense).

When ships or vehicles are in encounters, they should always track their current speed. A ship may be operating at any speed from 0 to its maximum; however, accelerating and decelerating take maneuvers to accomplish.

A starship or vehicle with a silhouette between 1 and 4 can benefit from one Pilot Only maneuver per round, and can benefit from a second Pilot Only maneuver if it suffers 2 system strain (Pilot Only maneuvers are ones that affect the movement of the ship itself, and ships may only move so fast and so far). If the starship has a single pilot, the pilot must also suffer 2 strain (or downgrade his action to a maneuver) to perform two maneuvers, as per combat rules. Some ships can have multiple pilots, in which case each can perform a Pilot Only maneuver, and only the ship suffers the strain. However, these ships are rare.

A starship or vehicle with silhouette 5 or higher can only benefit from one Pilot Only maneuver in a round.

## ACCELERATE/DECELERATE

**Pilot Only:** Yes
**Silhouette:** Any
**Speed:** Any
The pilot may increase or decrease the ship's or vehicle's current speed by one, to a minimum of 0 or a maximum of the ship's maximum speed rating.

**Pilot Only:** Yes
**Silhouette:** Any
**Speed:** Any
This starship maneuver reflects the simple act of moving the ship or vehicle closer or farther away from something at its current speed. The number of starship maneuvers required for a ship or vehicle to move through a given number of range bands (see **Planetary Scale Range Bands**, page 244) is dependent on its speed. It is important to remember that range is based on the moving ship's perspective, and is not a measure of actual physical distance. Moving between one range band and the next always takes two maneuvers regardless of speed, with the following exceptions detailed below:

- **Speed 0:** The ship or vehicle is not moving and cannot use this starship maneuver until it accelerates.

- **Speed 1:** One starship maneuver to move within close range of a target or object, or two starship maneuvers to move from close to short range or from short range to close range.

- **Speed 2–4:** One starship maneuver to move within close range of a target or object, or to move from close to short range or from short to close range. Two starship maneuvers to move from close to medium or medium to close range.

- **Speed 5–6:** One starship maneuver to move within close range of a target or object, or to move from close to medium range or from medium to close range. Two starship maneuvers to move from close to long or long to close range.

## EVASIVE MANEUVERS

**Pilot Only:** Yes
**Silhouette:** 1–4
**Speed:** 3+
Evasive Maneuvers reflects a pilot's efforts to avoid incoming fire, collision, or other calamity. Executing Evasive Maneuvers upgrades the difficulty of the dice pool once for all attacks made against the ship until the end of the pilot's next turn. While this makes the ship executing the starship maneuver harder to hit, it also makes it harder for the ship executing the starship maneuver to hit anything else. Executing Evasive Maneuvers likewise upgrades the difficulty of the dice pool once for all attacks made by the ship until the end of the pilot's next turn. Evasive Maneuvers can only be undertaken by ships and vehicles of silhouette 4 or lower. Anything larger is typically too slow or awkward to perform Evasive Maneuvers.

## STAY ON TARGET

**Pilot Only:** Yes
**Silhouette:** 1–4
**Speed:** 3+

This reflects a pilot's concentration and ability to shut out combat-related stresses and distractions to make sure a target is hit or an adversary destroyed. Until the end of the pilot's next turn, all combat checks from the vehicle or vessel executing this maneuver upgrade the ability of the dice pool once. Unfortunately, while he is concentrating so hard on his target, the pilot blocks out all other threats and is an easier target for opponents. Any combat checks made targeting a ship executing this starship maneuver also upgrade their ability once until the end of the pilot's next round. This starship maneuver is restricted to small vessels like starfighters and patrol boats; only ships and vehicles of silhouette 4 or lower can Stay on Target.

## PUNCH IT

**Pilot Only:** Yes
**Silhouette:** 1–4
**Speed:** Any

This maneuver allows a ship or vehicle to go immediately to its maximum speed rating from any other speed, by throwing the throttles to maximum and overloading the ship or vehicle's drives. While expeditious, it also puts undue strain on a ship or vehicle. When executing this starship maneuver, the ship or vehicle suffers one point of system strain for every point of speed between the ship's current speed and its maximum speed.

For example, the pilot of a YT-1300 light freighter is hiding from an Imperial Navy patrol at speed 0 in the lee of a large asteroid. Suddenly, he is set upon by a pair of TIE fighters, decides that discretion is the better part of valor, and Punches It. He immediately throws his throttles to their maximum setting, and the ship jumps to life. While he escapes unharmed and is able to jump to hyperspace, the sudden acceleration deals three points of system strain to his ship.

This starship maneuver is restricted to ships of silhouette 4 or lower, as larger vessels have too much mass to accelerate so quickly.

## ANGLE DEFLECTOR SHIELDS

**Pilot Only:** No
**Silhouette:** Any
**Speed:** Any

Using this maneuver, a crew member with access to the shield controls can reassign up to one point of defense from one defense zone to another. For example, a player could shore up a vessel's forward defense zone with a point from its aft defense zone. This maneuver only works if the ship or vehicle has defense that can be reassigned, as with deflector shields.

# ACTIONS

In combat involving starships or vehicles, there are some additional actions characters may perform that specifically apply to the ship or vehicle they are operating. Some of these actions are labeled as Pilot Only actions. A starship or vehicle may benefit from only one Pilot Only action per round, no matter how many crew members are aboard it. (Pilot Only actions are actions that affect the movement of the ship itself, and ships may only move so fast and so far.)

Remember, any of the actions listed starting on page 209 in **Chapter VI: Conflict and Combat** can also be performed in combats involving ships or vehicles, within the bounds of common sense.

## DAMAGE CONTROL

**Pilot Only:** No
**Silhouette:** Any
**Speed:** Any

As a ship's hull shakes and rattles beneath the abuse of an enemy's laser cannons, sparks fly and systems begin to fail. The Damage Control action is an attempt to mitigate such stress, whether it's caused by combat or accident. Using this action, any Player Character who makes a successful Mechanics check recovers one point of system strain per success. The difficulty of the Mechanics check is determined by the system strain the ship is currently suffering (see **Table 7–2: Damage Control Difficulty**). Damage Control can be attempted as many times as needed to reduce a ship's system strain to zero (with the caveat that a single character can still only perform one action per turn, of course).

Likewise, a skilled mechanic can repair some of the hull trauma dealt to a vehicle even during an ongoing fight, although this is much trickier. In general, PCs can only attempt one Damage Control check to reduce hull trauma (by one point per success) per encounter—there are only so many repairs that can be accomplished without the facilities of a proper shipyard. In addition, the GM is the final arbiter as to whether a PC can attempt repairs of hull trauma at all (a snubfighter pilot could not climb out of his cockpit during a dogfight to patch his wing, nor could a speeder biker reattach one of his control surfaces while driving through a forest).

Characters can also use this action to repair Critical Hits from which the ship is suffering. The difficulty of repairing a Critical Hit is listed on **Table 7–9: Critical Hit Result** on page 250. Checks to repair Critical Hits can be attempted multiple times, until the Critical Hit is repaired.

## TABLE 7-2: DAMAGE CONTROL DIFFICULTY

| Total Strain | Total Hull Trauma | Difficulty |
|---|---|---|
| System strain less than half system strain threshold. | Hull trauma less than half vehicle's hull trauma threshold. | Easy (◆) |
| System strain equal to or more than half vehicle's system strain threshold. | Hull trauma equal to or more than half vehicle's hull trauma threshold. | Average (◆◆) |
| System strain exceeds vehicle's system strain threshold. | Hull trauma exceeds vehicle's hull trauma threshold. | Hard (◆◆◆) |

## GAIN THE ADVANTAGE

**Pilot Only:** Yes
**Silhouette:** 1–4
**Speed:** 4+

This action reflects the constant, frantic give-and-take of a dogfight between small craft like starfighters and patrol boats or high-speed vehicles such as airspeeders. It allows a pilot to gain the upper hand over a single opponent so that he positions himself for a better attack during the following round. To execute this starship action, the pilot makes a Piloting check, the difficulty of which is determined by the relative speeds of the ships or vehicles involved in the attack. These difficulties are outlined in **Table 7–3: Speed Advantage Difficulty**. If the check succeeds, the pilot ignores all penalties imposed by his own and his opponent's use of the Evasive Maneuvers starship maneuver until the end of the following round. In addition, the pilot also chooses which defense zone he hits with his attack. If he fails his check, he fails to Gain the Advantage from the attempt and still suffers the effects of any Evasive Maneuvers.

Once the advantage has been gained, on the following turn the opponent may attempt to cancel out the advantage by using Gain the Advantage as well. This works as described earlier, but his check is one step more difficult for each time he or his opponent has successfully Gained the Advantage against the other.

## TABLE 7-3: SPEED ADVANTAGE DIFFICULTY

| Difference in Speed | Difficulty |
|---|---|
| Initiating ship is traveling at the same speed as the target ship. | Average (◆◆) |
| Initiating ship's speed is one or more higher than target ship. | Easy (◆) |
| Initiating ship's speed is one lower than target ship. | Hard (◆◆◆) |
| Initiating ship's speed is two or more lower than target ship. | Daunting (◆◆◆◆) |

## ADDITIONAL SHIP AND VEHICLE ACTIONS

**Pilot Only:** No
**Silhouette:** Any
**Speed:** Any

When aboard a vehicle in combat, those who are not piloting or firing weapons may still want to contribute to the encounter. Although the number of options open to them is limited only by a player's creativity, **Table 7–4: Additional Starship and Vehicle Actions** has a list of some of the actions passengers can attempt during encounters. The table lists the actions by name, the skill required, the check's attendant difficulty, and the results of a success (GMs should modify the difficulty of the check if they see fit, and can also keep PCs from using certain skills that may not make sense in a certain situation). These actions are all covered by the Perform a Skill Check action, and are by no means an exhaustive list. However, they do serve to provide a range of ideas.

## PERFORM A COMBAT CHECK WITH VEHICLE WEAPONS

**Pilot Only:** No
**Silhouette:** Any
**Speed:** Any

This is similar to the Perform a Combat Check action on page 210, with some minor differences in implementation due to the differences between vehicles and individuals. For this reason, the steps to perform a combat check are repeated here, with the differences for vehicle weapons listed in each step, instead of being listed without context.

Each weapon on a starship or vehicle may only be fired a maximum of once per round unless a rule specifically allows otherwise.

### 1. DECLARE AN ATTACK AND SELECT TARGETS

With the enemy ship lined up in his gun sights and the sound of his targeting systems in his ears, the character

## TABLE 7-4: ADDITIONAL STARSHIP AND VEHICLE ACTIONS

| Action | Skills and Difficulty | Results |
|---|---|---|
| Plot Course | **Average (◆◆) Astrogation** check or **Hard (◆◆◆) Perception check** | The crew member studies the terrain ahead and plots a course that should take the vehicle safely through it. On a successful check, each success reduces the ■ suffered for difficult terrain by one. |
| Co-Pilot | **Average (◆◆) Piloting check** | The crew member serves as the vehicle's co-pilot, managing systems and auxiliary equipment to allow the pilot to focus on flying or driving. On a successful check, each success downgrades the difficulty of the pilot's next piloting check by one. |
| Jamming | **Average (◆◆) Computers check** | The crew member uses the vehicle's systems to jam the communications of enemy vehicles. On a successful check, the enemy must make an Average (◆◆) Computers check to use its communication systems. The difficulty increases by one for each additional ✵ ✵, and the jamming affects an additional target for each ✪ spent. |
| Boost Shields | **Hard (◆◆◆) Mechanics check** | The crew member re-routes power from other systems to boost the defensive systems of a vehicle. This only works if the vehicle already has a defense rating. On a successful check, the vehicle suffers 1 system strain and increases the defense of one defense zone by one until the beginning of the crew member's next turn. Additional ✵ increase the duration by one round per ✵. |
| Manual Repairs | **Hard (◆◆◆) Athletics check** | In some cases, repairs can be as simple as a sturdy metal plate welded over a damaged system. If the GM allows it and the crew member has the proper tools for the job, the crew member can attempt to use the Damage Control action with Athletics rather than Mechanics. If successful, he may remove 1 point of hull trauma from the ship, plus 1 additional point for each additional ✵ ✵. Remember, this follows the limitations of the Damage Control action, and thus may only be attempted once per encounter. |
| Fire Discipline | **Hard (◆◆◆) Leadership** or **Discipline check** | The crew member forgoes fighting to analyze the opponents' tactics and direct his fellows to greater accuracy with their weapons fire. If successful, the next crew member firing a weapon aboard the ship can add □ to his check. Each additional ✵ ✵ grants this to an additional crew member. In addition, the crew member may spend ✪ ✪ ✪ to allow every hit from shipboard weapons to inflict 1 system strain on their target as well as regular hull trauma damage until the beginning of his next turn, as the carefully timed shots pummel shields and overload systems. |
| Scan the Enemy | **Hard (◆◆◆) Perception check** | The crew member uses the ship's scanners to study the enemy. If successful, he learns what weapons the ship has, its modifications, and its system strain and hull trauma thresholds. If he spends ✪ ✪ he can also learn its current system strain and hull trauma levels. |
| Slice Enemy's Systems | **Hard (◆◆◆) Computers check** | The crew member uses powerful shipboard computers to attempt to disrupt the systems of an enemy vehicle. If successful, he reduces the defense of one zone on the target vehicle for one round per ✵. A ⊕ may be spent to disable a weapon system for one round, and ✪ ✪ may be spent to inflict 1 system strain on the target vehicle. |
| "Spoof" Missiles | **Average (◆◆) Computers** check or **Hard (◆◆◆) Vigilance check** | The crew member tracks incoming attacks and uses vehicle systems to disrupt their tracking systems, or even times incoming missiles and drops flares and chaff at opportune moments. If successful, any attacks against the crew member's ship or vehicle using weapons with the Guided quality upgrade their difficulty by one (plus an additional upgrade for every additional ✪ ✪) until the start of the crew member's next turn. |

chooses to make an attack. He selects the skill he will use to make the attack (usually the Gunnery skill, although some vehicles may have weapons on them requiring the Ranged [Heavy] skill instead). Most combat checks aboard a starship or vehicle are made using the starship or vehicle's weapons. Remember, **a particular starship or vehicle weapon can only be used once per round**, no matter how many characters are aboard the ship.

## 2. ASSEMBLE THE DICE POOL

Before unleashing a barrage of laser fire at his target, the character must assemble a dice pool based on the skill used, its characteristic, and any applicable talents and abilities he possesses. Certain conditions, such as a Critical Injury's effect, a Critical Hit inflicted on the ship or vehicle, a vehicle's defense, or an environmental effect, may also contribute dice to the dice pool. See page 24 for more information on building a dice pool.

The difficulty of combat checks when firing from vehicles or starships is based on comparing silhouettes of the firing ship and the target (even if the target of the attack is not a vehicle or starship) and is outlined in **Table 7–5: Silhouette Comparison**. The listed difficulties reflect the fact that large ships find it challenging to hit small, fast vessels, and their bulk makes them easy targets for those same small craft. Thanks to the advanced targeting computers installed in most starships, the range of a shot has no bearing on the attack's difficulty; if the target is within range, a starship can hit it. The check is further affected by modifiers brought on by starship maneuvers, talents, or terrain, or by any other modifiers, at the Game Master's discretion.

When attacking a ship of silhouette 4 or lower, the defender chooses which defense zone the attack hits. Smaller ships are more agile and constantly in motion, meaning that during combat they are continually juking, dodging, evading, and generally positioning themselves so that their strongest defense zone is always facing their attacker. When attacking a ship of silhouette 5 or higher, the defense zone affected by the attack is determined by the positions of the ships

in combat. The relative positions of ships in combat is determined by both the Game Master's and the Player Characters' actions and is illustrated through the cinematic gameplay style inherent in FORCE AND DESTINY.

## TABLE 7–5: SILHOUETTE COMPARISON

| Difference in Silhouette | Difficulty |
|---|---|
| Firing vessel has the same silhouette as target, or the silhouette is 1 larger or smaller than the target. | Average (◆◆) |
| Firing vessel has a silhouette 2 or more points smaller than the target vessel. | Easy (◆) |
| Firing vessel has a silhouette 2 points larger than the target ship. | Hard (◆◆◆) |
| Firing vessel has a silhouette 3 points larger than the target ship. | Daunting (◆◆◆◆) |
| Firing vessel has a silhouette 4 or more points larger than target ship. | Formidable (◆◆◆◆◆) |

## 3. POOL RESULTS AND DEAL DAMAGE

Once the player rolls the dice pool for his character, he evaluates the results. As with any skill check, the check must generate more ✸ than ▼ to be successful.

When making a combat check, after calculating overall success, each remaining ✸ adds +1 damage to a successful attack. If the attack affects multiple targets, the additional damage is added to each target. Remember, most weapons on vehicles and starships deal damage on planetary scale, meaning each point of damage is the equivalent of ten points of damage on personal scale.

## 4. RESOLVE ❂ AND ⊕

As with every skill check, ❂ and ⊕ can be spent to gain incidental beneficial effects on a combat check. However, just as the rules governing encounters are somewhat more regimented than the rules governing narrative gameplay, some of the options governing the spending of ❂ and ⊕ during combat also are more clearly defined. In encounters, the player controlling the active character determines how his character spends ❂ and ⊕ unless the GM has a specific reason to decide for him instead.

The first way to spend ❂ and ⊕ in a starship or vehicle attack is to activate Critical Hits or active weapon qualities. As described on pages 165 and 249, each weapon has a critical rating that consists of a numeric value. The user can spend that many ❂ to inflict one Critical Hit on the target in addition to regular effects and damage. (If the target is an individual, it inflicts a Critical Injury as per page 223.) For more information on starship and vehicle Critical Hits, see page 249. Remember, the attack must deal damage past armor to inflict a Critical Hit.

A weapon's qualities are special effects and abilities that apply only when using that particular weapon. They come in two forms: active and

## TABLE 7-6: SPENDING ⟐ AND ⊕ IN STARSHIP AND VEHICLE COMBAT

| Cost | Result Options |
|---|---|
| ⟐ or ⊕ | Add □ to the next allied active character's Piloting, Gunnery, Computers, or Mechanics check. |
| | Notice a single important point in the ongoing conflict, such as a flaw in an enemy ship's course or a speeder's weak point. |
| | Inflict a Critical Hit with a successful attack that deals damage past armor (⟐ cost may vary). |
| | Activate a weapon quality (⟐ cost may vary). |
| ⟐ ⟐ or ⊕ | Perform an immediate free maneuver, provided the active character has not already performed two maneuvers in that turn. |
| | Add ■ to the targeted character's next Piloting or Gunnery check. |
| | Add □ to any allied character's next Piloting, Gunnery, Computers, or Mechanics check, including that of the active character. |
| ⟐ ⟐ ⟐ or ⊕ | When dealing damage to an opposing vehicle or ship, the shot temporarily damages a component of the attacker's choice rather than deal hull damage or system strain. The effects of this are up to the attacker and the GM, and should make sense. For example, damaging a ship's shield generator should drop its defense to 0 until the generator is repaired (with a Mechanics check). However, it should not be too debilitating. See **Tables 7–10** and **7–11**, on page 251, for some possible components to disable. |
| | Ignore penalizing terrain or stellar phenomena until the end of the active character's next turn. |
| | If piloting the ship, perform one free Pilot Only maneuver (provided it does not exceed the maximum number of Pilot Only maneuvers in a turn). |
| | Force the target ship or vehicle to veer off, breaking any Aim or Stay on Target maneuvers. |
| ⊕ | Upgrade the difficulty of the targeted character's next Piloting or Gunnery check. |
| | Upgrade any allied character's next Piloting, Gunnery, Computers, or Mechanics check. |
| | Do something vital to turning the tide of battle, such as destroying a capital ship's shield generator or losing a pursuing ship in an asteroid field. |
| ⊕ ⊕ | When dealing damage to an opposing vehicle or ship, have the shot destroy some important component of the attacker's choice rather than deal hull damage or system strain, leaving it completely inoperable until fully repaired. As with the above option for disabling a component, this should be agreed upon by the GM and player, but could include destroying the engines of a fleeing ship, taking out its hyperdrive, or blowing off weapons. See **Tables 7–10** and **7–11** on page 251 for some possible components to destroy. |

## TABLE 7-7: SPENDING ⊚ AND ▽ IN STARSHIP AND VEHICLE COMBAT

| Cost | Result Options |
|---|---|
| ⊚ or ▽ | If piloting a ship, sudden maneuvers force the ship to slow down by 1 point of speed. |
| | The active character loses the benefits of a prior maneuver (such as executing Evasive Maneuvers or Aim) until he performs the maneuver again. |
| | The active character's ship or vehicle suffers 1 system strain. (This option may be selected more than once.) |
| ⊚ ⊚ or ▽ | An opponent may immediately perform one free maneuver in response to the active character's check. |
| | Add □ to the targeted character's next Piloting or Gunnery check. |
| | The active character or an allied character suffers ■ on his next action. |
| ⊚ ⊚ ⊚ or ▽ | The Initiative slot being used by the active player drops to last in the Initiative order. |
| | The active character grants the enemy a significant advantage in the ongoing encounter, such as drifting straight into his line of fire, thereby decreasing the difficulty of any checks made against the active character's ship or vehicle by one until the beginning of that character's next turn. |
| ▽ | The primary weapon system of the active character's ship (or the particular weapon system he is manning if he is acting as a gunner) suffers the effects of the Component Hit Critical (see page 250). This does not count toward the ship's accumulated Critical Hits. |
| | Upgrade the difficulty of an allied character's next Gunnery, Piloting, Computers, or Mechanics check, including that of the current active character. |
| | The active character suffers a minor collision, either with one of his opponents within close range or with the stellar phenomena/terrain he is flying or driving through. |
| ▽ (plus failed check) | The active character suffers a major collision, either with one of his opponents within close range or with the stellar phenomena/terrain he is flying or driving through. |

passive. Active qualities require the user to spend a certain number of ⟐ to trigger them. Generally, this is ⟐ ⟐, although some qualities require more or less. Qualities can inflict effects on a target that, unless specified otherwise, apply in addition to other effects, Critical Hits and Injuries, and damage.

In addition to always counting as an additional ✬, ⊕ can be spent to activate these qualities as well. ⊕ may be spent to inflict one Critical Hit (no matter what the weapon's critical rating is) on a successful attack. In addition, ⊕ may be spent to activate one weapon quality, no matter how many ⟐ it would normally take to do so.

# VEHICLES AND MINIONS

When using starships and vehicles in combat, a GM can still use the rules for minions to streamline and speed up encounters. The process for using minion rules with single-pilot vehicles such as speeder bikes, airspeeders, and starfighters is very similar to the process for using minion rules with NPC minion groups. Simply combine two to four of the same vehicles (piloted by the same minion NPC profile) into a single minion group. This group of vehicles operates as a single entity, which can narratively be described as flying in formation or a loosely clustered mob. Just as with minion groups of NPCs, starship or vehicle minion groups attack once as a group (upgrading the skill check if the minion NPC profile's "group only" skills allow this) and take damage as a group. They all select the same maneuvers and move to roughly the same locations as well.

Larger capital ships or heavy vehicles are generally never treated as minions—nobody wants to have to fight a minion group of two to four Star Destroyers, after all. However, they can have minion groups operating within them. A capital ship with multiple weapons should have its weapons operated by minion gunners. Such a ship generally has multiple weapons of the same type firing in the same arc. A GM can group multiple weapons of the same type and with the same firing arc on the same vehicle or ship and have them fire as a single minion group. This means all the weapons fire as one at the same target, upgrading the check if the minion gunners have Gunnery as a group skill. This speeds up the turns of capital ships (since they generally have a large number of guns to fire) and represents the ability of capital ships to hit other vessels through sheer volume of fire.

Remember, however, when using minion groups on a single capital ship or vehicle, the vehicle is still what takes damage, not the minion group.

However, there are additional options for spending and in starship or vehicle combat. A list of the most common can be found on **Table 7–6: Spending and in Starship and Vehicle Combat**, on page 243. As in regular combat, this list is not intended to be absolute, but to provide guidelines for players and GMs.

### 5. RESOLVE AND

In the same fashion in which the controlling player determines how his character spends and in his combat check, the GM determines how to spend any and generated in the check. Although the GM does this by default, in some cases (such as checks made by NPCs) he may give the players the option to spend and instead.

While most weapon descriptions include options for spending and , most do not have specific options for spending and (although this is not always the case). Some particularly volatile or dangerous weapons do have these options, and if they do, the options are detailed in the weapon's description. Starship encounters, however, do include specific options for spending and . The most common of these can be found on **Table 7–7: Spending and in Starship and Vehicle Combat**. As with and , keep in mind that these are not intended to be the only options available. As always, GMs can invent other ways to spend and , depending on the specific circumstances of the encounter, and any option that the players and GM agree on can be viable.

### 6. REDUCE DAMAGE, APPLY TO HULL TRAUMA THRESHOLD, AND APPLY CRITICAL HITS

When a ship or vehicle suffers damage, it reduces that damage by its armor (fulfilling the same purpose as soak on individuals). If any damage remains after this reduction, the vehicle suffers that much hull trauma (applied against its hull trauma threshold). If the net result is zero or negative, the vehicle suffers no hull trauma. See page 248.

A successful attack can also generate a Critical Hit, which is similar to a Critical Injury. This can occur because the weapon's critical rating triggered or because the target accumulated hull trauma greater than its hull trauma threshold. When a Critical Hit is inflicted, the attacker rolls percentile dice on **Table 7–9: Critical Hit Result**, on page 250. The result of the dice roll indicates which Critical Hit is applied.

Some weapons and talents modify Critical Hit rolls, potentially making a Critical Hit more or less effective. In addition, the attacker can spend the critical rating cost multiple times on a single hit, adding +10 to the result for each additional Critical Hit beyond the first. Note that talents and qualities that specifically affect Critical Injuries do not affect Critical Hits (so the Vicious quality, for example, would have no effect on a ship or vehicle).

# PLANETARY SCALE RANGE BANDS

Like personal combat, starship and vehicle combat utilizes broad and abstract range measurements, referred to as **planetary scale range bands**. Planetary scale range bands follow the same rules as regular range bands, found on page 213. The only difference is that planetary scale range bands operate on a much larger scale.

As stated on page 216, close range on planetary scale picks up where personal scale leaves off. However, the scale is so much bigger that a single person could never use maneuvers to move next to a target that is "close" to him on a planetary scale—the distance may be up to several kilometers and take an hour of walking to cover. Further range bands on a planetary scale would be even more extreme.

This isn't to say that ships and vehicles (especially smaller vehicles such as landspeeders), can't operate in standard range bands. Any ship or vehicle able to move could cover the distance measured by standard range bands quickly, and individuals would measure their range to a vehicle or ship using standard range bands. However, because ships and vehicles can cover those distances so quickly, it makes little sense for them to measure distances in such (relatively) small increments. This is doubly true for starfighters and airspeeders, which can cover kilometers of distance in seconds.

Therefore, vehicles and starships use a second set of range bands, referred to as planetary scale range bands. As mentioned previously, the shortest range band in planetary scale, "close range," represents a larger distance than all range bands in personal scale, and therefore encapsulates all range bands in personal scale. This means a ship or vehicle able to move to a point within close range is also covering the equivalent of all five range bands' worth of distance in personal scale. This also means even the shortest-range starship and vehicle weapons have the range of the largest personal-scale ranged weapons.

## CLOSE RANGE

Close range in planetary scale is slightly farther than extreme range in personal scale, and it can cover everything from a few dozen meters up to several kilometers in distance between two points. This might seem like a great deal of space, but most vehicles can cover this distance in several minutes at worst and microseconds at best.

On the surface of a planet, most ground vehicles engage at close range, using their larger heavy blasters and laser cannons to hit targets a regular soldier would have trouble seeing, much less hitting. In the air

## PLANETARY SCALE IN SPACE AND ON THE GROUND

Planetary scale range bands can represent longer or shorter distances, depending on whether the encounter is taking place in space or on (or just above) a planet's surface. This is because space is a much larger environment than any ground-based environment. Without air friction and terrain to hinder movement, starships can move much faster than even the fastest airspeeder. This is why each planetary scale range band talks about the distances represented in space and on the ground.

and in space, close range is the metaphorical "knife fight" range, in which dogfights between snubfighters or high-performance airspeeders take place. Capital ships endeavor to stay out of close range of each other, as it is essentially point-blank for their weapon batteries. Two large warships slugging it out at close range can tear each other to bits in short order.

## SHORT RANGE

Short range in planetary scale is anything up to roughly several dozen kilometers away. On the surface of a planet, this is far enough that vehicles no longer engage each other with line-of-sight weaponry (although artillery weapons can still pound opponents with indirect fire).

In space, short range is just out of dogfighting range and beyond the range of most starfighter and patrol boat weapons. However, most self-propelled weapons can hit targets within short range, so these smaller vessels often carry concussion missiles and proton torpedoes to extend their reach. Short range is still uncomfortably close for capital ships, though not quite as brutally point-blank as close range.

## MEDIUM RANGE

On the surface of a planet or inside a planet's atmosphere, something is within medium range if it is within roughly fifty kilometers, distant enough that only the most powerful artillery weapons can engage it.

In space, something may be within medium range at a somewhat longer distance, up to a few hundred kilometers. This is far beyond the reach of most starfighter weapons, but at the ideal range of most of the big guns mounted on capital ships. Thus, most capital ship engagements happen at medium range, with starfighters dogfighting between them.

## LONG RANGE

Long range on a planet's surface can be anywhere from a hundred to two hundred kilometers away. Engagements never happen at this distance, at which enemies appear as flickering phantoms on the screens of each side's scanner systems.

In space, however, long range can be up to several thousand kilometers away. At this point, engagements between ships become rare, with only the largest capital ship weapons able to bridge the gulf.

## EXTREME RANGE

On a planet's surface, extreme range is the far edge of a vehicle's scanners, too far for most weapons to reach.

In space, extreme range is likewise beyond the range of almost all starship weapons, even those mounted on capital ships. At extreme range, opposing ships are still jockeying for position before engaging each other, and both sides still have the chance to break off and escape.

# STELLAR PHENOMENA OR TERRAIN

Space is full of obstacles, from simple asteroids and icy comets to strange gravitational anomalies, nebulae, and even dreaded black holes. When a ship passes near or through one of these treacherous obstacles, the pilot might need to make an appropriate Piloting check, even if he is attempting a starship maneuver that typically wouldn't require one. This starship maneuver's difficulty is based on the ship's speed (as it is generally easier to avoid an obstacle while traveling at a reduced speed) and silhouette (as it is usually easier to dodge something in a smaller ship than in a larger one).

These rules also apply to vehicles driving on the surface of a planet or flying in a planet's atmosphere. The basic concepts are the same: smaller, more agile vehicles are more likely to avoid a fatal collision with the local terrain than larger, cumbersome vehicles.

The difficulty of the Piloting check is equal to the vehicle or starship's current speed or half of its silhouette (rounded up), whichever is higher. The lower of the two values indicates how many times the difficulty of the check is upgraded. For example, the pilot of a TIE fighter flying through an asteroid field at top speed (speed 5) would make a Piloting check with a **Formidable (◆ ◆ ◆ ◆ ◆)** difficulty. He would then take half the ship's silhouette (base of 3, divided in half and rounded up to 2) and upgrade the difficulty of the check by that value. In the end, the poor TIE pilot has to make a check against ◆ ◆ ◆ ◆ ◆.

However, a Jawa sandcrawler with a speed of 1 and silhouette of 4 driving through a canyon would only be an **Average (◆ ◆) check**, with one die upgraded to a ◆. In this case, the slow speed of the sandcrawler works to the Jawa pilot's advantage, even though the vehicle is fairly large and unwieldy.

Failing these checks does not mean the ship or vehicle crashes (although failing and generating ▽ might well result in a crash). Instead, it means that the pilot has been unsuccessful in navigating through the situation. He drops his speed by one, and does not reach wherever he was attempting to go (if he was trying to reach a specific location at medium range from his ship or vehicle, for example, he remains at medium range from the location).

## NAVIGATION HAZARDS

While even the tiniest speck of debris can pose a threat to a starship hurtling through the void, not all astronomical features are created equal. Piloting a ship through a well-charted nebula is one thing, but threading a ship through a densely packed asteroid field while being chased by Imperial fighters is another matter entirely. If local space is hazardous enough, the Game Master can add ■ to a player's Piloting check.

## CELESTIAL HAZARDS AND DIFFICULT MANEUVERS

Ship captains or vehicle drivers might find themselves in situations where they are already in the thick of an asteroid field or nebula (or a swamp or scree-covered hillside) and need to perform an action that requires a Piloting check. In this case, the player makes the Piloting check as specified in the description of the action (not the check specified by his speed and silhouette). He does, however, add the specified number of ■ dictated by the difficulty of the obstacles; see **Table 7–8: Navigation Hazard Setback Dice** for reference. The Game Master can also choose to upgrade the difficulty of the check based on the speed of the vehicle or ship. In general, he should upgrade the difficulty once if the speed is 1, 2, or 3 and twice if the speed is 4, 5, or 6.

## TABLE 7–8: NAVIGATION HAZARD SETBACK DICE

| Number of ■ | Planetary Description | Space Description |
|---|---|---|
| – | Light terrain. Flat, clear terrain. Roads, firm fields, grassy plains, or (if flying) clear skies and good weather. Light urban ground or air traffic. | An easy, relatively unchallenging navigational situation. A broad, loosely packed asteroid field, for example, or a thin, calm nebula. |
| ■ | Medium terrain. Deep mud or standing water less than fifty centimeters deep, trees, dense undergrowth, heavy traffic, sand dunes, or windy weather. | A tricky but not seriously daunting set of obstacles. Flying over high mountains on a moon, or a thicker asteroid field or nebula. |
| ■ ■ | Heavy or dangerous terrain. Thick forests, flowing water a meter deep, rocky hills, or flying in atmosphere during a violent storm. Wheeled vehicles typically cannot pass this type of terrain, but tracked vehicles and walkers can. | A dangerous astronomical feature. Flying around or through a fracturing comet, dodging a gas giant's ring system, or navigating through a particularly dense and turbulent asteroid field. |
| ■ ■ ■ + | Very risky terrain. Sheer cliff faces, deep swamps, semi-cooled lava, and speeding through a canyon only just wide enough for the vehicle to fit through are all examples of this type of terrain. | An extremely dangerous situation calling on every ounce of a pilot's skill and coolness. Navigating the Maw, flying close to a deadly pulsar, flying through asteroid tunnels, or other foolhardy pursuits. |

# THE CHASE

There are some cases in starship and vehicular combat when two or more characters want to engage in a chase. In such cases, the standard rules for combat can be modified slightly to represent this.

The most important thing to remember in a chase is that a great deal of the action is going to be narrative in nature. Skill checks can and will resolve the outcome of the chase, but the action during the chase is mostly narrative, and therefore up to the GM and players to describe.

To resolve a chase, the GM first should determine how far away the two vehicles start from each other. If the chase consists of two ground vehicles, such as speeder bikes or landspeeders, the GM may want to use personal scale range bands. If, on the other hand, the chase consists of two airspeeders, starfighters, or even capital ships, he should probably use planetary scale range bands.

Once he's determined starting distance, the chased and the pursuer should make a **competitive Piloting check**, with the type of Piloting check (Planetary or Space) being dependent on the vehicles used. The difficulty of the check depends on the circumstances of the chase. A pursuit through clear space with no terrain could be a **Simple (–) check**. Conversely, if the terrain is actually a factor, then the difficulty should be set using the rules found on the previous page, which means pilots will likely need to balance their need for speed with the dangers of running into possibly fatal obstacles.

Once both parties have made their check, compare total successes (as with every competitive check). If the pursuer wins, he closes the distance between himself and his prey by one range band. If the chased wins, he opens the distance between himself and his pursuer by one range band. In addition, if the winner is traveling faster than the loser, he opens or closes the distance by an additional number of range bands equal to the difference in relative speeds.

It is up to the GM at what point the chase resolves, but in general, it should end if the pursuer is able to close the gap so that he is engaged (or at close range) with his prey, or if the chased is able to open the distance to beyond extreme range.

If the chase is taking place as part of a larger encounter (such as two characters on speeder bikes chasing each other while the rest of the group fights a larger battle), then the GM should have the parties involved in the chase make their competitive check at the beginning of the round, before anyone else takes their turn. Then all characters take their turns as normal, with those involved in the chase having a turn to boost their speed, attack the person they're pursuing, or even try to make emergency repairs while they continue their pursuit (however, they cannot use their turn to take maneuvers that would move their position relative to the other members of the chase until the chase is over). It's important to note that the positions of those involved in a chase are likely changing relative to the rest of the party, and it's up to the GM and players as to where they go. Remember, the chase rules represent how far away the members of a chase are from each other, not how far they travel or where they actually go. This part is the narrative aspect of a chase, discussed previously.

Finally, it's important to note that these rules can also be used to play out a foot chase, the only differences being that the difficulty of the chase would be a set difficulty, the speeds of all participants would be equal, and the competitive check would probably be Athletics.

# TAKING DAMAGE

As is the case with Player Characters in personal combat, there are two types of damage ships and vehicles suffer in FORCE AND DESTINY: system strain and hull trauma. System strain is similar to the strain suffered by Player Characters and reflects light, temporary damage caused by glancing blows or pushing a vessel to the limits of its capabilities. Hull trauma is more serious and, consequently, more life-threatening. This is actual, physical damage that makes its way past the ship's defenses and becomes hull trauma. Hull trauma is permanent until repaired.

## HULL TRAUMA

A ship or vehicle's hull trauma threshold is a measure of its sturdiness and build quality. When a ship suffers damage in excess of its armor, the excess converts into hull trauma. When hull trauma exceeds a ship or vehicle's hull trauma threshold, one of two things happens. For vehicles silhouette 3 or smaller and of no particular importance (a common TIE fighter or a landspeeder full of faceless thugs, for example), it simply explodes, killing the pilot and any passengers. Alternatively, at the Game Master's discretion, the vehicle could simply be disabled. For larger vehicles such as stock light freighters and anything silhouette 4 or larger (or a smaller ship such as a starfighter or a landspeeder with a Player Character inside it), the vehicle immediately suffers a Critical Hit from **Table 7–9: Critical Hit Result**, on page 250. Additionally, the ship's systems shut down, it reverts to emergency power, its sublight drives sputter out, and it is adrift. At this point, the ship is a near-lifeless hulk, effectively out of combat, and likely being evacuated.

If the pilot or crew of an incapacitated ship with hull trauma that exceeds its hull trauma threshold is particularly desperate or foolish, they may attempt some temporary repairs to either escape or rejoin the fray. By scavenging parts from ruined systems, raiding the hold for any spares, and bypassing damaged components, along with a **Hard (◆ ◆ ◆) Mechanics check**, the crew can bring the ship back to some semblance of life. The ship reduces its hull trauma to one point below its hull trauma threshold but suffers the following penalties: speed is reduced to 1, handling is reduced to –3, and all weapon systems are inoperable until fully repaired. If the ship reenters combat in this fragile state, any attack that inflicts hull trauma immediately generates a Critical Hit, with +30 added to the roll on **Table 7–9: Critical Hit Result**. All of these effects persist until the ship can be dry-docked and repaired.

There are occasions when vehicles or starships run into the terrain around them, or into another nearby vehicle or starship. In these cases, there are two possible types of collision: glancing blows (minor collisions) and head-on hits (major collisions). Collisions can be mitigated by a ship's defenses; particle shields in particular are specifically designed to absorb impacts.

In the case of a minor collision, all vehicles or starships involved suffer a single Critical Hit. Subtract the ship's defense times ten from the roll; if the result is zero, the ship's shields or other defenses have nullified the collision entirely, and the Critical Hit is canceled. In the case of a major collision, all vehicles or starships involved suffer a single Critical Hit as well. However, only subtract the ship's defense multiplied by five from the roll. If there are multiple defense values on multiple facings of the ship, the GM chooses which facing is hit, based on what the ship or vehicle was doing at the time.

At the GM's discretion, some particularly large vehicles and vessels might be able to ignore collisions with very small vehicles or vessels. However, larger ships and vehicles have a harder time avoiding collisions with larger asteroids or terrain features.

## SYSTEM STRAIN

System strain works the same way as strain suffered by characters. A vehicle that suffers strain in excess of its system strain threshold quickly finds itself in an untenable situation. Generators overload, reactors shut down, shields fall, engines go dead, electrical fires start, and all manner of electrical mayhem occurs as, one by one, essential systems go offline and the ship becomes unresponsive. Until the crew can make repairs, the ship becomes helpless, adrift in space or hurtling along a course from which it can neither deviate nor escape.

In game terms, when a ship or vehicle exceeds its system strain threshold, the ship's speed drops to zero during the following round. The majority of its systems (such as engines, weapons, and shields) cease operating as well. This means it cannot move, its weapons cannot shoot, and its defense drops to zero. This might be a relatively minor situation if this is a ship flying through deep space or a vehicle safely sitting on the ground—or a more dangerous situation if the ship is flying near something with a gravitational pull.

While the situation aboard a ship that has exceeded its system strain threshold is indeed dire, not all is lost. Any crew member can aid the ship in recovering strain by performing repairs and damage control such as rebooting systems, bypassing fried circuits, and putting out electrical fires. This is accomplished through the Damage Control action.

Ships and vehicles do recover from system strain slowly over time. For every full day a ship or vehicle spends without taking more system strain, it reduces its total system strain by one.

## CRITICAL HITS

Occasionally a lucky, well-placed shot or a collision with a particularly large or dangerous object does more to a ship than bounce harmlessly off the shields or scuff up the armor. Ion cannon blasts can short out systems; searing laser beams can pierce shields, armor, and hull alike to incinerate crew alive; and rogue asteroids can tear a ship's innards out, leaving it powerless and adrift in the cold dark of deep space.

These rare occurrences are reflected by the results on **Table 7–9: Critical Hit Result**. A number of factors can lead to a ship's suffering a Critical Hit. For example, it might suffer enough hull trauma to exceed its hull trauma threshold, or a successful combat check could generate enough ✪ or ✦ to trigger a weapon's critical rating. Remember, an attack's damage also has to exceed a target's armor to deal a Critical Hit, which is important when firing small arms at something using armor instead of soak. When an attacker generates a Critical Hit, he rolls on **Table 7–9: Critical Hit Result**, and his target suffers the listed effects. Critical Hits are divided into four color-coded severity levels, which dictate the difficulty of the check required to repair the Critical Hit, as listed in the table. These difficulties can be further modified at the GM's discretion.

Once a ship or vehicle suffers a Critical Hit, it counts as suffering that Critical Hit until it is repaired. This status counts even if the effects of the Critical Hit only last a single round. While a ship or vehicle is suffering the effects of a Critical Hit, any additional Critical Hits generated against it add +10 to the roll on **Table 7–9: Critical Hit Result** per existing Critical Hit.

## COMPONENT CRITICALS

Of all the Critical Hit results, **Component Hit Criticals** have the potential to be the most devastating (outside of those that completely destroy a vessel). Component Hit Criticals functionally disable, either temporarily or permanently, critical systems on a target vessel and can lead to a number of complications. There are two charts for Component Hit Criticals on page 251, one for small ships of silhouette 4 or lower, and one for large ships of silhouette 5 or higher. The effects of most of these Critical Hits stack, and a ship can suffer more than one Component Hit Critical.

## REPAIRING HULL TRAUMA

While system strain and the results of many Critical Hits are temporary, hull trauma is more permanent. Repairing hull trauma requires three things—proper facilities, money, and time—the latter two in abundance. Proper facilities have enough tools, light, parts, and workspace to make needed repairs to the vehicle. They could be anything from an orbital space station to a groundside spaceport (in the case of a starship) or simply a well-stocked garage (in the case of a walker or landspeeder).

Once a ship is in a slip or dry dock for repairs, each point of hull trauma restored costs roughly 500 credits. This cost is highly variable, however, and can fluctuate dramatically based on the Player Characters' reputation, the overall damage to the ship, the scarcity of parts, and countless other factors. The final cost for repairs, like many other aspects of FORCE AND DESTINY, is left to the Game Master's discretion. The time required is also variable and is left to the Game Master's discretion. A good rule of thumb is that light damage (up to a quarter of a ship's total hull threshold) should take an amount of time measured in days, while any damage over that takes weeks or even months to repair, depending on its severity.

If it proves imprudent or impossible to get to a proper maintenance facility, the GM might choose to allow the PCs to repair their vehicle using scavenged parts and their own ingenuity. However, these repairs should be somewhat inferior to the real thing, hard to perform (requiring several **Hard [◆ ◆ ◆]** or **Daunting [◆ ◆ ◆ ◆] Mechanics checks**) and time-consuming. In short, they should be an arduous plot point for the PCs to overcome, not a cheapskate way to avoid getting work done at proper facilities.

# TABLE 7-9: CRITICAL HIT RESULT

| d100 | Severity | Result |
|------|----------|--------|
| 01–09 | Easy (◆) | **Mechanical Stress:** The ship or vehicle suffers 1 point of system strain. |
| 10–18 | Easy (◆) | **Jostled:** A small explosion or impact rocks the vehicle. All crew members suffer 1 strain and are disoriented for one round. |
| 19–27 | Easy (◆) | **Losing Power to Shields:** Decrease defense in affected defense zone by 1 until the Critical Hit is repaired. If the ship or vehicle has no defense, suffer 1 point of system strain. |
| 28–36 | Easy (◆) | **Knocked Off Course:** A particularly strong blast or impact sends the ship or vehicle careening off in a new direction. On his next turn, the pilot cannot execute any maneuvers and must make a Piloting check to regain control. The difficulty of this check depends on his current speed. |
| 37–45 | Easy (◆) | **Tailspin:** All firing from the ship or vehicle suffers ■■ until the end of the pilot's next turn. All crew members are immobilized until the end of the pilot's next turn. |
| 46–54 | Easy (◆) | **Component Hit:** One component of the attacker's choice is knocked offline and is rendered inoperable until the end of the following round. For a list of ship components, see **Table 7–10: Small Ship or Vehicle Components** or **Table 7–11: Large Ship or Vehicle Components**, depending on target ship silhouette. |
| 55–63 | Average (◆ ◆) | **Shields Failing:** Reduce defense in all defense zones by 1 point until the Critical Hit is repaired. If the ship or vehicle has no defense, suffer 2 points of system strain. |
| 64–72 | Average (◆ ◆) | **Navicomputer Failure:** The navicomputer (or in the case of a ship without a navicomputer, its R2 unit) fails, and the ship cannot make the jump to hyperspace until the Critical Hit is repaired. If the ship or vehicle is without a hyperdrive, the vehicle or ship's navigation systems fail, leaving it flying or driving blind, unable to tell where it is or where it's going. |
| 73–81 | Average (◆ ◆) | **Power Fluctuations:** The ship or vehicle is beset by random power surges and outages. The pilot cannot voluntarily inflict system strain on the ship (to gain an extra starship maneuver, for example) until this Critical Hit is repaired. |
| 82–90 | Hard (◆ ◆ ◆) | **Shields Down:** Decrease defense in affected defense zone to 0, and decrease defense in all other defense zones by 1 until this Critical Hit is repaired. While the defense of the affected defense zone cannot be restored until the Critical Hit is repaired, defense from other zones can be assigned to protect that defense zone as usual. If the ship or vehicle has no defense, suffer 4 points of system strain. |
| 91–99 | Hard (◆ ◆ ◆) | **Engine Damaged:** The ship or vehicle's maximum speed is reduced by 1 point, to a minimum of 1, until the Critical Hit is repaired. |
| 100–108 | Hard (◆ ◆ ◆) | **Shield Overload:** The ship's shields completely fail. Decrease the defense of all defense zones to 0. This Critical Hit cannot be repaired until the end of the encounter, and the ship suffers 2 points of system strain. If the ship or vehicle has no defense, reduce armor by 1 until the Critical Hit is repaired. |
| 109–117 | Hard (◆ ◆ ◆) | **Engines Down:** The ship or vehicle's maximum speed is reduced to 0 until the Critical Hit is repaired, although it continues on its present course thanks to momentum. In addition, the ship cannot execute any maneuvers until the Critical Hit is repaired. |
| 118–126 | Hard (◆ ◆ ◆) | **Major System Failure:** One component of the attacker's choice is heavily damaged and is inoperable until the Critical Hit is repaired. For a list of ship components, see **Table 7–10: Small Ship or Vehicle Components** or **Table 7–11: Large Ship or Vehicle Components**, depending on target ship silhouette. |
| 127–133 | Daunting (◆ ◆ ◆ ◆) | **Major Hull Breach:** A huge, gaping tear is torn in the ship's hull, and the ship depressurizes. For ships and vehicles of silhouette 4 and smaller, the entire ship depressurizes in a number of rounds equal to the ship's silhouette. Ships and vehicles of silhouette 5 and larger tend to be highly compartmentalized and have many safeguards against depressurization. These ships don't completely depressurize, but parts do (the specifics regarding which parts depressurize is up to the GM; however, each section of the ship or vehicle that does lose air does so in a number of rounds equal to the vehicle's silhouette). Vehicles and ships operating in an atmosphere can better handle this Critical Hit. However, the huge tear still inflicts penalties, causing the vehicle to suffer the Destabilized Critical Hit instead (see next entry). |
| 134–138 | Daunting (◆ ◆ ◆ ◆) | **Destabilized:** The ship or vehicle's structural integrity is seriously damaged. Reduce the ship or vehicle's hull trauma threshold and system strain threshold to half their original values until repaired. |
| 139–144 | Daunting (◆ ◆ ◆ ◆) | **Fire!:** Fire rages through the ship. The ship or vehicle immediately takes 2 points of system strain, and anyone caught in the fire takes damage as discussed on page 220. A fire can be put out with some quick thinking and appropriate skill or Vigilance and/or Cool checks at the Game Master's discretion. Once going, a fire takes one round per 2 of the ship's silhouette points to put out. |
| 145–153 | Daunting (◆ ◆ ◆ ◆) | **Breaking Up:** The vehicle or ship has suffered so much damage that it begins to come apart at its seams, breaking up and disintegrating around the crew. At the end of the following round, the ship is completely destroyed, and the surrounding environment is littered with debris. Anyone aboard the ship or vehicle has one round to get to an escape pod, bail out, or dive for the nearest hatch before they are lost. |
| 154+ | – | **Vaporized:** The ship or vehicle is completely destroyed, consumed in a particularly large and dramatic fireball. Nothing survives. |

## TABLE 7-10: SMALL SHIP OR VEHICLE COMPONENTS

| Component | Description |
|---|---|
| Support Droid | Typically an astromech, the droid is knocked out of commission until it can be repaired. If this droid is a Player Character, it immediately suffers 10 strain. |
| Ejection System | The pilot and/or crew are unable to escape the ship in an emergency until this system resets or is repaired, depending on the severity of the Critical Hit. |
| Weapon System | One weapon system of the attacker's choice is knocked offline. |
| Sensors | Sensor range is reduced by one range band. If the ship's sensors are already limited to close range, they are knocked offline completely, and the ship is effectively blind until the sensors are rebooted or repaired, depending on the severity of the Critical Hit. |
| Comms | The comms are knocked offline, and the ship can neither send nor receive any electronic signals or data. |
| Sublight Engines | The engines are slightly damaged, and the ship's speed is reduced by 1 point. |
| Hyperdrive | Either the hyperdrive or navicomputer is damaged, and the ship cannot make the jump to hyperspace. |
| Shields | The ship's defense is reduced by 1 point in all defense zones. |

## TABLE 7-11: LARGE SHIP OR VEHICLE COMPONENTS

| Component | Description |
|---|---|
| Landing Gear | The ship's landing gear is stuck. Any attempt to land a ship that cannot deploy its landing gear results in 2 points of hull trauma and 2 points of system strain. This only applies to ships of silhouette 5 or less; anything larger is unable to enter a planet's atmosphere. |
| Weapon System | One weapon system of the attacker's choice is knocked offline. |
| Sensors | Sensor range is reduced by one range band. |
| Comms | The comms are knocked offline, and the ship can neither send nor receive any electronic signals or data. |
| Sublight Engines | The engines are slightly damaged, and the ship's speed is reduced by 1 point. |
| Hyperdrive | The hyperdrive is damaged, and the ship cannot make the jump to hyperspace. |
| Shields | The ship's defense is reduced by 1 point in all defense zones. |
| Landing Bay | One of the vessel's landing bays is knocked out of commission. The severity of the damage is ultimately left to the Game Master's discretion, and could result in anything from a temporary inability to launch or recover ships from this bay to a failure of the docking bay shield and a total decompression of the entire compartment. |
| Cargo Hold | The ship is hulled, and one of the cargo holds is exposed to vacuum. Cargo may be damaged or lost, and anyone in the cargo hold takes damage according to the Game Master's discretion. |
| Bridge | The bridge is damaged. No starship maneuvers or starship actions may be executed aboard the ship until the damage is repaired. In addition, the ship continues on its course at its current speed, and cannot be stopped or its course changed until the damage is fixed. |

# INTERSTELLAR TRAVEL

Despite the fact that the advent of the galaxy-shrinking hyperdrive has made travel between stars commonplace, the galaxy is still largely an unimaginably vast, empty void dotted here and there with tiny islands of civilization. The distances involved in space travel are much larger than those on a planet's surface. Where an overland trip of a thousand kilometers is considered quite long on a planet, traveling the same distance into space from the surface barely takes a ship into orbit. On the other hand, a trip of hundreds of thousands of kilometers, from a planet to its moon, for example, can be considered a short hop.

There are two types of starship travel: sublight travel and hyperspace travel.

## SUBLIGHT TRAVEL

Sublight travel happens in realspace while a ship is running under its sublight engines. Traveling from a planet's surface to one of its moons or flying between planets in the same system are trips that are undertaken at sublight speeds. These journeys are measured by hundreds of thousands or millions of kilometers. Even at the incredible speeds at which starships travel in realspace, such trips can require days to complete. **Table 7–12: Sublight Travel Times** presents examples of rough travel distances and times to help both the Game Master and the players estimate the time required for their trip and plan accordingly. These are simply guidelines, however, and should not be taken as hard fact. There are any number of obstacles or extenuating circumstances that could shorten or lengthen a trip, from exceedingly heavy traffic to a freak meteor shower to the appearance of an Imperial fleet in orbit. Ultimately, the Game Master should remember that the exact length of any trip at sublight speeds is left to his discretion, and such movement happens, essentially, at whatever speed the plot requires.

## Table 7-12: Sublight Travel Times

| Trip Time | Example |
| --- | --- |
| 5–15 minutes | Time needed to fly from a planet's orbit to a safe hyperspace jump distance. |
| 30–90 minutes | Time needed to fly from a planet's surface to one of its moons. |
| 6–12 hours | Time needed to fly from one planet to another within the same star system. This time varies a great deal depending on the relative position of the planets in question and any stellar phenomena between them. |
| 12–72 hours | Time needed to fly from the center of a star system to its farthest limits. Again, this time varies greatly depending on the size of the system and any obstacles or stellar phenomena encountered along the way. |

# HYPERSPACE TRAVEL

Whereas sublight travel is how ships move between the planets of a single star system, hyperspace travel is how they travel between the stars themselves. Essentially another dimension accessed through the fantastic technology of the hyperdrive, hyperspace allows starships to travel at many times the speed of light, shortening a trip that would take thousands of years at sublight speeds to a handful of days or weeks. Although it is a mature technology, and ships travel relatively stable hyperspace routes (information about which is updated constantly), traveling through hyperspace is still a dangerous proposition.

Although it has been studied and scrutinized for millennia, much of hyperspace remains a mystery. Scientists know that hyperspace is an alternate dimension that exists conterminously with realspace. This means that anything traveling through hyperspace is traveling the same direction in realspace. This conterminous nature allows for the mapping of hyperspace and the establishment of hyperspace routes. Objects, especially large objects with powerful gravity like planets and stars, cast a shadow in hyperspace, and thus they exist in both planes at once. For example, if a star exists at a certain location, its reflection exists in the same location in hyperspace. The hyperspace shadows possess the same mass and gravity in hyperspace as the objects that cast them possess in realspace. For all intents and purposes, they physically exist in hyperspace and present a serious and concrete obstacle in both planes.

Due to the existence of hyperspace shadows, there is no straight, fixed hyperspace route from one end of the galaxy to another. Ships moving through hyperspace must navigate around these obstacles as they do in realspace. This is why fixed, well-established hyperspace routes exist between major population centers in the galaxy, although "fixed" is a relative term due to the fact that the galaxy is constantly in motion and, therefore, so are its hyperspace lanes.

Navigating even the most well-documented hyperspace route entails a raft of incredibly complex calculations, which are largely handled by a ship's navicomputer. Although the navicomputer does the bulk of the work, a ship's captain (or in those ships large or lucky enough to have one, its astrogator) still needs to enter coordinates and double-check the computer's final calculations. Under ideal conditions, this requires an **Easy (◇) Astrogation check**. As conditions are rarely ideal for those fighting against the Empire, the Game Master should use the modifiers in **Table 7–13: Astrogation Modifiers** to increase the difficulty of the Astrogation check to reflect the circumstances under which it is being made.

Once a ship is actually in hyperspace, there is little for the crew and passengers to do but sit back and enjoy the ride. All hyperspace routes have an average duration, measured in hours or days, based on the time required for a ship equipped with a Class 1 hyperdrive to make the trip under ideal conditions. Again, conditions are rarely ideal when dealing with hyperspace travel; transit times can be shortened or lengthened due to any number of complications. As with sublight travel, the time it takes to travel between star systems is left to the Game

## Table 7-13: Astrogation Modifiers

| + ◇ | Description |
|---|---|
| +◆◆◆ | Damaged or missing astromech droid or navicomputer. |
| +◆ | Quick calculations or entry into hyperspace under duress, typically while escaping pursuit. |
| +◆ | Ship is lightly damaged. |
| +◆◆ | Ship is heavily damaged. |
| +◆ | Outdated, corrupt, or counterfeit navigation charts or navicomputer data. |

Master's discretion. When determining the length of time needed for any given trip through hyperspace, the GM should consult **Table 7-14: Hyperspace Travel Times** for general guidelines. These average times are modified by a ship's hyperdrive class, and they can be further modified by the Game Master at his discretion due to complications with the Astrogation check, fluctuations in the route, outdated charts, or any other reason he sees fit.

Of course, most starships (especially civilian vessels) do not have a Class 1 hyperdrive. To determine the actual travel time for a particular starship, first determine the hyperspace travel time. The GM should consult **Table 7-14**; then, using that information as a basis, he can estimate the actual travel time between the two points for a Class 1 hyperdrive. Next, he multiplies this travel time by the hyperdrive's class. So, the time for a Class 1 hyperdrive remains the same. However, a ship with a Class 2 hyperdrive would take twice as long to get somewhere, a Class 3 hyperdrive would take three times as long, and so on.

## FATAL ENCOUNTERS

Of all the well-documented hazards of traveling through hyperspace, none is more feared or more potentially devastating than a collision with a mass shadow. Although every hyperspace-capable ship is equipped with a number of sensors and failsafes designed to drop the ship immediately into realspace if it passes dangerously close to a gravity well or mass shadow, accidents do happen; there are many documented cases of a ship in hyperspace colliding with a planet or flying into a star. This, obviously, spells certain death for the starship and anyone aboard. In certain, very rare cases, the starship can even come out of hyperspace far too close to a planet's surface and crash at dangerous speeds. This could do considerable damage if it has the misfortune of impacting a city or other population center. It is the fear of both such occurrences that keeps a dedicated corps of explorers, astrogators, and cartographers busy keeping hyperspace charts up to date.

## Table 7-14: Hyperspace Travel Times

| Distance Traveled | Average Duration |
|---|---|
| Within a sector | Ten to twenty-four hours. |
| Within a region | Ten to seventy-two hours. |
| Between regions | Three days to one week. |
| Across the galaxy | One to three weeks. |

# VEHICLE PROFILES

**P**lanetary vehicles in FORCE AND DESTINY fall into four broad categories, which encompass a wide variety of landspeeders, walkers, airspeeders, and groundcars. Used in nearly every occupation and often a requirement for survival, a good, reliable vehicle is usually more than the sum of its parts.

## AIRSPEEDERS

Airspeeders are a common sight on worlds across the galaxy. Airspeeders are generally small-to-medium-sized atmospheric craft powered by a combination of high-thrust turbine engines and repulsorlifts. The repulsorlifts keep the airspeeders aloft, while the engines give airspeeders their signature speed, although most can't leave a planet's atmosphere. Airspeeders are used for a variety of purposes, including hauling cargo, transporting passengers, and even warfare.

### CIVILIAN AIRSPEEDER

Designed to carry passengers, cargo, or some combination of both, civilian airspeeders are ubiquitous throughout the galaxy. Designed for sport, commuting, or work, these civilian speeders are rarely armed and feature no armor or shields. The following profile represents a common civilian airspeeder of the type found on most civilized worlds.

| SILHOUETTE | SPEED | HANDLING | DEF: FORE/PORT/STARBOARD/AFT | | | | ARMOR |
|:---:|:---:|:---:|:---:|:---:|:---:|:---:|:---:|
| 2 | 3 | +0 | 0 | - | - | 0 | 0 |
| | | | HT THRESHOLD | | | SS THRESHOLD | |
| | | | 5 | | | 5 | |

**Vehicle Type/Model:** Airspeeder/Civilian.
**Manufacturer:** Various manufacturers.
**Maximum Altitude:** 1 kilometer.
**Sensor Range:** Short.
**Crew:** One pilot.
**Encumbrance Capacity:** 10–30.
**Passenger Capacity:** 1–6.
**Price/Rarity:** 10,000 credits/3.
**Customization Hard Points:** 1.
**Weapons:** None.

### UBRIKKIAN INDUSTRIES TALON I COMBAT CLOUD CAR

A sturdy, nimble, high-atmosphere cloud car designed specifically for combat and patrol duty, the Ubrikkian Industries' Talon I is utilized by planetary security from the Core Worlds to the Outer Rim. Filling the gap between starfighters and airspeeders, the Talon I is able to operate in virtually any atmosphere and comes equipped with armor plating and advanced weapon systems. The combat cloud car is commonly employed for patrol and scouting, as well as for customs enforcement and traffic control duties in busy spaceports such as those at Nar Shaddaa and Sleheyron.

| SILHOUETTE | SPEED | HANDLING | DEF: FORE/PORT/STARBOARD/AFT | | | | ARMOR |
|:---:|:---:|:---:|:---:|:---:|:---:|:---:|:---:|
| 2 | 4 | +2 | 0 | - | - | 0 | 3 |
| | | | HT THRESHOLD | | | SS THRESHOLD | |
| | | | 6 | | | 7 | |

**Type/Model:** Cloud Car/Talon I.
**Manufacturer:** Ubrikkian Industries.
**Maximum Altitude:** 100 kilometers.
**Sensor Range:** Short.
**Crew:** One pilot.
**Encumbrance Capacity:** 10.
**Passenger Capacity:** 0.
**Price/Rarity:** 36,000 credits/5.
**Customization Hard Points:** 2.
**Weapons:** Forward-mounted twin heavy blaster cannon (Fire Arc Forward; Damage 5; Critical 4; Range [Close]; Linked 1).

## LANDSPEEDERS

Landspeeders are the personal, commercial, and military vehicle of choice throughout the galaxy. They are produced in countless numbers by hundreds of well-respected manufacturers such as SoroSuub and Incom. With their low-powered repulsorlift generators, landspeeders have an average altitude of less than one hundred meters and typically carry a mix of passengers and cargo. Landspeeders are cheap, efficient, reliable transportation with designs that run the gamut from swoops and speeder bikes to small, two-person runabouts to massive freight transporters.

Speeders ignore hazards and the effects of terrain lower than their operating altitudes.

### PASSENGER LANDSPEEDER

Passenger landspeeders are the go-to personal transport vehicle throughout the galaxy. Produced in countless styles by SoroSuub, Trask, Mobquet, and others, they range from sporty two-seater hot rods to staid commuter vehicles to the opulent VIP landspeeders used to ferry around Imperial officials. Passenger landspeeders typically require one driver and can carry upwards of four passengers. Depending on their equipment and configuration, they can travel at various speeds and altitudes. They do not commonly come equipped with armor or weapons. The following profile represents a typical five-person landspeeder used for commuting and short-range planetary travel.

| | | | DEF. FORE/PORT/STARBOARD/AFT | | | | ARMOR |
|---|---|---|---|---|---|---|---|
| 3 | 1 | +0 | 0 | - | - | 0 | 0 |
| SILHOUETTE | SPEED | HANDLING | | | | | |
| | | | HT THRESHOLD | | SS THRESHOLD | | |
| | | | 8 | | 8 | | |

**Vehicle Type/Model:** Speeder truck/A-A3.
**Manufacturer:** Trast Heavy Transports.
**Sensor Range:** Close.
**Crew:** One pilot.
**Encumbrance Capacity:** 135 (without passengers in the bed).
**Passenger Capacity:** 2 in the cab, up to 8 in the bed.
**Price/Rarity:** 7,000 credits/2.
**Customization Hard Points:** 3.
**Weapons:** None.

### 85-XS ODYSSEY HEAVY SPEEDER BIKE

Aratech's Odyssey is a speeder bike built for adventure. Based on the reliable 74-Y speeder bike platform, this two-person speeder bike was designed for long-distance travel over rough terrain. Built with exploration in mind, the Odyssey features a reinforced frame, heavy-duty power systems, improved repulsorlift drives, and capacious storage for luggage and supplies. A compact and extremely powerful ground-following sensor suite mated to a navigation system makes handling the heavy vehicle easy for nearly any sentient. Not as common or popular as the 74-Y, the 85-XS enjoys slow-but-steady sales and can be found relatively easily on less-developed worlds where ruggedness and reliability take precedence over speed and handling.

| | | | DEF. FORE/PORT/STARBOARD/AFT | | | | ARMOR |
|---|---|---|---|---|---|---|---|
| 2 | 2 | +0 | 0 | - | - | 0 | 1 |
| SILHOUETTE | SPEED | HANDLING | | | | | |
| | | | HT THRESHOLD | | SS THRESHOLD | | |
| | | | 3 | | 4 | | |

**Vehicle Type/Model:** Speeder Bike/85-XS.
**Manufacturer:** Aratech Repulsor Company.
**Sensor Range:** Close.
**Crew:** One pilot.
**Encumbrance Capacity:** 15.
**Passenger Capacity:** 1.
**Price/Rarity:** 4,500 credits/5.
**Customization Hard Points:** 4.
**Weapons:** None.

# WHEELED AND TRACKED VEHICLES

Wheels and tracks remain some of the oldest means of locomotion in the galaxy. Many civilized worlds have long since replaced tires and treads with repulsorlifts and articulated walker legs. However, wheels and tracks do have one enduring advantage: they're simple to produce and even easier to maintain.

| | | | DEF. FORE/PORT/STARBOARD/AFT | | | | ARMOR |
|---|---|---|---|---|---|---|---|
| 2 | 2 | +0 | 0 | - | - | 0 | 0 |
| SILHOUETTE | SPEED | HANDLING | | | | | |
| | | | HT THRESHOLD | | SS THRESHOLD | | |
| | | | 4 | | 5 | | |

**Vehicle Type/Model:** Landspeeder/various.
**Manufacturer:** Various corporations.
**Sensor Range:** Close.
**Crew:** One pilot.
**Encumbrance Capacity:** 10.
**Passenger Capacity:** 4.
**Price/Rarity:** 3,500 credits/3.
**Customization Hard Points:** 4.
**Weapons:** None.

### A-A3 DRAY LIGHT SPEEDER TRUCK

Smaller and lighter than the heavy A-A5 speeder truck, the A-A3 Dray by Trast Heavy Transports is a common sight throughout the galaxy. Designed as a light duty speeder truck and marketed to craftsmen and contractors as work vehicles and light cargo haulers, Drays feature an enclosed cab that seats three abreast and a long, open bed that can carry cargo or passengers. Numerous aftermarket accessories for the Dray, such as soft and hard-top covers for the bed, cargo-handling systems, and reinforced structures, and the ease with which the speeder can be repaired and modified make the Dray a popular exploration and backcountry sporting vehicle as well as a reliable workhorse.

Wheeled vehicles suffer the effects of terrain as discussed in **Stellar Phenomena or Terrain**, page 246 while tracked vehicles treat any terrain as if it were one step lower in difficulty.

## GALLIS-TECH 48 ROLLER

Gallis-Tech's 48 Roller is a one-person wheel bike, a contraption where the pilot rides within a single, large wheel. Gallis-Tech decided to power its wheel bike with a pair of jet engines. This gives the Roller an impressive speed but makes it even harder to control. Skilled operators can steer the Roller by simply leaning in the direction they want to turn. Unskilled drivers, on the other hand, quickly find themselves smeared across the landscape. The Roller is often found on frontier planets on the Outer Rim, where, unsurprisingly, it's most popular among a civilization's youth.

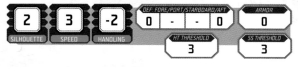

| SILHOUETTE | SPEED | HANDLING | DEF: FORE/PORT/STARBOARD/AFT | | | | ARMOR |
|---|---|---|---|---|---|---|---|
| 2 | 3 | -2 | 0 | - | - | 0 | 0 |
| | | | HT THRESHOLD | | SS THRESHOLD | | |
| | | | 3 | | 3 | | |

**Vehicle Type/Model:** Wheel Bike/48 Roller.
**Manufacturer:** Gallis-Tech.
**Sensor Range:** None.
**Crew:** One pilot.
**Encumbrance Capacity:** 5.
**Passenger Capacity:** 0.
**Price/Rarity:** 750 credits/5.
**Customization Hard Points:** 0.
**Weapons:** None.

## GROUNDCAR

The groundcar is as primitive as it is ubiquitous on poor or recently colonized worlds. Instead of using repulsorlifts or even tracks, it moves via four or more powered wheels. Groundcars typically have a slow top speed and are woefully hampered by terrain, tradeoffs that more than counterbalance their inexpensiveness and ease of maintenance.

| SILHOUETTE | SPEED | HANDLING | DEF: FORE/PORT/STARBOARD/AFT | | | | ARMOR |
|---|---|---|---|---|---|---|---|
| 2 | 2 | -1 | 0 | - | - | 0 | 0 |
| | | | HT THRESHOLD | | SS THRESHOLD | | |
| | | | 5 | | 3 | | |

**Vehicle Type/Model:** Groundcar/Various.
**Manufacturer:** Various manufacturers.

**Sensor Range:** None.
**Crew:** One pilot.
**Encumbrance Capacity:** 20.
**Passenger Capacity:** 3.
**Price/Rarity:** 1,500 credits/2.
**Customization Hard Points:** 2.
**Weapons:** None.

# WALKERS

Walkers are one of the more common transportation options in the galaxy, acting as something of a compromise between rugged but painfully primitive groundcars or crawlers and more expensive repulsorlift vehicles. Two or more articulated legs give walkers the ability to traverse most terrain, although not at any great speed. However, their engines and motive systems tend to be more reliable than repulsorlifts. Traditionally, walkers tend to be used in military forces. However, many colonists find these vehicles useful, and can purchase civilian models.

Like repulsorlift vehicles, walkers ignore penalties from light terrain and from difficult terrain composed of any hazard lower than half the vehicle's height.

## AT-HCT

A derivative of the popular AT-EST, Rothana Heavy Engineering's All Terrain Heavy Civilian Transport has served the needs of isolated colonies for decades. Designed for simplicity and versatility, the AT-HCT resembles an eight-legged beast of burden. A single driver controls the vehicle from a saddle-seat mounted off its front. Behind the driver, the rest of the AT-HCT consists of a single open-topped bed. The vehicle is not flashy, fast, or particularly combat-capable, but it is tough and durable, and it can carry a great deal of cargo over long distances.

| SILHOUETTE | SPEED | HANDLING | DEF: FORE/PORT/STARBOARD/AFT | | | | ARMOR |
|---|---|---|---|---|---|---|---|
| 3 | 1 | -1 | 0 | - | - | 0 | 0 |
| | | | HT THRESHOLD | | SS THRESHOLD | | |
| | | | 15 | | 15 | | |

**Vehicle Type/Model:** Walker/AT-HCT.
**Manufacturer:** Rothana Heavy Engineering.
**Sensor Range:** Medium.
**Crew:** One pilot.
**Encumbrance Capacity:** 200.
**Passenger Capacity:** 6.
**Price/Rarity:** 3,000 credits/3.
**Customization Hard Points:** 2.
**Weapons:** None.

# STARSHIP PROFILES

**S**tarships are produced in a dizzying array of shapes, styles, and sizes by dozens of highly respected shipwrights and industrial concerns throughout the galaxy. Some are famous, like Corellian Engineering Corporation's YT-series of light freighters, and some are notorious, like the Imperial Navy's unmistakable Star Destroyers. Starships have been used for personal transport, freight shipping, sport, smuggling, and waging war for tens of thousands of years. Nearly every spacefaring species has an indigenous starship design, and many species, like the Sullustans, Verpines, and Mon Calamari, are known more for their ships than for any other part of their culture or history. The following section provides a list of vessels that an itinerant Force user might encounter in his travels.

## STARFIGHTERS AND PATROL BOATS

Starfighters and patrol boats are the smallest hyperspace-capable starships found in the galaxy. While they share some overlapping missions, starfighters and patrol boats are generally quite different in their construction, load-out, and usage.

Starfighters are small, short-range, one- or two-person spacecraft used by both military and civilian organizations across the galaxy for patrol, escort, force projection, and reconnaissance duties. Powered by small reactors fueling multiple ion engines, with backup repulsorlift drives for atmospheric work, they are fast, agile, and often difficult to fly. Typically lightly armored, they carry minimal shields and possess little-to-no hyperspace capabilities, but pack considerable firepower. Due to their small size, short range, and, in many cases, lack of hyperspace capabilities, starfighters typically deploy from spaceports or are carried into battle by larger, sturdier ships acting as carriers.

Patrol boats are larger and sturdier vessels. Typically between a starfighter and a light freighter in size, patrol boats are designed for intrasystem patrols, interdiction, law and customs enforcement, and long-range reconnaissance. They generally carry a crew of between two and six, and are equipped with hyperdrives, navicomputers, and sophisticated communications and sensor suites. Patrol boats are usually slower than starfighters, but what they lack in speed they make up for with armor, shields, and firepower. Their larger size allows them to mount heavier weapons and more ordnance. The durability and hyperspace capabilities of patrol boats give these ships relatively long legs, allowing them to stay in space for weeks at a time.

### BTL-A4/BTL-S3 "Y-WING" ATTACK STARFIGHTER

Koensayr Manufacturing's BTL-A4 is a dedicated heavy attack and bomber starfighter designed primarily for disabling and destroying capital ships. Known affectionately as "the Wishbone" by its pilots, the Y-wing's fuselage consists of a central section flanked by two drive nacelles mounted to reinforced pylons. The central section houses a heavily armored one-person cockpit with full life support, and an astromech socket directly abaft it. The Novaldex power generator, along with the fighter's shield generator, hyperdrive, and numerous other essential systems, is mounted amidships in a reinforced section from which the engine nacelles extend. Each of these nacelles contains a powerful Koensayr-produced R200 ion engine, which provides a respectable amount of thrust. The most common variants are armed with a pair of light ion cannons in a turret mounted above the cockpit, a pair of nose-mounted laser cannons, and two proton torpedo launchers, a formidable load-out for such small vessels.

In their role as attack fighters, Y-wings have thick armor and heavy shields to protect them against withering fire from the weapon batteries of capital ships, their primary prey. With their slim cross sections, sturdy protection, and powerful weapons, they are well-suited to a role that requires them to fight their way to a target, deliver their ordnance, and fight their way back to base. Despite their reputation for reliability, Y-wings possess some quirks and minor design flaws that make them relatively high-maintenance. This has led to frustrated crews and technicians permanently removing the largely cosmetic hull plating for the convenience of constant access to the fighter's internal systems—it's a rare Y-wing that flies with its hull plates intact.

| SILHOUETTE | SPEED | HANDLING | DEF: FORE/PORT/STARBOARD/AFT | | | | ARMOR |
|---|---|---|---|---|---|---|---|
| 3 | 4 | +0 | 1 | - | - | 1 | 3 |
| | | | HT THRESHOLD | | | SS THRESHOLD | |
| | | | 12 | | | 10 | |

**Hull Type/Class:** Starfighter/BTL Y-wing.
**Manufacturer:** Koensayr Manufacturing.
**Hyperdrive:** Primary: Class 1, Backup: None.
**Navicomputer:** None—astromech droid socket.
**Sensor Range:** Close.
**Ship's Complement:** One pilot (one gunner in BTL-S3).
**Encumbrance Capacity:** 10.
**Passenger Capacity:** 0.
**Consumables:** One week.
**Price/Rarity:** 80,000 credits/4.
**Customization Hard Points:** 1.
**Weapons:** Turret-mounted twin light ion cannons (Fire Arc Forward [Fire Arc All for S3 variants]; Damage 5; Critical 4; Range [Close]; Ion, Linked 1).

Forward-mounted medium laser cannons (Fire Arc Forward; Damage 6; Critical 3; Range [Close]; Linked 1).

Forward-mounted proton torpedo launchers (Fire Arc Forward; Damage 8; Critical 2; Range [Short]; Blast 6, Breach 6, Guided 2, Limited Ammo 8, Linked 1, Slow-Firing 1).

## DELTA-6 SYSTEM DEFENSE STARFIGHTER

Small, fast, and agile, the Delta-6 *Sprite*-class starfighter was introduced by Kuat Systems Engineering in the decades leading up to the Clone Wars. Descended from earlier KSE designs and the Delta-X technology testbed, the Delta-6 was envisioned initially as a short-range point defense interceptor. An incredibly simple starfighter, the Delta-6 is a lightweight, single-seat interceptor with a narrow, arrowhead-shaped hull. Mounted all the way aft over the engines is a tiny, cramped cockpit with a bubble canopy, which gives the pilot a nearly 360-degree view of the surroundings. Standard armament consists of a pair of high-output Taim & Bak light laser cannons, with light armor and shields. As they are short-range fighters, these fighters have no hyperdrives, astromech ports, or navicomputers, and carry only minimal stores.

After its initial release and the first glowing reviews of its performance and efficiency, the Delta-6 caught the eye of the Jedi Order. The Order took delivery of several squadrons of Sprites, which quickly became the Jedi's go-to fightercraft. After decades of faithful service, the Sprite's short range and light armament were seen as outdated, and they were phased out in favor of the Delta-7 and Delta-7B. Today, Delta-6 interceptors are usually found only in the service of out-of-the-way planetary defense forces or small private concerns.

| SILHOUETTE | SPEED | HANDLING | DEF: FORE/PORT/STARBOARD/AFT | | | | ARMOR |
|---|---|---|---|---|---|---|---|
| 3 | 4 | +1 | 1 | - | - | 0 | 2 |
| | | | HT THRESHOLD | | | SS THRESHOLD | |
| | | | 6 | | | 5 | |

**Hull Type/Class:** Starfighter/Delta-6.
**Manufacturer:** Kuat Systems Engineering.
**Hyperdrive:** None.
**Navicomputer:** None.
**Sensor Range:** Close.
**Ship's Complement:** One pilot.
**Encumbrance Capacity:** 8.
**Passenger Capacity:** 0.
**Consumables:** One day.
**Price/Rarity:** 30,000 credits/4.
**Customization Hard Points:** 2.
**Weapons:** Forward-mounted twin light laser cannons (Fire Arc Forward; Damage 5; Critical 3; Range [Close]; Linked 1).

## DELTA-7 AETHERSPRITE INTERCEPTOR

Released with much fanfare three decades ago, Kuat Systems Engineering's Delta-7 *Aethersprite*-class light interceptor was a revolution in small starfighters. The Aethersprite was designed to replace the aging Delta-6 in military, paramilitary, and private defense forces. Like its Delta-6 forebear, the Delta-7 has a long, narrow, arrowhead-shaped hull with two forward-mounted medium laser cannons and an aft-mounted cockpit with bubble canopy. Longer than the old Sprite interceptor, the Aethersprite features more powerful engines, better maneuvering systems, a higher-resolution sensor suite, and improved targeting and life support systems. The most dramatic evident change is the inclusion of an astromech droid to handle fire control and hyperspace navigation duties. The droid allows the Delta-7 to interface with the Syliure-31 hyperspace docking ring, giving the tiny ship good medium-range hyperspace capabilities.

From the outset, the Delta-7 showed excellent promise as a light interceptor and reconnaissance starfighter. Purchased in large numbers by the Republic Judicial Department and fielded by the Jedi Order, the Delta-7 quickly proved its worth. Most Aethersprites were lost in action during the Clone Wars, and many that survived have languished for decades in hangars and scrapyards throughout the Outer Rim.

## DELTA-12 SKYSPRITE

The Delta-12 *Skysprite*-class is a rare two-seat version of the Delta-7 Aethersprite light interceptor. Designed by KSE as both a trainer and long-range reconnaissance fighter, the Skysprite features the same hull and internal systems, with an elongated cockpit that seats two individuals in tandem. Thanks to their speed, stores, and limited amenities, Skysprites were often used by the Jedi Order as VIP couriers.

Delta-12s feature stronger shields, stronger armor, and a more powerful sensor suite. The Delta-12s were stripped of their weapons, which made their sale to civilian organizations easier. The internal systems remained intact, however, and with a small amount of work and an upgrade to the ship's computer systems, the Skysprite can carry a respectable armament of light or even medium laser cannons.

| SILHOUETTE | SPEED | HANDLING | DEF: FORE/PORT/STARBOARD/AFT | | | | ARMOR |
|---|---|---|---|---|---|---|---|
| 3 | 5 | +2 | 1 | - | - | 0 | 2 |
| | | | HT THRESHOLD | | | SS THRESHOLD | |
| | | | 7 | | | 7 | |

**Hull Type/Class:** Starfighter/Delta-7.
**Manufacturer:** Kuat Systems Engineering.
**Hyperdrive:** None.
**Navicomputer:** None—astromech droid socket.
**Sensor Range:** Close.
**Ship's Complement:** One pilot, one astromech droid.
**Encumbrance Capacity:** 4.
**Passenger Capacity:** 0.
**Consumables:** 5 days.
**Price/Rarity:** 78,000 credits/6.
**Customization Hard Points:** 2.
**Weapons:** Forward-mounted twin medium laser cannons (Fire Arc Forward; Damage 6; Critical 3; Range [Close]; Linked 1).

| SILHOUETTE | SPEED | HANDLING | DEF: FORE/PORT/STARBOARD/AFT | | | | ARMOR |
|---|---|---|---|---|---|---|---|
| 3 | 4 | +1 | 1 | - | - | 1 | 3 |
| | | | HT THRESHOLD | | | SS THRESHOLD | |
| | | | 10 | | | 8 | |

**Hull Type/Class:** Starfighter/D-12.
**Manufacturer:** Kuat Systems Engineering.
**Hyperdrive:** None.
**Navicomputer:** None—astromech droid socket.
**Sensor Range:** Short.
**Ship's Complement:** One pilot.
**Encumbrance Capacity:** 8.
**Passenger Capacity:** 1.
**Consumables:** Two weeks.
**Price/Rarity:** 85,000 credits/8.
**Customization Hard Points:** 3.
**Weapons:** None.

## SYLIURE-31 HYPERSPACE RING

Designed by TransGalMeg in association with KSE, the Syliure-31 is a medium-range hyperspace sled made to provide hyperspace capabilities to the Delta-7, Delta-7B, and Delta-12 starfighters. The Syliure-31 is a simple affair consisting of two powerful ion engines and a medium-range Class 1 hyperdrive giving the Delta-series fighters respectable range and hyperspace capabilities. Docking with a hyperspace ring takes an **Easy (◇) Piloting (Space) check** as an action.

## LAMBDA-CLASS T4-A LONG-RANGE SHUTTLE

A common utility shuttle used by the Imperial Navy, the Sienar Fleet Systems *Lambda*-class shuttle is a common sight at Imperial installations. Slow and sturdy, these shuttles were designed to haul both passengers and cargo, and they can be configured as troop carriers, heavy cargo shuttles, or even luxury VIP shuttles for high-ranking Imperial officers and dignitaries. *Lambda*-class shuttles have a heavily armored square hull with a forward bridge section that vaguely resembles the cockpit of Koensayr's Y-wing starfighter. The ship has a single tall vertical stabilizer mounted to the dorsal part of the main hull and two long folding wings with an inverted gull-wing design that, when deployed, give the ship a cross section resembling an inverted letter Y.

*Lambda*-class shuttles are driven by two SFS-204 ion engines, with an SFS S/ig-37 hyperdrive providing long-range capabilities. Well-armed for a shuttle, the *Lambda* is equipped with a number of laser and blaster cannons in both forward and aft hard points, giving the ship excellent defensive fire coverage. Instead of standard escape pods, the ship's entire forward bridge section detaches from the hull as a lifeboat in case of emergency. Incredibly useful and surprisingly versatile for a bespoke military design, these ships are often the target of ship thieves and pirates and can, on occasion, be purchased at staggering cost on the black market.

| 4 | 3 | +0 | DEF: FORE/PORT/STARBOARD/AFT |  |  |  | ARMOR |
|---|---|----|----|----|----|----|----|
| SILHOUETTE | SPEED | HANDLING | 2 | - | - | 1 | 4 |
|  |  |  | HT THRESHOLD |  | SS THRESHOLD |  |  |
|  |  |  | 25 |  | 15 |  |  |

**Hull Type/Class:** Shuttle/Lambda.
**Manufacturer:** Sienar Fleet Systems and Cygnus Spaceworks.
**Hyperdrive:** Primary: Class 1, Backup: Class 10.
**Navicomputer:** Yes.
**Sensor Range:** Short.
**Ship's Complement:** One pilot, one co-pilot, one navigator, one gunner, one comms operator, one engineer.
**Encumbrance Capacity:** 200 (without passengers).
**Passenger Capacity:** 20.
**Consumables:** Two months.
**Price/Rarity:** 140,000 credits (R)/6.
**Customization Hard Points:** 2.
**Weapons:** Two forward-mounted twin light blaster cannons (Fire Arc Forward; Damage 4; Critical 4; Range [Close]; Linked 1).

Two forward-mounted twin light laser cannons (Fire Arc Forward; Damage 5; Critical 3; Range [Close]; Linked 1).

Aft-mounted twin light blaster cannons (Fire Arc Aft; Damage 4; Critical 4; Range [Close]; Linked 1).

## PATHFINDER SCOUT SHIP

When released during the final years of the Old Republic, Vangaard Industries' *Pathfinder*-class scout ship was considered on the bleeding edge of starship technology. A long, narrow vessel with a sharply pointed bow, steeply raked, aft-mounted stabilizers, and a planform like an arrow, the Pathfinder was designed as a long-range scout and courier vessel. The *Pathfinder*-class' reputation as a high-tech ship comes from both its advanced sensor suite and the fact that it was one of the first mass-produced vessels of its size to feature hyperspace capabilities. Essentially oversized starfighters, Pathfinder scout ships carry two sentients seated abreast in a small, cramped, but well-laid-out cockpit. Directly abaft the cockpit is a small area with a refresher, a bunk, and a small storage area for ship's provisions and emergency supplies. Everything abaft the cockpit and rest area is packed with sophisticated long-range sensors, shield generators, and the powerful twin drive engines.

Lightly armed and armored, Pathfinders have defensive armament comprising a single turret-mounted light laser cannon atop the hull just abaft of the cockpit. The shield generators are unique to the ship class, and the armor is typical for a light scout vessel. At the time of their introduction, Pathfinders were considered among the fastest scout vessels on the market, among other accolades. Their speed, handling, and powerful sensor suite, while relatively commonplace today, help maintain these tiny ships' popularity and drive their sales all these decades after their release.

| 4 | 4 | +1 | DEF: FORE/PORT/STARBOARD/AFT | | | | ARMOR |
|---|---|----|-----|---|---|---|----|
| SILHOUETTE | SPEED | HANDLING | 1 | - | - | 1 | 2 |
| | | | HT THRESHOLD | | | | SS THRESHOLD |
| | | | 16 | | | | 10 |

**Hull Type/Class:** Scout Ship/Pathfinder.
**Manufacturer:** Vangaard Industries.
**Hyperdrive:** Primary: Class 3, Backup: Class 15.
**Navicomputer:** Yes.
**Sensor Range:** Extreme.
**Ship's Complement:** One pilot, one co-pilot.
**Encumbrance Capacity:** 45.
**Passenger Capacity:** 2.
**Consumables:** Three months.
**Price/Rarity:** 45,000 credits/6.
**Customization Hard Points:** 2.
**Weapons:** Dorsal turret-mounted light laser cannon (Fire Arc All; Damage 5; Critical 3; Range [Close]).

## T-65B "X-WING" MULTI-ROLE STARFIGHTER

Incom's T-65B X-wing is the Rebel Alliance's primary force-projection starfighter. A powerful, capable, easy-to-fly starfighter, the X-wing combines speed and hitting power into a potent package. These new fighters were brought into the Alliance Fleet to replace the aging Koensayr Y-wings and to provide more versatility in starfighter operations for Alliance commanders.

The X-wing is a true multi-role fighter, extremely effective in missions ranging from reconnaissance to attack to ship-to-ship dogfighting. With its four powerful Incom 4L4 engines and advanced avionics, the X-wing is more than a match for the Imperial TIE fighters. Its load-out of four linked Taim & Bak laser cannons and proton torpedo launchers makes it a serious threat to gunboats and even larger vessels. In large battles, the X-wing acts as an escort fighter, keeping enemy fighters away from slower-moving attack fighters and bombers and protecting the precious Alliance capital ships. Thus far, the X-wing has proven to be

an incredible asset to the Alliance, and some Rebel tacticians suggest that it is the game changer the Alliance needs to succeed against the Empire. While the X-wing is seen as a symbol of the Rebellion, other organizations use it as well, meaning it can be found outside the Rebel Fleet.

| 3 | 5 | +1 | DEF: FORE/PORT/STARBOARD/AFT | | | | ARMOR |
|---|---|----|-----|---|---|---|----|
| SILHOUETTE | SPEED | HANDLING | 1 | - | - | 1 | 3 |
| | | | HT THRESHOLD | | | | SS THRESHOLD |
| | | | 10 | | | | 10 |

**Hull Type/Class:** Starfighter/T-65B X-wing.
**Manufacturer:** Incom Corporation.
**Hyperdrive:** Primary: Class 1, Backup: None.
**Navicomputer:** None—astromech droid socket.
**Sensor Range:** Close.
**Ship's Complement:** One pilot, one astromech droid.
**Encumbrance Capacity:** 10.
**Passenger Capacity:** 0.
**Consumables:** One week.
**Price/Rarity:** 120,000 credits/5.
**Customization Hard Points:** 1.
**Weapons:** S-foil-mounted medium laser cannons (Fire Arc Forward; Damage 6; Critical 3; Range [Close]; Linked 3).

Forward-mounted proton torpedo launchers (Fire Arc Forward; Damage 8; Critical 2; Range [Short]; Blast 6, Breach 6, Guided 2, Limited Ammo 6, Linked 1, Slow-Firing 1).

## TIE/LN STARFIGHTER

The primary space superiority fighter of the Imperial Navy, the tiny and fragile Twin Ion Engine fighter has been in service for years. Light, fast, and incredibly nimble, the iconic TIE fighter is a bare-bones, no-nonsense fightercraft that, in sufficient numbers, poses a threat to nearly any ship or installation it's deployed against. Consisting of a spherical, lightly armored command module with a large circular transparisteel viewport in its forward face attached to two massive hexagonal wing and solar panel assemblies, the TIE fighter possesses very few of the amenities featured in competing starfighters. In an almost obsessive quest to save weight, nearly every system common to starfighters around the galaxy was omitted from the TIE's design. The ship features no shields, no landing gear, no hyperdrive, few computerized systems, and, shockingly, no life-support system, requiring the pilots to wear fully sealed vacuum suits during flight. Only the lightest alloys are used in its construction, and even the pilots are specially selected for their small stature. Every bit of fat was trimmed from the initial design, resulting in a very dangerous, blisteringly fast, and astonishingly agile ship, although one that has a very high attrition rate.

Along with being very light, the ship is also incredibly simple, with few moving parts and a highly modular construction that allows it to be assembled and maintained with little effort by technicians with scant experience. It draws its power from a miniature version of Sienar Fleet Systems' I-a2b solar ionization reactor, which collects solar energy from the panels in the fighter's wing assemblies and converts it into energy. This generator powers the twinned, high-output SFS P-s4 ion engines, as well as the twin-linked laser cannons that make up the entirety of the ship's weaponry. Due to their lack of hyperdrives and life support, TIE fighters are necessarily short-range fighters.

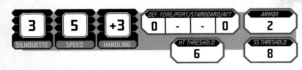

| SILHOUETTE | SPEED | HANDLING | DEF: FORE/PORT/STARBOARD/AFT | | | | ARMOR |
|:---:|:---:|:---:|:---:|:---:|:---:|:---:|:---:|
| 3 | 5 | +3 | 0 | - | - | 0 | 2 |
| | | | HT THRESHOLD | | SS THRESHOLD | | |
| | | | 6 | | 8 | | |

**Hull Type/Class:** Starfighter/TIE Series.
**Manufacturer:** Sienar Fleet Systems.
**Hyperdrive:** None.
**Navicomputer:** None.
**Sensor Range:** Close.
**Ship's Complement:** One pilot.
**Encumbrance Capacity:** 4.
**Passenger Capacity:** 0.
**Consumables:** Two days.
**Price/Rarity:** 50,000 credits (R)/4.
**Customization Hard Points:** 0.
**Weapons:** Forward-mounted medium laser cannons (Fire Arc Forward; Damage 6; Critical 3; Range [Close]; Linked 1).

# FREIGHTERS AND TRANSPORTS

The lifeblood of galactic commerce, transports and freighters carry the agricultural, industrial, and commercial bounty of the galaxy. Used by militaries, governments, and private concerns, these are spacious, generally slow vessels designed for the sole purpose of moving goods from production to market as efficiently and safely as possible.

Freighters are small, relatively fast vessels designed to carry small cargoes over medium distances. These ships require between two and six crew on average, and typically have accommodations for passengers as well as capacious cargo holds. Freighters are usually designed and built with an eye toward ease of modification; they have modular, easily upgraded systems that allow their owners to tailor the ships to specific roles. Incredibly versatile, freighters are commonly found in

the hands of small, independent shipping concerns or single owner-operators.

Transports are huge, lumbering ships designed to carry bulk cargo on long-haul trips throughout the galaxy. Staffed by relatively large crews, transports carry vast amounts of cargo in their cavernous holds. What they lack in dash they make up for in raw power and carrying capacity. Slow and ponderous, with little to nothing in the way of armor, weapons, or shields, they rely on armed escorts and strength in numbers to protect themselves from the predation of pirates, thieves, and overzealous Imperial customs officials. Transports are most likely to be found in the fleets of massive corporate entities, powerful shipping magnates, and the logistics corps of large navies.

### G9 RIGGER LIGHT FREIGHTER

Already considered an antique at the outset of the Clone Wars, Corellian Engineering Corporation's G9 *Rigger*-class light freighter is a rare sight in the modern spacelanes. A small, unremarkable craft, the G9 has a blocky, double-decked hull which resembles a speeder truck more than a starship. A single long, thin wing extends from the starboard side of the ship, and a short folding stabilizer is mounted to the vessel's ventral side. The forward third of the vessel contains the flight deck, engineering deck, and crew quarters on two spartan decks. The rest of the ship is given over to a single large cargo hold accessed by a large aft-loading ramp.

Designed as a utilitarian, short-to-medium-range hauler, the *Rigger*-class has little in the way of amenities and only the most basic of defensive systems. Armament consists of dorsal auto-blasters and two light blaster cannons. Shields are a simple low-output Novaldex system, and the ship's armor is basic carbon-durasteel. Little thought was given to speed or handling, and while these ships aren't dangerously slow or sluggish, they are not high-performance by any

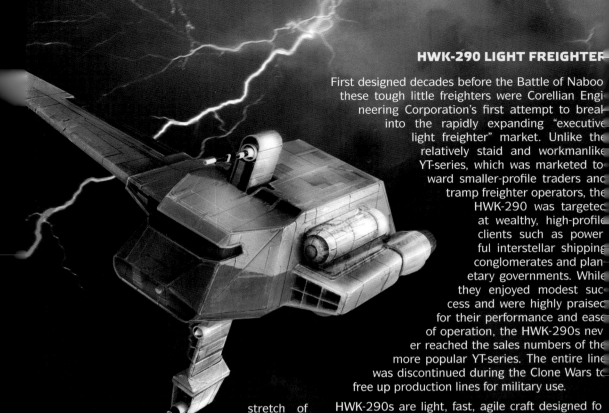

stretch of the imagination. What they lack in frills and comfort, however, these little ships more than make up for in reliability, sturdiness, and ease of repair. In fact, so well-built are these ancient freighters that many are still operating, and operating quite well, with much of their original equipment.

| 4 | 2 | -2 | DEF: FORE/PORT/STARBOARD/AFT | | | | ARMOR |
|---|---|---|---|---|---|---|---|
| SILHOUETTE | SPEED | HANDLING | 1 | - | - | 1 | 2 |
| | | | HT THRESHOLD 25 | | | | SS THRESHOLD 15 |

**Hull Type/Class:** Light Freighter/*Rigger*-class.
**Manufacturer:** Corellian Engineering Corporation.
**Hyperdrive:** Primary: Class 3, Backup: None.
**Navicomputer:** Yes.
**Sensor Range:** Medium.
**Ship's Complement:** One pilot, one co-pilot.
**Encumbrance Capacity:** 80.
**Passenger Capacity:** 6.
**Consumables:** One month.
**Price/Rarity:** 55,000 credits/5.
**Customization Hard Points:** 4.
**Weapons:** Dorsal auto-blasters (Fire Arc Forward; Damage 3; Critical 5; Range [Close]; Auto-fire).
Outrigger turret-mounted light blaster cannon (Fire Arc Forward, Starboard, and Aft; Damage 4; Critical 4; Range [Close]).
Ventral wing-mounted light blaster cannon (Fire Arc Forward; Damage 4; Critical 4; Range [Close]).

# HWK-290 LIGHT FREIGHTER

First designed decades before the Battle of Naboo these tough little freighters were Corellian Engineering Corporation's first attempt to break into the rapidly expanding "executive light freighter" market. Unlike the relatively staid and workmanlike YT-series, which was marketed toward smaller-profile traders and tramp freighter operators, the HWK-290 was targeted at wealthy, high-profile clients such as powerful interstellar shipping conglomerates and planetary governments. While they enjoyed modest success and were highly praised for their performance and ease of operation, the HWK-290s never reached the sales numbers of the more popular YT-series. The entire line was discontinued during the Clone Wars to free up production lines for military use.

HWK-290s are light, fast, agile craft designed for speed and comfort rather than heavy lifting. They are handsome vessels with lean, angular hulls and narrow, deeply tinted viewports which make them look fast and aggressive, even when parked in a hangar. While they were never designed to carry much cargo, the HWK-290s still has respectable lift capacity for vessels of their size; they are well suited for courier work and the transportation of small, highly valuable cargoes. They have light armor and were originally designed with no weapon systems, relying instead on raw speed and maneuverability for protection. Of course, being CEC products, they are extremely versatile and modular; most Hawks still plying the spacelanes are so heavily modified as to be nearly unrecognizable to their original designers.

| 3 | 4 | +1 | DEF: FORE/PORT/STARBOARD/AFT | | | | ARMOR |
|---|---|---|---|---|---|---|---|
| SILHOUETTE | SPEED | HANDLING | 1 | - | - | 1 | 2 |
| | | | HT THRESHOLD 18 | | | | SS THRESHOLD 18 |

**Hull Type/Class:** Freighter/HWK-290.
**Manufacturer:** Corellian Engineering Corporation.
**Hyperdrive:** Primary: Class 2, Backup: None.
**Navicomputer:** Yes.
**Sensor Range:** Short.
**Ship's Complement:** One pilot, one co-pilot.
**Encumbrance Capacity:** 75.
**Passenger Capacity:** 2.
**Consumables:** Three months.
**Price/Rarity:** 70,000 credits/7.
**Customization Hard Points:** 5.
**Weapons:** None.

## HT-2200 MEDIUM FREIGHTER

Solidly built and packed with state-of-the-art avionics and cargo-handling systems, the massive, slab-sided HT-2200 medium freighter is a relatively new ship design from Corellian Engineering Corporation (CEC). Shaped like a tuning fork or an oversized Y-wing, the ship houses its crew, weapons, and engineering sections in a central hull, with four spacetight cargo holds in the port and starboard booms which point forward along the ship's line of flight. The trademark CEC conical cockpit is located amidships between the booms, giving the pilot and co-pilot a nearly 180-degree view of their surroundings. Each of the four holds is shielded and reinforced, and each contains a number of modular cargo systems that allows it to be configured for different types of cargo. In addition, each hold has its own environmental systems, allowing the crew to adjust the temperature, atmospheric makeup, and gravity of each hold separately.

Once released, initial reviews of the vessel were favorable, and orders steadily came in from large shipping concerns in the Mid Rim and Outer Rim. As pilots and crews became more familiar with the ships, however, they reported a number of serious shortcomings. The ships' primary power generator was woefully underpowered. The cost-cutting measures extended to most of this ships' systems and included the use of cut-rate power couplings throughout, making the vessels' systems surprisingly susceptible to brownouts and short circuits. These issues, along with an unusually light weapons load-out of two turret-mounted laser cannons, made the new freighters easy pickings for pirates and commerce raiders. Despite all of their inherent flaws, HT-2200s remain in production, although not in the same numbers as their more popular siblings, thanks to their advanced cargo systems, sturdy hulls, and ease of modification.

| SILHOUETTE | SPEED | HANDLING | DEF: FORE/PORT/STARBOARD/AFT | ARMOR |
|---|---|---|---|---|
| 5 | 2 | -2 | 1 / 1 / 1 / 0 | 5 |
| | | | HT THRESHOLD 35 | SS THRESHOLD 14 |

**Hull Type/Class:** Freighter/HT-2200.
**Manufacturer:** Corellian Engineering Corporation.
**Hyperdrive:** Primary: Class 3, Backup: Class 15.
**Navicomputer:** Yes.
**Sensor Range:** Short.
**Ship's Complement:** One pilot, one co-pilot, one engineer, one loadmaster.
**Encumbrance Capacity:** 800.
**Passenger Capacity:** 8.
**Consumables:** Three months.
**Price/Rarity:** 140,000 credits/5.
**Customization Hard Points:** 5.
**Weapons:** One dorsal and one ventral turret-mounted medium laser cannon (Fire Arc All; Damage 6; Critical 3; Range [Close]).

## SIMIYIAR LIGHT FREIGHTER

One of the more popular ships to come out of the vaunted Mon Calamari Shipyards, the *Simiyiar*-class light freighter is a study in both form and function. A lovely ship by any standard, this small, nimble freighter shows all the hallmarks of the smooth-edged, quasi-organic styling for which the Mon Calamari shipwrights are so famous. A *Simiyiar*-class vessel is flat, low-slung, and single-decked, with a bulbous forward section, a narrow midships section, and a flaring, wing-like aft section. The entire forward third of the ship is given over to its cargo hold, a capacious modular space accessed by port and starboard cargo lifts and a ventral loading ramp. The midships section contains crew and passenger berthing and common areas, as well as a ladderway to the small, two-person command deck. In addition to its drive, most of the ship's power, weapons, and hyperspace systems are housed in the outboard wing sections or the flaring forward section, and a pair of escape pods are mounted directly aft, over the primary thrusters.

Relatively heavily armed for a vessel of its class, the Simiyiar is armed with a turret-mounted twin light laser cannon on the dorsal surface and a single light ion cannon in a fixed forward position. Speed and handling are a little above average, and the stout, ablative armor and well-tuned shields provide more than adequate protection. Although popular, *Simiyiar*-class light freighters suffer many of the downsides common to Mon Calamari ships. Each ship is unique, essentially hand-made, and there is little-to-no parts commonality from one to another. As such, they are among the most expensive light freighters on the market. They are very reliable, however, and achingly beautiful. These two traits alone are enough to explain the popularity of these fine little ships.

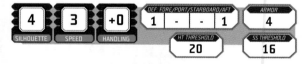

| SILHOUETTE | SPEED | HANDLING | DEF: FORE/PORT/STARBOARD/AFT | ARMOR |
|---|---|---|---|---|
| 4 | 3 | +0 | 1 / - / - / 1 | 4 |
| | | | HT THRESHOLD 20 | SS THRESHOLD 16 |

**Hull Type/Class:** Freighter/Simiyiar.
**Manufacturer:** Mon Calamari Shipyards.
**Hyperdrive:** Primary: Class 2, Backup: Class 15.
**Navicomputer:** Yes.
**Sensor Range:** Medium.
**Ship's Complement:** One pilot, one co-pilot.
**Encumbrance Capacity:** 90.
**Passenger Capacity:** 5.
**Consumables:** Two months.
**Price/Rarity:** 165,000 credits/6.
**Customization Hard Points:** 4.
**Weapons:** Dorsal turret-mounted twin light laser cannons (Fire Arc All; Damage 5; Critical 3; Range [Close]; Linked 1).

Forward-mounted light ion cannon (Fire Arc Forward; Damage 5; Critical 4; Range [Close]; Ion).

## ZH-25 QUESTOR LIGHT FREIGHTER

Spurred by the success of the Z-10 *Seeker*-class scout ship, the ZH-25 *Questor*-class is Starfeld Industries' first foray into the light freighter market. Essentially a Seeker writ large, the ZH-25 is a fast, reliable, easily modifiable freighter designed to compete against Corellian Engineering Corporation's YT- and YV-series freighters. With a hull that resembles a pair of magnoculars in planform, the ZH-25 consists of a central hull section of a vaguely hourglass shape with a CEC-style cockpit forward and a bank of powerful Novaldex JV-74 engines in the stern. The port and starboard hull sections contain crew quarters, common areas, and escape pods for crew and passengers. The aft two-thirds of the ship is given over to a massive open cargo hold equipped with all the usual modern cargo-handling systems. In addition, two external cargo pods are slung beneath the hull and serve to extend both the ship's cargo and storage capacity.

From the factory, Starfeld fits out the Questor with a single medium laser cannon in a ventral-mounted turret, good carbon-durasteel armor, and a reliable Sirplex shield generator, which together provide the vessel with respectable defensive capabilities. The crew and passenger areas, while utilitarian, are comfortable and designed to alleviate the stresses of long-distance travel in hyperspace. Like most light freighters from CEC, SoroSuub, and Ghtroc, the ZH-25 was built with an eye toward end-user modification and the use of aftermarket parts. To that end, these ships feature modular power fittings and numerous redundant systems that allow owners to easily customize their ships to their own tastes and needs. While still a relative newcomer to the freighter market, the ZH-25 is quickly gaining popularity among private shipping concerns, single owner-operators, and smugglers thanks to its reliability and smart design.

| 4 | 3 | -1 | DEF: FORE/PORT/STARBOARD/AFT | | | | ARMOR |
|---|---|----|------|---|---|---|-------|
| | | | 1 | - | - | 1 | 3 |
| SILHOUETTE | SPEED | HANDLING | HT THRESHOLD | | | SS THRESHOLD | |
| | | | 30 | | | 20 | |

**Hull Type/Class:** Freighter/Questor.
**Manufacturer:** Starfeld Industries.
**Hyperdrive:** Primary: Class 2, Backup: Class 15.
**Navicomputer:** Yes.
**Sensor Range:** Medium.
**Ship's Complement:** One pilot, one co-pilot.
**Encumbrance Capacity:** 100.
**Passenger Capacity:** 6.
**Consumables:** Three months.
**Price/Rarity:** 115,000 credits/6.
**Customization Hard Points:** 4.
**Weapons:** Ventral turret-mounted medium laser cannon (Fire Arc All; Damage 6; Critical 3; Range [Close]).

# CAPITAL SHIPS

In layman's terms, a capital ship is typically a large, heavily armed and armored warship designed to battle other ships of its type. Numerous types of ships fall under the definition of capital ship, from light and nimble corvettes to workhorse cruisers to the massive, terrifying Star Destroyers of the Imperial Navy. As a rule, capital ships have sturdy hulls, thick armor, robust shields, and the most powerful shipboard weapon systems in the galaxy.

## ADZ-CLASS DESTROYER

One of the smallest capital ships in the Imperial Navy's arsenal, the *Adz*-class destroyer is a relative newcomer to the galactic spacelanes. Produced by Kuat Drive Yards (KDY), the *Adz*-class is designed for long-range patrol duty. Best described as tall and angular, these vessels have a long, narrow, slab-sided hull flanked by port and starboard sponsons that house the primary thrusters and sensor systems. Their prows are steeply angled wedges rising to tall superstructures that house the ships' powerful soliton-wave antennae, which can sense the comings and goings of other vessels in hyperspace, and their attendant cooling systems. Thanks to state-of-the-art slave-circuit systems, these vessels have a very small crew for their size and can operate at peak efficiency with only a handful of officers and crew.

The ship has some issues: the foremost that the sensor suite suffers from being mated to the finicky, high-maintenance soliton antenna and is prone to brownouts, spoofing, and signal interference. In addition, the soliton antenna drains power at a ferocious rate. Despite these complaints, many *Adz*-class destroyers are already patrolling out-of-the-way parts of the Outer Rim.

| 5 | 2 | -2 | DEF. FORE/PORT/STARBOARD/AFT | | | | ARMOR |
|---|---|----|---|---|---|---|---|
| | | | 2 | 2 | 2 | 1 | 6 |
| SILHOUETTE | SPEED | HANDLING | HT THRESHOLD | | SS THRESHOLD | | |
| | | | 50 | | 35 | | |

**Hull Type/Class:** Destroyer/Adz.
**Manufacturer:** Kuat Drive Yards.
**Hyperdrive:** Primary: Class 2, Backup: Class 12.
**Navicomputer:** Yes.
**Sensor Range:** Extreme.
**Ship's Complement:** 30 officers, pilots, and crew.
**Starfighter Complement:** 6.

**Encumbrance Capacity:** 250.
**Passenger Capacity:** 8 troops.
**Consumables:** 3 months.
**Price/Rarity:** 4,450,000 credits (R)/7.
**Customization Hard Points:** 1.
**Weapons:** Two forward and one aft dorsal turret-mounted quad laser cannons (Fire Arc All; Damage 5; Critical 3; Range [Close]; Accurate 1, Linked 3).

Two port and two starboard turret-mounted light ion cannons (Fire Arc All; Damage 5; Critical 4; Range [Close]; Ion).

## CR90 CORVETTE

A versatile light capital ship, Corellian Engineering's CR90 corvette is a small, multi-purpose vessel. Long and sleek, the CR90 has a distinctive, wasp-waisted profile with a narrow midships section flanked by a massive bank of eleven Girodyne ion turbine engines aft and a broad, hammerhead bridge and crew section forward. This ship is remarkably fast and agile for a vessel of its size, and can be configured as a troop carrier, cargo hauler, passenger liner, consular ship, or even a heavily armed escort vessel.

In their standard configuration as lightly armed passenger and cargo liners, these corvettes mount a pair of Taim & Bak twin medium turbolasers in dorsal and ventral midships turrets as their main weapons. Along with the medium turbolasers are four light turbolasers, two to a side, mounted dorsally in turrets on the midships hull section. Thanks to their modular nature and high power output, CR90s can mount even more guns, which makes them well-suited as blockade-runners and heavy escorts for cash-strapped militaries.

**Hull Type/Class:** Corvette/CR90.
**Manufacturer:** Corellian Engineering Corporation.
**Hyperdrive:** Primary: Class 2, Backup: None.
**Navicomputer:** Yes.
**Sensor Range:** Long.
**Ship's Complement:** 30–165, depending on configuration.
**Encumbrance Capacity:** Up to 2,500, depending on configuration.
**Passenger Capacity:** Up to 600, depending on configuration.
**Consumables:** One year.
**Price/Rarity:** 1,200,000 credits/5.
**Customization Hard Points:** 4.
**Weapons:** One dorsal and one ventral turret-mounted twin medium turbolaser battery (Fire Arc All; Damage 10; Critical 3; Range [Long]; Breach 3, Linked 1, Slow-Firing 1).

Two port and two starboard turret-mounted light turbolasers (Fire Arc Port or Starboard; Damage 9; Critical 3; Range [Medium]; Breach 2, Slow-Firing 1).

### IR-3F-CLASS LIGHT FRIGATE

The predecessor to Republic Sienar Systems' *IPV-1-class* corvette, the *IR-3F*-class light frigate is an old and outdated patrol craft first introduced during the later decades of the Old Republic. Long and sleek, the IR-3F is a short-range patrol craft designed for intra-system picket and customs duty. Fitted from the ship-yard with a high-output power system and powerful sublight engines usually fitted to larger, cruiser-sized vessels, these ships had a reputation for blistering speed and relatively good maneuverability for vessels of their size. This, along with limited atmospheric capabilities, gives the *IR-3F*-class a well-deserved reputation as a dangerous and hard-to-elude ship, especially when handled by a competent crew.

While its speed and maneuverability are certainly respectable, this ship also carries a flexible and powerful array of weapons. Armed with a combination of medium laser cannons and light turbolaser batteries, the *IR-3F*-class punches well above its weight, allowing it to engage and defeat opponents considered impossible for a ship of its size.

It is lightly armored, a compromise made to wring more speed out of the vessel, but its Novaldex shield systems are quite robust and make up for any deficiencies in its armor. If this ship has a major flaw it is that, being designed as short-range craft, it has no hyperdrive or navicomputer. In addition, its power and

computer systems are designed in a way that makes retrofitting these systems quite difficult. Despite their advanced age, lack of hyperspace capabilities, and scarcity of parts, many of these ships are still serving throughout the galaxy.

**Hull Type/Class:** Frigate/IR-3F.
**Manufacturer:** Republic Sienar Systems.
**Hyperdrive:** None.
**Navicomputer:** None.
**Sensor Range:** Extreme.
**Ship's Complement:** 20 officers and enlisted crew.
**Starfighter Complement:** None.
**Encumbrance Capacity:** 1,800.
**Passenger Capacity:** 10 troops.
**Consumables:** One month.
**Price/Rarity:** 1,000,000 credits/6.
**Customization Hard Points:** 2.
**Weapons:** One ventral turret-mounted twin light turbolaser battery (Fire Arc Forward; Damage 9; Critical 3; Range [Medium]; Breach 2, Linked 1, Slow-Firing 1).

One dorsal turret-mounted twin light turbolaser battery (Fire Arc All; Damage 9; Critical 3; Range [Medium]; Breach 2, Linked 1, Slow-Firing).

One port and one starboard turret-mounted twin medium laser cannon (Fire Arc Port and Starboard; Damage 6; Critical 3; Range [Close]; Linked 1).

### VICTORY-CLASS STAR DESTROYER

Built during the height of the Clone Wars, the *Victory*-class was designed as an all-purpose heavy line-of-battle ship meant to support planetary landings and take part in fleet actions. While considered fine ships at the time, they were rushed to production after many delays and political wrangling within the Navy and Kuat Drive Yards, and the resulting ships required more maintenance and dry dock time than was considered acceptable even in the heavily bureaucratic Republic. They suffered from a rash of problems (from burned-out hyperdrive couplings to a disturbing tendency to electrocute crew in their bunks), and the entire class quickly gained a reputation as unlucky ships and spacegoing coffins.

Though *Victory*-class Star Destroyers have impressive hyperdrives allowing for quick response throughout the galaxy, their slow sublight speed limits the ability to fight in a modern space battle. The development of new heavy cruisers and the *Imperial*- and *Imperial II*-class Star Destroyers quickly rendered the old Victories obsolete despite their upgrades. Unloved by nearly everyone, many Victories were relegated to planetary garrison and light patrol duty in the farthest

reaches of the
Empire. Command
of or assignment to
one of the old Victories
was seen as death to a Navy officer's career. Other
Victory Star Destroyers were sold to private concerns such as the Corporate Sector Authority for
their private paramilitary forces.

However, as much as *Victory*-class Star Destroyers
are mocked and maligned, the ships are still
incredibly powerful and mount a devastating array
of dangerous weaponry. In the Outer Rim, the sudden arrival of a Victory can send pirates and smugglers fleeing for their lives before the iron fist of
the Empire.

| 8 | 1 | -3 | DEF: FORE/PORT/STARBOARD/AFT | | | | ARMOR |
|---|---|----|---|---|---|---|---|
| | | | 2 | 2 | 2 | 2 | 9 |
| SILHOUETTE | SPEED | HANDLING | | HT THRESHOLD 120 | | SS THRESHOLD 50 | |

**Hull Type/Class:** Star Destroyer/Victory.
**Manufacturer:** Kuat Drive Yards.
**Hyperdrive:** Primary: Class 1, Backup: Class 15.
**Navicomputer:** Yes.
**Sensor Range:** Long.
**Ship's Complement:** 6,107 officers, pilots, and en-
listed crew.
**Starfighter Complement:** Twenty-four starfighters.
**Vehicle Complement:** Numerous shuttles, landing
craft, utility vehicles, and AT-series walkers.

**Encumbrance Capacity:** 6,500.
**Passenger Capacity:** 1,600 troops.
**Consumables:** One year.
**Price/Rarity:** 50,000,000 credits (R)/6.
**Customization Hard Points:** 4.
**Weapons:** Five port and five starboard light quad tur-
bolaser batteries (Fire Arc Port and Forward or Star-
board and Forward; Damage 9; Critical 3; Range [Me-
dium]; Breach 2, Linked 3, Slow-Firing 1).

Ten forward-mounted twin medium turbolasers
(Fire Arc Forward; Damage 10; Critical 3; Range
[Long]; Breach 3, Slow-Firing 1).

Ten dorsal twin medium turbolasers (Fire Arc Forward; Damage 10; Critical 3; Range [Long]; Breach
3, Slow-Firing 1).

Twenty assault concussion missile launchers (Fire
Arc Forward; Damage 7; Critical 3; Range [Short];
Blast 4, Breach 5, Guided 2, Inaccurate 1, Slow-
Firing 1).

Ten hull-mounted heavy tractor beams (Fire Arc All;
Damage –; Critical –; Range [Short]; Tractor 6).

### ADDITIONAL RULES

**Massive 1:** When making an attack targeting this
starship, the critical rating of any weapons used
counts as 1 higher.

# SHIP AND VEHICLE MODIFICATIONS

For any band of wanderers in the *Star Wars* galaxy, a starship is much more than a simple means of transportation. As individuals live aboard it and get to know a ship's various attributes, they tend to make modifications to it to better suit their needs. Likewise, the owner of a beloved ground vehicle or speeder bike may tinker with his ride, tweaking the engine or handling characteristics, or even adding weapons to give it some punch in a fight. Many ships and vehicles can be improved in a wide variety of ways. These improvements can range from simple increases in armor, shields, or speed to more esoteric enhancements such as electronic countermeasures or hidden storage compartments.

## ATTACHMENTS

The following are a small selection of common attachments seen on the ships and vehicles used by characters in **Force and Destiny**. These modifications run the gamut from docking clamps and larger engines to hidden compartments and more powerful weapons. This is not intended to be a comprehensive list, as such a list is well outside the scope of this publication, but it is meant to be representative of what can be done to customize a spacecraft. Game Masters are encouraged to design their own attachments to fit their players' tastes and the needs of their campaigns. More options for attachments will appear in future supplements.

### ADVANCED TARGETING ARRAY

Advanced targeting arrays use sophisticated holo-imaging to present a pilot or gunner a detailed, three-dimensional view of his target. Installation of an ATA increases the accuracy of a ship's weapons and allows gunners to get more shots on target, increasing their effectiveness in combat.
**Models Include:** Taim & Bak LR-375a Sureshot Advanced Targeting Array, Fabritech KR-770 "Sharpshooter" Targeting Computer, Koensayr Manufacturing 840.z Holo-Targeting Suite.
**Base Modifiers:** Upgrades the ability of Gunnery checks when firing mounted weapons by 1.
**Modification Options:** 1 Additional upgrade Mod, 1 Innate Talent Mod (Sniper Shot), 1 Innate Talent Mod (True Aim).
**Hard Points Required:** 1.
**Price:** 4,000 credits.

### ELECTRONIC COUNTERMEASURES SUITE

Designed to blind and deafen enemy ships, an electronic countermeasures suite transmits a dense stream of white noise and junk data that fogs sensors and jams comms traffic within close range of the broadcasting ship. This may be applied to all starships and vehicles.
**Models Include:** Fabritech 995 Stormcloud ECM Suite, Miradyne 4x-Phantom Short-Range Sensor Jammer (starfighters only), KDY 220-SIG Tactical Combat Jammer (capital ships only).
**Base Modifiers:** Blocks all sensors within range, counting the ship or vehicle's silhouette as one step smaller when being fired at. Immediately notifies all ships in a star system, or within 100 kilometers if planetside, of the ship or vehicle's existence.
**Modification Options:** 1 Increase difficulty by 1 when making subsequent attacks with the Guided quality Mod.
**Hard Points Required:** 1.
**Price:** 3,000 credits.

### ENHANCED CARBON-DURASTEEL ARMOR

Produced by numerous starship manufacturers, these armor plates are made from a complex lattice of carbon nanotubes embedded with spun threads of durasteel. This modification may be applied to all starships and vehicles.
**Models Include:** Ferro-Magnesium Armor Plate, Cerro-Ablative Sheets.
**Base Modifiers:** Adds one point to starship armor and reduces starship handling by one.
**Modification Options:** None.
**Hard Points Required:** 2.
**Price:** 2,000 credits per point of starship or vehicle silhouette.

### HIGH-OUTPUT ION TURBINE

Upgraded engines increase a ship or vehicle's raw, straight-line speed at the cost of lower reliability. This

## TABLE 7–15: ATTACHMENTS

| Attachment | Price | Rarity | HP |
|---|---|---|---|
| Advanced Targeting Array | 4,000 | 4 | 1 |
| Electronic Countermeasures | 3,000 | 6 | 1 |
| Enhanced Armor | 2,000 x silhouette | 3 | 2 |
| High-Output Ion Turbine | 5,300 | 5 | 1 |
| Hydraulic Control Circuits | 1,000 | 7 | 2 |
| Hyperdrive Generator | 6,400 | 4 | 1 |
| Reinforced Shield Generator | 3,800 | 5 | 2 |
| Retrofitted Hangar Bay | 5,000 x silhouette | 3 | 2 |
| Smuggling Compartments | (R) 1,200 | 1 | 1 |
| Upgraded Comms Array | 4,800 | 6 | 1 |
| Upgraded Weapons | Varies | Varies | Varies |

## STARSHIPS, VEHICLES, AND MODS

Like personal equipment, starships and vehicles can benefit greatly by being modded. Ships and vehicles follow the rules for attachments and mods as discussed in **Chapter V: Gear and Equipment**. The only difference is that installing a mod on a ship or vehicle costs ten times as much due to their greater size and complexity.

modification may be added to any ship or vehicle.

**Models Include:** Girodyne Ter40 High-Output Ion Turbine, Sienar Fleet Systems SFS-220 Ion Drives, Koensayr Manufacturing R800 Ion Ramjet.

**Base Modifiers:** Adds 1 point to a ship's speed and reduces system strain threshold by 1.

**Modification Options:** None.

**Hard Points Required:** 1.

**Price:** 5,300 credits.

### HYDRAULIC CONTROL CIRCUITS

Hydraulic control circuits are a throwback to an earlier era of shipbuilding. Instead of using traditional conductive material pressed into composite wafer boards to transfer electromagnetic energy, HCCs use countless near-microscopic transparisteel tubes full of highly conductive liquid metal similar in its composition to mercury. Held under pressure and regulated by a series of minute valves, this metal controls the flow of energy. Bulky, antiquated, and difficult to work with, these circuits do have an incredible resistance to the effects of ion weapons, a fact that has not gone unnoticed among pilots and ship owners.

**Models Include:** Corellian Engineering Corporation Hydraulic Control Circuits, Santhe-Sienar Hardened Circuitry, Fabritech Insulated Circuitry.

**Base Modifiers:** Ships equipped with these attachments suffer half damage from weapons possessing the Ion quality after damage is reduced by soak. When installed, reduce handling and system strain threshold by 1.

**Modification Options:** 1 Defender chooses ship component affected by Ion item quality, as opposed to the attacker Mod. 1 increase system strain threshold by 1 Mod.

**Hard Points Required:** 2.

**Price:** 1,000 credits.

### HYPERDRIVE GENERATOR

Upgraded hyperdrive generators increase a vessel's speed through hyperspace, allowing it to complete journeys in a fraction of the usual time. Such devices are expensive; generally only high-quality couriers, smugglers, and government agents can afford them.

**Models Include:** Isu-Sim SSP05 Hyperdrive Generator, SFS S/ig-30 Hyperdrive System, KDY JumpStar Hyperdrive Generator.

**Base Modifiers:** Reduces a ship's hyperdrive rating by 1 to a minimum of 1.

**Modification Options:** 2 Reduce hyperspace rating by 1 to a minimum of .5 Mods.

**Hard Points Required:** 1.

**Price:** 6,400 credits.

### REINFORCED SHIELD GENERATOR

A good defense is crucial to keeping a starship intact when pursued by the Empire. Hardened shields upgrade a ship's stock particle and ray shielding, increasing its strength and making the shields easier to manage.

**Models Include:** KDY 880 Palisade Shield Generator, Phoah-Kingsmeyer 721a AEGIS Shield Generators, Sienar SH-2/a.Z Shield Reinforcement.

**Base Modifiers:** 1 additional point of defense to one defense zone of choice.

**Modification Options:** 2 One additional point of defense to one defense zone of choice Mods.

**Hard Points Required:** 2.

**Price:** 3,800 credits.

### RETROFITTED HANGAR BAY

Some starships and large vehicles can be modified to carry smaller vehicles (with a maximum silhouette of two smaller than the carrier) in a converted cargo hold or other compartment. The hangar bay modification includes launch and recovery systems as well as fueling, traffic control, and maintenance facilities. This is a common modification among the larger ships serving in the Rebel Alliance's ersatz navy. The Rebels have no access to purpose-built carriers and must make do with what they have to ferry their starfighters and gunboats into battle with the Empire. May only be used on ships or vehicles with a silhouette of 5 or more.

**Models Include:** None.

**Base Modifiers:** Allows a ship or vehicle to carry smaller vehicles (with a maximum silhouette of 2 smaller than the carrier) in a converted cargo hold or other compartment. The maximum capacity is calculated by adding together all of the carried vehicles' silhouettes. Carrier vehicles with silhouette 5 can carry a total silhouette of 5, silhouette 6 vehicles can carry a total silhouette of 20, and silhouette 7+ vehicles can carry a total silhouette of 60. Common sense and GM judgment apply when determining what vehicles can and cannot fit in a hangar bay.

**Modification Options:** 5 Additional +1 maximum silhouette capacity Mods.

**Hard Points Required:** 2.

**Price:** 5,000 credits per point of starship or vehicle silhouette.

## SMUGGLING COMPARTMENTS

Installed in starships, especially freighters and transports, for the transportation of contraband, smuggling compartments are used to hide goods (and occasionally, people) from the prying eyes of planetary customs agents and Imperial law enforcement. Designed to be incredibly hard to spot by blending into their surroundings, smuggling compartments are commonly installed beneath deck plates, behind heavy equipment, or in any of a thousand other bolt-holes throughout a vessel.

**Base Modifiers:** Stores items of up to 25 encumbrance per compartment. This still counts as part of the total encumbrance threshold of a ship. Increases difficulty of checks made to find compartments by +2.

**Modification Options:** 2 Additional storage (25 encumbrance) Mods.

**Hard Points Required:** 1.

**Price:** (R) 1,200 credits.

## UPGRADED COMMS ARRAY

Upgraded comms systems are powerful subspace comms arrays that can be fitted to most ships in the galaxy. They are typically equipped with both video and audio pickups and with the ability to interface quickly and easily with droid brains and other comms systems.

**Models Include:** Chedak Communications Frequency Agile Subspace Transceiver (FAST), SFS Ranger Long-Range Transceiver, Fabritech 44Q/r Multi-Band Transceiver.

**Base Modifiers:** Increases the range of shipboard communications by 1 range band.

**Modification Options:** 2 Additional comms range band Mods.

**Hard Points Required:** 1.

**Price:** 4,800 credits.

## TABLE 7-16: UPGRADING WEAPONS

| Weapon | Price/ Rarity | Compatible Silhouettes |
|---|---|---|
| Auto-Blaster | 3,000/3 | 2-10 |
| Blaster Cannon (Light) | 4,000/2 | 2-10 |
| Blaster Cannon (Heavy) | 5,000/3 | 3-10 |
| Concussion Missile Launcher | 7,500/5 | 3-10 |
| Ion Cannon (Light) | 5,000/5 | 3-10 |
| Ion Cannon (Medium) | 6,000/6 | 5-10 |
| Ion Cannon (Heavy) | 7,500/7 | 6-10 |
| Laser Cannon (Light) | 5,500/4 | 3-10 |
| Laser Cannon (Medium) | 7,000/4 | 3-10 |
| Laser Cannon (Heavy) | 7,500/5 | 4-10 |
| Proton Torpedo Launcher | (R) 9,000/7 | 3-10 |
| Quad Laser Cannon | 8,000/6 | 4-10 |
| Tractor Beam (Light) | 6,000/4 | 4-10 |
| Tractor Beam (Medium) | 8,000/5 | 5-10 |
| Tractor Beam (Heavy) | 10,000/6 | 5-10 |
| Turbolaser (Light) | (R) 12,000/7 | 5-10 |
| Turbolaser (Medium) | (R) 15,000/7 | 6-10 |
| Turbolaser (Heavy) | (R) 20,000/8 | 6-10 |
| Linking two or more weapons of the same type (this adds the Linked quality to the weapon with a value equal to the additional weapons added) | + half the cost of the weapon per additional weapon | As weapon |

## UPGRADED WEAPONS

The simple act of mounting more or heavier weapons on a starship or vehicle. The combinations of weapon load-outs are nearly endless, thanks to the diversity of weapon systems in the galaxy. Weapon choice is left up to the needs of the Player Characters and the availability, either legally or illegally, of weapon systems.

**Models Include:** Arakyd Flex Tube Proton Torpedo Launcher, ArMek SW-6 Heavy Ion Cannon.

**Base Modifiers:** See **Table 7-16: Upgrading Weapons** for a list of what weapons can be mounted to what kind of ship. This is not meant to be an exhaustive list, but it provides a series of guidelines that can be applied for other, non-standard weapons as well.

**Modification Options:** None.

**Hard Points Required:** 0 if replacing an existing system. 1 if adding a new weapon system. Weapon systems combining two or more weapons always cost 1 hard point, even if replacing an existing system.

**Price:** Varies.

# VIII

# THE FORCE

Although the galaxy is a vast place, 20,000 standard years of recorded hyperspace travel, technological progress, and exploration have uncovered many of its mysteries. Galactic civilization has spread across the stars. Its sciences have explained the physical laws governing the universe, and—some argue—swept away the need for primitive superstitions.

And yet, the galaxy has a fundamental mysticism that science cannot unravel. This power has always defied the attempts of skeptics to explain it away, and its influence is undeniable. Species and cultures have known this strange energy by a multitude of names, but the Jedi and Sith know it as the Force.

Sentient beings have known of the Force throughout galactic history. Historians have recorded the role of Force-sensitive beings in momentous events since the earliest days of the Old Republic. Force users fought in many pivotal conflicts, from the ancient and nigh-mythical battles between the Jedi and Sith to the recent conflicts in the galaxy-spanning Clone Wars. They have counseled governments and led Empires. They have brought both strife and peace to the galaxy.

Despite Imperial attempts to suppress knowledge of the Force, memories remain of the two great opposing traditions of Force users: the Jedi and the Sith. Each has sought to understand the Force in its own way, and myths and tales tell of their constant struggle throughout the ages. Perhaps because of the inherently mystical nature of their studies, both remain shrouded in legend. However, these two paths embody the duality of the Force, and comprise the major approaches for those who wish to manipulate its awesome power for good or ill.

Regardless of legend or rumor, such feats are almost unthinkable now in this era of galactic civil war and Imperial persecution. The Force remains, always, but its students are scattered and hidden. If they are to shape the course of galactic events once again, they must learn its ways and choose a path for themselves.

# THE NATURE OF
# THE FORCE

The Force simply is. It has existed as long as life has flourished in the galaxy, and will endure as long as life remains. It has been called an energy field, and in many ways this is true, though it cannot be measured by conventional or technological means. It binds the galaxy together, though in more than just a physical sense. Although it eludes the grasp of pure intellect, the rival traditions of Force users have learned much about its power over the millennia. Those who would use that power today must understand these lessons.

The Force consists of two related, but distinct, elements: the Living Force and the Cosmic Force. The Living Force is generated by the energy of living beings throughout the galaxy. This is the Force at its most immediate and instinctive level. It is this aspect of the Force that allows for many of the impressive abilities that have fueled the aura of legend around the Jedi and Sith, and that still excites the galaxy's imagination. The ability to trick the minds of other beings, to sense their presence, and to manipulate physical objects all come from the Living Force.

As life in all its myriad forms cycles endlessly, so does the Living Force. It can ebb and flow, growing stronger in some places than others, especially in locations of great significance for life or death. However, this sequence of renewal forms the foundation of the Force's other half—the Cosmic Force.

Ultimately, all energy from the Living Force passes into the Cosmic Force. This includes not only the energy of the Living Force at a particular point in time, but the energy of all things that have ever lived in the galaxy. For this reason, the Cosmic Force transcends normal conceptions of time and space. In this way, it also connects all things in the galaxy together: not only what is, but what was and what has yet to come.

The Cosmic Force is the more difficult of the two for a Force user to access. It requires meditation, openness, and harmony to attune oneself to its rhythms. It is also from here that perhaps the most powerful Force abilities come— to see distant places and events, and even to catch glimpses of myriad potential futures. These abilities are seldom featured in the derring-do of a holo-drama, but comprehending the deeper mysteries of the galaxy and possessing the gift of foresight is a route to power savored only by a few.

## MIDI-CHLORIANS

Midi-chlorians are micro-symbiont organisms that live within the bloodstreams of all living things. The Jedi of the Old Republic studied them, and believed them to be fundamental to the connection between life and the Force, though the exact nature of this relationship remains mysterious.

Testing an individual's midi-chlorian count is one of the few known ways to measure Force ability using technological means, as higher counts are associated with greater potential for Force sensitivity. However, as with many matters related to the Force, there are few absolutes. Unexpected individuals have been known to develop an affinity for the Force, regardless of testing results.

Since the fall of the Jedi, active study of midi-chlorians has become increasingly rare. The subject is treated with ridicule by disinterested scientists and with official discouragement by Imperial authorities.

This intimate link between life and the Force means that—despite rumors of Force-attuned technology—only living organisms can sense its presence. Sentient beings in particular can be born Force-sensitive or become so during the course of their lives. The Force is particularly strong within some individuals, and some say that this trait can be passed down in families. Indeed, certain family names have been associated with the most famous, or infamous, Force users in the galaxy's history.

The Force also appears to have its own will. Many powerful Force users have long hinted at this phenomenon, especially after communing with the Force or experiencing events of mystical significance. They believe not only that the Force derives its energy from life, but that it also guides the actions of the living.

Some have stated that it responds most strongly to actions taken by those who consciously seek to use it, and that it aids or opposes individuals according to its own remote designs. Given these observations, those sensitive to the Force understand that it has an undeniable role in the destiny of the galaxy.

# THE DUALITY OF THE FORCE

The Force reflects the patterns of life, and life seeks to perpetuate itself. Despite their endless variety throughout the galaxy, most life forms are driven by instinct to seek the necessities for survival. At the most primordial level, whether on a steaming jungle world or a sun-baked desert planet, life struggles to exist.

However alien their ecosystems may be from each other, all cycles of life encompass both creative and destructive impulses. On a grand scale, species arise and adapt, and then thrive for a time. Most are eventually extinguished, either by some cataclysm or a gradual fading as conditions change, and then are replaced by still others. To take a closer view, there are predators and prey, and many species that must be both, in order for life to continue. Life includes the act of birth, but also death.

As it is so intimately linked to life, the Force also has a duality that encompasses both creation and destruction. As long as sentient beings have been able to wield the power of the Force, they have been aware of this division, for it is an inherent part of its nature. They gave names to these opposed sides, taking their understanding from the most intuitive of relationships: that between light and dark.

## TOUCHING THE FORCE

Sentients have learned to build civilizations, to travel between the stars, and perhaps most importantly, to interact with the Force. They are able to make conscious choices and to desire more than mere survival. It is this ability to impose one's will on reality that gives a moral dimension to existence and to both the light and dark sides of the Force. The capacity for choice and intent in using the Force goes beyond the natural cycles of creation and destruction that feed it.

Those who draw upon the light side know it by the feelings that invite its presence: peace, understanding, compassion, and even love. In action, its use is closely associated with life-affirming and selfless motives. For those who have gained the deepest understanding, wielding the light side is less about imposing their own will than about allowing that of the Cosmic Force to shape destiny.

At the opposite end lies the dark side. Its users know that their strength flows from raw emotion. Fear, anger, jealousy, and hatred are all conduits to the power of the dark side. Those who believe they have gained mastery over it know, too, that it is most effectively bent to their will when used for destructive actions and focused by the burning need to fulfill personal desires.

The two great Force-using traditions of the galaxy—the Jedi Order and the Order of the Sith—each developed following the path of one side to the exclusion of the other. Though their exact origins are ancient and mysterious, they have remained enemies throughout galactic history. For this reason, some believe that the Jedi and Sith must share an ultimately common origin, and that their creation in the distant past embodies the opposition between the light and dark sides. As their relative power has increased or diminished over the centuries, it has only reinforced another deeply held belief about the Force: that it has a balance, and that this balance can shift over time.

Amid this discussion of the Jedi and Sith, it is worth noting that the Force is not set apart solely for interaction with those who can directly manipulate it. All sentient beings can choose to act in life-affirming or destructive ways. Most view their actions (and lapses) within the moral code of their species or world, or in keeping with some personal creed. This does not mean that they are not acted upon by the Force, or that their actions do not contribute to the balance between light and dark.

However, those who use the Force itself to further these competing moral ends operate on a different level. By embracing one side over the other, they are actively engaging in the unceasing struggle between the light and dark sides. More than any others, it is the Force-sensitive beings of the galaxy who have the greatest influence upon the balance of the Force.

Still, even the greatest of light side users can seek only to understand the will of the Force. In the twilight days of the Old Republic, the Jedi Council came to believe that the Force was dangerously out of balance. To them, the lessening of their contact with the Cosmic Force and the return of the Sith meant the dark side was growing dangerously ascendant.

You have learned much about the Force in a short time. Sometimes, we learn our best lessons from stories. So, I will tell you one: a story about losing one's way.

Once, three seekers traveled deep into space, following a mysterious distress call. A very old call. The first was a mighty warrior, fearless and impetuous in equal measure. The second had been the warrior's master; he was disciplined and wise, but detached. The third was the warrior's apprentice; she was passionate and loyal, but inexperienced. When they got to the source of the signal, they found only a great structure in space, like none they had ever seen before. It felt old, even more ancient than the signal they came for, and it pulled them inside.

The seekers awoke in another place. It was a beautiful world, and idyllic, but also alien. The natural laws of the galaxy didn't seem to operate the same there. Each of them was open to the Force, and they could sense that this place was extremely strong with it, and they could not leave.

They met others there. The first called herself Daughter. She was beautiful, too, in a luminous way, and not unkind, but she was also very serious, and stern. She offered to guide them, but the friends became separated, and only the warrior was able to follow.

The other two asked him to wait, but he was impatient, and they knew that he would go his own way, whatever they counseled.

A furious storm broke out, and the blooming plants they had journeyed past only hours earlier began to die. It was then that they met the Son. Where the Daughter was bright and aloof, he was dark and brooding. He asked them if their friend was truly the Chosen One. They responded with suspicion, for that prophecy was known only to a few, and among that number were their enemies. But the Son only warned them to take shelter from the storm, and left them there.

Now on his own, the warrior found his way to a building, a monastery in the hills of that place. Its symbolism was hauntingly familiar, but he sought answers, and so with little pause he went inside. There, he met the third being, wizened by untold experience, who called himself the Father.

They talked, and the Father said he and his children were called "Force Wielders." He said that he governed the balance between his family—and between the light and the dark—in that place. If he did not, their power could threaten the fabric of the universe. As the Son had hinted at earlier, the Father asked the warrior if he was the Chosen One.

It was a title the warrior did not believe in, and a mantle he did not seek. Still, the Father wanted to know the truth of this. So he sent his children to capture the warrior's friends, and he brought them to the monastery. There, with the warrior's old master threatened by the Daughter's light, and his apprentice by the Son's darkness, the Father told the warrior to choose which to save.

He would not choose. Drawing upon the Force that was all around them in that place, the warrior subdued both the Son and the Daughter and made them release his friends. However, the great power he displayed only reinforced the Father's conviction that he was the Chosen One.

The Father took the warrior aside, explaining that he was dying and that it was the Chosen One's destiny to take his place, and to maintain the balance. The warrior considered, but refused him. He had a life beyond that place, and a wife he loved passionately, though in secret, for their love was forbidden. The Father said he could not force the warrior to accept his destiny, but warned him that refusing it would bring suffering to the entire galaxy. The warrior would not be persuaded, and the seekers departed into the melancholy sky. Did the Father's warning come to pass? Well, perhaps I will tell you more of their fate another time.

The Jedi also believed in the prophecy of the Chosen One: that a being would emerge with the power to restore balance to the Force. Some within the council even claimed to have identified the One among the order's own members. Unfortunately, the Jedi soon fell to betrayal during the Clone Wars and were all but exterminated. To those who can sense it, the Force remains out of balance in the current era of the Galactic Civil War.

# THE WAYS OF THE FORCE

The Force still represents one of the greatest sources of power in the galaxy, for good or evil. It requires the will of a Force-sensitive being to use it and lacks the easy approachability of technology. To those with the necessary ability, it can be turned to a seemingly infinite number of uses. Individuals who are strong in the Force can enhance their own abilities, understand their surroundings on an intuitive level, or even use it to exert their will upon the physical matter around them.

## LEARNING ABOUT THE FORCE

Such ability is very rare. Though an individual may manifest sensitivity to the Force at any time, it is a talent that must be developed, rather than a skill that can be taught. In most species, it typically appears at a young age. Their gift often sets these individuals apart, as even untrained Force use can grant insights or physical capabilities far beyond those considered normal.

This keeps the communities of Force users small, and isolated from much of galactic society. In the days of the Jedi Order, members sought out children with Force potential for instruction. Today, exhibiting such ability is extremely dangerous. Rumors of it are likely to bring Imperial scrutiny and retribution down upon those thought to harbor a Force-sensitive, let alone upon the individual himself.

Even for those with the talent, discipline and training are necessary to fully open themselves to the Force and learn to use it. Finding a mentor to assist one in learning about the ways of the Force is difficult at best, for those with the greatest wisdom were the first to fall during the Empire's purges. Many of those since born with the gift remain unaware of it. Those who know are often best advised to hide it.

Still, there always remain those who will not be stopped from pursuing their destiny and realizing their potential. They are compelled to learn what they can about the Force, whether for themselves or the sake of others.

## THE POWERS OF THE FORCE

The power that the Force confers to a user can vary widely, but its capabilities are traditionally broken into three broad categories:

### POWERS OF THE BODY

Force users can control and harness the Living Force within themselves to heighten their own physical

prowess. Abilities of this type gave the Jedi and Sith their astounding agility and strength, among other talents such as healing from terrible injuries, or hibernating through long periods of deprivation.

## POWERS OF MANIPULATION

The second category of ability allows Force users to alter and manipulate the physical environment surrounding them. This allows for such feats as moving objects in seeming defiance of normal physical laws and directing or even projecting energy. This control can also involve the subtle manipulation of the minds of other beings. Those impressed with raw power—whether Force-sensitives or not—have always been drawn to this grouping of talents.

## POWERS OF THE MIND

The final category of ability encompasses those involved in sensing or gaining awareness of the greater galaxy around the Force user. As mentioned before, the highest levels of these abilities involve communing directly with the Cosmic Force. Though the present and future are always in motion, the Force has much influence over both, and an individual armed with knowledge can sometimes direct events to his own ends.

## LIGHTSABERS AND THE FORCE

There is one other arena in which Force sensitivity bestows a power not available to most individuals: the ability to wield the lightsaber, the ancient weapon of the Jedi and Sith. Rarely seen even at the height of the Old Republic, the lightsaber has all but disappeared with the Jedi, becoming a weapon of legend or an item of curiosity.

There are many who believe lightsaber prowess to be the signature attribute of an accomplished Force user, as it arguably draws upon all three of the areas of Force ability. Only those capable of supernaturally fine physical control can wield a lightsaber's massless blade without great risk to themselves. To be a truly effective combatant, they must also have a considerable degree of spatial awareness, gained through opening themselves to the Force. Finally, it is rumored that a lightsaber is best constructed by a Force user capable of making delicate manipulations to align its focusing crystals. Indeed, this act was considered a rite of passage for the Jedi.

# BEING A FORCE-SENSITIVE IN THE GALAXY

Following the ways of the Force has always been a lonely path. Few are granted the potential. Fewer still

### THE BALANCE OF THE FORCE

The tale of the warrior and the Force Wielders? No, it does not end with his departure. Yes, I know that would not make a good story. Remember, our lessons are not always comforting.

So, as the seekers attempted to leave, the Son tricked all of them, including the Father. He meant to break free of that realm and take control in the wider galaxy. He stole the warrior's apprentice and poisoned her mind against him. In their desperation, the warrior and his master turned to the Daughter, who led them to a sacred place and showed them a powerful dagger, which she said they could use against the Son. With no other choices, warrior and his master took it and set out to free the apprentice.

It was a trap. The apprentice fought with the warrior, and their conflict only fed the Son's powers. He captured the dagger and tried to kill the Father with it, so that he could escape. However, his plans were upset, too, for the Daughter intervened, sacrificing herself to save the wounded Father.

In a final attempt to escape, the Son showed the warrior a vision of his future. It was dark and filled with the pain of the terrible things he would do. The Son convinced the warrior that if he joined the Son's cause, he would be spared the tragedy of his fate. The warrior was afraid, and fell under the Son's control.

However, the Father was able to recover enough of his power to take action. He confronted the warrior with the hard truth that he alone could choose his own destiny, but banished the knowledge of the future from him. This broke the Son's hold over the warrior, and the Father determined to make a final sacrifice.

The Son came upon them all, believing his power complete and his way free. The Father warned him of the danger to the universe's balance, but the Son was heedless. Taking the dagger, the Father mortally wounded himself, in order to sever the Son's connection to the Force. The warrior then killed the Son.

As he lay dying, the Father's heart was heavy, for his family were all dead. But he gave the warrior cause for hope, telling him that he could still fulfill his destiny in another way, by continuing on his path. After that, he faded, and the three seekers finally departed.

Why do I pass this story on to you? For the same reason it was told to me. Yes, the Force is still out of balance. Yes, the dark side has grown in power, but there *is* still hope. Even those of us who are strongest in the Force cannot know *all* of our destiny. We can learn to embrace its will, and carry on in the belief that one day the prophecy will be fulfilled, and the balance restored.

can find the teaching and discipline to hone their potential into mastery.

This is truer now than ever. The Jedi Order may have kept the peace of the Republic for a thousand generations, but the Republic is no more, and the Jedi have been hunted to extinction. Dark times have come, and the Empire rules now. While the Sith appear victorious in their long struggle, they remain almost a rumor and are nearly as rare as their foe.

To be a Force user is to be unique, and to face choices. A galactic civil war rages, and the Force remains unbalanced. It compels those who would use it to make decisions of significance and propels them along the path they choose, forever altering their destiny. Soon enough, they will come to serve one side or the other in this conflict, for they are the heirs of the greatest power in the galaxy.

# THE FORCE IN FORCE AND DESTINY

By default, all characters playing a career from **Force and Destiny** are Force-sensitive. Being Force-sensitive is very different from being a Jedi, as only years of study in the techniques and teachings of the Order entitle a Force user to such an accolade. Most Force-sensitives would not be able to achieve the degree of skill necessary to become fully fledged Jedi Knights, and in the modern age, the Jedi have been so thoroughly expunged that finding a qualified teacher in their techniques is a practical impossibility. That being said, many of the characters in **Force and Destiny** have the opportunity to advance their abilities and hone their skills to the point where they could rival the Jedi of old. It is up to them as to whether they emulate the ancient guardians of the galaxy or supplant them.

In this game, the ability to use the Force is represented by a character's Force rating. Most Non-Player Characters have a Force rating of 0. This does not mean they are wholly cut off from the Force, as everything in the galaxy is affected by it, but it has no tangible impact on their day-to-day existence as they perceive it. Force-sensitive characters who do comprehend the

Force always have a Force rating. All of the Player Characters who use a career from **Force and Destiny** have a Force rating of 1 at character creation, and have chances to increase it as their characters grow.

## FORCE-SENSITIVE CHARACTERS

Being Force-sensitive allows a character to unlock certain special abilities and the means with which to activate and use Force powers, which are discussed later in this chapter.

**A Force-sensitive character is any character with a Force rating of 1 or higher.** A character must be Force-sensitive to select certain specialization trees and particular talents. In addition, certain talents and abilities may affect Force-sensitive characters in different ways than they affect characters who do not have a Force rating. There are some abilities that only affect Force-sensitive characters, and there are others to which Force-sensitives are effectively immune. When this is the case, it is noted in the description of the talent or ability in question.

### BECOMING FORCE-SENSITIVE

Generally, Player Characters using a career from **Force and Destiny** do not need to become Force-sensitive, since they start that way. A Player Character who uses one of **Force and Destiny**'s six careers gains Force rating 1 as a starting ability.

If a PC does not begin play with Force rating 1 (this generally will only happen if the player selects a career from **Age of Rebellion** or **Edge of the Empire**), the character will need to take one of the Force-sensitive universal specializations in those books to gain Force rating 1 and become a Force-sensitive.

## FORCE DICE

The twelve-sided, white Force die ⬡ is the seventh narrative die used in **Force and Destiny**. On it are white, circular symbols representing the light side of the Force ⬤ and black, circular symbols representing the dark side of the Force ◯.

The Force die is unique among the dice in **Force and Destiny** because, unlike the other dice, the Force die does not generate symbols that contribute toward success or failure. In addition, the Force die's Light Side and Dark Side symbols do not cancel each other out. Instead, the Force die generates resources in the form of Force points ◖ for Force-sensitive characters to spend to activate Force powers and other abilities.

# FORCE-SENSITIVE RULES

Force-sensitives gain access to certain unique powers and abilities via the Force. These abilities can take the form of **Force powers** or **Force talents**. Both Force powers and Force talents have a set of individual rules governing their use, as described later in this section. They also share certain universal rules.

Force powers and Force talents generally work in one of two ways:

- First, the PC can make a **Force power check**, rolling a number of Force dice ⬡ and using the results to generate Force points ◗. The character can spend these ◗ to activate and enhance abilities in a variety of ways, as described in the individual Force power or Force talent.

- Second, the PC can **commit** a number of Force dice. While Force dice are committed to a power (as described in the power), the PC counts his Force rating as one lower than normal for each Force die committed. Force dice can remain committed to a power or ability for multiple game rounds and, while committed, provide the PC with an ongoing effect.

## FORCE POWER CHECKS

Most Force powers and Force talents provide the user with a temporary effect—they accomplish something and then end. What they accomplish is detailed in the description of the power or talent. However, most powers and talents that provide a temporary effect require the character to spend one or more **Force points** ◗ to activate the power or ability.

Characters generate ◗ by making a Force power check, rolling one or more Force dice ⬡ and generating ◗ based on the results. When a Force-sensitive character attempts to activate a power or use certain Force talents, he creates a dice pool that—usually—consists solely of a number of Force dice. The ability sometimes specifies how many Force dice he uses; **however, the number of Force dice he adds to the pool can never exceed his current Force rating**. He then rolls the dice. Every Light Side result ◯ generates one Force point ◗ the character may spend to fuel the power's abilities. Every Dark Side result ● generates no Force points ◗ and is disregarded.

However, the dark side of the Force is always offering easy power, tempting a Force user to give in and accept its aid. A Force-sensitive character

may use one or more ● to generate one additional ◗ each—in addition to those generated by the ◯. The consequences that come with this choice can be dire, and can gravely affect the individual who gives in to this temptation. A Force-sensitive character in **FORCE AND DESTINY** who wishes to use one or more ● to provide Force points for a power must flip one Destiny Point from light to dark. If there are no light side Destiny Points to flip, he may not use ● at all. **He then suffers strain equal to the number of ● results he uses to generate ◗, and suffers Conflict equal to the number of ● results he uses to generate ◗.** A character may always choose to have a ◯ result or ● result not generate ◗.

Once the character determines how many ◗ he has generated, he consults the Force power or Force talent and determines how he may spend those ◗. Most powers and talents have abilities that require one or more ◗ to activate. Each ◗ can be spent only once. The character may spend as many or as few ◗ as he wishes; however, once he is finished spending ◗, any unspent ◗ are lost.

Once a Force power check has been resolved, this concludes the character's action. A Force power is always "successfully" activated, even if the check does not generate any Force points to spend on the power.

### COMBINED FORCE POWER CHECKS

Some Force powers and Force talents require the character to make a Force power check that is combined with a skill check. This generally

represents the character using Force abilities in conjunction with other skills. It also comes into play when the character's Force abilities may be opposed by the skills of his target.

When a character combines a Force power check with a standard skill check, he combines the ⬡ he would roll to make the Force power check with the dice he would roll to make the skill check. Relevant powers and talents specifically state when a combined check should take place. Such a check may also occur when a PC is dealing with particularly powerful characters (see the **Resisting Force Power Checks** sidebar, on page 283). Unless specifically stated otherwise, the character must generate enough ◐ to activate the Force talent or Force power's basic power (or appropriate control upgrades) *and* must generate at least one uncanceled ✵ for the check to succeed (see page 31 for more information on passing or failing checks).

This entire process counts as making a single check.

### SPENDING ◐ BEFORE RESOLVING CHECKS

Many combined Force power checks allow the character to spend ◐ before resolving the overall success or failure of a check. For example, a talent might allow the character to make a Force power check combined with a skill check, then spend ◐ to add additional ✵ to the check. In other cases, a Force power could require the character to generate enough ◐ to move an object toward a target but also require him to succeed at a skill check to hit the target with the moving object.

In these cases, although the entire check is made at one time, the character should generate and spend ◐ immediately after rolling the dice pool, before interpreting the results of the rest of the pool.

## ACTIVATING BASIC POWERS AND UPGRADES OF A FORCE POWER MULTIPLE TIMES

Each Force power has basic uses, as well as upgrades that can enhance and modify these uses. Unless the power states otherwise, a Force user can activate the basic use or upgrades of a power multiple times to increase the effects of the power. For example, the Influence power's basic use is "spend ◐ to inflict 1 strain on a target." A Force user can then spend additional ◐, each inflicting another strain on the target.

For convenience, however, most basic uses and upgrades have clarifying text indicating whether or not they can be activated multiple times as part of a single use of their Force power. Some basic uses and upgrades may not have this clarifying text because they are passive upgrades or because their specific effect would not change due to additional activations.

# COMMITTING FORCE DICE

Some Force powers and Force talents provide an ongoing effect—they give the character a benefit that lasts until he chooses to end it. What they do is detailed in the description of the power or talent. However, most powers or talents that provide an ongoing effect require the character to commit a number of Force dice.

To activate and fuel an ongoing effect, the Force-sensitive character **commits** a number of Force dice ⬡. The number of ⬡ that need to be committed is

There are no hard limits as to how long a ⬡ can remain committed to a Force power or Force talent. Some talents and powers impose penalties for every round the ⬡ remains committed, but other powers (such as Sense and Enhance) do not. Generally this is not a problem, but some players may choose to leave ⬡ committed to powers for multiple encounters, or even multiple sessions.

If players are abusing this, the GM can implement the following rule: If a player leaves ⬡ committed to his character's Force powers or talents for multiple encounters, the GM can stop his character from recovering strain at the end of each encounter. This limiter remains in play until the character uncommits all ⬡ and leaves them uncommitted until the next encounter begins.

listed in the effect; however, a character cannot commit more ⬡ than his current Force rating.

When a character has committed one or more ⬡, he counts his current Force rating as lower than his actual Force rating. For all mechanical purposes, the character's Force rating temporarily decreases by an amount equal to the number of ⬡ committed. This is the PC's **current Force rating**. When he ends the effect, the character no longer counts his Force rating as lower than usual, because the dice are no longer committed. However, a Force-sensitive character still counts as a Force-sensitive character, even if committing ⬡ has dropped his current Force rating to 0.

A character may end an ongoing effect at the end of any of his subsequent turns as an incidental. While an ongoing effect is active, the character may not activate that specific ongoing effect again (the character cannot be benefiting from two "copies" of the same ongoing effect).

## FORCE TALENTS

Force-sensitive characters have access to a number of unique talents, referred to as Force talents. Force talents are talents available only to individuals who possess a Force rating. They represent the Force's ability to aid an individual in minor ways, but they are not complex enough to be individual Force powers. Often, these talents represent the character's ability to unconsciously tap into the Force; they are his instinctual awareness of the Force and his surroundings.

Force talents follow all the rules for talents, with the caveat that they can only be used by characters who have a Force rating of 1 or higher. Note that non-Force-sensitive characters can purchase a Force talent, but they cannot use it or gain any benefit from it until they become Force-sensitive (and this includes talents that increase a character's Force rating). Characters may use Force talents if their current Force rating is 0 due to committing ⬡; however, many Force talents require characters to commit ⬡ or make Force power checks, which are based on the character's current Force rating.

Active Force talents state whether they require an action, maneuver, or incidental to activate.

## FORCE POWERS

The primary means by which a Force user manipulates the Force is not unconscious. A true Force user can deliberately tap into the Force to change and manipulate himself and his surroundings. The Force can allow someone to do things others may see as fantastic or even unbelievable: levitating items, blocking blaster shots with one's hands, controlling the minds of others, and even predicting the future.

Force powers are one of the means by which a Force-sensitive character accomplishes those tasks. In **FORCE AND DESTINY**, Force powers are broad and overarching abilities that allow Force-sensitive characters to perform impressive and fantastic feats.

Each Force power focuses on a particular task that can be performed through the manipulation of the Force. Force powers might require Force power checks to activate temporary effects, or they could require users to commit Force dice to activate ongoing effects. Some might be able to do both. In any case, unless the power's description specifically states otherwise, **using the power requires one action in structured time**.

The initial purchase of each Force power costs a certain amount of experience, which is listed in the power's entry. Once the power is purchased, the user may spend additional experience to further customize and enhance it.

Unless specified in the Force power description, Force powers can be purchased by any Force-sensitive character. Some powers have a prerequisite Force rating that a character must possess before he can purchase the power.

### FORCE POWER BREAKDOWN

Each Force power can be divided into two sections: the power's basic form and its upgrades. A Force-sensitive character who purchases a Force power immediately gains access to the most basic form of the power. This is represented in the first row of the power's Force power tree. The basic form is the Force power at its simplest, and it provides the foundation for all of the upgrades that accompany the Force power.

Force powers are designed to be simple and inclusive, so that what Player Characters can accomplish with a power is often limited only by their imaginations. However, when confronting a powerful adversary, even skilled Force users may find their abilities stymied by an opponent's formidable will.

When any character attempts to use a Force power against a Player Character (or a PC attempts to use a Force power against a powerful Non-Player Character, such as a nemesis or plot-important named rival), **the Force power check becomes an opposed check**, if it is not already an opposed check or a combat check. This **always** applies when a Force power targets a PC, and the GM can use his discretion as to when the rule applies to NPCs.

To make the check opposed, the GM consults with the player and determines a skill that the attacking character must use as part of the Force power check. The attacking character then assembles a dice pool combining the Force dice he would use to make the Force power check with the Ability and Proficiency dice he would use in the skill check.

The GM then determines what skill the defending character must use to oppose the check. This skill sets the difficulty of the check, as per the rules for opposed checks on page 33. The attacking player then makes the check. The check must generate sufficient ◑ to activate the power and must generate at least one uncanceled ✸ to successfully execute the action he is attempting with the Force power.

The skills used in the check are up to the GM and the players involved, and they depend on the circumstances of the check. Generally, the attacking character can default to using the Discipline skill, although in some cases, other skills may make sense. An opposed check involving the Seek power, for example, might have the attacking character use Vigilance, whereas a check involving the use of Influence in a social setting could use Deception or Charm.

Likewise, the skills used to oppose the check also depend on the situation. The defending character often can use Discipline to oppose a Force power check if that character is also a Force user. However, in an opposed check where the attacking character is trying to pull the weapon from the defending character's hand, the defending character might use Athletics (representing attempts to hold onto a weapon). Likewise, an attempt to use Move to throw a character around a battlefield could be opposed by Resilience, as the defending character resists with his raw physical strength.

Force power upgrades are the means by which players can customize the Force powers their characters can access, modifying them to serve their needs and their characters' personalities. Upgrades are purchased with experience points; an upgrade can be purchased only if it is connected to the basic form or to a previously purchased upgrade in its tree. The experience cost of each upgrade is listed in its box.

## UPGRADES

Force power upgrades are grouped into several different categories, as described below.

**Strength:** Strength upgrades amplify the basic effect of a power, making the power more potent.

**Magnitude:** Magnitude upgrades increase the number of targets affected by the power, allowing the user to affect multiple items or individuals with a single action.

**Duration:** Duration upgrades increase the length of time of the power's effects.

**Range:** Range upgrades increase the distance from which the Force power can affect its targets.

**Control:** Control upgrades add new effects to Force powers, or modify existing effects (adding or changing the way the Force-sensitive character spends Force points).

**Mastery:** Each Mastery upgrade allows an experienced Force user to unlock an extremely potent ability for the power.

These categories remain the same for each Force power, although how they modify the Force power depends on the power itself. For example, the Duration upgrade for Influence increases the length of Influence's effect by one minute or one round of combat per upgrade, whereas the Duration upgrade for Sense increases the number of times its ongoing effects can be triggered each round. Some Force powers do not have each category of upgrade, depending on the power and how it works.

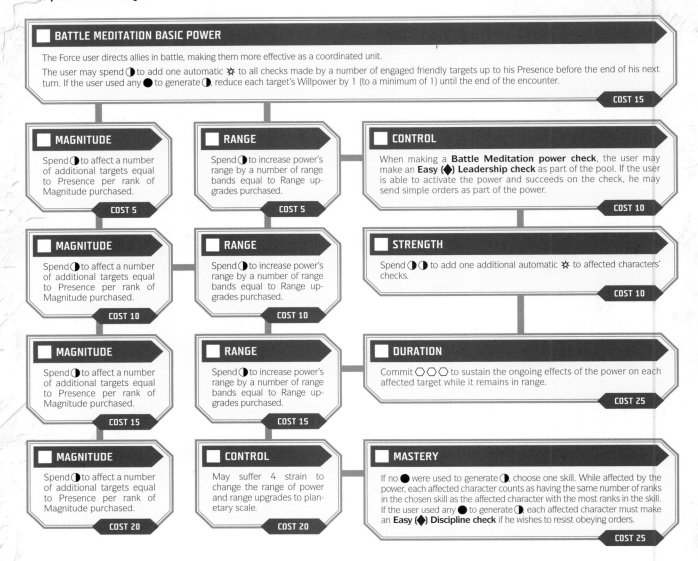

**BATTLE MEDITATION BASIC POWER**

The Force user directs allies in battle, making them more effective as a coordinated unit.

The user may spend ◐ to add one automatic ☼ to all checks made by a number of engaged friendly targets up to his Presence before the end of his next turn. If the user used any ● to generate ◐, reduce each target's Willpower by 1 (to a minimum of 1) until the end of the encounter.

COST 15

**MAGNITUDE**

Spend ◐ to affect a number of additional targets equal to Presence per rank of Magnitude purchased.

COST 5

**RANGE**

Spend ◐ to increase power's range by a number of range bands equal to Range upgrades purchased.

COST 5

**CONTROL**

When making a **Battle Meditation power check**, the user may make an **Easy (◆) Leadership check** as part of the pool. If the user is able to activate the power and succeeds on the check, he may send simple orders as part of the power.

COST 10

**MAGNITUDE**

Spend ◐ to affect a number of additional targets equal to Presence per rank of Magnitude purchased.

COST 10

**RANGE**

Spend ◐ to increase power's range by a number of range bands equal to Range upgrades purchased.

COST 10

**STRENGTH**

Spend ◐◐ to add one additional automatic ☼ to affected characters' checks.

COST 10

**MAGNITUDE**

Spend ◐ to affect a number of additional targets equal to Presence per rank of Magnitude purchased.

COST 15

**RANGE**

Spend ◐ to increase power's range by a number of range bands equal to Range upgrades purchased.

COST 15

**DURATION**

Commit ⬡⬡⬡ to sustain the ongoing effects of the power on each affected target while it remains in range.

COST 25

**MAGNITUDE**

Spend ◐ to affect a number of additional targets equal to Presence per rank of Magnitude purchased.

COST 20

**CONTROL**

May suffer 4 strain to change the range of power and range upgrades to planetary scale.

COST 20

**MASTERY**

If no ● were used to generate ◐, choose one skill. While affected by the power, each affected character counts as having the same number of ranks in the chosen skill as the affected character with the most ranks in the skill. If the user used any ● to generate ◐, each affected character must make an **Easy (◆) Discipline check** if he wishes to resist obeying orders.

COST 25

# FORCE POWER: BATTLE MEDITATION

Some Force users can telepathically guide allies around them, helping them to coordinate and achieve amazing feats. This guidance can easily become domination, however, and Force users must strive to maintain a balance between gentle guidance and outright tyranny. Meanwhile, individuals less concerned with trifling matters like "morality" and "the basic dignity of all sentients" use Battle Meditation to guide their disposable pawns to ignoble ends for their own selfish betterment.

### BASIC POWER

Battle Meditation's basic power allows the Force user to influence and coordinate large groups of allies, guiding their actions to help them work as a unified whole.

The basic power has one way of spending Force points:

- The user may spend ◐ to add one automatic ☼ to all checks made by a number of engaged friendly targets up to his Presence before the end of his next turn. If the user uses any ● to generate ◐ on this check, reduce each target's Willpower by 1 (to a minimum of 1) until the end of the encounter. The user may not activate this multiple times.

### UPGRADES

**Control Upgrade:** When making a **Battle Meditation power check**, the user may make an **Easy (◆) Leadership check** as part of the pool. If he generates enough Force points to activate the power and succeeds on the check, he can telepathically transmit a simple order to each character he affects with this power. This order is not mandatory, but the recipient comprehends it even if he does not understand the user's language.

**Control Upgrade:** Before attempting to activate this power, the user may suffer 4 strain to change the range of the Battle Meditation basic power to close on the planetary scale rather than engaged on the personal scale, for this use of the power only. If he does so, activating the range upgrades increases the range of the power by planetary scale range bands.

**Duration Upgrade:** The power gains the ongoing effect: Commit ⬡ ⬡ ⬡ after successfully activating the basic power. This power remains in effect on each affected target as long as the target stays within range of the power. If a target moves beyond the range of the power, the effects end for him, but not for any other targets of the power. The user may not activate this multiple times.

**Magnitude Upgrade:** Spend ◗ to increase the number of targets affected by an amount equal to the user's Presence multiplied by the number of Magnitude upgrades purchased. The user may activate this multiple times, increasing the number of targets by this number each time.

**Mastery Upgrade:** If no ● were used to generate ◗, the user may choose one skill; while under the effects of the power, each affected character counts as having the same number of ranks in the chosen skill as the affected character with the most ranks in that skill. If any ● were used to generate ◗ on this check, each target affected must make an **Easy (◆) Discipline check** if he wishes to resist obeying any orders given by the user as part of this power.

**Range Upgrade:** Spend ◗ to increase the maximum range at which the Force user can affect targets through this power by a number of range bands equal to the number of Range upgrades purchased. The user may activate this multiple times, increasing the range by this number each time.

**Strength Upgrade:** Spend ◗◗ to add one additional ✸ to all affected characters' checks. The user may activate this multiple times, adding one additional ✸ to all checks each time.

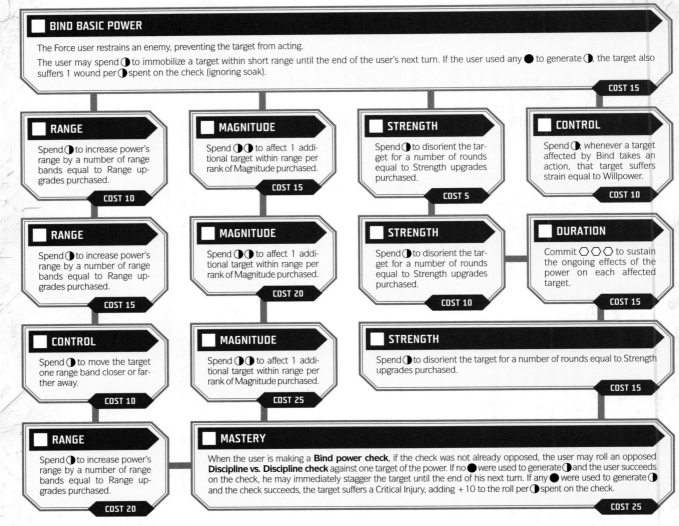

**BIND BASIC POWER**

The Force user restrains an enemy, preventing the target from acting.

The user may spend ◗ to immobilize a target within short range until the end of the user's next turn. If the user used any ● to generate ◗, the target also suffers 1 wound per ◗ spent on the check (ignoring soak).

**COST 15**

**RANGE**
Spend ◗ to increase power's range by a number of range bands equal to Range upgrades purchased.
**COST 10**

**MAGNITUDE**
Spend ◗◗ to affect 1 additional target within range per rank of Magnitude purchased.
**COST 15**

**STRENGTH**
Spend ◗ to disorient the target for a number of rounds equal to Strength upgrades purchased.
**COST 5**

**CONTROL**
Spend ◗, whenever a target affected by Bind takes an action, that target suffers strain equal to Willpower.
**COST 10**

**RANGE**
Spend ◗ to increase power's range by a number of range bands equal to Range upgrades purchased.
**COST 15**

**MAGNITUDE**
Spend ◗◗ to affect 1 additional target within range per rank of Magnitude purchased.
**COST 20**

**STRENGTH**
Spend ◗ to disorient the target for a number of rounds equal to Strength upgrades purchased.
**COST 10**

**DURATION**
Commit ◇◇◇ to sustain the ongoing effects of the power on each affected target.
**COST 15**

**CONTROL**
Spend ◗ to move the target one range band closer or farther away.
**COST 10**

**MAGNITUDE**
Spend ◗◗ to affect 1 additional target within range per rank of Magnitude purchased.
**COST 25**

**STRENGTH**
Spend ◗ to disorient the target for a number of rounds equal to Strength upgrades purchased.
**COST 15**

**RANGE**
Spend ◗ to increase power's range by a number of range bands equal to Range upgrades purchased.
**COST 20**

**MASTERY**
When the user is making a **Bind power check**, if the check was not already opposed, the user may roll an opposed **Discipline vs. Discipline check** against one target of the power. If no ● were used to generate ◗ and the user succeeds on the check, he may immediately stagger the target until the end of his next turn. If any ● were used to generate ◗ and the check succeeds, the target suffers a Critical Injury, adding + 10 to the roll per ◗ spent on the check.
**COST 25**

# FORCE POWER: BIND

Force users skilled in telekinetic powers can seize others from afar, preventing them from moving or attacking. When used with a calm heart, this power can be an extremely useful defensive tool, letting the Force user stop an enemy in his tracks without hurting him. Of course, once a foe is in the Force user's grip, it can be extremely tempting to simply crush him.

## BASIC POWER

Bind's basic power allows the Force user to restrain those nearby, preventing them from harming others and themselves. The basic power has one way to spend Force points:

- The user may spend ◗ to immobilize a target within short range until the end of the user's next turn. If the user used any ● to generate ◗ on this check, the target also suffers 1 wound (ignoring soak) per ◗ spent on the check. The user may not activate this multiple times.

## UPGRADES

**Control Upgrade:** Spend ◗ to immediately move the target one range band toward or away from the user. The user may not activate this multiple times.

**Control Upgrade:** Spend ◗, whenever a target affected by Bind takes an action, he suffers strain equal to the user's Willpower. The user may not activate this multiple times.

**Duration Upgrade:** The power gains the ongoing effect: Commit ◇◇◇ after successfully activating the basic power. If a target was immobilized or staggered by this power, he remains immobilized or staggered as long as ◇◇◇ remain committed and the target stays within range. If a target moves beyond the range of the power, the effects end for him, but not for any other targets of the power. The user may not activate this multiple times.

**Magnitude Upgrade:** Spend 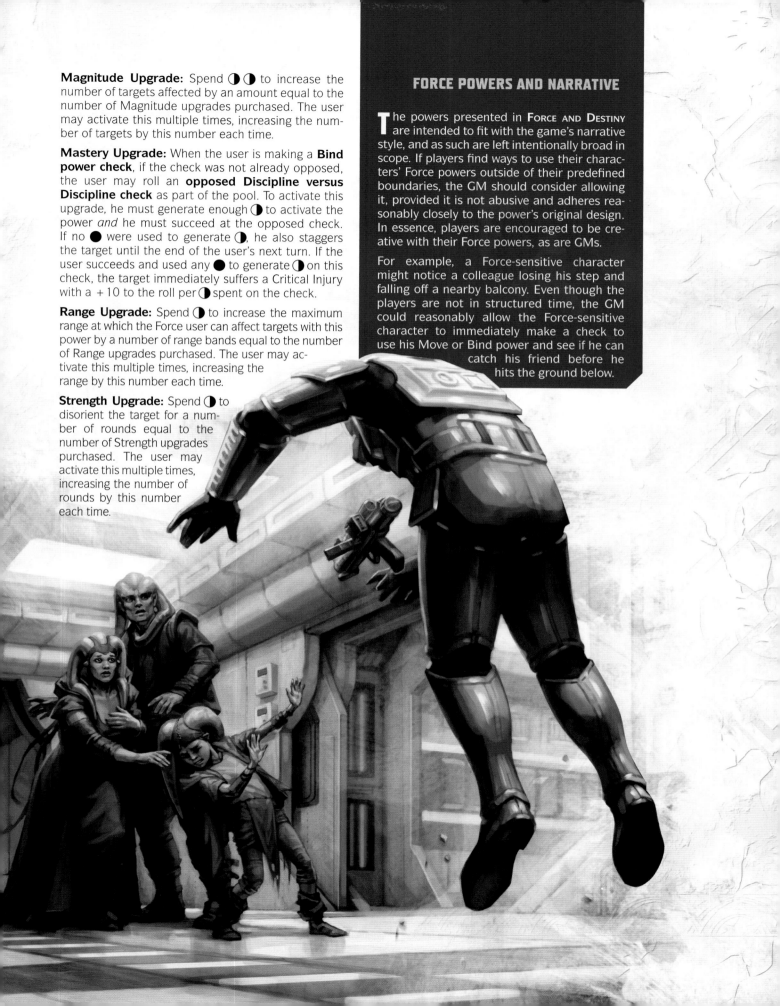◐◐ to increase the number of targets affected by an amount equal to the number of Magnitude upgrades purchased. The user may activate this multiple times, increasing the number of targets by this number each time.

**Mastery Upgrade:** When the user is making a **Bind power check**, if the check was not already opposed, the user may roll an **opposed Discipline versus Discipline check** as part of the pool. To activate this upgrade, he must generate enough ◐ to activate the power *and* he must succeed at the opposed check. If no ● were used to generate ◐, he also staggers the target until the end of the user's next turn. If the user succeeds and used any ● to generate ◐ on this check, the target immediately suffers a Critical Injury with a +10 to the roll per ◐ spent on the check.

**Range Upgrade:** Spend ◐ to increase the maximum range at which the Force user can affect targets with this power by a number of range bands equal to the number of Range upgrades purchased. The user may activate this multiple times, increasing the range by this number each time.

**Strength Upgrade:** Spend ◐ to disorient the target for a number of rounds equal to the number of Strength upgrades purchased. The user may activate this multiple times, increasing the number of rounds by this number each time.

## FORCE POWERS AND NARRATIVE

The powers presented in FORCE AND DESTINY are intended to fit with the game's narrative style, and as such are left intentionally broad in scope. If players find ways to use their characters' Force powers outside of their predefined boundaries, the GM should consider allowing it, provided it is not abusive and adheres reasonably closely to the power's original design. In essence, players are encouraged to be creative with their Force powers, as are GMs.

For example, a Force-sensitive character might notice a colleague losing his step and falling off a nearby balcony. Even though the players are not in structured time, the GM could reasonably allow the Force-sensitive character to immediately make a check to use his Move or Bind power and see if he can catch his friend before he hits the ground below.

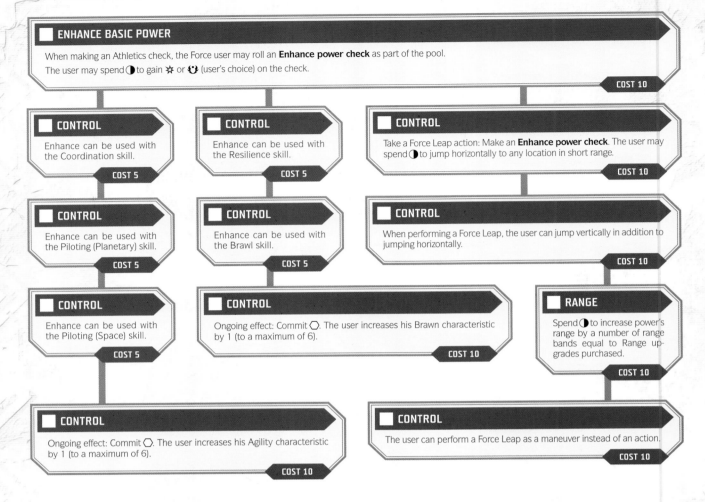

**ENHANCE BASIC POWER**

When making an Athletics check, the Force user may roll an **Enhance power check** as part of the pool. The user may spend ◐ to gain ✸ or ۞ (user's choice) on the check.

COST 10

**CONTROL**

Enhance can be used with the Coordination skill.

COST 5

**CONTROL**

Enhance can be used with the Resilience skill.

COST 5

**CONTROL**

Take a Force Leap action: Make an **Enhance power check**. The user may spend ◐ to jump horizontally to any location in short range.

COST 10

**CONTROL**

Enhance can be used with the Piloting (Planetary) skill.

COST 5

**CONTROL**

Enhance can be used with the Brawl skill.

COST 5

**CONTROL**

When performing a Force Leap, the user can jump vertically in addition to jumping horizontally.

COST 10

**CONTROL**

Enhance can be used with the Piloting (Space) skill.

COST 5

**CONTROL**

Ongoing effect: Commit ⬡. The user increases his Brawn characteristic by 1 (to a maximum of 6).

COST 10

**RANGE**

Spend ◐ to increase power's range by a number of range bands equal to Range upgrades purchased.

COST 10

**CONTROL**

Ongoing effect: Commit ⬡. The user increases his Agility characteristic by 1 (to a maximum of 6).

COST 10

**CONTROL**

The user can perform a Force Leap as a maneuver instead of an action.

COST 10

# FORCE POWER: ENHANCE

One of the most straightforward ways in which Force users utilize the power of the Force is to imbue their own bodies with energy and strength. Making leaps that might otherwise be deemed impossible, moving at high speeds, and harnessing physical strength well beyond the capacity of most sentient beings are all equally viable. In this way, the Force becomes an almost literal fuel for feats of endurance and power. Most Force users find it a relatively simple thing to use the Force in order to overcome their own physical limitations and shrug off the effects of fatigue. With a little practice, most Force users are able to expand the arenas in which they can use the Force beyond that of mere brute strength. They are able to concentrate the Force into assisting them with acts of dexterity and acrobatics.

## BASIC POWER

Enhance allows Force users to perform athletic feats beyond the original scope of their natural abilities. The basic power has one way of spending Force points:

- When making an Athletics check, the user may roll an **Enhance power check** as part of the pool. The user may spend ◐ to gain ✸ or ۞ (his choice) on the check. (Remember, this counts as a normal Force power check in every way—it is simply combined with the overall skill check.)

## UPGRADES

Upgrades to Enhance work in two distinct ways. Force users may choose to use the power to improve their natural abilities, enhancing existing skills and even improving their bodies' physical characteristics using the Force. Alternatively, Force users can employ the power to achieve physical feats not otherwise achievable by other beings, leaping long distances or incredible heights.

**Control Upgrade:** The user gains the ability to use Enhance with the Coordination skill.

**Control Upgrade:** Enhance can be used with the Piloting (Planetary) skill.

**Control Upgrade:** Enhance can be used with the Piloting (Space) skill.

**Control Upgrade:** This power gains the ongoing effect: Commit ⬡. The Force user increases his Agility characteristic by 1 (to a maximum of 6).

**Control Upgrade:** Enhance can be used with the Resilience skill.

**Control Upgrade:** Enhance can be used with the Brawl skill.

**Control Upgrade:** This power gains the ongoing effect: Commit ⬡. The Force user increases his Brawn characteristic by 1 (to a maximum of 6).

**Control Upgrade:** The user can take a Force Leap action to make an **Enhance power check**. He may spend ◐ to jump horizontally to any location within short range. He can use this to leap over obstacles or impassable terrain but cannot leap directly vertically. The user may not activate this multiple times.

**Control Upgrade:** When taking a Force Leap action, the user can leap to any location in range vertically as well as horizontally.

**Control Upgrade:** The user only needs to use a maneuver to perform a Force Leap, instead of an action.

**Range Upgrade:** Spend ◐ to increase the maximum range the user can jump by the number of Range upgrades purchased. The user may not activate this multiple times. Remember that the user must still spend Force points to activate the power's actual effects.

# Force Power Tree: Foresee

**Prerequisites: Force Rating 1 +**

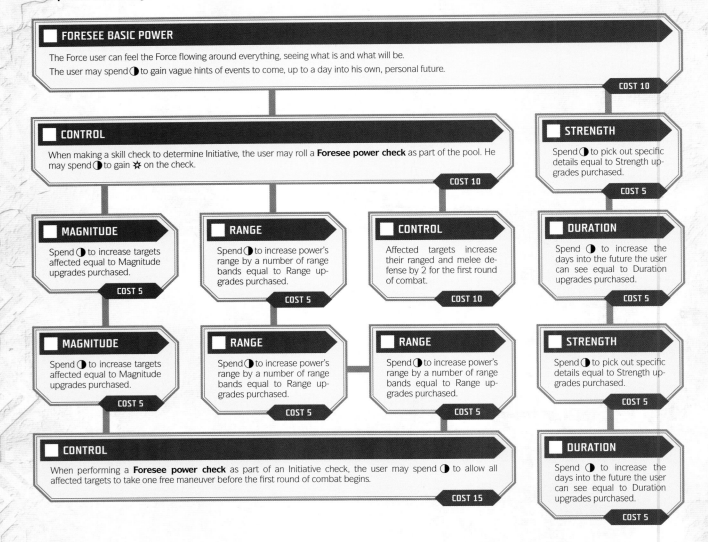

**FORESEE BASIC POWER**

The Force user can feel the Force flowing around everything, seeing what is and what will be.
The user may spend ◑ to gain vague hints of events to come, up to a day into his own, personal future.

COST 10

**CONTROL**

When making a skill check to determine Initiative, the user may roll a **Foresee power check** as part of the pool. He may spend ◑ to gain ✸ on the check.

COST 10

**STRENGTH**

Spend ◑ to pick out specific details equal to Strength upgrades purchased.

COST 5

**MAGNITUDE**

Spend ◑ to increase targets affected equal to Magnitude upgrades purchased.

COST 5

**RANGE**

Spend ◑ to increase power's range by a number of range bands equal to Range upgrades purchased.

COST 5

**CONTROL**

Affected targets increase their ranged and melee defense by 2 for the first round of combat.

COST 10

**DURATION**

Spend ◑ to increase the days into the future the user can see equal to Duration upgrades purchased.

COST 5

**MAGNITUDE**

Spend ◑ to increase targets affected equal to Magnitude upgrades purchased.

COST 5

**RANGE**

Spend ◑ to increase power's range by a number of range bands equal to Range upgrades purchased.

COST 5

**RANGE**

Spend ◑ to increase power's range by a number of range bands equal to Range upgrades purchased.

COST 5

**STRENGTH**

Spend ◑ to pick out specific details equal to Strength upgrades purchased.

COST 5

**CONTROL**

When performing a **Foresee power check** as part of an Initiative check, the user may spend ◑ to allow all affected targets to take one free maneuver before the first round of combat begins.

COST 15

**DURATION**

Spend ◑ to increase the days into the future the user can see equal to Duration upgrades purchased.

COST 5

## FORCE POWER: FORESEE

Force users often have precognitive flashes, experiencing waking dreams or visions about people and situations through their abilities. These powers are rarely so clear and obvious as to provide unequivocal visions of the future, but they are certainly enough to give Force users pause for thought when they have a "bad feeling about something."

The power of foresight has been used in countless different ways by countless different Force users throughout history. Some use it to gain vague images far into the future, while others use it to predict the movements of their foes or see an unexpected event soon to happen.

### BASIC POWER

The most basic form of Foresee allows the character to look into the Force to see vague hints of his near future. These hints may be blurry visual images, brief samples of sound, or simple emotions. The basic power has one way of spending Force points:

- The user may spend ◑ to gain vague hints of events to come in the next day of his own, personal future. The basic power cannot see further than one day.

### UPGRADES

Foresee's upgrades work in two distinct manners. The first set of upgrades serves to further enhance the character's ability to intuit the actions of oth-

## DISTURBANCES IN THE FORCE

Any form of rapid or violent change in the galaxy creates a disturbance in the Force. While death causes the greatest ripples, anything from the birth of a child to galactic cataclysms can trigger these tremors to ripple through the Force like a shockwave. Force users feel these disturbances as a sense of uneasiness or discomfort that suddenly takes hold of them. Though this feeling varies in intensity, no disturbance should be dismissed lightly. They are each a sign of a transformation occurring in the galaxy. It is also through sensing these disturbances that Force users is capable of detecting when he is in the presence of other Force-sensitive objects and beings.

**Magnitude Upgrade:** The user may spend  to affect engaged allies with the power as well as himself. This increases the number of people affected by the number of Magnitude upgrades purchased. The user may activate this multiple times, increasing the number of targets by this number each time.

**Range Upgrade:** The user may spend ◑ to increase the range at which he can affect his allies with this power by a number of range bands equal to the number of Range upgrades purchased. The user may activate this multiple times, increasing the range by this number each time.

**Strength Upgrade:** The Force user can spend ◑ to pick out a number of specific details from his vision equal to the number of Strength upgrades purchased. The user may activate this multiple times, recalling more details each time.

ers in the short term, particularly in combat rounds. Other, more esoteric, advantages of the power allow the Force user to reach further into the future, pulling specific details from events to come.

**Control Upgrade:** When making a skill check to determine Initiative, the user may roll a **Foresee power check** as part of the pool. He may spend ◑ to gain ✵ on his check, and may activate this multiple times.

**Control Upgrade:** When performing a Foresee power check as part of an Initiative check, the user may spend ◑ to allow all affected targets to take one free maneuver before the first round of combat begins. The user may not activate this multiple times.

**Control Upgrade:** When performing a Foresee power check as part of an Initiative check, all targets affected by the power increase their ranged and melee defense by 2 for the first round of combat.

**Duration Upgrade:** The user may spend ◑ to see a number of extra days into the future equal to the number of Duration upgrades purchased. The user may activate this multiple times, increasing the number of days by this number each time.

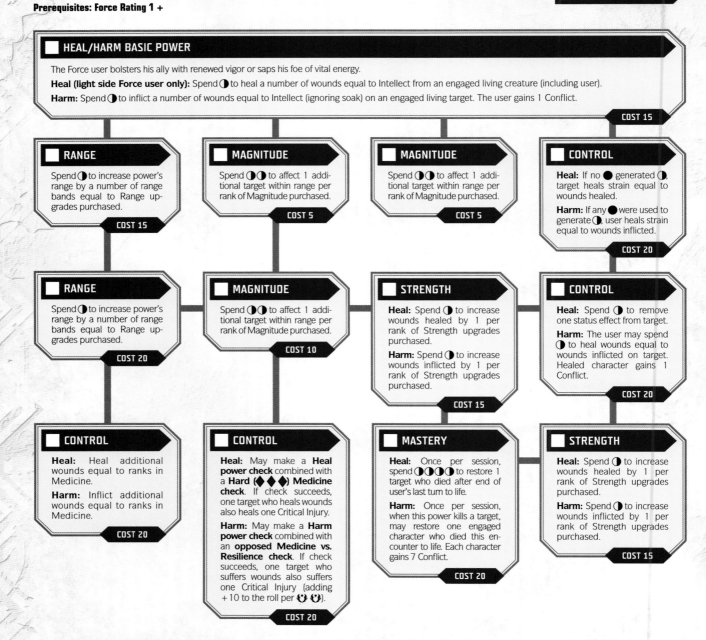

### HEAL/HARM BASIC POWER

The Force user bolsters his ally with renewed vigor or saps his foe of vital energy.

**Heal (light side Force user only):** Spend 🌑 to heal a number of wounds equal to Intellect from an engaged living creature (including user).

**Harm:** Spend 🌓 to inflict a number of wounds equal to Intellect (ignoring soak) on an engaged living target. The user gains 1 Conflict.

**COST 15**

### RANGE

Spend 🌓 to increase power's range by a number of range bands equal to Range upgrades purchased.

**COST 15**

### MAGNITUDE

Spend 🌑🌓 to affect 1 additional target within range per rank of Magnitude purchased.

**COST 5**

### MAGNITUDE

Spend 🌑🌓 to affect 1 additional target within range per rank of Magnitude purchased.

**COST 5**

### CONTROL

**Heal:** If no ⬤ generated 🌓, target heals strain equal to wounds healed.

**Harm:** If any ⬤ were used to generate 🌓, user heals strain equal to wounds inflicted.

**COST 20**

### RANGE

Spend 🌓 to increase power's range by a number of range bands equal to Range upgrades purchased.

**COST 20**

### MAGNITUDE

Spend 🌑🌓 to affect 1 additional target within range per rank of Magnitude purchased.

**COST 10**

### STRENGTH

**Heal:** Spend 🌓 to increase wounds healed by 1 per rank of Strength upgrades purchased.

**Harm:** Spend 🌓 to increase wounds inflicted by 1 per rank of Strength upgrades purchased.

**COST 15**

### CONTROL

**Heal:** Spend 🌓 to remove one status effect from target.

**Harm:** The user may spend 🌓 to heal wounds equal to wounds inflicted on target. Healed character gains 1 Conflict.

**COST 20**

### CONTROL

**Heal:** Heal additional wounds equal to ranks in Medicine.

**Harm:** Inflict additional wounds equal to ranks in Medicine.

**COST 20**

### CONTROL

**Heal:** May make a **Heal power check** combined with a **Hard (◆◆◆) Medicine check**. If check succeeds, one target who heals wounds also heals one Critical Injury.

**Harm:** May make a **Harm power check** combined with an **opposed Medicine vs. Resilience check**. If check succeeds, one target who suffers wounds also suffers one Critical Injury (adding +10 to the roll per 🌀🌀).

**COST 20**

### MASTERY

**Heal:** Once per session, spend 🌑🌑🌑🌑 to restore 1 target who died after end of user's last turn to life.

**Harm:** Once per session, when this power kills a target, may restore one engaged character who died this encounter to life. Each character gains 7 Conflict.

**COST 20**

### STRENGTH

**Heal:** Spend 🌓 to increase wounds healed by 1 per rank of Strength upgrades purchased.

**Harm:** Spend 🌓 to increase wounds inflicted by 1 per rank of Strength upgrades purchased.

**COST 15**

# FORCE POWER: HEAL/HARM

This power reflects a Force user's capacity to manipulate the living energy in things around him. It is the individual's choice, however, whether to use this gift to help others flourish, binding their injuries and making them whole, or to steal their vital essence, ripping the life from them to watch as they wither and die.

## BASIC POWER

Unlike many other Force powers, Heal/Harm has a basic power that can be used in two distinct ways (to heal or to harm). Heal allows the Force user to treat his comrades'

injuries, while Harm lets him drain the life from his foes. When a character purchases the basic power Heal/Harm, he gains access to both Heal and Harm. Each time a character uses the basic power, he must choose whether he is using Heal or Harm, and he receives only the effects associated with his choice. Each upgrade a character purchases improves both Heal and Harm, but some improve each power in a different way.

## HEAL (LIGHT SIDE FORCE USER ONLY)

The basic power for Heal lets a character mend wounds with a simple touch. Heal can only be used by light side Force-sensitive characters. The basic power has one way to spend Force points:

- The user may spend ◗ to heal a number of wounds equal to his Intellect on one engaged living creature (including himself). This counts as a use of a stimpack on the affected target (see page 227). This means a single target may only benefit from five uses of Heal over a twenty-four-hour period, and his uses of Heal also count against the limit on uses of stimpacks (and vice versa). The user may not activate this multiple times.

## HARM

The basic power for Harm lets a character drain the very life from a target with a touch. The basic power has one way to spend Force points:

- The user may spend ◗ to inflict a number of wounds (ignoring soak) equal to the Force user's Intellect on one engaged living creature. The user gains 1 Conflict. The user may not activate this multiple times.

## UPGRADES

**Control Upgrade:** This Control upgrade has different effects for Heal and for Harm.

- **Heal:** The user increases the number of wounds healed by this power by his ranks in Medicine.

- **Harm:** The user increases the number of wounds inflicted by this power by his ranks in Medicine.

**Control Upgrade:** This Control upgrade has different effects for Heal and for Harm.

- **Heal:** If the user used no ● to generate ◗ on the check, the target of Heal also heals an amount of strain equal to the wounds he recovered.

- **Harm:** If the user used any ● to generate ◗ the check, the user heals of an amount of strain equal to the wounds he inflicted on one target.

**Control Upgrade:** This Control upgrade has different effects for Heal and for Harm.

- **Heal:** The user may spend ◗ to immediately remove the staggered, immobilized, or disoriented condition from one target of the power. The user may activate this upgrade multiple times.

- **Harm:** The user may spend ◗ to heal a number of wounds on an engaged living creature (including himself) equal to the damage he inflicted on one target. This counts as a use of a stimpack on the target of the healing (see page 227). The character healed this way gains 1 Conflict. The user may activate this upgrade multiple times, but must select a different target to be healed each time.

**Control Upgrade:** This Control upgrade has different effects for Heal and for Harm.

- **Heal:** When the user is making a **Heal power check**, he may also roll a **Hard (◆◆◆) Medicine check** as part of the pool. If he heals one or more wounds on a target and succeeds on the Medicine check, he may also heal one Critical Injury that target is suffering.

- **Harm:** When the Force user is making a **Harm power check**, he may also roll an **opposed Medicine versus Resilience check** (if the check was not already opposed) as part of the pool. If he inflicts one or more wounds on a target and succeeds on the Medicine check, he may also inflict one Critical Injury on the target and may spend ۞ ۞ to add +10 to the roll (he may spend ۞ ۞ to increase the roll multiple times).

**Magnitude Upgrade:** The Magnitude upgrade improves both Heal and Harm in the same way. Spend ◗◗ to increase the number of targets affected by an amount equal to the number of Magnitude upgrades purchased. The user may activate this multiple times, increasing the number of targets by this number each time.

**Mastery:** The Mastery upgrade has different effects for Heal and for Harm.

- **Heal:** The user may spend ◗◗◗◗ to resuscitate one target of the power who died since the end of the Force user's last turn. Immediately remove the Critical Injury or other effect that killed the target. The Force user can only activate this once per session. Note that in this case, the user is pulling the target back from the brink of death, not actually bringing him back to life.

- **Harm:** When this power kills a sentient living target, the user may restore to life an engaged character who died this encounter. Immediately remove the Critical Injury or other effect that killed the target. The user and the character revived this way each gain 7 Conflict. Note that this Conflict gain is only for the perversion of nature that is returning a soul to its body after its time has come, and not for any associated acts of evil, such as killing an innocent to do it, which may generate additional Conflict (see page 324). The user may only activate this once per session.

**Range Upgrade:** The Range upgrade improves both Heal and Harm in the same way. Spend ◗ to increase the maximum range at which the Force user can affect targets with this power by a number of range bands equal to the number of Range upgrades purchased. The user may activate this multiple times, increasing the range by this number each time.

**Strength Upgrade:** The Strength upgrade has different effects for Heal and for Harm.

- **Heal:** The user may spend ◗ to heal 1 additional wound on the target per rank of Strength purchased. The user may activate this multiple times, increasing the number of wounds healed by this number each time.

- **Harm:** The user may spend ◗ to inflict 1 additional wound per rank of Strength purchased. The user may activate this multiple times, increasing the number of wounds inflicted by this number each time.

# Force Power Tree: Influence
**Prerequisites: Force Rating 1 +**

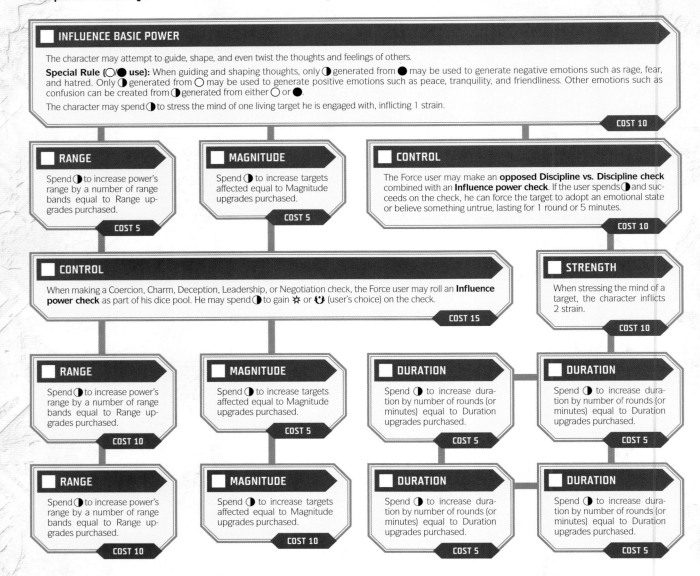

**INFLUENCE BASIC POWER**

The character may attempt to guide, shape, and even twist the thoughts and feelings of others.

**Special Rule (○/● use):** When guiding and shaping thoughts, only ◑ generated from ● may be used to generate negative emotions such as rage, fear, and hatred. Only ◑ generated from ○ may be used to generate positive emotions such as peace, tranquility, and friendliness. Other emotions such as confusion can be created from ◑ generated from either ○ or ●.

The character may spend ◑ to stress the mind of one living target he is engaged with, inflicting 1 strain.

COST 10

**RANGE**

Spend ◑ to increase power's range by a number of range bands equal to Range upgrades purchased.

COST 5

**MAGNITUDE**

Spend ◑ to increase targets affected equal to Magnitude upgrades purchased.

COST 5

**CONTROL**

The Force user may make an **opposed Discipline vs. Discipline check** combined with an **Influence power check**. If the user spends ◑ and succeeds on the check, he can force the target to adopt an emotional state or believe something untrue, lasting for 1 round or 5 minutes.

COST 10

**CONTROL**

When making a Coercion, Charm, Deception, Leadership, or Negotiation check, the Force user may roll an **Influence power check** as part of his dice pool. He may spend ◑ to gain ✸ or 🝔 (user's choice) on the check.

COST 15

**STRENGTH**

When stressing the mind of a target, the character inflicts 2 strain.

COST 10

**RANGE**

Spend ◑ to increase power's range by a number of range bands equal to Range upgrades purchased.

COST 10

**MAGNITUDE**

Spend ◑ to increase targets affected equal to Magnitude upgrades purchased.

COST 5

**DURATION**

Spend ◑ to increase duration by number of rounds (or minutes) equal to Duration upgrades purchased.

COST 5

**DURATION**

Spend ◑ to increase duration by number of rounds (or minutes) equal to Duration upgrades purchased.

COST 5

**RANGE**

Spend ◑ to increase power's range by a number of range bands equal to Range upgrades purchased.

COST 10

**MAGNITUDE**

Spend ◑ to increase targets affected equal to Magnitude upgrades purchased.

COST 10

**DURATION**

Spend ◑ to increase duration by number of rounds (or minutes) equal to Duration upgrades purchased.

COST 5

**DURATION**

Spend ◑ to increase duration by number of rounds (or minutes) equal to Duration upgrades purchased.

COST 5

# FORCE POWER: INFLUENCE

The ability to influence the minds of others is not something to be taken lightly. Misuse of the ability, colloquially known as a "mind trick," is a sure step on the path to the dark side. A powerful Force user can manipulate the minds of others to the point where he can convince them to believe things that are untrue, or calm an angry crowd. Conversely, he can rile the crowd into a murderous frenzy, or frighten a single soul into gibbering madness. This is where the danger of Influence lies.

However, Influence is not inherently evil. Many Force users have used Influence to protect the helpless or to deal with a threat in a way that avoids violence. It is much better to convince a guard to return to his post than to have to kill him.

Influence's most basic and arguably crudest ability allows the user to inflict strain on a living target, stressing his mind until he passes out. However, upgrades allow the Force user who specializes in Influence to perform much more subtle and impressive feats.

## BASIC POWER

The most basic form of Influence does not allow the Force user to guide or shape the thoughts of others. He can merely strain their mind, inflicting stress and exhaustion. The basic power has one effect that can be triggered multiple times on the same or different targets:

- The user spends ◑ to stress the mind of one living target he is engaged with, inflicting 1 strain. The user may activate this multiple times, increasing the strain inflicted by one each time.

When upgrading this power, the user can choose whether to influence and sway large crowds of people with his abilities, or to directly modify the thoughts or emotions of others.

**Control Upgrade:** To gain the ability to alter the thoughts and emotions of a living target with whom he is engaged, the user makes an **opposed Discipline check** against the target as part of the pool to activate the power. The user must spend ◑ *and* he must succeed on the check to force the target to adopt an emotional state such as fear, friendliness, or hatred, or to believe something untrue ("these are not the droids you are looking for"). The effect lasts for roughly five minutes, or one round in combat. If the Force user has the ability to affect multiple minds with this power (such as with the Magnitude upgrade), the Discipline check either must be opposed by the mind with the highest ranks in Discipline, or its difficulty must be set statically based on the number of minds (at the GM's discretion).

**Control Upgrade:** The user gains the ability to enhance his arguments and charisma via the Force. When making a Coercion, Charm, Deception, Leadership, or Negotiation check, the user may roll an **Influence power check** as part of the pool. He may spend ◑ to gain ✬ or ☯ (his choice) per point on the check.

**Strength Upgrade:** When stressing the mind of a target, the Force user inflicts 2 strain instead of 1.

**Duration Upgrade:** The user may spend ◑ to increase the time this effect lasts by a number of minutes or rounds in combat equal to the number of Duration upgrades purchased. The user may activate this multiple times, increasing the duration multiple times.

**Range Upgrade:** The user may spend ◑ to increase the range at which the character can touch minds by a number of range bands equal to the number of Range upgrades purchased. The user may activate this multiple times, increasing the range by this number each time.

## INFLUENCE SPECIAL RULE

When Influence is used to guide and shape thoughts and emotions, checks using ○ to generate ◑ may be used to create negative emotions such as rage, fear, and hatred, but may not be used to evoke positive emotions. Checks using ● to generate ◑ may create positive emotions such as peace, tranquility, and friendliness, but may not be used to generate negative emotions. More neutral emotions such as confusion can be elicited regardless of whether the check used ● or ○ to generate ◑. This rule applies in addition to the rule about using ● or ○ results to generate ◑. This means that to generate negative emotions, the average player aligned with the light side must first roll ○, then flip a Destiny Point and suffer strain to use it to generate at least one ◑ to spend.

**Magnitude Upgrade:** The user may spend ◑ to increase the number of minds being affected equal to the number of Magnitude upgrades purchased. The user may activate this multiple times, increasing the number of targets multiple times.

# Force Power Tree: Misdirect

**Prerequisites: Force Rating 1 +**

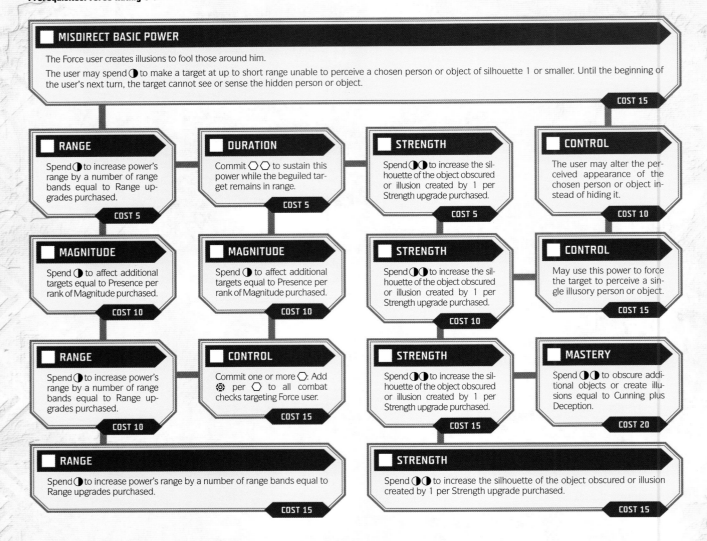

**MISDIRECT BASIC POWER**

The Force user creates illusions to fool those around him.

The user may spend ⬤ to make a target at up to short range unable to perceive a chosen person or object of silhouette 1 or smaller. Until the beginning of the user's next turn, the target cannot see or sense the hidden person or object.

COST 15

**RANGE**

Spend ◗ to increase power's range by a number of range bands equal to Range upgrades purchased.

COST 5

**DURATION**

Commit ◯◯ to sustain this power while the beguiled target remains in range.

COST 5

**STRENGTH**

Spend ◗◗ to increase the silhouette of the object obscured or illusion created by 1 per Strength upgrade purchased.

COST 5

**CONTROL**

The user may alter the perceived appearance of the chosen person or object instead of hiding it.

COST 10

**MAGNITUDE**

Spend ◗ to affect additional targets equal to Presence per rank of Magnitude purchased.

COST 10

**MAGNITUDE**

Spend ◗ to affect additional targets equal to Presence per rank of Magnitude purchased.

COST 10

**STRENGTH**

Spend ◗◗ to increase the silhouette of the object obscured or illusion created by 1 per Strength upgrade purchased.

COST 10

**CONTROL**

May use this power to force the target to perceive a single illusory person or object.

COST 15

**RANGE**

Spend ◗ to increase power's range by a number of range bands equal to Range upgrades purchased.

COST 10

**CONTROL**

Commit one or more ◯: Add ✸ per ◯ to all combat checks targeting Force user.

COST 15

**STRENGTH**

Spend ◗◗ to increase the silhouette of the object obscured or illusion created by 1 per Strength upgrade purchased.

COST 15

**MASTERY**

Spend ◗◗ to obscure additional objects or create illusions equal to Cunning plus Deception.

COST 20

**RANGE**

Spend ◗ to increase power's range by a number of range bands equal to Range upgrades purchased.

COST 15

**STRENGTH**

Spend ◗◗ to increase the silhouette of the object obscured or illusion created by 1 per Strength upgrade purchased.

COST 15

# FORCE POWER: MISDIRECT

Trickery is an important part of many Force users' arsenals, letting them tip the scales of battle in their favor or even avoid some conflicts entirely. Force users versed in shrouding techniques often walk unseen amidst their foes—a particularly useful ability for any Force-sensitive hiding from the Empire. Especially skilled crafters of illusions can even project visions onto those around them, baffling pursuers or terrifying enemies with horrific phantasms.

## BASIC POWER

The Misdirect power allows the user to manipulate the senses of others, beguiling his targets so that he can hide people and objects in plain sight or impose sensory illusions on those targets. The basic power has one way to spend Force points:

- The user may spend ◗ to deceive the senses of a living target at short range or closer. The target does not perceive one object or being of silhouette 1 or lower that is within his line of sight until the beginning of the Force user's next turn. The user may not activate this multiple times.

## UPGRADES

**Control Upgrade:** Instead of merely hiding an object or person from the target with this power, the user may alter the appearance of that object or person, making it appear to be something or someone else to the target.

**Control Upgrade:** Instead of hiding an object or person from the target with this power, the user may cause the target to see a vision of an illusory object, person, or creature where none exists. This phantasm can be silhouette 1 or smaller. To accomplish this, the Force

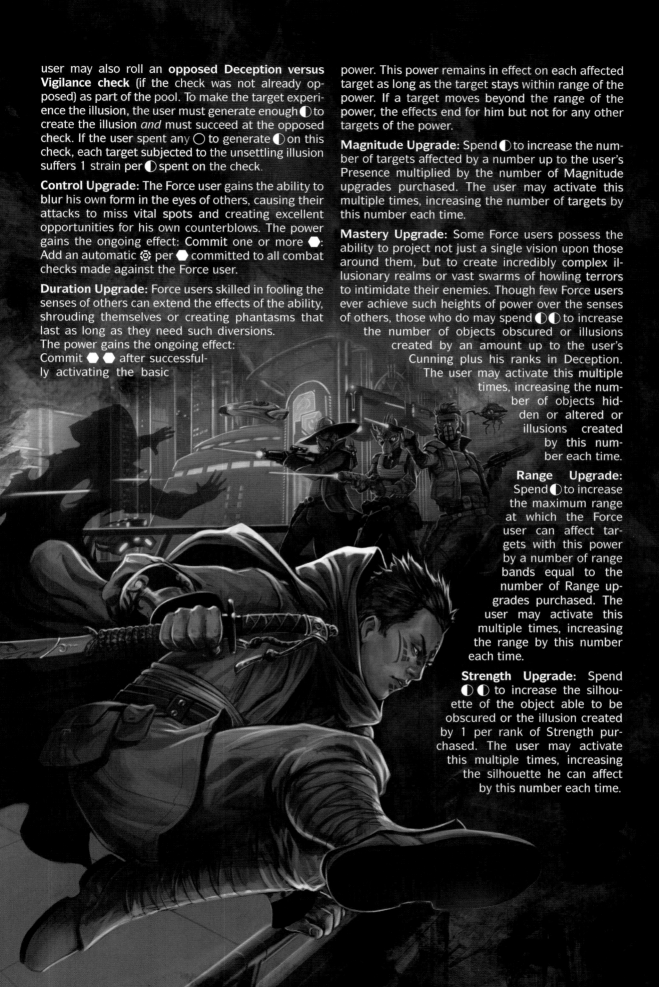

user may also roll an **opposed Deception versus Vigilance check** (if the check was not already opposed) as part of the pool. To make the target experience the illusion, the user must generate enough ◐ to create the illusion *and* must succeed at the opposed check. If the user spent any ○ to generate ◐ on this check, each target subjected to the unsettling illusion suffers 1 strain per ◐ spent on the check.

**Control Upgrade:** The Force user gains the ability to blur his own form in the eyes of others, causing their attacks to miss vital spots and creating excellent opportunities for his own counterblows. The power gains the ongoing effect: Commit one or more ◆: Add an automatic ۞ per ◆ committed to all combat checks made against the Force user.

**Duration Upgrade:** Force users skilled in fooling the senses of others can extend the effects of the ability, shrouding themselves or creating phantasms that last as long as they need such diversions. The power gains the ongoing effect: Commit ◆ ◆ after successfully activating the basic

power. This power remains in effect on each affected target as long as the target stays within range of the power. If a target moves beyond the range of the power, the effects end for him but not for any other targets of the power.

**Magnitude Upgrade:** Spend ◐ to increase the number of targets affected by a number up to the user's Presence multiplied by the number of Magnitude upgrades purchased. The user may activate this multiple times, increasing the number of targets by this number each time.

**Mastery Upgrade:** Some Force users possess the ability to project not just a single vision upon those around them, but to create incredibly complex illusionary realms or vast swarms of howling terrors to intimidate their enemies. Though few Force users ever achieve such heights of power over the senses of others, those who do may spend ◐◐ to increase the number of objects obscured or illusions created by an amount up to the user's Cunning plus his ranks in Deception. The user may activate this multiple times, increasing the number of objects hidden or altered or illusions created by this number each time.

**Range Upgrade:** Spend ◐ to increase the maximum range at which the Force user can affect targets with this power by a number of range bands equal to the number of Range upgrades purchased. The user may activate this multiple times, increasing the range by this number each time.

**Strength Upgrade:** Spend ◐ ◐ to increase the silhouette of the object able to be obscured or the illusion created by 1 per rank of Strength purchased. The user may activate this multiple times, increasing the silhouette he can affect by this number each time.

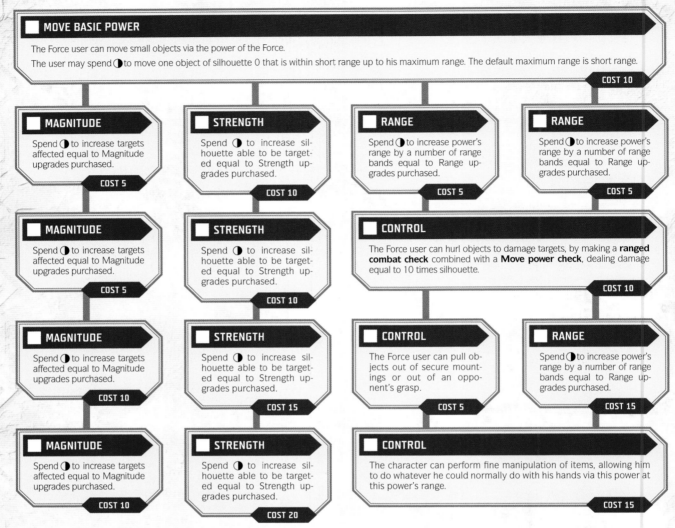

## MOVE BASIC POWER

The Force user can move small objects via the power of the Force.

The user may spend ◑ to move one object of silhouette 0 that is within short range up to his maximum range. The default maximum range is short range.

**COST 10**

### MAGNITUDE
Spend ◑ to increase targets affected equal to Magnitude upgrades purchased.
**COST 5**

### STRENGTH
Spend ◑ to increase silhouette able to be targeted equal to Strength upgrades purchased.
**COST 10**

### RANGE
Spend ◑ to increase power's range by a number of range bands equal to Range upgrades purchased.
**COST 5**

### RANGE
Spend ◑ to increase power's range by a number of range bands equal to Range upgrades purchased.
**COST 5**

### MAGNITUDE
Spend ◑ to increase targets affected equal to Magnitude upgrades purchased.
**COST 5**

### STRENGTH
Spend ◑ to increase silhouette able to be targeted equal to Strength upgrades purchased.
**COST 10**

### CONTROL
The Force user can hurl objects to damage targets, by making a **ranged combat check** combined with a **Move power check**, dealing damage equal to 10 times silhouette.
**COST 10**

### MAGNITUDE
Spend ◑ to increase targets affected equal to Magnitude upgrades purchased.
**COST 10**

### STRENGTH
Spend ◑ to increase silhouette able to be targeted equal to Strength upgrades purchased.
**COST 15**

### CONTROL
The Force user can pull objects out of secure mountings or out of an opponent's grasp.
**COST 5**

### RANGE
Spend ◑ to increase power's range by a number of range bands equal to Range upgrades purchased.
**COST 15**

### MAGNITUDE
Spend ◑ to increase targets affected equal to Magnitude upgrades purchased.
**COST 10**

### STRENGTH
Spend ◑ to increase silhouette able to be targeted equal to Strength upgrades purchased.
**COST 20**

### CONTROL
The character can perform fine manipulation of items, allowing him to do whatever he could normally do with his hands via this power at this power's range.
**COST 15**

# FORCE POWER: MOVE

Many Force users develop the ability to shift objects without physically handling them, moving matter with the power of the mind. Those with a modicum of training in the skill can cause small objects to slowly and painstakingly rise, fall, or travel in space. True masters of the Force are rumored to be able to hurl starships about or juggle heavy crates in the air. Other applications of the power allow for Force users to manipulate control panels or computer keyboards at a distance. There is thought to be no limit to what a Force user could move with the application of enough concentration.

When moving items, the default speed is slow and deliberate, not fast enough to inflict injury or accurate enough to allow for fine manipulation.

### BASIC POWER

At its most basic, Move allows the Force user to move small objects that are near him. It has one basic effect:

- The user may spend ◑ to move one object of silhouette 0 that is within short range up to his maximum range. The default maximum range is short range. The user may not activate this multiple times.

### UPGRADES

Move's upgrades include the ability to move a larger number of objects at once, to move increasingly large objects, and to move objects over greater distances. Some upgrades give the Force user different ways to use the power, though most are cumulative improvements to the abilities described by the basic power.

**Control Upgrade:** The user gains the ability to move objects fast enough so as to be both difficult to dodge and capable of inflicting damage. Resulting impacts deal damage to both the target and the object being moved. The user makes a Force power check and rolls a ranged attack (using the Discipline skill) as part of the pool. The attack's difficulty is equal to the silhouette of the object being thrown instead of the normal only succeeds if the user can also spend enough ◐ to move the object. Silhouette 0 objects deal 5 damage, while other objects deal damage equal to ten times their silhouette. The number of targets affected by a single object is up to the GM, but in general, a single object should only affect a single target, unless the object is particularly large. If the player wants to use multiple objects to hit multiple targets, he may do so by using the rules for hitting multiple targets with the Auto-fire quality. This attack follows all the rules for ranged attacks, including ranged defense and aiming.

**Control Upgrade:** The user gains the ability to pull objects off secure mountings or from an opponent's grasp.

**Control Upgrade:** The user gains the ability to perform fine manipulation of items, allowing him to do whatever he could normally do with his hands to a held item. If this power is used to manipulate something such as a control board, the controls count as an object of silhouette 0.

**Magnitude Upgrade:** Spend ◐ to increase the number of targets affected by an amount equal to the number of Magnitude upgrades purchased. The user may activate this multiple times, increasing the number of targets by this number each time. However, remember that the user must still spend Force points to activate the power's actual effects.

## MOVING AND DURATION

As written, the Move power does not have a set duration. This is intentional. During narrative gameplay, the duration can be as long as it needs to be; in general, users will be moving items from one point to another. If they do need to keep an item suspended for a short period of time, that's perfectly acceptable and does not require a second check. Of course, if they do need to keep an item suspended for a long period of time (more than several minutes), the GM can decide to require a second check, or start inflicting strain as the Force user attempts to maintain the power.

The same holds true for durations during encounters. Generally, Force users suspend items for a single round when they use the Move power. If they wish to lift an item for multiple rounds, the GM could treat that as an ongoing effect, requiring the Force user to commit ⬡ to maintain the power. For particularly large items (silhouette 2 or larger, for example), the GM can also inflict strain equal to the silhouette each round the Force user maintains the power. However, this is up to the GM, based on the circumstances of the encounter.

**Range Upgrade:** Spend ◐ to increase the maximum range at which the user can move objects by a number of range bands equal to the number of Range upgrades purchased. The user may activate this multiple times, increasing the range by this number each time. However, remember the user must still spend Force points to activate the power's actual effects.

**Strength Upgrade:** Spend ◐ to increase the maximum silhouette of objects a character can move by a number equal to the number of Strength upgrades purchased. The user may activate this multiple times, increasing the silhouette of the objects he can move by this number each time.

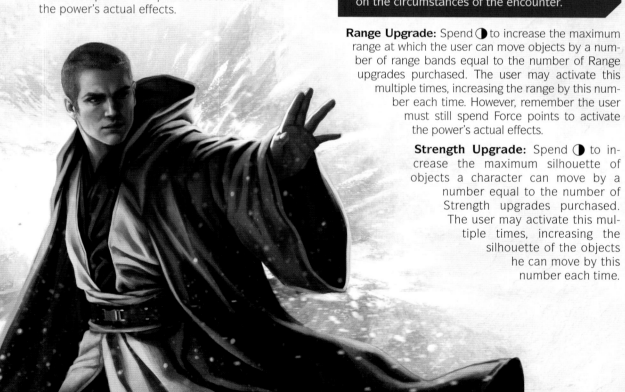

**Prerequisites: Force Rating 3 +**

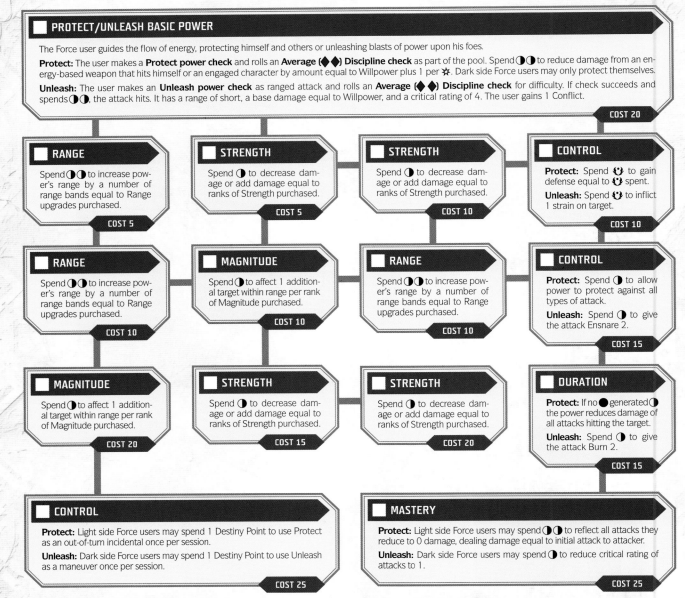

### PROTECT/UNLEASH BASIC POWER

The Force user guides the flow of energy, protecting himself and others or unleashing blasts of power upon his foes.

**Protect:** The user makes a **Protect power check** and rolls an **Average (◆◆) Discipline check** as part of the pool. Spend ○○ to reduce damage from an energy-based weapon that hits himself or an engaged character by amount equal to Willpower plus 1 per ✦. Dark side Force users may only protect themselves.

**Unleash:** The user makes an **Unleash power check** as ranged attack and rolls an **Average (◆◆) Discipline check** for difficulty. If check succeeds and spends ○○, the attack hits. It has a range of short, a base damage equal to Willpower, and a critical rating of 4. The user gains 1 Conflict.

COST 20

### RANGE
Spend ○○ to increase power's range by a number of range bands equal to Range upgrades purchased.

COST 5

### STRENGTH
Spend ○ to decrease damage or add damage equal to ranks of Strength purchased.

COST 5

### STRENGTH
Spend ○ to decrease damage or add damage equal to ranks of Strength purchased.

COST 10

### CONTROL
**Protect:** Spend 🜨 to gain defense equal to 🜨 spent.

**Unleash:** Spend 🜨 to inflict 1 strain on target.

COST 10

### RANGE
Spend ○○ to increase power's range by a number of range bands equal to Range upgrades purchased.

COST 10

### MAGNITUDE
Spend ○ to affect 1 additional target within range per rank of Magnitude purchased.

COST 10

### RANGE
Spend ○○ to increase power's range by a number of range bands equal to Range upgrades purchased.

COST 10

### CONTROL
**Protect:** Spend ○ to allow power to protect against all types of attack.

**Unleash:** Spend ○ to give the attack Ensnare 2.

COST 15

### MAGNITUDE
Spend ○ to affect 1 additional target within range per rank of Magnitude purchased.

COST 20

### STRENGTH
Spend ○ to decrease damage or add damage equal to ranks of Strength purchased.

COST 15

### STRENGTH
Spend ○ to decrease damage or add damage equal to ranks of Strength purchased.

COST 20

### DURATION
**Protect:** If no ● generated ○ the power reduces damage of all attacks hitting the target.

**Unleash:** Spend ○ to give the attack Burn 2.

COST 15

### CONTROL
**Protect:** Light side Force users may spend 1 Destiny Point to use Protect as an out-of-turn incidental once per session.

**Unleash:** Dark side Force users may spend 1 Destiny Point to use Unleash as a maneuver once per session.

COST 25

### MASTERY
**Protect:** Light side Force users may spend ○○ to reflect all attacks they reduce to 0 damage, dealing damage equal to initial attack to attacker.

**Unleash:** Dark side Force users may spend ○ to reduce critical rating of attacks to 1.

COST 25

# FORCE POWER: PROTECT/UNLEASH

Force users can harness the innate abilities of the Force to protect themselves and others from harm. However, that same power can be turned to terrible ends when the user infuses himself with the dark side. Dark siders can shoot lightning from their fingertips or envelop their targets in withering, murderous cold.

### BASIC POWER

Unlike many other Force powers, Protect/Unleash has a basic power that can be used in two very different ways. A character who purchases the basic power Protect/

Unleash gains access to both Protect and Unleash. Each time a character uses the basic power, he must choose whether to use Protect or Unleash and receives only the effects associated with that choice. Each upgrade a character purchases improves both Protect and Unleash, but some improve each power in a different way.

### PROTECT

The basic power for Protect lets a Force user shield himself or an ally against oncoming energy attacks. A dark side Force user cannot use Protect to defend allies (he can only use it to protect himself). The basic power has one way to spend Force points:

- The user chooses himself or one ally he is currently engaged with and makes a **Protect power check**, and rolls an **Average (◆ ◆) Discipline check** as part of the pool. To raise this Force barrier, he must spend ◑ ◑ to activate the power and he must succeed on the Discipline check. Once the power is activated, if the target of the power suffers a hit from a blaster shot, Force power, lightsaber, or other energy attack before the beginning of the user's next turn, the character may reduce damage by an amount equal to his Willpower characteristic plus the number of ✹ scored on the Discipline check. The power may only reduce damage from one hit during its duration. Dark side Force users may only protect themselves with Protect. The user may not activate this multiple times.

## UNLEASH

The basic power for Unleash lets a character blast an enemy with a surge of manifest emotion. The basic power has one way to spend Force points:

- The Force user makes a **Unleash power check** and rolls a ranged attack as part of the pool. The attack uses an **Average (◆ ◆) Discipline check** instead of the normal difficulty for ranged attacks, and only succeeds if the user also spends ◑ ◑. The attack has a range of short, a base damage equal to the user's Willpower, and a critical rating of 4. The user gains 1 Conflict. The user may not activate this multiple times.

## UPGRADES

**Control Upgrade:** This Control upgrade has different effects for Protect and for Unleash.

- **Protect:** The user may spend ۞ to gain ranged and melee defense equal to the ۞ spent until the beginning of his next turn.

- **Unleash:** The user may spend ۞ on his Discipline check to inflict 1 strain on the target (ignoring soak).

**Control Upgrade:** This Control upgrade has different effects for Protect and for Unleash.

- **Protect:** The user may spend ◑ to have the barrier protect against all types of attacks instead of only projecting against energy attacks. The user may not activate this multiple times.

- **Unleash:** The user may spend ◑ to have the attack gain the Ensnare 2 quality. The user may not activate this multiple times.

**Control Upgrade:** This Control upgrade has different effects for Protect and for Unleash.

- **Protect:** If he is a light side Force user, then once per game session, the user may spend a Destiny Point to use Protect as an out-of-turn incidental.

- **Unleash:** If he is a dark side Force user, then once per game session, the Force user may spend a Destiny Point to use Unleash as a maneuver.

**Duration Upgrade:** The Duration upgrade has different effects for Protect and for Unleash.

- **Protect:** If no ● were used to generate ◑, the Force barrier protecting the user's target shields against all energy attacks the target would otherwise suffer before the beginning of the user's next turn (instead of just the next energy attack).

- **Unleash:** The user may spend ◑ to give the attack the Burn 2 quality. The user may not activate this multiple times.

**Magnitude Upgrade:** The Magnitude upgrade has different effects for Protect and for Unleash.

- **Protect:** The user may spend ◑ to increase the number of targets affected by the power by an amount equal to the number of Magnitude upgrades purchased. The Force user may still only reduce damage from one hit among all affected targets. The user may activate this multiple times, increasing the number of targets by this number each time.

- **Unleash:** The user may spend ◑ to inflict one additional hit on a number of targets engaged with the original target equal to the number of Magnitude upgrades purchased. These hits deal the same damage as the initial hit. The user may activate this multiple times, increasing the number of additional hits by this number each time. Each target may only be hit once.

**Mastery:** The Mastery upgrade has different effects for Protect and for Unleash.

- **Protect:** This upgrade represents gaining the clarity of mind required to let energy and aggression flow harmlessly through the Force user and back to his attackers. A light side Force user may spend ◑ to reflect all attacks that would be reduced to 0 damage (before soak) by this power back upon their sources. Each attack reflected this way hits the attacker for the amount of damage it would have dealt to the user (before the reduction for Protect).

- **Unleash:** This upgrade represents mastering the ultimate dark side technique, the dreaded Force lightning. If the user is a dark side Force user, he may spend ◑ to reduce the attack's critical rating to 1.

**Range Upgrade:** The Range upgrade improves both Protect and Unleash in the same way. Spend ◑ ◑ to increase the maximum range at which the Force user can affect targets with this power by a number of range bands equal to the number of Range upgrades purchased. The user may activate this multiple times, increasing the range by this number each time.

**Strength Upgrade:** The Strength upgrade improves both Protect and Unleash. Spend ◑ to increase the damage reduced by Protect by 1 per Strength upgrade for this use, or spend ◑ to add 1 damage per Strength upgrade to the base damage of Unleash for this attack. The user may activate this multiple times.

# Force Power Tree: Seek

**Prerequisites: Force Rating 1 +**

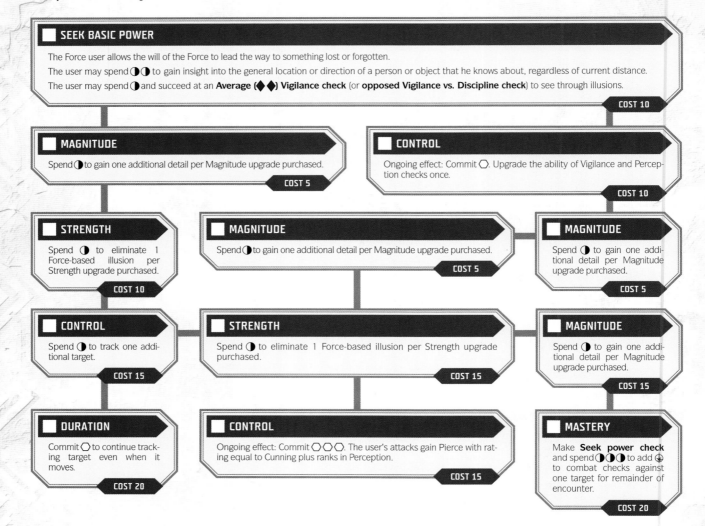

**SEEK BASIC POWER**

The Force user allows the will of the Force to lead the way to something lost or forgotten.

The user may spend ◐◐ to gain insight into the general location or direction of a person or object that he knows about, regardless of current distance.

The user may spend ◐ and succeed at an **Average (◆◆) Vigilance check** (or **opposed Vigilance vs. Discipline check**) to see through illusions.

COST 10

**MAGNITUDE**

Spend ◐ to gain one additional detail per Magnitude upgrade purchased.

COST 5

**CONTROL**

Ongoing effect: Commit ◯. Upgrade the ability of Vigilance and Perception checks once.

COST 10

**STRENGTH**

Spend ◐ to eliminate 1 Force-based illusion per Strength upgrade purchased.

COST 10

**MAGNITUDE**

Spend ◐ to gain one additional detail per Magnitude upgrade purchased.

COST 5

**MAGNITUDE**

Spend ◐ to gain one additional detail per Magnitude upgrade purchased.

COST 5

**CONTROL**

Spend ◐ to track one additional target.

COST 15

**STRENGTH**

Spend ◐ to eliminate 1 Force-based illusion per Strength upgrade purchased.

COST 15

**MAGNITUDE**

Spend ◐ to gain one additional detail per Magnitude upgrade purchased.

COST 15

**DURATION**

Commit ◯ to continue tracking target even when it moves.

COST 20

**CONTROL**

Ongoing effect: Commit ◯◯◯. The user's attacks gain Pierce with rating equal to Cunning plus ranks in Perception.

COST 15

**MASTERY**

Make **Seek power check** and spend ◐◐◐ to add ✦ to combat checks against one target for remainder of encounter.

COST 20

# FORCE POWER: SEEK

The Force user casts out with his mind's eye, searching for something lost, concealed, or forgotten. While countless different Force traditions across the galaxy have attached different practices and techniques to this power, from tribal cultures that use it to hunt prey-beasts to orders of assassins who seek out any who defy their orthodoxy, the basic ability remains the same: those who follow pathways of the Force can track down anything or anyone, regardless of the distance or eons that separate them from their quarry.

### BASIC POWER

Seek's basic power allows Force users to find faraway things and to shatter sensory tricks that might hide their quarry. The basic power has two ways to spend Force points:

- The user may spend ◐◐ to gain insight into the general location or direction of a person or object that he knows about, regardless of its current distance from him. The user may not activate this multiple times.

- The user may make an **Average (◆◆) Vigilance check** with the power check to see through all sensory misdirections confronting him, whether these come from technology or more esoteric sources. This power works against tricks such as cloaking fields, holograms, Force illusions, and even physical disguises, at the GM's discretion, but has no direct effect on spoken or written lies. To successfully see past the deception, the character must spend ◐ to activate the power *and* must succeed on the **Average (◆◆) Vigilance check** (or **opposed Vigilance versus Discipline check** if illusions are being created by another Force user). If the user succeeds, his supernatural senses pierce the falsehoods, letting him perceive the truth they conceal.

## UPGRADES

**Control Upgrade:** Spend ◗ to track up to one additional target when using this power. The user can activate this multiple times.

**Control Upgrade:** The Force user becomes increasingly attuned to the subtle cues in the world around him and is capable of sharpening his mind-senses to cut through all distractions that might conceal important details. The power gains the ongoing effect: Commit ◯. Upgrade the ability of all Perception and Vigilance checks the user makes once. The user may not activate this multiple times.

**Control Upgrade:** As it encompasses the lives of all things, so too does the Force contain the secrets of all ends. From time to time, a particularly perceptive Force user can spot these fault lines in the universe and, in doing so, uncover a unique opportunity or even an opponent's fatal flaw. To a Force user who has honed such an ability, all vulnerabilities and cracks in even the thickest armor are laid bare. The power gains the ongoing effect: Commit ◯ ◯ ◯. The user's attacks gain Pierce with a rating equal to the user's Cunning plus ranks in Perception (or increases existing Pierce rating by the same amount).

**Duration Upgrade:** The power gains the ongoing effect: Commit ◯ after successfully activating the basic power to find the direction of a person or object. Whenever the person or object moves, the Force user becomes aware of this movement and of the person or object's new general location or the direction he must follow to reach it.

**Magnitude Upgrade:** Spend ◗ to gain one additional helpful detail per rank of Magnitude about the location, direction, or path of the target when using the basic power to search for it. These details can include short flashes of phenomena including sights, sounds, smells, landmarks, or even brief visions, as determined by the GM. For instance, if the basic power reveals that the user's quarry was headed in the direction of the Yavin system, the GM might have this upgrade provide the user with an image of light falling through the leaves of large trees—giving the user an important hint as to which planet (or moon) in that system the target has chosen as a hiding place. The user can activate this multiple times.

**Mastery Upgrade:** The Force user scans the target with his mind, following the flow of energy to the flaw that will be the enemy's undoing. The Force user makes a Force check as an action and chooses an enemy he can perceive. If he spends at least ◗ ◗ ◗, the user adds one automatic ✷ to each combat check he makes against the target until the end of the encounter. The user may not activate this multiple times.

**Strength Upgrade:** Spend ◗ to completely eliminate one Force-based illusion per rank of Strength purchased instead of merely seeing through it when using the basic power. Force illusions banished this way stop working against all targets they previously affected and vanish like mist in the sun. The user can activate this multiple times.

# Force Power Tree: Sense

Prerequisites: Force Rating 1 +

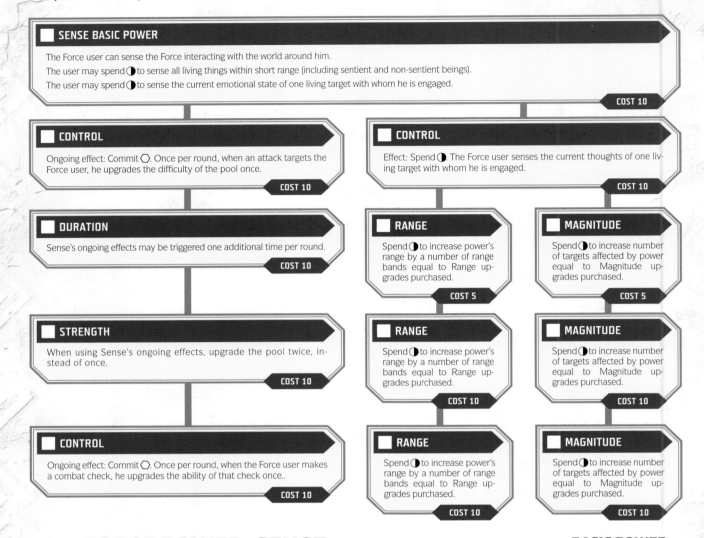

**SENSE BASIC POWER**

The Force user can sense the Force interacting with the world around him.

The user may spend ◐ to sense all living things within short range (including sentient and non-sentient beings).

The user may spend ◐ to sense the current emotional state of one living target with whom he is engaged.

COST 10

**CONTROL**

Ongoing effect: Commit ◯. Once per round, when an attack targets the Force user, he upgrades the difficulty of the pool once.

COST 10

**CONTROL**

Effect: Spend ◐. The Force user senses the current thoughts of one living target with whom he is engaged.

COST 10

**DURATION**

Sense's ongoing effects may be triggered one additional time per round.

COST 10

**RANGE**

Spend ◐ to increase power's range by a number of range bands equal to Range upgrades purchased.

COST 5

**MAGNITUDE**

Spend ◐ to increase number of targets affected by power equal to Magnitude upgrades purchased.

COST 5

**STRENGTH**

When using Sense's ongoing effects, upgrade the pool twice, instead of once.

COST 10

**RANGE**

Spend ◐ to increase power's range by a number of range bands equal to Range upgrades purchased.

COST 10

**MAGNITUDE**

Spend ◐ to increase number of targets affected by power equal to Magnitude upgrades purchased.

COST 10

**CONTROL**

Ongoing effect: Commit ◯. Once per round, when the Force user makes a combat check, he upgrades the ability of that check once..

COST 10

**RANGE**

Spend ◐ to increase power's range by a number of range bands equal to Range upgrades purchased.

COST 10

**MAGNITUDE**

Spend ◐ to increase number of targets affected by power equal to Magnitude upgrades purchased.

COST 10

## FORCE POWER: SENSE

By opening his mind, a Force user can commune with the world around him. He senses the endless movement of the Living Force, seeing beyond what his eyes allow. The actions of those around him are laid bare, as if the Force user had a bird's eye view of his surroundings, allowing him to anticipate attacks and better strike blows of his own, or even spot ambushes and lurking foes. Alternatively, he can sense the thoughts of others. Even a Jedi cannot read someone's mind completely, but a Force-sensitive being can detect his target's feelings and emotions, and even sense surface thoughts.

Unlike many other Force powers, Sense has a basic power that can be used in two very different ways. Users can rely on Sense to augment their defensive (and eventually offensive) abilities, or they can invest in the ability to read the emotions and feelings of others. They can even read their surface thoughts, which can be particularly valuable in a wide variety of situations.

### BASIC POWER

Sense's basic power allows the Force user to sense the living Force interacting with the world around him. This allows him to perceive life and read emotions. The basic power has two ways to spend Force points:

- The user may spend ◐ to sense all living things within short range of himself (including animals and sentient beings). The user may not activate this multiple times.

- The user may spend ◐ to sense the current emotional state of one living target with whom he is engaged. The user may not activate this multiple times.

### UPGRADES

Sense's upgrades are split into two groups: those that allow the Force user to protect himself from danger and augment his attacks, and those that allow him to detect the thoughts of others.

# USING SENSE IN THE GAME

**S**ense can be an extremely potent ability in a game. Arguably, it has the most potential to derail a game, as it can put the GM in the situation of being forced to divulge crucial information that can seriously undermine the tension of an adventure. Reading the thoughts of an opponent can reveal critical facts, such as the location of a hideout or his plans to double-cross the Player Characters at a later date. At the same time, however, the GM should not simply deny this information to the character. Thus, the GM has to walk a fine line between revealing relevant information and revealing too much information. When using this power, both players and GMs should keep the following guidelines in mind:

- Some species (and some individuals with particularly strong minds) are more resistant to powers such as Sense than others.

- Some species are completely immune.

- Sense does not work on communications over long distances.

- Sense allows a Force user to read only the emotional state and surface thoughts of a target. This means that characters can only obtain an imperfect snapshot of another's mind and cannot simply call up any specific piece of information they want on demand.

Overall, the GM should endeavor to allow PCs to use Sense to learn valuable information they would not normally know. However, this information should not allow them to automatically succeed in their goals, but instead provide a valuable clue or insight as they proceed. Simply put, it should help them with their work, but not do their work for them.

**Control Upgrade:** The user gains the ability to sense danger the moment before it strikes, allowing him to anticipate attacks and avoid incoming blows. This power gains the ongoing effect: Commit ◯. Once per round, when an attack targets the Force user, he upgrades the difficulty of the pool once. The user may not activate this multiple times.

**Control Upgrade:** The Force user's ability to anticipate danger allows him to anticipate the actions of his opponents while he takes the offensive, making his own blows harder to avoid. This power gains the ongoing effect: Commit ◯. Once per round, when the Force user makes a combat check, he upgrades the ability of the pool once. The user may not activate this multiple times.

**Control Upgrade:** The user gains the ability to detect the surface thoughts of the target. This power gains the effect: Spend ◑. The user senses the current thoughts of one living target with whom he is engaged. The user may activate this multiple times.

**Duration Upgrade:** Sense's ongoing effects may be triggered one additional time per round.

**Magnitude Upgrade:** Spend ◑ to increase the number of targets affected by the number of Magnitude upgrades purchased. The user may activate this multiple times, increasing the number of targets by this number each time.

**Range Upgrade:** Spend ◑ to increase the range at which the character senses living things by a number of range bands equal to the number of Range upgrades purchased. The user may activate this multiple times, increasing the range by this number each time.

**Strength Upgrade:** When using Sense's ongoing effects, the user may upgrade one additional die.

# IX

# THE GAME MASTER

*"What's in there?"*

*"Only what you take with you."*

–Luke Skywalker and Master Yoda

**W**elcome to the first step in becoming a **Force and Destiny** Game Master. Running a roleplaying game is fun and rewarding in ways that are different from playing an individual character. This chapter gives new and experienced Game Masters the tools needed to rise to the challenge and become accomplished and entertaining *Star Wars* GMs.

For Game Masters, it is fun to see the players engage in a story and make it their own. One Player Character mind-tricks a guard into letting his friends into a secure landing bay, while another uses the Force to shove a shuttle into the path of oncoming stormtroopers. Suddenly, all of them sense a disturbance in the Force just as an Inquisitor enters the bay with his red lightsaber ignited and ready. Now what do they do? Escaping the station was their plan, and retreat is the wiser move. Instead, the PCs draw their lightsabers and charge their hated enemy. Now what does the GM do? Smile at their bravado and think fast.

The Game Master has many responsibilities in a game session. He creates the overall storyline for the adventure. He interacts constantly with the players,

describing the details their characters need to understand the situation. The GM plays the part of everyone the characters meet and describes everywhere they go. He must think on his feet and be ready to improvise at any moment. The GM interprets the game rules in a fair and consistent manner.

This sounds like a lot, but fortunately, the GM need not be perfect in every respect. The GM's primary goal is to create an entertaining and memorable game. Running a roleplaying game for friends doesn't have to be like refereeing a sports event. When an unexpected situation requires a ruling on a game mechanic, it is best to make a quick judgment call and assess the results later. GM and player cooperation creates the best environment for an entertaining game.

This chapter focuses on the Game Master's role in the game. The first section introduces the practical aspects of running a game session, including character creation, player interaction, and experience points. The second section discusses adjudicating specific rules and options such as Morality and fear. The final section covers creating adventures and campaigns.

# HOW TO RUN A FORCE AND DESTINY GAME

Running a **FORCE AND DESTINY** game session requires players, planning, rules knowledge, and an interest in creating a great deal of fun. This section guides new and experienced Game Masters through a typical game, from the first game session onward. The first several sections, from **Recruiting Players** through **Continuing the Story**, are intended for beginner GMs. The advice in the remaining sections is intended for GMs with a session or two of experience and can be safely skipped by GMs preparing for their first game.

## RECRUITING PLAYERS

First and foremost, the game needs players. The GM should look first to his circle of friends. It's okay if they have never played a roleplaying game before. Thanks to the popularity of the *Star Wars* movies, it's likely they already have a basic understanding of the setting. This enables them to understand the overall motivations, locations, and major events much more quickly than they might in a standalone roleplaying game setting. Players may also be recruited from a local game club, game store, convention, or appropriate online gaming organization. The same holds true for players seeking a GM.

For the first session and short adventures, player chemistry is less important than in prolonged campaigns. However, GMs and players should try to recruit others with whom they get along and who mesh well together. It's helpful if they enjoy similar play styles and have similar expectations about the game and how it will be played. If the GM is running his first game, he should tell the other players. They'll be more forgiving while the GM learns the system. If they themselves are Game Masters, they may be able to give the new GM advice along the way.

## PREPARING TO RUN THE FIRST SESSION

Game preparation is one of the GM's key duties. Detailed advice is provided later in this chapter. For now, read the rules. The GM doesn't need to memorize all of them or understand all of their intricacies for the first game session. His familiarity with the rules will grow with every game he runs. Focus on character creation rules, as this is the first contact most players will have with the game mechanics. They will usually look to the GM for guidance.

The GM should start with **Chapter I: Playing the Game** for an overview of the core game mechanics.

In **Chapter II: Character Creation**, the GM should focus on the character creation rules, but does not need to read the descriptions of every single talent and piece of equipment (or the associated chapters in detail, initially). The GM should understand the basics of combat. Knowing the rules for Force usage is a must, given the focus of this game.

In preparing for the first game, the GM should learn the basic combat rules—attacks, movement, damage, and healing. Combat is likely in each game session. One of the GM's primary responsibilities is to play the part of all the adversaries, enemies, allies, and bystanders during the fight. Though the GM battles the Player Characters tactically, he is not their enemy. He must roleplay the combatants, making their tactical decisions based on what each one knows about the situation and what their goals are. While there are plenty of scenes where the bad guys will stop at nothing to eliminate the good guys, this isn't always the case. There are plenty of other entertaining ways to end a scene without necessarily killing everyone on one side.

Next, read the adventure. For the first game, using a published adventure, such as **Lessons from the Past**, found on page 423, is highly recommended. Using a published adventure allows the novice GM to focus on learning how to run the game without the pressure of creating a good plot line from scratch. The GM should highlight or jot down reminders about important plot points. Adventure and campaign creation is covered later in this chapter.

The GM should review any specific or unusual rules used in the adventure. He should take notes regarding their use, along with page numbers for quick reference. This helps to speed play. Everyone learns the

## FUN FIRST, RULES SECOND!

Always remember that everyone at the table is there to have a good time. Adjudicating the rules is important, but secondary to this goal. Don't let a rules question or interpretation derail the fun. Everyone wants to create a great tale with some wild moments. While the GM has primary control over the planned storyline, he should not overlook player ideas and actions for great, if unpredictable, results. If the GM and the players are enjoying the game, everyone is on the right track!

## DICE ETIQUETTE AND PROTOCOL

**D**ice rolling is central to playing FORCE AND DESTINY. The custom dice used in this game go beyond simply indicating success or failure. The GM and players use the results of the dice pool to inform the story.

Players should always roll the dice where everyone can see the results. While this prevents players from cheating, it also allows the GM to see the die symbol results. Not every roll needs creative interpretation, but it is fun and a helpful story guide. See **Interpreting the Dice Pool**, on page 316.

The GM normally rolls his dice in the open. Like the players' rolls, the GM's results are open to interpretation. More importantly, the players have ways to influence the dice pool, and therefore need to see it most of the time.

There are times where the GM may want to conceal the results. Occasionally, an adversary will try something that may affect the Player Characters, but they would only become aware of it if the roll doesn't go the adversary's way. In this case, the GM probably doesn't want to tip the adversary's hand by revealing the results.

Rolling dice in private affects the game in several ways. If the GM always conceals the roll, the players cannot influence rolls as the system expects. Often, GMs interpret rolls in the name of providing a better game experience for everyone at the table. This usually occurs when a Player Character faces death, or if one side suffers a string of poor results or other bad luck. This type of interpretation is allowed, built into, and expected in the FORCE AND DESTINY narrative dice system, making it much easier to roll in the open.

However, the GM should avoid fudging too many results. It detracts from gameplay and the players' sense of achievement. If they believe their successes and failure come only at the whim of the GM, they quickly lose interest in playing.

game more quickly by playing, so playing in a session run by another GM can improve practical application of the rules. It might also help the GM form ideas for how he may or may not want to run his own sessions.

The GM also prepares anything else needed at the table, such as maps or player handouts. The table itself should be big enough for everyone to have space to write and roll dice, with room in the center if the GM plans to use a map. It is always a good idea to have extra dice and blank character sheets around. The GM should consider creating a couple of Player Characters prior to play. These can be used by players who don't have one, don't want to create one, or arrive late. Extra characters can always be used as NPCs, if needed.

## CHARACTER CREATION

The GM should help the players create their characters. Before beginning, the GM needs to convey the type of story he anticipates for the adventure. This includes the starting location, time frame, backstory, and other details that could influence the selection of a character's career, specialization, species, and background.

The players usually have their own ideas about the characters they want to play. If the GM finds that a player's character concept significantly conflicts with the intended plot line or doesn't mesh well with the rest of the group, it is his call whether to allow the character in the adventure or campaign. However, most players are willing to adjust their character concepts enough to satisfy the needs of the story and work with the party.

It is useful to create characters around a group concept. FORCE AND DESTINY focuses on Force-centric campaigns, with an expectation that the Player Characters are all Force users. An example group concept is that they all escaped from an Imperial facility holding suspected Force users. The characters might start with their Force use a secret, but they might also already be known to authorities or certain individuals.

The character creation rules in **Chapter II: Character Creation** give the players ideas for basic backgrounds and starting points for their characters, along with ideas for their Morality and Motivation. The amount of information needed depends largely on the GM's play style. Backgrounds can be as detailed or as basic as the GM and players want them to be. The GM can and should use suggestions and plot points from the character backgrounds to tie them into the storyline.

Players throw unusual twists at every GM. One might want to play a secret Force user, dedicated to following the light side of the Force. Another might want to play a character willing to experiment with the dark side regularly as the character explores the limits and dangers of the Force without the benefit of Jedi knowledge or training. Backgrounds that conflict with each other can make for interesting storylines and drama, but the GM needs to be careful that it doesn't divide the party and the players so much that it ruins all enjoyment of the game.

Two aspects of character creation that should include GM involvement are Morality and how a character's personality fits into their Morality and their origins. When the player rolls on (or chooses from) **Table 2–1: Morality**, on page 50, the player and

GM should discuss and develop the character's backstory and personality based on the results. The backstory and the character's personality can be as short as a couple of evocative sentences or as detailed as the GM and player want to make it. In the first game session, the players can use a simple description. However, as the game goes on, a character's backstory and personality can and should become more detailed and expand in scope. Published adventures might include additional Morality guidance. See **Using Morality**, on page 322, for more information.

## LEARNING ON THE JOB

From the beginning, player and Game Master focus naturally falls on figuring out game system mechanics. As the GM and players become more proficient, everyone needs less time for rules discussion and learning, leaving more time for roleplaying and story advancement. Players will look to the GM for rules explanations and interpretations, but he shouldn't feel he must make a ruling in a vacuum. The GM may ask for the players' points of view, especially if everyone is learning the game at the same time. The GM should be fair and impartial, and should take the players' views into account. In the end, however, the GM's word is final.

## RUNNING THE FIRST SESSION

The first session normally begins with character creation. Some GMs use the entire first session to create characters. This gives the players ample opportunity to familiarize themselves with the character creation process and their options. It also allows them to discuss their character ideas in detail and to devise preliminary background histories, keeping their Morality and first Force use in mind. The GM should quickly review finished characters, primarily looking for obvious mistakes.

Starting the first adventure during the session is highly recommended, even if it is only to introduce the characters to each other and experience a quick encounter. As play progresses, the GM should try to move the story along and not get too hung up looking up rules for every action. Rules proficiency comes in time, and their intricacies become clearer with practice.

If the GM uses a published adventure, it guides the story. If the GM creates his own story, he should keep it simple. Introduce new actions and concepts a little bit at a time. Plan at least one personal-scale combat encounter, a roleplaying-focused encounter, an opportunity to use Force powers, and some time for the Player Characters to interact and get to know each other. Later on, the GM can add space combat and situations using other specialized rules. Note that it is natural for character creation and combat to run more slowly than usual the first few sessions. Play speed increases as everyone learns the rules.

## ROLL THE DICE

The *Star Wars* ROLEPLAYING DICE and symbols are often unfamiliar and can be intimidating to new players. Since EDGE OF THE EMPIRE and AGE OF REBELLION use the same dice as FORCE AND DESTINY, players familiar with those games can help new players during the session. Before the adventure, and perhaps before character creation, the GM should roll and explain to the players the following sample checks, using the stats from a pre-generated character or one of the adversaries in **Chapter XII: Adversaries**. The GM should read the **Dice Pool Evaluation: Success** and **Dice Pool Evaluation: Failure** sidebars, on pages 318 and 319, for sample dice pool interpretations.

- Melee Attack
- Ranged Attack
- Skill Checks
- Force Power Use
- Initiative
- Destiny Points

### THAT STAR WARS FEELING

A crucial aspect of running a *Star Wars* game is making it feel like something seen on the movie or TV screen. The game and plot should be fast-paced and entertaining, have a dash of humor, and feature moments of high drama or tension.

The GM should limit or avoid plots that run counter to expectations. Horror, for instance, is not normally a part of the core *Star Wars* experience. Gruesome scenes explained in graphic detail are not expected. That isn't to say they could never be used—there are occasional graphic moments in the movies—but they should not be the norm.

It is also worth noting that the Expanded Universe (official books and stories outside of the movies and TV shows) touches on a wider range of storytelling elements, including horror. GMs wanting to explore similar ideas might look to it for inspiration while keeping the *Star Wars* feel. GMs should also give the players an indication that their story may address non-traditional *Star Wars* themes, so that they are not caught off guard once play begins.

## CONTINUING THE STORY

Once the first adventure is completed, what happens next? First, the GM should find out if the players had fun and discuss how the next session might be improved. If the campaign is to continue, the GM should also award experience points (see page 320) and other rewards such as credits or equipment.

Next, the GM should give the players the opportunity to alter, rebuild, or scrap their characters if they so desire. Players should not be burdened with characters they do not like, especially when they are first learning the game. As players try out their characters, they may decide their original choices do not match their play style, see other options they like better, or simply find one more fun to play. Players may also wish to keep their overall character concept but completely rebuild the character mechanically. Players changing or creating new characters should not be penalized for doing so.

The GM is free to build on the storyline from the first adventure or to encourage the characters to move to a different story. This might be another published adventure or one of the GM's own creation. For more detail, see the **Creating Encounters, Adventures, and Campaigns** section, on page 330.

# MANAGING THE PARTY

Managing and maintaining a gaming group takes work, even when the players are friends. Sometimes schedules conflict with game times. Sometimes there are distractions during the game. Personality differences may come to the forefront due to differing play styles, or in reaction to issues brought up in an adventure's storyline. Players may become angry when things go badly for their characters, particularly if they feel they were the victim of another player's actions.

Most of the time, none of these issues are enough to derail a campaign or split up a group. However, it can happen. Conflict can still make for some uncomfortable sessions, even when properly addressed. This section contains advice to help prevent or diffuse these situations.

### TABLE RULES

Table rules are usually unwritten guidelines understood by all involved that Game Masters use to cover situations pertaining to player actions beyond the scope of the game itself. There are no hard-and-fast rules that pertain to every GM or every group. However, it is best to establish guidelines for some common situations, so the players know what to expect before they arise. The following are some suggested table rules; individual groups may invent others.

- **Off-Topic Discussions:** Gaming is a social gathering and an entertaining pastime. Players joke

and talk among themselves. While this is fine, it can derail a dramatic moment or otherwise disrupt gameplay. This is especially true when the GM is only focused on one or two players. The amount of discussion allowed or tolerated depends very much on the group, but players should be considerate of others if asked to turn their focus to the game at hand.

- **Distractions:** Much like off-topic discussions, distractions at the table should be minimized. This includes laptop computers, tablets, phones, music players, TVs, and anything else that draws the players' attention from the game.

- **Metagame Coordination:** Sometimes even game-related discussions become a distraction. During gameplay, particularly combat, players often attempt to coordinate their characters' actions. While some planning is acceptable, talk in the middle of a combat round should be discouraged if their characters are not in a situation that allows it. A secondary problem occurs when a player suggests actions to another player. While this can be helpful, and beneficial to new players, it can lead to unrealistic coordination. It may irritate other players at the table if it occurs every session. See also **Player Knowledge vs. Character Knowledge**, on page 317.

- **Morality Discussions:** Because Morality is a central theme of **Force and Destiny**, the Player Characters regularly encounter difficult or gray areas in the choices the group or individuals must make. It is acceptable, and should be encouraged, for players to discuss the moral consequences of their actions before actually deciding to take them. A player might also alert the other players when their character is about to take an action that is perfectly in character, but which other Player Characters might find reprehensible

## INTRODUCING NEW PLAYER CHARACTERS

Bringing a new player into an existing group can be exciting. It is often necessary to replace players who leave during a long campaign. The addition of a new character shakes up the group dynamics and brings out new or unexpected opportunities within the game. However, not all additions go smoothly, and considerations should be made regarding the storyline and the enjoyment of the group as a whole.

Before adding a new player, the group should discuss whether that person meshes well with the current game and group. The GM could discreetly discuss the situation with each player to minimize hurt feelings if some players object.

When the new player arrives at the table, the group and GM should bring him up to speed on the current story, table rules, and any house rules in use.

When the new character arrives in-game, there should be an accompanying story reason for him to join the group. The GM can create it, but it works best when it includes ideas from the new player and the existing group. The new character may be a friend, relative, or other associate of the PCs, or he might be introduced by an NPC. Introduction through an adventure specifically created to introduce the Player Character is a good way to integrate the new character with the existing storyline or campaign.

If the new player is also new to Force and Destiny or RPGs in general, he may need help learning the rules and terminology. While the GM can and should aid him, it is often better for a player to act as a mentor. This frees the GM to concentrate on the game and the entire group, while the individual player gets specific advice or instructions.

or counterproductive. The player might wish to make it clear that the character's actions aren't what he would condone in real life. This does not excuse a player who tries to use these actions to resolve conflicts with another *player*. The players may also discuss and plan how their characters might respond to the given action.

- **Note Passing:** There may be times when a character wants to act on knowledge that no other Player Character has, and wants to conceal that action. The player and GM may pass notes to each other to secretly progress that part of the storyline. Less common is note passing between players, bypassing the GM. Both are generally acceptable, but the GM should be careful not to let it dominate the game or overly frustrate players left out of the loop.

### GROUP DYNAMICS

There are two major group dynamics in play at the gaming table. One is between the players, while the second is between their characters. Both are important to having fun. Ideally, the players enjoy playing with each other, and their characters have enough in common to associate with each other without large amounts of unwanted tension. Disruptions in either of these cases can diminish the fun of playing.

### WHEN THE PARTY DISAGREES

Roleplaying is highly situational. As a story unfolds, the party often debates the desired course of action. This normally works itself out as the party discusses its options. Disagreements due to roleplaying individual characters can be great moments in the game, and the Morality system encourages tough moral positions and decisions. See **Morality Discussions** in the **Table Rules** section on the previous page. If a disagreement grows to the point that it disrupts the fun of the game, it's usually a good time to take a break. Breaks may last just a few minutes or may suspend the game until the next session.

Sometimes, the GM can alter the in-game situation enough to provide a more obvious or agreeable path forward. Compromise from the GM or other players to move the story along is normally acceptable and desirable, especially if the situation is making one or more players uncomfortable at the table. The party should be careful to avoid lingering disagreements, as they can lead to bad feelings and possibly break up the group.

### WHEN THE PARTY SPLITS UP

Sometimes the best course of action is for the party to split up in the game. This normally happens when the action is spread out and the party needs to be in more than one place at the same time. This can also be used to diffuse situations in which the party greatly disagrees on the correct course of action.

No matter the cause, splitting the party also splits the attention of the GM. This naturally focuses the GM's attention on one part of the group at a time, leaving the rest to wait until the spotlight returns to them. The GM must be careful not to let too much downtime pass between groups. In some cases, the players might leave the table and go to different rooms or areas to avoid overhearing or disrupting a scene that their characters are not part of and cannot influence. See **Player Knowledge vs. Character Knowledge**, on page 317.

Splitting the party is acceptable and expected for limited durations. It is least disruptive to the game as a whole if the GM keeps all players at the table. Splitting the party for longer-term situations can add to the story, but must be carefully managed. The GM might even consider running separate sessions in extreme cases.

### WHEN THE PARTY GOES OFF THE RAILS

One of the great attractions of roleplaying games for players is the freedom to play their characters as they see fit. The players almost always push the story in unexpected but perfectly logical directions. One of the joys and responsibilities of the GM is to keep the story moving when the unexpected happens.

Sometimes, the party's actions completely depart from the prepared storyline. How strictly the GM tries to keep to the envisioned storyline depends on the GM's philosophy. Most allow the characters to pursue their own course for a while, inserting clues, new NPCs, or events that eventually bring them back to the planned plot. More freewheeling GMs might jettison their storyline and react to the characters' new actions and goals. Flexibility within the story is one key to great gaming sessions. Neither approach is wrong, unless the players become unhappy with the outcome.

### ABSENT PLAYERS

A bsent and no-show players are a common problem. Such absences can disrupt or derail a storyline, so it is best if the GM plans ahead to deal with absences.

If the player isn't there, find a reason for the character to be offscreen during the session. There are a lot of plausible reasons: maybe he's sick, wounded, training, taking care of other business, fixing the ship, or even detained by the authorities.

If the absent player's character is central to the session at hand, someone else may run the character. If the character holds secret knowledge unknown to the rest of the group, the GM may run the character. Otherwise, it is recommended that someone from the group run the character. It is considered bad form to allow serious injury or death to occur to the character while being controlled by someone else.

If the character is absolutely critical to the storyline, sometimes it is best to cancel the session and play when everyone can attend. Obviously, this should be the last resort. However, when the story itself has a major event that everyone wants to be a part of, cancellation is often the best route to avoiding disappointment and hurt feelings by the absent player.

# PLANNING GAME SESSIONS

Planning each game session takes time and effort. While some GMs create highly detailed outlines and plans, others run their games free-form, with minimal notes. Each GM eventually settles on a method that works for him with the time he has. Different aspects of game planning rise and fall in importance as the GM's style, proficiency, and storytelling develop. The novice GM should start with the guidance given above about the first session and then integrate the following advice when the game or story requires it.

### STYLE OF PLAY

Different groups and GMs enjoy different ways of playing the game. The GM should learn his group's preferences and prepare sessions that enhance, if not cater to, their expectations. The GM should still feel free to use other play styles if a specific scene or encounter warrants it. Major play styles can be exploration and storytelling-focused or combat-focused. FORCE AND DESTINY adventures are often exploration-focused, but they still include action and combat. GMs usually settle on a combination of the two, alternating between story-based sessions and combat-intensive play.

Exploration and storytelling focus more on the overall plot and the characters' interaction with the fantastic locations, events, and adversaries of the larger *Star Wars* universe. Entire sessions or more may pass without firing a single blaster. Conflict comes more from the environment and NPC plans and reactions than from dodging fire. Plot lines may be more intricate or may tie into character backstories to a much greater degree.

Combat-focused play concentrates more on the tactical moments of the game, with combat in nearly every session. Fighting uses a significant portion of play time, limiting the depth and complexity of other scenes. The players generally like battling their foes directly by tactically outsmarting or overwhelming them. Large-scale combat with military ground forces and fleets is less typically common in FORCE AND DESTINY than in AGE OF REBELLION.

### STORYTELLING

The core of every roleplaying game is the storyline. The Player Characters are the main actors in a plot of the GM's devising. The complexity and depth of the story depends greatly on the desires of the gaming group as a whole. A good story is an entertaining one, not necessarily the most complex.

The GM needs to create at least a basic plot for the adventure he wants to run (or to understand it when using a published adventure). He should take

## USING THE *STAR WARS* EXPANDED UNIVERSE

**P**rior to 2015, anything officially licensed but not produced directly by Lucasfilm (i.e., outside of the movies and TV shows) is referred to as the EU (Expanded Universe), or Legends. With over thirty-five years of material, it is a huge resource for newcomers to get a handle on a complex universe. The materials in the Expanded Universe are extremely varied, and some have become irrelevant or disregarded as new movies have come out and the *Star Wars* universe has grown and matured. However, GMs can still use discarded or altered material in their own games.

When running a *Star Wars* game, the GM should decide early on whether to stick with *Star Wars* canon as his stories develop. In most cases, it is not a big issue. If the storyline does not involve notable characters and events from official stories, the game plot may peacefully co-exist with the universe at large.

However, some GMs and players feel constrained by the knowledge that their heroes aren't the center of the universe, or are unable to affect certain galactic events. It is the GM's prerogative to use as much or as little *Star Wars* canon he feels comfortable with. If the GM wants to run a game based on an alternate version of events, that is perfectly acceptable. However, he should inform his players.

ideas from the Player Characters' backgrounds to tie them closely into the storyline. For example, a character's response to an attacking Force wielder might be quite different if the attacker turns out to be a relative than if he is a hated enemy. Unexpected revelations, conflicts of interest, and more increase the complexity, and potential enjoyment, of the plot. See **Creating a FORCE AND DESTINY Adventure**, on page 330, and **Running a Full Campaign**, on page 334, for more detail on creating adventures.

### SOURCES OF INSPIRATION

The *Star Wars* Expanded Universe (or Legends) is enormous. With over thirty-five years of movies, comics, novels, games, sourcebooks, TV shows, and more, there is a vast wealth of information for GMs to draw upon when creating their own games. Of course, the *Star Wars* game lines from Fantasy Flight Games will continue to grow, providing rules and adventures for a variety of play experiences. However, GMs should feel free to draw upon any *Star Wars* publication or other source for story ideas. Many provide great visual references at the game table as well.

# RUNNING THE GAME

Running the game means more than managing the story. The GM must also attend to the mechanical means of keeping the game going. This section provides guidance on how to handle specific rules and other elements during the game session, and on how the rules and elements interact.

## RULES ADJUDICATION

The GM is the final arbiter of all rules discussions. It is important that he listen to points the players might argue for their side of an interpretation. However, rules discussions should not dominate playing time. After a short discussion, the GM should make a ruling to keep the game moving and should review the rule in detail later. If the ruling was incorrect, the GM may try to make it up to the player or group in question in a future session, or he may simply acknowledge the mistake and chalk it up as a lesson learned.

Sometimes the GM feels the rules are unclear or that he has an unusual situation. The GM may create a house rule to address the issue. He might also gain further insight from discussing the issue with other GMs or rules-proficient players, in person or in online gaming forums. However, rules lawyering—using the minutia of the rules to gain an unfair, unexpected, or unintended advantage in a game—should be avoided by both players and GMs.

## INTERPRETING THE DICE POOL

One of the GM's primary responsibilities is to interpret the results of the dice rolls. Given that the exact makeup of each dice pool varies wildly, the GM and the players have many opportunities to translate the results into narrative effects. During the heat of the game, the players may rapidly assess a roll of the dice only for success or failure then quickly pick up the dice for the next check. The GM should discourage this, especially if the story is at a critical juncture. While not every dice roll needs extensive interpretation, important moments should always be influenced by the dice results.

The die symbols generated by each check go well beyond the simple task of indicating success or failure. Success indicated by a ⬡ can mean something different than if it occurs on an ◆ or ☐. In the case of a ⬡, a success might indicate the character's skill overcame all other challenges. If the same result occurred using a ☐, fortune may have stepped in at the right moment. The GM should inform the story via the dice whenever possible.

☐ and ■ indicate the influence of fortune and misfortune in the results. Failure indicates that the inherent difficulties of the situation, terrain, or task at hand were too much to overcome. Success indicates that luck, the Force, or a beneficial circumstance affected the outcome.

◆ and ◆ represent the battle between a character's natural abilities and knowledge versus the inherent difficulty of the task at hand. Failure indicates that the task was just too hard to accomplish this time.

⬡ and ⬢ dice represent the character's trained skill versus the most difficult challenges. Similar to the ability and difficulty dice, success indicates the character's training has prevailed, while failure indicates the circumstances were just too difficult to surpass.

⚡ and ✦ indicators are often less clear-cut in their influence on the dice pool. Sometimes they may trigger certain talents, abilities, or effects. They give the GM or player the opportunity to describe how the results place the character in a better or worse position than before the action.

✦ and ▽ indicators should generate excitement at the game table. ✦ indicates a critical success that should also grant the character an advantage in the scene. ▽ indicates a critical failure, which should disrupt the character and make the situation much worse.

Instead of (or along with) a narrative effect, ⚡, ✦, ✦, and ▽ may be spent per **Table 6–2: Spending ⚡ and ✦ in Combat**, on page 212, and **Table 6–3: Spending ✦ and ▽ in Combat**, on page 212. See the similar tables on page 243 for spending these results in vehicle combat.

Usually, the makeup of the dice pool does not evenly align die types that are in direct opposition to each other. Instead, successes, failures, and other indicators are spread across different dice in different amounts. It is often up to the GM to decide which of the successes or failures is most relevant to the story interpretation.

## USING BOOST AND SETBACK DICE

Boosts and setbacks are basic GM tools for manipulating fortune and misfortune in the game. Beyond the normal guidelines for setting difficulty within the dice pool, ☐ and ■ enable the GM to allow characters to try unusual or outright insane ideas during play. The players enjoy the chance to try creative solutions within the game, and the GM can regulate the difficulty through adding more ■ instead of saying no to the idea. Note that ☐ and ■ dice are not normally upgraded to other die types.

Alternatively, ☐ may be used to reward a PC for good planning or creative thinking. ☐ may also be used in situations not covered by the rules. If the PC comes up with a good idea and the GM wants to allow it, he may add ☐. This is especially encouraged if the idea is in keeping with the spirit of the *Star Wars* movies and stories.

## USING MUSIC AND PROPS

One of the great advantages of running a game in the *Star Wars* setting is the availability of music. The movie soundtracks add instant atmosphere to a game session. Beginning an adventure with the opening fanfare and the main title track instantly sets an unmistakable and recognizable tone. Running the soundtracks at low volume in the background of the game session can add ambiance. A better approach is to play selected tracks at relevant moments to add to the situation at hand. Nothing fills the players with apprehension and says "the Empire is here" like playing "The Imperial March" just before announcing a Star Destroyer has arrived to ruin their day.

With the multitude of *Star Wars* toys, models, replicas, and other products available, it is easy to use them as props during the game. Starship models, books with detailed pictures, and toy weapons can be adapted for use at the table or serve as examples. However, not all toys set the appropriate mood. A highly accurate lightsaber replica with light and sound can add interesting details to an in-game discussion about the weapon. A cheap plastic knockoff won't have the same effect.

### USING STRAIN

Strain is a non-lethal way for characters to suffer physical and psychological effects. See page 222 for a complete description of strain. For the GM, strain represents an opportunity to add mechanical emphasis and consequences to narrative aspects of the scene or combat.

In combat, the GM should not (often) overwhelm the PCs with strain, so that they have the opportunity to voluntarily take on strain to make additional maneuvers or to use talents. This is especially significant for some lightsaber-wielding characters. Extreme environments or circumstances may occasionally increase the amount of strain the GM inserts into the encounter. Environmental strain should be less of a concern during the average combat.

Suffering strain emulates reacting to harmful environmental effects. Enduring long periods of exposure to heat, cold, radiation, or unusual weather like sandstorms may cause strain. Psychological pressure may also induce strain. It may come from strong emotional reactions to loss, extreme anger, frustration, or similar issues that distract a character from the task at hand.

Characters using certain talents combined with the Lightsaber skill may voluntarily suffer strain to mitigate damage and possibly other effects during combat. The details are described in each relevant talent description in **Chapter IV: Talents**. During lightsaber combat, spending ⚙ to inflict strain on a character represents the physical and mental fatigue of fighting. It is possible that a combatant becomes fatigued enough to abandon the fight, flee, or surrender, especially in a lightsaber duel. Lightsaber duels can also end abruptly if a character's strain threshold is exceeded. He is overwhelmed and his defense becomes ineffective, leaving him open to a final killing strike.

When assigning strain, the GM should consider how different sources may interact in an encounter or scene. Creating a scene in which strain is a primary component is perfectly fine, but having a scene accidentally become overwhelmed with strain can alter the narrative in unexpected ways. Typically, the GM should assign one or two points of strain for a given effect. When environmental conditions inflict strain, the amount of strain inflicted can serve as a good indicator of how dangerous the environment is.

### CHARACTER DEATH

Death is a significant part of the *Star Wars* universe. While Player Character death is unlikely to happen in most game sessions, the threat of death builds tension. How a player reacts to his character's demise depends largely on the player. Some take it in stride and are soon ready to create a new one. Other players may be disappointed, upset, or angry, especially those with a lot of time and effort invested into the character. The player may be particularly frustrated if the character's death is meaningless or cheap, or feels unfair. While the GM may try to prevent a character death through subtle or obvious means, such aid should be backed up by solid reasoning. Perceived favoritism in the GM's handling of different deaths between different Player Characters can lead to hurt feelings and angry players.

### PLAYER KNOWLEDGE VS. CHARACTER KNOWLEDGE

Players generally know a lot more about a given situation than the characters they are playing. It is important that they differentiate between information learned outside of the game and information that their characters are aware of. To aid in the suspension of disbelief, players should not use information their characters cannot logically know within the game.

This is particularly true when the party is split, with characters in different locations. For ease of play, the GM may allow all players to remain at the table while they play their individual scenes. However, the uninvolved players should not have their characters act on any information gained by listening to the interaction between the GM and the rest of the group. On the other hand, with a party of Force users, the GM might allow the PCs to act nominally on normally unknown

**W**hat do the following dice pool results have in common?

Pool 1 ◈

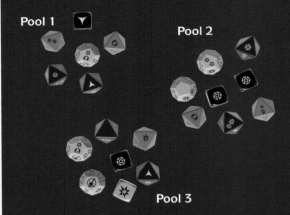

Pool 2

Pool 3

Each of these dice pools indicates a successful check. At least one uncanceled ✶ appears in each pool. Assume that each pool represents a Force-wielding Sentinel battling a Force-using Imperial Inquisitor. Below are example interpretations of these results.

**Dice Pool 1—Success with a Momentary Advantage:** The two ✶ appearing on the ◈ are cancelled by the ▼ showing on one ◇ and one □. The ❂ on the ◈ is cancelled by ◇ showing ✵. One ✶ and one ❂ appear on the ⬣ and are uncanceled. The Sentinel's lightsaber skill enables his attack to slip through the Inquisitor's defense, leaving the Sentinel in a slightly advantageous position.

"The Inquisitor defends himself vigorously, but your skillful technique gets a quick strike past his blade. You end up in a momentarily advantageous position."

**Dice Pool 2—Successful but Significantly Threatened:** The two ✶ on one ◇ and the two ✶ on one of the ⬣ are uncanceled, resulting in four net ✶. The ◇ showing one ❂ is canceled by one □ showing one ✵. One ⬣ is blank, and of no help or hindrance. However, the two ◇ one remaining □ has four additional ✵. The Sentinel lands a solid hit, but ends up very exposed or in a precarious position.

"Your slashing attack strikes the Inquisitor soundly, but your momentum swings you around awkwardly, leaving you wide open to a retaliatory strike."

**Dice Pool 3—A Triumphant Attack:** The ✶ on the □ is canceled by the ▼ on one ◇. One ⬣ has an ❂, canceled by the ✵ on the □. The remaining ◇ is blank and has no effect. This leaves the first ⬣ with an uncanceled ✶, the ◇ with another uncanceled ✶, and the other ⬣ has a ⊕! The Sentinel's attack damages the Inquisitor and produces a significant narrative result.

"With a mighty two-handed swing, you hit near the hilt of his lightsaber. The strike damages his hand, and the impact of the blow knocks his saber away. It shuts down as it hits the floor and rolls under a nearby control panel."

# DICE POOL EVALUATION: FAILURE

What do the following dice pool results have in common?

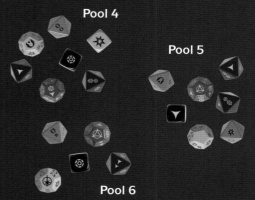

Pool 4

Pool 5

Pool 6

Each of these dice pools indicates an unsuccessful check. No uncanceled ☼ appears in any of these pools. The first is an opposed check, the second a fear check, and the last a standard skill check. Below are interpretations of these results.

**Dice Pool 4—Unconvincing:** The ▢ shows one ☼, but it is canceled by the ◇ showing a ▼. The ◇ and ⬡ show a total of three ☹, which are canceled by the ☐ and ◇ showing a total of three ✵. All that remains is the ⬡ showing a ▼ and uncanceled ✵. The Consular fails a Charm check versus a crime lord's Cool skill, and is unable to convince the crime lord to forgive a longstanding debt.

"The advantage and favor granted by rescuing the crime lord's prized pet has proven to be useless after your allies insulted the crime lord earlier. To make matters worse, you accidentally anger him when you mention a secret deal in front of his own allies. He refuses to cancel the debt."

**Dice Pool 5—A Frightening Reaction:** One ◇ shows the only ☼ result, which is canceled by the ▼ on one ◇. The ☹ on the remaining ◇ is canceled by one ✵ on the ◇, leaving one ✵ unaffected. The blank ⬤ has no impact either way. The ⬡ shows ☖! The Consular fails a fear check when a trio of Imperial Inquisitors bursts into his hideout.

"Three Inquisitors use the Force to blow open the door and hurl it across the room. The unexpected attack on your hideout takes you completely by surprise. Not only are you frozen in shock, but you also suffer 1 Conflict from fear."

**Dice Pool 6—Disastrous Results:** The ◇ showing ☼ and the success portion of the ✦ from the ⬤ are canceled by the ◇ showing two ▼. The ☹ on the same ◇ is canceled by the ✵ on the ■. The ☖ and the triumph portion of the ✦ remain. The Consular fails an Athletics check to jump between two buildings, and the combination of a simultaneous ✦ and ☖ provides interesting results.

"As you try to leap across to the other building, you trip over the parapet wall and fall toward the road below. Fortunately, a fabric canopy breaks your fall about halfway to the street. Unfortunately, you bounce off of it like on a trampoline, fly through the air, and smash through the Imperial Governor's office window. You crash headfirst into his desk. He is not amused."

events as a way to loosely emulate the precognitive qualities of some Force users.

Additionally, players may know a great deal about the *Star Wars* universe. While the use of such knowledge can add great details to the game, players must be careful not to use information their characters do not know about the universe or political situation. It is highly unlikely, for instance, for the characters to know the intimate history of Darth Vader, despite his depiction in the movies and elsewhere.

## PLAYING THE ROLE

GMs should always remember that they are playing the role of NPCs motivated by their own desires, fears, relationships, and orders. How far the GM goes in portraying and performing the character depends on the GM's comfort level in acting out the role. It is acceptable to speak in third person, such as "The dark side adept threatens to push your companion into the chasm unless you drop your lightsaber." However, it is more engaging and immersive to perform using an in-character voice or accent, speaking directly to the characters. The same line might be said as, "Drop that lightsaber or your friend is going to find the bottom of the chasm for us." Most GMs use a mixture of these two methods. However, if the GM's performance elicits unintended laughter in a dramatic situation, it is probably time to consider a different approach.

## IMPROVISING

Becoming a good GM requires a number of improvisational skills that are used throughout the game session. For the GM, improvisational acting occurs when he plays the roles of NPCs reacting to character questions and actions. Improvisational story changes occur regularly, as the GM makes constant behind-the-scenes adjustments in order to keep the plot moving forward. If the characters move in an unexpected yet logical direction, the GM must be able to create new scenes or characters on the fly. Fortunately, these skills improve with time and practice.

# AWARDING AND SPENDING EXPERIENCE POINTS

The GM should award experience points after every session. The target amount to award per session varies depending on how fast the GM wants the characters to advance. A slower rate of advancement is typically 10 to 15 XP per PC per session. This enables players to spend their XP about every other session. Moderately paced advancement sets the target at about 20 XP, which enables the player to buy a new talent, raise a skill, and so on once per game session. For the quickest advancement, the target is 25 XP. It is better suited for shorter campaigns and becomes hard to sustain in the long run.

The amount awarded each session is typically 10 to 20 XP per character (adjusted per the previous paragraph for moderate or fast rates of play) for a game of two or three major encounters and a handful of minor ones. An additional bonus of 5 XP may be granted for reaching key milestones or completing story arcs. Playing to a character's Motivation also grants 5 XP per session. The GM may consider awarding an extra point or two of XP for exceptional roleplaying or highly clever thinking. Published adventures may include recommended XP awards.

The GM should give the players an idea of the source of their XP. For example, they may receive 5 XP for avoiding a bounty hunter and another 5 XP for successfully transporting their cargo to their client. Any bonus XP that is awarded should definitely be explained to the players so they may aspire to those standards in future sessions.

## SPENDING EXPERIENCE POINTS

When awarding experience, the GM should keep in mind what players will be able to spend experience points on and how much those items cost. This is covered on page 102, but is reprinted here in **Table 9–1: Spending Experience** for convenience. This only covers spending experience after character creation.

## TABLE 9–1: SPENDING EXPERIENCE

| Options | Cost | Prerequisites |
|---|---|---|
| May spend experience to purchase ranks in any skill, up to rank 5. | Career skills cost five times the purchased rank in experience. Non-career skills cost five times the purchased rank in experience, plus 5 additional experience. | Whether for a career skill or non-career skill, each rank must be purchased sequentially (so rank 2 must be purchased before rank 3, and so on). |
| May spend experience to purchase talents within specializations. | Depends on talent's position within specialization talent tree. | Talents may only be purchased if they are on the first level of a specialization, or if they are connected by a bar to a talent already purchased. |
| May spend experience to purchase new specializations. | New specializations cost ten times the total number of specializations the character will have. Non-career specializations cost 10 additional experience. | None. |

## MANAGING RECORDS AND DOWNTIME

Between sessions, the GM and the players should maintain certain records. The GM should alter the group's current Morality after players note their changes. The players should update their character sheets, particularly if they increase their abilities or need to adjust their listed equipment. It is also helpful if the GM or a player keeps a journal or notes about each session. This makes it easier to remember the events of the story and track the movements and names of NPCs.

Not every new adventure picks up immediately where the previous one ends. Most should include downtime for the characters. This allows them to gain needed training and carry out tasks that don't need to be played out at the table. For instance, a Force user might learn and practice his abilities between adventures. There is no need to play out mundane events. The GM and players should be ready to summarize what has occurred during the downtime between adventures.

## ADVANCED CHARACTERS AND KNIGHT-LEVEL PLAY

Once Player Characters earns 150 XP or more after character creation, they are considered advanced characters. They are better equipped to handle tougher opponents and situations. In preparing for a game session with these characters, the Game Master needs to account for their greater abilities. The PCs should regularly face stronger adversaries (often with the Adversary talent). The GM could use rivals where minions might have previously been appropriate, and increase the abilities and danger of minions when they are required. Advanced minions should still be noticeably weaker than the characters. Regular minions can and should still be used on occasion, so that the players can see the results of their dedication to playing and advancing their characters. They should see the benefits of their advanced abilities over the average opponents or NPCs that were once dangerous to the PCs.

Unique to **FORCE AND DESTINY**, once PCs have earned 150 XP, the game assumes the PCs have had the chance to obtain a Lightsaber weapon of some type. Thus, the GM can pit the PCs against opponents who have lightsabers or weapons with the Cortosis quality and who have the ability to Parry or Reflect attacks. PCs uninterested in lightsaber combat should have the opportunity to obtain something comparable, such as additional XP to invest in Force powers or specialization trees.

### KNIGHT-LEVEL PLAY

In FORCE AND DESTINY, advanced characters and adventures are called "Knight level." Knight-level play represents PCs who are on the cusp of reaching the skill level of a Jedi Knight, while still giving them plenty of room to grow and improve. PCs may earn their way up to Knight level after beginning as starting characters. The GM may also opt to run a game that is Knight-level from character creation. This enables starting characters who want to use a lightsaber to be able to purchase talents and skills to make its use more effective. Starting Knight-level characters gain an additional 150 XP. The PCs must spend their extra XP after character creation is complete (and therefore cannot spend it on characteristics). See page 104 for additional Knight-level character creation guidance. Knight-level FORCE AND DESTINY characters are expected to have access to a lightsaber. Future FORCE AND DESTINY published adventures may include advice for modifying the adventures specifically for Knight-level play.

## FEEDBACK AND IMPROVEMENT

Constructive feedback is critical for GMs, particularly new GMs, to learn what they can do to improve gameplay for everybody. The GM should ask for feedback after every few sessions, or after any particularly difficult or dull game. Feedback may be taken with the group at the table, but many players find it easier to discuss difficult situations one on one with the GM. Feedback may reveal issues mishandled by the GM or players. However, it also helps the GM alter the game to better fit player expectations, or vice versa.

# GAME MASTER RULES AND OPTIONS

This section presents Game Master–specific rules, such as fear, and possible alternate versions of some rules. In addition, it discusses the adjudication of some of the common gray areas in certain rules, such as those involving Morality, Motivations, and Destiny Points.

## USING MORALITY

The Morality system essentially tracks how good or evil a Player Character acts. A PC's struggle with *being* good versus the temptation and power of the dark side manifests as Conflict points in the Morality system. A Player Character's Morality value changes how he interacts not only with the Force, but also with other characters in the game.

A PC is considered to be one of the "good guys" until his Morality drops below 30, after which he falls to the dark side. A PC's Morality may drop over the course of the adventure, or a player may choose to have his PC start as a dark side Force user voluntarily at the beginning of the game. If this occurs, the GM and player should work out how the character fell to the dark side and whether or not he is actively seeking redemption.

Challenging the PCs' moral choices is central to FORCE AND DESTINY. Sometimes, the consequences of a choice are very clear to the character. However, adventures should include at least one situation where the PCs' goal can be achieved more easily with less than noble actions. In other words, the GM offers an easier option that reduces the PCs' danger, effort, or increases wealth but ultimately hurts another character, ship, group, or other entity as a consequence.

## TRIGGERING MORALITY (OPTIONAL RULE)

Triggering Morality is an optional rule the GM can adopt if he wants inspiration for his adventures, or to make the players' moral choices take front and center in a game. If the GM wants to use this rule, he should make a list of everyone's current Morality value. Before each game session begins, the Game Master should roll a d100. He should then determine which PC has a Morality score closest to the result.

### EXAMPLE

At the start of the game session, Jim, who is the GM, rolls a d100. It comes up with a 73. He consults the character sheets for each of the players, and finds that Sarah's character has a 75 Morality. Because his die roll is closest to her Morality, Sarah's character has her Morality triggered.

When a character's Morality triggers, the GM and the player should make an effort to engage that character's emotional strength or emotional weakness (or both!) in a crucial encounter or decision during that session. The GM, for example, can tweak encounters that play to the character's emotional strengths and weaknesses. The player, in turn, can have his character make one or more crucial decisions based on his emotions rather than solely on logic.

### EXAMPLE

Sarah's character's Morality has an emotional strength of Compassion and an emotional weakness of Hatred. During the session, the GM planned on having the characters infiltrate a shadow market on an Outer Rim world. Now he introduces a pair of cruel Zygerrian slavers with a collection of helpless slaves. Sarah decides that her character saves the slaves (playing into her strength of Compassion), but although she has the option of sneaking out quietly, she instead kills both slavers (giving into her weakness of Hatred).

If the GM and the player agree that the player's character made at least one important decision or based an important action on the character's emotional strengths or weaknesses, then the character successfully engaged his triggered Morality. If he did not, then nothing happens. Note that the player can engage his character's triggered Morality via his character's emotional strength or his emotional weakness, and the mechanical result is the same (see the **Engaging a Triggered Morality** sidebar on page 51). However, his choices may have other repercussions as well.

## TRIGGERED MORALITY

When a character's Morality is triggered at the start of a game session, he gains a chance to do something particularly good or devastatingly evil, linked to his specific Morality. This might occur spontaneously during the game, or the GM can map out different possibilities for use at the right moment. For example, a character from a PC's past returns to help or hinder the PC. The GM should work this into the ongoing story, but if the triggered narrative is too disruptive for the events in the adventure, the narrative portion can be skipped. At a minimum, triggering doubles the Morality increase or decrease at the end of the game session.

## TABLE 9-2: COMMON CONFLICT POINT PENALTIES

| Conflict Received | Action |
|---|---|
| 1 | **Knowing Inaction:** The PC knows that an NPC or other PC will do something particularly bad (an action that would earn 5+ Conflict points) and chooses not to intervene. |
| | **Lying for Personal Gain:** The PC tells a lie for selfish reasons or to benefit himself. Some lies can be told without penalty to benefit others, such as avoiding a combat situation or protecting innocents. |
| | **Resorting to Violence as the First Solution:** When confronted with a problem, the PC defaults to violent acts to solve it, without exploring any other options. This penalty can be mitigated if the PC is the one being attacked. |
| 2 | **Coercion and Threatening with Violence:** The PC threatens someone with violence, or coerces the person to do his bidding against the person's will. |
| | **Inflicting Emotional Abuse:** The PC says something cruel or petty just to upset or cause mental torment in a person. |
| 2-3 | **Theft:** The PC steals something that does not belong to him. The Conflict point penalty can be mitigated in this case if the PC is stealing from a corrupt and/or wealthy authority (such as the Empire), and does so to give back to those who need it. The Conflict point penalty can be increased if the PC steals something from those who can particularly ill afford to lose it. |
| 3-4 | **Unnecessary Destruction:** The PC destroys objects, property, or other items willfully and without good cause. |
| 4-5 | **Unprovoked Violence or Assault:** The PC assaults, beats, or otherwise attacks an NPC for no reason. |
| 6-7 | **Unnecessary Cruelty to Non-Sapient Creatures:** The PC maliciously tortures or torments animals or droids with animal-level intelligence. |
| 10 | **Torture:** The PCs torture a character. |
| 10+ | **Murder:** The PCs murder a character. In this case, murder is killing someone who is helpless or no threat to the PCs. |

## BESTOWING CONFLICT

Players track their characters' Morality scores during play. A player may choose to keep his score secret from the other players, though the GM should always know everyone's score.

The GM bestows Conflict through game mechanics and narrative action. When Conflict is given to PCs, it is tracked as a discrete amount, such as 4 Conflict or 12 Conflict. Players track Conflict bestowed mechanically, since it results from specific, defined actions.

- A PC receives 1 Conflict per ● result used to generate ◗ during a Force power check.
- The GM bestows 1 to 10 (and sometimes even more) Conflict for narrative actions, depending on the severity of the PC's deeds. See **Table 9-2: Common Conflict Point Penalties**, above, for examples of Conflict awarded for common negative or evil actions. The GM can and should adjust the penalties to account for unusual actions or situations.

Character intent should influence the amount of Conflict awarded, as some actions may be considered good in one situation and evil in another. Obviously evil or overly selfish acts combined with the main transgression can add from 1 to 5 additional Conflict points. Gray areas, such as using ● results to generate ◗ for a selfish but not a truly evil action, receives a minimum of +1 Conflict, but possibly 2 to 5 more Conflict. The GM's determination and ruling is final.

## SESSION TALLY

At the end of each session, each player totals the amount of Conflict his character received and rolls 1d10. If the roll result is less than the number of Conflict points earned, he *decreases* his Morality by the difference between the number of points earned and his roll. If the roll is greater than the number of Conflict points, he *increases* his Morality by the difference between his roll and his Conflict points earned. (If the roll and Conflict earned are the same, Morality neither increases

### SECRECY AND MORALITY

Secrecy is key to the PCs' survival in Imperial space. Situations that threaten to reveal a character's Force abilities are one common way to challenge their Morality.

For example, an innocent bystander observes the PC using an obvious Force ability. Upon realizing this, the PC must choose how to react. He might do nothing, hoping that the individual won't report him, or he might plan to be long gone before Imperial authorities arrive. He might attempt to Charm the individual into keeping his secret. Things quickly take a darker turn if the PC intimidates or threatens the observer. Intimidation through violent means, or outright attacking the individual, is darker still. Worst of all would be killing the individual, blackmailing him with threats against his family, or similar actions.

nor decreases.) Since the roll potentially increases or decreases the score, it reduces player manipulation of the system. If the game session is unusually short, the GM might require the roll after the following session instead. (For an example of rolling, see page 51.)

## FALLING TO THE DARK SIDE

Falling to the dark side should be a major moment in any story. Given that Morality is adjusted *after* a session, no one usually knows for sure during play if the PC will fall. From a roleplaying standpoint, the GM and the player should emphasize any action that gains Conflict points and allow that to build tension between the character and his enemies and allies. The player could play out what seems to be a fall, then confirm it at the end of the session. If the PC doesn't fall, then the events he just experienced might be a close call that could suggest the character reconsider his path. Near misses are dramatic in their own way.

When a PC falls to the dark side, the GM and PC should discuss the events of the next session, making the fall the central theme. The reaction of the other PCs is important. If they remain on the light side while one falls, it might challenge the game going forward. Good PCs might avoid a fallen one, and may even attack him.

PC vs. PC combat is not typically encouraged due to the potential of hurt feelings among players. However, it replicates a common theme in the *Star Wars* movies, where former allies become enemies and fight in a tense and emotional battle. There can be equally dramatic scenes between the PCs, assuming the player dynamics can withstand potentially devastating results of losing or seriously damaging a character. The GM should be ready to halt the game if emotions start to get out of hand.

Players continuing their dark side characters (as well as GMs playing dark side characters) should be discouraged from playing out truly offensive acts or vile scenes. Some graphic and horrifying events occur in the *Star Wars* movies—but they happen offscreen. Once a character's intent is clearly implied, the story cuts away to another scene. The consequences are shown or communicated after the fact. Similar methods also work within the game, with play skipping over such details in session, or having the event occur between sessions. Typically, it is more fun for everyone playing to avoid these scenes altogether.

### REDEMPTION

Redemption from the dark side is not easy. Not only does it require a long climb back up the Morality track to a score of 70, but a character's redemption should also be challenging narratively. The character should face situations that tempt him to use dark side Force points. For instance, a character near his strain threshold might be unwilling or unable to risk exceeding the threshold by spending light side points on a Force

## HOW DARK?

The GM's discretion when bestowing Conflict gives him some control over the rate of gain. Regularly granting more points potentially pushes characters closer to the dark side more quickly. Granting fewer points gives a character more leeway, making it easier to atone. Consistency is important in bestowing Conflict so the players understand the potential severity of their actions.

Power. Instead, he might be tempted to use dark side points to use the Force to escape a dangerous situation. The story of redemption can be dramatic and the source of many adventures.

The specific mechanics for what happens to a PC who falls to the dark side, and how he can redeem himself, can be found on pages 52 and 281.

## LIGHT SIDE PARAGON THRESHOLD

When a Force user's Morality score is over 70, he crosses the paragon threshold and becomes a champion of good and the light side. Narratively, the paragon gains no specific abilities. However, the GM may play up the PC's status, such as by altering NPC actions or attitudes. The PC's reputation might precede him, making interactions easier or more difficult, depending on an NPC's background or the situation. Likewise, when in the presence of the PC, dark side users may sense the character's strong connection to the light side, and focus their attention or attacks on him.

# PLAYER MOTIVATIONS AND HOW TO USE THEM

Motivations are built-in story and roleplaying hooks. Players use Motivations to inform their characters' reactions to specific situations, offering a level of thought or detail beyond simply responding to the situation as presented. The GM uses PC Motivations to link the characters more intimately with the ongoing storyline. Players adhering to their characters' Motivations should be rewarded with additional XP.

## MANAGING MOTIVATIONS

The GM should note the PCs' Motivations to help plan interactions in an adventure. Motivations, especially those determined randomly, may conflict with the assumed Player Character adventure goals. Keeping this in mind when planning an adventure can help the GM avoid unexpected complications but also allow him to deliberately give the PCs a chance to make decisions based off their Motivations.

Players may keep their PCs' Motivations secret from other players. Secret Motivations add to the depth and tension of the game, but also entail possible story and party disruption when the secret is revealed. If the party has widely divergent Motivations, the GM should step in should player feelings be hurt when the Motivations are divulged.

The GM may simplify Motivation interaction by encouraging characters to combine their Motivations, when possible. The GM may de-emphasize Motivation for players disinterested in more complex storylines. Highlighting different Motivations can provide alternate adventures or encounters as a break from an ongoing campaign.

Characters rarely change their Motivations (see **Changing Motivations**, page 105). When they do, it should be for compelling story reasons, not because the bonus XP is too difficult to gain. Some Motivations naturally end when a character concludes a story integral to the Motivation. A Motivation may slowly be replaced by a new Motivation as the character's situation evolves.

## INCORPORATING MOTIVATIONS INTO THE STORY

The players dictate how important their characters' Motivations are in the game. Whereas Morality is a variable element that permeates character interaction, Motivation is part of a character's internal drive and should influence his life choices. The GM should reward players who play up Motivations with more story interactions specific to them.

Not all Motivations provide deep story hooks. It is fine if some players are more comfortable reacting to situations as they unfold. Some players rely on their Motivation to justify their actions.

The potential interactions arising from a character's Motivation and Morality can inspire complex storylines, complete with surprises from the past or unknown connections between characters. It is best if details trickle out during the adventure, adding mystery and foreshadowing revelations. An unexpected connection or reveal can add tension or surprise to a scene or story.

Motivation-related XP bonuses need not occur in every game session. Sticking to a Motivation should be a real choice. Actions that result in bonus XP might come at the cost of other rewards or cause difficulty with the group's goals. Sticking to a Motivation should be an interesting, and sometimes difficult, choice.

## REWARDING MOTIVATIONS

The standard experience point reward for utilizing Motivation is 5 XP per session, with one 10 XP reward for an exceptional session, which occurs once in the character's life. Additional bonus XP awards are not usually necessary.

Story-wise, Motivation rewards can include opportunities to use Motivation more often. An exceptionally good use of Motivation might grant a tangible, in-game item or advantageous situation. This might help compensate when adhering to Motivation was not in the party or another player's best interest.

Players should not be penalized for violating their Motivations. People and characters are complex entities, and it is sometimes difficult to anticipate when a character might find other forces more compelling than their normal internal drive. Usually, characters who act against their Motivations simply do not receive related XP rewards or story advantages.

## CREATING NEW MOTIVATIONS

Character Motivations extend conceptually beyond the categories and examples included in **Force and Destiny**. Additional Motivations are included in **Edge of the Empire**, **Age of Rebellion**, and other *Star Wars* roleplaying products.

In addition, GMs and players may create their own Motivations using the following guidelines:

- Check to see if the proposed Motivation fits within the Ambition, Cause, or Faith categories (or categories from other products, if available). If not, it is a new Motivation.

- Check to see if the proposed specific Motivation fits with any of the existing Motivations. If so, consider using the existing Motivation instead.

- Create a new category, if needed. Try creating a short list of related Motivations to test if the category is broad enough.

- Establish expected story types likely to work with the new Motivation, so the GM and player fully understand the intended driving force behind it.

- Make sure the new Motivation is something the character will have to work to maintain. Avoid Motivations that easily give up their XP rewards every session through actions a character might take in any game session, regardless of story.

- Offer the new Motivation to the other players, unless it is intended to remain secret in the game.

# FEAR

Fear takes a special role in **Force and Destiny**. Fear is a major path to the dark side. It is a weapon in the hands of the Sith and other dark side Force users. Careers and specializations such as the Aggressor also allow certain PCs to readily use fear. War, combat, intimidating adversaries, and environmental hazards may instill fear in anyone, anywhere. Fear can interfere with character actions and goals. It may reduce a character's effectiveness, make him hesitate, or even cause him to flee.

Within the game, fear is typically countered by the **Discipline** skill. If the character has time to prepare for the encounter, he may occasionally use the **Cool** skill instead, at the GM's discretion. The GM sets the difficulty of such checks and adds the appropriate dice to the character's dice pool. Interpreting the dice pool results is key to determining the effects of fear. The check result represents the character's ability to act in the face of fear, not necessarily the level of fear a character may feel.

### EXAMPLE

A character enters a vergence of the Force (see the **Adventuring in the Tree** sidebar on page 337) and is seemingly ambushed in a surprise attack by his most intimidating and lethal foe. The character makes a fear check by rolling a **Discipline check** with a difficulty set by the Game Master based on **Table 9–3: Fear Guidelines** on page 328. The result of the check is a failure ▼, compounded by uncanceled ✸. Checking the result in the **Effects of Fear** section, on page 328, indicates that the character suffers strain as he reels from the shocking surprise. His fear interferes with his ability to concentrate and fight, represented by adding ■ to each of his skill checks until he can overcome his fear or the encounter ends.

## WHEN TO MAKE A FEAR CHECK

Anytime Discipline or Cool is used to counter fear, it is called a fear check. Not every frightening situation requires a fear check. It should be restricted to unusual circumstances or the first time a character experiences a particularly frightening situation. A Sentinel fighting stormtroopers probably doesn't need to make a check. If Darth Vader appears and the Sentinel has never seen him personally, a check is appropriate.

The GM determines the frequency of checks. Typically, once a check is rolled, the GM should not require another check for the same source of fear during the same encounter, unless the circumstances change significantly. Stories highlighting fearful situations may require more checks.

## DETERMINING FEAR DIFFICULTY

The difficulty of a fear check is determined taking into account both the circumstance and the individual experiencing the fear. No two people respond the same way to a frightening situation. Where an untrained civilian might freeze in terror when a fight breaks out, a trained soldier may act with confidence and effectiveness. This is not to say that the soldier is unafraid; it simply means that he is better able to act in the face of fear.

Example circumstances and difficulties are shown on **Table 9–3: Fear Guidelines** on page 328. The listed difficulties reflect the fear levels of a person without prior experience in the given event. The difficulty of the check can be upgraded. Upgrades usually depend on the circumstances of the check, including details about the creature or character that causes the check.

For example, confronting a grim warrior in black armor and carrying a lightsaber could at the very least be a **Daunting (◆ ◆ ◆ ◆) check**. However, knowing that the warrior is Darth Vader, who hunted down and killed the Jedi and is a Dark Lord of the Sith, can upgrade the difficulty of the check three times. The GM may add ■ to represent other aspects of the situation, such as surprise. The GM may also add ☐ if the character's resolve is supported by powerful allies or other aids.

## TABLE 9-3: FEAR GUIDELINES

| State of Fear | Fear Check | Example |
|---|---|---|
| Minimally Afraid | Easy (◆) | Somewhat overmatched in combat, a minimally dangerous creature, a minor threat to one's safety. |
| Moderately Afraid | Average (◆◆) | Obviously overmatched in combat, a dangerously aggressive creature, a credible threat to one's safety and minimal threat to one's life. |
| Very Afraid | Hard (◆◆◆) | Battlefield combat, a pack of aggressive creatures, a major threat to one's safety and moderate fear for one's life. |
| Mortally Afraid | Daunting (◆◆◆◆) | Terrifyingly intense combat, confronting a large and dangerous creature such as a krayt dragon, overwhelming fear for one's life. |
| Utterly Terrified | Formidable (◆◆◆◆◆) | A hopeless and utterly terrifying situation, combat against things incomprehensible to one's mind, being attacked by a group of wampas, fear so crippling that sanity cracks. |
| Confronting something reputed to be dangerous. | 1 difficulty upgrade | Escaping a disintegrating starship, negotiating under direct threat of violence. |
| Confronting something known to be dangerous and very rare. | 2 difficulty upgrades | Confronting a Sith warrior or Inquisitor. |
| Confronting something known to be extremely dangerous and unique. | 3 difficulty upgrades | Fighting Darth Vader. |

## EFFECTS OF FEAR

The GM interprets the dice pool results and may create additional effects that reflect the details of the situation. Some creatures or talents requiring a fear check might also dictate the effects of a failed check. As in other types of checks, 🔅 and 🔆 carry effects regardless of success or failure. If multiple fear checks are needed, 🔅 and 🔆 of later rolls may cancel out effects from earlier rolls.

### Suggested minimum failure or negative effects:

- **Failure:** The character adds ■ to each action he takes during the encounter.

- **Threat:** The character suffers a number of strain equal to the number of ▼. If the check generates 🔅 🔅 🔅 or more, the character can be staggered for his first turn, instead.

- **Despair:** The character is incredibly frightened and increases the difficulty of all checks by one until the end of the encounter. In addition, the character accrues Conflict as detailed in the **Fear Leads to Anger...** section, below.

### Suggested success or positive effects:

- **Success or multiple successes:** The character avoids any fear effects, except those triggered by 🔅.

- **Advantage:** Add □ to the next character's fear check. If spending multiple 🔆, grant □ to an additional player's first check.

- **Triumph:** Can be spent to cancel all previous penalties from fear checks or to ensure the character need not make any additional fear checks during the encounter, no matter the source.

## FEAR LEADS TO ANGER...

Fear may affect characters with a Morality score in another way. Instead of the suggested failure or negative effects, the GM may bestow an amount of Conflict equal to the difficulty of the check for a failed check. When a PC suffers a 🔯 result on the check, this happens automatically and in addition to the normal effects of the 🔯. The Conflict points cannot be negated by a ✪ on a later fear check.

# ADJUDICATING DESTINY POINTS

Destiny Points (see page 35) represent the inherent connection between the characters, the villains, and the fate of the galaxy—or at least their part in it. Destiny Points are flexible and fickle, sometimes aiding the characters, sometimes hindering them. They also represent the influence of the light and dark sides of the Force on the characters' actions and lives. The flow of Destiny Points between the light and dark side pools represents the shifting balance of power between the light and dark side of the Force.

Mechanically, the Player Characters only spend light side Destiny Points, while the GM may only spend dark side Destiny Points. This holds true even if the PC is a dark side Force user. While this may seem a bit strange, having some PCs use dark side Destiny Points while others use light side Destiny Points breaks the system, and thus is strongly discouraged.

## ENCOURAGING DESTINY POINT USE

The flow of Destiny Points varies between different parties and GMs. Newcomers to the game may be reluctant to spend Destiny Points for fear of having them unavailable when a more important or critical situation arises. The GM should encourage Destiny Point use throughout the game. He should spend points regularly to replenish the light side pool, and to highlight the integral role of the Force and of Destiny in the *Star Wars* setting.

The players may ration Destiny Point use, and they are allowed to form strategies for Destiny Point expenditure. They might hoard them to prevent the GM from using them at critical moments. This is a good occasional tactic, but if it becomes a regular problem, the GM should balance things out by holding back a few points for his use at critical moments.

Ideally, there should be a free flow of Destiny Points throughout the game. While not every die roll needs to be influenced, the GM should use Destiny Points often when major NPCs are involved or critical moments arise. Overuse in lesser situations may annoy or demoralize the players, especially when using starting characters.

More subtly, the sudden use of Destiny Points against consecutive die rolls can highlight the difficulty of the Player Characters' current approach. Perhaps the dark side is stronger at this location. Perhaps the Player Characters have taken the wrong path, and this is the way the Force is telling them there might be a better approach. Using Destiny Points instead of ■ to fulfill this role hints at the influence of the Force over the situation instead of naturally occurring hindrances.

## DESTINY POINTS AS NARRATIVE AID

Destiny Points can influence the ongoing story narratively. The players may spend Destiny Points to improve their immediate situation. These expenditures are classified into three categories: dumb luck, reasonable extrapolation, and common sense.

### DUMB LUCK

Dumb luck comes into play when the players request something that might reasonably be expected to be absent in the current location or situation, but is somehow available. Examples include finding a password hidden in a desk, discovering a much needed piece of equipment in an abandoned mechanics shop, or even just recovering the right part in a junk pile. Dumb luck can explain a lot, but it should not be allowed when it stretches credulity too much. Salvaging exactly the right hyperdrive part from a dissimilar starship shouldn't normally work.

### REASONABLE EXTRAPOLATION

Reasonable extrapolation occurs when the players request something that could logically be available in the current location. Finding a medpac in an emergency vehicle, locating a secured comlink for an enemy's comm system on a high-ranking officer, and benefiting from an NPC's plans are examples of reasonable extrapolation. The characters usually should find what they are looking for. It may not be exactly what they want, but should be adaptable in some fashion.

### COMMON SENSE

Sometimes, common sense explains an item's availability. For example, fruit should be found on a fruit tree in season, a toolbox contains the proper common tool, or a freighter's computer system contains the shipping manifest. The item is expected to be there, but there is not a 100% chance, which makes the Destiny Point useful. If the requested item is nearly guaranteed to be there, the GM may grant the item without Destiny Point expenditure.

It is up to the GM to approve all Destiny Point uses to influence the narrative. In essence, the GM should decide if the request is reasonable given the circumstances and assess any impact on the adventure plot. Creativity should be rewarded whenever possible. However, the players should not be allowed to abuse the system to avoid paying for something they could otherwise afford or to circumvent prohibitions that would normally prevent them from acquiring the item or service. Likewise, the characters should not be allowed to use a Destiny Point to make up for unusual forgotten items or poor planning, or to give them something they purposely avoided or left behind.

If the Destiny Point use would derail the adventure plot, it should be denied or altered, even if it would be a reasonable request in other circumstances. For example, if the adventure purposely restricts the characters' resources, using a Destiny Point to find a needed item at just the right moment probably should not be allowed.

# CREATING ENCOUNTERS, ADVENTURES, AND CAMPAIGNS

Adventures are the heart of the roleplaying game experience. Most GMs and players use the same characters through multiple adventures that together form the overall campaign. The adventures might lead directly from one to the next, advancing a larger story arc or catering to the ambition and direction of the Player Characters. Adventures can also be relatively unrelated, with the PCs providing the common thread through the stories. This section discusses FORCE AND DESTINY adventure and campaign creation in detail.

## CREATING A FORCE AND DESTINY ADVENTURE

Creating new adventures can be one of the most exciting and enjoyable aspects of becoming a Game Master. Creating an interesting story that is also fun and mechanically compatible with the PCs is challenging. This section will help GMs create their own adventures, specifically ones that are thematically appropriate for FORCE AND DESTINY.

### USING PUBLISHED ADVENTURES

Using published adventures gives the GM a prime example of how a FORCE AND DESTINY–style adventure works. It also allows players from different gaming groups to have shared experiences, letting them compare both how the adventure developed and their differences in approach and final outcomes. While published adventures are useful, the GM needs to create his own adventures to extend the story or bridge gaps between official adventures.

## ASSEMBLING THE CAST

Every episode, adventure, and story needs a cast of memorable characters. Sometimes, the major characters are outlined first, with the story developing around their goals and actions. Sometimes the plot comes first, generating characters to fulfill certain roles or cover aspects of the story. Usually, the characters and plot are developed together and complement each other.

### STOCK NPCS

Stock NPCs are the unnamed masses the Player Characters encounter, battle, and negotiate with in most game sessions. They are often minions and rivals (see **Chapter XII: Adversaries**, page 399). Stock NPCs in a FORCE AND DESTINY adventure include the average stormtrooper, Imperial Security Bureau agents, inexperienced and untrained Force-wielding opponents, and so on. Many stock NPCs don't even need statistics, or can rely on standard stats provided in this product or others. Stock NPCs usually don't have much of a backstory, or at least not one that directly influences the adventure. They are usually short-term contacts or adversaries.

### RECURRING CHARACTERS

Recurring characters are those whom the PCs encounter on a regular basis. They usually have names, and often the GM will create specific stats for each. Recurring characters might be enemies or associates of the Player Characters. They can be anything from an ally who turns a blind eye to the character's Force use and suspicious actions to major villains out to get them. These characters are typically rivals or nemesis adversaries (see **Chapter XII: Adversaries**, page 400).

Recurring characters help make the galaxy a more familiar place. They also save the GM a lot of planning time. It's much easier to rely on an old favorite character than to come up with a new one for every session. GMs should find ways to integrate such characters into the storyline. Turning background characters into influential characters is a way to build a more layered and interesting story.

### FAMOUS CHARACTERS

*Star Wars* is filled with interesting characters famous within the galaxy far, far away. Not all of the characters made famous by the movies are actually well known within the galaxy itself. Many in the galaxy know who Darth Vader is. Fewer will recognize Ben Kenobi or a certain pair of common-looking droids.

The GM may use famous characters at his discretion. Part of this decision should be based on the GM's thoughts toward maintaining official continuity (see **Using The *Star Wars* Expanded Universe**, on page 315). Some characters are better than others at literally and figuratively surviving encounters with the Player Characters. If the GM wants to maintain continuity, it is not a good idea to place major movie characters in situations where the PCs could logically endanger them.

However, using recognizable characters is a great way to increase the *Star Wars* feeling of the game session. Being hauled before Darth Vader elevates a scene in the players' minds in ways that add layers of tension and information not easily conveyed with a new or lesser-known NPC. Higher-profile characters from the movies or other sources can assign missions or hire the PCs to fulfill specific requests. A character might also deal with the PCs from beyond their immediate reach, such as via holographic communications or view screens. The novelty of famous characters wears off quickly, so it's best to limit such encounters to special occasions.

## CREATING MEMORABLE NPCS

Creating an entertaining and memorable ally or enemy is challenging, but it is usually worth the extra effort. Ideally, players should enjoy interacting with the character, and recall him fondly well after the game is over.

There is no single formula for creating a successful character. Books and other resources that discuss characters in novels and stories are equally helpful when researching character creation. However, there are elements with which every GM can start:

- **Select the character's species and homeworld, and what he learned from it.** Sometimes making an NPC a species other than "stock" human can make that character more memorable. Even NPCs who move around the galaxy

are influenced by the attitudes or environment of their original or current home planet.

- **Select the character's profession and former professions.** Characters' professions influence their current actions. NPCs have pasts exploitable by the GM or the players.

- **Create the character's personality.** Personality traits run the gamut from arrogant and overbearing to kind and wise. Highlighting a few basic traits when interacting with the PCs makes a character more memorable. Personalities for allies should have at least one redeeming feature. In **FORCE AND DESTINY**, allies are often on the shady side. Enemies are often greedy and selfish, but these traits can be held in check by loyalty or fear of a leader.

- **Describe the character's physical appearance.** Characters in *Star Wars* have no shortage of tattoos, cybernetics, distinctive armor, signature clothing, scars, unusual hairstyles, and other memorable physical attributes. Major characters should have an immediately recognizable quality.

  - **Develop the character's "voice."** Selecting the accent, pitch, or tone of a character's voice is a crucial element in differentiating that character from others. A GM who is not comfortable with accents or voices should at least describe the character's voice from time to time.

  - **Consider the character's connection to the Force.** The Force is the major focus of **FORCE AND DESTINY**. The GM should consider how Force-using NPCs approach their situations. The GM should select the appropriate powers for such NPCs and note how close they are to falling to the dark side.

  - **Outline how the character treats others.** Plan how the NPC interacts not only with the Player Characters, but with friends and enemies as well. The NPC may not treat everyone the same or fairly, and the differences can reveal more layers of the character to the players.

  - **Create the character's stats.** Once the GM understands what the character is, he can develop game stats appropriate to the character.

# PRODUCING THE PLOT

Creating a good adventure means concocting an entertaining and plausible plot. Adventure ideas may come from innumerable sources, but it takes the GM to weave an idea into a playable game session. PC actions alter prepared plots almost immediately. Since players have a habit of moving the story in unexpected directions, it falls to the GM to create an adventure that is adaptable to change and can take multiple possible outcomes into account.

## THE STORY ARC

Much like a novel or other story, an adventure story arc should contain a beginning, middle, and climactic end. The beginning introduces the situation and the antagonists. The middle develops the events and character actions. The end ties up major plot points in a dramatic finish.

### BUILDING ENCOUNTERS

After outlining a plot and noting adversaries, the GM should divide the major plot points into encounters. Adventures usually handle encounters one of two ways. They can be highly linear in nature, with one encounter leading directly into the next, or they can be more free-form, with the next encounter dependent on the exact outcome of the one before it. Of the two types, the free-form variety allows for the most flexibility during the session. Highly linear adventures run the risk of making the players feel like they've been railroaded into specific situations, with no control over their own actions. Giving the players at least the illusion of free will is critical to maintaining the fun.

### PACING

*Star Wars* adventures should be fast paced. While there is a place for investigation, political intrigue, and slower events, they should be interspersed among chases, skirmishes, dramatic confrontations, and battle scenes. The GM should keep the action moving. Action doesn't always mean outright combat. The GM should dispense with any encounter or scene that feels overly mundane, especially if it can be explained in a narrative.

If the players are at a loss as to how to proceed, the GM can provide just enough additional information to move them to the next scene. If the players spend too long mulling over a certain situation or stalling out over a specific plot point, the GM can introduce something new to react to. This can be subtle. A Force user can be tipped off by the Force and "get a bad feeling about this," or receive hints to the correct decision. The "something new" can also be as blatant as thugs kicking down the door. Outside events that

## IN MEDIA RES

Latin for "in the middle of things," *in media res* is the time-honored technique of starting a story in the middle of the action. *Star Wars*: Episode IV *A New Hope* starts immediately with a Star Destroyer pursuing and blasting away at a Rebel blockade runner. Similar techniques can create an exciting start for a new adventure. The players are forced to deal with the immediate situation before delving into the underlying issues that created it in the first place.

The GM can combine this concept with one or more of the PCs' backgrounds. The Empire might already be pursuing the PCs or an associate for reasons other than their Force connections. They might start with a mysterious holocron spouting unexpected or dangerous advice. The action doesn't have to center on the Player Characters themselves; they might just be in the wrong place at the wrong time.

intrude on the Player Characters' plans can make the players feel like their PCs are part of a larger world that advances even when they do not.

### DRAMATIC ACTION

Not every scene or encounter involves high drama. However, major events should have a dramatic focus. The GM should create critical moments that significantly impact the overall storyline. The outcome of these encounters should have real consequences for the plot. The Imperial agent actually arrests PCs. The Empire readily throws the Player Characters in detention if they are suspected Force users or Rebels. Most dramatically, their characters might not make it through this encounter alive. If the players are truly concerned about the outcome of the encounter and its effects on their characters, it quickly raises the level of drama in the scene.

### CONTROLLING ENCOUNTER DIFFICULTY

Building a challenging encounter without overwhelming the PCs is an exercise in controlling adversaries, combat, and environmental difficulties. Not every encounter needs to be a fair fight, but most of the time, the Player Characters should have a decent chance of winning or escaping.

Adversaries in combat encounters consist of minions, rivals, and nemeses (see **Chapter XII: Adversaries**). When selecting adversaries, the GM must compare their attack skills and defenses with the Player Characters' abilities. If an adversary uses a dice pool comparable to the PCs' dice pools for the same skills, it is an appropriate individual opponent. If the PCs are outnumbered, their opponents should include more minions and rivals that are less of a threat individually, but are more effective in numbers. Individually, these opponents' combat abilities should be one or more dice lower than those of the PCs.

Balancing narrative scenes is less of a concern. If die rolls are needed, they usually involve skill checks. The GM simply needs to confirm that any adversaries have a roughly even chance of successfully opposing the Player Characters' skill checks. However, it is perfectly acceptable for opponents to have greater skill and abilities in these scenes, especially if it is important to the story.

## ENCOUNTER VARIETY

Each adventure includes a variety of encounter types, but FORCE AND DESTINY games should feature exploration and mystery to a greater degree. Characters of every career type need the opportunity to contribute significantly to the story. Most adventures should be a mixture of combat, roleplaying, exploration, and confrontation encounters. Some may mix in investigation, training, and other forms of play less common in the core Star Wars experience. Encounters should also vary in location and adversaries. See **Running a Full Campaign**, on page 334, for encounter location ideas.

## DIRECTING THE SESSION

FORCE AND DESTINY sessions feature the Player Characters' personal struggles learning, using, and hiding their Force abilities. It is them against a galaxy that fears their abilities, fears the consequences of associating with them, or both. While the PCs may be tempted and even encouraged to act heroic, the more open their heroism, the more trouble they will generate for themselves. GMs should keep this in mind when playing NPCs and improvising new characters and situations on the fly.

### LET THE PLAYERS SHINE

GMs must remember that the Player Characters are the stars of the show. No matter how complex or exciting the plot, the Player Characters should always feel they are the center of attention. Following this notion, each individual player should also get moments of glory within an adventure. It is common for players to create characters focused on roles they enjoy playing, often with an effort to diversify the group and make sure all potential bases are covered. When crafting an adventure, the GM should build in moments for each of those character types, or specific characters, to significantly contribute to the story. In short, give the players a chance to shine both in-game and out.

## PRIOR TO START OF PLAY

Character creation or adjustments should be completed before the start of play. Prior to a session, the GM can choose to trigger Morality (see page 323) and determine whether he is going to work a character's Morality into the session.

## THE OPENING SCROLL

Every Star Wars movie starts with scrolling text that explains the immediate situation to the audience. It gives a little bit of context to the opening scene and foreshadows major plot developments. The GM can write his own opening scroll for adventures he creates. It helps tie into the overall Star Wars feel and provides an easy introduction for the players. The GM should mimic the scroll style, limiting the text to the bare bones of what is required to set up the opening scene. Star Wars: Episode IV A New Hope does this in three long sentences. The GM should leave out detailed descriptions, working them in later as part of the first encounter.

## SCREEN WIPES

Star Wars movies use screen wipes to transition from scene to scene, jumping forward in time or changing locations. GMs can use metaphoric screen wipes to transition between encounters, especially if a lot of time has passed. These can be used to cover long periods of travel, switch between groups in a party that has split up for a long period of time, and cover mundane actions that have no effect on the plot.

## ENDING THE SESSION

Ending a session is different than ending the adventure. Ending a session can occur midstream, when the players do not have enough time to complete an adventure in one sitting. The players should note their characters' current status and write reminders about the exact situation they ended on so it is easier to recall at the start of the next session. Sessions can end on cliffhangers, leaving the players in suspense.

The GM awards Conflict, and the Player Characters apply the results to their Morality scores. (See page 48, and **Using Morality**, page 322.) Generally the GM also awards XP at the end of the session.

## ENDING THE ADVENTURE

An adventure is typically finished with the completion of the central story. When the adventure is part of a larger campaign, subplots or story elements may carry over to the next adventure. Campaign story arcs span many adventures. The GM should award XP and grant other rewards at the end of the adventure. Conflict points are awarded and applied to Morality just as they are at the end of a session. Player Characters are free to advance their characters between adventures.

# RUNNING A FULL CAMPAIGN

Campaigns are to adventures what the *Star Wars* saga is to individual movies. A campaign is a long-term story arc in which the action that occurs within the story of each adventure adds to the arc. Campaigns give the players time to play, develop, and advance their characters. Running a highly detailed campaign is not necessary; a GM might opt to run largely unconnected adventures with the Player Characters as the only constant. However, developing a larger story arc gives the players the chance to attain a greater goal than what can be accomplished in a single adventure.

## DEFINING THE CAMPAIGN

Above all else, FORCE AND DESTINY games feature the Force and Force users. How the PCs use the Force, for good or evil, makes morality a regular theme. Adventures should challenge the party's sense of right and wrong. The moral consequences of their choices should become apparent over the course of a campaign—both to the PCs and those around them.

FORCE AND DESTINY features exploration. The PCs explore their powers. They search out knowledge both academic and practical. They even search for hideouts. This leads them to unfamiliar places and situations, some safe, others dangerous. Trusting to the Force, or being manipulated by it, may lead PCs to a specific point or person, or bring someone to the PCs, and is one way to start a campaign.

FORCE AND DESTINY features the struggle between right and wrong. A central theme of this game is the PCs deliberately deciding to be good people, then facing the consequences of that choice. They must do good deeds, help the helpless, and fight oppression, all without any offered reward. The GM should confront his group with bad things happening to innocent people, and expect his group to do something about it.

## OUTLINING THE CAMPAIGN

Campaigns are made of multiple adventures, usually at least three or more, that require multiple game sessions to complete. Some campaigns may last weeks, months, or even years in real time. When creating a new campaign, the GM should outline the major events, locations, and characters of the story arc. It isn't necessary to understand every connection to every story idea from the beginning. A loose progression of events forms a skeletal plot that can be detailed as play proceeds. Much like adventures, campaigns usually have a beginning, middle, and end.

### LINEAR AND NON-LINEAR CAMPAIGNS

Like adventures, campaigns may use a linear or non-linear progression of stories. Linear progressions allow one story to build directly on the events of the previous adventure. They diminish Player Character freedom to take the story in unexpected directions. The GM must spend time and resources to keep the PCs on track, and the players might feel railroaded if it disrupts their illusion of choice too much.

A non-linear campaign takes more planning, but allows for more flexibility. In a non-linear campaign, the results of an adventure dictate which adventure comes next. When outlining the campaign, the GM creates a flowchart or tree of adventures in which a positive or negative (or other defined) outcome links up with an adventure that is based on that result. The PCs may skip some adventures completely, depending on the exact layout of the chart. GMs who like to give the players a lot of leeway in the direction of the campaign may find that the non-linear approach allows the story arc to evolve even if the circumstances or specifics change.

**Example Campaign Concept: Family Destiny.** A close-but-estranged relative of one (or more) of the Player Characters is killed in an Imperial raid on the PC's home. During the fight, the relative turns to the dark side and becomes something frighteningly evil. The PCs simultaneously investigate why she returned home and how to avoid her fate. They discover a secret family past that sends them to a distant world to find a holocron. The Empire pursues them relentlessly, eventually sending an Inquisitor to apprehend them and maybe find the ancient artifact.

**Sample Linear Campaign Basic Outline:**

- **Episode 1: Dark Arrival.** The PCs discover an estranged relative searching the family home. Just as she pulls a datachip out of a hidden compartment, an Imperial ISB agent and stormtroopers burst in. The relative defends herself with a pair of swords and the Force. She turns to the dark side, her eyes becoming yellow as she fights, enraged. The PCs grab the datachip when the relative drops it during the fight. The PCs are heavily outnumbered, but they escape as she is killed. The PCs must then elude Imperial patrols. If they tell anyone what happened, they are turned away or turned in.

- **Episode 2: Enemies Everywhere.** The PCs search for a way to decrypt the unusual datachip. They must get an uncommon data reader and expert advice or risk destroying the data. They search for a slicer in the underworld. The slicer sells them a decryption kit, but turns them in to the Imperials for a bounty. They must escape. They decrypt the chip and find a partial family history of hidden Force users—many of whom turned evil and were cast out by the family. They also find coordinates of a secret family-owned research outpost on a remote planet.

- **Episode 3: Hidden Outpost.** The PCs travel to the planet. The coordinates lead them to the abandoned outpost, now flooded by a river. The river is inhabited by dangerous water creatures. The PCs eventually find a case holding a holocron

# FAMILY DESTINY

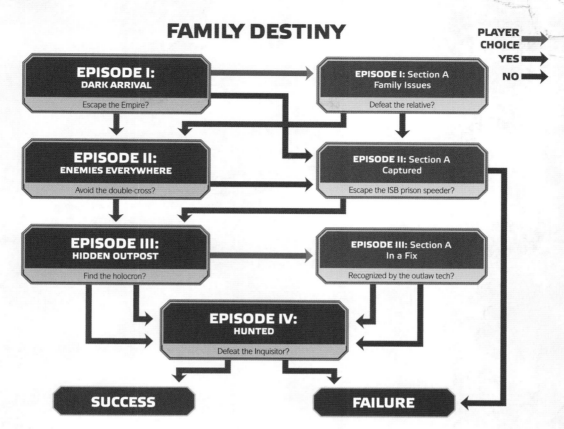

PLAYER CHOICE ➤
YES ➤
NO ➤

**EPISODE I:** DARK ARRIVAL
Escape the Empire?

**EPISODE I: Section A** Family Issues
Defeat the relative?

**EPISODE II:** ENEMIES EVERYWHERE
Avoid the double-cross?

**EPISODE II: Section A** Captured
Escape the ISB prison speeder?

**EPISODE III:** HIDDEN OUTPOST
Find the holocron?

**EPISODE III: Section A** In a Fix
Recognized by the outlaw tech?

**EPISODE IV:** HUNTED
Defeat the Inquisitor?

**SUCCESS**

**FAILURE**

in a flooded shuttlecraft. The holocron is damaged. Any successful repair not only fixes the holocron, but also immediately and unexpectedly activates it. It randomly turns on and off, spouting disjointed lessons about the Jedi and the Force. It dies after a few hours of disjointed advice.

- **Episode 4: Hunted.** Now that the PCs have obtained the holocron, they find themselves the target of Imperial attentions. An Imperial Inquisitor was already interested in them based on their prior interactions with the ISB. At the next civilized location they travel to, ISB agents locate the PCs and report them to the Inquisitor. The Inquisitor tracks them using the Force, confronting them as they try to leave the planet. The PCs try to protect the holocron, defeat the Inquisitor, and escape. Failure leads to arrest, incarceration, or death.

### Sample Campaign Flowchart/Tree Outline:

See the campaign tree, above, which builds off of the linear campaign and adds additional adventures:

- **Episode 1A: Family Issues.** The relative can survive and flee the PCs and Imperials empty-handed, and the PCs can choose to pursue her instead of following up on the chip immediately. The relative wants the chip, and she is willing to toy with the PCs instead of fighting them, at least at first. If any of the Force-using characters are morally conflicted, she tries to tempt them with the power of the dark side. She flees into the city but stays in touch with the PCs via their comlinks. If the PCs resist temptation,

she attempts to lure them into a trap to recover the datachip. The PCs can attempt to trick her by pretending to join her, can be lured into her trap, or can come up with another plan for dealing with her. Either way, they are forced to confront her one final time. They have a slim chance of convincing her to give up her evil ways, and if they fail, they must fight her. If they overpower her with words, she repents and leaves to start on the road to redemption. If the PCs defeat her in combat, she repents while dying. Otherwise, the relative leaves the defeated PCs to be captured by the Empire. (Proceed to Episode 2 if successful, Episode 2A if defeated.)

- **Episode 2A: Captured.** If the PCs are captured, they are loaded aboard an ISB transport speeder and sent to an ISB base in another city. Aboard the transport, the ISB does not realize what the PCs can do with the Force, and their unique abilities provide them opportunities to escape (perhaps by using Influence or Misdirect on the guards, or Move to grab a set of keys). If they do not escape before reaching the base, they may wind up confronting the Inquisitor and possibly being killed.

- **Episode 3A: In a Fix.** The PCs try to repair the holocron. If they fail, they try to find an expert outlaw tech on a civilized world. The outlaw tech gets it working, though some randomness remains. However, if the PCs generate too much ✶ or ▽ on interactions with him, he recognizes them and plans to sell them out to the ISB.

## THROW IN A MAJOR VILLAIN

Campaigns usually include at least one major villain. While the villain could be something generic, like the Empire, it is much more effective to make the villain an individual person or small group roughly equal in power to the PCs. This puts a face on the faction to which the villain belongs. The villain can be defeated, but the overall organization cannot. The villain may be known from the beginning, or may be discovered as the plot develops.

Major villains must be memorable (see **Assembling the Cast**, on page 330). They are most effective if their handiwork is seen in person by the PCs, even when the villain is not around. Villains must do evil, villainous things to motivate the Player Characters and set up a rivalry for good roleplaying. That's not to say every villain must be evil incarnate, but major villains should be worse than the average bad guy. Possible villains include Imperials of any sort, bounty hunters, crime lords, and competing groups.

## SELECTING LOCATIONS

The *Star Wars* galaxy is filled with fantastic locations and exotic environments. Spectacular locations are much more memorable than others. For example, Cloud City, floating above a gas giant planet; the city-sinkholes of Utapau; and the city-planets of Coruscant (Imperial Center) and Nar Shaddaa all offer very different and unique urban environments. While some types of adventures may be run at any of these locations, others will be enhanced by selecting one that complements the NPCs and envisioned plot. **Force and Destiny** locations tend to be where the Imperials are not. If the location itself isn't somewhat intimidating, then the characters inhabiting it, or the situation itself, often should be.

Selecting individual encounter locations is also important. They should be interesting in some fashion—in their location, layout, environmental effects or hazards, or even creatures supported. Avoid setting final battles or encounters in mundane locales or hallways. These should be epic locations that add greatly to the atmosphere and gameplay.

## ADVENTURES AND ENCOUNTERS INSPIRED BY MORALITY AND MOTIVATION

The campaign format allows GMs to insert adventures or encounters prompted by session-activated Morality or results of Motivation-inspired play. When planning the campaign, the GM should outline several encounters and a couple of adventures appropriate to the PCs' Moralities and Motivations. They should be adaptable and dropped in when needed.

If the GM prefers player decisions to dictate their adventures more than GM plotting, he should regularly mine the PCs' Moralities and Motivations for encounter ideas. The GM can construct entire adventures and campaigns around these ideas.

## PLANNING REWARDS

Every adventure in the campaign needs rewards. Rewards may be wealth, equipment, vehicles, knowledge, information, influence, or something less tangible but equally valuable to the PCs. Having a debt forgiven or receiving a favor, an introduction to an influential figure, or access to a safe area away from the Imperials are examples of intangible rewards. Tangible rewards may also be temporary, such as a useful but consumable item.

Story rewards are also a must for adventures. Completing an adventure should alter the characters' Morality, immediate situation, or both. Rewarding players for adhering to their PCs' Motivations also keeps the party happy.

Rewards at the end of a campaign should be impressive and grander in scale. They should significantly

The mystical nature of the Force manifests in unusual and unexpected ways. Force-focused mystical or supernatural encounters, adventures, and locations can provide an unusual break in the action, or become the center of a greater story. The tree in *Star Wars: The Empire Strikes Back* is an example of a mystical encounter that affects a single individual, whereas the Mortis trilogy in *The Clone Wars* illustrates an adventure-length story that encompasses a very large location and includes several individuals at once. These locations are called vergences in the Force.

While within a mystical vergence, it is difficult or impossible to tell illusion from reality. The GM is free to use this to challenge the characters in unexpected ways, such as when Darth Vader unexpectedly appeared with Luke in the tree.

A vergence may be focused on the light side or dark side. PCs with a Force rating can detect small vergences when within a few meters, though more powerful areas may be detected at far greater distances. What creates a vergence isn't known, though some locations are associated with the demise of a powerful Force user.

Vergence adventures or encounters have a metaphor or lesson to teach. These encounters provide a character with a glimpse of a possible (usually bad) future if he continues on his current path. The GM should map out such lessons ahead of time and craft them to the specific character or characters involved. Simple encounters may show the character turning to the dark side or using his abilities in less than noble causes. They might reflect a character's previous transgressions.

Characters usually remember their encounter within a vergence. However, they may return to the real world with no memory of what happened or why. This enables the encounter or adventure to act as an interlude or "what if" story to a larger campaign. However, GMs should craft this encounter for their groups. Since some players are not interested in the mystical nature of the Force, the GM should try to determine ahead of time if they would like to play with such unusual events.

help the PCs, though the GM needs to account for the rewards' effects on future sessions. Campaign rewards' values are much higher than adventure rewards.

## DEALING WITH PARTY CHANGES

Long-running campaigns increase the likelihood that players must leave before the campaign is finished. Fortunately, extended storylines provide multiple situations for a character to leave and a new character to be introduced. GMs should look for natural opportunities to do so, such as between adventures or when the characters are in a public location, where they can meet a new addition to the party.

Usually, a player leaves due to scheduling conflicts, as other life events influence playing time. However, if one or more player leaves because they are not enjoying the campaign, the GM should get feedback from them and the remaining players and consider altering the game. If the remaining players are okay with the direction, and there is little the GM can do to keep the departing players, there may not be much to change. However, if the players are not enjoying the campaign, and the GM can do something about it, he definitely should alter it. This applies to published adventures as well as original work.

## KEEPING THE CAMPAIGN ON TRACK

Keeping the campaign moving forward can be challenging when the players take the story in an unexpected direction. Most campaign outlines can withstand a lot of flexing and adjustment. An unexpected twist might require inserting a special encounter or session. If the players want their characters to follow a path that is completely tangential to the campaign, it is usually time to run an individual adventure or series of encounters to play out the situation.

## CONCLUDING THE CAMPAIGN

The conclusion of a campaign should be the highlight of the entire story arc. Being *Star Wars*, it should include an impressive skirmish or battle, along with a dose of personal drama for one or more characters. All major plots and subplots should be resolved logically and satisfactorily to the players.

Many campaigns end early due to unforeseen circumstances or player or GM fatigue. If interest is waning, the GM should end the game in a satisfying way, rather than letting it fall apart. Concluding a long-running campaign is often a major feat that the players and GM should rightly celebrate beyond the game.

# CROSS-GAME LINE COMPATIBILITY

ORCE AND DESTINY is an interesting and complex stand-alone game. However, it is also part of a much larger roleplaying experience. FORCE AND DESTINY is one of three fully compatible *Star Wars* roleplaying games alongside AGE OF REBELLION and EDGE OF THE EMPIRE. The three games are designed so that players can take elements from each of the three game lines and use them together with minimal effort. Thus, a lone Jedi in hiding can join a ragtag band of Rebels fighting against the Empire, or a smuggler can help his Force-sensitive friend and a couple of Rebel pilots destroy the greatest threat the galaxy has ever seen.

## CROSS-GAME PARTIES

When playing in the Force-centric stories of FORCE AND DESTINY, some players might want to explore the other facets of the Star Wars galaxy by playing characters from EDGE OF THE EMPIRE or AGE OF REBELLION. During character creation, players should feel free to select a character's species, career, and specialization from any of the three core rulebooks or their supplements. They may also take a career from one game line and then purchase additional specializations from another.

### MORALITY, DUTY, AND OBLIGATION

The primary difference between the characters from the three different game lines is Morality, Obligation, and Duty. Characters with Obligation from EDGE OF THE EMPIRE are indebted or otherwise affected by their dealings with the shady side of the galaxy. Characters with Duty from AGE OF REBELLION are focused on their status and impact within the Alliance. Characters with Morality from FORCE AND DESTINY are focused on their own personal balance between right and wrong.

When playing with a group including characters from two or more of these games, the three mechanics can be used in several different ways depending on the kind of game the group and GM want to run.

### CHOOSE MORALITY, DUTY, OR OBLIGATION FOR THE GROUP

The simplest option for a group is to select one of the three mechanics and use it, excluding the other two. Which mechanic the group decides to use depends on the adventure it wants to play.

Groups that want to focus on adventures in the galactic underworld and along the fringe of the galaxy should use Obligation. Groups that want to play a military-themed campaign focusing on war with the Galactic Empire should use Duty. Groups that want to play a more spiritual campaign featuring the struggle between good and evil should use Morality.

With this option, all PCs should use the step 2 of character creation from the appropriate core

rulebook: EDGE OF THE EMPIRE for Obligation, AGE OF REBELLION for Duty, and FORCE AND DESTINY for Morality. This mode of gameplay is best for games that primarily focus on one game experience over the others. (Note: PCs from FORCE AND DESTINY who are not using the Morality mechanic should ignore any Conflict they earn, and they cannot become dark side Force users or light side paragons as per page 52).

### CHOOSE MORALITY, DUTY, OR OBLIGATION FOR EACH PLAYER

In this type of game, each player uses Duty, Obligation, or Morality in accordance with whether his character has selected a career from EDGE OF THE EMPIRE, AGE OF REBELLION, or FORCE AND DESTINY. This means that some characters may be using one system while other characters may be using another system.

This option works best for groups who want to focus on broader adventures within the *Star Wars* universe, rather than adventures with a more focused theme. Groups with diverse characters from all three game lines may want to consider this option.

With this option, all PCs follow step 2 of character creation in the rulebook that contains their chosen career. This option is simple and easy for a group to use, because each player needs to track only one mechanic, and his character is guaranteed to be using the mechanical system designed for his career. However, the GM will have to do a little more bookkeeping to keep track of up to three different mechanical systems. The GM needs to create a separate chart for Duty and Obligation (players using Morality track that on their own).

When generating starting Duty or Obligation, the starting amount is determined by the number of Player Characters using that mechanic, *not* the total number of Player Characters in the group.

### COMBINING MORALITY WITH DUTY OR OBLIGATION

The third option for a group is to select Duty or Obligation and have any Force-sensitive Player Characters also use Morality. The group can choose Duty or Obligation based on the type of adventure it wants to play, while Force-sensitive PCs also have to struggle with the moral ramifications of their actions.

This option works best for groups who have one or two Force users, while the majority of the group is made up of non-Force users from EDGE OF THE EMPIRE or AGE OF REBELLION. It allows Force-using characters to explore the light and dark side of the Force, while the majority of the group focuses on adventures that explore EDGE OF THE EMPIRE or AGE OF REBELLION's unique themes.

In this option, all PCs should use the step 2 of character creation from the appropriate core rulebook, depending on whether the group chooses Obligation or

Duty. Then, any Force-sensitive PCs should also start with a Morality score of 50, as per step 2 of the **Force and Destiny** Core Rulebook. (They *do not* get to choose additional credits or XP; they can only do so by taking additional Obligation or sacrificing Duty. They also cannot change their starting Morality score.) If any PC becomes a Force-sensitive later in the adventure, the GM should also give him a Morality score of 50 and have him use the Morality mechanic as well.

## OTHER COMBINATIONS

The previous three options describe the easiest ways to combine Obligation, Morality, and Duty. However, this does not cover all the combinations of these three mechanics, which could include any pairing of the three, or even having every PC in the party using all three mechanics. When coming up with these combinations, use the following guidelines.

### ADDITIONAL STARTING CREDITS AND XP

No matter how many systems a character is using, he can never start with more than 2,500 additional credits and/or 10 additional starting experience points.

### ONE-ROLL TRIGGERS FOR MORALITY, DUTY, AND OBLIGATION

If characters in a group are using a combination of Morality, Duty, and Obligation, the GM can make a single d100 roll at the beginning of the session for all three mechanical systems to see if they trigger, applying the result to the Duty chart, Obligation chart, and list of player Morality values.

### CALCULATING STARTING DUTY OR OBLIGATION

Always use the number of PCs who are using Duty or Obligation, not the total number of PCs in the group, when calculating the starting values for these mechanics.

# BALANCING ITEMS

A lightsaber is an incredibly powerful weapon and an iconic one for Jedi and other Force users. Most **Force and Destiny** characters will expect to gain a lightsaber at some point in a campaign, and probably fairly early on so they get a chance to use it. So how does a GM balance this valuable reward if there are characters in the party (Force users or otherwise) who *don't* want lightsabers?

### ASYMMETRICAL ITEM REWARDS

One thing a GM can do to equally reward every member in a mixed group of Force users and non–Force users is balance the value of each reward based on its value to the Player Character, not its mechanical value. This can mean ignoring the listed price or rarity, and instead determining how central the reward is to the vision the player has for his Player Character.

For example, one player might make a Guardian from **Force and Destiny**. The GM could give his character a lightsaber at the end of an adventure. Meanwhile, another player is playing an Ace from **Age of Rebellion**. Instead of a weapon, the GM gives him an X-wing. A third player is playing a Technician from **Edge of the Empire**, and the GM gives that player an entire pit crew of repair droids. Each reward has wildly different uses and very different costs in credits. However, each is equally important to the character when it comes to realizing the character's goals, which means each player feels equally rewarded.

Even if the GM wants to hand out rewards that are roughly equivalent in cost, he should still consider taking the asymmetrical approach. For example, if one player gets a lightsaber for his PC, another PC shouldn't get a vibrosword (which is another close combat weapon that probably won't be as effective as the lightsaber). Instead, the GM could give the Shii-Cho Knight a lightsaber, the Sharpshooter could get a powerful sniper rifle, the Scoundrel could get a pair of fancy blaster pistols, and the Marauder could get some expensive battle armor and some extra credits to customize it. While each of these items will be useful in personal-scale combat encounters, they all play to the characters' strengths and allow them to focus on a different part of combat (melee combat, short-range shooting, long-range shooting, and surviving hits).

# BALANCING ENCOUNTERS

Gear rewards and character advancement are not the only game aspects that can be balanced asymmetrically. The philosophy of asymmetrical balance also holds true when GMs are designing encounters for challenging the party.

GMs should design their sessions with a mix of combat, social, and other encounters, with each encounter requiring the use of different skills and abilities. This helps ensure that each player has his own chance to show off his character. However, even if two characters are equally good at the same skill, the GM can change the encounter's narrative to feature one character over another. Even if a Smuggler and a Consular are both socially focused, the Smuggler is going to have a hard time relating to a monastery full of monks, and the Consular might be out of his depth making a deal with a local crime boss.

The same approach can be taken with the individual encounters. If a party includes a Sentinel with aspirations to knighthood, the GM should have him square off against a dark sider with a lightsaber. However, he should remember to throw in a bunch of stormtroopers for the Hired Gun to mow down at range, and perhaps an enemy bounty hunter with a disruptor that the Soldier can engage in a deadly snipers' duel.

### A FINAL THOUGHT...

Although this advice is intended to help players combining the three game lines, it can be just as valuable when addressing balance issues in *any* gaming group that has diverse and unique Player Characters.

# THE GALAXY

There are those who think of the galaxy as a settled and established place, linked together by tangled webs of hyperlanes and HoloNet nodes. However, it only takes one new hyperspace route opening up new territories and exotic alien civilizations to make the galaxy suddenly seem twice as big and strange as before. Of the nearly half-trillion stars in the galaxy, only a fraction have been surveyed, even fewer have been thoroughly explored, and even fewer still have been colonized. Even so, Imperial databases recognize over five million intelligent species and counting. In other words, it is impossible to go everywhere, see everything, and meet every alien species.

A spiral galaxy with five distinct arms, known space was once defined by spacers as a swath of stars referred to as "the Slice," a heavily surveyed, triangular expanse flaring eastward from galactic center across thousands of light years. Over millennia, the Republic expanded and divided known space into nine distinct regions. These regions are rough, concentric rings, flaring out from the center of the galaxy and into the scattered stars at its very edge.

The spherical center of the galaxy is a dense, roiling mass of black holes, stars, and shifting gravitational fields called the Deep Core. The Core Worlds are a flattened disc of stars encircling the Deep Core. The eastern quadrant of the Core, also known as the Arrowhead, is the ancestral cradle of humanity. The Colonies region is the next concentric ring outward, settled long ago by the generation and sleeper ships that defined early colonization efforts.

Improvements to hyperdrive technology created a three-thousand-year expansion boom called the Great Manifest Period. This era defined the Slice by blazing two Rimward trade routes from the Core: the Perlemian to the north, and the Corellian Run to the south. Expansion into the Inner Rim created another belt of inhabitable space beyond the Colonies. Soon after, as explorers abandoned the hyperspace cannon and beacon networks in favor of modern hyperdrive technology, the Republic opened the Expansion Region for settlement in hopes of discovering new resource-rich worlds.

Meanwhile, explorers in the center of the galaxy still had their hands full discovering new routes to uncharted stars right in their own stellar backyard. As they did so, they learned that most of the galaxy's galactic West was hidden and inaccessible behind a deadly web of hyperspacial anomalies. Ships that ventured into their roiling depths seldom made it through into the uncharted regions beyond, and even fewer returned. Explorers collectively referred to the unseen side of the galaxy opposite the Slice as the Unknown Regions, while the unsettled stars just beyond defined borders are called Wild Space. As exploration pushed westward, what was once Wild Space to the south settled and became the Trailing Sectors and the Western Reaches, and to the north, the Trans-Hydian Borderlands and the New Territories. As millennia wore on, exploration of the galaxy continued at a steady pace, necessitating the creation of two more belt-like regions, called the Mid Rim and Outer Rim, to satisfy the full radius of the galaxy.

While the explored regions of space represent over half the geography of the galaxy, vast pockets of space within them remain unexplored. The Core and Colonies regions possess an intricate web of hyperspace routes packed with inhabited worlds, but other regions have settlements only along major hyperspace routes. Whole swaths of the galaxy remain undiscovered, waiting for the footsteps of intrepid explorers.

# THE STATE OF THE GALAXY

The Galactic Empire rose from the ashes of the ineffective Republic in the wake of the Clone Wars. Clothed in absolute power, Emperor Palpatine rules a grateful populace in the Deep Core, Core Worlds, and Colonies, with strong control over the Inner Rim. However, in the Mid Rim and Outer Rim, his authority is much weaker and often relies on the barrel of a blaster or the looming presence of orbiting Star Destroyers.

The Hutts' domain has shrunk considerably in the decades since the Clone Wars, but they still control a significant swath of space in the Mid Rim and Outer Rim. Their empire of gangsters and crime lords relies on soft influence and political power rather than overt military might, and it can sometimes be hard to see where Hutt Space ends and the rest of the galaxy begins. Other independent and client states like Bothan Space and the Corporate Sector manage their own domains with minimal Imperial oversight, though they pay tribute to Coruscant and the Emperor in tithes, taxes, or political deference.

With the destruction of the Death Star at Yavin, the Alliance to Restore the Republic has catapulted itself onto the stage of galactic politics. Now the Rebel Alliance wages an all-out war with the larger and more powerful Galactic Empire, fighting fleet actions, ground battles, and conflicts of subversion or politics. The Empire, in turn, has directed more and more of its ponderous (but formidable) military might to wipe out these upstarts and crush the dream of democracy and freedom in the galaxy once and for all.

# THE GALACTIC EMPIRE

The Galactic Empire is by far the most powerful government in the known galaxy. Emperor Palpatine rules from his throne on Coruscant, also known as Imperial Center. He has recently disbanded the Imperial Senate, the final remnant of the representative democracy of the Old Republic.

In place of senators, the Emperor appoints trusted Moffs to rule entire sectors of Imperial space, and governors to oversee individual systems. Grand Moffs oversee clusters of priority sectors as needed. These regional politicians have varying styles of governance, but whether a governor favors the redroot or the stick, the might of the Imperial war machine gives weight to his words. Unfortunately, the way some exercise this might can create unrest and foment rebellion.

The Imperial military is split between the Army and Navy, which command the legions of troops, towering AT-ATs, waves of TIE fighters, and terrifying Star Destroyers. The dreaded Stormtrooper Corps remains independent of either branch of the military and loyal only to the Emperor, though they work with both when required. Palpatine also has an even more loyal unit of soldiers known as the Imperial Royal Guard, who act as his personal bodyguards.

Beyond his formidable military, the Emperor maintains a cadre of diverse and elite agents who answer to him and him alone. Little is known about these shadowy and mysterious individuals. Some are called Inquisitors, while others go by different titles, or by no moniker at all. One, the most feared of all, is a Dark Lord of the Sith. However, all are extensions of Emperor Palpatine's power and authority. In the Empire, they speak with the Emperor's voice, and Palpatine entrusts them with the most sensitive and difficult tasks. In the last few decades, many of these tasks have involved hunting down and eliminating the last surviving Jedi, and eliminating potential Force users before they can become threats to the Emperor's reign.

## GALACTIC BUREAUCRACY

The galaxy has had many centuries to build up countless bureaucratic agencies, not all of which are directly controlled by the Empire. Imperial Intelligence, the Imperial Security Bureau, and to a lesser extent COMPNOR (Commission for the Preservation of the New Order) constantly compete to root out the Empire's enemies. In matters unrelated to the Rebellion, the Sector Rangers and Imperial Office of Criminal Investigations coordinate with local police forces to standardize law enforcement across the Empire and police the gaps between civilized worlds.

The Bureau of Ships and Services, a bureaucracy commonly and aptly known as BoSS, continues to operate facilities, issue licenses and titles for starships, and validate arms load-out permits. The BoSS also maintains incredibly detailed records of hyperlanes, trade routes, and stellar phenomena. If it involves getting from one place to another, the BoSS likely oversees it.

The Emperor uses his bureaucracy to control the flow of information throughout the Empire. He nationalized the HoloNet for military use, isolating planets from independent news sources. Imperial HoloNet News is available across the galaxy, but those outside the Core region regard it as unreliable propaganda. Likewise, regulated HoloNet access can be obtained, but few blithely believe their messages and activities on it go unmonitored. In the absence of trusted information about the government, cynics assume the worst. Shadowfeeds have exploded in popularity, revealing Imperial atrocities throughout the Rim. Imperial heavy-handedness, along with a lack of representation, has driven countless individuals to openly rebel against the Empire.

# THE REBEL ALLIANCE

While individuals and even entire planets have rebelled against the Empire since its formation in the wake of the Clone Wars, a large-scale, organized rebellion is a recent development. Early attempts at defiance began with Separatist holdouts from the Clone Wars in the Outer Rim. The Empire overthrew entire civilizations and created new Imperial strongholds while crushing the resistance. The brutal display cowed most planets into submission.

The rebellion-minded remained patient until their disparate forces united to become the Rebel Alliance. These groups put aside their differences to dedicate themselves to freeing the entire galaxy. This selflessness was critical to claiming the moral high ground when recruiting like-minded resistance groups to their cause. Together they formed the Alliance to Restore the Republic, more commonly known as the Rebel Alliance or simply the Rebellion.

The Rebellion began by staging a daring series of successful guerrilla strikes against high-profile targets. Military success begat diplomatic success, as

the Rebellion added soldiers and materiel to its ranks and its list of supporters and sympathizers swelled. The destruction of the Death Star at the Battle of Yavin marked the Rebellion's most significant victory against the Empire. The Death Star had destroyed Alderaan along with Rebel leader Bail Organa and countless supporters. It was only through perseverance and desire for freedom that the Rebels kept fighting and turned the tide. Now, with the Death Star destroyed, the Rebel Alliance has reinforced its standing as a powerful and skillful military and political force.

The Rebel Alliance has two primary assets, the Rebel Fleet and the Army. The Fleet remains mobile, jumping across uninhabited regions to stay hidden from Imperial agents. Alliance High Command dispatches orders from the Fleet through a combination of courier agents and secure networks. However, the Fleet is ill-equipped to transport the entire Army, so the Rebellion requires at least one world to train and quarter its troops. The Rebels previously used hidden facilities at Yavin 4 and Dantooine, but they were forced to evacuate by the Empire. In the meantime, High Command has dispersed many of its soldiers until a new headquarters can be established.

In addition to the Rebellion's military forces, it has a number of sympathizers throughout the galaxy. These critical allies provide the Rebels with information, arms, equipment, ships, and even asylum. However, sympathetic worlds must assist in secret to avoid

brutal Imperial retaliation. The Rebels' guerrilla tactics have enraged the Empire, and most commanders salivate for a large, immobile target on which to vent their frustrations, leading to tragic atrocities and even massacres on sympathetic worlds. Despite recent victories, the Empire is far from defeated, and the Rebels still face a vastly more powerful adversary.

# OTHER DOMAINS

While the Empire and Rebellion are the two largest factions in the galaxy, other powers share the galactic stage. Some civilizations maintain their independence from the Empire through either negotiation or military demonstration. These allied regions and independent enclaves are potential havens for those evading the Empire. Criminal organizations and powerful corporations likewise wield enormous influence bought from ruling governments with their vast stores of wealth.

### THE HUTT CARTELS

The Empire rules several client states which receive a measure of independence as long as they contribute to Imperial coffers. The Hutt Cartels publicly submit to Imperial rule, but they still hold true power over Hutt Space, which, despite shrinking borders, still encompasses most of the Slice in the Outer Rim. The Hutts control a criminal empire that extends beyond their physical borders, and they keep their fingers in all sorts of questionable dealings.

### THE CORPORATE SECTOR AUTHORITY

The Corporate Sector Authority is the 500-year-old brainchild of a cabal of power brokers running the galaxy's largest corporations. For centuries, the Republic ignored strip-mining and slave labor practices within the CSA's Tingel Arm of the Outer Rim out of a desire for cheap raw materials to fuel the galactic economy. Many of these organizations supported the Separatists during the Clone Wars, and when the conflict ended, the Empire nationalized the region and put Empire-friendly corporations in charge. Now, the Corporate Sector is a region of space entirely under the control of corporate interests. In exchange for a share of the profits, the Empire leaves them to run hundreds of star systems as they see fit.

### HERGLIC SPACE

The Herglics of Giju are an ancient, galaxy-faring civilization that once controlled much of the southern Colonies and Inner Rim, and was among the most influential powers of the Southern Core. However, their trade empire imploded millennia ago and shrank to approximately forty star systems. The Empire nationalized Herglic Space's industrial and manufacturing worlds

early, but the Herglics resisted the young Empire, creating a political disaster. Now, the Empire leaves Herglic Space as nominally independent, though many nationalized assets still exclusively supply the Empire, and the Herglics know their limited freedoms depend on their willingness to cooperate.

## OTHER POWERS

There are additional forces that have galaxy-spanning influence. Other influential criminal organizations in the galaxy include the Crymorah, a massive multi-pronged criminal syndicate based out of Coruscant, and Black Sun, whose criminal agents are involved in myriad schemes throughout the galaxy. The Pykes are a notorious syndicate of spice dealers constantly jockeying for power in the volatile spice smuggling racket. The Bounty Hunters' Guild maintains outposts filled with skilled, galaxy-hopping hunters. The Zann Consortium is a new player on the galactic stage, and growing rapidly. The CEO of Kuat Drive Yards and Lord Raith Sienar of Sienar Fleet Systems are two of the most powerful beings in the galaxy, behind the Emperor. Each has almost limitless resources and access to more security, employees, and worlds than many governments.

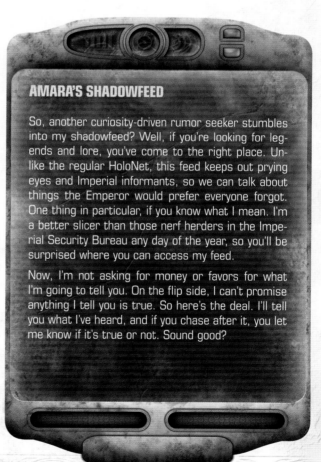

### AMARA'S SHADOWFEED

So, another curiosity-driven rumor seeker stumbles into my shadowfeed? Well, if you're looking for legends and lore, you've come to the right place. Unlike the regular HoloNet, this feed keeps out prying eyes and Imperial informants, so we can talk about things the Emperor would prefer everyone forgot. One thing in particular, if you know what I mean. I'm a better slicer than those nerf herders in the Imperial Security Bureau any day of the year, so you'll be surprised where you can access my feed.

Now, I'm not asking for money or favors for what I'm going to tell you. On the flip side, I can't promise anything I tell you is true. So here's the deal. I'll tell you what I've heard, and if you chase after it, you let me know if it's true or not. Sound good?

# THE GREAT HYPERLANES

Hyperspace is a superluminal parallel dimension that makes galactic civilization possible. Long ago, ancient human and Duros cultures reverse-engineered mysterious and pre-historical technology to create hyperspace cannons, hyperspace beacons, and, eventually, the modern hyperdrive. A trip that would take hundreds of thousands of years at sublight speeds takes only hours or days in hyperspace.

In these times, hyperspace travel is ubiquitous and taken for granted by most of the galaxy, but it is not without danger. Points in the alternate dimension have corresponding points in realspace, and objects with enough mass in realspace (such as stars and planets) cast mass shadows in hyperspace. A collision with one of these mass shadows usually spells doom for travelers. What's worse, objects that are navigable in realspace can prove deadly obstacles in hyperspace. Even something as benign as a nebula can create an impenetrable mass shadow. This is why established routes along well-explored areas of space are essential to intergalactic travel.

## MAJOR HYPERLANES

The prevalence of mass shadows throughout the galaxy necessitated a concerted effort to chart safe routes between worlds to encourage interplanetary trade and commerce. Five major hyperlanes connect the disparate regions of the galaxy. Fast, safe passage along each of these routes is critical to keep intergalactic goods and services flowing. If pirates or Rebels were to control even a small portion of a major hyperlane, it would generate a perception of weakness in the Empire. The Imperial Navy fields heavy patrols along the major hyperlanes to mitigate this risk as much as possible. Innumerable smaller routes branch off from the major lanes, connecting the known galaxy.

### HYDIAN WAY

The Hydian has only reached its full potential as the longest hyperspace route in the galaxy during the last few millennia. Explorers stitched the route together from myriad smaller routes, and it now spans the entire way from the Corporate Sector Authority at the northern edge of the galaxy through the Core and South into the Western Reaches and Wild Space.

**Notable Locations:** The Corporate Sector Authority, Telos, Bogden, Brentaal, Denon, Eriadu, Mustafar, Terminus.

### PERLEMIAN TRADE ROUTE

One of the first hyperlanes, the Perlemian loosely follows a route taken by early colonists from Coruscant all the way to the Tion Cluster and beyond to Wild Space. This route forms the northern border of the Slice and the southern edge of the Northern Dependencies and the Trans-Hydian Borderlands. Key branches wind their way to Hutt Space, Mon Calamari Space, and the Corporate Sector.

**Notable Locations:** Coruscant, Chandrila, Rhinnal, Brentaal, Raithal, Taanab, Lantillies, Roche, Abhean, the Wheel, Centares, and Lianna.

### CORELLIAN RUN

The Corellian Run is as old as the Perlemian Trade Route, and initially only linked Coruscant to Corellia. Eventually, the trail was blazed southeast to Ryloth and beyond into Wild Space. The Corellian Run forms the southern border of the Slice and the northern border of the Trailing Sectors, and was long ago settled predominantly by Corellians. Key junctions connect the Corellian Run to the Ag Circuit and Hutt Space.

**Notable Locations:** Coruscant, Corellia, Nubia, Loronar, Byblos, Denon, Milagro, Falleen, Ando, Christophsis, and Ryloth.

### CORELLIAN TRADE SPINE

Though it began as a small route connecting Corellia to Duro, the Trade Spine grew through the Southern Core, crosses the Western Reaches to Terminus. From there, the route crosses paths with the Hydian Way and extends into Wild Space.

**Notable Locations:** Corellia, Duro, Devaron, Foless, Bestine IV, Mechis, Yag'Dhul, Harrin, Kinyen, Bespin, Gentes, and Terminus.

### RIMMA TRADE ROUTE

Discovered by the nobles of the Tapani sector, the Rimma Trade Route runs from the rugged trade world Abregado-rae through the Southern Core and south to Wild Space. The Rimma Trade Route forms the border between the Trailing Sectors and the Western Reaches. A bypass route connects the Rimma Trade Route to Fondor and Mrlsst of the Tapani sector.

**Notable Locations:** Abregado-rae, Dentaal, Herglic Space, Ghorman, Thyferra, Yag'Dhul, Wroona, Sullust, Eriadu, Clak'dor VII, Sluis Van, Dagobah, Elrood.

# THE DEEP CORE

The bright center of the galaxy is also perhaps its most mysterious location, as its densely packed stars and massive black holes cause hyperspace routes to shift or even collapse daily. The Empire fiercely protects the few stable routes with mass shadow mines, *Interdictor*-class cruisers, and coded access to navigational updates, strictly limiting access to the region.

There are, however, a few inhabited worlds in the Deep Core. Historians have traced much of human galactic exploration back to the carbonite-rich Empress Teta system. Colonists used carbon-freeze techniques to hibernate during their protracted journeys to potentially habitable worlds. While Empress Teta has waned in galactic influence in the modern era of hyperdrives, it remains an old and established civilized world, and the gateway to the Deep Core. The Koros Trunk Line, which runs from Empress Teta to Coruscant, is one of the few publicly accessible hyperspace routes in all the Deep Core. However, the world features a major Imperial presence; travelers who wish to head further into the Deep Core must obtain permits from the Bureau of Ships and Services and the Imperial Security Bureau.

## HYPERSPACE SECURITY

Those granted access to the Byss Run or one of the other Deep Core routes must suffer an endless string of checkpoints. Imperial patrols verify credentials and update navigational data at each stop. The imposing number of warships at each checkpoint ensure spacers are on their best behavior. This network of patrols and security is known as the Deep Core Security Zone, and it nearly accomplishes the seemingly impossible task of locking down an entire region of the galaxy. Though there are holes in the net, they are small, shifting, and difficult to find and exploit.

Regional security is ultimately the responsibility of Grand Moff Gann, who governs from Odik II. Situated on the Byss Run, the Odik system serves as headquarters to the Empire's Fifth Army, the notorious Shadow Hand Command. Created during the Clone Wars, the Fifth has always functioned as a strategic reserve. Currently, Moff Gann has deployed Shadow Hand Command throughout the Deep Core in defense of the many fortresses and resource-rich worlds along the Byss Run.

Perhaps because of the strict security, countless rumors have spread throughout the galaxy about what goes on in the Deep Core. The theories break down into two basic categories: those centered on the Empire, and those concerning the now-extinct Jedi Order. Speculators suggest the Imperials have secret prisons, shipyards, fortress worlds, and more, while the Jedi allegedly hid treasures, historical texts, and even secret academies long forgotten.

Fringe researchers believe a number of mythical worlds, like Tython and Had Abbadon, exist somewhere within the Deep Core's swirling maelstrom of ever-shifting gravitational forces. The promises of fortune and glory draw explorers and archaeologists from across the galaxy to search for these and other lost worlds. However, exploring the Deep Core is dangerous. Those cleared to continue rarely return, leading the Empire to ban most expeditions.

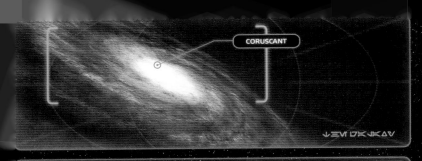
CORUSCANT

# THE GALAXY

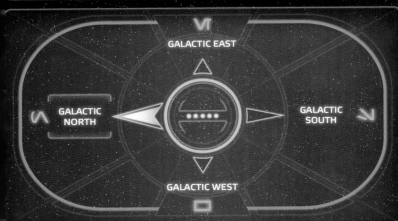

VI
GALACTIC EAST

GALACTIC NORTH

GALACTIC SOUTH

GALACTIC WEST

## MAJOR TRADE ROUTES OF THE GALAXY:

1. Perlemian Trade Route
2. Corellian Run
3. Corellian Trade Spine
4. Rimma Trade Route
5. Hydian Way

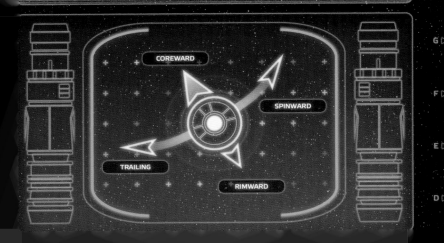

COREWARD

SPINWARD

TRAILING

RIMWARD

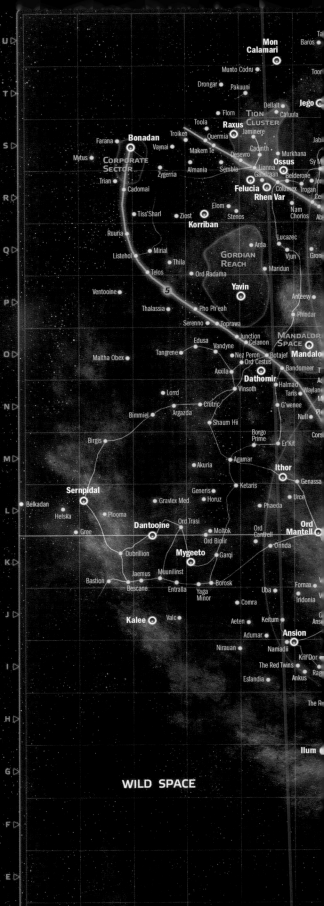

WILD SPACE

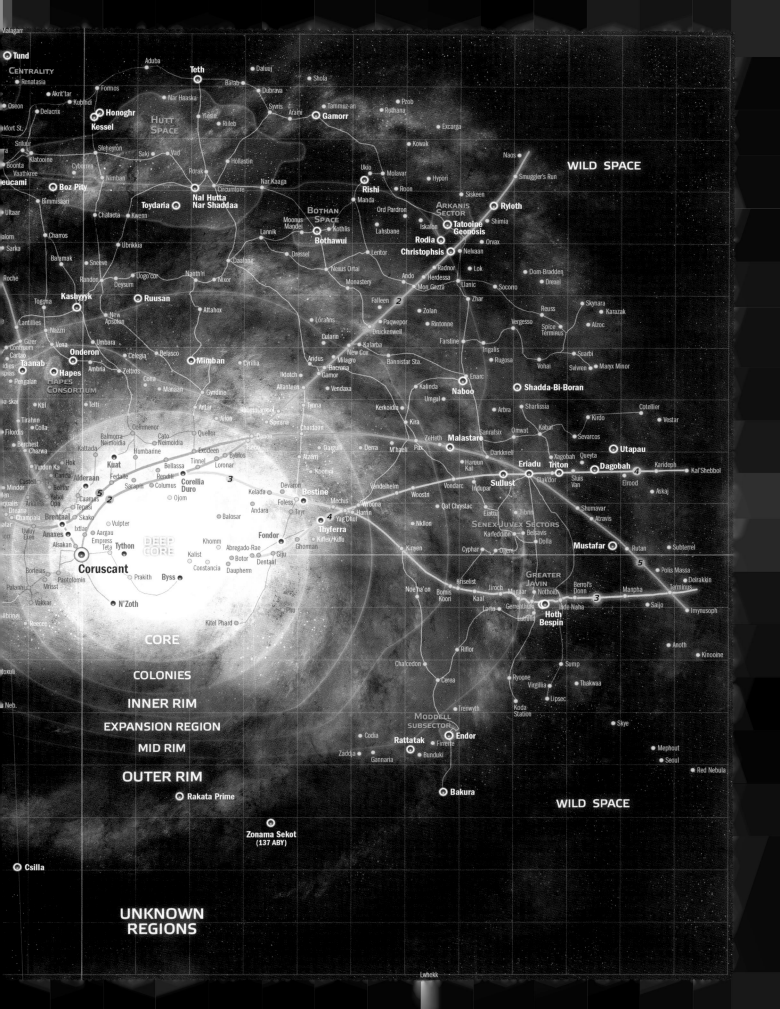

# NOTABLE LOCATIONS

The following are areas of interest within the Deep Core, during or before Imperial rule.

**Byss:** Also known as the Emperor's retreat, Byss is home to a massive Imperial citadel that nearly rivals the Imperial Palace on Coruscant. The nigh inaccessible world is an auxiliary throne world for Palpatine in the unlikely event Coruscant is lost. Byss is the most secure planet in all the Empire, defended by a combination of secrecy, misinformation, and some of the largest ships in the Imperial fleet.

**Byss Run:** The Byss Run is a secret hyperspace route with countless Imperial checkpoints from the Empress Teta system through Prakith and on to Byss. Advanced non-mass S-thread boosters hold the fragile hyperlane in place.

**Empress Teta (Koros Major):** Renamed millennia ago for a popular ruler, Empress Teta is famous as the galaxy's leading exporter of carbonite, a substance once vital to colonization efforts, now used for gas mining and other industrial processes in the Outer Rim. Other than the carbonite mines, the entire planet of Empress Teta is urbanized.

**Had Abbadon:** Experts believe it is possible the mythical world of Had Abbadon exists somewhere in the Deep Core. Rumors and legends connected to the planet claim it is anything from the birthplace of the dark side of the Force to the secret lair of a Jedi cabal that survived the attempted coup.

**Jerrilek:** Jerrilek is a tropical world favored by Imperial nobility and high-ranking military officers alike for its resorts and private retreats. The archipelago city of Graleca is a massive agricultural and manufacturing center built to support the world's tourism trade.

**Koros Trunk Line:** The Koros Trunk Line is one of the only hyperspace routes into the Deep Core free and open to public travel. Early in the Republic, bulk freighters hauled carbonite toward Coruscant and Corellia for colony sleeper ships. While carbonite is still exported today, most traffic is passing through from Coruscant to other worlds in the Deep Core.

**Prakith:** Colonized around the time of the Clone Wars, the Empire converted Prakith into a fortress world under Moff Foga Brill. Rumors persist of a dark citadel nestled in the mountains used by Imperial Inquisitors as a training facility, prison, or headquarters for directing a number of mysterious excavation projects.

## THE FORCE'S SONG

So you want some information on the Deep Core? Well, if you think you can get through the checkpoints and patrols, who am I to stop you?

There's a lot of rumors floating around the Deep Core, from tales of the Emperor's hidden pleasure palace to stories about that so-called Citadel Inquisitorius that I don't even feel comfortable talking about on a private shadowfeed. But here's one that's so crazy, there might just be something to it. It comes with a half-corrupted set of coordinates, as likely to send you into a black hole as get you anywhere. Maybe you can figure them out.

**<<Transferring data fragment—The following excerpt is attributed to Scout Ley Neetels. Archive data corrupted: dating procedures indicate fragment at least 3,000 years old.>>**

Every Jedi perceives the Force in a manner unique to their species, background, personality, and training. It is hard to describe, but for me, and perhaps this is because I am a Pa'lowick, the Force is a cacophony of notes emanating from everything, everywhere, that I have spent my life learning to hear. When the Force is in balance, the notes create a beautiful harmony of life. As a Jedi and an explorer, it is my sacred duty to seek out new worlds, that they might add a movement to the galaxy's great symphony.

It was maybe a month ago during an investigation on Jerrilek that I heard a low, mournful call tugging at my consciousness. I have heard variations of the song many times, and recognized it as a cry from something wishing to be found, to join the great cosmic orchestra in song. As I took the *Wandering Diva* into orbit, other notes joined the first and formed a simple theme. I let the song of the Force fill me and guide my hands over the controls. The tempo increased, and my fingers flitted across the navicomputer as if it were an ivory nalargon. I pulled the lever and shot the *Diva* into hyperspace, trusting in the Force to protect me.

By reversion to realspace, the theme had evolved into a rich melody, picking up flourishes as the Force guided me through jump after jump. I could feel the song coursing through my veins and the beat thumping in my bones. I was getting closer and things were beginning to happen faster, the jumps and course corrections keeping time. I felt the song building as I flew, and I dropped out of hyperspace as it hit its crescendo.

I have never felt so alive, dancing to the great, universal song. A blue-green orb with two moons, one light, one dark, filled the viewport, and the Force sang a triumphant fanfare reintroducing a long-lost planet to the galaxy.

**<<Data fragment ends.>>**

# THE CORE

There is a popular saying, "All routes lead to Coruscant." While the majority of major trade routes do funnel to Coruscant, the intended meaning is that no matter what happens in the galaxy, trace the events or credits back far enough, and the trail ends in the Core. Though this is usually meant as a positive remark on the Core's influence on the galaxy, Rim Worlders have often used it to air their displeasure with anything from government policy to a product's durability.

## HEART OF THE EMPIRE

The Core Worlds are among the galaxy's most powerful and prestigious planets, and they have been the seat of galactic government for millennia. While this power historically has been concentrated on Coruscant, worlds like Corellia, Kuat, Brentaal IV, and Chandrila wield enormous influence. With this long-held status has come unimaginable wealth and cultures that influence the galaxy. Long generations of inherited fortunes have given many Core Worlders the financial freedom to pursue the arts and sciences with unparalleled passion. Since the end of the Clone Wars, the Empire has wielded the stature and authority of the Core with ruthless precision to advance Palpatine's agenda.

The Empire has absolute power in the Core Worlds, and those living in the region are overwhelmingly loyal and supportive of all things Imperial. For those in the Core, the Galactic Civil War raging throughout the Rim Worlds is an almost abstract concept, something being fought "over there," thanks to Emperor Palpatine. The social elite of the Core have a deep, underlying fear that the filthy Rim-folk of the Rebellion are coming for their homes and riches, and they rely on the Empire to safeguard their privileged status. It is only the Emperor wielding the mighty Imperial war machine that keeps the Rebels at bay.

Many Core Worlders are obsessed with nobility and ancestry, some tracing their lines back hundreds of generations to famous explorers, politicians, and warriors. Among the Core's most influential families are the Ketos, Mottis, Organas, Prajis, Tagges, and Valorums. Beings from around the galaxy recognize these ancient names as key power brokers and trendsetters, though many epitomize Core World snobbery at its worst. It is also interesting to note that all of these families are human. While no alien species is exactly out of place in the diverse populations of the Core, there are few planets in the region with native non-humans that have spread beyond their system of origin, excepting Duro and Skako. This is likely because human colonization of the Core wiped out most native species, and those that survived are often insular and xenophobic.

## THE LOST HISTORY OF THE GALAXY

One thing players should keep in mind is that the *Star Wars* galaxy is *old*. Before the formation of the Empire, the Galactic Republic was around for tens of thousands of years, and groups such as the Hutts have been present even longer. Oldest of all organizations are the Jedi, who have existed in some form or another since before recorded history. However, age clouds the records of the galaxy, leaving much of early history cloaked in myth and legend and faded by time. In addition, the Empire has systematically eradicated information from public records relating to the Jedi Order or the Force in general since the end of the Clone Wars.

Openly researching the Jedi is a quick way to attract the attention of Imperial Intelligence or an Imperial Inquisitor, so wise seekers of lore conduct their inquiries in secret. PCs can also acquire this privileged information as a mission reward, as loot from a defeated enemy, or even while slicing a computer system or droid that might reasonably have such information.

## NOTABLE LOCATIONS

The following are areas of interest within the Core, during or before Imperial rule.

**Brentaal IV:** Brentaal IV is located at the intersection of the Hydian Way and the Perlemian Trade Route, which makes it one of the most vital trade hubs in the entire galaxy. Brentaal's warehouse district features massive facilities of major corporations across the galaxy.

**Chandrila:** A founder of the Republic and its very first agriworld, Chandrila is an idyllic paradise committed to democracy, peace, and harmony with nature. Chandrila's gardens in the Gladean State Parks are beloved throughout the galaxy.

**Corellia:** Corellia is home to the Corellian Engineering Corporation, a popular shipbuilder that produces fast, customizable ships. Corellia has also achieved a measure of infamy for the wanderlust of its natives. Many have gone on to become heroes or outlaws, and sometimes both.

**Coruscant:** Also known as "Triple Zero," in reference to its galactic coordinates, Coruscant has always been considered the center of the galaxy, and it is home to Emperor Palpatine's throne. The planet is a never-ending cityscape, with kilometers-tall skyscrapers dominating the skyline.

**J't'p'tan:** Still called Doornik-628E on some star charts, J't'p'tan is a sparsely populated world at the easternmost end of the Metellos Trade Route. H'kig

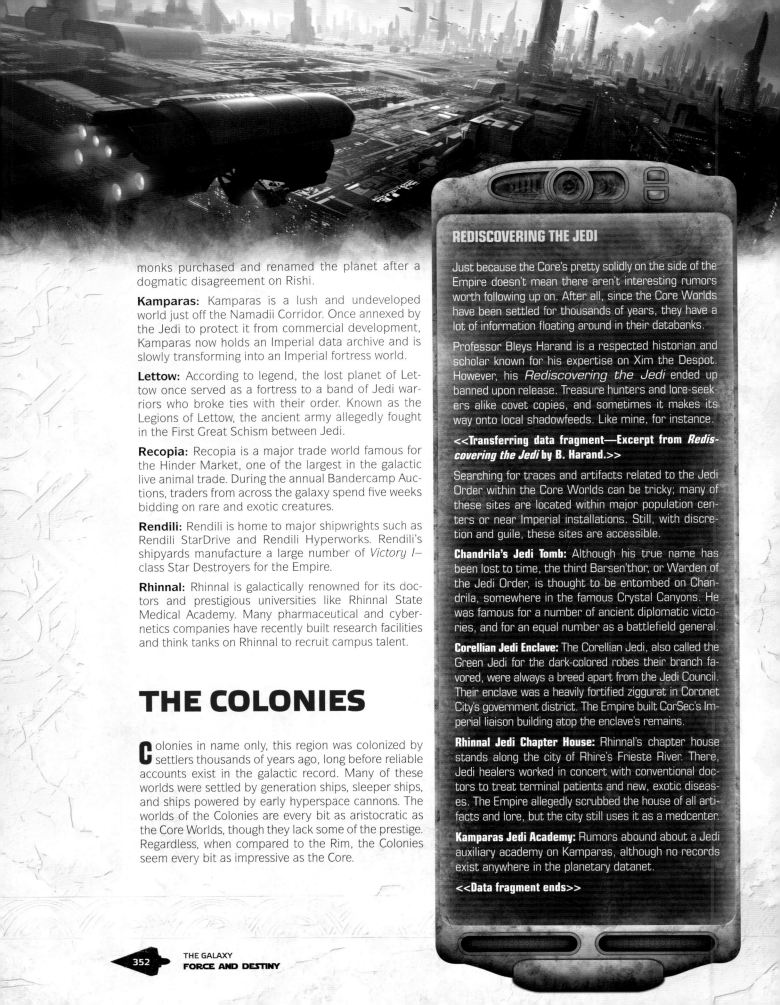

monks purchased and renamed the planet after a dogmatic disagreement on Rishi.

**Kamparas:** Kamparas is a lush and undeveloped world just off the Namadii Corridor. Once annexed by the Jedi to protect it from commercial development, Kamparas now holds an Imperial data archive and is slowly transforming into an Imperial fortress world.

**Lettow:** According to legend, the lost planet of Lettow once served as a fortress to a band of Jedi warriors who broke ties with their order. Known as the Legions of Lettow, the ancient army allegedly fought in the First Great Schism between Jedi.

**Recopia:** Recopia is a major trade world famous for the Hinder Market, one of the largest in the galactic live animal trade. During the annual Bandercamp Auctions, traders from across the galaxy spend five weeks bidding on rare and exotic creatures.

**Rendili:** Rendili is home to major shipwrights such as Rendili StarDrive and Rendili Hyperworks. Rendili's shipyards manufacture a large number of *Victory I–*class Star Destroyers for the Empire.

**Rhinnal:** Rhinnal is galactically renowned for its doctors and prestigious universities like Rhinnal State Medical Academy. Many pharmaceutical and cybernetics companies have recently built research facilities and think tanks on Rhinnal to recruit campus talent.

# THE COLONIES

Colonies in name only, this region was colonized by settlers thousands of years ago, long before reliable accounts exist in the galactic record. Many of these worlds were settled by generation ships, sleeper ships, and ships powered by early hyperspace cannons. The worlds of the Colonies are every bit as aristocratic as the Core Worlds, though they lack some of the prestige. Regardless, when compared to the Rim, the Colonies seem every bit as impressive as the Core.

## REDISCOVERING THE JEDI

Just because the Core's pretty solidly on the side of the Empire doesn't mean there aren't interesting rumors worth following up on. After all, since the Core Worlds have been settled for thousands of years, they have a lot of information floating around in their databanks.

Professor Bleys Harand is a respected historian and scholar known for his expertise on Xim the Despot. However, his *Rediscovering the Jedi* ended up banned upon release. Treasure hunters and lore-seekers alike covet copies, and sometimes it makes its way onto local shadowfeeds. Like mine, for instance.

**<<Transferring data fragment—Excerpt from *Rediscovering the Jedi* by B. Harand.>>**

Searching for traces and artifacts related to the Jedi Order within the Core Worlds can be tricky; many of these sites are located within major population centers or near Imperial installations. Still, with discretion and guile, these sites are accessible.

**Chandrila's Jedi Tomb:** Although his true name has been lost to time, the third Barsen'thor, or Warden of the Jedi Order, is thought to be entombed on Chandrila, somewhere in the famous Crystal Canyons. He was famous for a number of ancient diplomatic victories, and for an equal number as a battlefield general.

**Corellian Jedi Enclave:** The Corellian Jedi, also called the Green Jedi for the dark-colored robes their branch favored, were always a breed apart from the Jedi Council. Their enclave was a heavily fortified ziggurat in Coronet City's government district. The Empire built CorSec's Imperial liaison building atop the enclave's remains.

**Rhinnal Jedi Chapter House:** Rhinnal's chapter house stands along the city of Rhire's Frieste River. There, Jedi healers worked in concert with conventional doctors to treat terminal patients and new, exotic diseases. The Empire allegedly scrubbed the house of all artifacts and lore, but the city still uses it as a medcenter.

**Kamparas Jedi Academy:** Rumors abound about a Jedi auxiliary academy on Kamparas, although no records exist anywhere in the planetary datanet.

**<<Data fragment ends>>**

# FALSE ARISTOCRACY

Most Rim World nerf herders see little difference between the Core Worlds and the Colonies, but those living there are all too aware of the distinction. The Colonies have something of an inferiority complex when it comes to the Core Worlds, craving acceptance and a sense of equality, but never quite measuring up to the exacting Core World standards of culture and breeding.

Desperate for acceptance by the Core, the populations of the Colonies are notoriously staunch Imperial supporters, eager to inform on suspicious offworlders (particularly if they have the look of the Outer Rim to them). The Colonies look to the success of Commenor as a model to follow for achieving the kind of cultural status the Core respects. Many Colonies open new museums, art galleries, opera houses, and monument parks in hopes of endorsements from influential nobles of the Core.

Interstellar travel through the Colonies is more or less open and free, in stark contrast to the Core's incessant checkpoints and regulations. However, many worlds in the region take exception to scoundrels and Rim-folk. Long, hooded robes or a dirty spacer vest and worn trousers may arouse notice on an affluent Colony world, and a blaster worn openly on the hip may attract unwanted attention from the local authorities.

# NOTABLE LOCATIONS

The following are areas of interest within the Colonies, during or before Imperial rule.

**Arkania:** Arkania's icy tundras dominate the adopted homeworld of the tall, pale Arkanians. They are infamous across the galaxy as amoral geneticists of the highest order, and the Arkanian economy suffers from an Imperial ban on the export of cloning technology. Still, the planet has a wealth of diamond mines, worked by Arkanian offshoot subspecies genetically engineered long ago.

**Carida:** This planet was once a Republic military outpost, home to space station Valor and an extensive agricultural industry. While Carida still exports food, the galaxy knows it better as one of the largest military academies in the Empire. Carida trains stormtroopers for combat in extreme environments, and it is said to create the most disciplined officers in the galaxy.

**Commenor:** Commenor is the largest trading hub in the Colonies, and those from the region consider it the pinnacle of culture and status, equal to any world in the Core. While part of the Empire, Commenor retains an independent, though hardly rebellious, spirit.

**Commenor Run:** The Commenor Run connects half a dozen worlds between Commenor and Brentaal. The route is still profitable for spacers despite the destruction of Alderaan, though its use has since waned.

**Fondor:** Fondor, a member of the Freeworlds region of the Tapani Expanse, boasts some of the galaxy's

## COLONIAL TROUBLE

Given what you're interested in, I'd be careful when you're poking around the Colonies. Pro-Imperial sentiments plus jealousy of the Core Worlds means some of the planets enforce Imperial law more rabidly than Coruscant.

For example, I intercepted a mandate from officials on Carida ordering that all records in their military academies pertaining to the history of the Clone Wars undergo "review for intellectual purity" by a dozen COMPNOR agents. While I can just guess what kind of intellectual purity COMPNOR wants to enforce, it's got me wondering if there's some information about events in the Clone Wars that they're worried someone might read.

On the other side of the Colonies, the Imperial liaison on Fondor just sent out an arrest warrant for a pair of individuals, a human and an Ithorian, hiding out in the construction debris fields orbiting the planet. Nothing strange there, except that the warrant describes the human as "able to throw heavy objects using invisible repulsorlift technology."

premiere shipyards. Once a bustling commercial yard, Fondor now serves the Empire exclusively, often constructing top-secret capital ship prototypes.

**Giju:** Giju is the capital of Herglic Space, a trade empire encompassing over forty systems. Once ruled by the proud Herglics, a large species of cetacean bipeds, Giju has had its assets forcibly nationalized by the Empire.

**Koensayr:** This Gran colony is home to Koensayr Manufacturing, one of the largest producers of starship components in the galaxy. The Gran have industrialized most of the planet, though lower latitudes feature a small, seaside tourism industry famous for vibrant, colorful sunsets.

**Loronar:** Loronar is a former Corellian colony turned Imperial stronghold. The planet is effectively ruled by the Loronar Corporation, a galactic mega-corporation that manufactures all manner of products, most notably drone barges, patrol craft, and scout ships.

**Procopia:** Procopia is a temperate, island-spotted world that functions as the capital of the Tapani Expanse. Almost every noble in the sector maintains a lavish estate on Procopia and enjoys frequent business retreats there to negotiate with other noble houses, make laws, arrange marriages, and hunt baranda.

**Raithal:** If Carida's academy graduates the toughest Imperial officers, Raithal turns out the smartest. An otherwise unremarkable ice ball, Raithal has been among the galaxy's top military academies for centuries.

# THE INNER RIM

A region struggling for identity, the Inner Rim is seen by denizens of the Core as an uncouth backwater, while those Rimward see it as a haven of spineless Imperial appeasers. Most worlds of the Inner Rim aspire to the refined culture and wealth of the Core and feel fortunate their worlds have moved past the lawlessness still present in Rimward regions. However, the Inner Rim is just as disgusted by the soft, blue-blooded, trust-funded, data-juggling nobility of the Core. What the Inner Rim truly values is an entrepreneurial spirit and an environment with social mobility on a level playing field.

## THE TAMED WILDERNESS

Over the millennia, the Inner Rim has traded its status as the wild edge of civilization for a reputation as a manufacturing and trade hub. The factories of the Inner Rim utilize the raw materials of the outlying sectors to create products for the mass consumerism of the Core. While lacking the quality of the Core and Colonies' artistic and cultural centers, the Inner Rim does rival its cosmopolitan cousins in matters of commerce. There is an independent, can-do work ethic throughout the Inner Rim, and a great respect for any rags-to-riches story. Unlike those in the Core, Inner Rimmers respect wealth that comes from hard work rather than an accident of birth.

Perhaps the most valuable resource of the region is medicine. The Inner Rim world of Thyferra is a provider of the so-called "miracle cure," bacta. The Zaltin and Xucphra Corporations were hand-selected by the Emperor to manage Thyferra, ensuring a steady flow of bacta to Imperial forces. Conversely, the Empire nationalized the kolto market shortly after occupying Manaan, centralizing distribution.

The Inner Rim also has a number of key hyperspace intersections that bolster trade across the region. Yag'Dhul sits at a junction between the Corellian Trade Spine and the Rimma Trade Route. Denon joins the Corellian Run and the Hydian Way, funneling materials from throughout the Outer Rim back toward the Core. In addition, the Inner Rim contains a bridge between the Lesser Lantillian Route and the Trellen Trade Route, which, through a winding series of routes, links both Hutt Space and the Centrality with the Core by way of Kashyyyk.

## NOTABLE LOCATIONS

The following are areas of interest within the Inner Rim, during or before Imperial rule.

**Antar 4:** The fourth moon of Antar suffers severe tides, electromagnetic storms, and weeks-long eclipses. This extreme environment gave birth to the horn-headed Gotal species. Antar 4 is also the birthplace of the Antarian Rangers, a resistance movement that seeks a return of the Jedi Knights.

**Berchest:** Berchest was once a major tourist destination, thanks to its famed crystal cities, which a nasty series of groundquakes tragically damaged just before the Clone Wars. Just as rebuilding efforts were completed, the rise of the Empire devastated the tourist trade throughout the sector. To stabilize its economy, Berchest opened up trade markets that exploited its proximity to the Perlemian Trade Route.

**Bogden:** Bogden's twenty moons are a haven for criminal scum, bounty hunters, and rebels. Some orbit each other so close their atmospheres kiss, allowing airspeeder transit between moons. The lunar surfaces have rapidly shifting gravity, allowing pubtenders throughout the galaxy to accuse customers of "stumbling like an Anx on Bogden" after one too many Corellian ales.

**Denon:** Denon is a major trade hub heavily defended by the Empire at the intersection of the Hydian Way and Corellian Run. The half-trillion sentients of the planetwide city work in its myriad corporate headquarters and field offices.

**Foless:** Situated at the intersection of the Corellian Trade Spine and the Shipwrights' Trace, Foless is a large trading center that features a massive stellar-class starport. The rest of the planet is an endless panorama of mountains and forests teeming with ferocious predators.

**Lesser Lantillian Route:** This route is a key hyperspace corridor that runs through the Inner Rim and on to Commenor, all the way to the Centrality, beyond the Outer Rim. It includes stops on planets such as Ambria, Onderon, Togoria, and Bimmisaari.

**Onderon:** Tensions between the colonists of Onderon's capital city Iziz and a faction of exiles in the wilds and highlands have led to millennia of civil war, often escalated by outside forces. The Imperials currently support Iziz with Jyrene Base, an Imperial supply depot also responsible for forces along the Lesser Lantillian Route.

**Phateem:** High above the clouds that water the bamboo swamps of Phateem, in the crags of the Ashlendu Mountains, are the Halls of Knowledge. The Jedi library and storehouse was once one of the twenty wonders of the galaxy, but the Jedi abandoned and emptied the halls long before the Clone Wars, leaving the site to decay.

**Taanab:** An agriworld troubled by pirates, Taanab exports food all along the Perlemian Trade Route. Hex-shaped farms and vast denta fields cover the planet. Ranchers herd bantha, nerf, staga, and, most famously, roba.

**Thyferra:** Located on the Rimma Trade Route, Thyferra is the swampy homeworld of the insectoid Vratix, creators of the cure-all known as bacta. Emperor Palpatine appointed the Xucphra and Zaltin corporations to manage the planet and ensure a steady supply of bacta to Imperials.

## RUINED TEMPLES, FORGOTTEN FANES

One thing I keep hearing is that Inner Rim worlds are rife with the ruins of age-old Jedi chapter houses, many destroyed during the rise of the Empire. Stories say that a group called the Jedi Service Corps typically operated the chapter houses, which once functioned as embassies and forward operating bases for traveling Jedi Knights. But if you dig deeper, you find records hinting that the Inner Rim may also be home to even older establishments as well. Here are a few of the more interesting ones.

**Ambria Jedi Enclave:** What little information exists on the Ambrian Enclave comes from ancient epic poetry relating the tragedy of Ulic Qel-Droma. Jedi Master Thon allegedly instructed future Jedi Grand Master Nomi Sunrider in the ways of the Force on Ambria. The enclave was near both a meditative canyon and Lake Natth, populated by hordes of hssiss, a species of lizard tainted by the dark side. Unfortunately, the exact location is lost to history, and while epic poetry is long on flowery descriptions, it's lacking in useful details.

**Bogden Jedi Chapter House:** Just before the Clone Wars, the Jedi Order built a small chapter house on the third moon of Bogden to accommodate Jedi younglings awaiting training space on Coruscant. At the end of the Clone Wars, the facility suffered an explosion and burned to the ground in an alleged act of Jedi terrorism. The Bounty Hunters' Guild, which has constructed a nearby lodge, rebuffs any attempt to examine the site.

**Truuine Jedi Praxeum:** An ancient Jedi parable over four thousand years old tells of a Gotal named Kith Kark and his quest to become a Jedi Knight. While the Jedi likely created the tale to teach initiates Jedi values, Master Jassa's Praxeum may have been real. According to texts, it was located deep within the mountains of Truuine's polar region, with a commanding view of glaciers shedding icebergs into the ocean.

**Truuine:** Patrolian and Karkarodon settlers have colonized ocean-covered Truuine's equatorial belt of islands. Many spacers have sworn off the planet after witnessing firsthand the violent contention between the two factions for fishing and trade rights.

# THE EXPANSION REGION

The Expansion Region has three distinct sub-regions: the Slice to the east, the Trailing Sectors to the south, and the Outer Expansion Zone to the north. The Slice is the oldest explored area, but thousands of years of strip mining, war, and slavery have devastated the region. The Outer Expansion Zone is widely considered a disaster, rife with more of the same practices that decimated the Slice before it. Other than the Trailing Sectors, corporations consider the entire region a waste of time and credits, though the Empire is attempting to reverse the trend. The Corellians of the Trailing Sectors control much of the region's wealth, tied mostly to powerful trade worlds like Bacrana, Milagro, and Arrgaw.

## SPOILED SLICE

Prospectors and settlers alike have long considered the northern and eastern Expansion Region a cursed, barren wasteland. However, the Empire has invested trillions of credits to revitalize the area. The Empire has also encouraged resettlement on a number of Expansion Region worlds in the Slice, especially those along major trade routes.

Imperial efforts have rebuilt agriworlds like Bovo Yagen, Charra, and Reytha by bestowing valuable Imperial contracts. Funded colonies on Attahox and in the Ishanna system search for resources previous strip miners overlooked. Others, like Iktotch, Trammen, Tarhassan, and Zaloriis are now Imperial staging areas. The resettlement campaigns have increased commerce, which has revitalized trade worlds like Prazhi and Cyrillia.

However, a world that greatly benefited from the Empire is Fabrin, home to the Fabritech Corporation, which has lucrative contracts to supply the Imperial war machine with sensors. The torrent of Imperial credits flowing to Fabrin has bolstered commerce along the entire Nanth'ri Route.

## NOTABLE LOCATIONS

The following are areas of interest within the Expansion Region, during or before Imperial rule.

**Almas:** A world in the Cularin system mysteriously terraformed with kaluthin grass, Almas supports a small colony named Forard. Most colonists relish their

## EVALUATION

Now here's something interesting. You don't know what I had to go through to intercept *this* message.

### <<Transferring data fragment>>

Subject: Advanced Training—Code Level Alpha Sigma

Inquisitor, your orders are to proceed to the following locations throughout the Expansion Region to explore ruins and to observe and train with local sects. I believe some of them to have associated traditions that may link to the Force. Learn anything of value, and then evaluate them for acquisition, annihilation, or isolation.

**Almas:** The ruins of both Darth Rivan's fortress and a Jedi Academy are near the Forard settlement. Be cautious; other Inquisitors sent to investigate the ruins never returned. Cultists, dark lizards, t'salaks, maalraas, and even a k'kayeh dragon are purported to stalk the grounds and guard a cache of holocrons.

**Alpheridies:** The prevalence of Force sensitivity among Miraluka led the Jedi to establish a large academy on Alpheridies, which the Empire destroyed after Order 66. The Luka Sene Force tradition focuses on enhancing Miralukan Force sight. Investigate the ruins and abilities of the Luka Sene. They may be useful in rooting out the Emperor's hidden enemies.

**Umbara:** Umbara was home to a powerful Sith Academy centuries ago. The Umbaran shadow assassins appropriated the academy's temple after the defeat of the Sith. Rumors suggest they are masters of stealth, able to bury their presences in the Force. Seek them out and evaluate their usefulness.

Do this, and the Emperor will be most pleased.

### <<Data fragment ends>>

quiet lives on the plains, but a cabal of universities is determined to unlock the secrets of the kaluthin grass and sponsor a research station near Forard.

**Alpheridies:** Alpheridies, an agriworld near the Veil Nebula, is the adopted homeworld of the eyeless Miraluka species. The world is also home to the Alpheridians, though they constitute a small percentage of the global population.

**Arrgaw:** A major trade world linking the Hydian Way and the Harrin Trade Corridor, Arrgaw is one of the wealthiest planets in the Expansion Region. Arrgaw's infinite sprawl of warehouses and corporate administrative spires pales in comparison to its famed orbital trade rings.

**Dorin:** The Kel Dor homeworld of Dorin is an unremarkable dust ball flanked by two black holes. Unsafe for most humanoids without rebreathers, Dorin has robust customs and trade stations at the edge of the system.

**Fabrin:** Fabritech owns and operates the entire planet of Fabrin and is the galaxy's largest producer of starship sensor units. Fabrin's manufacturing districts dominate the plains with thousands of colossal, droid-operated factories, each dedicated to a single product and managed by working-class overseers. Programmers live and work on luxurious beach resorts with every imaginable amenity.

**Gyndine:** Gyndine is an Imperial fortress world and the seat of Governor Essada's rule over the Circarpous sector. Situated at the intersection of the Ootmian Pabol and the Nanth'ri Trade Route, Gyndine supports its own shipyards, where Kuat Drive Yards conducts research and development.

**Kinyen:** A tranquil agriworld and home of the docile Gran, Kinyen is at the crossroads of the Corellian Trade Spine and Great Gran Run. As Kinyen had been a supporter of the Separatists, the Empire cracked down on it harshly and nationalized its food production.

**Milagro:** Milagro is a thriving trade and manufacturing world at the intersection of the Corellian Run and Harrin Trade Corridor. Although the Empire maintains a large Clone Wars-era base there, noble houses rule Milagro, claiming ancestral lineage to the original Corellian colonists.

**Reytha:** Known as the Breadbasket of the Empire, Reytha feeds nearly ten percent of the Imperial war machine. Situated along the Ootmian Pabol, just Rimward of Gyndine, Reytha has only a token defense force, commanded by Governor Belladar.

**Shili:** The brightly colored Togrutas hail from Shili, a planet of expansive plains and prairies covered in tall turu-grass. Located near the Hydian Way, Shili's capital city of Corvala is focused on trade and is renowned for its masters of holistic medicine.

**Teya IV:** This rural planet of rolling hills and still meadows is home to the Strak, a species of green-skinned humanoids whose heads feature a long pair of dorsal, curving horns. Throughout history, the Strak have opened their planet to small groups of refugees, inviting them into their small villages.

**Umbara:** Located within the Ghost Nebula, Umbara is plunged in near-eternal darkness; visitors to Umbara require UV goggles to see. The native Umbarans rival the Bothans in their thirst for secrets and intrigue, and Imperial Intelligence often employs Umbaran spies and assassins.

# THE MID RIM

Many Mid Rim worlds have small settlements that function as agriworlds and manufacturing centers, populated by simple folk trying to get by. The region has vast pockets of unexplored space where hyperspace scouts ply their trade, hoping to blaze new junction routes and bypasses.

## FRINGE OF THE EMPIRE

Piracy has plagued the Mid Rim for millennia, and while traders have increased their own defenses, the raids had often gone unpunished until the formation of the Empire. These worlds have little to offer individually, but they are sometimes small enough that a single pirate band can take over for days, even weeks, before an Imperial response. The Imperial presence has become increasingly militarized as a result, though military might has suffered as the Empire continues to draw off forces to combat the Rebellion.

Many Mid Rim worlds are relatively sparsely occupied, with populations ranging from a few million to half-a-trillion spread between just a few settlements. Such places might be "company towns," with the entire world's population focused around a single type of industry (or even a single company), or agriworlds like Balamak, Fengrine, Qiilura, or Uyter. The people on these planets often live simple lives, and families frequently remain on one planet for generations. Of course, the Mid Rim has been settled long enough that more populous and cosmopolitan worlds exist. Trade hubs like Daalang and Nexus Ortai are scattered through the region, taking the goods and resources of their neighbors and distributing them across the galaxy.

The proximity to raw materials from the Rimward regions makes the Mid Rim popular with shipbuilders as well. Major independent shipyards in the Mid Rim include Contruum, Lantillies, Roche, and Ubrikkia, plus hundreds of smaller repair yards and custom shipwrights. The Empire has reserved several major shipyards in the region for its exclusive use.

Freedom from religious persecution was one of the larger incentives for a number of Mid Rim colonial efforts. Disciples of the Akol, Vianism, Psusan, and Pius Dea religions colonized countless Mid Rim worlds as pilgrims, particularly in the Slice. Most of these religions faded generations later, but groups like the Aqualish Barralenal pilgrims, the B'omarr Order, and the Order of Ffib still practice their beliefs in their adopted homes.

# NOTABLE LOCATIONS

The following are areas of interest within the Mid Rim, during or before Imperial rule.

**Abhean:** Lord Felmas is the chief designer and CEO of Abhean Shipyards, the creator of some of the galaxy's largest bulk freighters. While Abhean used to hold contracts with the Jedi Order to build custom academy

## CAPTAIN'S LOG

Here's an undiscovered treasure. I've gotten the copy of a captain's log from a modified G-9 Rigger light freighter up for auction on Garqi. I think the owner may have been a Jedi, though there's no way to know if it's legit.

### <<Transferring data fragment>>

**11:17:9 GRS Haruun Kal:** It is hard to believe Master Windu was born here; everyone is so…not like him. Master Bowspritz's report on the akk dogs is accurate, but incomplete. It is true they are large, fierce, and they can bond with their masters through the Force. However, they're not mindless familiars: they're family members. The akks are joyous, gentle beasts, only violent if abused or defending their pack or herd. Touching their minds is like getting your face licked by their long, black tongues.

**14:9:19 GRS Kashyyyk:** Kashyyyk might be the most beautiful planet in the galaxy. It's not just the views—it's how this place feels in the Force. It's so alive and raw and connected, but at the same time in harmony. I feel so centered here. Still, there are dark places, deep in the Shadowlands. Yesterday I went down with Lovvrenk, hoping to spot a shadow keeper, but a terentatek found us instead. It took Lovvrenk's leg before I could even draw my lightsaber. I was able to wound it and drag Lovvrenk to safety. Tomorrow we'll form a hunting party.

**18:5:25 GRS Abhean:** The Jedi Purges have me looking over my shoulder and avoiding old friends, worried the Imperials or bounty hunters are watching them. Still, dangle the right bait, and even I'll bite. One of my contacts found a taozin in a shipyard maintenance shaft, feeding on borcatu. Taozin are reportedly extinct, but they live long lives underground. Their scales render them, or a wearer, invisible in the Force. That might help me avoid the Inquisitors.

**21:4:08 GRS Aleen:** I think this used to be a Jedi chapter house used by the old ExplorCorps, but my poking around turned up nothing but long-burned wreckage. Apparently, orbital bombardments destroyed the house just after the Clone Wars. However, Aleen construction favors a balance of levels above and below the surface, meaning some Jedi lore and artifacts may remain intact. Now, the site's home to a temple, where the locals worship a subterranean goddess who they claim causes groundquakes and protects the forests. That seems to hint that there might be something below the surface worth finding, but good luck convincing the Aleena to let you poke around in their sacred temple. I didn't get anywhere talking to them.

### <<Data fragment ends>>

vessels, today they build and maintain container vessels almost exclusively for the Imperial Supply Corps.

**Alaris Prime:** A moon of the gas giant Alaris, Alaris Prime was terraformed over the millennia by Wookiee colonists to resemble Kashyyyk. The Empire and Trandoshan Slavers Guild maintain a slave-processing center there to crew Imperial construction projects.

**Aleen Minor:** Aleen Minor is a lush world famous for its countless arenas. In addition to their love of speed and sport, the small, reptilian Aleena have built a reputation as master crafters of artisanal laroon wood, marble, and granite furniture.

**Chalacta:** Once an uninhabited planet of jagged mountains and dry, dusty valleys, Chalacta was colonized by the peaceful pilgrims of the Chalactan Adepts. The Temple of Illumination, the largest of their many temples, is just outside the valley town of Jordir.

**Enarc:** This key trade world sits at the confluence of several hyperlanes that connect Mid Rim worlds between the Hydian Way and Corellian Run. Enarc was a Trade Federation regional headquarters until Imperials nationalized its assets and transformed it into an Imperial Army transport and supply command.

**Ithor:** Sometimes referred to as the Garden of the Galaxy, Ithor is famous for its unspoiled botanical beauty and a sentient forest of bafforr trees in the Cathor Hills. Only the highest-ranking Ithorian shamans may walk the planet's surface, a provision enforced by the Empire. Ithorians and tourists instead occupy floating herd cities drifting several kilometers above the surface.

**Iridonia:** A historically war-torn world near several key hyperspace routes in the New Territories, Iridonia is one of many worlds controlled by the militant Zabrak. The ritually tattooed Zabrak have been quietly, but violently, resisting Imperial rule on Iridonia for years.

**Kashyyyk:** Kashyyyk is almost an organic reflection of Coruscant, with kilometers-tall wroshyr trees and endless forests in place of skyscrapers and cityscapes. The highest branches intertwine to form cities for the shaggy Wookiees. Like Coruscant, the lower levels are dangerous to the uninitiated, being full of savage predators.

**Krant:** Krant features colorful forests that would draw tourism from many nearby worlds were it not for a local insurrection. The native, pale-skinned Krantians are openly rebelling against Moff Yittreas and his Imperial forces.

**Lantillies:** Located at the junction of the Perlemian Trade Route and the Randon Run, Lantillies is a historically important center of trade and shipbuilding. The Lantillian Spacers' Brotherhood is one of the largest merchant guilds, with guild houses across the galaxy. By the time of Imperial rule, the Tagge family had absorbed many Lantillian corporations and shipbuilders to wield enormous influence across the planet.

**Naboo:** The unspoiled expanse of Naboo's verdant hills and cliffs define beautiful landscapes for the rest of the galaxy, while its murky swamps hide the submerged cities of the amphibious Gungans. Naboo is the capital of the Chommell sector and homeworld of Emperor Palpatine.

# THE OUTER RIM

The Outer Rim is the edge of the settled galaxy, populated by colonists, criminals, and aboriginal species hardy enough to resist colonization, or isolated enough to avoid it. While the Empire sends fleets to combat piracy, counter rebellion, and flaunt its authority, the Outer Rim is far too vast for even the Empire to control without a symbol of absolute power like the Death Star. Much of the region remains unexplored.

## THE WILD FRONTIER

The Outer Rim is home to countless sentient nonhuman species, and human cultures tend to be less common. Alien cultures run the spectrum from primitive xenophobes to advanced, trade-friendly civilizations. Some, like the Mon Calamari, have colonized entire sectors, but most count themselves lucky if they remain in control of their homeworld. Indigenous natives or colonists govern most planets, but Imperial governors, slavers, pirates, or crime lords rule others, usually with a cruel hand.

Those working outside the law often make their home in the Outer Rim, which includes innumerable worlds where smugglers, con artists, and criminals can ply their illicit trades far from Imperial eyes. The Empire, Rebellion, Black Sun, Hutts, and countless other interests fight over worlds with strategic resources or locations. While all the factions provide opportunities for outlaws, it is the spaces along and in-between the battle lines where the independent criminal element thrives. In many cases, criminals play more than one side of a conflict, stealing a cache of weapons from the Rebels on behalf of Black Sun, only to deliver new weapons from the Hutt Cartels days later. When the offended parties catch on, criminals can flee to an almost infinite number of bolt-holes absent from official star charts.

## INQUISITOR EVALUATION

Heads up. Just managed to swipe this off an encrypted HoloNet transmission. If you're headed into the Outer Rim, be careful. Looks like some dangerous people may be watching it.

### <<Transferring data fragment>>

Subject: Evaluation Report—Code Level Beta Sigma

My Lord, I have done as you asked. Here is my report.

**Bosph:** The Bosph describe the Force as the Yentarr, and most of their leaders, healers, and best warriors are Ela'b'Yentarr, or Followers of Yentarr. The accuracy of their "farseers" and prowess of their "sickhealers" is impressive. Their numbers are great and could pose a danger if militarized. Immediate Base Delta Zero recommended.

**Gand:** The insectoid Gand findsmen are well-respected trackers among those who stalk big game and clever bounties. The findsmen meditate with ritual incense and smoky mist to reveal the future. Though their traditions are likely just nonsense, I suspect there may be an unconscious link to the Force through their rituals. However, they have no galactic ambitions, and if some of them are sensitive, they themselves do not realize it. I recommend they be ignored, or possibly used as trackers for our needs.

**Voss:** The planet Voss has a native species once ruled by an order of mystics with advanced precognition and healing Force techniques. The mystics are no longer in power, but they have a base hidden in the Nightmare Lands. They are marginalized by Voss society and small in number, but far too dangerous to operate unchecked. They should join us or die.

### <<Data fragment ends>>

The Rebels have a number of bases in the Outer Rim, thanks to the vast swaths of unexplored space between hyperlanes, which makes the region the target of concentrated Imperial searches for Rebel forces. However, not all planets cooperate with disruptive and heavy-handed Imperial investigations, resulting in escalating tensions that can spiral out of control. The Empire is accused of a multitude of atrocities throughout the region, including genocides, orbital bombardments, conscription, and enslavement. These destructive tactics often create as many Rebel recruits as they destroy.

## NOTABLE LOCATIONS

The following are areas of interest within the Outer Rim, during or before Imperial rule.

**Bespin:** The gas giant of Bespin is a galactic source of Tibanna gas located along the Ison Corridor. While the world hosts numerous mining and refinery operations in the floating cities of its human-habitable cloud layers, Cloud City is the largest, and perhaps the most famous, thanks to its casinos, hotels, and restaurants.

**Cathar:** Cathar is an endless, rolling savannah, and home to sentient cat-like humanoids of the same name. Massive city-trees dot the surface, each housing hundreds of Cathar.

**Ciutric IV:** Ciutric IV is both the capital and trade hub for the aristocratic Ciutric Hegemony. Ruled by Imperial Grand Vizier Sate Pestage's family for generations, most consider the Hegemony a model Imperial state.

**Eriadu:** Believed to be the busiest trade port in the Outer Rim, Eriadu sits at the nexus of several hyperspace routes, including the Rimma Trade Route and the Hydian Way. Pollution and urbanization dominate the surface of the planet as it races to become a Coruscant-like planet-city.

**Florrum:** A desert world of rocky canyons and sulfuric geyser ranges, Florrum is just devoid enough of resources to function as the perfect hideout for pirates, smugglers, and outlaws.

**Gand:** The mist-shrouded world of Gand has an ammonia-based atmosphere toxic to most humanoids. Trade stations are set up in orbit to prevent accidents, but many spacers find it frustrating to develop contacts among the locals, thanks to odd cultural taboos regarding egotistical use of pronouns.

**Gentes:** Gentes's surface is predominantly swampland broken up by lone volcanoes. A few diminutive porcine natives known as Ugnaughts still inhabit the planet during Imperial governorship, though most surviving clans dispersed after General Grievous's sacking of Gentes during the Clone Wars.

**Mandalore:** Centuries ago, Mandalore was the capital of an expansive and proud warrior state. Boundless warfare transformed Mandalore's forests and arable fields into radioactive deserts of white sand. Many natives have adopted a pacifist outlook from within their domed cities, almost as a penance for the arid wasteland their actions had wrought. However, other factions seek a return to more traditional values.

**Mon Calamari (Dac, Mon Cala):** Mon Calamari is a water-covered world known for its shipyards. The oceans are home to two species, the Quarren, who work in Imperial shipyards, and the Mon Calamari, who are enslaved as Imperial aides and servants throughout the galaxy.

**Sullust:** A volcanically active world with a native species of nearly hairless, rodent-like humanoids called the Sullustans, most of Sullust's population centers are underground in warren-like cave networks. The Sullustan-operated SoroSuub Corporation employs half the planet's population in the manufacture and distribution of a variety of goods. Once a major member of the Commerce Guild, SoroSuub is now an ally of the Empire, providing Imperials with arms and equipment.

**Taris:** Long ago, Taris was a vast ecumenopolis rivaling Denon, and was famous for its swoop races. An orbital bombardment during an ancient battle between the Jedi and the Sith destroyed much of the landscape, and Taris still bears scars despite millennia of reconstruction efforts.

**Tund:** Tund is a barren, radioactive wasteland, thanks to an unexplained incident that obliterated all life on the planet less than a decade ago. The world was once home to a vibrant colony of Toongs and, allegedly, the Sorcerers of Tund, a legendary (and possibly completely mythical) order of mystics and evil sorcerers.

**Utapau:** Utapau is an arid planet of dry, cracked crust punctuated by deep sinkholes, which are home to the administrative Pau'ans and the working-class Utai. Under Imperial control since the formation of the Empire, Utapau's mineral deposits have made it of prime importance to the Imperial war machine. Many of its citizens been evicted and now roam the galaxy as refugees.

**Vjun:** Vjun is a graveyard of sprawling noble estates abandoned over two decades ago. Rumors explaining the vanished populace abound, each more horrifying than the next. The most popular theory is that an experimental pathogen that caused murderous psychosis got loose, an idea strengthened by the Imperial quarantine blockade around the system.

**Voss:** Voss is a member of the Allied Tion sector, and its native Voss and Gormak species are slowly vanishing into extinction. The Empire is building an industrial infrastructure on Voss to rival Lianna, but it faces opposition from Tionese nobles.

**Zygerria:** Homeworld of the red-furred Zygerrians in the Chorlian sector, Zygerria is famous for its slave auctions. A major supporter of the Separatists during the Clone Wars, the Zygerrian Slavers Guild now provides the Empire with disposable laborers for a number of construction projects.

**Mustafar:** Mustafar is a volcanically active world covered in igneous rock and lava flows, which droids skim for molten ores. An Imperial garrison on Mustafar trains stormtroopers to fight in volcanic environments. It is a major strategic staging point for the Imperial fleets that scour the Outer Rim for seditious activity.

**Nal Hutta:** Also known as Hutta, Nal Hutta translates to "Glorious Jewel" in Huttese. The planet is the adopted homeworld of the Hutts and the center of their criminal empire, filled with kajidics' palaces and endless swampland. The Hutts and the Empire have an uneasy truce that affords the Hutts their independence, for now.

**Rhen Var:** Rhen Var is a mountainous, ice-covered planet just off the Perlemian Trade Route near the Tion Cluster. Rhen Var has countless ancient ruins predating the Republic and is home to a small Imperial listening outpost.

**Ryloth:** Ryloth suffers from recurrent heat storms, harsh terrain, and most of all from the slave trade. The native Twi'leks live in caves, hoping to avoid most dangers, but they are often sold into slavery by their own clans to work as laborers, servants, and entertainers.

**Socorro:** Socorro is a world of endless black sands and jagged mountain ranges colonized by Corellians three thousand years ago. Its remote location makes it a haven for independent spacers, smugglers, and thieves.

# WILD SPACE AND THE UNKNOWN REGIONS

The two most dangerous, lawless regions of the galaxy are Wild Space and the Unknown Regions. Wild Space encompasses the edge of the galaxy beyond the Outer Rim. While it has not yet been officially explored, a number of smugglers, outlaws, and exiles have discovered bolt-holes and encountered strange alien civilizations at the very edges of the galaxy. The Empire rarely ventures this far Rimward, leaving the trackless expanses of empty space to those with the courage to explore it.

While Wild Space is the outermost edge of the galaxy, the Unknown Regions are a large wedge of unexplored space running from the edge to the core, and makes up much of the galaxy's western expanse. In theory, this region should constantly shrink as exploration charts its stars and hyperlanes. However, in practice, the Unknown Regions are surrounded by strange and formidable hyperspatial distortions and gravitational eddies. Hyperspace routes into the Unknown Regions are hard to find and harder to map, and they tend to fade and vanish over time. So far, very few explorers have ventured into the Unknown Regions, and even fewer have returned.

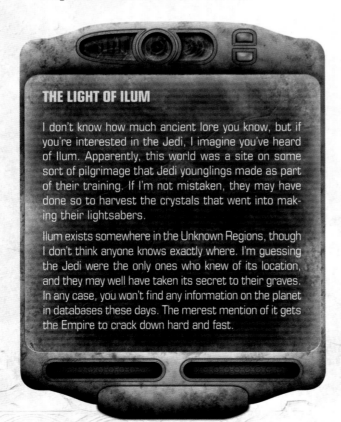

## THE LIGHT OF ILUM

I don't know how much ancient lore you know, but if you're interested in the Jedi, I imagine you've heard of Ilum. Apparently, this world was a site on some sort of pilgrimage that Jedi younglings made as part of their training. If I'm not mistaken, they may have done so to harvest the crystals that went into making their lightsabers.

Ilum exists somewhere in the Unknown Regions, though I don't think anyone knows exactly where. I'm guessing the Jedi were the only ones who knew of its location, and they may well have taken its secret to their graves. In any case, you won't find any information on the planet in databases these days. The merest mention of it gets the Empire to crack down hard and fast.

## WILD SPACE

In theory, reaching Wild Space is easy enough. A traveler just needs to find the bright center of the galaxy, and travel away from it. Sooner or later, that traveler ends up in Wild Space. Of course, things are a lot more complicated in practice.

First and foremost, travelers in Wild Space have to deal with astrogation information that's out of date, incomplete, or simply non-existent. Would-be explorers can spend days trying to calculate a single hyperjump to the next star, or weeks working out a course through a vast and previously undiscovered asteroid field. Pirates and smugglers hide among the moons and planets in Wild Space, using the lawless region as a safe haven from law enforcement. Explorers might even run into an unknown alien civilization, perhaps one that might prove hostile and dangerous.

So why travel to Wild Space at all? Most people do so because the opportunities equal or outweigh the risks. New worlds full of precious ores or valuable natural resources, untouched planets ripe for colonization, or undiscovered alien species willing to trade can all make the discoverer a very wealthy person. For this reason, corporations, governments, and even exceedingly rich individuals all finance explorations into Wild Space. In addition, Wild Space is fully beyond the bounds of the Empire. There are few better places to go for those attempting to evade Imperial law.

## THE UNKNOWN REGIONS

If Wild Space is a rough set of star charts, the Unknown Regions are a blank space on the map. While the region remains behind a nigh-impenetrable barrier of hyperspatial anomalies, explorers can only dream about what wonders they could find among its uncharted stars.

However, no matter how ambitious an adventurer's dreams, an explorer must face up to cold reality. The hyperspace barrier takes the form of a tangled maze of hyperspace routes, punctuated by gravitational anomalies and deadly pitfalls. Most of the ships that jump into hyperspace through the barrier simply vanish, without any explanation why.

However, a few plucky explorers have made it through the hyperspatial barrier and returned to tell the tale. They speak of strange new stars, unspoiled worlds, and unique and wondrous alien species not yet known to the galaxy. Sometimes, they return bearing cargos of exotic goods that fetch commanding prices in the Galactic Core.

Legends say that some Jedi possess the ability to perform complex astrogation calculations with the help of the Force. If so, it is possible that a Force sensitive may succeed in finding a path into the Unknown Regions where so may others have failed.

# NOTABLE LOCATIONS

The following are areas of interest within Wild Space and the Unknown Regions, during or before Imperial rule.

**Bakura:** Bakura briefly, but infamously, served as headquarters for Separatist leader Count Dooku during the Clone Wars. Today, Bakura is Wild Space's top repulsorlift manufacturer and exporter under the rule of Imperial Governor Nereus. For many, it is the last civilized stop on the road into the unexplored frontier.

**Csilla:** Only a few high-level diplomats, military personnel, and fringe traders know of the icy world of Csilla. Even so, most only know it as the capital of the Chiss Ascendency, a xenophobic, militant domain with advanced technology. The blue-skinned Chiss are rare, though not unheard of in the Outer Rim. Within the Empire, they are considered an exotic curiosity.

**Diab 6:** Diab 6 is one of six moons orbiting Diab, a planet of intense electrical storms just outside the Dreighton Nebula in Wild Space. The storms wreak havoc with even distant sensors elsewhere in the system.

**Ilum:** The journey to Ilum was a mystical pilgrimage once undertaken by the Jedi. While the Jedi Order kept Ilum's location secret, researchers believe it is somewhere in Wild Space. Claims of its rediscovery and rumors of Jedi treasure inside Ilum's mountainside citadels are common among spacers.

**Kalee:** Kalee is a Wild Space planet that is home to the Kaleesh, a species of highly skilled hunters and warriors. Kalee has a variety of climates and terrains, and the Kaleesh hunt and fight in all of them.

**Kamino:** Kamino is a water-covered world deep in Wild Space—so deep that it can be found in territory outside the galaxy proper. The cloners of Kamino are most famous for producing the clones of the Grand Army of the Republic during the Clone Wars. Its importance during the conflict afforded Kamino representation in the Senate, but the Empire's shift away from clone troopers after the Wars quickly marginalized the world and its importance.

**Kro Var:** A colony ship crashed in the Unknown Regions on Kro Var long ago, unable to make its true destination. Those that survived the volcanic planet devolved into a feudal state over the centuries before their relatively recent rediscovery by the Republic.

**Rhand:** Rhand is a prairie planet dotted with massive stone fortresses within the Unknown Regions' Dreighton Nebula. Few know safe routes through the nebula, but rumors abound of gems and precious metals for the taking.

**Yanibar:** Yanibar functions as a last thread of civilization on the border between the Outer Rim and Wild Space. Yanibar's Tho Yorla Spaceport is home to crazy and desperate spacers and explorers plying their trade at the edge of the galaxy.

# FORGOTTEN SECRETS OF THE FORCE

The galaxy is large, old, and mysterious, and civilization has forgotten more about the Force than even Emperor Palpatine could ever hope to learn. Planets once home to powerful Jedi Masters, Sith Lords, or Force adepts have been lost due to shifting hyperspace routes and the ravages of time. Innumerable artifacts imbued with the power of the Force lie scattered throughout the galaxy. Entire regions of space once ruled by powerful masters of the Force lie hidden behind dense nebulae in the Rim and shifting mass shadows in the Deep Core. Those growing in their attunement to the Force would do well to spend time seeking the wealth of these lost places of ancient power.

# SITH SPACE

Sith Space and its hyperlanes have long been lost to history and devolved into myth. However, the Stygian Caldera, the feature that allegedly surrounds Sith Space, is a recognized nebula in the Outer Rim's Esstran sector. According to some shadowfeeds, the Empire may have found, explored, and perhaps even blockaded four of the worlds within: Begeren, Khar Shian, Moraband, and Jaguada. It is possible that these worlds are four ancient homeworlds of the Sith.

Pieced together from mythic parables and legends, the history of the Sith stretches back before the Republic. Some say the Sith were red-skinned humanoids who could tap into the dark side of the Force, empowering themselves with rage and aggression. Others claim the Sith were humans, or even that a Sith could be one of any species. Whatever the truth, the ancient Sith Empire was said to encompass hundreds of stars around the Stygian Caldera. Republic history texts indicate it may have grown to envelop much of the galaxy on occasion, as it fought to conquer the galaxy against Republic fleets and the Jedi Knights.

Today, the Sith Empire has long since crumbled into dust and ash. Their worlds may remain, but they are dead places of tombs and the ghosts of the ancient past.

## NOTABLE LOCATIONS

The following are potential areas of interest within Sith Space. Few are sure if they actually exist, or are creations of myth and allegory. However, there may be some truth in the stories.

**Athiss:** Thousands of years ago, the fields, forests, and canyons of Athiss were allegedly home to Sith Lord Vodal Kressh and his vassals. Though the Republic apparently destroyed him and his followers, it is believed a dark cult of worshippers still protect his tomb and follow his teachings.

**Begeren:** Begeren is a desert world with a number of mountain ranges rich in gemstones and punctured with ancient mineshafts. Begeren is one of the few publicly known worlds that are allegedly a part of Sith Space, making it the chief starting point for those chasing Sith fortunes. The Rebels and Imperials fought over Begeren's mines early in the Galactic Civil War.

**Bosthirda:** Bosthirda was a legendary knowledge repository of the Sith. The massive temples were said to contain countless holocrons, scrolls, texts, and artifacts.

**Daragon Trail:** An ancient parable claims that siblings Gav and Jori Daragon blazed this legendary lost hyperspace route from Koros Major to Korriban over five thousand years ago. Some scholars speculate that their actions may have unleashed the Sith on the Republic for the first time.

**Dromund system:** The Dromund system was a key population center in Sith Space located at the heart

## SECRETS OF SITH SPACE

Well, this is certainly interesting—and maybe a little scary. One of my friends who maintains a waystation along the Hydian Way has been keeping tabs on some very large Imperial ship movements through his sector of space. Now, that wouldn't be so strange if they were headed on up towards the Corporate Sector, but the convoys are breaking off from the Hydian at Listehol and following some little-known hyperroute into deep space.

He doesn't know where they're headed, but when one of the convoys came back, it had to stop at his station for unscheduled repairs. The ship—and we're talking a Star Galleon, here—looked like something tore a fair-sized chunk of hull off the aft end. Maybe, just maybe, something with *teeth*. The crew wouldn't talk to anyone, and the captain told my friend that while he was making repairs, any attempts to look inside the cargo hold would get his entire station blown to bits.

Now, I don't know where that ship came from, but my friend said convoys are still headed out that way. If you're brave or foolish enough, you might be able to follow one.

**Kalsunor:** Kalsunor is said to have grotesquely mutated silooth beasts which stalk the world's deep canyons.

**Khar Delba:** A rumored stronghold of legendary Sith Lord Naga Sadow, Khar Delba is said to have held his palace and power base. However, other texts suggest this was a false target provided for his many enemies, and that his true palace was on its icy moon, Khar Shian.

**Krayiss II:** An important world to the ancient pureblood Sith, Krayiss II once housed a grand and enormous library-temple that hosted the sum total of Sith knowledge.

**Moraband (Korriban):** Moraband is a world dedicated to the dead that has sometimes acted as capital of the Sith Empire. The Valley of the Dark Lords holds the remains of deceased leaders of the Sith Empire, locked away within booby-trapped (and some say haunted) crypts.

**Rhelg:** This planet was the stronghold of infamous Sith Lord Ludo Kressh, a political rival of Naga Sadow. Unlike most worlds of the Sith Empire, Rhelg had vast expanses of arable land, making it one of the only agriworlds in the region.

**Ziost:** Ziost has been the capital of the Sith Empire under both King Adas and Jedi Exile Ajunta Pall, as well as their successors. As with most planets of Sith Space, war and the dark side stripped life from the planet until it became a barren ball of lifeless rock.

of the Stygian Caldera. It had a number of habitable worlds and moons, and was a center of Sith political power. Though the system is generally thought to be a legend, rumors flitting around the shadowfeeds claim that the Empire may know of its location.

**Dromund Fels:** Dromund Fels is an arid wasteland that was home to a number of Sith Lord estates and training camps. Darth Igrol allegedly maintained a lavish estate on Dromund Fels four thousand years ago.

**Dromund Kaas:** Dromund Kaas was once the capital of the Sith Empire, an honor it has traded with Korriban and Ziost throughout history. According to legend, the swamp-covered planet is littered with temple ruins, Sith treasures, and dark side vergences.

# FORGOTTEN TEMPLES

During the history of warfare between the Jedi Order and the various incarnations of the Sith Empire, countless temples, outposts, and storehouses were constructed, raided, destroyed, and rebuilt across the galaxy. The Emperor's secret archives contain information on thousands of sites with ties to the ages-old conflict, most of which remain uninvestigated. Countless more remain undiscovered. Many of these sites are unnaturally strong with Force energy.

## A POWERFUL VERGENCE

Most adepts refer to a nexus of strong Force energy as a vergence. These vergences can be linked to an object or even a person, but they are most frequently associated with places. Force adepts can sense these wellsprings of Force energy, sometimes from vast distances, and can draw upon their power to enhance their control over the Force. These properties have made vergences desirable locations for meditation, temples, and pilgrimages.

While no one knows why vergences in the Force occur, there are many theories on how they form. It is possible that the death of a powerful Force adept can sometimes leave behind a vergence at the location of the adept's demise. The vergence is often inherently light or dark based on the deceased. Other vergences may be caused by dark rituals—the type that often ends in the mass murder of countless sentients. Sometimes a large enough collection of Force-imbued artifacts can leave a

faint vergence in the Force behind, even after removing said artifacts. Still other vergences seem to spring from the will of the Force itself, without apparent cause.

### PLACES OF POWER...AND MYSTERY

Some vergences have been known to the Jedi for centuries. Far more were known once but have long since been lost. And some vergences are known to neither Jedi nor Sith, but have instead been discovered by those who cannot comprehend their power. Local religious cults, superstitious space pirates, and even unwary travelers can discover a vergence and cower in awe before its supernatural nature without understanding they are witnessing the Force at work.

In some cases, these vergences are places shunned as the domain of evil spirits, or are hallowed as the sacred homes of ancestors. Those who find vergences often turn them into places of worship, ranging from sites where cautious smugglers pour out a measure of liquor to appease the "gods of hyperspace" to full-fledged temples where teeming throngs of the faithful worship their deities. Just as likely, vergences might be declared taboo by those who find them, either as sacred or as defiled ground. Sometimes, the punishment for trespassing is death.

In any case, most vergences that have become places of veneration present a tricky prospect for a traveler. Those who worship or fear such locations seldom welcome outsiders attempting to "despoil" them.

## NOTABLE LOCATIONS

The following are areas of alleged vergences and locations of interest to those who can touch the Force, largely drawn from myth and legend.

**Ambria:** The deserts of Ambria are said to conceal a major dark vergence at Lake Natth, where hssiss dragons spawn from the dark energies. There is also a minor light vergence within a nearby canyon.

**Arbra:** A forested world in the Outer Rim used only by smugglers and outlaws, Arbra was once home to a fortress of the ancient Sith. A hidden geothermal cave with massive crystalline power rods contains a major vergence in the Force.

**Bardotta:** A mountainous planet ruled by the spiritual Dagoyan Masters, Bardotta is also said to be the mythical homeworld to the legendary Frangawl Cult.

**Byss:** The rumored and hidden private world of the Emperor, Byss (if it exists) is said to possess the unmistakable taint of evil. It is even possible that the planet itself could be a vergence for the dark side.

**Coruscant:** The Jedi Temple that once stood proudly near Coruscant's government district was said to have a major vergence in the Force at its base. Now, the Jedi Temple has been claimed by Palpatine as his Imperial Palace, restricting access to this powerful well-spring of Force energy.

**Darkknell:** Capital of a forgotten Sith Empire in the Western Reaches, Darkknell features a minor vergence in the Force in the ruins of a hexagonal palace in the city of Xakrea.

**Dathomir:** Dathomir is a jungle world which is home to a matriarchal society of Force users who weave their understanding of the Force with shamanistic traditions. The Nightsisters of Dathomir embrace certain aspects of the dark side of the Force.

**Florrum:** During the Clone Wars, pirates shot down a millennium-old corvette-sized Jedi training ship called the *Crucible* on Florrum. The ship contained a droid with vast stores of knowledge about the Jedi and advanced knowledge of lightsaber construction. What information may remain within the wreck of the *Crucible* is yet unknown.

**Lettow:** The First Great Schism of the Jedi had its origins on Lettow. According to legend, the Jedi Xendor and his lover were denied permission to study Force traditions other than those of the Jedi, leading them to form their own academy. Xendor's Legionnaire Academy trained like-minded adepts in a wider view of the Force, which eventually led to open warfare with the Jedi. The world has become lost to time, but if discovered, ruins, lore, and artifacts wait to be found.

**Mortis:** The legendary Mortis is allegedly the home of powerful Force beings known as the Father, the Son, and the Daughter. Though it is most certainly a major vergence in the Force, no one is sure whether Mortis is an artificial station, a location within the Chrelythiumn system, or even a place beyond the comprehension of mortal minds.

**Nathema:** Once known as Medriaas, Nathema was an agriworld of the Sith Empire at a time when the Sith also controlled the Chorlian sector. An ancient Dark Lord of the Sith named Darth Vitiate destroyed all life on Nathema with a ritual designed to grant him immortality. A transcription of the ritual was recorded by Darth Revan and served as the inspiration for Lord Kaan's thought bomb on Ruusan.

**Obroa-skai:** Obroa-skai is home to an ancient library, which the Empire has recently transformed into a data archive. The Jedi Order had an academy here that featured enormous storerooms of Jedi artifacts and lore, which have created a minor light vergence. While the Empire cleared the vaults, it is possible they missed something amid the temple ruins.

**Prakith:** While the major dark vergence on Prakith remains hidden within archaeological ruins, it was once the foundation of Darth Andeddu's Keep. Andeddu was said to be a powerful Sith Lord consumed with the hunt for immortality.

**Recopia:** On this trade world of sulfuric oceans is a small island named Mallif Cove, reputedly home to the Seyugi Dervishes, a centuries-old order of assassins armed only with the Force. Though the Jedi are said to have wiped the order out, rumors persist that some of the assassins survived.

**Rekkiad:** Rekkiad is a world of vicious storms sweeping across snow-covered plains and icy mountains in the Outer Rim's Chorlian sector. On this world is said to be the tomb of Dramath the Second, a powerful Sith Lord from ancient times. An allegorical epic claims his tomb was only accessible from the top of one of the Twin Spears, a pair of kilometers-tall columns of ice.

**Rhen Var:** A contested planet during the Galactic Civil War, Rhen Var was the location of fabled fallen Jedi Ulic Qel-Droma's exile, redemption, and death. The planet has several temples, ruins, and caves, some already ancient during Ulic's exile. There are a number of powerful vergences in the Force scattered across the planet.

**Ruusan:** Ruusan's Valley of the Jedi is the location of the final Battle of Ruusan, where the Brotherhood of Darkness and Army of Light were killed en masse by a powerful thought bomb. The valley is a major vergence in the Force, believed to be among the most powerful in the galaxy.

**Thule:** The Sith colony of Thule was filled with cold, barren deserts, wide savannahs, and a colony of Chiss, who have since spread themselves thinly throughout the galaxy. The world is the final resting place of a powerful Sith weapon able to consume life through dark manipulations of the Force to power itself.

**Vjun:** Deep within Bast Castle, Darth Vader's secret retreat on Vjun, there is a dark vergence in the Force. The castle possesses many automated defenses both technical and mystical; it is a dangerous place to explore even if the Dark Lord isn't at home.

**Yavin 4:** It is said that the temples that dot the surface of the jungle moon were constructed by Massassi warriors, possibly to honor a long-forgotten Sith Lord. These same temples were later used by the Rebel Alliance to launch the starfighters that destroyed the Death Star.

**Zigoola:** The rocky wastes of Zigoola create a desolate vista, permeated by a planetwide dark vergence in the Force. Large hoards of dark artifacts are hidden somewhere beneath the ruins of a Sith Temple destroyed by Jedi General Obi-Wan Kenobi during the Clone Wars.

# CEREA

**Astronavigation Data:** Cerean system, Semagi sector, Mid Rim region

**Orbital Metrics:** 386 days per year / 27 hours per day

**Government:** Cerean Council of Elders

**Population:** 450,000,000 (Cereans 85%, humans 7%, Ithorians 4%, other 4%)

**Languages:** Basic, Cerean

**Terrain:** rural villages, farmland, rolling hills, forests

**Major Cities:** Tecave City

**Areas of Interest:** Outsider Citadels

**Major Exports:** foodstuffs

**Major Imports:** technology

**Trade Routes:** Great Gran Run, Cerean Reach, Spar Trade Route

**Special Conditions:** offworlders must remain in Outsider Citadels unless granted special permission

**Background:** Cerea is a small, backwater agriworld and home to the cone-headed Cereans. Its endless hills and forests provide ample farmland for all Cereans, who prefer to maintain a simple, rustic existence. Cereans usually build their houses from local materials, and they run their farms without any industrialization. The fact that Cereans have two hearts is well known, and most say the first is for the family, but the second is for Cerea itself. For fear of pollution and industrialization of their verdant homeworld, Cereans have outlawed most technology. However, the policy does not apply to the local Imperial garrison and those in Outsider Citadels, as long as they keep their tech on the premises.

The Outsider Citadels are large, top-heavy towers located a day's ride outside Tecave City so as not to mar the horizon. Each citadel contains tens of thousands of traders, farmhands, negotiators, and merchants. While the citadels are very necessary for the export of foodstuffs, most Cereans are against their increasing presence; their numbers have been on the rise for decades. To most locals, Outsider Citadels are a source of crime, pollution, and contraband technology.

While Imperial Governor Andreo Tagge brings vast expertise in agriworld management, the Empire allows the Cerean Council of Elders to govern the planet. The council is an annual convocation of five hundred representatives from villages across the planet, led by a president. A small portion of the council remains in Tecave City year-round to address time-sensitive issues.

Tecave City is a white-columned wonder of squat spires and bronzed domes handcrafted without the aid of droids or industrial equipment. While most farmers and farmhands live on the land they work, a number of support industries are centralized. At Tecave's markets, Cereans can purchase riding aryxes, plowing moofs, oorg meat, or any variety of metalwork they might need. Most farmers sell their crops to intermediaries in Tecave, who put a portion on the local market and bring the rest to an Outsider Citadel to negotiate its sale to offworld markets.

## RISING TENSIONS

Governor Tagge continues to annex and industrialize more of Cerea's arable land each year in blatant violation of Cerea's terms of surrender. A growing offworlder presence has increased the prevalence of small technological items among Cerea's youth, including datapads, glow rods, and other trinkets. These have become points of tension between the Imperials and the Council of Elders, and have caused strife within many Cerean families. The council has filed a number of formal complaints and launched investigations, but to no effect, leading to growing discontent with Imperial rule.

# CORUSCANT

**Astronavigation Data:** Coruscant system, Corusca sector, Core region

**Orbital Metrics:** 368 days per year / 24 hours per day

**Government:** Imperial dictatorship

**Population:** 1 trillion (humans 78%, other 22%)

**Languages:** Basic

**Terrain:** dense, multilevel, planetwide urban cityscape

**Major Cities:** Imperial City

**Areas of Interest:** Imperial Palace (formerly the Jedi Temple), Galactic Museum, Imperial Senate, Column Commons, Monument Plaza, The Works

**Major Exports:** culture

**Major Imports:** foodstuffs, medicinal goods

**Trade Routes:** Corellian Trade Spine, Perlemian Trade Route, Namadii Corridor

**Special Conditions:** none

**Background:** Coruscant is among the most ancient of the galaxy's civilized worlds. Coruscant's life and civilization predate the Republic, as well as the ancient Rakata Infinite Empire, by tens of thousands of years. As the system of hyperspace routes grew across the galaxy, Coruscant benefited significantly from its location. Coruscant's political and economic power and influence became dominant. It grew to become the capital of the Republic, a world that every galactic government must ultimately control to be considered legitimate.

As the planet developed, the needs of the economic powerhouse and galactic government brought with it a massive boost in population. The world was already covered by layers of urban cityscape, and it kept growing. As the city stretched higher into the sky, the population stratified. The wealthy and powerful literally rose to the top, leaving the lower levels to the poor.

As the seat of Imperial power, the planet is protected by formidable fleets of Star Destroyers, numerous orbital defense platforms, and powerful planetary shields. The Emperor rules from the Imperial Palace, and many of Coruscant's districts house the machinery of Imperial bureaucracy.

In general, the citizens of the mid and upper levels are among the staunchest Imperial supporters in the Empire. Most benefit daily from Imperial economic activity, from the largest of suppliers to maintenance workers and others living on Imperial wages. Rebel activity is to be feared, and associating with Rebels risks damage to reputation as well as Imperial arrest.

## THE JEDI TEMPLE

For centuries, the Jedi Order maintained its headquarters on Coruscant. The Jedi Temple was an impressive and imposing structure topped by five lofty spires. Within it, the Jedi trained their younglings and Padawans, maintained the histories and resources of their Order, and meditated on the mysteries of the Force. The temple was the heart of the Jedi Order—and one of the first places targeted by Emperor Palpatine when he set out to destroy it.

At Palpatine's command, Darth Vader led an army into the temple and slaughtered everyone he found. Now, Imperial banners hang from the temple's walls, and to make his victory complete, the Emperor has turned the Jedi Temple into his palace. Few know what goes on within its walls, though what is certain is that few enter the Imperial Palace without the Emperor's blessing, and even fewer leave alive.

# DAGOBAH

**Astronavigation Data:** Dagobah system, Sluis sector, Outer Rim region

**Orbital Metrics:** 341 days per year / 23 hours per day

**Government:** none

**Population:** none

**Languages:** none

**Terrain:** bayous, bogs, jungles, swampland

**Major Cities:** none

**Areas of Interest:** Dark Side Cave, Mount Dagger

**Major Exports:** none

**Major Imports:** none

**Trade Routes:** Rimma Trade Route

**Special Conditions:** none

**Background:** The Force is particularly strong on Dagobah, though why the Force might be stronger on some planets than others is a mystery the Jedi never quite unraveled. While planets that exhibit abundant flora and fauna often have a strong presence in the Force, something more is at work within the swamps of Dagobah. The world is a vergence in the Force, a place where time seems to stand still. To a Force user in meditation there, the secrets of the universe seem to lay themselves bare. It is places like Dagobah where the boundaries of time, space, life, and death seem to intertwine.

Gnarltrees dominate the murky swamps, their thick canopies blocking out what little sunlight makes it through the persistent fog. The gnarltrees grow in hauntingly twisted shapes, with airborne trunks that sit atop seven or eight major roots, leaving a hollow underneath. Each hollow is a miniature ecosystem packed with a variety of flora and fauna.

The gnarltrees are among the strangest life forms on Dagobah in that they spend their infancy as a mobile organism called a knobby white spider. The carnivorous creatures can reach up to two meters in height as they wander and feed. When a spider reaches adulthood, it plants its legs as roots and becomes a gnarltree. Eventually, a gnarltree root fattens and cracks, releasing a knobby white spider to begin the cycle anew.

The wild bayou teems with life, from the smallest rootworms to the massive swamp slugs. Bogwings, often mistaken for mynocks, feed on small rodents. Jubba birds are colorful, Force-sensitive hunters with a pleasant song that calms their prey, which includes anything from insects and rodents to knobby white spiders. The undisputed alpha predator of Dagobah is the dragonsnake, which is up to six meters of blaster-resistant scales, razor-sharp fins, and dagger-like fangs. It prefers to stalk coastal prey and drag them deep underwater. Once the dragonsnake is certain its prey is dead, it swallows it whole.

## THE DARK SIDE CAVE

Deep within the swamps of Dagobah, beneath an ancient gnarltree, a cave marks the final resting place of a dark threat that ended long ago. The stain of death has scarred the Force itself within the cave, and those sensitive to the Force who approach can sense it as a cold, unnatural presence.

Force users who dare to venture into the cave encounter hyperrealistic visions of their greatest fears or failures, or their darkest possible futures. Those unable to endure the visions without lashing out or recoiling in horror reveal a susceptibility to fear. Observing, questioning, or engaging the visions in conversation often leads adepts to newly discovered truths about themselves. This is often a crucial step toward avoiding a dark future and overcoming deep-seated fears.

has a strong presence at the edge of the system in order to tax hyperspace traffic changing course at Dorin, but it usually ignores intrasystem traffic. However, despite Dorin's lucrative location, few spacers make landfall on the planet.

Two hazardously proximal black holes dim the already-faint light of Dorin's orange star; and most species find it a dark, depressing place. The atmosphere has such little oxygen that most species have to wear breathers. Vicious storms plague Dorin year round. Kel Dor architecture consists of squat domes and ziggurats built to withstand Dorin's powerful winds. Most homes and buildings need underground shelters in the event of a mega-storm. These conditions have limited Dorin's potential as a trade hub but have also afforded it limited autonomy.

Imperial Moff Sticrie is ostensibly in charge, but he governs the sector from Myomar and avoids Kel Dor politics unless there is an interruption in tax collection. While the locals are generous, their commitment to justice is absolute. Dorin's natives deny Sticrie the customary bribes, privileges, and diplomatic immunity Imperial officials receive elsewhere. Convictions are difficult to get in Kel Dor courts, but once the court reaches a verdict, there are few chances for appeals or reprieves. Justice comes within days, and the punishments are typically more severe than a simple fine or prison sentence.

Outsiders often compare Kel Dor cities to the backs of bony hutta toads, with their evenly spaced grid of mismatched horns and bumps. Though the cities are thought of as ugly from above, most spacers change their minds after a trip through town. Almost every building is awash with animated lights in soothing colors designed to cut through the murky atmosphere and attract clientele. An emergency program can override the lighting protocols to direct everyone to safety in the event of a storm.

## THE BARAN DO SAGES

An ancient order of seers that grew out of a necessity to predict lethal storms, the Baran Do helped govern Dorin until its discovery by the Republic. Eventually, the sages faded to the background of Dorin society. The marginalization of the Baran Do is the only reason they escaped destruction during Order 66.

Those offered a permanent home with the Baran Do learn to use the Force through the lens of the natural elements. The Sages organize their Force techniques into three categories: the Hassat-Birr, Hassat-Durr, and Hassat-Worl, or the guided wind, lightning, and stream. The Sages are not militant, though many train in the martial arts. The quarterstaff is popular among the Baran Do, as the walking stick is a common sight in the face of Dorin's strong winds.

# ILUM

**Astronavigation Data:** Ilum system, 7G sector, Unknown Regions

**Orbital Metrics:** 1,078 days per year / 66 hours per day

**Government:** none

**Population:** 5,200 (support crew 45%, temporary researchers 30%, military 20%, other 5%)

**Languages:** none

**Terrain:** frozen lakes, mountains, ice steppes

**Major Cities:** none

**Areas of Interest:** Jedi Temple, excavation sites, various ruins

**Major Exports:** Ilum crystals (formerly)

**Major Imports:** none

**Trade Routes:** none

**Special Conditions:** frigid conditions require cold-weather gear, and some vehicles and equipment may require cold-weather modifications

**Background:** Historically famous as a secret Jedi pilgrimage site, icy Ilum is home to the crystal caves. A visit to these caves was a milestone in the training of tens of thousands of hopeful Jedi throughout the ages. The Jedi Order kept the hyperspace routes to Ilum a secret from the galaxy at large, though researchers currently believe Ilum is somewhere west of the Negs in the Unknown Regions. The clarion call of Ilum's presence in the Force is so strong as to almost be audible to Force adepts traveling west of the Namadii Corridor. A number of Jedi accounts mention Metellos as a jumping-off point in Force-assisted hyperspace jumps to Ilum.

Shortly after the Clone Wars, the Empire discovered Ilum's location in the archives of the conquered Jedi on Coruscant and blockaded the planet—a blockade that remains to this day. Dotting the planet's ice sheets and mountains are a number of excavation sites and Imperial research outposts, their personnel searching for relics of the past and secrets of the Jedi.

The planet is far from safe. Native and transplanted predators abound, including lisks, guids, and gorgodons. The lisks are pack hunters that lay in wait beneath fresh snowfall to ambush unsuspecting creatures wandering past. Transplanted to the world long ago, the guids stalk Ilum's caves. However, the violent gorgodons are among the most dangerous creatures

on the planet. Despite their classification as reptiles, the hulking gorgodons have simian-like bodies covered in shaggy grey fur. Gorgodon hides are almost blaster-proof, and they possess sharp claws and three rows of razor-sharp teeth. However, the creature has a soft, vulnerable spot at the back of its neck.

## ILUM'S JEDI TEMPLE

The Jedi built a massive, ornate entrance into the side of a large mountain that sits above a powerful Force vergence and a vast network of crystal caves. The interior was gigantic, with a spiraling walkway that led to meditation chambers with striking views of Ilum's frozen landscape. The facility could have supported thousands of Jedi, but it rarely accommodated more than a dozen at any given time.

The Jedi used the dizzying cave network to obtain crystals suitable for lightsaber construction. The search for the right crystal was more ritual than physical labor, though the Force often presented difficulties to test Jedi and younglings. The children would often be confronted with a test that forced them to face their own weaknesses—fear, anger, overconfidence, or recklessness, for example—and overcome them.

# MORABAND (KORRIBAN)

**Astronavigation Data:** Horuset system, Esstran sector (Stygian Caldera), Outer Rim region

**Orbital Metrics:** 780 days per year / 28 hours per day

**Government:** none

**Population:** none

**Languages:** Basic, Sith

**Terrain:** mountains, canyons, ruins

**Major Cities:** Dreshdae ruins

**Areas of Interest:** Valley of the Dark Lords, Valley of Golg, shyrack caves

**Major Exports:** Sith artifacts

**Major Imports:** foodstuffs

**Trade Routes:** Daragon Trail, Nache Bhelfia, Kamat Krote

**Special Conditions:** none

**Background:** Moraband is the homeworld of the Sith, who knew it as Korriban. According to legend, the ancient Sith Empire, populated by a species of long-extinct red-skinned aliens, was a proud civilization that spread throughout the Stygian Caldera around the same time that the earliest known documents relating to the Galactic Republic were recorded. In bygone times, a group of fallen Jedi, exiled from the Republic, crash-landed on Moraband.

These fallen Jedi dominated the Sith and eventually set themselves up as the ruling elite. Over time, presumably through some form of Sith alchemy, the former Jedi bred with the Sith to continue their lines. Eventually, these new Sith and the Republic Jedi clashed, resulting in full-scale war. The vicious conflicts between these two Force-using sects unleashed unimaginable devastation upon the galaxy, and Moraband did not escape unscathed. The planet saw repeated bombardment in the ongoing wars: its surface was blasted of life and its inhabitants fled or died.

Moraband itself is now an abandoned, dry, dull rock filled with canyons and caverns. Fierce, Sith-spawned predators like the tuk'ata hounds, terentatek, and bat-like shyracks populate the world. All across the planet are ruins of monuments to the exploits of ancient Sith Lords, who are entombed in even larger crypts. Exotic Sith-spawned creatures often guard the tombs, and ancient texts suggest the dead Sith Lords haunt their own catacombs, seeking one last victim.

While most structures on Moraband were designed to house only the dead, the planet did have some areas for the living. Moraband once hosted the Sith's most prestigious academy, which, in a morbid parody of the Jedi Order, was also home to their Dark Council. A small spaceport called Dreshdae supplied the academy. However, the Sith abandoned both the academy and the city long ago, and the world is now populated only by the marooned and insane.

## VALLEY OF THE SLEEPING KINGS

The Valley of the Dark Lords is a long, winding canyon where the most powerful of Sith kings are entombed, allegedly dating back to King Adas, an ancient Sith ruler who helped his people colonize Sith Space. Each king and Dark Lord of the Sith created a vast crypt, following a Sith belief in a Force-powered immortal afterlife. When a Sith Lord died, servants placed him in a Sith sarcophagus with his most prized possessions and sealed him in his crypt. Internal conflicts and war with the Jedi have resulted in the valley's destruction several times throughout history (and perhaps far more). It was rebuilt and re-excavated each time, though nobody knows what the valley is like today.

# OSSUS

**Astronavigation Data:** Adega system, Auril sector, Outer Rim region

**Orbital Metrics:** 231 days per year / 31 hours per day

**Government:** Ysanna tribal government

**Population:** 3,750,000 (Ysanna 99%, other 1%)

**Languages:** Ysannan, Basic

**Terrain:** hills, forests, mountains, caves

**Major Cities:** Knossa

**Areas of Interest:** Imhar Canyon, Eocho Mountains, Jedi ruins

**Major Exports:** none

**Major Imports:** technology

**Trade Routes:** none

**Special Conditions:** none

**Background:** The rolling hills and stubby mountains of Ossus give way to green forests that surround the overgrown ruins of Jedi outposts. Until almost five thousand years ago, the entire planet was an oasis of life, and for two millennia, the Great Jedi Library had been the largest repository of Jedi knowledge and artifacts in the galaxy. Scholars and pilgrims from across the galaxy would come to Ossus seeking wisdom. All Jedi made the pilgrimage to Ossus at least once in their life, to meditate and bask in the natural harmony between the Force and the corporeal world. It was not to last.

As a consequence of the ancient war between the Sith and the Jedi, a supernova scorched the surface of the planet. The Jedi had warning and were able to evacuate most inhabitants, lore, and artifacts offworld. However, there were far too many treasures and far too little time to move everything, and much was lost. The supernova blocked hyperspace access to the planet for generations.

Once it was accessible again, Ossus became a favored site for archaeologists hoping to rediscover ancient knowledge and for treasure hunters seeking priceless caches of Jedi artifacts. The planet's plant life has since recovered, and small tribes of primitive humans roam the hills. Known as the Ysanna, these tribes have a high percentage of Force-sensitive members, and the Jedi believed they were descendants of a band of Jedi trapped during the evacuation. Unfortunately, when the Jedi arranged for Ossus to be classified as a protected historical site to cut down on loot-

ers, this action denied the Jedi their right to test and recruit the Ysanna for Jedi training. Instead, the Jedi focused on excavation projects and artifact recovery as late as the Clone Wars. When the Empire emerged as the galactic power at the end of the Clone Wars, it immediately blockaded Ossus, restricting access to only those cleared by the Emperor's office.

## LOST ARTIFACTS OF OSSUS

A number of powerful artifacts are believed to still exist on Ossus. If they do, they would be impressive (and dangerous) finds.

**Ajunta Pall's Lightsaber:** It is said that the Jedi Master Ajunta Pall was the leader of a group of fallen Jedi who crash-landed on Moraband. According to lore, the lightsaber he used was taken by the Jedi Council and later moved to the Great Jedi Library on Ossus.

**The Relle Talisman:** Sith Lady Zoiya Relle was among the best fighters in the Sith Empire, but she had little charisma or guile. To compensate, she created a talisman that could dominate the minds of others. She later became one of the few women to rule the Sith. It is thought a Sith carrying her talisman fell on Ossus.

# WEIK

**Astronavigation Data:** Weik system, Wild Space

**Orbital Metrics:** 248 days per year / 30 hours per day

**Government:** feudal/tribal

**Population:** 260,000,000 (humans 58%, Twi'leks 14%, Duros 11%, Zabrak 9%, Lanniks 8%)

**Languages:** numerous local dialects derived from Basic

**Terrain:** mountains, forests, plains

**Major Cities:** Vossport, Skyholme, Sunrace Citadel, Fume

**Areas of Interest:** Crysifal Peak, the Madlands, Rimesea, the Adamite Tower

**Major Exports:** none

**Major Imports:** none

**Trade Routes:** none

**Special Conditions:** isolation from galactic civilization

**Background:** Weik is a world far removed from the rest of the galaxy. Its star orbits in the distant reaches of Wild Space, beyond charted hyperspace lanes. Few have visited the world, and the rest of the galaxy doesn't know it exists. However, this isolation has led to a fascinating culture involving the Force.

In millennia past, a colony vessel from the Core Worlds crash-landed on Weik. Though the ship did not survive the landing, most of the passengers and crew did. These shipwrecked survivors—a mix of several species including Duros, humans, Twi'leks, and several others—attempted to make the most of their predicament, and settled the rugged world they found. Luckily, Weik proved habitable, a mix of towering, icy mountains, thick forests, and windswept plains.

Over the centuries, most of the technology the survivors salvaged from the wreck broke down, and records and memories of the wider galaxy faded. Eventually, the planet's society reverted to a feudal state, where fire-forged steel and wind power were the height of technology. Those species that survived tended to separate into their own enclaves only mixing in cosmopolitan trading centers like bustling Vossport on the shores of the chilly Rimesea.

Though Weik is ruled by kings and queens, Force-sensitives are the true power on the planet. A cadre of Jedi accompanied the ancient colony ship, and over the years its bloodlines mingled with the settlers'. The ability to touch the Force is rare, but not unheard-of. However, these inhabitants do not understand the Force, cloaking their powers in ritual and superstition and adopting the mantle of mages and shamans. Those who remain pure in spirit tend to be advisors, community healers, or wandering knights, while those who fall to the dark side may become tyrannical despots or raider warlords. However, neither light nor dark has ever gained the upper hand on Weik, ensuring the conflict continues to this day.

## TECHNO-RELICS

Though most of Weik's tech base has long been lost to history, some examples of technology endure, or are brought to the planet by the extremely rare trader or traveler. Generally these "relics" are highly durable and simple technology, and without fail are considered "magical" by their owners. A few warlords have ruled by the strength of their "light throwers" or used an "orb of destruction" to bring down an enemy stronghold.

However, one item that has endured for all of Weik's history is the lightsaber. Still extremely rare, a handful of these weapons have survived the ages due to the extreme simplicity and durability of their construction. Weik folklore tells many tales of these blades, inevitably mythologizing them as magic swords that find their way into the hands of heroes or villains who perform the deeds of ages.

# THE JEDI AND THE SITH

*"For over a thousand generations, the Jedi Knights were the guardians of peace and justice in the old Republic."*

—Obi-Wan Kenobi

For centuries, the crackling clash of lightsabers meant imminent death and destruction. A blur of energy blades signaled war and the renewal of what seemed a never-ending conflict between the Jedi and the Sith. Yet, at last, the continual fighting halted, in what was said to have been the apocalyptic culminating battle of a vicious war between Sith and Jedi. The Jedi won at great cost, and thought they had defeated the Sith for all time.

By the final decades of the Republic, the average galactic citizen had no knowledge of the Sith. The Jedi Order held sway over public knowledge of the Force, but its relatively small numbers meant that Jedi were rarely, if ever, encountered by the average galactic citizen. Even the Jedi remained mysterious and isolated to most citizens; the Sith were almost entirely forgotten by the galaxy. Those few historians who knew of the Sith thought of them as a footnote in ancient history, long lost to time.

However, the Sith had persevered. At least one Sith Lord survived that ancient war and, in the wake of it, hid from galactic civilization. He established the Rule of Two: that there would always be two Sith, a master and an apprentice. The master would teach the apprentice the knowledge of the Sith, and eventually, the apprentice would slay his master and take on his own apprentice so the cycle could begin anew.

The Sith had survived for centuries adhering to the Rule of Two and hiding from the public and the Jedi. Working from the shadows, the Sith undermined the Jedi Order and the Republic itself. Both fell, destroyed by the Sith. With the rise of the Galactic Empire, the Sith and Jedi reversed roles. The Jedi became enemies of the state, and the populace turned against them. The Sith controlled the government and the galaxy, while the few remaining Jedi went underground, relentlessly pursued and purged from the galaxy.

The Emperor destroyed the reputation of the Jedi along with the Order and its allies. The general public saw the Force as more myth than reality. The historical records of the Jedi were lost or locked away. By the time Luke Skywalker destroyed the Death Star, Jedi history and beliefs were as muddled and half-remembered as the ancient tales.

# STORIES AND LEGENDS OF THE JEDI

W ith Jedi serving throughout the galaxy for thousands of years, maintaining a complete historical record was impossible. Though the Jedi archives held reports, recordings, holocrons, and data from throughout their history, the archives also contained incomplete information, inaccuracies, half-remembered stories, omissions, and outright falsehoods. For all that the Jedi retained, they also lost innumerable records. Centuries of war, schisms, sabotage, competing philosophies, and uncounted disasters left major gaps in Jedi history. Some of the remaining old tales were so outlandish that many considered them myths, or at least wildly exaggerated. Of course, with the Force involved, wild tales, great evil, and fantastic deeds could have been perfectly true. Even false or exaggerated stories still may prove useful as parables and inspiration.

## THE RELIABILITY OF LEGENDS

Many tales have been told of the Jedi and the Sith, but the truth about their origins and early adventures has yet to be revealed. The tales within this section should be treated merely as inspiration for Game Masters and players who want to use this material to establish a deep history for their characters' universe, and should not be treated as canonical truth.

the Empire and allied institutions and individuals keep watch over almost all known material related to the Force, Jedi, or Sith. Searching for certain subjects or showing a concerted interest in any of these topics could prompt an Imperial investigation. Truly useful information seems to mysteriously disappear shortly after discovery. Occasionally, the discoverer disappears as well.

Here are some of the tales that have survived the millennia, whatever their accuracy might be:

## MYTHS OF TYTHON

Some say that Tython is the birthplace of the Je'daii, the group that would evolve to become the Jedi Order. The ancient history of the Jedi is as murky as any past civilization's, but some myths and stories have survived in holocrons, texts, and other sources.

Tython is the name of a star system and planet said to exist in the Deep Core region of the galaxy, where dangerous and difficult hyperspace routes open and collapse without warning, isolating the planet for years, decades, and even centuries. According to the lore, Tython is so heavily influenced by the Force that Force storms manifest on its surface. It is a chaotic and violent place, with dangerous creatures attuned to the Force living among its extreme landscapes. The Tython system, if the legends are true, is located within what is now the Imperial Deep Core Security Zone, making it extremely dangerous and nearly impossible for outsiders to reach the planet.

The inhabitants of Tython are rumored to have been transplanted from planets across the galaxy, yielding a mix of sentient species including humans,

Through the years, the Force users developed the Je'daii Rangers to help maintain order and peace. Said to be the precursors of the Jedi Order, the Je'daii Rangers carried out missions within the Tython system, much like later Jedi Knights. Unlike the Jedi, the Je'daii were not strictly servants of the light side of the Force. The Je'daii believed in keeping a balance between light and dark, and that balance was everything. (See **The Je'daii**, page 382.)

As legend has it, Tython's two moons represented (and, some believe, embodied) the two sides of the Force. Ashla was the light side, while Bogan was the dark. Those Force users who leaned too far toward the dark side were marooned on Bogan, and those who strayed too far toward the light side were left on Ashla, to isolate them and allow them to rediscover their balance. It also got them off of Tython, preventing them from endangering others by throwing nearby portions of the planet out of balance—whether accidentally or on purpose.

The path of the Je'daii from Tython back to the rest of the galaxy is clouded in legend. Stories tell of a lost Gree-designed hypergate that was ancient even then. It reportedly facilitated jumps to other worlds. Other tales say the system was reconnected to the galaxy after a ship from the Rakata Infinite Empire crashed on the world. Eventually, understanding of the benefits and consequences of focusing on the light and dark sides led Tython to the first battles between the adherents of each side, known as the Force Wars. Such battles have been repeated unendingly in the millennia since.

Tython's location and even the knowledge of its existence has passed in and out of galactic history and legend. Likewise, its sentient population has risen and fallen many times. Tales suggest the ancient Gree once used the world and then disappeared. The Je'daii arrived centuries later, but eventually moved on to the rest of the galaxy, abandoning the world. Legendary figures are said to have rediscovered and lost the system several times. The instability of the Deep Core hyperspace routes could, and did, cut Tython off from the rest of the galaxy many times, contributing to its repeated loss. After the loss of the Jedi Temple in the Sith Empire's infamous Sacking of Coruscant, the Jedi returned and used Tython as their new home and training grounds.

## ANCIENT WARS

Thousands of years after the Je'daii emerged from Tython, the Old Republic entered a time of great turmoil. Invaders struck the Republic many times over many generations. The Sith and the Mandalorians, sometimes together, other times alone, sought to seize control of the Republic through military means.

By this time, the Jedi Order had become well established in the Republic, though it was often divided in its philosophy, teachings, and methodology. The Jedi usually joined the Republic in beating back invaders. The earliest conflicts were the Hundred-Year Darkness, the Great Hyperspace War, and the Great Sith War, the latter two being Sith invasions of the Republic. See **The Ancient Sith**, on page 381, for information on these historic battles.

## REVAN, THE MANDALORIANS, AND THE JEDI CIVIL WAR

Devastated in the Great Sith War, the Mandalorians spent much of the next few decades recovering and rebuilding. A new idealism overtook the old Mandalorian ways, and the Neo-Crusader leadership reformed Mandalorian society. The Mandalorians remained nomadic, but recruited from all beings as they moved through the galaxy. Once their forces were strong enough, they started forays against the Republic's Outer Rim worlds, drawing the Republic military beyond its normal defensive zones. After a year of such tactics, they launched their main invasion, striking at worlds in Republic space which had defenses weakened by the deployment of ships to the Outer Rim.

With its military suffering humiliating defeats, the Republic asked the Jedi Order for aid. Still recovering from its losses in the Great Sith War more than two decades before, the Jedi leadership refused to help. However, during this time, the Jedi Council did not hold total control over the Jedi. Jedi Enclaves and training facilities were scattered throughout the galaxy, with many masters and mentors teaching their own versions of Jedi ideals and methodologies. Rivalries extended so far as to foster the formation of secret Jedi groups and covenants that operated independently, either on their own initiative or influenced by members of the Jedi Order and Jedi Council. Such infighting among the Jedi further disrupted the order during the Mandalorian invasions.

Not all Jedi were content to follow council orders and simply stand by as Republic worlds crumbled under the Mandalorian onslaught. One Jedi, named Revan, gathered other Jedi who wanted to defend the Republic directly. They engaged the Mandalorians and turned the tide of several battles. As more Jedi joined Revan's forces, the Republic gave them command over many Republic military units. As the Jedi reclaimed Republic worlds, Revan and his apprentice, Malak, were cheered as heroes. Finally, the Mandalorians were beaten back to Malachor V, where Revan and the Jedi nearly wiped them out.

Instead of returning to the Republic victorious, Revan and his fleet disappeared into the Unknown Regions. Years of warfare had changed the Jedi and his followers. Months later, their fall to the dark side was revealed when a much larger fleet reappeared: a Sith armada led by Darth Revan and his apprentice, Darth Malak. Having learned Sith ways, they immediately seized Moraband (Korriban), the traditional Sith homeworld. Revan and Malak expanded their territory rapidly, occupying many Republic systems to establish a new Sith Empire.

Even as a Dark Lord of the Sith, Darth Revan benefited from his hero's reputation among the Jedi and the Republic. Jedi, Republic military, beings of all ages and ranks, and entire star systems strongly believed in his leadership and willingly joined the Sith Empire. The Republic and the Jedi defended their territory, but they found they were often fighting their own former allies and comrades. As such, the battle against this new Sith Empire became known as the Jedi Civil War.

A Jedi attack on Darth Revan's and Darth Malak's starship radically changed the war. Taking Sith tradition and ideals to heart, Malak took advantage of the attack and tried to kill Revan and claim command of the Empire. The Jedi saved Revan and took him back to the Republic. The Jedi Council decided to try to rehabilitate the Sith Lord by erasing his memories. From there, the histories are incomplete, as Revan's journey was personal and mostly unrecorded. Details are murky at best, but it is believed that Revan found his way back to the source of the Sith's military power deep in the Unknown Regions and ultimately defeated Malak. Some say he returned to the light side; others believe he returned to evil.

In any case, the Sith Empire soon fell apart. A few short years later, three remaining Sith Lords joined

### TEMPLES AND ENCLAVES

After leaving Tython, the early Jedi reportedly settled on the planet Ossus. Ossus became the center of Jedi lore and teaching until a supernova induced by the Sith destroyed its surface during the Great Sith War. Afterward, the Jedi relocated to Coruscant, having already dedicated themselves to supporting Republic safety and ideals. There, they established a Jedi enclave and the Jedi Temple, though the teaching of Padawans was not yet centralized. Other temples and enclaves were scattered through the galaxy. Most followed the lead of the Jedi Council, but not all. Many had their own variations of Jedi philosophies. Through the centuries, with the fortunes of the Jedi rising and falling with the Republic, most of these centers were destroyed, closed, or abandoned, and eventually centralized on Coruscant.

forces to create the Sith Triumvirate. Darth Nihilus, Darth Sion, and Darth Traya targeted the Jedi Order directly with assassins and other agents. For a time, the order fell apart, its few survivors scattering across the galaxy. Extraordinary tales suggest that one such survivor tracked down and killed all three Sith Lords, shattering the Sith for many years.

It would not last. Hundreds of years later, though still thousands of years before the present day, the Sith returned from the shadows to create another new empire. They demonstrated their power by sacking the Republic capital world of Coruscant and destroying the Jedi Temple. Though this forced the Jedi to rebuild on Tython and elsewhere, the Jedi and the Republic eventually prevailed.

# THE ANCIENT SITH

The evolution of the Sith through galactic history is long and convoluted. Much has been lost or altered. Originally, the Sith were an actual species native to Moraband (Korriban). They were among the species transported to Tython and part of the early Je'daii Order. The Sith eventually sought the power of the dark side, reportedly inciting the First Great Schism—the first struggle between light and dark siders, the Jedi and the Sith. As like-minded individuals joined them over time, the name Sith expanded to cover all believers in their philosophy.

The Sith have a disconnected history. As the years passed, their philosophies about power and advancement led to internal strife and widespread warfare that decimated the Sith on more than one occasion. No matter how complete their destruction, the Sith always seem to rise from the ashes. Sometimes, the new Sith had no direct connection to the past Sith beyond discovering and learning from ancient works

and adopting their philosophies. Multiple Sith Empires rose and fell in ancient eras. The cycle continued for centuries until Darth Bane remade the Sith and instituted the Rule of Two (see page 386).

## THE HUNDRED-YEAR DARKNESS

Well after the early years on Tython, the tales say, the Jedi battled dark Jedi in the Hundred-Year Darkness. The dark Jedi had discovered how to use the Force to create mutant creatures to be used as warriors, mounts, and battlefield terrors, like the Leviathans. The Jedi exiled the dark siders and their teachings, and the situation quickly escalated to war. In the end, the Jedi won and succeeded in long-term banishment of the surviving dark siders. In exile, the dark siders discovered a planet called Korriban (now known as Moraband), and the savage Sith species native to it. The dark siders gained control over the Sith, becoming their lords and masters. It was nearly two thousand years later when they reemerged and returned to Republic space as the Sith.

## THE GREAT HYPERSPACE WAR

The days when hyperspace travel was far more dangerous set the stage for the Great Hyperspace War. Even the historical records of the Republic do not date from so far, but some fragmented stories do remain today. Legend has it that a pair of hyperspace explorers accidentally found a route deep into the heart of the Stygian Caldera, in the center of Sith Space. At the time, the Sith were divided between two powerful Sith Lords who were vying to replace their recently deceased leader, Dark Lord of the Sith Marka Ragnos. Ludo Kressh was content with current Sith holdings, while Naga Sadow advocated expansion. Sadow allowed one explorer to escape, having placed a tracking beacon on his ship, which led the Sith to the Republic. Sadow prevailed and led a massive Sith invasion fleet to strike the Koros system (currently known as the Empress Teta system). Sadow's forces failed and retreated back to the Sith Empire. Upon their return, Ludo Kressh's forces attacked Sadow's battered fleet. Republic pursuers arrived and smashed both fleets. Though thought to have been destroyed with his ship, Sadow actually escaped with his Massassi followers and vanished.

## THE GREAT SITH WAR

The wide-ranging and convoluted Great Sith War changed the galaxy and the Republic. It began with the formation and appearance of the Krath (see the next page), a group of spoiled aristocrats turned Sith adherents. They arrived on Onderon when the Jedi were relocating the fallen Jedi Freedon Nadd's sarcophagus to the moon Dxun. In a complicated series of events involving the aging King of Onderon, the Krath, the famous Jedi Ulic Qel-Droma, and the appearance of Nadd's spirit within the king, Nadd ultimately returned to his corpse, and the Krath fled back to the Empress Teta system with a cache of Sith artifacts. Nadd's sarcophagus was entombed in a secret location on Dxun.

That was just the beginning. The Krath staged an attempted coup in their home system. News of their Sith magic attracted the attention of the Jedi, who joined the Republic in battling the Krath. The fighting eventually spread far across the galaxy.

At the same time, the Jedi Exar Kun had taken an interest in the dark side. He located and broke into Nadd's tomb, releasing Nadd's spirit once again. Nadd led him to Korriban and manipulated the Jedi into falling to the dark side. Kun ultimately vanquished Nadd, and he believed he would bring about a new Golden Age of the Sith. As such, he set out to eliminate the Krath, whom he saw as rivals to his destiny.

By then, the fallen Jedi Ulic Qel-Droma led the Krath. Kun engaged him in combat, but the form of the long-deceased Dark Lord of the Sith Ragnos appeared and convinced the two to join forces. The war shifted with the alliance, and more combatants entered the fray. The Mandalorians joined the Krath. The Krath tried to occupy Coruscant. Allies betrayed each other. Ossus was decimated, unlivable for centuries. Ulic tried to redeem himself. Ultimately, the Sith were divided, betrayed each other, and defeated one by one. Exar Kun remained and met the Jedi and the Republic in his final battle, in which he unleashed

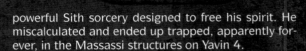

### SITH ALCHEMY

Some Sith transformed the dark side's power to educe spell-like effects. These individuals were adept at Sith alchemy—creating powerful items imbued with the dark side of the Force. Many of these items granted wearers or wielders temporary boosts to their Force abilities. They also corrupted the individual over time, whether or not the person was Force-sensitive.

Sith alchemy was difficult to learn, unless the individual had a natural talent for it. Even those with the necessary aptitude could be proficient at wildly different effects. For example, some were experts at forming spells that affected individual minds, whereas others used Sith alchemy to craft great illusions affecting many people at a time. Due to the dark side connection to alchemy, the Jedi did not approve of its use.

Some practitioners developed their own powers, whereas others acquired their skills from Sith texts or masters. The ancient Krath movement learned Sith alchemy from Sith artifacts and records. The Nightsisters of Dathomir, on the other hand, are expert alchemists with their own self-taught traditions.

powerful Sith sorcery designed to free his spirit. He miscalculated and ended up trapped, apparently forever, in the Massassi structures on Yavin 4.

In the end, a battered Republic managed to survive, aided by the Jedi. Peace would reign for many years, until the Mandalorian Wars.

## EARLY TRADITIONS

Before widespread and fast hyperspace travel, the isolation of many systems led to the formation of localized traditions.

### THE JE'DAII

Among the earliest mythical accounts of ancient Force traditions is that of the Je'daii. Believed by many to be the ancient precursors of the Jedi themselves, these practitioners hailed from the planet of Tython (see **Myths of Tython**, on page 378). Living on the tumultuous, Force-saturated world indoctrinated a strict belief in maintaining the balance of the Force within their members. They didn't adhere to following only the light or dark sides, as being out of balance on Tython often caused Force storms and led to a quick death. The so-called Je'daii Rangers resembled later Jedi Knights, carrying out critical missions or intervening in political or military conflicts. Apprentices were called Journeyers, after the great, dangerous journey that each was required to make, traveling around Tython to its various Je'daii Temples.

The inception of the Je'daii preceded the invention of the lightsaber. Instead, they carried strong, elegantly forged alloy swords that they could infuse with the Force. Eventually, they came to know of an early energy-bladed weapon called a forcesaber. It arrived on Tython with the Force hounds—bodyguards and warriors of high-ranking Rakata from the Rakata Infinite Empire—after they located the system. These forcesabers are thought to have been some of the earliest examples of lightsabers.

## THE KRATH

The Krath exemplify how dark side and Sith-related groups manifested without directly descending from the Sith themselves. In the Empress Teta system, cousins Satal and Aleema Keto were among other rich and spoiled aristocrats who decided to teach themselves elements of Sith sorcery. Their station gave them access to captured Sith artifacts and tomes from the thousand-year-distant Great Hyperspace War (see page 381). The cousins were lured deeper into Sith culture when they were drawn to the planet Onderon, where followers of the ancient Sith Lord Freedon Nadd (see the prior page) for Nadd's history) were rebelling. They discovered that the spirit of Freedon Nadd still existed and was working with the King of Onderon to continue Sith culture. When support for the king collapsed, Nadd promised to guide the cousins into a new Golden Age of the Sith.

The Krath supplemented their research on Sith artifacts, magic, and techniques with occasional direct guidance from Sith spirits such as Nadd. They studied anything that drew their interest, unconcerned with the dangers of the dark side. Using artifacts, advanced illusions, and ancient knowledge to great effect, they caused great pain in the galaxy.

When the cousins returned to the Empress Teta system, they attempted to seize control. The population resisted, and war engulfed the system. The Krath fought using all manner of their newfound powers of Sith sorcery to create impossibly large illusions. They engaged Republic and Jedi forces, and war spread into the greater galaxy. (See **The Great Sith War**, on the prior page.) In the end, the Krath were defeated and scattered into the galaxy, where they dwindled away.

## THE SORCERERS OF TUND

The Sorcerers of Tund presented Force use as though they had mastered magical powers and spells. They lived on the Outer Rim planet Tund. The Sorcerers were well-known to the ancient Jedi and equaled them in skill with the Force. The Jedi attempted, but failed, to recruit them into the order in a bid to teach them that the Force existed without the guise of magic. The Jedi periodically visited the Sorcerers, fearing that their teachings might eventually follow a darker path, but no one knows if they ever engaged in open conflict.

Though the Jedi reportedly last visited the Sorcerers well before the Battles of Ruusan, the legend survived the centuries into the Imperial era. However, Tund is now a dead world, recently decimated by an unknown catastrophic event. Some rumors say the one surviving Sorcerer, called Rokur Gepta, was granted command of an Imperial warship and held sway over Imperial forces in the region for a time. Exactly how and why he was allowed to do this is not public knowledge, but it implies important connections to the highest ranking Imperials. Other rumors blame him for Tund's destruction, while some whisper that Rokur Gepta died in the midst of his tyrannical rule.

## JAL SHEY

One of the oldest known Force-using cultures, the Jal Shey observed and studied the Force scientifically, rather than spiritually. Their origin and fate have been lost to history. The Jal Shey were highly nomadic, searching out areas where they might learn more about the Force and then moving on. They were highly skilled arbiters and negotiators, as well as honorable diplomats, the equal of any in the galaxy. Adept at imbuing the Force into weapons and items, they were able to do so in such a manner that any wielder (not just the creator, as is more common) could benefit from the specific improvements imparted by its creator. As they moved through the galaxy, the Jal Shey used their advancing knowledge to aid society.

Even in the Jal Shey's own era, other individuals were more likely to have encountered a Jal Shey item than the order itself. The Jal Shey's stringent recruiting requirements kept their membership small. They were divided into three groups: neophytes, advisors, and mentors. Neophytes were essentially apprentices, studying with mentors before advancing to carry out their own missions as advisors. The Jal Shey used basic lightsaber defense forms, but given their lack of combat focus and skill, they often created armor, belts, and other defensive items to boost their abilities.

# JEDI OF THE REPUBLIC

**M**ost Imperial citizens' minimal knowledge of the Jedi stems from memories, stories, and reports of the last decades of the Republic and the Clone Wars. Older citizens remember Jedi exploits and might have even met one or more. However, their views and opinions about the order are likely colored by the final days of the Clone Wars and how they feel about the Empire. (See page 388 for **The Fall of the Jedi**.) Below are elements the GM might use either as memories older NPC citizens could relate if questioned by the PCs, or as information that might still be found in public histories or private records. Since most people didn't follow the Jedi, their memories are likely hazy. The GM should omit facts, introduce confusing statements, or embellish as needed when roleplaying NPCs.

## JEDI KNIGHTS, MASTERS, AND APPRENTICES

The most common circumstance under which a citizen might have met or seen a Jedi was when a Jedi Knight, accompanied by an apprentice, or Padawan learner, was on a mission. Some older citizens might remember the different levels of Jedi, but most simply called them all Jedi Knights. Meeting a Jedi was normally a life experience not easily forgotten.

The Jedi had four basic levels of experience and knowledge. When deemed ready to advance, they were required to prove their aptitude and abilities, whether by test, trial, or extraordinary experience.

**Initiates** were the children, or younglings, sent to the temple to train to become a Jedi. Some citizens have heard falsehoods of Jedi forcibly taking Force-using children to the temple for training.

**Padawans** were adolescents and young adults apprenticed to a specific Jedi Knight.

**Jedi Knights** were the most common. They carried out missions assigned by the Jedi High Council, sometimes at the behest of the Republic Senate or Chancellor. During the Clone Wars, they served as commanders and generals over clone trooper units and were often seen in the midst of battle. People might remember specific Jedi exploits in famous battles.

**Jedi Masters** were older Jedi who proved through experience and extraordinary aptitude their mastery of the Force. The Masters oversaw all Jedi training and education. They carried out their own research. They sat on the Jedi Councils, though there were far more Masters than Council seats. They commanded entire armies during the Clone Wars, and the public viewed them as powerful and the wisest of Jedi.

**The Grand Master**, also called the Master of the Order, was the elected head of the Jedi High Council. Only Masters of unique skill and experience received the title, and even then, only one existed at a time.

## THE JEDI COUNCILS

Four councils governed the Jedi Order. Each council would meet within one of the five spires atop the Jedi Temple and typically comprised several Jedi Masters, the exact number varying over the years. The average citizen was likely to have heard of the Jedi Council, usually meaning the High Council, but probably none of the others.

**The High Council** oversaw all others and was the guiding authority of the Jedi Order. It dealt directly with the Republic Senate, the Chancellor, other public authorities, and outside institutions. It directed and coordinated Jedi assignments and missions when deployed with clone troopers during the Clone Wars. The High Council naturally held great influence and commanded respect, even among its political enemies on Coruscant.

**The Council of First Knowledge** maintained and protected the Jedi Archives. It oversaw knowledge and information passed along to Initiates and Padawans during their training. Public contact was restricted to archive acquisitions and special requests from the public or government agencies.

**The Council of Reconciliation** served as the Jedi diplomatic corps. It oversaw missions of arbitration

THE JEDI CODE

The Jedi Code encompassed the central philosophies that the Jedi were expected to study, understand, and adhere to. It provided a guide when circumstances and events exceeded expectations or experience. Interpreting the code was difficult to do in the moment, so the Jedi discussed and assessed possible reactions and situations throughout their training and career.

While the Jedi have essentially disappeared from the Galactic Empire, their code remains in many holocrons, texts, and records. A character successfully researching the Jedi should eventually discover a copy of the code, as it is not secret and is referenced in the historical records of many worlds. Even the Empire cannot completely purge it from all memory sources.

*There is no emotion, there is peace.*

*There is no ignorance, there is knowledge.*

*There is no passion, there is serenity.*

*There is no chaos, there is harmony.*

*There is no death, there is the Force.*

and negotiation in which Jedi served as peacemakers or impartial judges in conflicts throughout the galaxy. It had daily contact with many of the galaxy's troubled governments and corporations.

**The Council of Reassignment** administered the Jedi Service Corps, which oversaw the assignment, promotion, and development of Jedi who failed to pass their Initiate or Padawan trials. The Corps maintained the Jedi Temple, equipment, and all Jedi installations.

Corps members with particular aptitudes in non-combat Force use were also occasionally sent to aid others, such as missions of healing or rebuilding after conflict.

## JEDI ARCHIVES AND HOLOCRONS

The Jedi Archives are an irreplaceable cache of Jedi and galactic history. They contain most of the history of the Jedi Order, though many original records were destroyed in various wars and other actions against the order. After the fall of the Jedi, Emperor Palpatine took personal control over the temple and its vast stores of ancient artifacts. Of particular interest to Darth Sidious were the captured Sith holocrons and dark side artifacts the Jedi had confiscated over the centuries and locked away. One division of the Jedi actually pursued leads on any reported artifacts in order to retrieve them and keep them out of the hands of dark side users, as well as to prevent the artifacts from corrupting other individuals.

Holocrons were the ultimate information storage device for transferring knowledge and training from one generation of Jedi or Sith to the next. Holocrons could survive centuries of use. Each had its own "guardian," who served as the interface and guide between the user and the knowledge held within. The guardian typically resembled the form and personality of the holocron's creator. Though very realistic, and able to respond conversationally to a user, the guardian was simply a highly advanced electronic interface and hologram. The guardians often made holocron users prove that they were worthy of the knowledge contained therein, typically through verbal tests of knowledge and personality. Jedi holocrons were typically cube or dodecahedron-shaped. Sith holocrons were nearly always in the form of a four-sided pyramid.

# THE HIDDEN HISTORY OF THE SITH

Until the arrival of Darth Vader on the galactic stage, few citizens would have recalled any useful knowledge of the Sith, beyond the meager content in galactic history classes and some events of the Clone Wars. Modern Sith hid themselves and their actions so effectively that most of the galaxy believed them to be long extinct. To most, it appears Vader is the only one. Extremely few individuals know of the Emperor's true power, and those are his closest and most loyal allies.

The history of the Sith is even more unknown, obscure, muddled, and distorted than that of the Jedi. Once the Rule of Two was established, the master didn't always keep detailed histories, beyond the tales and

cache of knowledge required to pass on to the apprentice. Most hid their deeds, lest they alert the Jedi. Given the Sith's nature and beliefs, fabricated and exaggerated stories are certainly intermixed with information on actual events. A few Sith Lords recorded their own dark side holocrons and wrote treatises to advance their personal ideas and goals. The Emperor hoards and hides all Sith and Jedi knowledge he possesses and finds. Obviously, none of this is accessible to galactic historians.

## THE RULE OF TWO

The Rule of Two defined Sith existence for centuries. It was a plan with several goals: survival, the destruction of the Jedi, and seizing control of the galaxy. Only two Sith could exist at any one time—a master to wield power, and an apprentice to desire it.

The Rule of Two created a balance of power between the master and apprentice. The master should train, educate, and continually test his personally selected would-be successor. The apprentice needed to learn everything the master knew about the Force, Sith history, Sith power, and how to survive in hiding, in order to gain more personal and economic power and advance Sith goals. If the apprentice was too weak, he would fall during the master's instructions and tests. If the master deemed the apprentice unworthy of the title of Sith Lord, he would kill the apprentice and start again.

The apprentice had to survive and demonstrate to his master his improving skills and complete dedication to the Sith. As the apprentice gained knowledge and proficiency, he would eventually become the master's equal or better. The balance of power would be upset, and the apprentice had to challenge his master for the title. If the master showed any sign of weakness due to age, ailment, or injury, the apprentice might strike early, to ensure the strength of the Sith did not weaken or fail. Sometimes, an apprentice identified a likely apprentice of his own, before

dueling to the death. If the apprentice failed, the apprentice-in-waiting might succeed him, or the Sith Lord might deem him unsuitable and destroy him.

## DARTH BANE AND THE RULE OF TWO

The Sith of the ancient past once numbered in the thousands and more. They fell into a self-destructive pattern. The Sith gathered power, grew in numbers, and struck at the Jedi and the Republic, followed by shattering defeats at their hands. The survivors retreated—or fled—back to the shadows and distant reaches of the galaxy to begin again. The Sith notion that the strongest are meant to survive combined with their tradition that advancement comes through killing those above them made Sith Lords as much of a threat to each other as any Jedi or Republic soldier. Entire Sith invasions crumbled when their dominating leader fell to an apprentice or other being out to claim leadership. Sith strength often only lasted as long as their most powerful Sith Lord lived. After centuries of struggle and many defeats, one Sith Lord realized that their continued existence relied on drastically changing the equation.

Darth Bane had a new plan for the Sith.

Darth Bane is shrouded in myths, legends, supposed histories, and outright deceptions (many of his own making to confuse the Jedi and other pursuers). While some tales have survived the centuries in Jedi histories and the trappings of Sith lore, details are severely muddled and highly questionable.

Darth Bane realized that the continuous cycle of Sith Lord deaths, especially where lesser underlings massed together to defeat more powerful Sith Lords, severely weakened the Sith cause over time. Great leaders and assets were replaced by victorious but often weaker successors. Bane set out to permanently change that path.

Having survived the near-extinction of the Sith ranks by the Jedi, Bane and his apprentice were the first pair to follow his Rule of Two. From then on, the Sith virtually vanished from the galaxy and worked from the shadows and darkness. They avoided the Jedi and hid their existence. Ultimately, Bane's plan produced more powerful Sith Lords with each generation.

## DARTH PLAGUEIS, DARTH SIDIOUS, AND DARTH MAUL

The Rule of Two culminated in the success of Darth Sidious, a thousand years later. Darth Plagueis selected the skilled politician Palpatine as his apprentice. He guided Palpatine through his rise to power within the Galactic Senate. Following the tradition of his predecessors, Palpatine killed Plagueis and seized the mantle of master. Sidious took his own apprentice, the powerful warrior Darth Maul. Palpatine manipulated his homeworld of Naboo, the Trade Federation, and the Jedi to bring about his election as Chancellor of the Republic. It was not without cost. Events forced Darth Maul to reveal his existence to the Jedi, which ultimately resulted in his apparent death. As Chancellor, Palpatine achieved one Sith goal—control of the Republic—but he had not destroyed it or the Jedi.

## THE CLONE WARS

Sidious's schemes concocted the conditions and forces needed to create a galactic secessionist movement and to manipulate its adherents into waging war against the Republic. He created the need for a Republic army, and he secretly manipulated others into creating a massive clone force that was available just in time. As Chancellor Palpatine, he commanded Republic forces. As Darth Sidious, he was the power behind the generals and leaders of the Separatist movement. He took a new apprentice, in the form of fallen Jedi Count Dooku, called Darth Tyranus. Dooku was the face and primary instigator of the Separatist movement.

During the war, a number of dark side Force users appeared and nominally supported the Separatists. Asajj Ventress sought to become Darth Tyranus's apprentice. Though Tyranus added to her considerable Force skills and used her against the Jedi, she never attained that goal. When he had no more use for her, the leader of the Nightsisters, Mother Talzin, provided him with a new warrior: the powerful and brutal Savage Opress, brother of Darth Maul.

After Savage fell out of favor with Tyranus, he set out on a path that ultimately led him to find his brother, who had barely survived his apparent death at the hands of Obi-Wan Kenobi. With Mother Talzin's help, Maul was rehabilitated, somewhat, and the brothers set out on their own paths. Opress became Maul's apprentice. Darth Maul sought to set up his own power base, manipulating the Mandalorian Death Watch, Hutts, Black Sun, and other criminal syndicate resources to temporarily take control of the planet Mandalore.

With Maul still alive, the Rule of Two was temporarily broken. Maul's seizure of Mandalore made him a rival Sith who could not be ignored or tolerated. Unbeknownst to the galaxy, Darth Sidious personally crushed Maul and Opress, restoring the Rule of Two.

As the war waned, Sidious had his eye on a new apprentice. Under his guise as Chancellor Palpatine, he manipulated Jedi Knight Anakin Skywalker into killing Dooku for him. As the war waned, Sidious simultaneously achieved all of the goals of the ancient Sith. In his bid to turn Skywalker to the dark side, he finally revealed himself to the Jedi.

Horrified by the revelation that the Chancellor and the Sith Lord were one and the same, the Jedi Council attempted to arrest and overthrow Chancellor Palpatine and take control of the Republic. Though they may have had no choice in their actions, this played right into Darth Sidious's plans. With the help of the fallen Jedi Anakin Skywalker, Sidious defeated the Jedi sent to arrest him, then announced to the Senate that the Jedi Order had attempted a coup. He announced sadly that the only way he could protect the Republic was to declare himself Emperor and assume absolute power, a move the terrified Senators agreed to wholeheartedly.

Even as he claimed the mantle of Emperor, Sidious moved to eliminate his enemies completely. He took Anakin Skywalker as his new apprentice, naming him Darth Vader and a Dark Lord of the Sith. Vader assaulted the Jedi Temple, massacring all he found there. Meanwhile, Sidious issued Order 66, a secret instruction to the clone armies of the Republic. The Order warned the clone troopers that the Jedi were attempting to seize power and instructed them to eliminate all Jedi immediately. Except in a few very rare cases, the clones succeeded; many of the Jedi died by the guns of their own forces without ever knowing why.

And thus with one swift blow, the Sith smashed the Jedi Order and took control of the galaxy.

# THE FALL OF THE JEDI

**W**hile the fall of the Jedi and the Republic might have seemed abrupt to the average citizen, both events occurred only after centuries of secret Sith preparations, interference, and undermining. Working from the shadows, the Sith manipulated events throughout the galaxy to weaken the Republic, encourage corruption, and stoke the fires of dissent and opposition. Senator Palpatine and his allies deftly manipulated the Senate, orchestrating his own rise to the Chancellorship. Through contrived emergencies, he ultimately was able to declare himself Emperor.

For much of Republic history, the Jedi commanded a great deal of respect among the Senate and the populace. Though they often shouldered the blame for ancient struggles and galactic-scale wars with the Sith, centuries of duty to the Republic built them a reputation for fairness and loyalty. As the Republic descended into corruption and division in its last decades, the Jedi struggled to maintain the ideals the Republic's own leadership disregarded or twisted to their own profit.

The average citizen never met a Jedi. Many learned of the Jedi through school and history, or inevitably heard of their exploits in the news; however, Jedi numbers were too few compared to the vastness of the Republic and its billions of beings to be particularly visible. Further, the Jedi tended to seclude themselves in their temples and training centers, away from public view. Most citizens simply had no personal connection to, or experience with, a Jedi, and understood the Force even less.

The Clone Wars brought the Jedi to the daily public news, as they took command of clone military units and battled the Separatists. The worlds they saved regarded them as heroes. The Separatists saw them as one more problem with the Republic. Jedi commanders became a hated enemy of Separatist forces. The public saw Jedi exploits daily—the good and the bad—but the Jedi still stood apart and aloof from most.

Chancellor Palpatine manipulated Jedi missions during the war, sometimes setting them up for failure or exposing less honorable Jedi actions in the process. He befriended Anakin Skywalker and chipped away at the young Jedi's faith and trust in the Jedi Order and Council. As the Jedi changed from peacekeepers to warriors over the years, they lost some of their luster in the public eye. Palpatine's master stroke manipulated the Jedi attempt to arrest and expose him as a Sith Lord into the appearance of an attempted coup, and he used it as the final justification for declaring himself Emperor. Close Jedi allies were shocked by the accusation and watched, unable to stop Palpatine from achieving his long-suspected goals—total power and control over the galaxy.

The public, however, was more than willing to believe his tales. Scenes of clone troopers willingly firing on their own Jedi commanders convinced many that Palpatine's accusations must be true. As soldiers across the galaxy carried out Order 66, Darth Vader and his clone troopers seized the Jedi Temple so quickly that Jedi supporters had little time to understand what had happened, let alone render aid.

## MEMORIES OF THE JEDI

Decades of Imperial rule and propaganda against the Jedi and their "traitorous" ways further vilified the Jedi Order. Citizens born after the fall of the Republic regarded the Jedi cause and goals with suspicion. Loyal Imperial followers denigrated Jedi exploits and reported suspected surviving Jedi and other Force users to Imperial authorities. The few Jedi and Force users left remained in hiding (see **Force-Sensitives**, below). Even belief in the Force, a mainstay of galactic civilization for millennia, diminished and disappeared altogether on some worlds. Imperial loyalists purged records of the Jedi and the Force from databases, histories, and other records.

Despite the propaganda, misinformation, and accusations, some citizens have retained their belief in, and loyalty to, the Jedi. Dissidents, anti-Imperial organizations, and resistance fighters have to counter the propaganda when they can. They hope some Jedi have survived and will someday return to battle the Empire.

Older individuals who remember or witnessed Jedi exploits often notice discrepancies, outright lies, and distorted facts purported to apply to the Jedi and their actions. For some, this reinforces their doubt in or hatred of Imperial rule. It inspires some to resist, or to become more likely to sympathize with the Rebel cause. They try to pass their stories on to the later generations, in hopes of keeping the truth alive.

# FORCE-SENSITIVES

Throughout modern Republic history, the Jedi tried to adopt and take in any being in the Republic who was born Force-sensitive. Force-sensitive children were identified and tested at or near birth. Those meeting certain criteria, usually related to midi-chlorian levels, were turned over to the Jedi for oversight of their development. The Jedi and the Republic government believed that only formal, guided training could ensure that Force users would not fall to the dark side. To leave any on their own was to risk releasing powerful monsters into the world, ready to exploit their powers, light or dark, at the expense of, and immense risk to, others.

While many children taken to the Jedi Temple eventually became Jedi Knights, not everyone had the skill to pass the Jedi trials. These individuals were not released, but assigned to the Jedi Service Corps.

Such safeguards were not foolproof, and there would always be some Force-sensitives who slipped through the cracks. The galaxy is a big place, and some children would never be noticed and tested. In some cases, parents might even refuse to let their children be adopted by the Order. Such cases were rare but painful, with the Order caught between respecting the wishes of the parents and needing to do what was best for the child.

Jedi reach was not universal. Worlds outside of Republic space were also outside Republic law. Additionally, some species and worlds had their own Force traditions that were unrelated to the Jedi or Sith. While the Jedi tried to bring such groups into the fold, many preferred to stay separate. As long as they did not cause trouble and avoided the dark side, the Jedi usually left them to their own pursuits. Such traditions typically had few Force-sensitive individuals, and even fewer who could match a fully trained Jedi or Jedi Master. However, the Jedi would stay in contact and keep a watchful eye—or farseeing—over the group, stepping in if they detected trouble.

## IMPERIAL THREATS

The rise of the Empire completely changed the lives of all Force users in Imperial space. The fall of the Jedi also elicited suspicion and even anger about their purported actions at the end of the Clone Wars. Imperial propaganda completely villianized the Order, framing the Jedi as traitors to the Chancellor and the Senate. The Empire abandoned formal testing and suppressed all knowledge about the Force. (See **The Force in the Empire**, on page 393, for more details about Imperial actions and responses regarding Force users.)

## LIFE AS A FORCE-SENSITIVE

In Imperial space, Force-sensitives live a life of secrecy and deception. Most slowly discover that there is something different about them that no one else seems to share or discuss. They might have limited precognitive abilities, amazing reflexes, or rudimentary telekinesis. Some may reveal their powers to relatives

Playing a Force user in the Imperial era brings unique challenges, compared with earlier eras. Force-using Player Characters generally understand their limitations—that they must conceal their Force abilities to survive. Storylines must take this reality into account. The **Force-Sensitives** section, starting on page 389, covers Force users' lives and struggles under Imperial rule in more detail.

Sooner or later, a PC will use a Force power in public out of foolishness or necessity, or allies or enemies will witness or deduce a PC's powers. In civilized space, such exposure could happen at any time the character is in public view.

Before a game session begins, the Game Master should briefly review the areas the PCs are likely to visit or operate in. The GM should note (or determine) what local general attitudes are toward Force use and what NPC reactions are likely to be if they discover a characters' secret. Possible reaction ideas are presented in the **Force-Sensitives** and **The Force in the Empire** sections (on pages 389 and 393, respectively).

The attitudes and probable reactions of the primary villains and allies should be prepared by the GM in more detail. Some NPCs won't understand what they thought they saw. Occasionally, an observer is revealed as a kindred spirit, sympathizer, or other understanding ally. Some may recoil in fear. Underhanded NPCs might try to cut a deal or blackmail the PCs. Others may try to immediately alert the authorities, or try to cash in on standing bounties for Force users. A few might attack the character immediately.

The GM also needs to note how exposure alters the story, lest a sudden ill-advised action or indiscretion completely derail an encounter or adventure. Some mistakes are easily hidden, explained away, or otherwise disposed of quickly. Others are impossible to hide or explain.

By preparing reactions and a few phrases the NPCs are likely to use ahead of time, the GM can casually drop them into the scene. He might also prepare special encounters for just such a revelation. Exposure of Force use or powers should be a big event in most campaigns and adventures. The GM should maximize NPC character reactions to reinforce the seriousness of the breach of secrecy. Different NPCs won't always have exactly the same reactions in the same scenes—mixing these reactions can add uncertainty and excitement to the scene.

or friends. If their confidants happen to also be Force-sensitive, they might provide limited guidance in concealing their abilities, and slight help in developing and discovering their powers. However, many are not, so Force-sensitives might be rightly hesitant to reveal their powers for fear of being turned over for Imperial arrest, or simply rejection in a society that fears and hates Jedi.

### A SECRET LIFE

Those who choose to conceal their powers are on their own to understand and develop them. Resisting the temptations of the dark side is much more difficult when an individual doesn't understand the danger. The differences between the Living Force and the Cosmic Force and their impacts are rarely immediately obvious. Even the limits of their power and potential for growth are difficult for isolated Force-sensitives to understand.

Force-sensitives do have some advantages, however. Concealing the Force from the average being isn't difficult, and many practitioners may succeed for many years without a compromising incident. Some are wise enough to discern and avoid the dangers of the dark side. Even so, the temptations of the mind trick and other manipulative powers are often too much to resist. Even strong light side adherents may fall victim to their personal goals and desires.

Isolated Force-sensitives also run the risk of believing errant theories about the Force, whether due to their personal experiences or sources of bad information. Even worse, they are vulnerable to outright frauds or unscrupulous sensitives passing themselves off as knowledgeable teachers when they are really no better than any other untrained Force user. The relief and excitement from encountering another Force user can override a person's good sense.

In the end, secret Force-sensitives are most afraid of discovery and are driven to conceal their true nature. This naturally leads to lies and deception, a path filled with dark side temptations and dangers. Some do not hesitate to use violence, blackmail, threats, bribes, and more to protect themselves. Others succeed in remaining on the light side, even if they are not as noble or honest as they might wish to be.

### SECRET SEARCHERS

Force-sensitives driven to learn and advance their power to the maximum extent possible soon discover that they must travel to truly unlock its secrets. The secrets of the Force are rarely readily at hand, unless the Force user is on Coruscant, Moraband (Korriban), or another

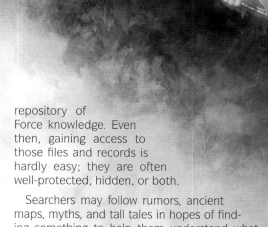

repository of Force knowledge. Even then, gaining access to those files and records is hardly easy; they are often well-protected, hidden, or both.

Searchers may follow rumors, ancient maps, myths, and tall tales in hopes of finding something to help them understand what is happening to them and how to control it. Their paths could lead almost anywhere in the galaxy, such as remote planets, academic centers, or ancient ruins. They might find and join up with other Force sensitives along the way, or simply take what knowledge the others can provide and move on. They might discover ancient Force traditions or splinter groups, or even isolated and hidden current traditions other than those of the Jedi that survive despite Imperial scrutiny.

However, not all knowledge is useful or safe. It may be recorded in forgotten languages or heavily encrypted. It might be fragmented, leading to easy misinterpretation. It might be rife with the dark side. The Force might draw or lead the seeker to a vergence, a location where the Force is naturally stronger or more active—whether light or dark.

More travel also means more risk of exposure. Force users might be discovered by Imperial spies and agents watching for any return of the Jedi. They might accidentally cross paths with Imperial Inquisitors, who may be drawn to the same target they are pursuing. Gathering knowledge also means storing it: creating records of one's own which can be stolen, discovered, or used against the untrained Force-sensitive.

## DISCOVERY AND ARREST

It is difficult for Force-sensitives to remain completely hidden. Once discovered by the Empire, they can expect to be endlessly pursued, to the fringes of the galaxy or society, if necessary. Low-level suspicion or observation by Imperial informants typically warrants an investigation by the Imperial Security Bureau (ISB) in civilian areas, and by intelligence and internal security officers in military venues.

Investigators might try to observe their targets prior to apprehension, but most simply arrest such individuals and let the Imperial bureaucracy handle the situation. ISB agents backed up by stormtroopers and Imperial officers are the most common arresting team. Detained individuals are usually held in an ISB facility, but may instead be held in detention areas of everyday law enforcement if needed. Detainees are held until their investigation is complete, and there are no guarantees as to how long that will take.

Depending on the strength of the evidence, suspected individuals might successfully beat or discredit their accusers. Powerful politicians, criminals, and businesspeople, as well as other influential individuals, might get charges dismissed through bribes or political pressure. As a last resort, detainees might escape on their own or be rescued by sympathetic allies. In any case, once an individual is identified as a potential Force user, the suspicion is never removed from his Imperial record without substantial effort or political orders.

Using the Force in public draws the quickest and most powerful response from Imperial authorities. Stormtroopers are immediately dispatched and ordered to apprehend the individual. Depending on the capabilities of the local force, they may be backed up by specialized squads or powerful vehicles. Truly powerful displays might also draw the attention of the Imperial Inquisitors. They are mysterious Force users in their own right. Those who know of their existence regard them as powerful, frightening, and merciless. (See **The Force in the Empire** on the next page for more information.)

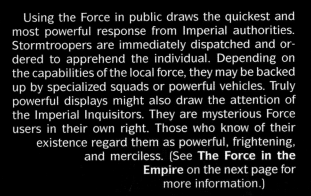

## LONG-TERM INVESTIGATIONS

Sometimes, Force-sensitives become the target of a lengthy investigation by an Imperial agency or opportunistic bounty hunter who suspects their secret. These investigations attempt to confirm whether such individuals are Force users, whether they know any other Force-sensitives or Jedi, and whether anyone is aiding them in concealing their secret. Individuals who are also suspected of involvement in the Rebel Alliance garner even more attention. Long-term investigations also help track down suspected or known Force user escapees.

Long-term investigations typically have a lead ISB agent. The agent knows and follows the details of the case, even if not actively in the field every day. Agents bucking for a promotion or notoriety may pursue such targets themselves, hoping to personally bring them in and expose their allies. The more important the target, the bigger the interest from higher levels of the ISB.

# FORCE-SENSITIVE GROUPS

Sometimes, Force-sensitive individuals band together in towns, living quarters, starships, or the like. Some groups are families in which Force sensitivity passes from one generation to the next. Others are completely unrelated, bound only by their common abilities. These groups may grow over time as they discover like-minded allies.

However, such congregations are extremely dangerous for everyone involved. Groups of Force-sensitives, especially those poorly trained, can accidentally give away their existence through the Force. Even if an Imperial Inquisitor never visits, the group might still be exposed by informant neighbors or careless displays of Force use. When discovered by the Empire, these groups and their allies are typically arrested and imprisoned. In populated areas, these arrests typically occur in public, and they are widely publicized as an example of what happens to those who oppose the Empire and conspire to revive the Jedi, whether it is true or not.

# THE FORCE IN THE EMPIRE

The destruction of the Jedi Order marked an end to widespread daily use of the Force to maintain peace in the galaxy. All security and investigative authority moved to the Imperial bureaucracy and military, which use conventional means. The Imperial Senate, while it existed, had no analog or replacement for the Jedi and what they had provided to the Republic Senate. Force use has been essentially outlawed, and much of the Imperial populace regards it as dangerous. It has become a threat to the Imperial order that superseded the chaos of the Clone Wars.

In reality, use of the Force to maintain control over galactic events has moved behind the scenes, out of public view. The Emperor's powers remain hidden. Darth Vader displays the most obvious use of the Force, through which he carries out the Emperor's commands to maintain control over the galaxy. Imperial Inquisitors (see page 394) actively carry out special missions.

After a generation without the Jedi and with unceasing Imperial propaganda against their methods and ideals, belief in the Force has waned in mainstream society. Vader is regarded as something of a relic of a past time, even among some of the highest ranking Imperial officers and Moffs. Fearsome and intimidating to be sure, but the last of a nearly dead religion whose last public action was to try to overthrow the popular and powerful Chancellor Palpatine. This final Jedi act still weighs heavily on Imperial memory and has undermined the Jedi's reputation for years.

However, not every Imperial citizen celebrates the loss of the Jedi Order. Even though its numbers have dwindled, believers and sympathizers are scattered throughout much of the Empire. Nevertheless, since vocalizing support is tantamount to treason, few are willing to risk arrest and imprisonment to support a defunct organization.

## INTO THE SHADOWS

While public displays of the Force are largely the purview of Darth Vader, he is far from the only adherent to the dark side within the Imperial government. Over the years, the Emperor has secretly recruited a cadre of dark side followers, agents, and advisers. He continues to clandestinely research the dark side and the Force. Furthermore, the creation of the Inquisitorius has provided a useful way to limit, watch, and exploit the dark side powers of more talented Force-sensitives. While their numbers are far smaller than the Jedi Order was, the dark siders serve some of the same functions as living enforcers of law and order, Imperial style.

### THE EMPEROR

Emperor Palpatine, secretly known as Darth Sidious, remains the most powerful Sith Lord and dark side adherent in the galaxy. His power may be unparalleled in the history of the Sith. His political skill is enhanced by his power to see into the future, adding to his reputation for being all-seeing and all-knowing. Beyond his Force powers, the Emperor skillfully manipulates the Imperial bureaucracy and makes use of a private, uncoordinated network of allies and spies outside of official channels. His powers of persuasion are often enhanced by the power of the Force.

To the general public, Palpatine is simply a fantastically skilled politician and fearsome Emperor. His obvious Sith attributes are concealed or explained away as injuries caused by the Jedi attack on him during their purported coup attempt. His secret identity remains intact.

Privately, many upper-level Imperial officials suspect there is more to the Emperor than anyone knows. They whisper about his creation of the Deep Core Security Zone and his interest in several planets in the Deep Core, including the rumored (but always discounted) planet of Byss. Some see the Emperor's tolerance of dark side adepts but hatred of the Force-wielding Jedi as hypocritical or suspicious. However, as anyone who looks too closely into the Emperor's affairs seems to mysteriously disappear, most officials are willing to remain comfortably ignorant. They prefer to play the complex political games necessary to secure their own power bases.

### DARTH VADER

As the Emperor's extension of personal power into specific galactic incidents and affairs, Vader enjoys a special position in the Imperial government. He holds great power and authority to carry out the direct orders of the Emperor. While he sometimes appears subservient to Grand Moffs and other officials, it is only at the Emperor's command. Vader strikes fear in his subordinates, often using the Force to threaten or eliminate failing underlings. Political foes are another matter entirely, handled with appropriate care or action.

As Darth Sidious's apprentice, Vader continues to expand his knowledge and the power of the dark side. He carries out a personal vendetta against surviving Jedi, though the Emperor often diverts his attention to what the ruler deems more important tasks. Vader is thoroughly dedicated to his current mandate to destroy the Rebel Alliance.

## THE IMPERIAL INQUISITORS

Few Imperials are feared more than the secretive Imperial Inquisitors. Adept at using the dark side of the Force, the intimidating Inquisitors pursue rogue Force users throughout Imperial space and beyond. They carry on Vader's search for any surviving Jedi, whom they arrest or destroy. The Inquisitors take charge of any Jedi artifacts that resurface, especially holocrons and lightsabers.

Though the galaxy is rife with rumors about them, the Inquisitors are mysteries to most Imperials, until they personally arrive to investigate a situation. They count on this secrecy to intensify fear in any who deal with them, whether friend or foe. Inquisitors tend to be highly skilled interrogators. Only the most hardened or disciplined victim can block or deflect their efforts, and usually only for a short time.

The Inquisitors operate semi-autonomously, doing whatever it takes to pursue their assigned target. Some have Imperial starships, stormtroopers, or other Imperial agents under their command. However, there is little understanding as to their place in the Imperial hierarchy, aside from the fact that they are entitled to any help they require. No one save the Emperor is even sure how many Inquisitors exist.

Inquisitors usually work alone, employing methods as varied as their origins. Some carry red-bladed lightsabers of unknown origin, while others may prefer different or even more exotic weapons. Their recruitment and training is held in secret, as are their past lives. Some are believed to be fallen Jedi or skilled Force users turned to Imperial service, but that is mere speculation. What is known is that few targets escape an Inquisitor for long, let alone defeat one in combat.

## IMPERIAL SECURITY BUREAU

The Imperial Security Bureau, or ISB, reinforces Imperial police and security efforts throughout the Empire. They investigate high-profile crimes, Rebel attacks, rumors of Force users and political dissidents, and even cases of Imperial corruption (when it suits their superiors). ISB agents operate in uniform, undercover, or in secret, as their assignment requires. Typically, a suspected Rebel or insurgent group is assigned one or more agents, making those agents ideal recurring characters in a campaign. Additionally, if the PCs defeat or kill an agent pursuing them, there are always more to replace him.

ISB agents vary widely in competency and skill. The lower-level agents might find themselves quickly outclassed by highly trained combatants. They might give themselves away while undercover or keeping the PCs under surveillance. However, ISB agents at moderate or higher levels of authority are much more likely to be razor-sharp and ready to counter PC plans.

## ORPHNE OF ALEEN

Some Force users have access to unusual powers beyond the teachings of the Jedi or Sith. Orphne of Aleen is a mystical being who lives beneath the surface of the planet Aleen. Though not of the species herself, she helps protect the Kindalo underworld beings against threats from the surface, such as the infiltration of surface air, which is poisonous to those who dwell below. She has the extraordinary ability to burst into thousands of points of mystical light to swarm and safely travel the labyrinth-like underworld. Her guardianship is not unlike that of the Jedi protecting those in need. She controls access to the planet's underworld, requiring proof that those seeking entrance are knowledgeable enough to deserve it. Her guidance often comes in the form of riddles.

Occasionally, an ISB agent may be assigned a case or posting due to political considerations. Such agents might be highly competent up-and-coming officers on the fast track to promotion, or they might have been granted a plum assignment as a favor to someone who is important to the Imperials. Many agents demonstrate complete dedication to the Imperial order or aggressiveness in completing high-profile assignments, while some agents may simply be skating by thanks to others who protect their position. The GM should feel free to embellish the personality of any ISB agents used in a campaign, especially if there is an opportunity to make them recurring characters important to the plot—or at least, interesting and worthy opponents.

## CITIZEN RESPONSES

Most Imperial citizens have completely bought into the notion that Force users are dangerous to themselves and the Empire. They are quite willing to immediately report suspected Force users and Rebels to the authorities. Even those who harbor sympathetic feelings are likely to succumb to the fear of arrest or reprisal should they fail to follow Imperial law.

Further threats come from the Commission for the Preservation of the New Order, or COMPNOR. This complex civilian organization operates in radical support of the Emperor and his New Order. Where private citizens might look the other way when it comes to the Rebellion or Force users, COMPNOR keeps a wary eye on all. Its agents and influence on social attitudes cannot be underestimated, even if they are disliked by the greater public.

# OTHER FORCE TRADITIONS

**D**espite the dominance of Jedi and Sith philosophies of the Force, they are not the only ones in the galaxy. Other practitioners hold different priorities and opinions as to the best use of the Force and the nature of the light and dark sides. These alternate traditions may be based around a certain philosophy, a charismatic leader, or a breakaway group. Some traditions arose in isolation on worlds where the Jedi and Sith are unknown, and a few traditions greatly impacted galactic history.

## BARAN DO SAGES

This native Force tradition of the Kel Dor species exemplifies Force use formed separately from the Jedi and Sith philosophies. The Baran Do Sages specialized in predicting danger by controlling visions that allowed them to see distant locations along with critical events in the future and past. Their control over and the accuracy of their visions were exceptional, allowing them to investigate criminal activities and foresee future disasters. They eventually became deeply integrated into Kel Dor business and government. Access to the Jedi Order eventually deprived the Baran Do of recruits, and the tradition faded almost completely on their homeworld of Dorin. In the Imperial era, this is fortunate, for they seem to have escaped Palpatine's purge of Force users. (See page 371 for more on the Baran Do Sages.)

## THE DAGOYAN MASTERS

The Dagoyan Masters are a strong Force-wielding monastic order that oversees the planet Bardotta. They run their world under a queen who is also a master Force user. Though their connection to the Force is strong, they connect passively. They are not warriors, and they sense the Force through intuition, knowledge, and the harmony of the universe. Jedi are not welcome on Bardotta, as the Dagoyan Masters have accused them of "stealing" Bardotta children. Though passive, the Dagoyan Masters are not immune to the dark side. One clan once worshiped Malmoural, an ancient demon of their faith, and elements of this clan may still exist in hiding.

## FORCE WITCHES OF DATHOMIR

Throughout the early history of the galaxy, many species developed the ability to use the Force without understanding its nature and dangers, or how best to control it. On some worlds, these native emerging Force users were called Force witches, or similar names. Force witches attributed their powers to magic and often believed that they or their group were unique in possessing them. Most discovered the light and dark sides of the Force, and some began to adhere to one or the other, depending on their morality and goals. Force witches who delved into the dark side to learn and study its unique alchemy soon fell to the dark side, making them extraordinarily dangerous to any who opposed them.

As galactic civilization spread, so too did the ideals and teachings of the Jedi and Sith. Force users gravitated toward one or the other, giving up their early traditions for the power and knowledge of advanced practitioners. Eventually, the Force witches all but disappeared from most Republic worlds and technologically advanced societies.

However, isolated pockets remained oblivious to the Jedi, or simply opposed their ideals, especially those about the dark side. After thousands of years of development, some of these groups became extremely advanced in the alchemical uses of the Force as well as other powers. When Jedi discovered such groups, they normally tried to recruit the witches into the Jedi Order, to educate them on dangers they might not have learned or understood, or at least to observe the group for signs of falling to the dark side.

## NIGHTSISTERS OF DATHOMIR

The best known enclave of Force witches is the Nightsisters of the planet Dathomir (see page 366). Their exact history is hazy, as are their numbers, but some believe that their early clans emerged from a rogue Jedi exiled on the planet at some point in the time of the Republic. The Nightsisters' leader, or "Mother," shows extraordinary skill at manipulating the Force through alchemical means and magic-like spells and incantations, wrapped up in the trappings of mysticism and ceremony.

During the Clone Wars, the Nightsisters and their companion clan, the Nightbrothers, played key roles in many important events. Their powerful leader, Mother Talzin, manipulated and arranged for her underlings and allies to aid the Separatists and Count Dooku for a time. (See page 387 for more on the Clone Wars.) Her skill and her Nightsisters' skill with the dark side engendered many great feats. They could manifest items from nothing and could transform and enhance living beings. They even defended themselves against a Separatist attack of revenge by animating their dead. Further, Mother Talzin saved Darth Maul from death and madness, "magically" building new mechanical legs for him after his years of isolation that followed his near-death at the hands of Obi-Wan Kenobi.

When Talzin and her assassin, Asajj Ventress, attempted to kill Count Dooku, the Sith Lord retaliated, sending his Separatist armies to wipe out the Nightsisters. It is yet uncertain how many of the Nightsister traditions survived the war, although rumors abound that both Talzin and Ventress escaped death. In any case, few individuals are willing to risk traveling to Dathomir to attempt to discover the Nightsister's current status, as the planet remains a dark and haunted place.

# LOST ARTIFACTS OF THE FORCE

Almost from the moment adepts discovered the Force, they sought ways to store and harness its energy through the creation of artifacts. The Jedi, Sith, and many isolated sects have all experimented with Force-powered items, of which many remain hidden throughout the galaxy in tombs, museums, and vaults. The Emperor is believed to have vast storehouses of Force artifacts dating from before the founding of the Republic.

Artifacts come in a variety of categories. Holocrons, Sith scrolls, and Sith spellbooks store information for future generations. Amulets and armor enhance an adept's connection to the Force and grant additional, unique powers. Force-imbued weapons have increased effectiveness and are often indestructible. Force crystals could be used to create other artifacts, forming the heart of amulets, armor, and weaponry.

## HOLOCRONS

Holocrons are Force-powered information display and storage devices capable of holding massive amounts of data. The devices are used by both the Jedi and Sith. An adept accesses a holocron through a holographic gatekeeper, which retains some of the Force essence of the holocron's creator. The gatekeeper relays the information to those he deems worthy, often requiring tests of character or attunement to the Force before revealing information.

## THE DUCTAVIS HOLOCRON

More than eleven thousand years ago, Jedi Grand Master and Supreme Chancellor of the Republic Biel Ductavis created his holocron, which was stored on Ossus after his death. Unfortunately, Jedi evacuating Ossus four thousand years ago were unable to access its special vault, and it has been lost ever since. The Ductavis Holocron contains historical accounts of the ancient Republic. Researchers think of it as a potential keystone that might rewrite ancient galactic history and rediscover mythical planets like Had Abbadon, Lettow, and Tython.

## AMULETS, MEDALLIONS, AND MORE

Many Force traditions have a rich history of imbuing jewelry and other crafted items with the Force. Artisans have imbued amulets, crowns, helms, masks, medallions, and talismans with the Force in an effort to achieve a specific effect when worn. While a wide variety of abilities have been tied to such artifacts, they are most associated with telepathic powers:

specifically, illusory and mind-control effects. The Nightsisters of Dathomir and Tyia adepts were particularly skilled at the creation of amulets.

## THE AMULET OF INFLUENCE

This artifact is a relatively simple amulet for dark side practitioners to create, given instruction. Whoever wears the amulet unquestionably obeys the commands of whoever gives it to him. Darth Tyranus created such an amulet during the Clone Wars from a simple necklace of Gungan design. One of Dooku's agents gave the necklace to Gungan Boss Lyonie, suggesting it would make him a better leader. Count Dooku's subsequent machinations almost enabled the Separatists to conquer Naboo.

## FORCE ARMOR

Armor strengthened by the Force has long been a tradition of the Sith, and has been used by other Force traditions throughout time. Force armor can provide enhanced protection from harm and, in some cases, a variety of other effects similar to those provided by amulets. Force armor can refer to an entire suit of armor or anything worn on the hands or arms, such as rings, armbands, bracers, gauntlets, and even traditional Jedi robes.

## THE GAUNTLET OF CRASSUS

Created by an ancient Sith Lord known for his avarice, the Gauntlet of Crassus is worn on the left hand. While worn, the wearer's grip is unbreakable, and when the wearer uses the Force to pull an item to his grasp, his telekinetic strength allegedly increases tenfold. The Gauntlet of Crassus is thought to be buried within Lord Crassus's lost tomb in the Valley of the Dark Lords.

## SITH SCROLLS

The ancient Sith technique for creating a holocron was long and arduous, and not known to every Sith Lord. A much more tried-and-true method of storing information was to etch it into a Force-imbued stone tablet. This technique was later refined to include scrolls, often organized into larger spellbooks and grimoires.

Such scrolls telepathically confer the pertinent knowledge to the reader when held and read aloud. With this knowledge comes not just an academic understanding, but a measure of inherited practical experience. Adepts can use scrolls to learn new Force techniques or how to create Force-powered artifacts.

## BROODICA'S GRIMOIRE

According to legend, Dark Lord Broodica was one of the original founders of the ancient Sith Empire. Broodica was obsessed with the power contained in ancient Sith scrolls. Once the exiles controlled Ziost, she began collecting as many scrolls and tablets as she could, transferring them into a large grimoire. A special lock of Broodica's design that functions similarly to a holocron gatekeeper seals the book.

## FORCE-IMBUED WEAPON

The lightsaber has been the preferred weapon of the Jedi and Sith orders for most of recorded history. Part of its ritual creation includes a long period of meditation in the Force, which makes the weapon an extension of its wielder. Many alternate Force traditions have developed a related metallurgical process to imbue the power of the Force into more conventional arms, most typically swords. These Force-forged weapons are strong enough to deflect blaster fire and parry lightsabers, and are possessed of an unnatural sharpness.

## GRAND MASTER PINA'S BLADES

A legendary pair of blades honed in the ancient forges of Vur Tepe, Awdrysta Pina's blades were long, thin, slightly curving swords with green crystals set in the hilts. The blades emitted a faint emerald glow. They were said to have cut down Xendor himself, the leader of the Legions of Lettow. The blades and Master Pina were lost when Pina went missing while tracking down remnants of the Legionnaires in the Unknown Regions.

## FORCE CRYSTAL

Force-powered crystals can be both naturally occurring and, in some very rare instances, synthetically created by practitioners. These crystals are most often used in the construction of lightsabers, and some can provide a Jedi with additional benefits beyond powering the weapon. Force crystals are also important in the creation of artifacts, as most Force-imbued items focus their power through such a crystal. Powerful Force crystals have been referred to as crystal balls, eyes, and shards, and they have been set into wands and scepters. However, some crystals are artifacts all on their own. The Jedi made use of healing crystals, and the Sith and the Witches of Dathomir made extensive use of crystals for a variety of purposes. Most notably, crystals have been used as a type of battery for absorbing, storing, and releasing Force energy, often acquired through mass murder.

## MOTHER TALZIN'S CRYSTAL BALL

The powerful Nightsister leader was said to use a crystal sphere roughly the size of a shockball for certain arcane and ritualistic practices. The crystal appeared to contain writhing tendrils of glowing orange energy. As Mother Talzin peered into its depths, she could see the future yet to come and events transpiring far across the galaxy.

# XII
# ADVERSARIES

*"He's more machine now than man. Twisted and evil."*

-Obi-Wan Kenobi

The galaxy is an unimaginably vast place, home to a stunning variety of sentient beings living on millions of inhabitable worlds. Many of these civilizations have journeyed to the stars, and from the greatest world-spanning metropolises of the Core to the seediest backwater shadowports of the Rim, the sheer variety of lifeforms one encounters amazes even the most seasoned galactic travelers. Beings of every shape and size work, scheme, and play side-by-side, but while many are able to overcome their vast differences in the name of peace or profit, just as many are quick to take up blaster, blade, or more exotic arms when things do not go their way. Conflict is a fact of life in the galaxy.

The freewheeling adventurers who frequent the Rim region, monstrous beasts out of a xenologist's worst nightmare, the tyrannical forces of the Imperium, desperate criminals both petty and organized: all these and more may be encountered by those who travel the hyperlanes. Any given interaction has the potential to turn deadly, and the wise know to be ready for the eventuality—some would say the inevitability—of violence.

In Force and Destiny, there are three different broad types of opponents that characters encounter in the galaxy. Although some variation is to be expected, the broad categories comprise minions, rivals, and nemeses.

## MINIONS

Minions are the most common NPCs encountered in the *Star Wars* universe. These are nameless individuals who provide muscle to flesh out encounters. Their only real threat is in numbers; a minion is not expected to stand toe-to-toe with a Player Character.

Minions are not major threats when encountered alone. Unfortunately, they tend to operate in small groups to increase their effectiveness. Minions are rarely more than a minor obstacle to most parties of characters, a delaying tactic that can stand in the way of achieving a goal that a more powerful enemy wishes to see prevented. Minions also have lower wound thresholds than other NPCs, making it very likely they'll drop in one or two hits.

GMs can use minions as adversaries either as individuals or in groups. However, unless the minion has relevant characteristics of 3 or higher, an individual minion is more likely to fail than succeed on all but the simplest combat checks. GMs should only use individual minions if they wish to pit the Player Characters against an easy combat challenge. The more typical way to use minions involves deploying them in groups, as described later in this section.

### MINION RULES

Minions have several unique rules that reflect their status as disposable adversaries.

- **Unless otherwise specified, minions do not suffer strain.** Anything that deals strain to a minion inflicts an equivalent number of wounds instead. They also cannot voluntarily suffer strain. This means that when a minion is taken out of combat due to exceeding his wound threshold, it is up to the GM whether he was incapacitated or killed, depending on the circumstances.

- **Minions do not possess ranks in skills.** One thing that makes minions significantly weaker than Player Characters is their lack of ranks in skills. They can compensate for this by operating as a group. Minion profiles list several skills in which they can gain ranks when acting as a group.

- **Minions can fight as a group.** As noted previously, the GM does not have to deploy minions in groups. However, deploying them in a group has several advantages. It simplifies combats and makes minions more dangerous while allowing GMs to include large numbers of adversaries. Minions are only deployed in groups of the same minion type. The minion group has a single wound threshold, shared by all members of the group. This wound threshold is equal to the sum of the wound thresholds of every member of the group. (For example, a group of three stormtroopers—each with a wound threshold of 5—has a wound threshold of 15.) Each time any member of the group suffers wounds, the wounds are applied to the group's wound threshold. Individual members of the group are defeated one at a time, each time the total wounds suffered exceeds that group member's share of the wound threshold. For example, when the stormtrooper group passes 5 wounds, one stormtrooper is defeated. When characters attack a group, they attack the group as a whole, not an individual. Likewise, minions make one attack per group, not per individual. Working as a group allows minions to use skills. A minion group gains one skill rank for each member of the group beyond the first, if that skill is on the minion's list. So, a group of four stormtroopers would count as having three ranks (for the three troopers after the first) in any checks the group is called on to make.

- **Minions are killed by Critical Injuries.** If a minion suffers a Critical Injury, it is immediately incapacitated. If a group of minions suffers a Critical Injury, it suffers one minion's worth of wounds (so that one of the minions in the group is incapacitated).

## RIVALS

**Rivals** are more dangerous than minions but still inferior to most Player Characters. Rivals are very similar to Player Characters in many respects, being generally more innately gifted and well-trained than minions. They possess skills and operate individually rather than in groups. They are generally less skilled than the PCs, however, seldom possessing more than two or three ranks in any one skill.

### RIVAL RULES

Rivals follow most of the same rules as Player Characters do, except as noted here.

- **Rivals suffer Critical Injuries normally.** However, when a rival exceeds his wound threshold, he can be killed outright (instead of incapacitated) at the GM's discretion.

- **Rivals cannot suffer strain.** When a rival is dealt strain, he suffers an equivalent number of wounds instead. He can, however, use abilities or invoke effects that would cause him to suffer strain; this simply causes him to suffer wounds instead. Remember, because he does not suffer strain, he cannot recover it either. Like minions, if a rival is incapacitated, the GM can determine whether he was killed or rendered unconscious based on the circumstances.

GMs can decide to track strain on certain rivals, even though this is not the norm. This does create extra bookkeeping for the GM but also allows some additional granularity for rivals that might prove important to the plot. In essence, this allows the GM to create nemesis-class characters with weaker than average statistics.

## NEMESES

The **nemesis** is the opposite of the Player Character. Nemeses are identical to PCs in virtually every respect and may, in fact, be more powerful. This is necessary to ensure that they are able to pose a threat to an entire party. Nemeses frequently possess a number of talents, as well as high characteristics and skills, and their equipment can often rival that of even the most well-supplied parties. Nemeses suffer strain and wounds normally and do not have any special rules governing their operations.

# ADVERSARY LIST

The following is a list of adversaries GMs can use in their adventures. These adversaries are divided into several groups, depending on their affiliations and motives. Each adversary's profile is also broken down into several discrete sections:

- **Name:** The adversary's name or type, plus whether it is a minion, rival, or nemesis.
- **Description:** A section describing the adversary.
- **Characteristics:** The ratings of the adversary's six basic characteristics.
- **Soak/Defense and Thresholds:** These are the adversary's soak, its defense (listed in both melee and ranged values), and its wound and strain thresholds. Only nemeses have listed strain thresholds. If a GM wishes to give a rival a strain threshold, it should have the same value as the listed wound threshold.
- **Skills:** Skills (if any) possessed by the adversary. If the adversary is a minion, these skills only apply in a group.

- **Talents:** Talents (if any) possessed by the adversary.
- **Abilities:** These are special abilities that are not skills or talents.
- **Equipment:** This is the adversary's equipment. The entry only lists important equipment such as weapons, armor, and vital pieces of gear. Items such as clothing, comlinks, spare change, glow rods, and so forth are not listed but are still present if it makes sense (and at the GM's discretion). Any bonuses from equipment are already added to the profile.

It is important to note that adversaries do not always follow the same rules that Player Characters do. These profiles are generated for simplicity and ease of use, so non-essential information can be omitted. For example, the Gand findsman has a soak higher than his Brawn, even though he does not wear armor. This is due to the findsman's innate resilience—however, this is not indicated by a unique rule. The higher soak value is sufficient.

# RIM WORLDERS

For Core Worlders, the very mention of the Rim conjures up visions of lawlessness and danger. The idea that the Rim is nothing but a wild frontier is not wholly true. Still, there are plenty of freebooters, smugglers, adventurers, and ne'er-do-wells populating the fringes. For every Imperial or corporate-run world in the Rim, there are a dozen backwater planets rife with opportunity and risk for those who dare face the many dangerous denizens that make the far reaches of the galaxy their home.

## BIG GAME HUNTER [NEMESIS]

The Rim's many dangerous worlds are home to countless frightening creatures, and big game hunters prey on the largest and most menacing of these. Frequently operating at the edges of civilization, these beings explore the deepest jungles, penetrate the harshest deserts, and even venture into the bottomless depths of ocean worlds to track and kill or capture the fiercest animals known to the galaxy. Some take contracts from settlements or rancher barons to eliminate dangerous predators. Others help fill the galaxy's fighting pits and gladiatorial arenas with a never-ending supply of exotic threats. Finally, some hunt for sport, savoring the rush of adrenaline at every kill. Big game hunters are deadly combatants, especially when circumstances require them to hunt the deadliest game: other sentients.

| BRAWN | AGILITY | INTELLECT | CUNNING | WILLPOWER | PRESENCE |
|-------|---------|-----------|---------|-----------|----------|
| 3 | 3 | 2 | 3 | 2 | 2 |

| SOAK VALUE | W. THRESHOLD | S. THRESHOLD | M/R DEFENSE |
|------------|--------------|--------------|-------------|
| 5 | 18 | 14 | 1   1 |

**Skills:** Cool 3, Knowledge (Xenology) 2, Melee 3, Perception 3, Piloting (Planetary) 2, Ranged (Heavy) 4, Stealth 3, Survival 4.

**Talents:** Adversary 2 (upgrade difficulty of all combat checks against this target twice), Hunter's Quarry (take Hunter's Quarry action: make a **Hard (◆ ◆ ◆) Survival check** to upgrade the ability of all attacks against one target at long range until the end of the big game hunter's next turn), Natural Hunter (once per session, may reroll any one Perception or Vigilance check).

**Abilities:** Animal Combatant (upgrade ability of checks when fighting wild creatures once), Wilderness Valor (add □□ to resist fear against wild creatures).

**Equipment:** Scoped long-range blaster rifle (Ranged [Heavy]; Damage 9; Critical 3; Range [Extreme]; reduce difficulty of combat checks at long and extreme range by one), oversized combat knife (Melee; Damage 5; Critical 3; Range [Engaged]), armored clothing (+1 soak, +1 defense), utility belt, extra reloads, survival kit.

## BITH MUSICIAN [MINION]

Native to the Rim world of Clak'dor VII, the highly evolved, humanoid Bith have spent millennia developing their minds to enhance abstract thinking skills such as language, logic, mathematics, and music, while at the same time diminishing their capacity to exhibit fear and aggression. This has resulted in a biological destiny of pacifism, and has made them sought after throughout the galaxy as computer programmers, engineers, and musicians. The Bith do not sleep, needing only brief periods of meditation to rest their bodies. This quality has proven especially useful to those among them who follow careers as performers in the round-the-clock cantinas and nightclubs of the Rim. Bith musicians may be encountered anywhere sentients gather to be entertained.

| BRAWN | AGILITY | INTELLECT | CUNNING | WILLPOWER | PRESENCE |
|:---:|:---:|:---:|:---:|:---:|:---:|
| 1 | 3 | 3 | 2 | 2 | 3 |

| SOAK VALUE | W. THRESHOLD | M/R DEFENSE |
|:---:|:---:|:---:|
| 1 | 4 | 0 \| 0 |

**Skills (group only):** Charm, Cool, Perception.
**Talents:** None.
**Abilities:** Keen Senses (add ☐ to all Perception checks).
**Equipment:** Musical instrument.

## HYPERLANE SCOUT [RIVAL]

As vast as the Empire is, it is dwarfed by the galaxy as a whole. Though many hyperlanes great and small have been established, there are countless more routes between the stars waiting to be discovered. It is in the unknown spaces at the edges of the charts and beyond that hyperlane scouts ply their trade. These brave souls are always looking for the next unexplored planet or unmapped star route, and many of them are willing to go to any length to be the first to stake his claim to the rights-of-discovery of new ways or worlds.

| BRAWN | AGILITY | INTELLECT | CUNNING | WILLPOWER | PRESENCE |
|:---:|:---:|:---:|:---:|:---:|:---:|
| 2 | 3 | 3 | 2 | 2 | 2 |

| SOAK VALUE | W. THRESHOLD | M/R DEFENSE |
|:---:|:---:|:---:|
| 3 | 12 | 0 \| 0 |

**Skills:** Astrogation 3, Gunnery 2, Knowledge (Outer Rim) 2, Mechanics 2, Piloting (Space) 3, Ranged (Light) 1.
**Talents:** Galaxy Mapper 3 (hyperlane scouts remove ■ ■ ■ from all Astrogation checks; Astrogation checks take 50% less time).
**Abilities:** None.
**Equipment:** Blaster pistol (Ranged [Light]; Damage 6; Critical 3; Range [Medium]; Stun setting), datapad, scout ship.

## PLANETARY DEFENSE TROOPER [MINION]

Most planets, even those that are part of the Empire, maintain a cadre of militia or local defense forces. Not as well-trained or equipped as members of the Imperial Army, these troops nonetheless stand ready to drive off pirates or other raiders. Some handle local policing duties, while others may be expected to conduct full-scale combat operations.

| BRAWN | AGILITY | INTELLECT | CUNNING | WILLPOWER | PRESENCE |
|:---:|:---:|:---:|:---:|:---:|:---:|
| 2 | 2 | 2 | 2 | 2 | 2 |

| SOAK VALUE | W. THRESHOLD | M/R DEFENSE |
|:---:|:---:|:---:|
| 3 | 5 | 0 \| 0 |

**Skills (group only):** Brawl, Discipline, Ranged (Light), Ranged (Heavy).
**Talents:** None.
**Abilities:** None.
**Equipment:** Blaster carbine (Ranged [Heavy]; Damage 9; Critical 3; Range [Medium]; Stun setting), 2 frag grenades (Ranged [Light]; Damage 8; Critical 4; Range [Short]; Blast 6, Limited Ammo 1), blast vest (+1 soak).

## PODRACER PILOT [RIVAL]

Podracer pilots risk death every time they strap themselves into their antigravity repulsorcraft towed by enormous turbine engines. The highly dangerous races see Podracers streaking along remote courses at blistering speeds. Outlawed by the Empire, Podracing is a clandestine activity that makes its participants criminals by definition.

| 2 | 3 | 2 | 3 | 2 | 2 |
|---|---|---|---|---|---|
| BRAWN | AGILITY | INTELLECT | CUNNING | WILLPOWER | PRESENCE |

| SOAK VALUE | W. THRESHOLD | M/R DEFENSE |
|---|---|---|
| 3 | 11 | 0 / 0 |

**Skills:** Cool 3, Mechanics 3, Piloting (Planetary) 4, Streetwise 2.
**Talents:** Full Throttle (take a Full Throttle action and make a **Hard [◆◆◆] Piloting (Planetary or Space) check** to increase a vehicle's top speed by 1 for three rounds), Skilled Jockey 1 (remove ■ from all Piloting [Planetary] and Piloting [Space] checks).
**Abilities:** None.
**Equipment:** Holdout blaster (Ranged [Light]; Damage 5; Critical 4; Range [Short]; Stun setting), tool kit, Podracer.

## PROVINCIAL LAW ENFORCEMENT OFFICER [MINION]

The day-to-day enforcement of laws does not generally fall on the armored shoulders of stormtroopers. Instead, most regions and municipalities rely on local talent, drawn from their own populations, to keep the peace, investigate criminal activity, and protect the citizenry from any threats that might arise. Though the details of their organizations and degrees of competence are as varied as the worlds they patrol, in general, provincial law enforcement officers are lightly armed and armored, with their most powerful weapons the comlinks they carry to call for backup when needed.

| 3 | 2 | 2 | 2 | 2 | 2 |
|---|---|---|---|---|---|
| BRAWN | AGILITY | INTELLECT | CUNNING | WILLPOWER | PRESENCE |

| SOAK VALUE | W. THRESHOLD | M/R DEFENSE |
|---|---|---|
| 4 | 4 | 0 / 0 |

**Skills (group only):** Coercion, Perception, Ranged (Light), Vigilance.
**Talents:** None.
**Abilities:** None.
**Equipment:** Blaster pistol (Ranged [Light]; Damage 6; Critical 3; Range [Medium]; Stun setting), truncheon (Melee; Damage 5; Critical 3; Range [Engaged]; Disorient 2), police armor (+1 soak), comlink (handheld).

## GAND FINDSMAN [RIVAL]

While seldom seen beyond their homeworld, Gand findsmen are some of the most skilled trackers and hunters in the galaxy. Their almost supernatural ability to track targets through the ammonia mists of Gand leaves many to mutter that the findsmen have a connection to the Force. In reality, most findsmen benefit from keen senses combined with an analytical mind, not a mystical

sensing ability. This lets them read their targets' intentions in the smallest clues, from a single footprint to a broken branch.

| 3 | 3 | 2 | 3 | 3 | 1 |
|---|---|---|---|---|---|
| BRAWN | AGILITY | INTELLECT | CUNNING | WILLPOWER | PRESENCE |

| SOAK VALUE | W. THRESHOLD | M/R DEFENSE |
|---|---|---|
| 4 | 16 | 0 / 0 |

**Skills:** Athletics 2, Coordination 2, Melee 2, Perception 3, Ranged (Heavy) 2, Survival 3, Vigilance 2.
**Talents:** Adversary 1 (upgrade difficulty of all combat checks against this target once), Expert Tracker 2 (remove ■ ■ from checks to find or follow tracks; Survival checks made to track targets take 50% less time than normal).
**Abilities:** Ammonia Breather (breathes ammonia; must use a respirator, and if exposed to oxygen, treats it as a dangerous atmosphere with rating 8).
**Equipment:** Scoped blaster rifle (Ranged [Heavy]; Damage 9; Critical 3; Range [Long]; reduce difficulty of combat checks at long range by 1, Stun setting), vibroblade (Melee; Damage 4; Critical 2; Range [Engaged]; Pierce 2, Vicious 1), macrobinoculars.

## TOYDARIAN MERCHANT [RIVAL]

Though they are most commonly encountered in Hutt Space, Toydarians may be found in nearly any spaceport in the Rim, wheeling, dealing, and facilitating trade. These ungainly looking bipeds sport outsized proboscises and wings that seem unlikely to support the girth of the typical Toydarian, but they are usually to be found hovering above the ground nonetheless. The secret to their buoyancy is in the abundance of natural gases absorbed in their frames. Toydarians are famed as merchants and traders, and they tend to have a reputation as shrewd and clever negotiators.

**Skills:** Charm 2, Cool 2, Deception 3, Negotiation 2, Perception 3, Streetwise 2.
**Talents:** Natural Negotiator (once per session, the character may reroll any one Cool or Negotiation check), Nobody's Fool 1 (upgrade the difficulty of any Charm, Coercion, or Deception checks attempted against the Toydarian merchant once).
**Abilities:** Hoverer (Toydarians do not have to spend additional maneuvers when navigating difficult terrain), Silhouette 0.
**Equipment:** Holdout blaster (Ranged [Light]; Damage 5; Critical 4; Range [Short]; Stun setting), loaded chance cubes, dataslate.

## UGNAUGHT MECHANIC [MINION]

Indefatigable workers, Ugnaughts have been taken to the ends of the galaxy by slavers who exploit their work ethic. Even enslaved, the Ugnaughts have not forgotten the customs of their society, relying on a rich oral tradition to keep their heritage alive.

**Skills (group only):** Athletics, Mechanics, Resilience.
**Talents:** None.
**Abilities:** Silhouette 0, Stubborn and Dependable (remove ■ from all checks Ugnaught mechanics perform).
**Equipment:** Durable clothing (+1 soak), giant hydrospanner (Melee; Damage 3; Critical 4; Range [Engaged]; Knockdown), tool kit, utility belt.

# GALACTIC UNDERWORLD

Even a galaxy held in the iron fist of tyranny has its dark corners, and, in those shadowy spaces, the underworld thrives. Every spaceport hosts conniving small-time hoods, while organized crime is so successful that the upper echelons of the Black Sun Syndicate live and work much like "legitimate" corporate plutocrats. Smuggling, slavery, and the spice trade make up a black-market economy that some say rivals the legitimate business of the Empire in scope.

## CON ARTIST [RIVAL]

The charismatic, smooth-talking con artist is the subject of many a holodrama, but in reality, those who live by the art of the grift would rather not be noticed at all. The cons they run range from simple games of chance on a street corner to elaborate schemes involving dozens of operatives, deft disguises, and false credentials. However, the goal is always the same—swindle as many credits as possible, preferably with the marks never realizing they've been conned.

**Skills:** Charm 2, Cool 2, Deception 3, Perception 3, Skulduggery 2.
**Talents:** Convincing Demeanor 1 (remove ■ from any Deception or Skulduggery checks), Nobody's Fool 1 (upgrade the difficulty of any Charm, Coercion, or Deception checks made against the Con Artist once).
**Abilities:** None.
**Equipment:** Holdout blaster (Ranged [Light]; Damage 5; Critical 4; Range [Short]; Stun setting), comm jammer, disguise kit.

## GUILDED BOUNTY HUNTER [RIVAL]

Compassionate souls are not drawn to bounty hunting. While many hunters make a good living working for the Empire, just as many, if not more, choose instead to work for corporations, private citizens, or criminal organizations. Most bounty hunters see a Force-sensitive as a quick and easy paycheck, and have no compunctions about turning him over to the Empire.

**Skills:** Cool 2, Melee 1, Ranged (Light) 2, Perception 2, Stealth 1, Streetwise 2, Survival 2.
**Talents:** Expert Tracker (removes ■ ■ from checks to find or follow tracks; Survival checks made to track targets take 50% less time than normal), Quick Draw (may draw or holster a weapon as an incidental).
**Abilities:** None.
**Equipment:** Disruptor pistol (Ranged [Light]; Damage 10; Critical 2; Range [Short]; Vicious 4), 2 stun grenades (Ranged [Light]; Damage 8; Critical 4; Range [Short]; Blast 8, Disorient 3, Limited Ammo 1, Stun damage),

bolas (Ranged [Light]; Damage 2; Range [Short]; Ensnare 3, Knockdown, Limited Ammo 1), armored clothing (+1 defense, +1 soak), jetpack, utility belt.

## HUTT SLAVE DEALER [NEMESIS]

There are few races in the galaxy as hated and feared as the Hutts. These massive beings have a stranglehold on the criminal underworld in the Outer Rim. Hutt slave dealers are particularly despised by most decent peoples for their traffic in sentient life. Generally surrounded by lackeys and bodyguards, Hutt slave dealers are formidable opponents, and their incredibly potent wills make them nearly immune to Force powers.

| BRAWN | AGILITY | INTELLECT | CUNNING | WILLPOWER | PRESENCE |
|---|---|---|---|---|---|
| 6 | 1 | 4 | 5 | 5 | 3 |

| SOAK VALUE | W. THRESHOLD | S. THRESHOLD | M/R DEFENSE |
|---|---|---|---|
| 10 | 30 | 30 | 0 \| 0 |

**Skills:** Charm 2, Coercion 3, Cool 4, Deception 4, Discipline 3, Knowledge (Outer Rim) 2, Knowledge (Underworld) 4, Melee 3, Negotiation 5, Ranged (Light) 3, Resilience 8, Streetwise 5.
**Talents:** Durable 3 (subtract 30 from Critical Injury rolls made against the Hutt), Intimidating 3 (Hutt slave dealers may suffer up to 3 strain to downgrade the difficulty of a Coercion check a number of times equal to the strain suffered; when targeted by Coercion, they may suffer up to 3 strain to upgrade the difficulty of the opponent's check a number of times equal to the strain suffered).
**Abilities:** Awkward (Hutts have great physical strength, but their bulk imposes severe limitations in flexibility and agility; they add ■■■ to all Brawl, Melee, and Coordination checks), Ponderous (Hutts can never spend more than one maneuver moving per turn).
**Equipment:** Generally none; if a Hutt needs something, he usually has an attendant to carry and use it. However, Hutts can wield weapons such as vibroaxes (Melee; Damage 9; Critical 2; Range [Engaged]; Pierce 2, Sunder, Vicious 3) and large-bore blaster pistols (Ranged [Light]; Damage 8; Critical 3; Range [Medium]; Stun setting, Hutt Only).

## SPICE PUSHER [RIVAL]

Perhaps no other underworld figure rivals the spice pusher in terms of sheer antisocial tendencies. Preying on the weak, the helpless, and the addicted, spice pushers are completely without conscience, demanding ever-higher payments for substances that eventually destroy the lives of those who purchase them.

| BRAWN | AGILITY | INTELLECT | CUNNING | WILLPOWER | PRESENCE |
|---|---|---|---|---|---|
| 2 | 3 | 3 | 3 | 2 | 1 |

| SOAK VALUE | W. THRESHOLD | M/R DEFENSE |
|---|---|---|
| 3 | 12 | 0 \| 0 |

**Skills:** Deception 3, Negotiation 3, Ranged (Light) 2, Skulduggery 3, Streetwise 4.
**Talents:** None.
**Abilities:** None.
**Equipment:** Heavy blaster pistol (Ranged [Light]; Damage 7; Critical 3; Range [Medium]; Stun setting), vibroknife (Melee; Damage 3; Critical 2; Range [Engaged]; Pierce 2, Vicious 1), avabush spice, death sticks, glitterstim, or other black-market drugs.

## STREET TOUGH [MINION]

Petty criminals and hired thugs exist throughout the galaxy, tending to congregate in seedy spaceports and shadowy slums. Street toughs comprise everyone from pickpockets and muggers to gang enforcers and murderers. Generally, they all tend to be short on brains, which they make up for with violent streaks a parsec wide.

| BRAWN | AGILITY | INTELLECT | CUNNING | WILLPOWER | PRESENCE |
|---|---|---|---|---|---|
| 3 | 2 | 2 | 2 | 1 | 1 |

| SOAK VALUE | W. THRESHOLD | M/R DEFENSE |
|---|---|---|
| 4 | 5 | 0 \| 0 |

**Skills (group only):** Melee, Ranged (Light) or Ranged (Heavy), Skulduggery.
**Talents:** None.
**Abilities:** None.
**Equipment:** Blaster pistol (Ranged [Light]; Damage 6; Critical 3; Range [Medium]; Stun setting) or slugthrower rifle (Ranged [Heavy]; Damage 7; Critical 5; Range [Medium]; Cumbersome 2), truncheon (Melee; Damage 5; Critical 5; Range [Engaged]; Disorient 2), heavy clothing (+1 soak).

# IMPERIAL FORCES

The Galactic Empire is a vast domain ruled by a single individual—Emperor Palpatine. However, its servants are legion, ranging from harried local officials to some of the deadliest beings in the galaxy. Whoever and wherever they may be, they all make common cause when Imperial interests are threatened. Whatever problem may arise, the Imperial way is to respond with overwhelming, and frequently deadly, force.

### GOVERNMENT BUREAUCRAT [RIVAL]

The machinery of the Galactic Empire runs on bureaucracy, and legions of bureaucrats keep those wheels turning at all times. Generally dour, punctual, and boring, many of these individuals manage to accomplish the near-impossible task of being more reviled than Imperial stormtroopers.

| BRAWN | AGILITY | INTELLECT | CUNNING | WILLPOWER | PRESENCE |
|:-:|:-:|:-:|:-:|:-:|:-:|
| 2 | 2 | 3 | 2 | 2 | 1 |

| SOAK VALUE | W. THRESHOLD | M/R DEFENSE |
|:-:|:-:|:-:|
| 2 | 8 | 0 / 0 |

**Skills:** Coercion 2, Computers 1, Discipline 2, Knowledge (Core Worlds) 2, Knowledge (Education) 2, Negotiation 3.
**Talents:** Nobody's Fool 2 (when targeted by Coercion or Deception checks, upgrade difficulty twice).
**Abilities:** None.
**Equipment:** Datapad of Imperial regulations.

### IMPERIAL ASSASSIN [NEMESIS]

The shadowy corps of Imperial assassins exercises the Emperor's will by eliminating any sentient its master wishes. No matter the target, an Imperial assassin tirelessly pursues him across the galaxy until he can get close enough for a kill. In their travels throughout the galaxy, Imperial assassins are hidden in plain sight, often taking on disguises to grant them easier access to their prey. The waiter at the tapcafé, the harried merchant across the counter, even the carefully vetted bodyguard—any of these may be assassins waiting to strike.

| BRAWN | AGILITY | INTELLECT | CUNNING | WILLPOWER | PRESENCE |
|:-:|:-:|:-:|:-:|:-:|:-:|
| 3 | 3 | 3 | 3 | 3 | 2 |

| SOAK VALUE | W. THRESHOLD | S. THRESHOLD | M/R DEFENSE |
|:-:|:-:|:-:|:-:|
| 3 | 18 | 20 | 1 / 1 |

**Skills:** Athletics 2, Cool 3, Coordination 3, Discipline 3, Melee 4, Perception 4, Piloting (Space) 2, Ranged (Heavy) 4, Stealth 4, Vigilance 4.
**Talents:** Adversary 2 (upgrade difficulty of all combat checks against this target twice), Parry 3 (when struck by a melee attack but before applying soak, suffer 3 strain to reduce damage by 5), Indistinguishable 2 (upgrade difficulty of checks to identify Imperial assassin twice).
**Abilities:** Neurotoxin Doses (the Imperial assassin has multiple doses of neurotoxin, which he can introduce into food or drink as a maneuver or apply to a Melee weapon as a maneuver; if he applies the neurotoxin to a weapon, it lasts for the remainder of the encounter; if a target ingests poisoned food or drink, or suffers wounds from a poisoned Melee weapon, the target must make an **Average [◆ ◆] Resilience check**; the target suffers 5 wounds if he fails, plus 1 strain per ☼; ▽ means the target must test against the poison again at the start of his next turn).
**Equipment:** Disruptor rifle (Ranged [Heavy]; Damage 10; Critical 2; Range [Long]; Cumbersome 2, Vicious 5, when the disruptor inflicts a Critical Injury, the minimum result is 96–100, "Crippled," unless it would be worse), combat vibroblade (Melee; Damage 5; Critical 2; Range [Engaged]; Pierce 2, Vicious 2).

## IMPERIAL DUNGEONEER [MINION]

Imperial dungeoneers are soldiers tasked with overseeing the prisoners confined to the Empire's many dungeon ships, detention facilities, and prison worlds. Despite the sensitive nature of their task, those chosen as guards for the Empire's enormous population of incarcerated sentients are usually those who couldn't make the grade in the regular Imperial Army. Considered lowly turnkeys by their compatriots, dungeoneers tend to be bitter and cruel, taking their resentment over their miserable existence out on their helpless charges.

| BRAWN | AGILITY | INTELLECT | CUNNING | WILLPOWER | PRESENCE |
|-------|---------|-----------|---------|-----------|----------|
| 3 | 2 | 2 | 2 | 2 | 1 |

| SOAK VALUE | W. THRESHOLD | M/R DEFENSE |
|-----------|--------------|-------------|
| 5 | 5 | 0  0 |

**Skills (group only):** Coercion, Melee, Ranged (Heavy), Vigilance.
**Talents:** None.
**Abilities:** None.
**Equipment:** Riot gun (Ranged [Heavy]; Damage 7; Critical 3; Range [Medium]; Auto-fire, Stun setting), truncheon (Melee; Damage 5; Critical 5; Range [Engaged]; Disorient 2), binders, comlink, padded armor (+2 soak).

## IMPERIAL ROYAL GUARD [NEMESIS]

Numbering among the deadliest of the Emperor's servants, his elite, crimson-garbed Imperial Royal Guards enjoy a reputation for preternatural combat skills and absolute, unwavering loyalty to their master. Only the most skilled and dependable fighters are chosen from the many branches of Imperial service to undergo Royal Guard training, and only a few survive this training to be inducted into the ranks of these elite warriors.

| BRAWN | AGILITY | INTELLECT | CUNNING | WILLPOWER | PRESENCE |
|-------|---------|-----------|---------|-----------|----------|
| 3 | 3 | 3 | 2 | 2 | 2 |

| SOAK VALUE | W. THRESHOLD | S. THRESHOLD | M/R DEFENSE |
|-----------|--------------|--------------|-------------|
| 5 | 16 | 12 | 1  1 |

**Skills:** Athletics 2, Discipline 3, Melee 4, Perception 3, Ranged (Light) 3, Vigilance 4.
**Talents:** Adversary 2 (upgrade difficulty of all combat checks against this target twice), Heightened Awareness (allies of Imperial Royal Guards within close range add □ to Perception and Vigilance checks; allies engaged with them add □ □ instead), Parry 4 (when struck by a melee attack but before applying soak, suffer 3 strain to reduce damage by 6).
**Abilities:** None.
**Equipment:** Cortosis-plated force pike (Melee; Damage 6; Critical 2; Range [Engaged]; Cortosis, Pierce 2, Stun setting), heavy blaster pistol (Ranged [Light]; Damage 7; Critical 3; Range [Medium]; Stun setting), heavy battle armor (+2 soak, +1 defense).

## IMPERIAL STORMTROOPER [MINION]

Stormtroopers serve as a constant reminder of Imperial might and to many sentients, they are the visible symbol of the Empire. Stormtroopers are not part of the Imperial Army, but are a separate corps of dedicated shock troops. With high-quality equipment and an absolute disregard for anything other than achieving their objectives, stormtroopers are implacable foes on the battlefield and perform missions regular Army troops would be unable or unwilling to accomplish.

| BRAWN | AGILITY | INTELLECT | CUNNING | WILLPOWER | PRESENCE |
|-------|---------|-----------|---------|-----------|----------|
| 3 | 3 | 2 | 2 | 3 | 1 |

| SOAK VALUE | W. THRESHOLD | M/R DEFENSE |
|-----------|--------------|-------------|
| 5 | 5 | 0  0 |

**Skills (group only):** Athletics, Discipline, Melee, Ranged (Heavy).
**Talents:** None.
**Abilities:** None.
**Equipment:** Blaster rifle (Ranged [Heavy]; Damage 9; Critical 3; Range [Long]; Stun setting), vibroknife (Melee; Damage 4; Critical 2; Range [Engaged]; Pierce 2, Vicious 1), 2 frag grenades (Ranged [Light]; Damage 8; Critical 4; Range [Short]; Blast 6, Limited Ammo 1), stormtrooper armor (+2 soak), utility belt, extra reloads. Individuals or groups of two may be armed with light repeating blasters with slings (Ranged [Heavy]; Damage 11; Critical 3; Range [Long]; Auto-fire, Cumbersome 3, Pierce 1).

## IMPERIAL STORMTROOPER SERGEANT [RIVAL]

Imperial stormtroopers are calculating, fearless individuals with a reputation for efficiency and an absolute lack of mercy and any emotion in the execution of their duties. Stormtrooper sergeants, who command squads of eight such individuals, are expected to exemplify those traits and show an increased grasp of tactics and abilities. Stormtrooper sergeants tend to be extremely motivated and self-assured individuals who place the mission above all else, sacrificing anything necessary to achieve the objective at hand. They can also carry more powerful weaponry than the rank-and-file.

**Skills:** Athletics 2, Discipline 2, Leadership 3, Melee 2, Ranged (Heavy) 2, Ranged (Light) 2, Resilience 2, Vigilance 2.
**Talents:** Adversary 1 (upgrade difficulty of all combat checks against this target once).
**Abilities:** Tactical Direction (may spend a maneuver to direct one Imperial stormtrooper minion group within medium range; the group may perform an immediate free maneuver or add ☐ to its next check).

**Equipment:** Heavy blaster rifle (Ranged [Heavy]; Damage 10; Critical 3; Range [Long]; Auto-fire, Cumbersome 3), vibroknife (Melee; Damage 4; Critical 2; Range [Engaged]; Pierce 2, Vicious 1), 2 frag grenades (Ranged [Light]; Damage 8; Critical 4; Range [Short]; Blast 6, Limited Ammo 1), stormtrooper armor (+2 soak), utility belt, extra reloads.

## TIE PILOT [MINION]

Pilots produced by the Empire's starfighter training programs are head-and-shoulders above any other equivalent force in the galaxy, according to Imperial propaganda. However, in reality, much like their starfighters, TIE pilots are something of an expendable resource for the Imperial Navy. Those few who manage to survive combat in their lightly armed-and-armored starfighters can strive to become ace pilots, but most never get the chance.

**Skills (group only):** Gunnery, Piloting (Space).
**Talents:** None.
**Abilities:** None.
**Equipment:** Light blaster pistol (Ranged [Light]; Damage 5; Critical 4; Range [Medium]; Stun setting), flight suit.

# DROIDS

Droids are as common a sight in the greater galaxy as starships or blasters. Alterations to their structure and programming allow them to function in virtually every conceivable environment. The vast majority are simply machines, laboring in the background to complete the tasks an advanced society requires to function. A smaller portion are much more advanced, capable of interacting with living beings with a semblance of the independence and creativity that the organic enjoy. And, of course, there are those few that are more than simple tools and instead can become tremendous allies or terrifying opponents.

Droids are typically divided into five broad categories depending on their function. These designations, referred to as "Class I" through "Class V," convey a general idea of what a droid from a given category can be expected to do, what capabilities it has, and what behaviors it is likely to exhibit. Class I includes perhaps the most advanced droids among its ranks, designed for medical and health-related purposes. Many Class II droids are designed for engineering and maintenance tasks, and are more like self-aware tools, though they

## PURCHASING DROIDS

Droids occupy a unique position in FORCE AND DESTINY, as they can be commodities for purchase but also sentient NPCs or adversaries. Therefore, they are presented in this chapter. However, if players wish to purchase these droids, they can consult the following chart for rarity and prices.

### TABLE 12-1: DROID PRICES

| Droid Type | Cost | Rarity |
|---|---|---|
| Analysis Droid | 7,500 | 5 |
| IG-100 MagnaGuard | (R) 90,000 | 10 |
| Interrogation Droid | (R) 9,600 | 8 |
| Medical Droid | 12,000 | 4 |
| Probe Droid | (R) 13,700 | 7 |
| Protocol Droid | 8,000 | 5 |

can develop quirky personalities. Class III droids, designed to interact with organic beings in a variety of fashions, range from the protocol droids frequently employed in diplomatic circles to the governess droids that the especially wealthy rely upon to care for their children. Class IV droids are by far the most restricted and heavily controlled, because they are designed for use in combat. Finally, Class V droids tend to be the simplest, generally handling straightforward, non-electronic repairs and menial labor. Class V droids usually have the least advanced processors and cognitive functions.

## ANALYSIS DROID [MINION]

Almost always found working in groups, analysis droids have served governments, corporations, wealthy private individuals, and even the defunct order of Jedi Knights. Most manufacturers make analysis droids, but the enduring popularity of Cybot Galactica's SP-4 and JN-66 models make them the category leaders. All analysis droids come equipped with a sophisticated sensory suite and a set of onboard analysis protocols that make them invaluable in aiding research, analyzing data, and performing experiments.

| BRAWN | AGILITY | INTELLECT | CUNNING | WILLPOWER | PRESENCE |
|---|---|---|---|---|---|
| 1 | 1 | 4 | 1 | 1 | 1 |

| SOAK VALUE | W. THRESHOLD | M/R DEFENSE | |
|---|---|---|---|
| 3 | 3 | 0 | 0 |

**Skills (group only):** Computers, Knowledge (Education).
**Talents:** Technical Aptitude 2 (analysis droids reduce the amount of time to complete computer-related tasks by 50%).
**Abilities:** Droid (does not need to breathe, eat, or drink and can survive in vacuum and underwater; immune to poisons and toxins), Silhouette 0.
**Equipment:** Datapad.

## IG-100 MAGNAGUARD [NEMESIS]

Thankfully rare, IG-100 MagnaGuard droids are relics of the Clone Wars, during which they served as elite bodyguards and shock troops for Separatist leaders. Though most were destroyed during the wars, some examples of the type are still active in the galaxy. Most such survivors are bound to the service of criminal overlords, Imperial Moffs, or other power brokers. More terrifying are those few who have been manumitted, haunting the hyperlanes alone or in pairs, following unknowable agendas. MagnaGuards are fearless combatants and reject ranged weapons out of hand, preferring to swiftly close with their opponents and engage them with their deadly electrostaves, which emit tendrils of energy designed to incapacitate and disorient foes.

| BRAWN | AGILITY | INTELLECT | CUNNING | WILLPOWER | PRESENCE |
|---|---|---|---|---|---|
| 4 | 4 | 2 | 3 | 1 | 1 |

| SOAK VALUE | W. THRESHOLD | S. THRESHOLD | M/R DEFENSE | |
|---|---|---|---|---|
| 8 | 20 | 14 | 1 | 1 |

**Skills:** Athletics 3, Brawl 3, Coordination 4, Melee 3, Perception 3, Vigilance 3.
**Talents:** Adversary 1 (upgrade difficulty of all combat checks against this target once), Parry 4 (when struck by a melee attack but before applying soak, suffer 3 strain to reduce damage by 6), Pin (as an action, upon a successful opposed Athletics check against an engaged opponent, immobilize that opponent until the end of the MagnaGuard's next turn; may spend any ⨁ on check to increase duration one round).
**Abilities:** Droid (does not need to breathe, eat, or drink and can survive in vacuum and underwater; immune to poisons and toxins).
**Equipment:** Electrostaff (Melee; Damage 8; Critical 3; Range [Engaged]; Cortosis, Cumbersome 3, Linked 1, Stun setting, Unwieldy 3), built-in armor plating (+2 soak, +1 defense).

## INTERROGATION DROID [RIVAL]

The interrogation droids designed by the Imperial Department of Military Research are among the most feared weapons in the Emperor's vast arsenal. These floating black spheres bristle with instruments of torture. Just the sight of them has been known to elicit confessions and coax out carefully guarded secrets from even the most steadfast of prisoners.

**Skills:** Coercion 4, Medicine 3, Perception 2, Ranged (Light) 3.
**Talents:** None.
**Abilities:** Droid (does not need to breathe, eat, or drink and can survive in vacuum and underwater; immune to poisons and toxins), Hoverer (interrogation droids have repulsorlifts that allow them to hover slightly off the ground; when hovering, they do not have to spend additional maneuvers when navigating difficult terrain), Silhouette 0.
**Equipment:** Built-in acid jet (Ranged [Light]; Damage 5; Critical 2; Range [Short]; Burn 2), built-in sonic torture device (Ranged [Light]; Damage 5; Critical –; Range [Short]; Concussive 3, Slow-Firing 1, Stun Damage), built-in interrogation drug syringe.

## MEDICAL DROID [RIVAL]

Medical droids take a variety of forms, from simple attendant droids capable of dressing flesh wounds or diagnosing basic illnesses up to the elaborate and incredibly advanced surgical droids that can be found on military starships and major urban centers throughout the galaxy.

**Skills:** Discipline 1, Medicine 3, Perception 2.
**Talents:** None.
**Abilities:** Droid (does not need to breathe, eat, or drink and can survive in vacuum and underwater; immune to poisons and toxins).
**Equipment:** Built-in diagnostic and surgical tools (count as medpac as well as stimpack that can be used once per session).

## PROTOCOL DROID [RIVAL]

With hundreds of thousands of intelligent races scattered across millions of planets throughout the galaxy, communication can be a significant problem when diplomacy is required. Protocol droids are designed to solve this problem; the advanced computer brains of these automatons retain millions of languages at a time. As their name indicates, the droids are not only translators but also serve to prevent misunderstandings by ensuring cultural problems do not arise. It is for this reason that, if these droids are left without a memory wipe and begin to develop a personality, they tend to be highly anxious and nervous.

**Skills:** Charm 2, Knowledge (Education) 3, Knowledge (Xenology) 3, Negotiation 2, Perception 1.
**Talents:** None.
**Abilities:** Droid (does not need to breathe, eat, or drink and can survive in vacuum and underwater; immune to poisons and toxins), Etiquette and Protocol (protocol droids allow allies to add ☐ to any Negotiation checks or other checks made to negotiate or mediate).
**Equipment:** None.

## VIPER PROBE DROID [RIVAL]

When searching the most remote regions in the galaxy, Imperial authorities often make use of probe droids to scout out remote planets and scour distant locations for signs of whatever, or whomever, is being sought. Probe droids travel to their destinations inside one-way hyperspace pods and communicate with their programmers via encrypted holo-channels. When the quarry may be on any of a thousand worlds, the best solution is often to disperse a thousand probe droids.

**Skills:** Cool 1, Perception 2, Ranged (Light) 2, Survival 2, Vigilance 2.
**Talents:** None.
**Abilities:** Droid (does not need to breathe, eat, or drink and can survive in vacuum and underwater; immune to poisons and toxins), Hoverer (probe droids do not have to spend additional maneuvers when navigating difficult terrain), Self-destruct Mechanism (should the probe droid's mission become compromised, it may self-destruct as an out of turn incidental; this explosion does 10 damage to engaged characters).
**Equipment:** Built-in blaster (Ranged [Light]; Damage 6; Critical 3; Range [Medium]; Stun setting), long-range holonet communicator, life form scanner, long-range sensor array.

# FORCE USERS

Despite Order 66 and the Empire's Inquisitors relentlessly hunting those with Force-sensitivity, there are still those throughout the galaxy who are born with the ability to harness the Force. Some of them are not even aware that their exceptional abilities are anything more than natural talent; others understand their Force-sensitivity makes them targets and hide their powers at any cost. None of them have undergone any sort of formal training. In a bygone era, they might have been recruited as potential Jedi. Now, they try to fit in as best they can—and avoid the Inquisitors at all costs.

## ACCOMPLISHED MECHANIC [RIVAL]

Force-sensitive mechanics instinctually know their way around machines and can coax them back to life long after other mechanics would have given up hope. Mechanics are a welcome addition to a smuggler's crew or a pirate band, where they're likely to avoid the watchful eye of Imperial Inquisitors. Occasionally, Force-sensitive mechanics will be found working legitimate jobs in respectable shops on civilized planets. Those who do are almost always unaware that their amazing ability to assess and repair machines is anything other than a natural talent.

**Skills:** Computers 2, Mechanics 2, Survival 1, Vigilance 1.
**Talents:** Gearhead (remove ■ from Mechanics checks), Force Rating 1, Imbue Item (spend a maneuver to commit ◯ and grant one weapon at short range +1 damage or decrease critical rating of weapon by one).
**Abilities:** None.
**Equipment:** Holdout blaster (Ranged [Light]; Damage 5; Critical 4; Range [Short]; Stun setting), tool kit, emergency repair kit.

## CAUTIOUS SMUGGLER [RIVAL]

Smuggling is a dangerous profession, requiring a mixture of luck, skill, and panache. Those smugglers with Force-sensitivity can detect a potential trap, come up with plausible cover stories for suspicious Imperial patrols, and know exactly when to dump their cargo (and when to pick it up later). Force-sensitive smugglers who get too cocky about their abilities often find themselves on the wrong end of the Imperial Inquisitorius, so those who realize what their sensitivity might mean keep it as quiet as possible.

Generally, Force-using NPCs have one or two primary Force abilities. However, the GM can allow these NPCs to have other basic Force powers to make the characters feel more well rounded. Each NPC's Force rating is provided for this purpose.

**Skills:** Charm 3, Cool 2, Deception 2, Ranged [Light] 2, Piloting (Space) 2, Skulduggery 2, Streetwise 2.
**Talents:** Force Rating 1, Intuitive Evasion (as a maneuver, suffer 1 strain and commit ◯ to upgrade the difficulty of all combat checks targeting pilot's vehicle once, until the beginning of pilot's next turn), Skilled Jockey 2 (remove ■ ■ from any Piloting checks).
**Abilities:** Force Power: Influence (may make an Influence power roll as part of a Coercion, Charm, Deception, Leadership, or Negotiation check. May spend ◑ to add 😡 or ☼ [cautious smuggler's choice] per ◑ spent to the check).
**Equipment:** Blaster pistol (Ranged [Light]; Damage 6; Critical 3; Range [Medium]; Stun setting).

## CSA INTRUSION SPECIALIST [RIVAL]

The Corporate Sector Authority's vast holdings make it an attractive target for slicers. The CSA's Security Police, commonly referred to as the Espos, employ a number of slicers to counter these threats. Elite slicers seem to have a natural ability to foil security protocols, guess passwords, and find backdoors in computer code. Their abilities seem almost supernatural, and in a few rare cases, maybe they are.

**Skills:** Computers 3, Cool 2, Skulduggery 2.
**Talents:** Bypass Security (remove ■ from any Computers or Skulduggery checks to bypass security), Force Rating 1.
**Abilities:** Computer Affinity (the Intrusion Specialist may add ◯ to any Computers check or Skulduggery check to analyze or infiltrate a security system. Spend ◑ to add 😡 to the check. Spend ◑◑ to add ☼ to any Computers check).
**Equipment:** Holdout blaster (Ranged [Light]; Damage 5; Critical 4; Range [Short]; Stun setting), slicer gear.

## DANDY GAMBLER [RIVAL]

Force-sensitive individuals have a distinct advantage at games of strategy and chance. Some choose to become professional gamblers. As with any successful gambler, these galactic dandies never find themselves in one casino for too long, lest those who lost credits to them come looking for reparation. These lucky individuals are always on the move, searching for the next big game.

| 2 | 2 | 2 | 4 | 1 | 2 |
|---|---|---|---|---|---|
| BRAWN | AGILITY | INTELLECT | CUNNING | WILLPOWER | PRESENCE |

| SOAK VALUE | W. THRESHOLD | M/R DEFENSE |
|---|---|---|
| 2 | 12 | 0  0 |

**Skills:** Charm 2, Cool 3, Deception 2, Perception 3, Skulduggery 3, Streetwise 2.

**Talents:** Force Rating 1, Second Chances 2 (once per encounter, the dandy gambler may choose 2 positive dice in one check he makes and reroll them).

**Abilities:** All the Luck in the Galaxy (when making a check to gamble, a Deception check, or a Negotiation check, add ⬡ to the check. Each ◯ result automatically adds ✸ to the check. ⬤⬤ results automatically add ⬦ to the check).

**Equipment:** Holdout blaster (Ranged [Light]; Damage 5; Critical 4; Range [Short]; Stun setting).

## FALLEN APPRENTICE [RIVAL]

For every Force user who sees the myths of the ancient Jedi as an ideal to live up to, someone else decides to follow a darker path. Sometimes, these deviants seek out apprentices who will aid and emulate them. Such apprentices are often weak-willed, eager for the easy power their new master promises.

| 2 | 3 | 2 | 3 | 2 | 1 |
|---|---|---|---|---|---|
| BRAWN | AGILITY | INTELLECT | CUNNING | WILLPOWER | PRESENCE |

| SOAK VALUE | W. THRESHOLD | M/R DEFENSE |
|---|---|---|
| 3 | 14 | 0  0 |

**Skills:** Coercion 2, Discipline 3, Lightsaber 3, Resilience 2, Stealth 2.

**Talents:** Adversary 1 (upgrade difficulty of all combat checks against this target once), Force Rating 1, Soft Spot (after a successful attack with a non-starship/vehicle weapon, the fallen apprentice may spend a Destiny Point to add 3 damage to one hit).

**Abilities:** Dark Side Force User (uses Dark Side results instead of Light Side results, see page 281).

**Equipment:** Basic lightsaber (Lightsaber; Damage 6; Critical 2; Range [Engaged]; Breach 1, Sunder), black robes (+1 soak).

## FALLEN MASTER [NEMESIS]

While not true Jedi or Sith, there are those who stylize themselves as "masters" of the Force. If these individuals turn to the dark side, they can be incredibly dangerous and terrifyingly savage. Some may even track down old relics from a bygone era such as lightsabers. In the hands of a fallen master, these blades often taste the blood of innocents.

| 3 | 3 | 3 | 3 | 4 | 3 |
|---|---|---|---|---|---|
| BRAWN | AGILITY | INTELLECT | CUNNING | WILLPOWER | PRESENCE |

| SOAK VALUE | W. THRESHOLD | S. THRESHOLD | M/R DEFENSE |
|---|---|---|---|
| 4 | 18 | 18 | 1  1 |

**Skills:** Athletics 2, Coercion 3, Discipline 4, Knowledge (Lore) 2, Leadership 2, Lightsaber 4, Resilience 3.

**Talents:** Adversary 2 (upgrade difficulty of all combat checks against this target twice), Force Rating 3, Hawk Bat Swoop (the fallen master may perform a Lightsaber [Agility] melee combat check against one target within short range and add ⬡⬡⬡ to the pool. He may spend ◗ before resolving the success or failure of the check to engage the target immediately as an incidental, and may spend ◗ to add 🗲 to the check. If the fallen master cannot move to engage the target, the attack automatically misses). Improved Reflect (when the fallen master suffers a hit from a Ranged [Light], Ranged [Heavy], or Gunnery check that generates ⬦ or ✸✸✸ and uses the Reflect incidental to reduce damage from that hit, after resolving the attack he may spend those results to inflict one hit on a target within medium range, dealing the same damage as the hit from the initial ranged attack.), Parry 5 (when struck by a hit from a melee attack but before applying soak, suffer 3 strain to reduce damage by 7), Reflect 5 (when struck by a hit from a ranged attack but before applying soak, suffer 3 strain to reduce damage by 7).

**Abilities:** Dark Side Force User (uses Dark Side results instead of Light Side results, see page 281).

**Equipment:** Double-bladed mephite lightsaber (Lightsaber; Damage 8; Critical 2; Range [Engaged]; Breach 1, Linked 1, Sunder, Unwieldy 3), black robes (+1 soak).

## MURDEROUS FUGITIVE [NEMESIS]

Without the benefit of Jedi training, some Force-sensitive individuals who might otherwise have been able to control their abilities are left confused and overwhelmed. They find delight in murder and inflicting pain, especially when using their Force-sensitivity to fuel their urges. Often hunted for these crimes, these individuals are extremely dangerous to everyone they encounter.

| BRAWN | AGILITY | INTELLECT | CUNNING | WILLPOWER | PRESENCE |
|:---:|:---:|:---:|:---:|:---:|:---:|
| 3 | 4 | 2 | 4 | 3 | 1 |

| SOAK VALUE | W. THRESHOLD | S. THRESHOLD | M/R DEFENSE | |
|:---:|:---:|:---:|:---:|:---:|
| 3 | 15 | 14 | 0 | 0 |

**Skills:** Brawl 2, Discipline 2, Melee 4, Perception 2, Stealth 2, Vigilance 3.

**Talents:** Adversary 2 (upgrade difficulty of all combat checks against this target twice), Force Rating 3, Soft Spot (after making a successful attack with a non-starship/vehicle weapon, flip a Destiny Point to add 4 damage to one hit of the successful attack).

**Abilities:** Dark Side Force User (uses Dark Side results instead of Light Side results, see page 281), Force Power: Unleash (the fugitive makes a Force power check targeting one enemy at short range, and rolls a ranged attack as part of the pool, using **Average (◆ ◆) Discipline check** instead of normal difficulty. If the check is successful and generates ◖◖, the attack deals 3 damage with a critical rating of 4, plus 1 additional damage per ☼. May spend ◖ to increase damage by 3, and ◖ to increase range to medium).

**Equipment:** Serrated vibroknife (Melee; Damage 5; Critical 2; Range [Engaged]; Pierce 2, Vicious 2).

## SCARRED GLADIATOR [NEMESIS]

Sometimes the most effective way to hide your Force-sensitivity is to hide it in plain sight. The Scarred Gladiator discovered that his combat skills could make him a lot of money in the arena. He's the veteran of hundreds of battles and has the scars to prove it. He is deeply invested in the criminal underworld, and there are too many people who make money off his skills for anyone to turn him over to the authorities. He doesn't flaunt his Force-sensitivity, but he enjoys his notoriety as a deadly and feared fighter. He knows

there may be a day when it all comes crashing down. Until that day comes, he's more than content to use his abilities to live life to the fullest.

| BRAWN | AGILITY | INTELLECT | CUNNING | WILLPOWER | PRESENCE |
|:---:|:---:|:---:|:---:|:---:|:---:|
| 4 | 3 | 2 | 2 | 2 | 3 |

| SOAK VALUE | W. THRESHOLD | S. THRESHOLD | M/R DEFENSE | |
|:---:|:---:|:---:|:---:|:---:|
| 6 | 19 | 16 | 2 | 0 |

**Skills:** Athletics 2, Brawl 4, Coordination 1, Medicine 3, Melee 3, Streetwise 2, Survival 2, Vigilance 2.

**Talents:** Adversary 2 (upgrade difficulty of all combat checks against this target twice), Force Rating 2.

**Abilities:** Dark Side Force User (uses Dark Side results instead of Light Side results, see page 281), Force Power: Harm (the Gladiator may make a Harm Force power check against one engaged target. Spend ◖ to inflict 2 wounds on the target, ignoring soak. Spend ◖ to increase wounds inflicted by 2 [may activate this multiple times], and spend ◐ to heal wounds equal to wounds inflicted).

**Equipment:** Vibro-trident (Melee; Damage 5; Critical 2; Range [Engaged]; Defensive 2, Pierce 4, Vicious 3), gladiatorial leathers (+2 soak).

# CREATURES

A multitude of exotic creatures can be found across the galaxy. While some species remain unique to their homeworld, others are seen far and wide, serving as pets, gladiatorial opponents, or working animals. The following species are some more interesting examples.

### STALKING ACKLAY [NEMESIS]

Acklays are ferocious, three-meter-tall, six-legged predators native to the planet Vendaxa. These non-sentient hunters evolved in the crucible of Vendaxa's harsh ecosystem to become finely honed killing machines. An acklay's high metabolism gives it a great deal of energy, especially when hunting. Acklays are thick-shelled crustaceans that can live underwater or on land. The acklay's three eyes can see in almost-total darkness, and each of its legs ends in an enormous claw it uses to pin or slash at prey. Because of their combat prowess, acklays are used across the galaxy in gladiatorial arenas.

| 5 | 3 | 1 | 3 | 3 | 1 |
|---|---|---|---|---|---|
| BRAWN | AGILITY | INTELLECT | CUNNING | WILLPOWER | PRESENCE |

| SOAK VALUE | W. THRESHOLD | S. THRESHOLD | M/R DEFENSE |
|---|---|---|---|
| 12 | 25 | 15 | 2 0 |

**Skills:** Athletics 4, Brawl 4, Coordination 2.
**Talents:** Adversary 1 (upgrade difficulty of all combat checks against this target once).
**Abilities:** Amphibious (acklays breathe underwater and do not suffer movement penalties in water), Six-armed (the acklay gains □ on all Brawl checks and may spend ☾ ☾ on a successful melee attack to hit a second target engaged with it, dealing the same damage as dealt to the original target), Silhouette 2.
**Equipment:** Large claws (Brawl; Damage 10, Critical 2; Range [Engaged]; Knockdown, Pierce 3).

### JAKOBEAST [MINION]

The colonization of the Outer Rim required hardy creatures that could withstand extreme environments and defend themselves against dangerous, and often unanticipated, predators. Jakobeasts were introduced on hundreds of ice planets across the galaxy and still roam many of these worlds today. Large, shaggy, feline creatures approximately two meters tall and three meters from nose to tail, jakobeasts are easily domesticated herd animals kept for meat, milk, and fur. Both male and female jakobeasts sport large tusks, primarily used for self-defense or establishing dominance. Though it is not widely known, as a group, jakobeasts can generate waves of Force energy to defend their herds from predators, although an individual does not have this ability if separated from its herd.

| 4 | 1 | 1 | 1 | 1 | 1 |
|---|---|---|---|---|---|
| BRAWN | AGILITY | INTELLECT | CUNNING | WILLPOWER | PRESENCE |

| SOAK VALUE | W. THRESHOLD | M/R DEFENSE |
|---|---|---|
| 3 | 9 | 0 0 |

**Skills (group only):** Athletics, Brawl, Resilience, Survival.
**Talents:** None.
**Abilities:** Silhouette 2, Strong as a Jakobeast (jakobeasts have an encumbrance threshold of 20), Force Power: Move (a minion group of three or more jakobeasts may attempt to shove enemies away with the Force. As an action, roll ⬡ ⬡. Each ☽ generated may be spent to move one silhouette 1 enemy within short range to medium range).
**Equipment:** Tusks (Brawl; Damage 6; Critical 4; Range [Engaged]).

## JUVENILE CREATURES

Certain Player Characters (notably those with the Pathfinder specialization) may be able to form a bond with a creature. This has mechanical as well as narrative benefits. However, since the size of the creature the PC can bond with depends on the PC's Force rating, the PC may gain the ability to bond with a mechanically superior creature, but not want to give up the creature he has already bonded with due to narrative reasons. To prevent this, GMs may use the following rules to delineate a young version of a creature, which can later "grow up" as the PC gains the ability to control the full-sized version.

To represent a juvenile version of a creature, the GM should apply the following changes:

- Decrease the creature's silhouette by 1, to a minimum of 0.

- Decrease the creature's wound and strain threshold (if applicable) to half normal (rounding up).

- Decrease the damage of any weapons or attacks the creature possesses to half normal (rounding up).

If and when the PC gains the ability to control a larger version of the creature, the GM can simply restore the creature to its original profile, explaining that it has grown in size and ability over the intervening time. However, use of this rule is strictly subject to GM approval.

### JUBBA BIRD [RIVAL]

Jubba birds are found in marketplaces, palaces, and the homes of wealthy merchants and upwardly mobile criminals throughout the galaxy, although they are native to the swamps of Dagobah. Brightly colored avians with reptilian features, jubba birds are prized for their red, yellow, and purple plumage as much as for their beautiful, haunting song. The jubba bird's whistling call is actually an instinctual ability to tap into the Living Force, and it produces a peaceful sensation in those who hear it. Jubba birds have small bodies but large wings, and they fare poorly in cages. Luckily, if an owner feeds his bird regularly, it is more than content to remain on a roost or perch and refrain from terrorizing a household or attempting to hunt other pets. On Dagobah, jubba birds hunt small prey such as rodents or other birds, but in captivity, a well-fed jubba bird will fight only to defend itself. Most importantly, if the jubba bird is not content, it refuses to sing.

Few owners realize that jubba birds are deceptively intelligent. While not as smart as most sapient species, they possess a level of cunning and a capacity for comprehension that dwarfs most animal species. Some researchers suspect that jubba birds deliberately pretend to be less intelligent when interacting with other species. These suspicions are only reinforced by rumors that, when paired with owners they trust and care for, jubba birds can act with more deliberation and foresight.

| BRAWN | AGILITY | INTELLECT | CUNNING | WILLPOWER | PRESENCE |
|---|---|---|---|---|---|
| 1 | 2 | 2 | 2 | 1 | 3 |

| SOAK VALUE | W. THRESHOLD | M/R DEFENSE |
|---|---|---|
| 1 | 3 | 0 / 0 |

**Skills:** Charm 2.
**Talents:** Sense Emotions (add ☐ to all Charm checks unless the target is immune to Force powers).
**Abilities:** Flyer (jubba birds can fly, see page 208), Soothing Song (the jubba bird may make an **Average (◆ ◆) Charm check** to heal 1 strain per ✪ from all creatures within medium range), Silhouette 0.
**Equipment:** Claws (Brawl; Damage 2; Critical 5; Range [Engaged]).

### KAATEN [RIVAL]

The kaaten is a one-and-half-meter, bipedal, semi-intelligent predator found on Felucia. It is a mimic, able to use the Force to appear to its prey as someone familiar to the individual the kaaten is hunting. Kaaten are solitary, with well-defined territorial lines that are crossed only when they mate. Therefore, they have not developed any kind of social structure or language. A kaaten can appear as a lost loved one, a companion or friend, or a member of its prey's species if the kaaten is hunting something non-sentient. Once the kaaten has lured its prey close, it strikes with its claws, attempting to quickly incapacitate its unsuspecting quarry.

| BRAWN | AGILITY | INTELLECT | CUNNING | WILLPOWER | PRESENCE |
|---|---|---|---|---|---|
| 2 | 2 | 2 | 3 | 1 | 1 |

| SOAK VALUE | W. THRESHOLD | M/R DEFENSE |
|---|---|---|
| 5 | 12 | 0 / 0 |

**Skills:** Charm 3, Deception 3, Stealth 3.
**Talents:** None.

**Abilities:** Force Mimic (at the GM's discretion, the kaaten may make **an opposed Charm or Deception versus Vigilance check** as an action to pretend to be a friend, companion, loved one, or of the same species as its target. When doing so, add ○ to the check; ◑ generated from ○ results add ✸ to Charm checks, while ◑ generated from ● results add ✸ to Deception checks. If the check succeeds, the illusion is successful, though what effect this has on gameplay depends on the situation and can be determined by the GM. Targets immune to Force powers are immune to these effects.)
**Equipment:** Claws (Brawl; Damage 7; Critical 4; Range [Engaged]; Pierce 2).

## KOUHUN [MINION]

Kouhuns are small, multi-legged, venomous arthropods approximately thirty centimeters long, with gray, segmented bodies and large mandibles. Kouhun bites deliver a fast-acting and fatal neurotoxin, making them a favorite "weapon" of many assassins. On their home planet of Indoumodo, they are simple predators who track prey by heat. Their tiny size makes them adept at slipping through ventilation systems, windows, cracks in masonry, and other tight spaces. When cornered, kouhuns can also use a sharp, non-venomous tail spine to defend themselves.

| 1 | 2 | 1 | 1 | 1 | 1 |
|---|---|---|---|---|---|
| BRAWN | AGILITY | INTELLECT | CUNNING | WILLPOWER | PRESENCE |

| SOAK VALUE | W. THRESHOLD | M/R DEFENSE | |
|---|---|---|---|
| 1 | 3 | 0 | 0 |

**Skills (group only):** Brawl.
**Talents:** None.
**Abilities:** Neurotoxin (if a target suffers wounds from a kouhun's mandible attack, the target must make an **Average (◆◆) Resilience check**. The target suffers 5 wounds if he fails, plus 1 strain per ۞. ۞ means the target must check against the poison again at the start of his next turn.), Silhouette 0.
**Equipment:** Spine (Brawl; Damage 2; Critical 4; Range [Engaged]; Pierce 5), Mandibles (Brawl; Damage 2; Critical 3; Range [Engaged]; Pierce 2).

## MAALRAA [RIVAL]

The maalraa is a non-sentient, feline pack hunter that uses the Force to cloak itself from its prey. Although once found throughout the galaxy and sometimes domesticated as guard animals, maalraas are now extremely rare, found only in a handful of the galaxy's forgotten places and in the seediest corners of the criminal underworld. The maalraa's ability to cloak itself makes it almost impossible to spot among the shadows, al-

though those who are sensitive to the Force can sometimes detect its presence. When it strikes, the maalraa uses its huge fangs to latch onto its prey and hold it inert, slowly crushing it, while other members of the pack finish the unfortunate creature.

| 3 | 3 | 1 | 2 | 2 | 1 |
|---|---|---|---|---|---|
| BRAWN | AGILITY | INTELLECT | CUNNING | WILLPOWER | PRESENCE |

| SOAK VALUE | W. THRESHOLD | M/R DEFENSE | |
|---|---|---|---|
| 4 | 12 | 0 | 0 |

**Skills:** Brawl 3, Stealth 4.
**Talents:** None.
**Abilities:** Cloak (add ■■■ to all checks made to spot or track the maalraa [this can include Vigilance checks made for Initiative if the maalraa ambushes a character]. Force-sensitive characters ignore this ability.)
**Equipment:** Fangs (Brawl; Damage 6; Critical 3; Range [Engaged]; Ensnare 2).

## MATURE TUSK CAT [RIVAL]

Tusk cats are feline predators that can grow up to two meters high and three meters long. Named for the two distinct tusks growing from their lower jaws, these mammals are social creatures who mate for life and form prides. They even can "guard" herds of prey animals, eating one every so often while protecting the rest of the herd from other predators. These instincts make them surprisingly easy to domesticate, and they are large enough that they can be ridden by most humanoid sapients. Many an Outer Rim wanderer relies on the keen eyes and sensitive nose of his trusted tusk cat companion.

| BRAWN | AGILITY | INTELLECT | CUNNING | WILLPOWER | PRESENCE |
|---|---|---|---|---|---|
| 4 | 4 | 1 | 3 | 1 | 3 |

| SOAK VALUE | W. THRESHOLD | M/R DEFENSE |
|---|---|---|
| 4 | 17 | 1 \| 1 |

**Skills:** Brawl 2, Coordination 2, Perception 2, Stealth 2, Vigilance 2.
**Talents:** Adversary 1 (upgrade difficulty of all combat checks against this target once).
**Abilities:** Leap (tusk cats add ☐ ☐ to all Athletics checks made to perform vertical or horizontal jumps), Silhouette 2.
**Equipment:** Tusks and claws (Brawl; Damage 6; Critical 2; Range [Engaged]; Pierce 2).

### VORNSKR [RIVAL]

Vornskrs are lanky, canine predators native to the planet Myrkr, but found throughout the galaxy as domesticated hunting animals, pets, and guards. They use a mild poison in their whiplike tails to stun prey, then kill it with their teeth or claws. Vornskrs are Force-sensitive, a result of hunting prey with Force-sensitivity on their homeworld. A vornskr immediately focuses on any Force-sensitive creatures or individuals in its presence as soon as it senses them, and generally attacks without hesitation. Mercenary Jedi hunters and Imperial Inquisitors have been known to use vornskrs to help ferret out Force-sensitive fugitives.

| BRAWN | AGILITY | INTELLECT | CUNNING | WILLPOWER | PRESENCE |
|---|---|---|---|---|---|
| 3 | 3 | 1 | 2 | 2 | 1 |

| SOAK VALUE | W. THRESHOLD | M/R DEFENSE |
|---|---|---|
| 5 | 12 | 1 \| 0 |

**Skills:** Athletics 1, Brawl 1, Perception 2, Resilience 1, Survival 1, Vigilance 2.
**Talents:** None.

**Abilities:** Detect Force-Sensitivity (the vornskr may make an **Average (◆ ◆) Perception check** to detect all Force-sensitive creatures or characters with a Force rating within medium range; this ability functions regardless of intervening terrain or material), Force Hunter (gain ☐ to all combat checks made against Force-sensitive creatures or characters with a Force rating).
**Equipment:** Tail (Brawl; Damage 4; Critical 5; Range [Engaged]; Stun 4), Teeth (Brawl; Damage 6; Critical 3; Range [Engaged]; Vicious 2).

### YSALAMIR [MINION]

Ysalamiri evolved on Myrkr, where one of their chief predators was the Force-sensitive, Force-detecting vornskr. As a result, ysalamiri developed an unusual defense: a natural "bubble" around them that negates other creatures' ability to influence the Force. These docile, tree-dwelling creatures resemble half-meter-long furred lizards and live deep within the forests of Myrkr, where they have claimed the canopy as their own. They are herbivores, feasting on the sap of the trees in which they live, and they use only their teeth to defend themselves if attacked. As a result of their Force-negating abilities, ysalamiri are highly valued as pets and companions by anyone who fears those who use the Force.

| BRAWN | AGILITY | INTELLECT | CUNNING | WILLPOWER | PRESENCE |
|---|---|---|---|---|---|
| 1 | 0 | 1 | 2 | 2 | 1 |

| SOAK VALUE | W. THRESHOLD | M/R DEFENSE |
|---|---|---|
| 1 | 2 | 0 \| 0 |

**Skills (group only):** None.
**Talents:** None.
**Abilities:** Negate Force Powers (an adult ysalamir creates a spherical zone extending out to short range, inside which Force-sensitive characters and creatures cannot exert influence over the Force. Inside this zone, any Force powers, Force talents, or other abilities that the GM decides work via the Force do not function. Likewise, such powers may not affect or detect anything within this zone.), Sessile (this creature is unable to perform Move maneuvers), Silhouette 0.
**Equipment:** Teeth (Brawl; Damage 1; Critical 5; Range [Engaged]).

# GALACTIC ODDITIES

The galaxy is an enormous and diverse place where there is no end to the variety of species and individuals. A few of the stranger varieties are detailed here.

### BESALISK ADVENTURER [RIVAL]

A common figure in the cantinas and sabacc dens of the Outer Rim is the wandering Besalisk adventurer. These bulky four-armed avians are known for their generosity, loyalty, and fearless approach to any dangers they might face in their travels. Gregarious, clever, and sharply observant, they can prove to be a valuable source of obscure information. However, many Besalisks hide their own agenda beneath their genial demeanor, and those who interact with them would do well to remember it.

| 3 | 2 | 2 | 3 | 3 | 2 |
|---|---|---|---|---|---|
| BRAWN | AGILITY | INTELLECT | CUNNING | WILLPOWER | PRESENCE |

| SOAK VALUE | W. THRESHOLD | M/R DEFENSE |
|---|---|---|
| 3 | 12 | 0 \| 0 |

**Skills:** Brawl 2, Ranged (Light) 2, Survival 2, Vigilance 2.
**Talents:** None.
**Abilities:** Four-armed (the Besalisk gains ☐ on all Brawl checks and may spend ⟡ ⟡ on a successful melee attack to hit a second target engaged with it, dealing the same damage as dealt to the original target).
**Equipment:** Blaster pistol (Ranged [Light]; Damage 6; Critical 3; Range [Medium]; Stun setting), brass knuckles (Brawl; Damage 4; Critical 4; Range [Engaged]; Disorient 3), utility belt.

## CHISS MERCENARY [NEMESIS]

The blue-skinned, red-eyed Chiss seldom venture beyond their hidden homeworld deep in the Unknown Regions. Thus is it unsurprising that when one does encounter a Chiss, it is often among the worlds of the Outer Rim. When leaving their homes, some Chiss wanderers take to the hyperlanes to find adventure, trading on their cool and calculating demeanors to become skilled mercenaries. Professional soldiers for hire, Chiss mercenaries are too few to be found together in numbers; one can rarely find more than a single Chiss in an entire star system.

| 2 | 3 | 4 | 3 | 2 | 1 |
|---|---|---|---|---|---|
| BRAWN | AGILITY | INTELLECT | CUNNING | WILLPOWER | PRESENCE |

| SOAK VALUE | W. THRESHOLD | S. THRESHOLD | M/R DEFENSE |
|---|---|---|---|
| 4 | 18 | 13 | 1 \| 1 |

**Skills:** Coercion 2, Cool 1, Coordination 2, Discipline 3, Melee 3, Ranged (Heavy) 4, Resilience 3, Vigilance 4.
**Talents:** Adversary 2 (upgrade difficulty of all combat checks against this target twice), Lethal Blows 2 (add +20 to any Critical Injury results inflicted on opponents), Quick Strike 2 (when performing a combat check, add ☐ ☐ against any target that has not yet acted in the encounter).
**Abilities:** Infravision (remove ■ imposed due to lighting conditions).
**Equipment:** Blaster rifle (Ranged [Heavy]; Damage 9; Critical 3; Range [Long]; Stun setting), cortosis sword (Melee; Damage 4; Critical 3; Range [Engaged]; Cortosis), heavy battle armor (+2 soak, +1 defense), stimpack.

## MUSTAFARIAN MINER [RIVAL]

Hailing from the young, volcanic world of Mustafar, the Mustafarians are the first species there to evolve to sentience, which is remarkable considering the violent nature of their homeworld.

These bipedal humanoids stand almost two-and-a-half meters tall, and are very much at home in some of the harshest planetary conditions in the galaxy. Mustafar's immense mineral resources have made the Mustafarians quite wealthy, and they have traded for technology and equipment to help them occupy even the harshest corners of their home planet. They quietly support the Galactic Empire in exchange for Imperial protection, happily exchanging their mineral wealth for relative privacy and advanced technology.

| 3 | 2 | 2 | 2 | 2 | 2 |
|---|---|---|---|---|---|
| BRAWN | AGILITY | INTELLECT | CUNNING | WILLPOWER | PRESENCE |

| SOAK VALUE | W. THRESHOLD | M/R DEFENSE |
|---|---|---|
| 4 | 14 | 0 \| 0 |

**Skills:** Athletics 2, Brawl 3, Melee 1, Resilience 2, Vigilance 1.
**Talents:** Adversary 1 (upgrade difficulty of all combat checks made against this target once).
**Abilities:** Heat Resistance (remove up to ■ from any checks due to hot or arid environmental conditions).
**Equipment:** Vibro-ax (Melee; Damage 8; Critical 2; Range [Engaged]; Pierce 2, Sunder, Vicious 3).

# THE INQUISITORIUS

Few people in the galaxy are aware of the existence of the Imperial Inquisitorius, but all who know of it rightfully fear it. Founded by the Emperor in the wake of the destruction of the Jedi at the beginning of the Imperial era, this shadowy organization tasks its members with hunting down Force users and either bending them to the will of the Emperor or destroying them utterly. Originally, Inquisitors hunted the few remaining Jedi, but now their remit extends to any and all Force users who come to their attention. Almost all Inquisitors are themselves Force users, and rumors abound that fallen Jedi can be found among their ranks.

Because members of the Inquisitorius may be of any species, age, or gender, game statistics are not provided for particular individuals. Instead, Game Masters should follow the seven step process below to generate Inquisitors who fit the needs of their story. This process is designed to create an Inquisitor who can stand up to an entire party of Player Characters, and thus is a formidable opponent.

## UNIQUE INQUISITORS

Although this process is designed to help GMs quickly create interesting Inquisitor characters, the GM should not feel bound by it if he has another idea in mind. Instead, he should feel free to design his terrifying NPC as he sees fit, and if that means bending the rules a little bit, then so be it!

## STEP 1: NPC TYPE

All Inquisitors are nemeses and follow all the rules for this NPC type (see page 400).

## STEP 2: CHARACTERISTICS

The GM takes the following values and assigns one value to each of the Inquisitor's characteristics. Each value can only be assigned once (when the 5 is assigned to one characteristic, for example, it cannot be used again). The values are as follows: 5, 4, 3, 3, 3, and 2.

## STEP 3: WOUNDS AND STRAIN

Every Inquisitor starts with a wound threshold of 20 and a strain threshold of 20. Game Masters should then add the Inquisitor's Brawn score to the Inquisitor's wound threshold and his Willpower score to his strain threshold. These are the Inquisitor's final wound threshold and strain threshold.

## STEP 4: SKILLS

All Inquisitors are highly skilled, and most are able to handle themselves equally well on and off the battlefield. Thus, when determining the Inquisitor's skills, use the following steps.

### COMBAT SKILLS

When determining the Inquisitor's ranks in combat skills, the GM takes the following values and assigns each value to a combat skill of the GM's choice. Each value can only be assigned once, and all skills that do not get a value assigned to them have rank 0. The values are as follows: 4, 3, and 2.

### KNOWLEDGE SKILLS

Inquisitors must be extremely educated individuals to carry out their duties, even if this knowledge is not readily apparent. The Inquisitor has two ranks in each Knowledge skill.

### GENERAL SKILLS

As stated previously, the GM is free to give his Inquisitor whatever skills he sees fit. However, the following are skill packages intended to speed up the process. If the GM chooses, he may select one package and apply those skill ranks to the Inquisitor.

- **The Acolyte:** Deception 1, Discipline 4, Leadership 2, Perception 2, Survival 3, Vigilance 3.
- **The Assassin:** Cool 2, Coordination 3, Deception 3, Medicine 1, Stealth 4, Vigilance 2.
- **The Brute:** Athletics 3, Coercion 3, Discipline 2, Resilience 4, Streetwise 1, Vigilance 1.
- **The Investigator:** Computers 2, Perception 4, Skulduggery 3, Streetwise 3, Survival 2, Vigilance 2.
- **The Mastermind:** Charm 2, Computers 4, Cool 2, Deception 3, Mechanics 1, Negotiation 1.
- **The Traveler:** Astrogation 2, Computers 1, Cool 2, Mechanics 3, Piloting (Planetary and Space) 4.
- **The Warlord:** Coercion 2, Discipline 3, Leadership 4, Perception 2, Piloting (Planetary) 1, Vigilance 2.

## STEP 5: TALENTS

All Inquisitors have the Adversary 3 talent (upgrade difficulty of all combat checks against this target three times) and may, at the Game Master's discretion, possess a Force rating of 3. In addition, the Game Master may add no more than two of the talents listed here. Some of these options are multiple ranks of a ranked talent. In these cases, they still count as a single choice.

- **Crippling Blow:** The Inquisitor increases the difficulty of his next combat check by one. If the check deals damage, the target suffers 1 strain whenever he moves for the remainder of the encounter.
- **Drive Back:** The Inquisitor may spend ⬦ or ❂ ❂ ❂ on a missed Brawl, Melee, or Lightsaber

# USING IMPERIAL INQUISITORS

Imperial Inquisitors are ready-made Force-wielding villains suitable for almost any FORCE AND DESTINY campaign. They may pursue the characters personally, or they may rely on legions of agents. Inquisitors should inspire awe and fear. They don't play fair, and they are out to destroy any Force user or troublesome Rebel in their sights. They may set traps for their targets, or they may bring overwhelming force to bear. When an Inquisitor appears, the PCs should quickly learn the extreme danger they are in.

Inquisitors are likely to be more skilled in the Force than the PCs, at least early in the PCs'

careers. They may have lightsabers or other exotic and dangerous weapons. Inquisitors tend to be trusted agents of the Emperor, and defeating one should be very different (possibly the climax of a campaign). Inquisitors are also canny and clever foes who should always be willing to flee to fight another day if the fight goes against them.

Captured PCs may be subject to interrogation before imprisonment or execution. This is especially true for active Rebel agents and Force users. Inquisitors may even try to turn or corrupt the prisoners to become their agents.

combat check to force his target to make a move maneuver in a direction of the Inquisitor's choice.

- **Improved Parry:** When the Inquisitor suffers a hit from a Brawl, Melee, or Lightsaber check that generates ▽ or ⚙ ⚙ ⚙ and the Inquisitor uses the Parry incidental to reduce damage from that hit, after resolving the attack, he may spend those results to inflict one hit on the attacker with a wielded Brawl, Melee, or Lightsaber weapon, inflicting the weapon's base damage. The Inquisitor must also take the Parry talent to use this.

- **Intense Focus:** The Inquisitor performs the Intense Focus maneuver, suffering 1 strain and upgrading the ability of his next skill check once.

- **Lethal Blows 2:** The Inquisitor adds +20 to any Critical Injury rolls inflicted on opponents.

- **Parry 4:** When struck by a melee attack but before applying soak, the Inquisitor may perform Parry as an out-of-turn incidental. He suffers 3 strain, then reduces the damage by 6.

- **Pressure Point:** When making a Brawl check against a living opponent, the Inquisitor may choose to forgo dealing damage as wounds, instead dealing the equivalent damage as strain, plus additional strain equal to his ranks in Medicine. These checks cannot be made with any weapons, but this strain damage is not reduced by soak.

- **Reflect 4:** When struck by a ranged attack but before applying soak, the Inquisitor may perform Reflect as an out-of-turn incidental. He suffers 3 strain, then reduces the damage by 6.

- **Scathing Tirade (Improved):** The Inquisitor may take the Scathing Tirade action, making an **Average (◆ ◆) Coercion check**. For each ✯, one enemy within short range suffers 1 strain and ■ on all skill checks for a number of rounds equal to the Inquisitor's ranks in Coercion. The Inquisitor may spend ☻; for every ☻ spent, one target already affected suffers 1 additional strain.

## STEP 6: ABILITIES AND FORCE POWERS

Every Inquisitor possesses two abilities and/or Force powers (if the Inquisitor is a Force user) chosen from the following list.

- **Aura of Command:** The Inquisitor may spend a maneuver to allow one allied minion group at medium range to immediately perform one maneuver or action. Add □ to any actions they perform.

- **Lightsaber Mastery:** Choose a characteristic. When making a check using the Lightsaber skill, the Inquisitor may use the chosen characteristic instead of Brawn.

- **Imperial Valor:** The Inquisitor may perform a maneuver to cause all ranged attacks targeting him to instead hit one ally or helpless enemy he is engaged with until the beginning of his next turn.

- **Intimidating Presence:** All enemies at short range of the Inquisitor add ⚙ to all skill checks they make.

- **Terrifying:** At the beginning of an encounter, each of the Inquisitor's enemies must make a **Hard (◆ ◆ ◆) fear check** (see page 326).

- **Harm:** *Force Power.* As an action, the Inquisitor may make a Force power check against one engaged target. The Inquisitor may spend ◗ to inflict a number of wounds on the target (ignoring soak) equal to the Inquisitor's Intellect. The Inquisitor may spend ◗ to heal an equal number of wounds on an engaged ally or himself. The Inquisitor may spend ◗ to increase the range of the power by one range band and may spend ◖ to increase the number of affected enemies by one. (he may activate the range and number upgrades multiple times).

- **Unleash:** *Force Power.* The Inquisitor makes a Force power check targeting one enemy at short range, and rolls a ranged attack as part of the pool, using an **Average (◆ ◆) Discipline check** instead of normal difficulty. If the check is successful and generates ⬤◗, the attack deals damage equal to the Inquisitor's Willpower with a critical rating of 4, dealing 1 additional damage per ✵. The Inquisitor may spend ◗ to increase the range by one range band, may spend ◗ to affect one additional target within range, and may spend ◗ to cause the attack to deal 3 additional damage (he may activate all of these upgrades multiple times).

- **Move:** *Force Power.* The Inquisitor may spend ◗ to move one silhouette 0 object within short range to another location within short range. He may spend ◗ to increase the range of the power by one band, spend ◗ to increase the silhouette of the object he can move by 1, and spend ◗ to increase the number of objects he moves at one time by 2 (he may activate all of these upgrades multiple times). Finally, he may hurl objects at opponents by making a Force power check and rolling a ranged attack as part of the pool. The attack's difficulty is equal to the silhouette of the object being thrown instead of the normal difficulty for ranged attacks, and only succeeds if the user can also spend enough ◗ to move the object. The attack deals damage equal to the silhouette of the object times ten (silhouette 0 objects deal 5 damage) plus one per ✵. If the Inquisitor wants to throw multiple objects, he must generate enough ◗ to move multiple objects, and must use the rules for Auto-fire to determine difficulty and targeting.

- **Influence:** *Force Power.* The Inquisitor may spend ◗ to inflict 2 strain (ignoring soak) on one engaged target (and may activate this multiple times). He may make an **opposed Discipline versus Discipline check** combined with an **Influence power check**. If successful, he may spend ◗ to cause the target to adopt an emotional state of rage, fear, or hatred or believe one untrue statement for one round or five minutes. He may spend ◗ to increase the duration by two additional rounds or ten additional minutes.

## STEP 7: EQUIPMENT

Game Masters should equip Inquisitors according to the needs of their story. Remember, Inquisitors have access to the limitless resources of the Galactic Empire. However, the GM should avoid over-equipping an Inquisitor. One or two weapons, some armor (if appropriate), and perhaps a piece of thematically appropriate gear should be enough. The GM can choose any gear from **Chapter V**, but here are a few suggestions:

- **Lightsaber or Pair of Lightsabers:** (Lightsaber; Damage 6; Critical 2; Range [Engaged]; Breach 1, Sunder).

- **Double-bladed Lightsaber:** (Lightsaber; Damage 6; Critical 2; Range [Engaged]; Breach 1, Linked 1, Sunder, Unwieldy 2).

- **Electrostaff:** (Melee; Damage +4; Critical 3; Range [Engaged]; Cortosis, Cumbersome 3, Linked 1, Stun setting, Unwieldy 3).

- **Heavy Blaster Rifle:** (Ranged [Heavy]; Damage 10; Critical 3; Range [Long]; Autofire, Cumbersome 3).

- **Heavy Blaster Pistol or Pair of Heavy Blaster Pistols:** (Ranged [Light]; Damage 7; Critical 3; Range [Medium]; Stun setting).

- **Armored Clothing:** (soak +1, defense +1).

- **Armored Robes:** (soak +2, defense +1).

### ADDITIONAL COMBAT TURNS

A single nemesis can have a hard time standing up to a large party of PCs, simply because the PCs have many more turns than the nemesis. If an Inquisitor is facing a PC group of 4 or more, the GM can choose to allow him to take a second turn each round. The GM should add one additional NPC slot to the Initiative order at the very end of the order. The Inquisitor may act in this turn and one other NPC initiative slot of his choice each round. Any effects that are supposed to end during his subsequent turn should end during his subsequent turn in the following round, instead. The GM should not use these rules if the Inquisitor has Improved Parry.

# LESSONS FROM THE PAST

*"By erasing the past, we ensure the success of the future."*

—Proctor Eren Garai

T housands of years ago, soured by ceaseless warfare, Jedi Master Val Isa gave up her lightsaber for a paintbrush, trading the life of a warrior for that of an artist. However, a vision of a Jedi Temple covered in blood compelled her to repurpose an old *Hammerhead*-class cruiser into a mobile hospital and temple. Her goal was to ensure that no matter what might befall the Jedi, their traditions could live on.

Meanwhile, Mandalorian warrior clans took up arms against the Republic. They struck deep into Republic territory, annexing planets in the Outer Rim and ravaging planets in the Core. Val Isa wanted to avoid battle as much as possible and used her ship to provide rescue and medical services. As the violence worsened, she attempted to hide her ship, the *Sanctuary*, in the Koler system. However, a Mandalorian strike force discovered and assaulted the vessel. The attack left the ship a half-destroyed hulk.

Val Isa perished on the *Sanctuary*, but her spirit somehow lived on in a talisman she had worn around her neck. The talisman came into the possession of a smuggler who ran afoul of the Empire and now sits in a crate, forgotten, at an Imperial university. That talisman, and Val Isa's spirit, patiently waits for a brave and worthy person to carry on the legacy of the Jedi.

## ADVENTURE SUMMARY

**Lessons from the Past** is an adventure designed to present a group of novice Force users with a wider view of the powers they wield. Specifically, it sets the PCs on the path to constructing their own lightsabers and honing their Force abilities. It also can be used to establish them in opposition to the Empire and as the catalyst for future adventures.

If the GM has a copy of the FORCE AND DESTINY GAME MASTER'S KIT, this adventure can be linked to the adventure presented there. Combined, the two adventures give any PC who wishes them the materials needed to construct a lightsaber, and noncombatant PCs a chance to enhance their own abilities. If the GM prefers to keep the two adventures separate, the rewards at the end of this adventure can be adjusted to reflect that.

As **Lessons from the Past** begins, the PCs learn of a collection of Republic artifacts at a university on the Outer Rim world Eriadu—artifacts that include Val Isa's talisman. However, Eriadu's university is guarded by an intelligence agent named Eren Garai.

Upon arrival, the PCs find their friend, a scholar named Ashur Sungazer. The scholar, both an optimist and a skeptic, wants to believe in the Jedi, but he has not yet discovered proof of their miraculous powers. As they avoid the watchful eyes of Eren Garai, the PCs and Ashur uncover the location of a lost Jedi training vessel, adrift in a dead system called Koler.

Koler is a violent red supergiant at the center of a debris field of dead ships and asteroids that hides the wreck of the *Sanctuary*. The PCs must reach the wreck and escape with Val Isa's gift: an ancient holocron that instructs the PCs in the ways of the Jedi. By inheriting her legacy, they complete a millennia-old cycle and embark on their first steps toward becoming Jedi Knights.

As the adventure begins, the GM can read the following opening crawl to the PCs:

> It is a dark time in the galaxy.
>
> Though the brave heroes of the REBEL ALLI-ANCE fight against the tyranny of the GALACTIC EMPIRE, countless worlds still tremble under the shadows of evil. The JEDI, guardians of order and justice, are gone, and at their passing the forces of darkness gather unimpeded.
>
> But all is not lost. In a distant corner of the galaxy, a small band of adventurers seeks to rediscover the legacy of the Jedi. If they are successful, perhaps hope can be restored to the galaxy once again....

## GETTING INVOLVED

This adventure assumes the PCs have a relationship with a scholar named Ashur Sungazer. Here are some suggestions on how to establish that relationship:

- In a previous adventure, they helped him out of some form of trouble. Ashur frequently travels the Outer Rim on research missions and has more curiosity and daring than common sense. The PCs saved him when he traveled with a con artist to a supposed ancient Jedi Temple, which in reality housed bandits waiting in ambush.

- Ashur and one of the PCs are family or close friends from the same planet. Both of them grew up hearing the legends of the Jedi, except Ashur considered them mere children's stories, while the PC sought them out as truth.

- The PCs don't know Ashur, but they experience a vision of the scholar hiding the talisman in a library-like archive surrounded by guards. The talisman glows brilliantly until a black-gloved hand envelopes it, plunging the vision into darkness. The hand clenches, the talisman cracks and crumbles, and the resultant sand dribbles down onto a planet, Eriadu.

If the PCs know Ashur, they receive a holomessage from him. The message resolves into a portly, bookish man with bright eyes and an innate enthusiasm. Read aloud or paraphrase the following:

> "Hello, my friends. It has been some time since we've last spoke. However, I've come across something you may find interesting."

The holomessage pans out to show various bric-a-brac laid out on examination tables among which Ashur is walking. He pauses in front of a stone talisman, and the holomessage zooms in closely, bringing it into sharper focus. He then picks up the stone and tilts it in such a way that tiny veins of color appear on the surface. In a conspiratorial whisper, he says the following:

> "I found this in the Archive at Phelar University. The crystallization in the stone reminds me of stories about lightsaber crystals, and the engravings may be several thousand years old.
>
> "I'd prefer not to speak more here; the Empire tends to censor our communications. But if you can meet me on Eriadu, I can show you this in person. Make sure you obtain some credentials; the relic cannot be removed from the University Archive, and you need to be an accredited scholar to gain access. Not that it'll prove to be a problem for you, I think." Ashur grins briefly. "Come quickly, my friends. We have much to discuss."

## THE IMPERIAL COMPLICATION

What Ashur does not know is that Imperial censors did tag his message, and they passed it to Imperial Security Bureau Agent Eren Garai for review. Garai is the head of ISB operations at Phelar University. The ISB installed him as a "University Proctor" to keep a secret watch for subversive activity.

Ashur's message certainly seems suspicious, and Garai is keeping a close eye on the scholar as a result. However, in this particular instance, Garai is actually hampered by Imperial propaganda. He sincerely believes the Jedi are a myth or a trick; thus, while he suspects the PCs may be some sort of subversives, at this stage he does not even consider the fact that they may be Force-sensitives.

The message ends with a comlink number. The PCs can use this to communicate with Ashur once they reach Eriadu.

### ASHUR SUNGAZER [RIVAL]

Ashur Sungazer is an accredited and accomplished human scholar specializing in galactic history. Though he traveled in his youth, now that he is entering middle age he has settled into a new career on Phelar. Even though Ashur grew up under Imperial rule and knows no other life, he found himself drawn to the stories and legends of the Jedi. His natural curiosity drove him to travel across the Outer Rim on research missions several years ago, and the galaxy's cruelty has not dulled his optimism.

Ashur is unsure whether the Jedi really existed, as he was only a child when the Clone Wars ended. The rational part of his mind believes Imperial propaganda, accepting that those who called themselves Jedi were likely charlatans or simply deluded. However, another, purer part of him wants to believe in the myths of heroic Jedi paladins of virtue and light.

**Skills:** Computers 2, Cool 1, Discipline 2, Knowledge (All) 3, Perception 1, Vigilance 1.
**Talents:** None.
**Abilities:** None.
**Equipment:** Breath mask, datapad, stylus.

---

## BACKGROUND: ERIADU

The PCs automatically know that Eriadu is an active trade center in the Outer Rim. They may also make an **Average (◇◇) Knowledge (Outer Rim) check** to learn the following information:

- ☼: An industrial Outer Rim world located in the Seswenna sector, Eriadu hosts over twenty billion souls, primarily humans, living under a miasma of haze and smog from rampant pollution. Its government of five noble houses resides in its capital, Eriadu City, presided over by a planetary governor. Its primary spaceport is the city of Phelar.

- ✪: The planet's industry focuses primarily on manufacturing, computer technology, droids, and servicing the Imperial drydock in orbit. The whole planet chokes on class inequalities;

power politics, wealthy titled families, and bureaucratic corruption dominate day-to-day life on Eriadu.

- ✪ ✪: The spaceport city of Phelar's primary university holds a massive collection of artifacts called the Archive, located on the Phelar University campus. The Archive possesses a surprising amount of security and only allows accredited scholars entry. The Archive has made Phelar a more diverse city, with all manner of species coming and going.

- ⊕: The late Grand Moff Tarkin came from Eriadu. Tarkin was very popular on his home planet, and his death means there is little love for Rebels and subversives here.

# ACT I: A WEALTH OF KNOWLEDGE

Traveling to the Eriadu system should not prove to be difficult for the PCs. If the PCs have their own vessel, then they can travel there directly. Since Eriadu relies heavily on trade, customs enforcement is nearly non-existent. If the PCs do not have a ship, they can hitch a ride on a passing freighter, which can get them to Eriadu in a few days. Once the group lands on Eriadu, read aloud or paraphrase the following:

> As you step off the ship, you see a bustling urbanized planet covered in industrial sprawl. Crowds of people move past the spaceport, beneath the ominous gaze of stormtroopers standing on the corners of major streets. The smog-filled air compels the people to wear decorative breath masks along with their fashionable turbans.

Once on the surface of the planet, the PCs may use the local comm grid to contact Ashur. He is happy to hear from the PCs, and is more than happy to talk with them. He agrees to meet them off campus if asked, but he points out that the artifact he wants to show them is locked in the University Archive and that it might be easier if the PCs simply gain access to the Archive and meet him there.

If the PCs want to meet Ashur before entering the Archive, Ashur suggests a small tapcafé off campus. When they meet, he tells them what he knows about the talisman (which isn't much; see page 430), but he reminds the PCs that they really should see it for themselves.

If the PCs want to meet Ashur in the University Archive, he tells them he can be found in office 182, on the 35th floor. He also reminds them they'll need identichips to prove they are accredited scholars to gain access to the Archive.

Unfortunately, Ashur cannot help the PCs obtain the identichips. The PCs can forge their own identichips by successfully making an **Average (◆ ◆) Computers check**. If they go to a forger instead, they must pay 100 credits per chip and succeed on an **Easy (◆) Streetwise check** to find someone reliable and trustworthy on Eriadu. If the PCs generate ۞ ۞ on either check, they obtain working identichips, but flaws in the design either impose ■ on checks the PCs make to deceive Eriadu security personnel or grant □ to those personnel if they interrogate or scrutinize the PCs.

If the PCs fail in their attempts to obtain an identichip, they must figure out another way to gain access to the Archive. At this point, the GM should allow the players to implement any plans that seem to have a reasonable chance of success. A few possibilities could be pretending to be a cleaning crew,

knocking out some of the security staff and posing as new recruits, or even sneaking into the Archive (if they choose this option, see page 429).

## BAD AIR

The air quality on Eriadu is poor enough that it can cause long-term health problems. Hopefully, the PCs won't be on the planet long enough to suffer long-term effects, but any PC without a rebreather (except those who don't need to breathe at all) suffers □ to all Brawn- and Agility-based checks when outdoors.

## A SHEEP AMONG WOLVES (OPTIONAL ENCOUNTER)

While the PCs are gathering identichips and wandering around campus, the GM can use this optional encounter to give them a chance to make some moral decisions, and possibly even make some new friends. Read aloud or paraphrase the following:

> As you wander the campus, you notice two security guards grab the arms of a tall, scrawny scholar and pull him behind a building, out of sight of the public. The scholar struggles, and one guard stuns him with a quick jab to his gut.

If the PCs follow the guards, they see the following:

> The guards shove the scholar onto the ground, but the scholar shouts defiantly, "I wasn't the one who sent your brother to prison. He sent himself. He shouldn't have been selling contraband."
>
> Other scholars notice the one-sided fight, but from their hurried strides and averted gazes, you can sense their fear of getting involved.

If the PCs don't intervene, the guards give the scholar, Psyrel Capanus, a sound beating, leaving him bleeding and battered in the alley. **The PCs each earn 1 Conflict for their inaction.** If the PCs intervene, they have several options to get the guards to back down, some of which can earn Conflict for the PCs.

If the PCs attempt to reason with the guards or bluff them (perhaps suggesting their superior is approaching), they must succeed on an **Average (◆ ◆) Charm** or **Deception check**. Success means the guards back off. Failure means they laugh at the PCs and tell them to get lost. The PCs can also attempt to threaten the guards, with an **Average (◆ ◆) Coercion check**. If they succeed, the guards back down, but if they fail, the guards attack the PCs for threatening them. Either way, the PC who makes the check earns 2 Conflict. Finally, the PCs can attack the guards without warning, although this results in 4 Conflict per PC, and 10 Conflict per PC if they kill the guards instead of incapacitating them. (The profile for the guards is on page 428).

If the PCs help, Psyrel conveys gratefulness that there are still "good citizens in the Empire." Psyrel, like a typical citizen of Eriadu, has wealth and ambition but remains nearsighted with regard to the faults of the Empire and is very provincial with regard to his planet. He won't hesitate to turn the PCs in to Garai if he suspects lawbreaking. However, if the PCs pass themselves off as visiting scholars and ask him for a reference to get into the Archives, he won't hesitate to provide it, adding ☐ to checks made to deceive the Archive's security forces.

# A TRIP TO THE LIBRARY

The Phelar University Archive, a relatively new, ugly, and towering skyscraper, dominates the campus. The other dozen or so buildings, while tall and imposing, sport design flourishes from the time of the Republic. Student housing surrounds those buildings, and a large security wall with over a dozen open gateways encompasses the university. Atmosphere scrubbers dot the campus, lending an odd near-subsonic hum. Various streetlamps remain lit even during the day due to the smog, issuing a misty, brownish-yellow glow.

counter. Remember, the quality of the Player Characters' identichips may add bonuses or setbacks to this encounter.

## SECURITY CHECKPOINT

To enter the Archive, the PCs must first pass a checkpoint with sensors, identichip scanners, and two security guards. Luckily for them, these guards haven't seen any real danger in years, and their monotonous questions, outdated scanners, and lax process make boredom the PCs' ally.

If the PCs' identichips don't identify them as scholars, the two security guards immediately turn them away. If they do have proper identichips, the bored security guards run through a list of basic questions: "Are you carrying any contraband or restricted materials? Are you armed, and if so, do you have a permit for your weapon?" and "Do your studies require restricted research materials?" Depending on their answers, each PC must make an **opposed Cool versus Vigilance (◆ ◆) check** to proceed through the security checkpoint unnoticed. If the PCs try to sneak in a weapon or other small object, the object should have an encumbrance no greater than 2, and the PC should make an **opposed Stealth versus Perception (◑ ◆) check** instead. If the PCs tell any significant lies during the questioning, they should make an **opposed Deception versus Discipline (◆ ◆) check** instead. Finally, if more than one of these circumstances applies, the GM should select which check is the most appropriate based on the PC's actions; generally, he should avoid having the PCs make more than one check in this en-

| 2 | 2 | 2 | 2 | 2 | 2 |
|---|---|---|---|---|---|
| BRAWN | AGILITY | INTELLECT | CUNNING | WILLPOWER | PRESENCE |

| SOAK VALUE | W. THRESHOLD | M/R DEFENSE |
|---|---|---|
| 4 | 4 | 0  0 |

**Skills (group only):** Brawl, Coercion, Melee, Perception.
**Talents:** None.
**Abilities:** None.
**Equipment:** Comlink (handheld), truncheon (Melee; Damage 4; Critical 5; Range [Engaged]; Disorient 2), padded armor (+2 soak).

If any Player Character fails the check, the GM can have the guards bar that PC from entry unless one of his quick-thinking comrades can come up with an explanation or excuse for his behavior. If the PCs succeed with ✹ ✹ or ▽, the guards let them through, but they flag them as suspicious individuals and send a report to Garai.

## ISB AGENT EREN GARAI

Any new scholars arriving at the Archive must meet with University Proctor Eren Garai for a short orientation briefing. This briefing is ostensibly to instruct the scholars in the proper procedures for handling materials and requesting restricted items while at the Archive. Of course, Eren Garai is actually an ISB agent, and he uses his position to subtly review new arrivals without drawing undue attention. Once the Player Characters pass through the security checkpoint, read aloud or paraphrase the following:

> *A thin, wiry man with a shaved head and a cybernetic brain implant approaches you wearing a dull gray and semi-official suit. He smiles pleasantly as he reaches out to shake your hands. "Welcome to Phelar and our university here! I am Proctor Eren Garai. Before we let you delve into our research materials, the university would like to give you a quick orientation tutorial. I know it sounds tedious, but we do have a certain way we like things done here."*

The PCs can attempt to convince Garai to postpone their orientation by passing an **opposed Charm** or **Deception versus Discipline (⬡ ⬡ ◆) check**. However, Garai does approach them at a later point to insist on the orientation briefing (and the GM should ensure this happens at an awkward time for the PCs: perhaps when they're deep in the middle of researching Ashur's talisman). However, if the guards at the Archive entrance flagged the PCs as suspicious, he politely but firmly insists on conducting the orientation briefing now, and cannot be dissuaded.

| 3 | 3 | 3 | 3 | 3 | 3 |
|---|---|---|---|---|---|
| BRAWN | AGILITY | INTELLECT | CUNNING | WILLPOWER | PRESENCE |

| SOAK VALUE | W. THRESHOLD | S. THRESHOLD | M/R DEFENSE |
|---|---|---|---|
| 3 | 14 | 15 | 0  0 |

**Skills:** Brawl 2, Charm 2, Coercion 2, Cool 2, Deception 2, Discipline 2, Knowledge (Education) 1, Knowledge (Xenology) 1, Perception 3, Ranged (Light) 2, Streetwise 2, Vigilance 2.
**Talents:** Adversary 2 (upgrade difficulty of all combat checks against this target twice).
**Abilities:** None.
**Equipment:** Breath mask, cybernetic brain implant, hand scanner, hidden disruptor pistol (Ranged [Light]; Damage 10; Critical 2; Range [Short]; Vicious 4, always generates a Crippled Critical Injury unless the injury would otherwise be worse).

When the PCs agree to the briefing, Garai brings them to a small, semicircular theater lecture room. In the center, a computer desk gives the lecturer several screens for manipulating a holographic projector above. Garai taps a screen, and a display of the Archive appears, rotating in the center of the projector. If the PCs were flagged as suspicious by the Archive guards, two campus security guards take up positions at the entrance to the theater lecture room. Read aloud the following:

> *"Phelar University is a major center for advanced learning in the sector, and our Archive is crucial to that effort. For that reason, we take great pains to maintain proper procedure for research efforts. Some of our artifacts are tens of thousands of years old. This knowledge must be protected, preserved, and understood."*

Garai continues in this vein for some time, discussing the proper procedures for requesting information, checking out datapads, analyzing artifacts, and reporting findings. In appearances, this should come across as a dull but informative orientation briefing. At the end of the briefing, Garai transitions into asking the PCs about their studies and areas of expertise.

Garai listens patiently to their responses, recording interviews for future analysis. At the end of the briefing, each PC must make an **opposed Charm or Deception versus Discipline (⬤⬤◆) check** or an **opposed Knowledge (Education or Xenology) versus Knowledge (Education or Xenology) (⬤◆◆) check** to convince him of the PC's scholarly background. The PCs should add ■ to the check if they mention Ashur Sungazer by name, have already been identified as his associates, or were flagged as suspicious.

Succeeding at the check indicates that Garai has no immediate desire to track and follow that particular PC. (Although by nature, he remains suspicious of everyone.) ✷ ✷ ✷ or more indicates Garai's interest in grooming that PC as a contact, mole, or agent, although he will not approach the PC about this currently, and he may not have the chance to do so before the PCs out themselves.

If a PC fails the check, Garai assigns a plainclothes agent (use the **Campus Security Guard** template, on the previous page) to accompany that PC at all times. A ▽ result changes the guard to the **Armed Security Guard** template (see page 430). Each ⬡ ⬡ adds an additional agent. The guards won't interfere with the PC's day-to-day dealings at the university, but do catalog his activities. When the group gets ready to leave Eriadu, these agents may hold the PC for further questioning.

At the end of the briefing, if everything goes well, Garai merely says:

> "If there is anything you need, please contact me. I want your stay to be both pleasant and illuminating. Good luck on your research!"

# BREAKING IN

The PCs might avoid running through the checkpoint and instead break into the Archive. If they do this, they may have to contact Ashur beforehand and get him to meet them inside after their break-in (since Ashur can enter the Archive on his own). Since the PCs remain free to walk around the university, they have the time to talk to scholars and to scout out the campus grounds. If the PCs succeed on an **Average (◆◆) Skulduggery check**, they learn the following:

- ✷: Only four armed security guards patrol the outside of the Archive during the night, on regular, four-hour shifts, watching the cargo entrance and the main entrance.
- ✷ ✷: Eight additional armed security guards patrol the interior during the night, on four-hour shifts.
- ⟁ ⟁: There are four additional emergency exits that lead into the Archive. They are locked, but not guarded.

## BEHIND THE MASK

With his gift for memorizing names and faces, Garai screens the Empire's next generation of instructors, scholars, and academics for potential sedition, "incorrect thinking," or recruitment. Garai has one blind spot: he truly believes the Empire's propaganda on the Jedi and the Force. He thinks the Jedi are merely children's stories.

If, for any reason, the PCs become suspicious of Garai, they can attempt to slice into university records and find out more about him. A successful **Daunting (◇◇◇◇) Computers check** reveals that Garai's university employment profile is false and was probably installed by a government organization. Failure means the profile looks legitimate, though any ⟁ generated on a failed check can reveal that his employment profile is too sparse for a longtime employee. ⬡ ⬡ ⬡ or ▽ can mean that the PCs' electronic intrusion is noticed by Garai.

- ⟁ ⟁ ⟁ or ✦: On the last night shift, the one before dawn, the bored and tired guards get sloppy. Decrease the difficulty of checks to break in by one.

To get inside, the PCs must slice one of the Archive entrances by succeeding on an **Average (◆◆) Computers check**. Any ⟁ generated can be spent to deactivate the following:

- Internal sensors assist the guards with regular heat signature and motion sensor sweeps.
- The guards use the building's own internal network to coordinate with each other. PCs can scramble the network and prevent them from coordinating, but the guards still can call for backup with a silent alarm.
- The interior guards can trigger a silent alarm to summon not only the security guards outside, but also Garai himself (with his own complement of **Tactical Assassin Droids**; see page 440).

If the PCs attempt to sneak past the guards at the main entrance or cargo entrance, each must succeed on an **Average (◆◆) Stealth check** to avoid being seen by the guards. However, the doors are unlocked so the guards can access the building's interior.

Once inside, each PC must make at least one additional **Easy (◆) Stealth check** to avoid being seen or heard by the roaming internal security patrols. If he fails, he is spotted by a pair of armed security guards and must deal with them in some manner. If a PC generates ⬡ ⬡ or ▽, he makes a noise and two of the guards hear and come to investigate.

## ARMED SECURITY GUARD [MINION]

The Archive's armed security forces are a subset of regular campus security. Their main difference is that they are authorized to carry weapons. However, they are under strict instructions to leave their blasters on stun unless they are confronted with deadly force.

| 2 | 2 | 2 | 2 | 2 | 2 |
|---|---|---|---|---|---|
| BRAWN | AGILITY | INTELLECT | CUNNING | WILLPOWER | PRESENCE |

| SOAK VALUE | W. THRESHOLD | M/R DEFENSE |
|---|---|---|
| 4 | 4 | 0   0 |

**Skills (group only):** Coercion, Melee, Perception, Ranged (Light).
**Talents:** None.
**Abilities:** None.
**Equipment:** Comlink (handheld), truncheon (Melee; Damage 4; Critical 5; Range [Engaged]; Disorient 2), light blaster pistol (Ranged [Light]; Damage 5; Critical 4; Range [Medium]; Stun setting), padded armor (+2 soak).

# MEETING ASHUR

When the PCs make it past the checkpoint and into the Archive proper, read or paraphrase the following:

> *In contrast to the bustling city and campus, the tall, ominous Archive building remains still and silent as a tomb. Noise suppressors keep the scattered conversations muffled, the lights remain dim, and the scent of dust and ancient things permeates the otherwise perfectly filtered air.*

The Archive contains over one hundred floors, not including the basements filled with power generators, computer cores, high-security storage units, hidden prison rooms, Garai's indoctrination and training facilities, and underground access corridors into Phelar. The outside appears dull, monolithic, and imposing.

Each floor contains the artifact storage shelves, which are rolling crates stacked neatly on top of each other. Overworked maintenance droids constantly shelve, re-shelve, and reorganize the crates on each floor. Scholars log their requests with a droid, take the received contents of the crates on plastic trays, and walk to various tables and desks to study them closely. Each desk and table has an interface by which the scholars may access the computer core.

The Archive refers not only to the building, but also to the building's vast database containing all research of the past two decades as well as the catalog of the artifacts stored in those crates. This database has no connection to the HoloNet. Each crate should have a label noting when the objects were discovered, by whom, where, and any other important information, but most are incomplete or missing.

The PCs find Ashur Sungazer waiting for them in the foyer past the security checkpoint. If the PCs have a relationship with him, Ashur gives his friends a hearty embrace and says:

> *"I'm so glad you got inside! I've been going out of my mind waiting for a chance to share in this discovery. I have a feeling about this talisman. It's not just a piece of jewelry. It's special. I know it."*

The conversation should be modified if Ashur has already met with the PCs. If the PCs don't know Ashur, they must succeed on an **opposed Charm versus Cool (⬤◆) check** to convince him they mean to help. Add ▢ due to his trusting nature. Failure means that he reports them to Garai, mistaking them as thieves.

After the introductions, Ashur takes them to the Ilum Talisman (the talisman he showed them in the message). As they walk through the Archive, he whispers the following:

> *"So, there're two problems with this talisman. Besides not knowing enough about what it is, I'm not sure where it came from, either! The university receives dozens of cultural artifacts from across the galaxy every day. They get put into storage immediately for cataloguing. Unfortunately, a lot of the paperwork is incomplete or just missing. It did come with some starship wreckage, but who knows if it's from the same dig site." Ashur smiles ruefully. "It's as frustrating as it is exciting."*

# INVESTIGATING THE ARTIFACT

The Archive has several repositories of artifacts, each of which is a large room with a single entrance. At each entrance is a window through which scholars can receive crates of artifacts from a custodian droid. Ashur checks out a crate from a droid using a long alphanumeric code. Then, he leads the PCs down another hall to a research room with a series of long tables, desks, computer terminals, and a supply of archaeological research equipment. He opens the crate and sets out a series of artifacts. The Player Characters have opportunities to investigate each of these artifacts. The GM can spend ◉ ◉ or ▽ generated on any checks made to investigate the artifacts to have Garai notice their ongoing research in the course of his routine surveillance and take an additional interest in the PCs. Remember, Garai is already keeping an eye on Ashur. He uses the Archive's surveillance systems (hidden holocams and a flagging system that tracks what artifacts each researcher checks out of the Archive) to watch him, and if the PCs' actions catch his attention, he'll use the same systems to keep tabs on them.

### AN ANCIENT HELMET CUT IN HALF

If the PCs succeed on an **Average (◆ ◆) Knowledge (Outer Rim) check**, they remember that this style of helmet came from wars with the Mandalorians waged thousands of years ago. With ❂ or ✷, they discover the following:

- The cut was made by a lightsaber.
- The Mandalorians pushed deep into Republic territory during the onslaught, getting as far as Onderon and down through to Corellia and Duro.

### AN OLD TRANSPONDER

With a successful **Average (◆ ◆) Mechanics check**, the PCs can extract an old transponder code and the name of the ship, the *Astral Jester*. With a successful **Easy (◆) Knowledge (Core Worlds) check**, the PCs remember several folktales about a modern captain of the *Astral Jester*, who claimed he knew secret hyperspace lanes through the Deep Core but never returned from one of his travels there.

### A STORMTROOPER OFFICER'S REPORT

The report notes the "acquisition" of these artifacts a little over four years ago. When played, the recording projects the following:

> *"Lieutenant TK-575 reporting. All useful cargo has been confiscated and added to our stores. The smuggler has been judged and sentenced."* You then hear the sounds of blaster fire. *"All other cargo, a transponder, helmet, electronics, and some sort of necklace, will be delivered to Eriadu. Nothing else to report."*

### AN ANCIENT DROID CONTROL CORE

PCs who succeed at a **Hard (◆ ◆ ◆) Knowledge (Core Worlds) check** discover that the partially functioning control core belongs to a Basilisk war droid. With additional ❂, the PCs can learn the following:

- The Mandalorians once rode these hulking, four-legged machines like tauntauns.
- Basilisks were semisentient.
- No one manufactures these droids anymore. The knowledge of their construction is lost to time.

Note that the control core won't help the PCs learn more about Val Isa, the Ilum Talisman, the *Sanctuary*, or Koler, but it serves as an alternate means to defeat the Basilisk. See **The Lair of the Beast**, on page 437.

### THE ILUM TALISMAN

The last object in the crate, a roughly teardrop-shaped stone chip about two-and-a-half centimeters long, with distinct but unrecognizable carvings on one side, radiates power to any Force-sensitive nearby. Tiny veins of crystals, seen only when held up to the light, give the stone an almost organic, living quality. A hole has been carved into the top and a thread woven through it so the talisman can be worn around the neck.

Succeeding on a **Hard (◆ ◆ ◆) Knowledge (Lore) check** allows the PC to recall that a Jedi Master known as Val Isa wore this charm, the Ilum Talisman. This was unusual for Jedi, since they eschewed jewelry. Additional ❂ can reveal the following:

- Val Isa guarded a "traveling sky temple."
- The talisman is also called "the weight of our history."
- This stone came from Ilum.

In addition, a successful **Hard (◆ ◆ ◆) Knowledge (Education) check** reveals that the unrecognizable carvings are actually an ancient proto-Republic dialect, spelling out "Val Isa, Jedi Master."

Using the Sense Force power allows a PC to discern the spirit of a once-living being in the talisman. Read the following aloud:

> The talisman feels like a living thing. It exudes calm and serenity. But you also sense sadness, loss, guilt, and mourning. You intuit a wish to do better, to be better, and you feel that the talisman will help you achieve this goal.

The first Force-sensitive to put the talisman on experiences a vision: the last moments of Val Isa. The GM should read aloud or paraphrase the following, shortening or elaborating as he sees fit.

> You find yourself on a stone dais, staring at a hidden safe embedded in the floor. A holocron sits nestled in the safe's center. The safe's lid, a stone block the size of an astromech droid, lies off to one side.
>
> The dais stands in the middle of a large chamber made of dark stone, perhaps thirty meters wide and just as tall. Stone walkways arc in circular patterns around the chamber.
>
> Even as you lift the stone block into place over the hidden safe, the chamber shudders and you hear distant explosions rumble. You turn to your students and the crew of your starship. One, wearing an officer's uniform, looks up from his comlink. "Master Isa. The Mandalorians have breached the hull!"
>
> You nod firmly. "Go. I will hold them here. You can still escape in the Sanctuary's shuttle."
>
> Your students protest, but you accept no argument. In a moment they've fled, leaving you alone. You kneel down on the dais, your lightsaber sitting on the stone before you. Soon, the sounds of combat fill the halls, and a pack of armored warriors bursts into the chamber. You look at them calmly. "I do not seek a fight."
>
> The warriors howl and leap at you, weapons drawn. You wait calmly, until they are moments away. Then your lightsaber flies into your hand, and you spring forward to fight your last battle.

As the vision fades, the PC senses Val's parting words:

> "Do not follow my example. Jedi cannot retreat from the world. They must struggle, succeed, and fail with the rest of the galaxy."

Nobody else who puts on the talisman will experience the vision.

# PUTTING CLUES TOGETHER

At this point, the PCs have just enough information to ask the right questions, and with a large repository of galactic knowledge at their fingertips, they can get answers quickly. Whatever subjects they wish to explore, present to them the Archive's many well-researched theses with a mix of factual history and blatant propaganda. Use the following as examples:

- **If the PCs research the *Sanctuary*:** The Archive has hundreds of documents on the fleet sizes of the Republic. The Archive does have a flight record from the *Sanctuary*, a "support ship," which lists the following worlds and systems: **Fedalle** (an industrial world in the Core), **Rendili** (an industrial world in the Core known for its stardrives), **Koler** (a red supergiant system), **Duro**, and **Exodeen** (an Imperial planet in the Colonies).

- **If the PCs research the *Astral Jester*:** A hundred years ago, the captain of the *Astral Jester* filed dozens of well-documented erroneous flight plans, hoping to establish a claim for a Deep Core hyperspace lane. The flight plans detail lanes from **Coruscant** to **Fedalle**, **Koler**, **Khomm** (a Deep Core planet with a genetically modified biosphere), and **Mauphin** (a minor Core system trailing Daupherm).

- **If the PCs research the Mandalorian Wars or the planet of Mandalore:** A good number of papers document the losses the Republic took on **Churr** (a minor farming world near Quellor), **Commenor** (a wealthy planet in the Colonies), **Duro**, and **Koler**.

- **If the PCs research the Basilisk war droid or the planet of Basilisk:** The Archive and the Empire officially believe the Basilisk war droids to be myth. Research missions to the Basilisk system have revealed only a primitive reptilian species. Fabled sightings of war droids occurred on worlds including **Basilisk** (an environmentally damaged Core World), **Gefthaine** (a primitive forest world near Mandalore), **Koler**, and **Mandalore** (the Outer Rim world where the Mandalorian clans originated).

- **If the PCs research Lieutenant TK-575:** The Archive contains records of older, declassified military mission reports. The PCs can discover TK-575's tour of duty, which included a winding path from **Commenor** to **Exodeen**, **Empress Teta** (near Koler), and **Lamman** (an asteroid system trailing Duro) hunting for criminals, smugglers, and contraband.

- **If the PCs research Val Isa:** The highly redacted records around Val Isa depict her as a mad, reclusive painter and any associations with Jedi powers as merely children's stories. Curiously, there are no images of her paintings and only one mention of specific titles, these being "**Bespin: air**," "**Dantooine: stone**," "**Koler: fire**," and "**Mon Calamari: water**."

- **If the PCs research Ilum:** The few, highly redacted papers suggest that the Jedi believed crystals contained nature spirits. Other papers suggest that the crystals of **Ilum** possess toxins that caused hallucinations, giving rise to the myths of the Jedi's supernatural powers. No scholar managed to set foot on Ilum; all the papers borrow heavily from Imperial ground and survey reports.

- No information on the **Ilum Talisman** exists in the Archive.

- **If a PC uses Seek:** If any PC uses the Seek power successfully, the power points him in the direction of the Core.

- **If the PCs research Koler:** The PCs don't find mention of Koler besides its pseudo-legendary status as a system of lost ships, but due to the instability of hyperspace lanes in the Deep Core, every system in that section of space has that reputation. As a red supergiant star system, it likely has no inhabitable planets.

This is a process-of-elimination puzzle for the players. All of the above entries have Koler in common; this is the PCs' next destination and the resting place of the *Sanctuary*. If the PCs need additional help figuring this out, the GM can have one make an **Average (◆ ◆) Discipline check** while meditating on the problem. Success means the PC's mind fixates on the "Koler: fire" painting by Val Isa.

---

### THE ILUM TALISMAN

The Ilum Talisman can do more than guide Force users to the wreck of the *Sanctuary*. It can also help a Force user calm himself and use his abilities. This talisman has no price associated with it; Force users may find it priceless, but most people see it as a curio. However, when a Force-sensitive character wears it, once per session he may add ◗ to any one check.

---

# FLEEING THE ARCHIVE

When the PCs decide to leave the Archive to head to Koler, Ashur immediately volunteers to accompany them. The PCs can attempt to convince him to stay. However, Ashur is very excited, and the PCs must succeed at an **opposed Charm versus Cool (◆ ◆) check** (or **opposed Coercion versus Discipline (◆ ◆) check** if they want to threaten) to convince him to stay.

The larger problem the PCs face is how to deal with Garai's surveillance. How difficult it is to elude the ISB agent depends on how much the PCs have aroused his suspicions over the course of their activities. The PCs could have provoked his interest if they acted suspiciously when entering the Archives, if they generated too many ✹ when interacting with him or during the course of their research, or if they generated too many ✹ when researching Garai directly. How suspicious these activities have made Garai is up to the GM (who should base Garai's suspicions on how often the PCs have drawn his attention).

For simplicity's sake, the GM should select one of three possibilities: Garai is mostly oblivious to the PCs' intentions, Garai is moder-

ately suspicious of the PCs, or Garai is convinced the PCs are seditionists and is waiting to arrest them.

If Garai is oblivious to the Player Characters' true intentions, the PCs have a good chance of sneaking out of the Archives unimpeded and escaping offworld before Garai realizes that they've gone. Each PC should make an **Easy (◆) Deception, Stealth,**

## IN THE BELLY OF THE BEAST

At several points during this adventure, the PCs may fail to evade Garai's grasp, and some or all may be captured.

While that result lies beyond the scope of this adventure, it does not necessarily mean the PCs are doomed. They still have two minor but significant advantages. First, while knowledgeable about the Empire's cultural enemy, Garai does not believe in the Jedi or the Force. Second, he believes that anyone and everyone can be corrupted.

The PCs have a chance to escape if they can convince Garai that they are mere criminals. A successful **opposed Charm** or **Deception versus Perception check** means that Garai takes them "under his wing" as potential Imperial agents.

Also, if only some of the party are captured, the GM has the option of having Garai bring them along with him as he pursues their friends to Koler. This may provide the captured PCs with a chance to escape at the climax of the adventure.

or **Cool check** to leave the Archive unnoticed (the type of check depends on whether they lie their way out, sneak out, or brazenly walk out without generating suspicion). The check represents the possibility that Garai or a guard notices something strange about the PCs at the last minute. Add ■ to any PC's check if that PC attempts to leave with an artifact. If any of the PCs fail the check, proceed to **Facing the Music,** below. Otherwise, they make it to the spaceport.

If Garai is moderately suspicious, the PCs must make a **Hard (◆ ◆ ◆) Deception**, **Stealth**, or **Cool check** to leave unnoticed. Add ■ ■ to the check of any PC who tries to leave with an artifact. If they fail, Garai notices them leaving. He already planned to stop them for questioning, and he moves to apprehend them. Proceed to **Facing the Music**.

If Garai is convinced the PCs are Rebels or seditionists, the PCs cannot escape unnoticed. As soon as they attempt to leave the Archive, Garai, leading a group of armed security guards, attempts to apprehend them. Proceed to **Facing the Music**.

## FACING THE MUSIC

If the PCs are noticed while leaving the Archive and Garai has reason to try to apprehend them, read aloud or paraphrase the following as soon as the PCs leave the Archive building.

*The campus lights suddenly take on an ugly, off-yellow tint: the signal that the university is on alert. You notice the crowds of scholars tense up as they look about to find the source of trouble.*

*On various computer monitors, both public and personal, you see your images, (assumed) names, and identichip numbers displayed, along with the text "wanted for questioning."*

If Garai was moderately suspicious or certain the PCs were seditionists, the PCs should immediately spot a squad of six armed security guards (two minion groups of three) pushing their way through the crowd

toward them. The encounter begins with the PCs and guards at medium range. The guards attempt to close with the PCs and attack with their truncheons and blaster pistols set to stun. However, the crowds mean both groups must treat the area as difficult terrain for the first two rounds (at which point the crowd scatters and leaves the area clear).

If Garai was oblivious to the PCs' intentions, the GM should have the PCs noticed by four campus security guards (page 428) rather than six armed guards. Read or paraphrase the following encounter instead.

*"Hey, you!" You look to see a group of four campus security guards heading toward you. The one in front has his baton out and is pointing in your direction. "I need you to come with us!"*

In either encounter, the PCs can attempt to flee or fight, depending on their preference. If they manage to move to extreme range, they flee into the surrounding city. Likewise, if they manage to defeat the guards, they have a few minutes to flee before reinforcements arrive.

If the PCs appear to be losing, an air purity warning sounds and the haze thickens. The PCs can now attempt to lose the guards in the miasma, weaving through the overworked air purifiers and alleyways in-between the academic buildings and dorms. Each PC must succeed on an **opposed Stealth versus Perception (◇ ◇) check** to get lost in the haze.

If a PC fails the check, then he runs into a single armed security guard at short range who immediately moves to subdue with a truncheon. After a couple of rounds, have the PC make another **opposed Stealth versus Perception (◇ ◇) check** to get lost in the haze.

Even when they escape, the PCs still haven't eluded Garai's grasp. The intelligence agent doesn't want to risk a high-speed chase through the streets of the capital, so he simply calls ahead to the spaceport to put all ships on lockdown. The Archive becomes inaccessible to them, although a friendly NPC may still do research on their behalf. See the section **Traveling to Koler**, on the following page for information on the lockdown.

# TRAVELING TO KOLER

Reaching the spaceport should not prove very difficult. However, if the Player Characters have their own ship, they must make it to the spaceport before Garai issues a lockdown order for any ships that could possibly belong to the PCs. They must pass an **Easy (◆) Piloting (Planetary) check** with ■ due to traffic or must each pass an **Average (◆◆) Athletics check** (depending on whether they're on foot or in a speeder) to reach the spaceport before the lockdown order. If they succeed, they may lift off before the order goes through. Proceed to **Act II: The Wreck of the Sanctuary**, below.

If the PCs cannot reach the spaceport in time, they still have several chances to escape. Garai cannot lock down every ship in a busy commercial spaceport, and he is unsure which ship belongs to the PCs. He must settle for interdicting any light freighters that have arrived in the last several days. The spaceport complies, using ground-based tractor beams to hold the starships in their landing pads while spaceport security goes from ship to ship investigating each in turn. The PCs have a half hour before security reaches theirs.

Each spaceport dock consists of a cylindrical blast wall with an open ceiling and doors and hatches large enough for freight transports and foot traffic. Inside the dock, the ship sits in the middle of some basic maintenance equipment and refueling stations. Upon lockdown, the blast doors and hatches seal shut, and a tractor beam keeps the ship grounded. To rescind or defeat the lockdown, the PCs have several options:

- They can access the spaceport data-net via their landing bay terminal. By passing a **Hard (◆◆◆)** **Computers check** with ■, they can override the lockdown and shut off the tractor beam that secures their ship to the dock.

- A quick trip to one of the adjoining landing bays reveals a light freighter cleared to leave. A successful **Average (◆◆) Skulduggery check** or any Force power that allows a PC to read thoughts can obtain the starship's takeoff clearance. The PCs can use that clearance code to rescind their own lockdown and leave. The PC who does so gains 2 Conflict.

- When the security patrol (two minion groups of three armed security guards [page 430]) arrives, the PCs can attempt to deceive it into thinking they are not the fugitives Garai is looking for. An **opposed Deception versus Discipline (◆◆) check** or a Force power that influences people's thoughts can accomplish this. Otherwise, the PCs can attempt to incapacitate the security patrol, then bluff spaceport control by using the patrol's comlinks. This simply requires an **Average (◆◆) Deception check** once the patrol is disabled.

Finally, if the PCs arrived on the planet without a ship of their own, the GM can give the PCs a chance to procure passage on another freighter or steal a starship. The GM can have the PCs use any of the previous encounters to represent obtaining clearance for a charted freighter, or for stealing an Imperial shuttle.

Once the PCs escape, Garai begins an immediate pursuit. He follows the PCs closely in a shuttle (he has no time to call for backup), staying just far away enough not to be noticed. He returns in the adventure climax.

# ACT II: THE WRECK OF THE *SANCTUARY*

Koler, a system on the edge of the Deep Core, contains an ancient red supergiant slowly shedding its atmosphere, a few rocky planets (once gas giants) in unstable orbits, an asteroid field, and the debris of destroyed starships. The wreck of the *Sanctuary* sits in the middle of a cluster of asteroids, so battered and ancient that it has become nearly indistinguishable from the tumbling rocks around it.

Getting to Koler requires an **Average (◆◆) Astrogation check** at minimum, barring exacerbating circumstances such as pursuit, damage, and navicomputer problems. Since the system sits in the Deep Core, the check has a ■■ penalty. Failure means the PCs' ship suffers a Critical Hit as it comes out of hyperspace into a clutch of asteroids or the edges of a solar flare, as per rules for minor collisions (page

248). Success means that the ship arrives at their destination without suffering damage.

## LOCATING THE SANCTUARY

The PCs need to make a **Piloting (Space) check**, adding ■■■ due to the asteroids, old starship debris, and high-radiation solar wind, and with a difficulty set as per the rules in **Stellar Phenomena and Terrain** (page 246). ✷ means they reach the *Sanctuary*. ▼ means they must try again. ⊙ can inflict system strain on the ship, while ⊙ ⊙ ⊙ or ▽ can have the PCs notice a high-speed asteroid or plasma wavefront on a collision course with their ship. They must succeed on an **Average (◆◆) Piloting (Space)** or **Gunnery check**, or suffer a major collision as per the rules on page 248.

# THE WRECK

Only half of the *Sanctuary* survived the attack and subsequent secondary explosions, which split it roughly down the middle from bow to stern. Now, it looks like a gothic tower with twisted structural beams for spires and electrical arcs for lanterns. The *Sanctuary* still has a thin atmosphere, since repair systems and long-dead droids patched up the hull breaches after the battle.

If the PCs succeed on an **Average (◆ ◆) Perception check**, they find the **Sternward Airlock**. If they fail, they find the **Forward Airlock** instead. Any PC who experienced the vision from the Talisman automatically knows of the **Sternward Airlock** near the central dome structure and the **Jedi Training Room**.

# SANCTUARY LAYOUT

The *Sanctuary*, an old *Hammerhead*-class cruiser retooled as an emergency rescue cruiser, retained some of its basic armaments, but Val Isa wanted the ship to be a bastion of learning, meditation, and Jedi practice. She had hoped the ship's mobility would let it avoid a destructive end, but the assault by the Mandalorians proved her wrong.

As the PCs explore the wreck, the GM can heighten the tension by describing the creepy atmosphere and ancient desolation, and by calling on the PCs to make fear checks. The GM can have the PCs make an **Easy (◆) fear check** as a plasma wavefront buffets the ship, causing it to creak and moan alarmingly. Failure can cause the PCs to be disoriented for the rest of the encounter, and ⊛ can inflict strain. Partway through the exploration, the GM can have the PCs make an **Average (⬡ ◆) fear check** with one difficulty upgrade as they hear a bone-chilling howl from the Basilisk war droid. Failure here can cause the PCs to cower in terror or suffer more severe effects, as detailed on page 326. ▽ should inflict 2 Conflict.

Notable features, from bow to stern, include:

### BRIDGE SUPPORT

The actual bridge, now gone, used to sit one deck above this one. This room handled sensors and communications. The sensors, long fried from exposure to solar radiation, cause random power spikes. An ancient protocol droid, plugged into the communications system, has lost its mobility and independence. For all intents and purposes, the droid simply acts as a voice for the comms system. With an **Easy (◆) Computers check**, the PCs can transmit a scrambled signal to attract the Basilisk to this location (which may be useful for luring it into a trap). Each ⊛ inflicts 1 strain from the electrical shocks. If the PC fails the check, he still rigs up the signal, but he suffers 3 wounds from a particularly unpleasant jolt.

### TURBOLASER BATTERY ROOM

A pressure hatch at the rear of bridge support leads to the cramped battery control room directly behind it. The independent power cells of the battery still function. A clever PC can rig these power cells to overload and explode in two rounds with a successful **Average (◆ ◆) Mechanics check**. Upon detonation, everything in the room gets vaporized (PCs can be incapacitated with a +50 Critical Injury roll at the GM's discretion), and the explosion bursts into bridge support. Any being in bridge support must make a successful **Average (◆ ◆) Coordination check** or suffer 8 wounds. Even with a successful check, if the check generated ⊛ ⊛ ⊛, the being still suffers 4 wounds from the blast.

### FORWARD AIRLOCK AND FREIGHT ELEVATOR

A functioning airlock is located close to bridge support. A freight elevator takes up the whole of the airlock's interior but remains non-functional.

### HOSPITAL/MEDICAL LABS

This section is open to space. Nothing of value survived the vacuum and exposure to Koler's unrelenting solar winds.

### REPAIR BAY AND GENERAL STORAGE

This section once supported the hangar in the deck below, but Val Isa converted it into a repair bay, general storage, and a hospital. Over the centuries, the Basilisk and the repair droid have ripped out wiring, bulkheads, and infrastructure for raw material for repairs. As such, this section is now a junk pile of spaceship hulls, droid parts, and even a single oil bath tank full of black, rancid, murky oil.

The repair droid barely functions, having taken parts from itself to maintain the Basilisk. If the PCs succeed on an **Average (◆ ◆) Computers check**, they can give it instructions to install the control core on the Basilisk war droid. See **The Lair of the Beast**, on the next page.

If the PCs entered through the forward airlock, they find the Basilisk in this room.

### JEDI TRAINING ROOM

See the section **Hero's Legacy**, on page 439.

### STERNWARD AIRLOCK

This functioning airlock is located near the science labs. A freight elevator takes up most of the interior but remains non-functional.

### CREW QUARTERS

The crew quarters on this deck are forward of the Jedi training room. During the first hull breach, several bulkhead doors closed and sealed off the crew quarters from the rest of the ship. Without power, the PCs need to manually crank open the bulkheads through a successful **Average (◆ ◆) Mechanics check** just to traverse this section. If they fail the check, the PCs suffer 3 strain due to the time and effort.

## SCIENCE LABS 1 AND 2

This section once housed several small laboratories, some of which supported the hospital and others which were devoted to pure science. Equipment, beakers, and machinery lie scattered and shattered throughout both labs.

In Lab 1, the PCs find a still-functioning electromagnet. With an **Average (◇ ◇) Mechanics check**, they can rig it to fire once before burning out. If the electromagnet fires, everyone in the room must make an **Average (◇ ◇) Resilience check** or suffer 4 strain (12 strain if a droid) and temporarily lose their metallic possessions, as the metallic items fly into the magnet. Any computer systems, such as datapads and comlinks, stop functioning for twenty minutes due to being shorted out by the electromagnetic pulse.

In Lab 2, the PCs find a still-functioning particle accelerator. With a **Hard (◇ ◇ ◇) Mechanics check**, they can jury-rig the accelerator into a one-shot blaster cannon (Ranged [Heavy]; Damage 15; Critical 2; Range [Short]; Ammo 1, Cumbersome 5).

## ENGINEERING

In this ravaged section, split in half by a giant bulkhead door, a single surviving power plant still powers the malfunctioning gravity generators. If the PCs wish, they can put the power plant and gravity generators on a feedback loop that will cause the ship to collapse in on itself and explode, providing excellent cover for their escape. This requires an **Average (◇ ◇) Computers** or **Mechanics check**. The explosion occurs after about five minutes. Each 🝑 can subsequently double or halve the time, depending on which is more advantageous to the PCs. See **Escaping Koler**, page 440.

## STARBOARD ENGINEERING ANNEX

A narrow service corridor connects engineering to this annex. The controls no longer function; its associated engine is long destroyed. However, the PCs might be able to salvage parts to repair their ship. If they make an **Average (◇ ◇) Mechanics check**, each ☆ or 🝑 provides about 500 credits' worth of material to repair hull trauma.

# THE LAIR OF THE BEAST

During the assault on the *Sanctuary*, a Mandalorian warrior perished, and her Basilisk war droid refused to leave her corpse behind. Over the centuries, the Basilisk has maintained a relatively low power profile, activating every so often to patrol the wreck.

A little over four years ago, a salvage ship accidentally jumped into the system. The ship docked with

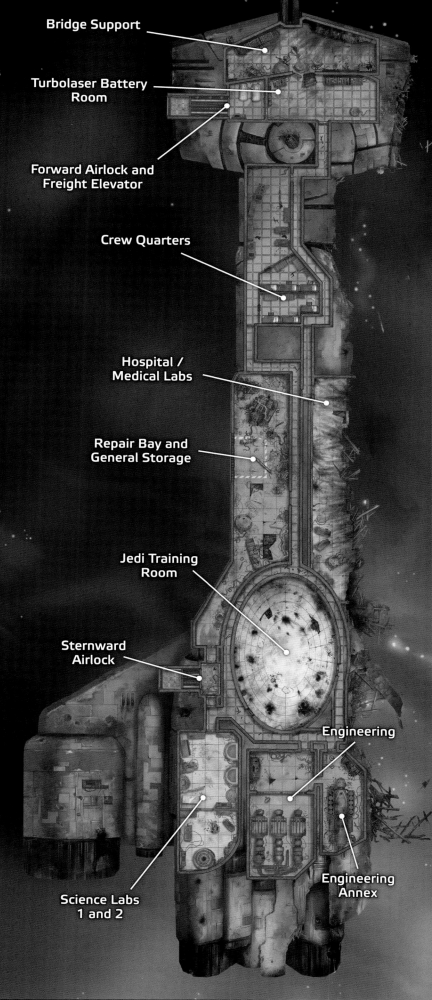

Bridge Support

Turbolaser Battery Room

Forward Airlock and Freight Elevator

Crew Quarters

Hospital / Medical Labs

Repair Bay and General Storage

Jedi Training Room

Sternward Airlock

Engineering

Engineering Annex

Science Labs 1 and 2

the *Sanctuary*, and the Basilisk immediately attacked its crew. This salvager managed to grab various bits and parts, including the Ilum Talisman, and left his crew to die on the *Sanctuary*. He escaped only to soon meet his fate at the hands of a stormtrooper firing squad. The Basilisk still hunts the *Sanctuary* hallways, expecting either its masters to return or new enemies to arrive.

It is up to the GM as to where the PCs may encounter the Basilisk war droid for the first time, but he should allow them some time to explore the wreck beforehand. When the PCs first encounter the Basilisk, read or paraphrase the following aloud:

> *Old servos and ancient mechanisms simulate labored breathing as a massive, four-legged metal beast creeps out from the shadows. Though it once must have been symmetrical, centuries of patchwork repairs using the parts of other droids have turned this powerful mechanized creature into an ugly, hulking nightmare of metal and rust. It growls and gets ready to pounce.*

If the PCs are not too busy running or fighting for their lives, they can make a **Daunting (◇ ◇ ◇ ◇) Knowledge (Lore) check** to identify the creature as a Basilisk war droid.

### DAMAGED BASILISK [NEMESIS]

In the ancient days of the Mandalorian Wars, the Mandalorians rode into battle on nightmarish war droids called Basilisks. More sentient than most droids, Basilisks were heavily armed and could even fly through space. Most were destroyed when the Mandalorians lost the war thousands of years ago, and most of the galaxy has mercifully forgotten they exist.

| BRAWN | AGILITY | INTELLECT | CUNNING | WILLPOWER | PRESENCE |
|-------|---------|-----------|---------|-----------|----------|
| 5 | 2 | 1 | 3 | 1 | 1 |

| SOAK VALUE | W. THRESHOLD | S. THRESHOLD | M/R DEFENSE | |
|-----------|--------------|--------------|-------------|---|
| 7 | 22 | 22 | 0 | 0 |

**Skills:** Melee 2, Vigilance 3.
**Talents:** Adversary 1 (upgrade difficulty of all combat checks against this target once), Crippling Blow (increase the combat difficulty by one; if the target suffers wounds, then the target suffers 1 strain each time he moves for the rest of the encounter), Knockdown (may spend ⊕ to knock target prone with successful melee attack).
**Abilities:** Droid (does not need to breathe, eat, or drink, and can survive in vacuum and underwater; immune to poisons and toxins), Silhouette 2.
**Equipment:** Claws (Melee; Damage 7; Critical 2; Range [Engaged]; Vicious 1).

The Basilisk has a larger silhouette than the PCs. It traverses the *Sanctuary* through the main corridors, but the PCs can utilize smaller service corridors and crawlspaces to escape. Evading the Basilisk this way requires a successful **opposed Athletics** or **Coordination versus Athletics (◇ ◇ ◇ ◇ ◇) check**.

### COMBINING THIS ADVENTURE WITH THE GAME MASTER'S KIT

This adventure is designed to be used before or after the GAME MASTER'S KIT adventure, **Hidden Depths**. In that adventure, the Player Characters have the opportunity to gather their own crystals with which to build their lightsabers. The GAME MASTER'S KIT also describes how to build a lightsaber hilt, and the PCs can find this information in Val Isa's holocron.

However, if the GM does not want to combine the adventures, he can choose to instead make lightsabers available to the PCs at the climax of **Lessons from the Past** instead. If he does so, he can put two basic lightsabers in the vault and have Val Isa's lightsaber found as well. See page 176 for a basic lightsaber profile.

If the PCs kept the control core from the Archive, they can use it to help them weaken the Basilisk. A successful **Average (◇ ◇) Mechanics check** makes the core semi-operational. If a PC manages to install the core in the droid (a **Hard (◇ ◇ ◇) Coordination check** while engaged), the droid suffers □ □ to all actions as it eats up processing power. Due to age and damage, the core cannot be used to directly control a droid. Each ⚉ ⚉ represents additional bad code that adds another □ to the Basilisk's checks.

If the PCs reprogram the repair droid in the repair bay, they can have it install the core when the Basilisk returns from its patrol. See **Repair Bay and General Storage**, page 436.

# HERO'S LEGACY

When the PCs find the Jedi training room, read or paraphrase the following aloud:

*The room appears almost exactly like it did in your vision. However, only a few sections of the winding walkways and platforms remain intact. Instead, the now wide-open chamber has a cathedral-like stillness, and rubble surrounds the central dais.*

*The Jedi robes of Val Isa lie sprawled in the middle of the dais over the location of the safe in your vision. Surrounding the robes lie the remnants of her foes; armor is scattered all about, and the ground is covered in the dust of stone, metal, and the long-decayed and deteriorated remnants of the deceased.*

SANCTUARY'S REWARDS

## SANCTUARY'S REWARDS

The holocron of the *Sanctuary* contains a mnemonic imprint of Val Isa's personality, recorded before her death. Her personality manifests itself as a serene older human woman with a hint of impish humor about her. Of course, while very lifelike, the holocron's personality is not truly sentient, though it may be hard to tell this at times.

The holocron of the *Sanctuary* is intended to be a tool the PCs can use to learn about the ancient Jedi Order. It is not an unlimited fount of information, of course, and its knowledge is several thousand years old (so it knows nothing of current events). However, it contains a great deal of basic Jedi instruction, which allows the GM and players to explain how the PCs are able to learn Jedi Force practices and train with lightsabers, for example.

The holocron also grants the following mechanical benefits to the party:

- Each PC may count Discipline and Medicine as career skills as long as the group possesses the holocron.

- When making a Knowledge (Lore) check to learn about the Jedi, the PCs may use the holocron to make an assisted check. The holocron counts as having three ranks in Knowledge (Lore).

Searching the robes reveals very little. Val Isa's lightsaber is missing. The floor appears seamless, and no handle or markings hint at the existence of the safe. If a PC who experienced the vision tries to find it, he can do so with a successful **Average (◇ ◇) Perception check**. If he did not experience the vision, the check becomes **Daunting (◇ ◇ ◇ ◇)**. The GM can allow players to retry the check at a later point in the adventure, after a prolonged search, if they fail the first time.

The easiest way to open the safe requires a PC to use the Move Force power. Originally designed as a Jedi exercise, the block over the safe has silhouette 1. The block can also be removed manually with a successful **Hard (◇ ◇ ◇) Athletics check**. Failing the check means suffering 3 strain.

Inside the safe, the PCs find a single holocron (see the **Sanctuary's Rewards** sidebar).

If the PCs haven't encountered the Basilisk yet, it appears here.

# GARAI'S ARRIVAL

**W**hen the PCs discover the Jedi training room or if they spend an inordinate amount of time exploring the *Sanctuary*, Garai arrives at Koler in an ISB covert ops ship, a *Simiyiar*-class light freighter called the *Starhound*. Garai has four tactical assassin droids in the cargo hold, ready to board the wreck of the *Sanctuary*.

If the PCs docked their ship to the wreck of the *Sanctuary*, Garai misses it on his first scans and moves to board the *Sanctuary*. If the PCs left their ship in the open, or if someone is still aboard, Garai moves to disable it with ion cannons first. If there is an NPC pilot aboard the PC's ship, the GM can have the NPC move the ship deeper into the asteroid field while Garai focuses on the wreck of the *Sanctuary*, which he correctly guesses is the true prize. If the GM needs the profile for the *Starhound*, use the *Simiyiar* profile on page 264.

At this point, Garai moves to board the *Sanctuary*. Instead of using an airlock, he adheres the *Starhound* directly to the hull and cuts through into the interior. He then boards the ship with his droids. He leaves the *Starhound*'s three command crew (use the TIE Pilot profile, on page 408) to guard the ship. He stays with his droids and hunts through the *Sanctuary*, looking for the PCs. He would like to take at least one PC alive, but if the PCs use deadly force, he responds in kind.

## TACTICAL ASSASSIN DROID [RIVAL]

| 3 | 3 | 1 | 2 | 1 | 1 |
|---|---|---|---|---|---|
| BRAWN | AGILITY | INTELLECT | CUNNING | WILLPOWER | PRESENCE |

| SOAK VALUE | W. THRESHOLD | M/R DEFENSE | |
|---|---|---|---|
| 5 | 14 | 0 | 0 |

**Skills:** Melee 2, Ranged (Light) 1, Vigilance 3.
**Talents:** None.
**Abilities:** Droid (does not need to breathe, eat, or drink, and can survive in vacuum and underwater; immune to poisons and toxins).
**Equipment:** Force pike (Melee; Damage 6; Critical 2; Range [Engaged]; Pierce 2, Stun setting [if Stun setting is used, Pierce does not apply]), integral wrist blaster (Ranged [Light]; Damage 5; Critical 3; Range [Medium]; Stun setting).

## CONFRONTING GARAI

How the GM manages the confrontation between the PCs and Garai depends on the PCs' prior actions, and whether the PCs take immediate action upon his arrival.

If the PCs took a long time to defeat the Basilisk and explore the wreck, or if they do not respond to Garai's arrival immediately, Garai has time to locate the PCs and attack them with his full force. In this case, Ga-

rai confronts the PCs in one of the locations of the GM's choosing, backed up by all four tactical assassin droids. If the PCs have three or fewer players, reduce the number of tactical assassin droids to two. If the PCs have five or more players, add another tactical assassin droid.

If the PCs dealt with the basilisk right away, explored the wreck quickly, or immediately took steps to deal with Garai when he arrived, they can deal with his forces in two groups instead of one. The first group they encounter has two tactical assassin droids. The second group has Garai and the remaining tactical assassin droids.

Besides fighting Garai directly, there are several options canny PCs could use to deal with him, including:

- **Getting the Basilisk to attack Garai:** Once Garai boards the *Sanctuary*, he becomes fair game for the Basilisk (if it is still active). If the PCs wish to lure the droid toward Garai to pit them against each other, have one of the PCs and Garai make a **competitive Perception check** to represent the PC trying to avoid the Basilisk while Garai tries to search for the PCs. The loser ends up confronting the Basilisk.

- **Boarding Garai's ship:** The PCs can hijack Garai's ship if they manage to evade him in the wreck. The hardest part is getting inside the vessel, as the lock on the outer hatch requires a **Hard (◆ ◆ ◆) Computers check** to open. Once inside, they must fight the ship's command crew.

## ESCAPING KOLER

Luckily, if the PCs eliminate the powerful ISB agent, the *Starhound*'s command crew detach from the wreck and flee immediately.

If the PCs wish to flee instead of confronting Garai and they make it off the wreck, they can make an **Average (◆ ◆) Astrogation check** as soon as their ship leaves the wreck. Success means they can jump after three rounds, and each 😊 reduces the time to jump by one round. In this scenario, the *Starhound* starts within long range of the PCs' ship and attempts to close the distance and engage it.

### EXPERIENCE REWARDS

Besides the usual XP rewards granted for each session, the GM can give additional XP for the following:

- +10 XP for escaping Phelar without arousing Garai's suspicions.

- +10 XP for defeating the Basilisk.

- +5 XP for recovering the holocron.

# INDEX

## PLAYTESTERS

Fantasy Fight Games would like to thank the following people for their hard work playtesting FORCE AND DESTINY. "Tuesday Night Follies" Chris Carlson with Howard Bein, Norm Carlson, Bill Cheesman, Pat Hall, Jason Orman, Julia Trimboli, and Daniel Walker. "Anozira Sector Rangers" Vincent Schelzo with Ian Dimitri and Jim Stone. "Low Rollers" Jay Wantland with Djinn Ferguson, Sean Leary, Brittany Thomas, and Teresa Wantland. "HK2" Jason Keeping with Harrison Keeping and Holly Keeping. "It's Worse" John "Drew" Hamilton with Kirsten Dahlberg, Mark Daube, Jason Gilbertson, Tim Haldane, and Kyle Traylor. "Death Star Contractors" Craig Atkins with Mark Charlesworth, Josh Jupp, Doug Ruff, and

Nathan Wilkinson. "Corellia's Finest" Rainer Winstel with Matthias Jelinek, Manuel Vögele, Matthias Vögele, Erik Winstel, and Timo Winstel. "Dark Side Cookies" Katrina Ostrander with Alex Guenther, Will Herrmann, Josh Lease, and James Quam. "Conflict In Action" Sam Stewart with Justin Baller, Max Brooke, Daniel Lovat Clark, Tim Flanders, Michael Gernes, Zoë Robinson, and Jonathan Ying. "Plausibly Deniable" Joshua Callaway, Grace Holdinghaus, Harrison Lavin, James Meier, Alexandar Ortloff, and Mark Underwood. William Coughlan. Dominic Tauer. Alex Zemanek.

In addition, FFG would like to thank those who participated in the FORCE AND DESTINY Beta Test.

## CHARACTER

**CHARACTER NAME**

SPECIES

CAREER

SPECIALIZATION TREES

FORCE RATING

### STAR WARS™
# FORCE
## AND DESTINY
### ROLEPLAYING GAME

PLAYER

| SOAK VALUE | WOUNDS | | STRAIN | | DEFENSE | |
|---|---|---|---|---|---|---|
| | THRESHOLD | CURRENT | THRESHOLD | CURRENT | RANGED | MELEE |

## CHARACTERISTICS

| BRAWN | AGILITY | INTELLECT | CUNNING | WILLPOWER | PRESENCE |
|---|---|---|---|---|---|

## SKILLS

| GENERAL SKILLS | CAREER? | RANK |
|---|---|---|
| Astrogation (Int) | | |
| Athletics (Br) | | |
| Charm (Pr) | | |
| Coercion (Will) | | |
| Computers (Int) | | |
| Cool (Pr) | | |
| Coordination (Ag) | | |
| Deception (Cun) | | |
| Discipline (Will) | | |
| Leadership (Pr) | | |
| Mechanics (Int) | | |
| Medicine (Int) | | |
| Negotiation (Pr) | | |
| Perception (Cun) | | |
| Piloting - Planetary (Ag) | | |
| Piloting - Space (Ag) | | |
| Resilience (Br) | | |
| Skulduggery (Cun) | | |
| Stealth (Ag) | | |
| Streetwise (Cun) | | |
| Survival (Cun) | | |
| Vigilance (Will) | | |

| COMBAT SKILLS | CAREER? | RANK |
|---|---|---|
| Brawl (Br) | | |
| Gunnery (Ag) | | |
| Lightsaber (Br) | | |
| Melee (Br) | | |
| Ranged - Light (Ag) | | |
| Ranged - Heavy (Ag) | | |

| KNOWLEDGE SKILLS | | |
|---|---|---|
| Core Worlds (Int) | | |
| Education (Int) | | |
| Lore (Int) | | |
| Outer Rim (Int) | | |
| Underworld (Int) | | |
| Xenology (Int) | | |
| Other: | | |

| CUSTOM SKILLS | | |
|---|---|---|
| | | |
| | | |
| | | |
| | | |
| | | |

## WEAPONS

| WEAPON | SKILL | DAMAGE | CRIT | RANGE | SPECIAL |
|---|---|---|---|---|---|
| | | | | | |
| | | | | | |
| | | | | | |
| | | | | | |
| | | | | | |
| | | | | | |

TOTAL XP

# CHARACTER SHEET

AVAILABLE XP

## MOTIVATIONS

TYPE: _____

TYPE: _____

## CHARACTER DESCRIPTION

GENDER: _____

AGE: _____

HEIGHT: _____

BUILD: _____

HAIR: _____

EYES: _____

NOTABLE FEATURES:

## MORALITY

EMOTIONAL STRENGTH: _____

EMOTIONAL WEAKNESS: _____

CONFLICT: _____

MORALITY: _____

## CRITICAL INJURIES

| SEVERITY: | RESULT: |
|-----------|---------|
|           |         |
|           |         |
|           |         |
|           |         |
|           |         |
|           |         |

## EQUIPMENT LOG

CREDITS

WEAPONS & ARMOR

PERSONAL GEAR

## TALENTS AND SPECIAL ABILITIES

| NAME | PAGE # | ABILITY SUMMARY |
|------|--------|-----------------|
|      |        |                 |
|      |        |                 |
|      |        |                 |
|      |        |                 |
|      |        |                 |
|      |        |                 |
|      |        |                 |
|      |        |                 |
|      |        |                 |
|      |        |                 |
|      |        |                 |
|      |        |                 |

FORCE POWER: _____

FORCE POWER: _____

FORCE POWER: _____

VEHICLE

NAME

MAKE / MODEL

HARD POINTS

ENCUMBRANCE CAPACITY

STAR WARS FORCE AND DESTINY ROLEPLAYING GAME

PLAYER

## CHARACTERISTICS

SILHOUETTE

SPEED

HANDLING

DEFENSE

FORE

PORT

STARBOARD

AFT

ARMOR

HULL TRAUMA

THRESHOLD | CURRENT

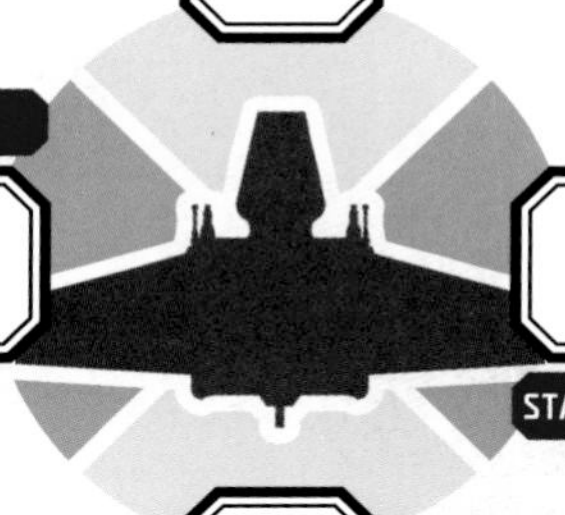

SYSTEM STRAIN

THRESHOLD | CURRENT

## WEAPONS

| WEAPON | FIRING ARC | DAMAGE | RANGE | CRIT | SPECIAL |
|---|---|---|---|---|---|
| | | | | | |
| | | | | | |
| | | | | | |
| | | | | | |
| | | | | | |
| | | | | | |
| | | | | | |

## ATTACHMENTS

| NAME | HARD POINTS REQUIRED | BASE MODIFIERS | MODIFICATIONS |
|---|---|---|---|
| | | | |
| | | | |
| | | | |
| | | | |
| | | | |
| | | | |
| | | | |

## CARGO HOLD

CREW

PASSENGERS

CONSUMABLES

HYPERDRIVE

SENSOR RANGE

# VEHICLE SHEET

GROUP

# BASE OF OPERATIONS

LOCATION

DESCRIPTION

## GROUP MORALITY

| MORALITY VALUE | PLAYER/CHARACTER | EMOTIONAL STRENGTH AND WEAKNESS | LIST OF MOTIVATIONS |
|---|---|---|---|
| | | | |
| | | | |
| | | | |
| | | | |
| | | | |

## GROUP RESOURCES

## GROUP POSSESSIONS

## GROUP CONTACTS

| LIGHT SIDE | DESTINY POOL | DARK SIDE |
|---|---|---|

# GROUP SHEET